FROM THE LIBRARY OF
THE DWIGHT VOGELS

CRITIQUES

and

ESSAYS IN CRITICISM

1920-1948

REPRESENTING THE ACHIEVEMENT OF MODERN BRITISH AND AMERICAN CRITICS

Selected By

ROBERT WOOSTER STALLMAN

UNIVERSITY OF CONNECTICUT

WITH A FOREWORD BY

CLEANTH BROOKS

THE RONALD PRESS COMPANY · NEW YORK

5

Library of Congress Catalog Card Number: 49-7475
PRINTED IN THE UNITED STATES OF AMERICA

FOR V. S.

PREFACE

CRITIQUES AND ESSAYS IN CRITICISM 1920-1948 is designed for courses in modern criticism, æsthetics, and, as a correlative text, for courses offering a critical approach to recent American and British literature, particularly the poetry and the drama. To supplement and enlarge the scope of this selection, I have included a comprehensive bibliography on the criticism of criticism, poetry, fiction, and aesthetics.

The purpose of this book is to consolidate and to make accessible the contemporary achievement in criticism. Much of this material has not received previous book publication, is available only in books and journals which are now out of print, or appears here for the first time.

"A bird's-eye view of criticism at the present day—its mechanism and conventions, not its exceptional individuals—shows a panorama of unbelievable muddle, futility, perversion." So wrote a critic in 1927. And other critics, taking the same bird's-eye view two decades later, describe the critical landscape in similar terms: it is a panorama of Alexandrian decadence, waste, muddlement. In actuality, what these critics are describing is the landscape of twenty years ago, for, as the materials presented in this book demonstrate, modern criticism is not confused, is not disunified. Here, for the first time, this criticism is embodied as a structure in itself; collectively these essays manifest the conception of criticism as an integral. Throughout the four parts of this schematic selection, the essays link one to another into a unified structure; they have ordered themselves into their own framework of issues and relevancies, created their own pattern of interrelationships—parallelisms in ideas and methods, crosscurrents of influences or collaborations.

This book is a selection of the best critical writings of those who created, promoted, or followed in the development of the critical movement inaugurated by T. S. Eliot in *The Sacred Wood* (1920) and by I. A. Richards in *The Principles of Literary Criticism* (1924). While on the one hand these critics have opened new approaches to literature by exploring new fields of inquiry, on the other they have restricted the scope of criticism and, by confining their strategy to the literary work itself, illuminated its center. In the main, the critics represented here assume or express a strict conception of the special nature and methods of poetry. Modern criticism was created to establish a new poetic convention, to explain it, and to make it prevail. Its central concern has been with methodology and techniques, poetic and critical. And it is this interest which forms, accordingly, the core of this book.

In making this selection I have asked: Of what use is this essay to the student or apprentice in criticism? The most fundamental tests established for this winnowing were to provide him (1) with specimens of evaluated texts, of critical positions and problems, and of techniques in critical procedure; and (2) with statements which elucidate the critical background, past and present. Values carefully considered in making individual selections were: first, historical-critical importance (especially in terms of the object of the criticism and of the intrinsic value of the criticism itself); second, literary quality; and finally, above all, teachableness.

My prime interest being the achievement of modern criticism rather than its history, I have ordered these essays into a critical framework in place of the more usual historical one. Instead of a broad representation of differing critical positions or of evaluated texts, I have emphasized coherence and critical procedure.

Considered in its entirety, this critical achievement has not been equalled by critics in any period of our literary history. Clearly this criticism has its defects and limitations. One charge that may be brought is that it neglects the creative process. It preoccupies itself almost wholly with the means and ends of poetry rather than with its sources, with the nature of the poem in relation to the reader rather than with the relation of the poem to the poet or maker. Analyses of poetic creation have been attempted by only a few of our poet-critics—Herbert Read, Allen Tate, Robert Graves, W. H. Auden, Robert Nichols, and Stephen Spender. Of these, Spender's "The Making of a Poem" seems to me most useful to the beginning practitioner of the craft.

But there are more serious limitations to this criticism, particularly its narrow range of evaluations. It has neglected the novel and the motion picture, and it has dealt only incidentally with literature in relation to the Fine Arts. It is only now beginning to advance beyond the investigation of poetic and dramatic methodology into the analysis of the newer forms and techniques of fiction. (One of the best of these is Joseph Frank's "Spatial Form in Modern Literature.") It is here, I think, that the immediate future of criticism lies—in the direction of the novel. The way has been prepared in technical criticism by such critics as Martin Turnell, R. P. Blackmur, Harry Levin, F. R. Leavis, Joseph Warren Beach, Malcolm Cowley, and Morton D. Zabel.

The new criticism, in sum, has limited its center of interest to the genres of poetry, drama, and criticism itself. The poem is foremost in these critical discourses, the seventeenth and twentieth century poem in particular. It was the School of Donne that furnished our epoch with the foundations for our revolution in the conception of poetry—a revolution accompanied by strategic onslaughts against two poets: Milton and Shelley. Of these two repudiations I have chosen to represent the case against Shelley because here, especially as F. R. Leavis presents it, we obtain a much sounder criticism. Also, in the general attack on Shelley there has been an almost solid front of agreement, whereas the allegations against Milton have been challenged even by critics from within the ranks. The case against Milton has been the work of a single critic, Eliot being solely responsible for Milton's dislodgment and again for his recent reinstatement.

Though the new critics have practiced their equipment upon medieval and early Elizabethan poetry (e.g., *Piers Plowman,* Chaucer, Wyatt, and the Scots literary tradition), they have done so only in isolated instances. Through such critics as T. S. Eliot, G. Wilson Knight, William Empson, and D. A. Traversi, criticism has extended its range of evaluations to the drama (Shakespeare and the Elizabethans, Dryden and the Restoration dramatists, Corneille, Racine, Molière) and to French and Italian poetry (Baudelaire and the French symbolists, Dante and the Italian modernists). As for eighteenth and late seventeenth century poetry, criticism has revised our attitude towards satire and thereby re-established the reputations of Pope and Dryden—notably through such revaluations as those by F. R. Leavis, Cleanth Brooks, and Austin Warren. To indicate this revised attitude I have used, in place of a specific study of Pope, a more general study of satire: Edgell Rickword's "The Use of 'Negative' Emotions," in which homage is paid particularly to Swift and Churchill.

The poets who here receive specific evaluations are Shelley, by F. R. Leavis; Hopkins, by W. H. Gardner; Hardy, by Delmore Schwartz; the later Yeats, by R. P. Blackmur; and the Eliot of *The Four Quartets,* by Helen L. Gardner. Used for incidental analyses by other critics are poems of Donne and the Metaphysicals, Swift's *The Lady's Dressing Room,* Landor's *Rose Aylmer,* Tennyson's *Maud,* Thomson's *The Vine,* Eliot's *The Waste Land,* Pound's *Cantos,* and Yeats's *Sailing to Byzantium.* The plays here analyzed include Elizabethan and Restoration plays, by William Empson, and four Shakespeare plays—*Macbeth,* by G. Wilson Knight; *Coriolanus,* by D. A. Traversi; *King Lear,* by Robert B. Heilman; and *Hamlet,* by T. S. Eliot and by Kenneth Burke.

Of the essays marking important stages in the development of modern criticism, the outstanding ones are T. E. Hulme's notes on Romanticism and Classicism; T. S. Eliot's pronouncements on Tradition, on the Metaphysical poets, and on Hamlet; I. A. Richards' studies of Belief and of Meaning; D. G. James's critique of I. A. Richards; F. R. Leavis' criticism of Shelley; and G. Wilson Knight's essay on Shakespeare. These essays have importance, however, not only on historical but also on critical grounds; they possess a permanent place in our critical interest. For example, Knight's analysis of *Macbeth* represents this critic at his best—the early Knight who inaugurated a new development in Shakespeare interpretation and criticism.

The new analytical method which this essay employs has long-range implications. It is applicable to all literary art.

Here, then, are the general determining considerations by which this selection has been made, the organizing principles by which it is integrated.

Eliot's essay "The Social Function of Poetry" has here its first American publication. Brooks's Foreword and Elder Olson's "An Outline of Poetic Theory" have their first appearance here. Essays which have not had previous book publication are those by Heilman, Schwartz, Traversi, Turnell, Vivas, and Wimsatt and Beardsley. Nothing of Rickword and Traversi has been published previously in America. Burke's "Lexicon Rhetoricae" is now reprinted for the first time; his *Counter-Statement,* out of print, cannot be obtained. (The same holds true for a number of other essays.) The final two sections of Burke's five-part "Lexicon" are omitted; Section II is abridged, III is not complete. Some abridgments have been made in the essays by Empson, James, Turnell, Wimsatt and Beardsley, and Wellek. Of Frank's three-part essay, I have reprinted Part I. Dupee's essay and Wilson's contain some revisions; my own essay appears here in wholly revised form.

More than half of all the critics in this book are poets as well as critics. Their publications in poetry are listed in the Biographical Notes, by which the Bibliography is thereby supplemented.

I wish to thank the several persons who examined the prospectus of this selection and, in conversation or in correspondence, provided criticism or information by which this book has benefited: Professors Eric Bentley, Cleanth Brooks, Kenneth Burke, Ronald S. Crane, Samuel Monk, William Van O'Connor, Monroe K. Spears, Allen Tate, Lionel Trilling, Dorothy Van Ghent, Austin Warren, and Morton D. Zabel.

R. W. STALLMAN

Lawrence, Kansas
December, 1948

ACKNOWLEDGMENTS

Grateful acknowledgment is made to the following authors and publishers for permission to reproduce these essays:

To R. P. Blackmur for two essays, "The Later Poetry of W. B. Yeats," reprinted from *The Expense of Greatness* (Arrow Editions, New York, 1940), and "The Enabling Act of Criticism," reprinted by permission of the author from *American Issues, II* (J. B. Lippincott Co., Philadelphia, 1941); F. W. Dupee, for "The Americanism of Van Wyck Brooks," reprinted from *The Partisan Reader* (Dial Press, Inc., New York, 1946); T. S. Eliot, for his special permission to reprint "The Social Function of Poetry," which appeared in the July 1945 issue of *The Adelphi;* Joseph Frank, for "Spatial Form in Modern Literature," which appeared (Part One) in the Spring 1945 issue of the *Sewanee Review;* Miss Helen L. Gardner, for "Four Quartets: A Commentary," reprinted by arrangement with the author and the publishers from *T. S. Eliot: A Study of His Writings by Several Hands* (*Focus Three*), ed. B. Rajan (Dennis Dobson, Ltd., London, 1947; and Funk & Wagnalls Co., New York, distributors of *Focus Three* in this country, 1948); W. H. Gardner, for "The Religious Problem in G. M. Hopkins," which first appeared in the June 1937 issue of *Scrutiny;* Robert B. Heilman, for "The Unity of *King Lear,*" which appeared in the Winter 1948 issue of the *Sewanee Review;* Elder Olson, for "An Outline of Poetic Theory," which is to appear in a volume on *General Criticism and the Shorter Forms of Poetry;* Edgell Rickword, for "The Use of 'Negative' Emotions," reprinted from *Towards Standards of Criticism,* ed. F. R. Leavis (Wishart Books, Ltd., London, 1933); Delmore Schwartz, for "Poetry and Belief in Thomas Hardy," which appeared in the Summer 1940 issue of the *Southern Review;* Stephen Spender, for "The Making of a Poem," which appeared in the Summer 1946 issue of the *Partisan Review;* D.. A. Traversi, for "Coriolanus," which appeared in the June 1937 issue of *Scrutiny;* Martin Turnell, for "Literary Criticism in France," which appeared in the September and December 1939 issues of *Scrutiny;* Eliseo Vivas, for "The Objective Correlative of T. S. Eliot," which appeared in the Winter 1944 issue of the *American Bookman;* Robert Penn Warren, for "Pure and Impure Poetry," which appeared in the Spring 1943 issue of the *Kenyon Review;* William K. Wimsatt, Jr. and Monroe C. Beardsley, for "The Affective Fallacy," which is to appear in the Winter 1949 issue of the *Sewanee Review.* Special thanks are due to Dorothy Van Ghent and Monroe K. Spears for their translations from the French of quotations used in the essay by Martin Turnell.

"The Language of Paradox" is reprinted from *The Well Wrought Urn* by Cleanth Brooks, copyrighted 1947 by Reynal & Hitchcock, New York. (This essay first appeared in *The Language of Poetry,* ed. Allen Tate, Princeton University Press, Princeton, N. J., 1942.) "Psychology and Form" and "Lexicon Rhetoricae" are reprinted from *Counter-Statement* by Kenneth Burke, copyrighted 1931 by Harcourt, Brace & Co., Inc., New York. ("Psychology and

Form" first appeared in *The Dial,* 79, July, 1925.) "The Metaphysical Poets," "Tradition and the Individual Talent," and "Hamlet and His Problems" are reprinted from *Selected Essays 1917–1932* by T. S. Eliot, copyrighted 1932 by Harcourt, Brace & Co., Inc. ("Metaphysical Poets" first appeared in the *Times Literary Supplement,* 1031, October 20, 1921; reprinted in *Homage to John Dryden,* Hogarth Press, Ltd., London, 1924. "Tradition and the Individual Talent" first appeared in *The Egoist,* 6, September and November, 1919; "Hamlet and His Problems" first appeared in the *Athenaeum,* 4665, September 26, 1919. These two essays were reprinted in *The Sacred Wood,* Methuen & Co., Ltd., London, 1920; Alfred A. Knopf, Inc., New York, 1921.) "Double Plots" is reprinted from *English Pastoral Poetry* by William Empson, copyrighted 1937 by W. W. Norton & Co., Inc., New York, first published under the title *Some Versions of Pastoral,* by Chatto & Windus, Ltd., London, 1935. "The Religious Problem in G. M. Hopkins" is reprinted by permission of Martin Secker & Warburg, Ltd., London, publishers of *Gerard Manley Hopkins* by W. H. Gardner, Vol. I, 1944, 1948; American publication by the Yale University Press, New Haven, Conn., 1948. "Romanticism and Classicism" by T. E. Hulme, is reprinted from *Speculations,* ed. Herbert Read, published 1924, by George Routledge and Kegan Paul, Ltd., London. "I. A. Richards," reprinted from *Scepticism and Poetry: An Essay on the Poetic Imagination* by D. G. James, is a retitling of Ch. 2: "A Denial of the 'Prime Agent'; And the Consequences." *Scepticism and Poetry* was published 1937 by George Allen & Unwin, Ltd., London. "The Milk of Concord: An Essay on Life-Themes in Macbeth" is reprinted from *The Imperial Theme* by G. Wilson Knight, published 1931 by Oxford University Press, London. It is here reproduced by permission of Methuen & Co., Ltd., under whose copyright (1948) the book is being reissued. "Shelley" is reprinted from *Revaluation: Tradition and Development in English Poetry* by F. R. Leavis, published 1936, by Chatto & Windus, Ltd. It is here reprinted by permission of George W. Stewart, Publisher, Inc., New York, under whose copyright (1947) the book has been published in the United States. (It first appeared in *Scrutiny,* 4, September, 1935.) "Poetry: A Note on Ontology" is reprinted from *The World's Body* by John Crowe Ransom, copyrighted 1938 by Chas. Scribner's Sons, New York and London, reprinted by permission of the publishers. (This essay first appeared in *The American Review,* 1, May, 1934.) "Poetry and Beliefs" is reprinted from *Science and Poetry* by I. A. Richards, copyrighted 1926 by W. W. Norton & Co., Inc. "The Bridle of Pegasus," from *Coleridge on Imagination* by I. A. Richards is here reprinted by permission of George Routledge and Kegan Paul, Ltd., who published the book in 1934. (It was published 1935 in the United States by Harcourt, Brace & Co., Inc.) "The Use of 'Negative' Emotions" by Edgell Rickword, which first appeared in *The Calendar of Modern Letters* (1, May, 1925), is reprinted from *Towards Standards of Criticism,* ed. F. R. Leavis (Wishart Books, Ltd., 1933). It is here reproduced by arrangement with Lawrence & Wishart, Ltd. "The New Critics," which originally appeared under the title "The New Criticism and the Southern Critics" in *A Southern Vanguard,* the John Peale Bishop Memorial Volume, ed. Allen Tate, copyrighted 1947 by Prentice-Hall, Inc., New York, is reprinted by permission of the publishers. "Tension in Poetry" is from *Reason in Madness: Critical Essays* by Allen Tate, published 1941, by G. P. Putnam's Sons, New York. It is here reproduced by permission of the Swallow Press-William

Morrow Co., Inc., New York, under whose copyright (1948) the essay appears in *On the Limits of Poetry: Selected Essays: 1928-1948* by Allen Tate. (This essay first appeared in the *Southern Review,* 4, Summer, 1938.) "The Mode of Existence of a Literary Work of Art" by René Wellek is from *The Theory of Literature* by René Wellek and Austin Warren, copyrighted 1948 by Harcourt, Brace & Co., Inc. (The essay first appeared in the *Southern Review,* 7, Spring, 1942.) "Historical Criticism" by Edmund Wilson is here reprinted by special arrangement with the author. The essay appears in *The Triple Thinkers,* published by the Oxford University Press, 1948. (It first appeared, under the title "The Historical Interpretation of Literature," in *The Intent of the Critic,* ed. Donald A. Stauffer, Princeton University Press, 1941.) "Preliminary Problems" by Yvor Winters is from *The Anatomy of Nonsense,* copyrighted 1943 by New Directions, Norfolk, Conn. It is here reproduced by permission of the Swallow Press-William Morrow Co., Inc., under whose copyright the essay appears in *In Defense of Reason* by Yvor Winters, 1947. "A Deep Sworn Vow," "The Second Coming," "Leda and the Swan," and "Sailing to Byzantium" by W. B. Yeats are from *The Collected Poems of W. B. Yeats,* copyrighted 1919, 1921, 1928, by The Macmillan Co. and used with their permission. "Bells for John Whiteside's Daughter" by John Crowe Ransom is from *Selected Poems* by John Crowe Ransom, copyrighted 1924, 1945, by Alfred A. Knopf, Inc., and used with their permission. "The Windhover" by Gerard Manley Hopkins is from *Poems of Gerard Manley Hopkins,* edited by W. H. Gardner, third edition, copyrighted 1948 by the Oxford University Press and used with their permission. "The Oxen," "The Masked Face," and "A Drizzling Easter Morning" by Thomas Hardy are from *Collected Poems of Thomas Hardy,* copyrighted 1911, 1922, 1925, by The Macmillan Co. and used with their permission.

Further acknowledgment is made to the editors of critical journals:

To Joseph T. Shipley, editor of the *American Bookman,* for the essay by Eliseo Vivas; to John Middleton Murry, editor of *The Adelphi,* for T. S. Eliot's essay "The Social Function of Poetry"; to John Crowe Ransom, editor of the *Kenyon Review,* for the essay by Robert Penn Warren; to the editors of the *Partisan Review,* for essays by F. W. Dupee and Stephen Spender; to F. R. Leavis, editor of *Scrutiny,* for contributions by W. H. Gardner, D. A. Traversi, and Martin Turnell; to John Palmer, editor of the *Sewanee Review,* for essays by Joseph Frank, Robert B. Heilman, and by W. K. Wimsatt, Jr. and M. C. Beardsley; and to the editors of the *University of Kansas City Review,* for the excerpt from Elder Olson's essay on "Sailing to Byzantium," used here as appendix to his present essay. I wish to thank F. R. Leavis for his many kindnesses, particularly in the matter of permissions to use *Scrutiny* selections.

R. W. S.

CONTENTS

PART IV

KINDS OF CRITICS AND CRITICISM

APPENDIX

FOREWORD

"MODERN CRITICISM, through its exacting scrutiny of literary texts, has demonstrated with finality that in art beauty and truth are indivisible and one." So writes Mark Schorer in a recent essay on criticism, and he continues as follows: [1]

> The Keatsian overtones of these terms are mitigated and an old dilemma solved if for beauty we substitute form, and for truth, content. We may, without risk of loss, narrow them even more, and speak of technique and subject matter. Modern criticism has shown us that to speak of content as such is not to speak of art at all, but of experience; and that it is only when we speak of the *achieved* content, the form, the work of art as a work of art, that we speak as critics. The difference between content, or experience, and achieved content, or art, is technique.
>
> When we speak of technique, then, we speak of nearly everything. For technique is the means by which the writer's experience, which is his subject matter, compels him to attend to it; technique is the only means he has of discovering, exploring, developing his subject, of conveying its meaning, and, finally, of evaluating it.

I subscribe to all that is said here. It is an admirable summary of what modern criticism has achieved. But I envy Schorer his boldness of tone: "Modern criticism has demonstrated with finality," "Modern criticism has shown us," etc. For I am conscious that nearly every statement that he makes has been, and continues to be, challenged; and further, that some of those who would accept his summary as a statement of the accomplishment of modern criticism, place a very different value on the accomplishment. Modern criticism has been blamed for strangling the creative impulse, for producing an arid intellectualization of our poetry, for perverting literary studies. If one is to provide a really serviceable introduction to such a volume as this, he had better not leave such charges out of account. Ignored, such charges confuse the issues on every level.

There is something to be said, then, for a general stock-taking, and particularly at the present time. The recent publication of books like Stanley Hyman's *The Armed Vision,* and Eric Bentley's *The Importance of Scrutiny,* or of essays like R. P. Blackmur's *A Burden for Critics* and of Schorer's *Technique as Discovery,* already mentioned—all suggest the sense of a period's having been fulfilled. The criticism characteristic of our time has come to fruition, or has arrived at a turning point, or, as some writers hint, has now exhausted its energies.

[1] From *The Hudson Review,* 1 (Spring, 1948), 67.

For those who would dwell upon this darker note there are further corroborative signs: the increasing tendency to talk about the "methods" of the "new" criticism; the growing academic respectability of the new criticism; the attempt to codify the new critics and to establish their sources and derivations. As it consolidates its gains, the new criticism ceases to be "new" and thus loses its romantic attractiveness, and with that, some of its more callow proponents. But, by the same token, it risks gaining the allegiance of another set of followers who hope to exploit it mechanically.

Yet, though a general stock-taking is in order, I shall not attempt it here. In the first place, it could hardly be done satisfactorily in a short introduction. In the second place, as a contributor to this volume, I do not wish to seem to sit in judgment upon my peers, defining what is central to the new criticism and what is peripheral. Suffice it to recognize that there is a large area of agreement among the critics represented in this volume. But they do not constitute a school—much less a guild. I have no wish to minimize their varying emphases and their active disagreements. It is even a question whether they are accurately described under a common name, and most of all under the name which has caught on— the "new criticism."

I suppose that when John Crowe Ransom chose the phrase a few years ago, he meant it to be a neutral and modest designation; i.e., the modern criticism, the contemporary criticism. Despite such intent, the name has hardly proved a happy choice. It has seemed to stress, perhaps arrogantly, the relative novelty of the criticism; and many popular reviewers and professors have been quick to sense in it a dangerous novelty. The typical professor of English is naturally and constitutionally opposed to change; the popular reviewer, in so far as his critical principles are concerned, only less so. Both have what amounts to a vested interest in a more desultory and less strenuous discussion of literature.

Yet much more than vested interests is of course involved. The misconceptions about modern criticism are too widespread and too persistent to be accounted for in such a fashion. They are very stubbornly rooted indeed. They are rooted, I believe, in an essentially romantic conception of poetry. This conception tends to take quite literally the view that poetry is the spontaneous overflow of emotion, and that its appreciation is best served by a corresponding overflow of emotion on the part of the reader. It conceives of the function of the intellect as only officious and meddling. The creation of poetry is magical, and if the intellect is brought into play at all in examining a poem, this is an attempt to expose the magic and thus do away with it.

Critical activity is therefore interpreted as somehow inimical to the creation of a robust poetry. Our own age, it is argued, is "Alexandrian," overingenious, self-conscious, and therefore cannot create anything but a kind of sophisticated intellectual poetry. The position is rarely argued: its strength is that it does not need to be argued. It is enough to catcall "Alexandrian." But a little argument may serve to take some of the sting out of the epithet. If ours is a critical age, it is not because of this fact an uncreative age. Measured against the poetry of the Victorians, say, the poetry of the twentieth century compares very favorably indeed. That will be the consensus, I think, even of those who are worried about what they take to be the twentieth century's excessive interest in criticism. As for those who would dispute the achievement of the twentieth century in poetry, they might be reminded that they dispute it on the basis of a critical judgment of their own, and so are begging the very question which they are deciding.

In brief, what is important about a "critical" age is the soundness of its criticism—the matter of whether its criticism is good or bad—and not the mere fact that the age is interested in criticism. Everything else being equal, the production of a great deal of criticism probably argues for an intense interest in the arts, and normally goes hand in hand with creative activity. For criticism does not compete with creative activity. The critic is not in his arrogance offering a scheme which explains the construction of poetry, a formula by which poems are to be written. Nor is he, on the other hand, concerned with reducing the poem to an intellectual scheme in order to "explain" the poem—that is, to explain the poem away—expose the magic—kill the emotional response.

In referring such misconceptions of criticism to a naively romantic view of the arts, I have perhaps made them seem overnaive—too simple to be held by practising writers. In that case it may be well to illustrate from a recent review which appeared in one of our metropolitan bookpages. Alfred Kazin, the reviewer, is concerned about the impersonality and technicality of the sort of criticism contained in this volume. Its very "expertness," for him, is damning: [2]

> In our day the real princelings of criticism have been those who can manage, in some way or other, to sound like impersonal experts, and for whom the work before them is always an occasion for technical analysis or some sovereign re-definition of our lot. In one sense they have even set themselves up as the rivals to the works before them, and have sought by their expertness to replace them with their own. This is not . . . entirely due to the presumption of critics. We live in a time when an overwhelming sense of having come to the end of a period in man's total history has put a premium on intellectual revaluation rather than on the literature of "real" experience. But it certainly leads to arid intellectual pride, and even, as there is no lack of examples around us to prove, patronage of artists themselves.

[2] From *Books* (*New York Herald Tribune*), May 30, 1948, p. 5.

Now the temptation of pride is a constant one, and in a fiercely competitive age like our own, men, including literary men, can never too often be warned against it. But to imply that the critics at whom Kazin points his finger are somehow especially susceptible as other critics (social, historical, etc.) are not, or, for that matter, as poets, novelists, and Saturday Reviewers of Literature are not, seems to me absurd. For the impersonality of the critic can just as fairly be interpreted as modesty rather than as arrogance—as an unwillingness to interpose his own personality between the reader and the work itself. Furthermore, the concern for technical analysis looks like a wholesome preoccupation with the work of art; that is, the critic is content to describe the work as sensitively as he can rather than to dilate upon his emotional response to it. Rivalry with the work of art is in fact more likely to be instituted by a critic who is anxious to stress his personal response or to use the work he discusses as a peg upon which to hang his own commentary on morals or politics.

I cannot therefore accept Kazin's suggestion that the new critics are on principle arrogant; but his other suggestion, namely, that the pressures of our age have something to do with the characteristic development of criticism in our time, seems to me quite true. I should prefer, however, to state the matter in somewhat different fashion—certainly not as the result of some "overwhelming sense of [our] having come to the end of a period in man's total history." I should prefer to put the case more modestly, and, I think, more specifically, thus: the raveling out of the Victorian poetic conventions coincided with the final breakdown of the current theory of poetic statement, itself some centuries old. It coincided also with the near collapse of linguistic training in our schools and colleges. All three are doubtless aspects of a general breakdown of the means of communication, but it may be serviceable to notice them separately.

The going to seed of a particular literary period may seem unimportant. But in this case it was special and significant, for the Victorian conventions represented what could be salvaged from a pre-scientific age, or represented compromises with the new scientific symbolism which had undercut the older poetic symbols. The Victorian conventions were thus the product of a poetics which had come dangerously close to relegating the specifically poetic uses of language to decoration and embellishment. This general impoverishment was, and is, abundantly reflected in the educational system—whether in the elementary grades or in the graduate school.

It would be unfair to say that the new poetry impinged upon an audience of illiterates. But the discovery that it lacked an audience that could read it soon raised a further and more fundamental question: whether that same audience could read any poetry, including the poetry of the past. The audience, of course, assumed that it could; but in that case, what did the typical reader derive from the poetry of the past—if he read it, and when he read it? Noble sentiments? Ethical doctrine? An escape from a dull and stale world? He read poetry for pleasure, to be sure. But pleasure becomes an even more ambiguous term in a day of mass-produced entertainment. If he answered "for truth," that term too, in an age overawed by the tremendous structure of science, called for elaborate definition and qualification. How could methods so notoriously unscientific as those of poetry yield anything resembling truth?

Questions of this sort are not, of course, new. But in our time it has become increasingly difficult to evade answering them. Partial solutions will no longer work. Compromises which apparently served the nineteenth century are no longer practical. This is not to say that the twentieth century has found the answers: it is to explain why it has had to canvass such questions thoroughly and *de novo*.

Thus far I have dealt with criticism as related to the impact of poetry on the modern world. But the problem has to be seen in broader terms. The rise of modern criticism is part of a general intensification of the study of language and symbolism. The development of semantics, symbolic logic, cultural anthropology, and the psychology of Jung and Freud may all be taken as responses to the same general situation. How they are specifically related to each other and what contributions these studies have made, or may make, to criticism are topics that I shall not attempt to discuss here. Suffice it that they all bear upon the problem of symbolism (logical and extra-logical) and represent attempts to recover symbolic "languages" whose real importance has become evident to us only as the supporting cultural pattern breaks down.

It is no accident, therefore, that a great deal of modern criticism has occupied itself with the problem of how language actually works and specifically how it works in a piece of literature. Because of this, there is a tendency to identify the new criticism with "close textual reading" and to assume that it is limited to problems of what used to be called "diction." The essays here collected should supply a corrective to such a view. Modern critics, it is perfectly true, tend to force attention back to the text of the work itself: that is, to look at the poem as a poem, not as an appendage to the poet's biography, nor as a reflection of his reading, nor as an illustration of the history of ideas. Such an emphasis naturally stresses a close reading of the text, and, since poems are written in words, careful attention to language. But, though the text must provide the ultimate sanction for the meaning of the work, that does not mean that close textual reading is to be conceived of as a sort of verbal piddling. Words open out into the larger symbolizations on all levels—for example, into archetypal symbol, ritual, and myth. The critic's concern for "language" need not be conceived narrowly, even if his concern leads to an intensive examination: it can be extended to the largest symbolizations possible. A renewed respect for words and a sense of their complexities are matters for congratulation. The alternative does not liberate: it leads away from literature altogether.

I have dealt with some of the honest and some of the willful misunderstandings of modern criticism. But these are probably calculated to do less damage than extravagant claims made for criticism. I shall cite only one example, though I think that it is a significant one. Stanley Hyman writes: [3] "... modern criticism for the most part no longer accepts its traditional status as an adjunct to 'creative' or 'imaginative' literature...." "'No exponent of criticism... has, I presume, ever made the preposterous assumption that criticism is an autotelic art,' T S. Eliot wrote in 1923, in 'The Function of Criticism.' Whether or not anyone had made that 'preposterous assumption' by 1923, modern criticism, which began more or less formally the following year with the publication of I. A. Richards's *Principles of Literary Criticism,* has been acting on it since."

I disagree. True, we can define art (Hyman suggests any "creation of meaningful patterns of experience") broadly enough to include criticism. But I think that we lose more than we gain. In any case, we risk confusing the issues, and, as has been pointed out, the issues are sufficiently confused as it is. Better to assign to literary criticism a more humble and a more specific function: let us say that the task of literary criticism is to put the reader in possession of the work of art.

To read a work of art successfully involves, of course, a process of imaginative reconstruction. The good reader thus necessarily makes use of a process related to that by which the author has constructed the work. If the poet is a maker, the critic is at least a remaker; and I suppose that the successful critic is entitled to claim that his work is imaginative in this sense. (He had certainly better not be lacking in imagination!) But I do not think that the critic is entitled to claim more, nor do I think that he wishes to claim more.

To put the reader into possession of the work of art. Is this a mere reading of the work or is it a judgment of it? Frankly, I do not see how the two activities can be separated. For to possess the work implies a knowledge of it as a work of art, not merely the knowledge of it as a document (political, philosophical, etc.), nor merely the knowledge of something abstracted from it (a logical scheme or paraphrase). The critic inevitably judges, but how explicit he is to make his judgment will obviously depend upon the circumstances. In some cases, and for some readers, he may think it enough to show the pattern of tensions in the work and the way in which they are resolved, or the failure to resolve them. In other cases, he may wish to make his judgment very explicit. But if a full reading of a work implies a judgment on it, a responsible judgment on it ought to imply that a full reading

[3] From *The Armed Vision* (New York: Alfred A. Knopf, 1948), p. 7.

lies behind the judgment, and if called for, can be set forth. The attempt to drive a wedge between close reading of the text and evaluation of the work seems to me confused and confusing.

The essays collected in this volume provide more than a mere sampling of modern criticism. They have not been chosen at random. If they show a real diversity, they also suggest a unity, making as they do a collective comment on the central problems of criticism. They represent an achievement, and taken even at the lowest discount, a worthy achievement.

I have little to say about the future of criticism. I shall not say that the future of criticism is immense. But I think that I can point out something that needs to be done (and is in process of being done): that is, to discriminate more closely among the various problems with which criticism in the large is concerned. To give an example: Beardsley and Wimsatt have pointed out that the genesis of the work (how it was composed, what went into its making, etc.) constitutes a problem distinct from what may be called the analysis of the work in terms of its formal properties. This latter problem has in turn to be distinguished from the further problem which has to do with the actual effect of the work on various kinds of people and at various periods. All three problems are intimately related, and all may be worth discussion; but unless they are distinguished we shall get into trouble. For example, it is one thing to discuss *Uncle Tom's Cabin* in terms of its formal properties as a novel. It is a rather different thing to ask how Harriet Beecher Stowe came to write it, how it was shaped by the pressures of the time. It is still another thing to account for the way in which it affected men in the past, and to try to predict what further effects (if any) it may have in the future. Here the discriminations seem easy; but many who concede them here in this instance refuse to recognize them when we substitute for *Uncle Tom's Cabin, Paradise Lost,* or *Moby Dick,* or *The Four Quartets.*

To insist on a clearer marking of boundary lines, of course, may suggest more specialization, more technicalities, and the segregation of the critic into an even narrower compartment. But clearly marked boundary lines do not imply fences, barricades, or tariff walls. Nobody wants to restrict free trade—between scholarship and criticism, and least of all, between the various areas of criticism. But if the distinctions are real—if they actually exist—muddling of the boundary markers remedies nothing: it merely begets confusion. To indicate the boundaries clearly is actually to encourage free passage across them; for, as it is, we too often line up to defend them as national borders in the spirit of troops repelling an invasion. The critic occupied with the formal analysis of a work is damned for having offered an obviously inadequate account of the social pressures which played upon the author of the work, or for having left out of account the importance of the work as a political document, or he is reproached for having (or for not having) accounted for the composition of the work.

The ways in which we can view a poem or novel or drama are very nearly infinite. Some of them are of the highest importance. Some of them in our day have hardly got the attention which they deserve. But instead of pining for the perfect critic who will do everything, it might be more sensible to see what the critics have actually done—to discriminate among the various "criticisms" in their proper relations to each other. Interrelated, they certainly are; but the ability to discriminate among them might allow us to make better use of the actual and limited, flesh-and-blood critics that we have.

CLEANTH BROOKS

PART I

THE NATURE AND FUNCTION OF POETRY

INTRODUCTORY COMMENT

THE OBJECT of the criticism in Part I is the poem considered in terms of theory. Hulme lays down a philosophical basis for the nature of poetry; Ransom, pushing on into metaphysics, studies poetry for a poetics; Tate furnishes an æsthetic of poetry; Warren analyzes the ingredients of the poem; Eliot deals with the social role of the poet and the social function of poetry, etc. The criticism here concerns itself with the poem in relation to the poet (Spender), the poem in relation to the objective values of the literary convention or culture (Hulme, Eliot, Rickword, Tate), and the poem as a thing in itself—with the internal relationships and with the techniques by which its parts are formed into an intrinsic whole.

These essays revaluate the poetic tradition; they define contemporary poetic techniques and values; they provide standards or points of reference for the practitioner of the craft. They analyze the stuff of which the poem is made—the components of imagery and idea (Hulme, Ransom), concretion and abstraction (Tate), thought and feeling (Eliot, Hulme), emotion (Rickword), paradox or irony (Brooks). No one of these elements is regarded as exclusive of another; a poem is the fusion of these elements.

Throughout the four-part division of this book the essays overlap by virtue of their interrelated critical positions, concepts, methods and problems. They are schematically linked by a unified cluster of ideas and recurrent key critical terms. Of these, together with some of the authors who use them, the main ones include:—tension (Tate); intention (Eliot, Wellek, Vivas); meaning (Warren in Part I and Richards and other critics in Part III); thought and feeling (Hulme, Eliot, Leavis, Winters); myth (Blackmur); ambiguity and irony (Brooks, Rickword, Warren, Empson); catharsis (Rickword, Olson, W. H. Gardner) ; suspense and symbol (Burke); etc.

ROMANTICISM AND CLASSICISM

(1913) [1]

T. E. Hulme

I want to maintain that after a hundred years of romanticism, we are in for a classical revival, and that the particular weapon of this new classical spirit, when it works in verse, will be fancy. And in this I imply the superiority of fancy—not superior generally or absolutely, for that would be obvious nonsense, but superior in the sense that we use the word good in empirical ethics—good for something, superior for something. I shall have to prove then two things, first that a classical revival is coming, and, secondly, for its particular purposes, fancy will be superior to imagination.

So banal have the terms Imagination and Fancy become that we imagine they must have always been in the language. Their history as two differing terms in the vocabulary of criticism is comparatively short. Originally, of course, they both mean the same thing; they first began to be differentiated by the German writers on æsthetics in the eighteenth century.

I know that in using the words "classic" and "romantic" I am doing a dangerous thing. They represent five or six different kinds of antitheses, and while I may be using them in one sense you may be interpreting them in another. In this present connection I am using them in a perfectly precise and limited sense. I ought really to have coined a couple of new words, but I prefer to use the ones I have used, as I then conform to the practice of the group of polemical writers who make most use of them at the present day, and have almost succeeded in making them political catchwords. I mean Maurras, Lasserre and all the group connected with *L'Action Française.*

At the present time this is the particular group with which the distinction is most vital. Because it has become a party symbol. If you asked a man of a certain set whether he preferred the classics or the romantics, you could deduce from that what his politics were.

The best way of gliding into a proper definition of my terms would be to start with a set of people who are prepared to fight about it—for in them you will have no vagueness. (Other people take the infamous attitude of the person with catholic tastes who says he likes both.)

[1] Date of writing. This essay was first published in 1924. [*Editor's note.*]

About a year ago, a man whose name I think was Fauchois gave a lecture at the Odéon on Racine, in the course of which he made some disparaging remarks about his dullness, lack of invention and the rest of it. This caused an immediate riot: fights took place all over the house; several people were arrested and imprisoned, and the rest of the series of lectures took place with hundreds of gendarmes and detectives scattered all over the place. These people interrupted because the classical ideal is a living thing to them and Racine is the great classic. That is what I call a real vital interest in literature. They regard romanticism as an awful disease from which France had just recovered.

The thing is complicated in their case by the fact that it was romanticism that made the revolution. They hate the revolution, so they hate romanticism.

I make no apology for dragging in politics here; romanticism both in England and France is associated with certain political views, and it is in taking a concrete example of the working out of a principle in action that you can get its best definition.

What was the positive principle behind all the other principles of '89? I am talking here of the revolution in as far as it was an idea; I leave out material causes—they only produce the forces. The barriers which could easily have resisted or guided these forces had been previously rotted away by ideas. This always seems to be the case in successful changes; the privileged class is beaten only when it has lost faith in itself, when it has itself been penetrated with the ideas which are working against it.

It was not the rights of man—that was a good solid practical war-cry. The thing which created enthusiasm, which made the revolution practically a new religion, was something more positive than that. People of all classes, people who stood to lose by it, were in a positive ferment about the idea of liberty. There must have been some idea which enabled them to think that something positive could come out of so essentially negative a thing. There was, and here I get my definition of romanticism. They had been taught by Rousseau that man was by nature good, that it was only bad laws and customs that had suppressed him. Remove all these and the infinite possibilities of man would have a chance. This is what made them think that something positive could come out of disorder, this is what created the religious enthusiasm. Here is the root of all romanticism: that man, the individual, is an infinite reservoir of possibilities; and if you can so rearrange society by the destruction of oppressive order then these possibilities will have a chance and you will get Progress.

One can define the classical quite clearly as the exact opposite to this. Man is an extraordinarily fixed and limited animal whose nature is absolutely constant. It is only by tradition and organisation that anything decent can be got out of him.

This view was a little shaken at the time of Darwin. You remember his particular hypothesis, that new species came into existence by the cumulative effect of small variations—this seems to admit the possibility of future progress. But at the present day the contrary hypothesis makes headway in the shape of De Vries's mutation theory, that each new species comes into existence, not gradually by the accumulation of small steps, but suddenly in a jump, a kind of sport, and that once in existence it remains absolutely fixed. This enables me to keep the classical view with an appearance of scientific backing.

Put shortly, these are the two views, then. One, that man is intrinsically good, spoilt by circumstance; and the other that he is intrinsically limited, but disciplined by order and tradition to something fairly decent. To the one party man's nature is like a well, to the other like a bucket. The view which regards man as a well, a reservoir full of possibilities, I call the romantic; the one which regards him as a very finite and fixed creature, I call the classical.

One may note here that the Church has always taken the classical view since the defeat of the Pelagian heresy and the adoption of the sane classical dogma of original sin.

It would be a mistake to identify the classical view with that of materialism. On the contrary it is absolutely identical with the normal religious attitude. I should put it in this way: That part of the fixed nature of man is the belief in the Deity. This should be as fixed and true for every man as belief in the existence of matter and in the objective world. It is parallel to appetite, the instinct of sex, and all the other fixed qualities. Now at certain times, by the use of either force or rhetoric, these instincts have been suppressed—in Florence under Savonarola, in Geneva under Calvin, and here under the Roundheads. The inevitable result of such a process is that the repressed instinct bursts out in some abnormal direction. So with religion. By the perverted rhetoric of Rationalism, your natural instincts are suppressed and you are converted into an agnostic. Just as in the case of the other instincts, Nature has her revenge. The instincts that find their right and proper outlet in religion must come out in some other way. You don't believe in a God, so you begin to believe that man is a god. You don't believe in Heaven, so you begin to believe in a heaven on earth. In other words, you get romanticism. The concepts that are right and proper in their own sphere are spread over, and so mess up, falsify and blur the clear outlines of human experience. It is like pouring a pot of treacle over the dinner table. Romanticism then, and this is the best definition I can give of it, is spilt religion.

I must now shirk the difficulty of saying exactly what I mean by romantic and classical in verse. I can only say that it means the result of these two attitudes towards the cosmos, towards man, in so far as it gets reflected in verse. The romantic, because he thinks man infinite, must always be talking about the infinite; and as there is always the bitter contrast between what you think you ought to be able to do and what man actually can, it always tends, in its later stages at any rate, to be gloomy. I really can't go any further than to say it is the reflection of these two temperaments, and point out examples of the different spirits. On the one hand I would take such diverse people as Horace, most of the Elizabethans and the writers of the Augustan age, and on the other side Lamartine, Hugo, parts of Keats, Coleridge, Byron, Shelley and Swinburne.

I know quite well that when people think of classical and romantic in verse, the contrast at once comes into their mind between, say, Racine and Shakespeare. I don't mean this; the dividing line that I intend is here misplaced a little from the true middle. That Racine is on the extreme classical side I agree, but if you call Shakespeare romantic, you are using a different definition to the one I give. You are thinking of the difference between classic and romantic as being merely one between restraint and exuberance. I should say with Nietzsche that there are two kinds of classicism, the static and the dynamic. Shakespeare is the classic of motion.

What I mean by classical in verse, then, is this. That even in the most imaginative flights there is always a holding back, a reservation. The classical poet never forgets this finiteness, this limit of man. He remembers always that he is mixed up with earth. He may jump, but he always returns back; he never flies away into the circumambient gas.

You might say if you wished that the whole of the romantic attitude seems to crystallise in verse round metaphors of flight. Hugo is always flying, flying over abysses, flying up into the eternal gases. The word infinite in every other line.

In the classical attitude you never seem to swing right along to the infinite nothing. If you say an extravagant thing which does exceed the limits inside which you know man to be fastened, yet there is always conveyed in some way at the end an impression of yourself standing outside it, and not quite believing it, or consciously putting it forward as a flourish. You never go blindly into an atmosphere more than the truth, an atmosphere too rarefied for man to breathe for long. You are always faithful to the conception of a limit. It is a question of pitch; in romantic verse you move at a certain pitch of rhetoric which you know, man being what he is, to be a little highfalutin. The kind of thing you get in Hugo or Swinburne. In the coming classical reaction that will feel just wrong. For an example of the opposite thing, a verse written in the proper classical spirit, I can take the song from *Cymbeline* beginning with "Fear no more the heat of the sun." I am just using this as a parable. I don't quite mean what I say here. Take the last two lines:

Golden lads and girls all must,
Like chimney sweepers come to dust.

Now, no romantic would have ever written that. Indeed, so ingrained is romanticism, so objectionable is this to it, that people have asserted that these were not part of the original song.

Apart from the pun, the thing that I think quite classical is the word lad. Your modern romantic could never write that. He would have to write golden youth, and take up the thing at least a couple of notes in pitch.

I want now to give the reasons which make me think that we are nearing the end of the romantic movement.

The first lies in the nature of any convention or tradition in art. A particular convention or attitude in art has a strict analogy to the phenomena of organic life. It grows old and decays. It has a definite period of life and must die. All the possible tunes get played on it and then it is exhausted; moreover its best period is its youngest. Take the case of the extraordinary efflorescence of verse in the Elizabethan period. All kinds of reasons have been given for this—the discovery of the new world and all the rest of it. There is a much simpler one. A new medium had been given them to play with—namely, blank verse. It was new and so it was easy to play new tunes on it.

The same law holds in other arts. All the masters of painting are born into the world at a time when the particular tradition from which they start is imperfect. The Florentine tradition was just short of full ripeness when Raphael came to Florence, the Bellinesque was still young when Titian was born in Venice. Landscape was still a toy or an appanage of figure-painting when Turner and Constable arose to reveal its independent power. When Turner and Constable had done with landscape they left little or nothing for their successors to do on the same lines. Each field of artistic activity is exhausted by the first great artist who gathers a full harvest from it.

This period of exhaustion seems to me to have been reached in romanticism. We shall not get any new efflorescence of verse until we get a new technique, a new convention, to turn ourselves loose in.

Objection might be taken to this. It might be said that a century as an organic unity doesn't exist, that I am being deluded by a wrong metaphor, that I am treating a collection of literary people as if they were an organism or state department. Whatever we may be in other things, an objector might urge, in literature in as far as we are anything at all—in as far as we are worth considering—we are individuals, we are persons, and as distinct persons we cannot be subordinated to any general treatment. At any period at any time, an individual poet may be a classic or a romantic just as he feels like it. You at any particular moment may think that you can stand outside a movement. You may think that as an individual you observe both the classic and the romantic spirit and decide from a purely detached point of view that one is superior to the other.

The answer to this is that no one, in a matter of judgment of beauty, can take a detached standpoint in this way. Just as physically you are not born that abstract entity, man, but the child of particular parents, so you are in matters of literary judgment. Your opinion is almost entirely of the literary history that came just before you, and you are governed by that whatever you may think. Take Spinoza's example of a stone falling to the ground. If it had a conscious mind it would, he said, think it was going to the ground because it wanted to. So you with your pretended free judgment about what is and what is not beautiful. The amount of freedom in man is much exaggerated. That we are free on certain rare occasions, both my religion and the views I get from metaphysics convince me. But many acts which we habitually label free are in reality automatic. It is quite possible for a man to write a book almost automatically. I have read several such products. Some observations were recorded more than twenty years ago by Robertson on reflex speech, and he found that in certain cases of dementia, where the people were quite unconscious so far as the exercise of reasoning went, that very intelligent answers were given to a succession of questions on politics and such matters. The meaning of these questions could not possibly have been understood. Language here acted after the manner of a reflex. So that certain extremely complex mechanisms, subtle enough to imitate beauty, can work by themselves—I certainly think that this is the case with judgments about beauty.

I can put the same thing in slightly different form. Here is a question of a conflict of two attitudes, as it might be of two techniques. The critic, while he has to admit that changes from one to the other occur, persists in regarding them as mere variations to a certain fixed normal, just as a pendulum might swing. I admit the analogy of the pendulum as far as movement, but I deny the further consequence of the analogy, the existence of the point of rest, the normal point.

When I say that I dislike the romantics, I dissociate two things: the part of them in which they resemble all the great poets, and the part in which they differ and which gives them their character as romantics. It is this minor element which constitutes the particular note of a century, and which, while it excites contemporaries, annoys the next generation. It was precisely that quality in Pope which pleased his friends, which we detest. Now, anyone just before the romantics who felt that, could have predicted that a change was coming. It seems to me that we stand just in the same position now. I think that there is an increasing proportion of people who simply can't stand Swinburne.

When I say that there will be another classical revival I don't necessarily anticipate a return to Pope. I say merely that now is the time for such a revival. Given people of the necessary capacity, it may be a vital thing; without them we may get a formalism something like Pope. When it does come we may not even recognise it as classical. Although it will be classical it will be different because it has passed through a romantic period. To take a parallel example: I remember being very surprised, after seeing the Post Impressionists, to find in Maurice Denis's account of the matter that they consider themselves classical in the sense that they were trying to impose the same order on the mere flux of new material provided by the impressionist movement, that existed in the more limited materials of the painting before.

There is something now to be cleared away before I get on with my argument, which is that while romanticism is dead in reality, yet the critical attitude appropriate to it still continues to exist. To make this a little clearer: For every kind of verse, there is a corresponding receptive attitude. In a romantic period we demand from verse certain qualities. In a classical period we demand others. At the present time I should say that this receptive attitude has outlasted the thing from which it was formed. But while the romantic tradition has run dry, yet the critical attitude of mind, which demands romantic qualities from verse, still survives. So that if good classical verse were to be written to-morrow very few people would be able to stand it.

I object even to the best of the romantics. I object still more to the receptive attitude. I object to the sloppiness which doesn't consider that a poem is a poem unless it is moaning or whining about something or other. I always think in this connection of the last line of a poem of John Webster's which ends with a request I cordially endorse:

> End your moan and come away.

The thing has got so bad now that a poem which is all dry and hard, a properly classical poem, would not be considered poetry at all. How many people now can lay their hands on their hearts and say they like either Horace or Pope? They feel a kind of chill when they read them.

The dry hardness which you get in the classics is absolutely repugnant to them. Poetry that isn't damp isn't poetry at all. They cannot see that accurate description is a legitimate object of verse. Verse to them always means a bringing in of some of the emotions that are grouped round the word infinite.

The essence of poetry to most people is that it must lead them to a beyond of some kind. Verse strictly confined to the earthly and the definite (Keats is full of it) might seem to them to be excellent writing, excellent craftsmanship, but not poetry. So much has romanticism debauched us, that, without some form of vagueness, we deny the highest.

In the classic it is always the light of ordinary day, never the light that never was on land or sea. It is always perfectly human and never exaggerated: man is always man and never a god.

But the awful result of romanticism is that, accustomed to this strange light, you can never live without it. Its effect on you is that of a drug.

There is a general tendency to think that verse means little else than the expression of unsatisfied emotion. People say: "But how can you have verse without sentiment?" You see what it is: the prospect alarms them. A classical revival to them would mean the prospect of an arid desert and the death of poetry as they understand it, and could only come to fill the gap caused by that death. Exactly why this dry classical spirit should have a positive and legitimate necessity to express itself in poetry is utterly inconceivable to them. What this positive need is, I shall show later. It follows from the fact that there is another quality, not the emotion produced, which is at the root of excellence in verse. Before I get to this I am concerned with a negative thing, a theoretical point, a prejudice that stands in the way and is really at the bottom of this reluctance to understand classical verse.

It is an objection which ultimately I believe comes from a bad metaphysic of art. You are unable to admit the existence of beauty without the infinite being in some way or another dragged in.

I may quote for purposes of argument, as a typical example of this kind of attitude made vocal, the famous chapters in Ruskin's *Modern Painters,* Vol. II, on the imagination. I must say here, parenthetically, that I use this word without prejudice to the other discussion with which I shall end the paper. I only use the word here because it is Ruskin's word. All that I am concerned with just now is the attitude behind it, which I take to be the romantic.

> Imagination cannot but be serious; she sees too far, too darkly, too solemnly, too earnestly, ever to smile. There is something in the heart of everything, if we can reach it, that we shall not be inclined to laugh at. . . . Those who have so pierced and seen the melancholy deeps of things, are filled with intense passion and gentleness of sympathy. (Part III, Chap. III, § 9.)
>
> There is in every word set down by the imaginative mind an awful undercurrent of meaning, and evidence and shadow upon it of the deep places out of which it has come. It is often obscure, often half-told; for he who wrote it, in his clear seeing of the things beneath, may have been impatient of detailed interpretation; for if we choose to dwell upon it and trace it, it will lead us always securely back to that metropolis of the soul's dominion from which we may follow out all the ways and tracks to its farthest coasts. (Part III, Chap. III, § 5.)

Really in all these matters the act of judgment is an instinct, an absolutely unstateable thing akin to the art of the tea taster. But you must talk, and the only language you can use in this matter is that of analogy. I have no material clay to mould to the given shape; the only thing which one has for the purpose, and which acts as a substitute for it, a kind of mental clay, are certain metaphors modified into theories of æsthetic and rhetoric. A combination of these, while it cannot state the essentially unstateable intuition, can yet give you a sufficient analogy to enable you to see what it was and to recognise it on condition that you yourself have been in a similar state. Now these phrases of Ruskin's convey quite clearly to me his taste in the matter.

I see quite clearly that he thinks the best verse must be serious. That is a natural attitude for a man in the romantic period. But he is not content with saying that he prefers this kind of verse. He wants to deduce his opinion like his master, Coleridge, from some fixed principle which can be found by metaphysic.

Here is the last refuge of this romantic attitude. It proves itself to be not an attitude but a deduction from a fixed principle of the cosmos.

One of the main reasons for the existence of philosophy is not that it enables you to find truth (it can never do that) but that it does provide you a refuge for definitions. The usual idea of the thing is that it provides you with a fixed basis from which you can deduce the things you want in æsthetics. The process is the exact contrary. You start in the confusion of the fighting line, you retire from that just a little to the rear to recover, to get your weapons right. Quite plainly, without metaphor this—it provides you with an elaborate and precise language in which you really can explain definitely what you mean, but what you want to say is decided by other things. The ultimate reality is the hurly-burly, the struggle; the metaphysic is an adjunct to clear-headedness in it.

To get back to Ruskin and his objection to all that is not serious. It seems to me that involved in this is a bad metaphysical æsthetic. You have the metaphysic which in defining beauty or the nature of art always drags in the infinite. Particularly in Germany, the land where theories of æsthetics were first created, the romantic æsthetes collated all beauty to an impression of the infinite involved in the identification of our being in absolute spirit. In the least element of beauty we have a total intuition of the whole world. Every artist is a kind of pantheist.

Now it is quite obvious to anyone who holds this kind of theory that any poetry which confines itself to the finite can never be of the highest kind. It seems a contradiction in terms to them. And as in metaphysics you get the last refuge of a prejudice, so it is now necessary for me to refute this.

Here follows a tedious piece of dialectic, but it is necessary for my purpose. I must avoid two pitfalls in discussing the idea of beauty. On the one hand there is the old classical view which is supposed to define it as lying in conformity to certain standard fixed forms; and on the other hand there is the romantic view which drags in the infinite. I have got to find a metaphysic between these two which will enable me to hold consistently that a neo-classic verse of the type I have indicated involves no contradiction in terms. It is essential to prove that beauty may be in small, dry things.

The great aim is accurate, precise and definite decription. The first thing is to recognise how extraordinarily difficult this is. It is no mere matter of carefulness; you have to use language, and language is by its very nature a communal thing; that is, it expresses never the exact thing but a compromise—that which is common to you, me and everybody. But each man sees a little differently, and to get out clearly and exactly what he does see, he must have a terrific struggle with language, whether it be with words or the technique of other arts. Language has its own special nature, its own conventions and communal ideas. It is only by a concentrated effort of the mind that you can hold it fixed to your own purpose. I always think that the fundamental process at the back of all the arts might be represented by the following metaphor. You know what I call architect's curves—flat pieces of wood with all different kinds of curvature. By a suitable selection from these you can draw approximately any curve you like. The artist I take to be the man who simply can't bear the idea of that "approximately." He will get the exact curve of what he sees whether it be an object or an idea in the mind. I shall here have to change my metaphor a little to get the process in his mind. Suppose that instead of your curved pieces of wood you have a springy piece of steel of the same types of curvature as the wood. Now the state of tension or concentration of mind, if he is doing anything really good in this struggle against the ingrained habit of the technique, may be represented by a man employing all his fingers to bend the steel out of its own curve and into the exact curve which you want. Something different to what it would assume naturally.

There are then two things to distinguish, first the particular faculty of mind to see things as they really are, and apart from the conventional ways in which you have been trained to see them. This is itself rare enough in all consciousness. Second, the concentrated state of mind, the grip over oneself which is necessary in the actual expression of what one sees. To prevent one falling into the conventional curves of ingrained technique, to hold on through infinite detail and trouble to the exact curve you want. Wherever you get this sincerity, you get the fundamental quality of good art without dragging in infinite or serious.

I can now get at that positive fundamental quality of verse which constitutes excellence, which has nothing to do with infinity, with mystery or with emotions.

This is the point I aim at, then, in my argument. I prophesy that a period of dry, hard, classical verse is coming. I have met the preliminary objection founded on the bad romantic æsthetic that in such verse, from which the infinite is excluded, you cannot have the essence of poetry at all.

After attempting to sketch out what this positive quality is, I can get on to the end of my paper in this way: That where you get this quality exhibited in the realm of the emotions you get imagination, and that where you get this quality exhibited in the contemplation of finite things you get fancy.

In prose as in algebra concrete things are embodied in signs or counters which are moved about according to rules, without being visualised at all in the process. There are in prose certain type situations and arrangements of words, which move as automatically into certain other arrangements as do functions in algebra. One only changes the X's and the Y's back into physical things at the end of the process. Poetry, in one aspect at any rate, may be considered as an effort to avoid this characteristic of prose. It is not a counter language, but a visual concrete one. It is a compromise for a language of intuition which would hand over sensations bodily. It always endeavours to arrest you, and to make you continuously see a physical thing, to prevent you gliding through an abstract process. It chooses fresh epithets and fresh metaphors, not so much because they are new, and we are tired of the old, but because the old cease to convey a physical thing and become abstract counters. A poet says a ship "coursed the seas" to get a physical image, instead of the counter word "sailed." Visual meanings can only be transferred by the new bowl of metaphor; prose is an old pot that lets them leak out. Images in verse are not mere decoration, but the very essence of an intuitive language. Verse is a pedestrian taking you over the ground, prose—a train which delivers you at a destination.

I can now get on to a discussion of two words often used in this connection, "fresh" and "unexpected." You praise a thing for being "fresh." I understand what you mean, but the word besides conveying the truth conveys a secondary something which is certainly false. When you say a poem or drawing is fresh, and so good, the impression is somehow conveyed that the essential element of goodness is freshness, that it is good because it is fresh. Now this is certainly wrong, there is nothing particularly desirable about freshness *per se*. Works of art aren't eggs. Rather the contrary. It is simply an unfortunate necessity due to the nature of language and technique that the only way the element which does constitute goodness, the only way in which its presence can be detected externally, is by freshness. Freshness convinces you, you feel at once that the artist was in an actual physical state. You feel that for a minute. Real communication is so very rare, for plain speech is unconvincing. It is in this rare fact of communication that you get the root of æsthetic pleasure.

I shall maintain that wherever you get an extraordinary interest in a thing, a great zest in its contemplation which carries on the contemplator to accurate description in the sense of the word accurate I have just analysed, there you have sufficient justification for poetry. It must be an intense zest which heightens a thing out of the level of prose. I am using contemplation here just in the same way that Plato used it, only applied to a different subject; it is a detached interest. "The object of æsthetic contemplation is something framed apart by itself and regarded without memory or expectation, simply as being itself, as end not means, as individual not universal."

To take a concrete example. I am taking an extreme case. If you are walking behind a woman in the street, you notice the curious way in which the skirt rebounds from her heels. If that peculiar kind of motion becomes of such interest to you that you will search about until you can get the exact epithet which hits it off, there you have a properly æsthetic emotion. But it is the zest with which you look at the thing which decides you to make the effort. In this sense the feeling that was in Herrick's mind, when he wrote "the tempestuous petticoat" was exactly the same as that which in bigger and vaguer matters makes the best romantic verse. It doesn't matter an atom that the emotion produced is not of dignified vagueness, but on the contrary amusing; the point is that exactly the same activity is at work as in the highest verse. That is the avoidance of conventional language in order to get the exact curve of the thing.

I have still to show that in the verse which is to come, fancy will be the necessary weapon of the classical school. The positive quality I have talked about can be manifested in ballad verse by extreme directness and simplicity, such as you get in *On Fair Kirkconnel Lea*. But the particular verse we are going to get will be cheerful, dry and sophisticated, and here the necessary weapon of the positive quality must be fancy.

Subject doesn't matter; the quality in it is the same as you get in the more romantic people.

It isn't the scale or kind of emotion produced that decides, but this one fact: Is there any real zest in it? Did the poet have an actually realised visual object before him in which he delighted? It doesn't matter if it were a lady's shoe or the starry heavens.

Fancy is not mere decoration added on to plain speech. Plain speech is essentially inaccurate. It is only by new metaphors, that is, by fancy, that it can be made precise.

When the analogy has not enough connection with the thing described to be quite parallel with it, where it overlays the thing it described and there is a certain excess, there you have the play of fancy—that I grant is inferior to imagination.

But where the analogy is every bit of it necessary for accurate description in the sense of the word accurate I have previously described, and your only objection to this kind of fancy is that it is not serious in the effect it produces, then I think the objection to be entirely invalid. If it is sincere in the accurate sense, when the whole of the analogy is necessary to get out the exact curve of the feeling or thing you want to express—there you seem to me to have the highest verse, even though the subject be trivial and the emotions of the infinite far away.

It is very difficult to use any terminology at all for this kind of thing. For whatever word you use is at once sentimentalised. Take Coleridge's word "vital." It is used loosely by all kinds of people who talk about art, to mean something vaguely and mysteriously significant. In fact, vital and mechanical is to them exactly the same antithesis as between good and bad.

Nothing of the kind; Coleridge uses it in a perfectly definite and what I call dry sense. It is just this: A mechanical complexity is the sum of its parts. Put them side by side and you get the whole. Now vital or organic is merely a convenient metaphor for a complexity of a different kind, that in which the parts cannot be said to be elements as each one is modified by the other's presence, and each one to a certain extent is the whole. The leg of a chair by itself is still a leg. My leg by itself wouldn't be.

Now the characteristic of the intellect is that it can only represent complexities of the mechanical kind. It can only make diagrams, and diagrams are essentially things whose parts are separate one from another. The intellect always analyses—when there is a synthesis it is baffled. That is why the artist's work seems mysterious. The intellect can't represent it. This is a necessary consequence of the particular nature of the intellect and the purposes for which it is formed. It doesn't mean that your synthesis is ineffable, simply that it can't be definitely stated.

Now this is all worked out in Bergson, the central feature of his whole philosophy. It is all based on the clear conception of these vital complexities which he calls "intensive" as opposed to the other kind which he calls "extensive," and the recognition of the fact that the intellect can only deal with the extensive multiplicity. To deal with the intensive you must use intuition.

Now, as I said before, Ruskin was perfectly aware of all this, but he had no such metaphysical background which would enable him to state definitely what he meant. The result is that he has to flounder about in a series of metaphors. A powerfully imaginative mind seizes and combines at the same instant all the important ideas of its poem or picture, and while it works with one of them, it is at the same instant working with and modifying all in their relation to it and never losing sight of their bearings on each other—as the motion of a snake's body goes through all parts at once and its volition acts at the same instant in coils which go contrary ways.

A romantic movement must have an end of the very nature of the thing. It may be deplored, but it can't be helped—wonder must cease to be wonder.

I guard myself here from all the consequences of the analogy, but it expresses at any rate the inevitableness of the process. A literature of wonder must have an end as inevitably as a strange land loses its strangeness when one lives in it. Think of the lost ecstasy of the Elizabethans. "Oh my America, my new found land," think of what it meant to them and of what it means to us. Wonder can only be the attitude of a man passing from one stage to another, it can never be a permanently fixed thing.

THE MAKING OF A POEM

(1946)

STEPHEN SPENDER

Apology

IT WOULD be inexcusable to discuss my own way of writing poetry unless I were able to relate this to a wider view of the problems which poets attempt to solve when they sit down at a desk or table to write, or walk around composing their poems in their heads. There is a danger of my appearing to put across my own experiences as the general rule, when every poet's way of going about his work and his experience of being a poet are different, and when my own poetry may not be good enough to lend my example any authority.

Yet the writing of poetry is an activity which makes certain demands of attention on the poet and which requires that he should have certain qualifications of ear, vision, imagination, memory and so on. He should be able to think in images, he should have as great a mastery of language as a painter has over his palette, even if the range of his language be very limited. All this means that, in ordinary society, a poet has to adapt himself, more or less consciously, to the demands of his vocation, and hence the peculiarities of poets and the condition of inspiration which many people have said is near to madness. One poet's example is only his adaptation of his personality to the demands of poetry, but if it is clearly stated it may help us to understand other poets, and even something of poetry.

Today we lack very much a whole view of poetry, and have instead many one-sided views of certain aspects of poetry which have been advertised as the only aims which poets should attempt. Movements such as free verse, imagism, surrealism, expressionism, personalism and so on, tend to make people think that poetry is simply a matter of not writing in metre of rhyme, or of free association, or of thinking in images, or of a kind of drawing room madness (surrealism) which corresponds to drawing room communism. Here is a string of ideas: Night, dark, stars, immensity, blue, voluptuous, clinging, columns, clouds, moon, sickle, harvest, vast camp fire, hell. Is this poetry? A lot of strings of words almost as simple as this are set down on the backs of envelopes and posted off to editors or to poets by the vast army of amateurs who think that to be illogical is to be poetic, with that fond question. Thus I hope that this discussion of how poets work will imply a wider and completer view of poets.

Concentration

The problem of creative writing is essentially one of concentration, and the supposed eccentricities of poets are usually due to mechanical habits or rituals developed in order to concentrate. Concentration, of course, for the purposes of writing poetry, is different from the kind of concentration required for working out a sum. It is a focussing of the attention in a special way, so that the poet is aware of all the implications and possible developments of his idea, just as one might say that a plant was not concentrating on developing mechanically in one direction, but in many directions, towards the warmth and light with its leaves, and towards the water with its roots, all at the same time.

Schiller liked to have a smell of rotten apples, concealed beneath the lid of his desk, under his nose when he was composing poetry. Walter de la Mare has told me that he must smoke when writing. Auden drinks endless cups of tea. Coffee is my own addiction, besides smoking a great deal, which I hardly ever do except when I am writing. I notice also that as I attain a greater concentration, this tends to make me forget the taste of the cigarette in my mouth, and then I have a desire to smoke two or even three cigarettes at a time, in order that the sensation from the outside may penetrate through the wall of concentration which I have built round myself.

For goodness sake, though, do not think that rotten apples or cigarettes or tea have anything to do with the quality of the work of a Schiller, a de la Mare, or an Auden. They are a part of a concentration which has already been attained rather than the causes of concentration. De la Mare once said to me that he thought the desire to smoke when writing poetry arose from a need, not of a stimulus, but to canalize a distracting leak of his attention away from his writing towards the distraction which is always present in one's environment. Concentration may be disturbed by someone whistling in the street or the ticking of a clock. There is always a slight tendency of the body to sabotage the attention of the mind by providing some distraction. If this need for distraction can be directed into one channel—such as the odor of rotten apples or the taste of tobacco or tea—then other distractions outside oneself are put out of competition.

Another possible explanation is that the concentrated effort of writing poetry is a spiritual activity which makes one completely forget, for the time being, that one has a body. It is a disturbance of the balance of body and mind and for this reason one needs a kind of anchor of sensation with the physical world. Hence the craving for a scent or taste or even, sometimes, for sexual activity. Poets speak of the necessity of writing poetry rather than of a liking for doing it. It is spiritual compulsion, a straining of the mind to attain heights surrounded by abysses and it cannot be entirely happy, for in the most important sense, the only reward worth having is absolutely denied: for, however confident a poet may be, he is never quite sure that all his energy is not misdirected nor that what he is writing is great poetry. At the moment when art attains its highest attainment it reaches beyond its medium of words or paints or music, and the artist finds himself realizing that these instruments are inadequate to the spirit of what he is trying to say.

Different poets concentrate in different ways. In my own mind I make a sharp distinction between two types of concentration: one is immediate and complete, the other is plodding and only completed by stages. Some poets write immediately works which, when they are written, scarcely need revision. Others write their poems by stages, feeling their way from rough draft to rough draft, until finally, after many revisions, they have produced a result which may seem to have very little connection with their early sketches.

These two opposite processes are vividly illustrated in two examples drawn from music: Mozart and Beethoven. Mozart thought out symphonies, quartets, even scenes from operas, entirely in his head—often on a journey or perhaps while dealing with pressing problems—and then he transcribed them, in their completeness, onto paper. Beethoven wrote fragments of themes in note books which he kept beside him, working on and developing them over years. Often his first ideas were of a clumsiness which makes scholars marvel how he could, at the end, have developed from them such miraculous results.

Thus genius works in different ways to achieve its ends. But although the Mozartian type of genius is the more brilliant and dazzling, genius, unlike virtuosity, is judged by greatness of results, not by brilliance of performance. The result must be the fullest development in a created æsthetic form of an original moment of insight, and it does not matter whether genius devotes a lifetime to producing a small result if that result be immortal. The difference between two types of genius is that one type (the Mozartian) is able to plumb the greatest depths of his own experience by the tremendous effort of a moment, the other (the Beethovenian) must dig deeper and deeper into his consciousness, layer by layer. What counts in either case is the vision which sees and pursues and attains the end; the logic of the artistic purpose.

A poet may be divinely gifted with a lucid and intense and purposive intellect; he may be clumsy and slow; that does not matter, what matters is integrity of purpose and the ability to maintain the purpose without losing oneself. Myself, I am scarcely capable of immediate concentration in poetry. My mind is not clear, my will is weak, I suffer from an excess of ideas and a weak sense of form. For every poem that I begin to write, I think of at least ten which I do not write down at all. For every poem which I do write down, there are seven or eight which I never complete.

The method which I adopt therefore is to write down as many ideas as possible, in however rough a form, in note books (I have at least twenty of these, on a shelf beside my desk, going back over fifteen years). I then make use of some of the sketches and discard others.

The best way of explaining how I develop the rough ideas which I use, is to take an example. Here is a Notebook begun in 1944. About a hundred pages of it are covered with writing, and from this have emerged about six poems. Each idea, when it first occurs is given a number. Sometimes the ideas do not get beyond one line. For example No. 3 (never developed) is the one line:—

A language of flesh and roses.

I shall return to this line in a few pages, when I speak of inspiration. For the moment, I turn to No. 13, because here is an idea which has been developed to its conclusion. The first sketch begins thus:—

a) There are some days when the sea lies like a harp
Stretched flat beneath the cliffs. The waves
Like wires burn with the sun's copper glow
[*all the murmuring blue*
every silent]

Between whose spaces every image
Of sky [*field and*] hedge and field and boat
Dwells like the huge face of the afternoon.
[*Lies*]

When the heat grows tired, the afternoon
Out of the land may breathe a sigh
[*Across these wires like a hand. They vibrate*
With]
Which moves across those wires like a soft hand
[*Then the vibration*]
Between whose spaces the vibration holds
Every bird-cry, dog's bark, man-shout
And creak of rollock from the land and sky
With all the music of the afternoon.

Obviously these lines are attempts to sketch out an idea which exists clearly enough on some level of the mind where it yet eludes the attempt to state it. At this stage, a poem is like a face which one seems to be able to visualize clearly in the eye of memory, but when one examines it mentally or tries to think it out, feature by feature, it seems to fade.

The idea of this poem is a vision of the sea. The faith of the poet is that if this vision is clearly stated it will be significant. The vision is of the sea stretched under a cliff. On top of the cliff there are fields, hedges, houses. Horses draw carts along lanes, dogs bark far inland, bells ring in the distance. The shore seems laden with hedges, roses, horses and men, all high above the sea, on a very fine summer day when the ocean seems to reflect and absorb the shore. Then the small strung-out glittering waves of the sea lying under the shore are like the strings of a harp which catch the sunlight. Between these strings lies the reflection of the shore. Butterflies are wafted out over the waves, which they mistake for the fields of the chalky landscape, searching them for flowers. On a day such as this, the land, reflected in the sea, appears to enter into the sea, as though it lies under it, like Atlantis. The wires of the harp are like a seen music fusing seascape and landscape.

Looking at this vision in another way, it obviously has symbolic value. The sea represents death and eternity, the land represents the brief life of the summer and of one human generation which passes into the sea of eternity. But let me here say at once that although the poet may be conscious of this aspect of his vision, it is exactly what he wants to avoid stating, or even being too concerned with. His job is to recreate his vision, and let it speak its moral for itself. The poet must distinguish clearly in his own mind between that which most definitely must be said and that which must not be said. The unsaid inner meaning is revealed in the music and the tonality of the poem, and the poet is conscious of it in his knowledge that a certain tone of voice, a certain rhythm, are necessary.

In the next twenty versions of the poem I felt my way towards the clarification of the seen picture, the music and the inner feeling. In the first version quoted above there is the phrase in the second and third lines

The waves
Like wires burn with the sun's copper glow.

This phrase fuses the image of the sea with the idea of music, and it is therefore a key-phrase, because the theme of the poem is the fusion of the land with the sea. Here, then are several versions of these one and a quarter lines, in the order in which they were written:—

b) The waves are wires
Burning as with the secret song of fires

c) The day burns in the trembling wires
With a vast music golden in the eyes

d) The day glows on its trembling wires
Singing a golden music in the eyes

e) The day glows on its burning wires
Like waves of music golden to the eyes.

f) Afternoon burns upon its wires
Lines of music dazzling the eyes

g) Afternoon gilds its tingling wires
To a visual silent music of the eyes

In the final version, these two lines appear as in the following stanza:—

h) There are some days the happy ocean lies
Like an unfingered harp, below the land.

Afternoon gilds all the silent wires
Into a burning music of the eyes.

On mirroring paths between those fine-strung fires
The shore, laden with roses, horses, spires,
Wanders in water, imaged above ribbed sand.

Inspiration

The hard work evinced in these examples, which are only a fraction of the work put into the whole poem, may cause the reader to wonder whether there is no such thing as inspiration, or whether it is merely Stephen Spender who is uninspired. The answer is that everything in poetry is work except inspiration, whether this work is achieved at one swift stroke, as Mozart wrote his music, or whether it is a slow process of evolution from stage to stage. Here again, I have to qualify the word "work," as I qualified the word "concentration": the work on a line of poetry may take the form of putting a version aside for a few days, weeks or years, and then taking it up again, when it may be found that the line has, in the interval of time, almost rewritten itself.

Inspiration is the beginning of a poem and it is also its final goal. It is the first idea which drops into the poet's mind and it is the final idea which he at last achieves in words. In between this start and this winning post there is the hard race, the sweat and toil.[1]

Paul Valéry speaks of the *"une ligne donnée"* of a poem. One line is given to the poet by God or by nature, the rest he has to discover for himself.

My own experience of inspiration is certainly that of a line or a phrase or a word or sometimes something still vague, a dim cloud of an idea which I feel must be condensed into a shower of words. The peculiarity of the key word or line is that it does not merely attract, as, say, the word "braggadocio" attracts. It occurs in what seems to be an active, male, germinal form as though it were the

[1] See Rosamond E. M. Harding's *An Anatomy of Inspiration* (W. Heffer, 1948). See also *Poets at Work* (Harcourt, Brace, 1948). Compare with Allen Tate's "Narcissus as Narcissus," in *Reason In Madness* (Putnam's, 1941). [*Editor's note.*]

centre of a statement requiring a beginning and an end, and as though it had an impulse in a certain direction. Here are examples:—

A language of flesh and roses

This phrase (not very satisfactory in itself) brings to my mind a whole series of experiences and the idea of a poem which I shall perhaps write some years hence. I was standing in the corridor of a train passing through the Black Country. I saw a landscape of pits and pitheads, artificial mountains, jagged yellow wounds in the earth, everything transformed as though by the toil of an enormous animal or giant tearing up the earth in search of prey or treasure. Oddly enough, a stranger next to me in the corridor echoed my inmost thought. He said: "Everything there is man-made." At this moment the line flashed into my head

A language of flesh and roses.

The sequence of my thought was as follows: the industrial landscape which seems by now a routine and act of God which enslaves both employers and workers who serve and profit by it, is actually the expression of man's will. Men willed it to be so, and the pitheads, slagheaps and the ghastly disregard of anything but the pursuit of wealth, are a symbol of modern man's mind. In other words, the world which we create—the world of slums and telegrams and newspapers—is a kind of language of our inner wishes and thoughts. Although this is so, it is obviously a language which has got outside our control. It is a confused language, an irresponsible senile gibberish. This thought greatly distressed me, and I started thinking that if the phenomena created by humanity are really like words in a language, what kind of language do we really aspire to? All this sequence of thought flashed into my mind with the answer which came before the question: *A language of flesh and roses.*

I hope this example will give the reader some idea of what I mean by inspiration. Now the line, which I shall not repeat again, is a way of thinking imaginatively. If the line embodies some of the ideas which I have related above, these ideas must be further made clear in other lines. That is the terrifying challenge of poetry. Can I think out the logic of images? How easy it is to explain here the poem that I would have liked to write! How difficult it would be to write it. For writing it would imply living my way through the imaged experience of all these ideas, which here are mere abstractions, and such an effort of imaginative experience requires a lifetime of patience and watching.

Here is an example of a cloudy form of thought germinated by the word *cross,* which is the key word of the poem which exists formlessly in my mind. Recently my wife had a son. On the first day that I visited her after the boy's birth, I went by bus to the hospital. Passing through the streets on the top of the bus, they all seemed very clean, and the thought occurred to me that everything was prepared for our child. Past generations have toiled so that any child born today inherits, with his generation, cities, streets, organization, the most elaborate machinery for living. Everything has been provided for him by people dead long before he was born. Then, naturally enough, sadder thoughts colored this picture for me, and I reflected how he also inherited vast maladjustments, vast human wrongs. Then I thought of the child as like a pin-point of present existence, the moment incarnate, in whom the whole of the past, and all possible futures *cross*. This word *cross* somehow suggested the whole situation to me of a child born into the world and also of the form of a poem about his situation. When the word *cross* appeared in the poem, the idea of the past should give place to the idea of the future and it should be apparent that the *cross* in which present and future meet is the secret of an individual human existence. And here again, the unspoken secret which lies beyond the poem, the moral significance of other meanings of the word "cross" begins to glow with its virtue that should never be said and yet should shine through every image in the poem.

This account of inspiration is probably weak beside the accounts that other poets might give. I am writing of my own experience, and my own inspiration seems to me like the faintest flash of insight into the nature of reality beside that of other poets whom I can think of. However, it is possible that I describe here a kind of experience which, however slight it may be, is far truer to the real poetic experience than Aldous Huxley's account of how a young poet writes poetry in his novel *Time Must Have a Stop*. It is hard to imagine anything more self-conscious and unpoetic than Mr. Huxley's account.

Memory

If the art of concentrating in a particular way is the discipline necessary for poetry to reveal itself, memory exercised in a particular way is the natural gift of poetic genius. The poet, above all else, is a person who never forgets certain sense-impressions which he has experienced and which he can re-live again and again as though with all their original freshness.

All poets have this highly developed sensitive apparatus of memory, and they are usually aware of experiences which happened to them at the earliest age and which retain their pristine significance throughout life. The meeting of Dante and Beatrice when the poet was only nine years of age is the experience which became a symbol in Dante's mind around which the *Divine Comedy* crystallized. The experience of nature which forms the subject of Wordsworth's poetry was an extension of a childhood vision of "natural presences" which surrounded the boy Wordsworth. And his decision in later life to live in the Lake District was a decision to return to the scene of these childhood memories which were the most important experiences in his poetry. There is evidence for the importance of this kind of memory in all the creative arts, and the argument certainly applies to prose which is creative. Sir Osbert Sitwell has told me that his book *Before the Bombardment,* which contains an extremely civilized and satiric account of the social life of Scarborough before and during the last war, was based on his observations of life in that resort before he had reached the age of twelve.

It therefore is not surprising that although I have no memory for telephone numbers, addresses, faces and where I have put this morning's correspondence, I have a perfect memory for the sensation of certain experiences which are crystallized for me around certain associations. I could demonstrate this from my own life by the overwhelming nature of associations which, suddenly aroused, have carried me back so completely into the past, particularly into my childhood, that I have lost all sense of the present time and place. But the best proofs of this power of memory are found in the odd lines of poems written in note books fifteen years ago. A few fragments of unfinished poems enable me to enter immediately into the experiences from which they were derived, the circumstances in which they were written, and the unwritten feelings in the poem that were projected but never put into words.

> . . . Knowledge of a full sun
> That runs up his big sky, above
> The hill, then in those trees and throws
> His smiling on the turf.

That is an incomplete idea of fifteen years ago, and I remember exactly a balcony of a house facing a road, and, on the other side of the road, pine trees, beyond which lay the sea. Every morning the sun sprang up, first of all above the horizon of the sea, then it climbed to the tops of the trees and shone on my window. And this memory connects with the sun that shines through my window in London now in spring and early summer. So that the memory is not exactly a memory. It is more like one prong upon which a whole calendar of similar experiences happening throughout years collect. A memory once clearly stated ceases to be a memory, it becomes perpetually present, because every time we experience something which recalls it, the clear and lucid original experience imposes its formal beauty on the new experiences. It is thus no longer a memory but an experience lived through again and again.

Turning over these old note books, my eye catches some lines, in a projected long poem, which immediately re-shape themselves into the following short portrait of a woman's face:—

> Her eyes are gleaming fish
> Caught in her nervous face, as if in a net.

Her hair is wild and fair, haloing her cheeks
Like a fantastic flare of Southern sun.
There is madness in her cherishing her children.
Sometimes, perhaps a single time in years,
Her wandering fingers stoop to arrange some flowers—
Then in her hands her whole life stops and weeps.

It is perhaps true to say that memory is the faculty of poetry, because the imagination itself is an exercise of memory. There is nothing we imagine which we do not already know. And our ability to imagine is our ability to remember what we have already once experienced and to apply it to some different situation. Thus the greatest poets are those with memories so great that they extend beyond their strongest experiences to their minutest observations of people and things far outside their own self-centredness (the weakness of memory is its self-centredness: hence the narcissistic nature of most poetry).

Here I can detect my own greatest weakness. My memory is defective and self-centred. I lack the confidence in using it to create situations outside myself, although I believe that, in theory, there are very few situations in life which a poet should not be able to imagine, because it is a fact that most poets have experienced almost every situation in life. I do not mean by this that a poet who writes about a Polar Expedition has actually been to the North Pole. I mean, though, that he has been cold, hungry, etc., so that it is possible for him by remembering imaginatively his own felt experiences to know what it is like to explore the North Pole. That is where I fail. I cannot write about going to the North Pole.

Faith

It is evident that a faith in their vocation, mystical in intensity, sustains poets. There are many illustrations from the lives of poets to show this, and Shakespeare's sonnets are full of expressions of his faith in the immortality of his lines.

From my experience I can clarify the nature of this faith. When I was nine, we went to the Lake District, and there my parents read me some of the poems of Wordsworth. My sense of the sacredness of the task of poetry began then, and I have always felt that a poet's was a sacred vocation, like a saint's. Since I was nine, I have wanted to be various things, for example, Prime Minister (when I was twelve). Like some other poets I am attracted by the life of power and the life of action, but I am still more repelled by them. Power involves forcing oneself upon the attention of historians by doing things and occupying offices which are, in themselves, important, so that what is truly powerful is not the soul of a so-called powerful and prominent man but the position which he fills and the things which he does. Similarly, the life of "action" which seems so very positive is, in fact, a selective, even a negative kind of life. A man of action does one thing or several things because he does not do something else. Usually men who do very spectacular things fail completely to do the ordinary things which fill the lives of most normal people, and which would be far more heroic and spectacular perhaps, if they did not happen to be done by many people. Thus in practice the life of action has always seemed to me an act of cutting oneself off from life.

Although it is true that poets are vain and ambitious, their vanity and ambition is of the purest kind attainable in this world, for the saint renounces ambition. They are ambitious to be accepted for what they ultimately are as revealed by their inmost experiences, their finest perceptions, their deepest feelings, their uttermost sense of truth, in their poetry. They cannot cheat about these things, because the quality of their own being is revealed not in the noble sentiments which their poetry expresses, but in sensibility, control of language, rhythm and music, things which cannot be attained by a vote of confidence from an electorate, or by the office of Poet Laureate. Of course, work is tremendously important, but, in poetry, even the greatest labor can only serve to reveal the intrinsic qualities of soul of the poet as he really is.

Since there can be no cheating, the poet, like the saint, stands in all his works before the bar of a perpetual day of judgment. His vanity of course is pleased by success, though even success may contribute to his understanding that popularity does not confer on him the favorable judgment of all the ages which he seeks. For what does it mean to be praised by one's own age, which is soaked in crimes and stupidity, except perhaps that future ages, wise where we are foolish, will see him as a typical expression of this age's crimes and stupidity? Nor is lack of success a guarantee of great poetry, though there are some who pretend that it is. Nor can the critics, at any rate beyond a certain limited point of technical judgment, be trusted.

The poet's faith is therefore, firstly, a mystique of vocation, secondly, a faith in his own truth, combined with his own devotion to a task. There can really be no greater faith than the confidence that one is doing one's utmost to fulfil one's high vocation, and it is this that has inspired all the greatest poets. At the same time this faith is coupled with a deep humility because one knows that, ultimately, judgment does not rest with oneself. All one can do is to achieve nakedness, to be what one is with all one's faculties and perceptions, strengthened by all the skill which one can acquire, and then to stand before the judgment of time.

In my note books, I find the following Prose Poem, which expresses these thoughts:

> Bring me peace bring me power bring me assurance. Let me reach the bright day, the high chair, the plain desk, where my hand at last controls the words, where anxiety no longer undermines me. If I don't

reach these I'm thrown to the wolves, I'm a restless animal wandering from place to place, from experience to experience.

Give me the humility and the judgment to live alone with the deep and rich satisfaction of my own creating: not to be thrown into doubt by a word of spite or disapproval.

In the last analysis don't mind whether your work is good or bad so long as it has the completeness, the enormity of the whole world which you love.

Song

Inspiration and song are the irreducible final qualities of a poet which make his vocation different from all others. Inspiration is an experience in which a line or an idea is given to one, and perhaps also a state of mind in which one writes one's best poetry. Song is far more difficult to define. It is the music which a poem as yet unthought of will assume, the empty womb of poetry for ever in the poet's consciousness, waiting for the fertilizing seed.

Sometimes, when I lie in a state of half-waking half-sleeping, I am conscious of a stream of words which seem to pass through my mind, without their having a meaning, but they have a sound, a sound of passion, or a sound recalling poetry that I know. Again sometimes when I am writing, the music of the words I am trying to shape takes me far beyond the words, I am aware of a rhythm, a dance, a fury, which is as yet empty of words.

In these observations, I have said little about headaches, midnight oil, pints of beer or of claret, love affairs, and so on, which are supposed to be stations on the journeys of poets through life. There is no doubt that writing poetry, when a poem appears to succeed, results in an intense physical excitement, a sense of release and ecstasy. On the other hand, I dread writing poetry, for, I suppose, the following reasons: a poem is a terrible journey, a painful effort of concentrating the imagination; words are an extremely difficult medium to use, and sometimes when one has spent days trying to say a thing clearly one finds that one has only said it dully; above all, the writing of a poem brings one face to face with one's own personality with all its familiar and clumsy limitations. In every other phase of existence, one can exercise the orthodoxy of a conventional routine: one can be polite to one's friends, one can get through the day at the office, one can pose, one can draw attention to one's position in society, one is—in a word—dealing with men. In poetry, one is wrestling with a god.

Usually, when I have completed a poem, I think "this is my best poem," and I wish to publish it at once. This is partly because I only write when I have something new to say, which seems more worth while than what I have said before, partly because optimism about my present and future makes me despise my past. A few days after I have finished a poem, I relegate it to the past of all my other wasted efforts, all the books I do not wish to open.

Perhaps the greatest pleasure I have got from poems that I have written is when I have heard some lines quoted which I have not at once recognized. And I have thought "how good and how interesting," before I have realized that they are my own.

In common with other creative writers I pretend that I am not, and I am, exceedingly affected by unsympathetic criticism, whilst praise usually makes me suspect that the reviewer does not know what he is talking about. Why are writers so sensitive to criticism? Partly, because it is their business to be sensitive, and they are sensitive about this as about other things. Partly, because every serious creative writer is really in his heart concerned with reputation and not with success (the most successful writer I have known, Sir Hugh Walpole, was far and away the most unhappy about his reputation, because the "highbrows" did not like him). Again, I suspect that every writer is secretly writing for *someone,* probably for a parent or teacher who did not believe in him in childhood. The critic who refuses to "understand" immediately becomes identified with this person, and the understanding of many admirers only adds to the writer's secret bitterness if this one refusal persists.

Gradually one realizes that there is always this someone who will not like one's work. Then, perhaps, literature becomes a humble exercise of faith in being all that one can be in one's art, of being more than oneself, expecting little, but with a faith in the mystery of poetry which gradually expands into a faith in the mysterious service of truth.

Yet what failures there are! And how much mud sticks to one; mud not thrown by other people but acquired in the course of earning one's living, answering or not answering the letters which one receives, supporting or not supporting public causes. All one can hope is that this mud is composed of little grains of sand which will produce pearls.

POETRY: A NOTE IN ONTOLOGY

(1934)

JOHN CROWE RANSOM

A POETRY may be distinguished from a poetry by virtue of subject-matter, and subject-matter may be differentiated with respect to its ontology, or the reality of its being. An excellent variety of critical doctrine arises recently out of this differentiation, and thus perhaps criticism leans again upon ontological analysis as it was meant to do by Kant. The recent critics remark in effect that some poetry deals with things, while some other poetry deals with ideas. The two poetries will differ from each other as radically as a thing differs from an idea.

The distinction in the hands of critics is a fruitful one. There is apt to go along with it a principle of valuation, which is the consequence of a temperament, and therefore basic. The critic likes things and intends that his poet shall offer them; or likes ideas and intends that he shall offer them; and approves him as he does the one or the other. Criticism cannot well go much deeper than this. The critic has carried to the last terms his analysis of the stuff of which poetry is made, and valued it frankly as his temperament or his need requires him to value it.

So philosophical a critic seems to be highly modern. He is; but this critic as a matter of fact is peculiarly on one side of the question. (The implication is unfavorable to the other side of the question.) He is in revolt against the tyranny of ideas, and against the poetry which celebrates ideas, and which may be identified—so far as his usual generalization may be trusted—with the hateful poetry of the Victorians. His bias is in favor of the things. On the other hand the critic who likes Victorian verse, or the poetry of ideas, has probably not thought of anything of so grand a simplicity as electing between the things and the ideas, being apparently not quite capable of the ontological distinction. Therefore he does not know the real or constitutional ground of his liking, and may somewhat ingenuously claim that his predilection is for those poets who give him inspiration, or comfort, or truth, or honest metres, or something else equally "worth while." But Plato, who was not a modern, was just as clear as we are about the basic distinction between the ideas and the things, and yet stands far apart from the aforesaid conscious modern in passionately preferring the ideas over the things. The weight of Plato's testimony would certainly fall on the side of the Victorians, though they may scarcely have thought of calling him as their witness. But this consideration need not conclude the hearing.

I. PHYSICAL POETRY

The poetry which deals with things was much in favor a few years ago with the resolute body of critics. And the critics affected the poets. If necessary, they became the poets, and triumphantly illustrated the new mode. The Imagists were important figures in the history of our poetry, and they were both theorists and creators. It was their intention to present things in their thinginess, or *Dinge* in their *Dinglichkeit;* and to such an extent had the public lost its sense of *Dinglichkeit* that their redirection was wholesome. What the public was inclined to seek in poetry was ideas, whether large ones or small ones, grand ones or pretty ones, certainly ideas to live by and die by, but what the Imagists identified with the stuff of poetry was, simply, things.

Their application of their own principle was sufficiently heroic, though they scarcely consented to be as extreme in the practice as in the theory. They had artistic talent, every one of the original group, and it was impossible that they should make of poetry so simple an exercise as in doctrine they seemed to think it was. Yet Miss Lowell wrote a poem on *Thompson's Lunch Room, Grand Central Station;* it is admirable if its intention is to show the whole reach of her courage. Its detail goes like this:

> Jagged greenwhite bowls of pressed glass
> Rearing snow-peaks of chipped sugar
> Above the lighthouse-shaped castors
> Of gray pepper and gray-white salt.

For most of us as for the public idealist, with his "values," this is inconsequential. Unhappily it seems that the things as things do not necessarily interest us, and that in fact we are not quite constructed with the capacity for a disinterested interest. But it must be noted even here that the things are on their good behavior, looking rather well, and arranged by lines into something approaching a military formation. More technically, there is cross-imagery in the snow-peaks of sugar, and in the lighthouse-shaped castors, and cross-imagery involves association, and will presently involve dissociation and thinking. The metre is but a vestige, but even so it means something, for metre is a powerful intellectual determinant marshalling the words and, inevitably, the things. The *Dinglichkeit* of this Imagist specimen, or the realism, was therefore not pure. But it was nearer pure than the world was used to in poetry, and the exhibit was astonishing.

For the purpose of this note I shall give to such poetry, dwelling as exclusively as it dares upon physical things, the name Physical Poetry.

It is to stand opposite to that poetry which dwells as firmly as it dares upon ideas.

But perhaps thing *versus* idea does not seem to name an opposition precisely. Then we might phrase it a little differently: image *versus* idea. The idealistic philosophies are not sure that things exist, but they mean the equivalent when they refer to images. (Or they may consent to perceptions; or to impressions, following Hume, and following Croce, who remarks that they are pre-intellectual and independent of concepts. It is all the same, unless we are extremely technical.) It is sufficient if they concede that image is the raw material of idea. Though it may be an unwieldy and useless affair for the idealist as it stands, much needing to be licked into shape, nevertheless its relation to idea is that of a material cause, and it cannot be dispossessed of its priority.

It cannot be dispossessed of a primordial freshness, which idea can never claim. An idea is derivative and tamed. The image is in the natural or wild state, and it has to be discovered there, not put there, obeying its own law and none of ours. We think we can lay hold of image and take it captive, but the docile captive is not the real image but only the idea, which is the image with its character beaten out of it.

But we must be very careful: idealists are nothing if not dialectical. They object that an image in an original state of innocence is a delusion and cannot exist, that no image ever comes to us which does not imply the world of ideas, that there is "no percept without a concept." There is something in it. Every property discovered in the image is a universal property, and nothing discovered in the image is marvellous in kind though it may be pinned down historically or statistically as a single instance. But there is this to be understood too: the image which is not remarkable in any particular property is marvellous in its assemblage of many properties, a manifold of properties, like a mine or a field, something to be explored for the properties; yet science can manage the image, which is infinite in properties, only by equating it to the one property with which the science is concerned; for science at work is always *a science,* and committed to a special interest. It is not by refutation but by abstraction that science destroys the image. It means to get its "value" out of the image, and we may be sure that it has no use for the image in its original state of freedom. People who are engrossed with their pet "values" become habitual killers. Their game is the images, or the things, and they acquire the ability to shoot them as far off as they can be seen, and do. It is thus that we lose the power of imagination, or whatever faculty it is by which we are able to contemplate things as they are in their rich and contingent materiality. But our dreams reproach us, for in dreams they come alive again. Likewise our memory; which makes light of our science by recalling the images in their panoply of circumstance and with their morning freshness upon them.

It is the dream, the recollection, which compels us to poetry, and to deliberate æsthetic experience. It can hardly be argued, I think, that the arts are constituted automatically out of original images, and arise in some early age of innocence. (Though Croce seems to support this view, and to make art a pre-adult stage of experience.) Art is based on second love, not first love. In it we make a return to something which we had wilfully alienated. The child is occupied mostly with things, but it is because he is still unfurnished with systematic ideas, not because he is a ripe citizen by nature and comes along already trailing clouds of glory. Images are clouds of glory for the man who has discovered that ideas are a sort of darkness. Imagism, that is, the recent historical movement, may resemble a naïve poetry of mere things, but we can read the theoretical pronouncements of Imagists, and we can learn that Imagism is motivated by a distaste for the systematic abstractedness of thought. It presupposes acquaintance with science; that famous activity which is "constructive" with respect to the tools of our economic role in this world, and destructive with respect to nature. Imagists wish to escape from science by immersing themselves in images.

Not far off the simplicity of Imagism was, a little later, the subtler simplicity of Mr. George Moore's project shared with several others, in behalf of "pure poetry." In Moore's house on Ebury Street they talked about poetry, with an after-dinner warmth if not an early-morning discretion, and their tastes agreed almost perfectly and reinforced one another. The fruit of these conversations was the volume *Pure Poetry*. It must have been the most exclusive anthology of English poetry that had yet appeared, since its room was closed to all the poems that dallied visibly with ideas, so that many poems that had been coveted by all other anthologists do not appear there. Nevertheless the book is delicious, and something more deserves to be said for it.

First, that "pure poetry" is a kind of Physical Poetry. Its visible content is a thing-content. Technically, I suppose, it is effective in this character if it can exhibit its material in such a way that an image or set of images and not an idea must occupy the foreground of the reader's attention. Thus:

> Full fathom five thy father lies
> Of his bones are coral made.

Here it is difficult for anybody (except the perfect idealist who is always theoretically possible and who would expect to take a return from anything whatever) to receive any experience except that of a very distinct image, or set of images. It has the configuration of image, which consists in being sharp of edges, and the modality of image, which consists in being given and non-negotiable, and the density, which consists in being full, a plenum of qualities. What is to be done with it? It is pure exhibit; it is to be contemplated; perhaps it is to be enjoyed. The art of poetry depends more frequently on this faculty than on any other in its repertory; the faculty of presenting images so whole and clean that they resist the catalysis of thought.

And something else must be said, going in the opposite direction. "Pure poetry," all the same, is not as pure as it is claimed to be, though on the whole it is Physical Poetry. (All true poetry is a phase of Physical Poetry.) It is not as pure as Imagism is, or at least it is not as pure as Imagism would be if it lived up to its principles; and in fact it is significant that the volume does not contain any Imagist poems, which argues a difference in taste somewhere. Imagism may take trifling things for its material; presumably it will take the first things the poet encounters, since "importance" and "interest" are not primary qualities which a thing possesses but secondary or tertiary ones which the idealist attributes to it by virtue of his own requirements. "Pure poetry" as Moore conceives it, and as the lyrics of Poe and Shakespeare offer it, deals with the more dramatic materials, and here dramatic means human, or at least capable of being referred to the critical set of human interests. Employing this sort of material the poet cannot exactly intend to set the human economists in us actually into motion, but perhaps he does intend to comfort us with the fleeting sense that it is potentially our kind of material.

In the same way "pure poetry" is nicely metred, whereas Imagism was free. Technique is written on it. And by the way the anthology contains no rugged anonymous Scottish ballad either, and probably for a like reason; because it would not be technically finished. Now both Moore and de la Mare are accomplished conservative artists, and what they do or what they approve may be of limited range but it is sure to be technically admirable, and it is certain that they understand what technique in poetry is though they do not define it. Technique takes the thing-content and meters and orders it. Metre is not an original property of things. It is artificial, and conveys the sense of human control, even if it does not wish to impair the thinginess of the things. Metric is a science, and so far as we attend to it we are within the scientific atmosphere. Order is the logical arrangement of things. It involves the dramatic "form" which selects the things, and brings out their appropriate qualities, and carries them through a systematic course of predication until the total impression is a unit of logic and not merely a solid lump of thing-content. The "pure poems" which Moore admires are studied, though it would be fatal if they looked studious. A sustained effort of ideation effected these compositions. It is covered up, and communicates itself only on a subliminal plane of consciousness. But experienced readers are quite aware of it; they know at once what is the matter when they encounter a realism shamelessly passing for poetry, or a well-planned but blundering poetry.

As critics we should have every good will toward Physical Poetry: it is the basic constituent of any poetry. But the product is always something short of a pure or absolute existence, and it cannot quite be said that it consists of nothing but physical objects. The fact is that when we are more than usually satisfied with a Physical Poetry our analysis will probably disclose that it is more than usually impure.

II. PLATONIC POETRY

The poetry of ideas I shall denominate: Platonic Poetry. This also has grades of purity. A discourse which employed only abstract ideas with no images would be a scientific document and not a poem at all, not even a Platonic poem. Platonic Poetry dips heavily into the physical. If Physical Poetry tends to employ some ideation surreptitiously while still looking innocent of idea, Platonic Poetry more than returns the compliment, for it tries as hard as it can to look like Physical Poetry, as if it proposed to conceal its medicine, which is the idea to be propagated, within the sugar candy of objectivity and *Dinglichkeit*. As an instance, it is almost inevitable that I quote a famous Victorian utterance:

> The year's at the spring
> And day's at the morn;
> Morning's at seven;
> The hill side's dew-pearled;
> The lark's on the wing;
> The snail's on the thorn:
> God's in his heaven—
> All's right with the world!

which is a piece of transparent homiletics; for in it six pretty, co-ordinate images are marched, like six little lambs to the slaughter, to a colon and a powerful text. Now the exhibits of this poetry in the physical kind are always large, and may take more of the attention of the reader than is desired, but they are meant mostly to be illustrative of the ideas. It is on this ground that idealists like Hegel detect something unworthy, like a pedagogical trick, in poetry after all, and consider that the race will abandon it when it has outgrown its childishness and is enlightened.

The ablest arraignment of Platonic Poetry that I have seen, as an exercise which is really science but masquerades as poetry by affecting a concern for physical objects, is that of Mr. Allen Tate in a series of studies recently in *The New Republic*.[1] I will summarize. Platonic Poetry is allegory, a discourse in things, but on the understanding that

[1] "Three Types of Poetry." Reprinted in *Reactionary Essays* (1936). Reprinted in *On the Limits of Poetry* (1948). [*Editor's Note.*]

they are translatable at every point into ideas. (The usual ideas are those which constitute the popular causes, patriotic, religious, moral, or social.) Or Platonic Poetry is the elaboration of ideas as such, but in proceeding introduces for ornament some physical properties after the style of Physical Poetry; which is rhetoric. It is positive when the poet believes in the efficacy of the ideas. It is negative when he despairs of their efficacy, because they have conspicuously failed to take care of him, and utters his personal wail:

I fall upon the thorns of life! I bleed!

This is "Romantic Irony," which comes at occasional periods to interrupt the march of scientific optimism. But it still falls under the category of Platonism; it generally proposes some other ideas to take the place of those which are in vogue.

But why Platonism? To define Platonism we must remember that it is not the property of the historical person who reports dialogues about it in an Academy, any more than "pure poetry" is the property of the talkers who describe it from a house on Ebury Street. Platonism, in the sense I mean, is the name of an impulse that is native to us all, frequent, tending to take a too complete possession of our minds. Why should the spirit of mortal be proud? The chief explanation is that modern mortal is probably a Platonist. We are led to believe that nature is rational and that by the force of reasoning we shall possess it. I have read upon high authority: "Two great forces are persistent in Plato: the love of truth and zeal for human improvement." The forces are one force. We love to view the world under universal or scientific ideas to which we give the name truth; and this is because the ideas seem to make not for righteousness but for mastery. The Platonic view of the world is ultimately the predatory, for it reduces to the scientific, which we know. The Platonic Idea becomes the Logos which science worships, which is the Occidental God, whose minions we are, and whose children, claiming a large share in His powers for patrimony.

Now the fine Platonic world of ideas fails to coincide with the original world of perception, which is the world populated by the stubborn and contingent objects, and to which as artists we fly in shame. The sensibility manifested by artists makes fools of scientists, if the latter are inclined to take their special and quite useful form of truth as the whole and comprehensive article. A dandified pagan worldling like Moore can always defeat Platonism; he does it every hour; he can exhibit the savor of his fish and wines, the fragrance of his coffee and cigars, and the solidity of the images in his favorite verse. These are objects which have to be experienced, and cannot be reported, for what is their simple essence that the Platonist can abstract? Moore may sound mystical but he is within the literal truth when he defends "pure poetry" on the ground that the things are constant, and it is the ideas which change—changing according to the latest mode under which the species indulges its grandiose expectation of subjugating nature. The things are constant in the sense that the ideas are never emancipated from the necessity of referring back to them as their original; and the sense that they are not altered nor diminished no matter which ideas may take off from them as a point of departure. The way to obtain the true *Dinglichkeit* of a formal dinner or a landscape or a beloved person is to approach the object as such, and in humility; then it unfolds a nature which we are unprepared for if we have put our trust in the simple idea which attempted to represent it.

The special antipathy of Moore is to the ideas as they put on their moral complexion, the ideas that relate everything to that insignificant centre of action, the human "soul" in its most Platonic and Pharisaic aspect. Nothing can darken perception better than a repetitive moral earnestness, based on the reputed superiority and higher destiny of the human species. If morality is the code by which we expect the race to achieve the more perfect possession of nature, it is an incitement to a more heroic science, but not to æsthetic experience, nor religious; if it is the code of humility, by which we intend to know nature as nature is, that is another matter; but in an age of science morality is inevitably for the general public the former; and so transcendent a morality as the latter is now unheard of. And therefore:

> O love, *they* die in yon rich sky,
> *They* faint on hill or field or river;
> *Our* echoes roll from soul to soul,
> And grow forever and forever.

The italics are mine. These lines conclude an otherwise innocent poem, a candidate for the anthology, upon which Moore remarks: "The Victorian could never reconcile himself to finishing a poem without speaking about the soul, and the lines are particularly vindictive." Vindictive is just. By what right did the Laureate exult in the death of the physical echoes and call upon his love to witness it, but out of the imperiousness of his savage Platonism? Plato himself would have admired this ending, and considered that it redeemed an otherwise vicious poem.

Why do persons who have ideas to promulgate risk the trial by poetry? If the poets are hired to do it, which is the polite conception of some Hegelians, why do their employers think it worth the money, which they hold in public trust for the cause? Does a science have to become a poetry too? A science is the less effective as a science when it muddies its clear waters with irrelevance, a sermon becomes less cogent when it begins to quote the poets. The moralist, the scientist, and the prophet of idealism think evidently that they must establish their conclusions in poetry, though they reach these conclusions upon quite other evidence. The poetry is likely to destroy the conclusions with a sort of death by drowning, if it is a free poetry.

When that happens the Platonists may be cured of Platonism. There are probably two cures, of which this is the better. One cure is by adversity, by the failure of the ideas to work, on account of treachery or violence, or the contingencies of weather, constitution, love, and economics; leaving the Platonist defeated and bewildered, possibly humbled, but on the other hand possibly turned cynical and worthless. Very much preferable is the cure which comes by education in the fine arts, erasing his Platonism more gently, leading him to feel that that is not a becoming habit of mind which dulls the perceptions.

The definition which some writers have given to art is: the reference of the idea to the image. The implication is that the act is not for the purpose of honest comparison so much as for the purpose of proving the idea by image. But in the event the idea is not disproved so much as it is made to look ineffective and therefore foolish. The ideas will not cover the objects upon which they are imposed, they are too attenuated and threadlike; for ideas have extension and objects have intension, but extension is thin while intension is thick.

There must be a great deal of genuine poetry which started in the poet's mind as a thesis to be developed, but in which the characters and the situations have developed faster than the thesis, and of their own accord. The thesis disappears; or it is recaptured here and there and at the end, and lodged sententiously with the reader, where every successive reading of the poem will dislodge it again. Like this must be some plays, even some play out of Shakespeare, whose thesis would probably be disentangled with difficulty out of the crowded pageant; or some narrative poem with a moral plot but much pure detail; perhaps some "occasional" piece by a Laureate or official person, whose purpose is compromised but whose personal integrity is saved by his wavering between the sentiment which is a public duty and the experience which he has in his own right; even some proclaimed allegory, like Spenser's, unlikely as that may seem, which does not remain transparent and everywhere translatable into idea but makes excursions into the territory of objectivity. These are hybrid performances. They cannot possess beauty of design, though there may be a beauty in detailed passages. But it is common enough, and we should be grateful. The mind is a versatile agent, and unexpectedly stubborn in its determination not really to be hardened in Platonism. Even in an age of science like the nineteenth century the poetic talents are not so loyal to its apostolic zeal as they and it suppose, and do not deserve the unqualified scorn which it is fashionable to offer them, now that the tide has turned, for their performance is qualified.

But this may be not stern enough for concluding a note on Platonic Poetry. I refer again to that whose Platonism is steady and malignant. This poetry is an imitation of Physical Poetry, and not really a poetry. Platonists practise their bogus poetry in order to show that an image will prove an idea, but the literature which succeeds in this delicate mission does not contain real images but illustrations.

III. METAPHYSICAL POETRY

"Most men," Mr. Moore observes, "read and write poetry between fifteen and thirty and afterwards very seldom, for in youth we are attracted by ideas, and modern poetry being concerned almost exclusively with ideas we live on duty, liberty, and fraternity as chameleons are said to live on light and air, till at last we turn from ideas to things, thinking that we have lost our taste for poetry, unless, perchance, we are classical scholars."

Much is conveyed in this characteristic sentence, even in proportion to its length. As for the indicated chronology, the cart is put after the horse, which is its proper sequence. And it is pleasant to be confirmed in the belief that many men do recant from their Platonism and turn back to things. But it cannot be exactly a *volte-face*, for there are qualifications. If pure ideas were what these men turn from, they would have had no poetry at all in the first period, and if pure things were what they turn to, they would be having not a classical poetry but a pure imagism, if such a thing is possible, in the second. The mind does not come unscathed and virginal out of Platonism. Ontological interest would have to develop curiously, or wastefully and discontinuously, if men through their youth must cultivate the ideas so passionately that upon its expiration they are done with ideas forever and ready to become as little (and pre-logical) children. Because of the foolishness of idealists are ideas to be taboo for the adult mind? And, as critics, what are we to do with those poems (like *The Canonization* and *Lycidas*) which could not obtain admission by Moore into the anthology but which very likely are the poems we cherish beyond others?

The reputed "innocence" of the æsthetic moment, the "knowledge without desire" which Schopenhauer praises, must submit to a little scrutiny, like anything else that looks too good to be true. We come into this world as aliens come into a land which they must conquer if they are to live. For native endowment we have an exacting "biological" constitution which knows precisely what it needs and determines for us our inevitable desires. There can be no certainty that any other impulses are there, for why should they be? They scarcely belong in the biological picture. Perhaps we are simply an efficient animal species, running smoothly, working fast, finding the formula of life only too easy, and after a certain apprenticeship piling up power and wealth far beyond the capacity of our appetites to use. What will come next? Perhaps poetry, if the gigantic effort of science begins to seem disproportionate to the reward, according to a sense of diminishing returns. But before this pretty event can come to pass, it is possible that every act of attention which is allowed us is conditioned by a gross and selfish interest.

Where is innocence then? The æsthetic moment appears as a curious moment of suspension; between the Platonism in us, which is militant, always sciencing and devouring, and a starved inhibited aspiration towards innocence which, if it could only be free, would like to respect and know the object as it might of its own accord reveal itself.

The poetic impulse is not free, yet it holds out stubbornly against science for the enjoyment of its images. It means to reconstitute the world of perceptions. Finally there is suggested some such formula as the following:

Science gratifies a rational or practical impulse and exhibits the minimum of perception. Art gratifies a perceptual impulse and exhibits the minimum of reason.

Now it would be strange if poets did not develop many technical devices for the sake of increasing the volume of the percipienda or sensibilia. I will name some of them.

First Device: metre. Metre is the most obvious device. A formal metre impresses us as a way of regulating very drastically the material, and we do not stop to remark (that is, as readers) that it has no particular aim except some nominal sort of regimentation. It symbolizes the predatory method, like a sawmill which intends to reduce all the trees to fixed unit timbers, and as business men we require some sign of our business. But to the Platonic censor in us it gives a false security, for so long as the poet appears to be working faithfully at his metrical engine he is left comparatively free to attend lovingly to the things that are being metered, and metering them need not really hurt them. Metre is the gentlest violence he can do them, if he is expected to do some violence.

Second Device: fiction. The device of the fiction is probably no less important and universal in poetry. Over every poem which looks like a poem is a sign which reads: This road does not go through to action; fictitious. Art always sets out to create an "æsthetic distance" between the object and the subject, and art takes pains to announce that it is not history. The situation treated is not quite an actual situation, for science is likely to have claimed that field, and exiled art; but a fictive or hypothetical one, so that science is less greedy and perception may take hold of it. Kant asserted that the æsthetic judgment is not concerned with the existence or non-existence of the object, and may be interpreted as asserting that it is so far from depending on the object's existence that it really depends on the object's non-existence. Sometimes we have a certain melancholy experience. We enjoy a scene which we receive by report only, or dream, or meet with in art; but subsequently find ourselves in the presence of an actual one that seems the very same scene; only to discover that we have not now the power to enjoy it, or to receive it æsthetically, because the economic tension is upon us and will not indulge us in the proper mood. And it is generally easier to obtain our æsthetic experience from art than from nature, because nature is actual, and communication is forbidden. But in being called fictive or hypothetical the art-object suffers no disparagement. It cannot be true in the sense of being actual, and therefore it may be despised by science. But it is true in the sense of being fair or representative, in permitting the "illusion of reality"; just as Schopenhauer discovered that music may symbolize all the modes of existence in the world; and in keeping with the customary demand of the readers of fiction proper, that it shall be "true to life." The defenders of art must require for it from its practitioners this sort of truth, and must assert of it before the world this dignity. If jealous science succeeds in keeping the field of history for its own exclusive use, it does not therefore annihilate the arts, for they reappear in a field which may be called real though one degree removed from actuality. There the arts perform their function with much less interference, and at the same time with about as much fidelity to the phenomenal world as history has.

Third Device: tropes. I have named two important devices; I am not prepared to offer the exhaustive list. I mention but one other kind, the device which comprises the figures of speech. A proper scientific discourse has no intention of employing figurative language for its definitive sort of utterance. Figures of speech twist accidence away from the straight course, as if to intimate astonishing lapses of rationality beneath the smooth surface of discourse, inviting perceptual attention, and weakening the tyranny of science over the senses. But I skip the several easier and earlier figures, which are timid, and stop on the climactic figure, which is the metaphor; with special reference to its consequence, a poetry which once in our history it produced in a beautiful and abundant exhibit, called Metaphysical Poetry.

And what is Metaphysical Poetry? The term was added to the official vocabulary of criticism by Johnson, who probably took it from Pope, who probably took it from Dryden, who used it to describe the poetry of a certain school of poets, thus: "He [John Donne] affects the metaphysics, not only in his satires, but in his amorous verses, where nature only should reign. . . . In this Mr. Cowley has copied him to a fault." But the meaning of metaphysical which was common in Dryden's time, having come down from the Middle Ages through Shakespeare, was simply: supernatural; *miraculous.* The context of the Dryden passage indicates it.

Dryden, then, noted a miraculism in poetry and repudiated it; except where it was employed for satire, where it was not seriously intended and had the effect of wit. Dryden himself employs miraculism wittily, but seems rather to avoid it if he will be really committed by it; he may employ it in his translations of Ovid, where the responsibility is Ovid's and not Dryden's, and in an occasional classical piece where he is making polite use of myths well known to be pagan errors. In his "amorous" pieces he finds the reign of nature sufficient, and it is often the worse for his amorous pieces. He is not many removes from a naturalist. (A naturalist is a person who studies nature not because he loves it but because he wants to use it, approaches it from the standpoint of common sense, and sees it thin and not thick.) Dryden might have remarked that Donne himself had a change of heart and confined his miraculism at last to the privileged field of a more or less scriptural revelation. Perhaps Dryden found his way to accepting Milton because Milton's miraculism was mostly not a contemporary sort but classical and scriptural, pitched in a time when the age of miracles had not given way to the age of science. He knew too that Cowley had shamefully recanted from his petty miraculism, which formed the conceits, and turned to the scriptural or large order of miraculism to write his heroic (but empty) verses about David; and had written a Pindaric ode in extravagant praise of "Mr. Hobs," whose naturalistic account of nature seemed to render any other account fantastic if not contrary to the social welfare.

Incidentally, we know how much Mr. Hobbes affected Dryden too, and the whole of Restoration literature. What Bacon with his disparagement of poetry had begun, in the cause of science and protestantism, Hobbes completed. The name of Hobbes is critical in any history that would account for the chill which settled upon the poets at the very moment that English poetry was attaining magnificently to the fullness of its powers. The name stood for common sense and naturalism, and the monopoly of the scientific spirit over the mind. Hobbes was the adversary, the Satan, when the latter first intimidated the English poets. After Hobbes his name is legion.

"Metaphysics," or miraculism, informs a poetry which is the most original and exciting, and intellectually perhaps the most seasoned, that we know in our literature, and very probably it has few equivalents in other literatures. But it is evident that the metaphysical effects may be large-scale or they may be small-scale. (I believe that generically, or ontologically, no distinction is to be made between them.) If Donne and Cowley illustrate the small-scale effects, Milton will illustrate the large-scale ones, probably as a consequence of the fact that he wrote major poems. Milton, in the *Paradise Lost,* told a story which was heroic and miraculous in the first place. In telling it he dramatized it, and allowed the scenes and characters to develop of their own native energy. The virtue of a long poem on a "metaphysical" subject will consist in the dramatization or substantiation of all the parts, the poet not being required to devise fresh miracles on every page so much as to establish the perfect "naturalism" of the material upon which the grand miracle is imposed. The *Paradise Lost* possesses this virtue nearly everywhere:

> Thus *Adam* to himself lamented loud
> Through the still Night, not now, as ere man fell,
> Wholsom and cool, and mild, but with black Air
> Accompanied, with damps and dreadful gloom,
> Which to his evil Conscience represented
> All things with double terror: On the ground
> Outstretcht he lay, on the cold ground, and oft
> Curs'd his Creation, Death as oft accus'd
> Of tardie execution, since denounc't
> The day of his offence. Why comes not Death,
> Said hee, with one thrice acceptable stroke
> To end me?

This is exactly the sort of detail for a large-scale metaphysical work, but it would hardly serve the purpose with a slighter and more naturalistic subject; with "amorous" verses. For the critical mind Metaphysical Poetry refers perhaps almost entirely to the so-called "conceits" that constitute its staple. To define the conceit is to define small-scale Metaphysical Poetry.

It is easily defined, upon a little citation. Donne exhibits two conceits, or two branches of one conceit in the familiar lines:

> Our hands were firmly cemented
> By a fast balm which thence did spring;
> Our eye-beams twisted, and did thread
> Our eyes upon one double string.

The poem which follows sticks to the topic; it represents the lovers in precisely that mode of union and no other. Cowley is more conventional yet still bold in the lines:

> Oh take my Heart, and by that means you'll prove
> Within, too stor'd enough of love:
> Give me but yours, I'll by that change so thrive
> That Love in all my parts shall live.
> So powerful is this my change, it render can,
> My outside Woman, and your inside Man.

A conceit originates in a metaphor; and in fact the conceit is but a metaphor if the metaphor is meant; that is, if it is developed so literally that it must be meant, or predicated so baldly that nothing else can be meant. Perhaps this will do for a definition.

Clearly the seventeenth century had the courage of its metaphors, and imposed them imperially on the nearest things, and just as clearly the nineteenth century lacked this courage, and was half-heartedly metaphorical, or content with similes. The difference between the literary qualities of the two periods is the difference between the metaphor and the simile. (It must be admitted that this like other generalizations will not hold without its exceptions.) One period was pithy and original in its poetic utterance, the other was prolix and predictable. It would not quite commit itself to the metaphor even if it came upon one. Shelley is about as vigorous as usual when he says in *Adonais:*

> Thou young Dawn,
> Turn all thy dew to splendour...

But splendor is not the correlative of dew, it has the flat tone of a Platonic idea, while physically it scarcely means more than dew with sunshine upon it. The seventeenth century would have said: "Turn thy dew, which is water, into fire, and accomplish the transmutation of the elements." Tennyson in his boldest lyric sings:

> Come into the garden, Maud,
> For the black bat, night, has flown.

and leaves us unpersuaded of the bat. The predication would be complete without the bat, "The black night has flown," and a flying night is not very remarkable. Tennyson is only affecting a metaphor. But later in the same poem he writes:

> The red rose cries, "She is near, she is near";
> And the white rose weeps, "She is late";
> The larkspur listens, "I hear, I hear";
> And the lily whispers, "I wait."

and this is a technical conceit. But it is too complicated for this author, having a plurality of images which do not sustain themselves individually. The flowers stand for the lover's thoughts, and have been prepared for carefully in an earlier stanza, but their distinctness is too arbitrary, and these are like a schoolgirl's made-up metaphors. The passage will not compare with one on a very similar situation in *Green Candles,* by Mr. Humbert Wolfe:

> "I know her little foot," gray carpet said:
> "Who but I should know her light tread?"
> "She shall come in," answered the open door,
> "And not," said the room, "go out any more."

Wolfe's conceit works and Tennyson's does not, and though Wolfe's performance seems not very daring or important, and only pleasant, he employs the technique of the conceit correctly: he knows that the miracle must have a basis of verisimilitude.

Such is Metaphysical Poetry; the extension of a rhetorical device; as one of the most brilliant successes in our poetry, entitled to long and thorough examination; and even here demanding somewhat by way of a more ontological criticism. I conclude with it.

We may consult the dictionary, and discover that there is a miraculism or supernaturalism in a metaphorical assertion if we are ready to mean what we say, or believe what we hear. Or we may read Mr. Hobbes, the naturalist, who was very clear upon it: "II. The second cause of absurd assertions I ascribe to the giving of names of 'bodies' to 'accidents,' or of 'accidents' to 'bodies,' as they do that say 'faith is infused' or 'inspired,' when nothing can be 'poured' or 'breathed' into anything but body . . . and that 'phantasms' are 'spirits,' etc." Translated into our present terms, Hobbes is condemning the confusion of single qualities with whole things; or the substitution of concrete images for simple ideas.

Specifically, the miraculism arises when the poet discovers by analogy an identity between objects which is partial, though it should be considerable, and proceeds to an identification which is complete. It is to be contrasted with the simile, which says "as if" or "like," and is scrupulous to keep the identification partial. In Cowley's passage above, the lover is saying, not for the first time in this literature: "She and I have exchanged our hearts." What has actually been exchanged is affections, and affections are only in a limited sense the same as hearts. Hearts are unlike affections in being engines that pump blood and form body; and it is a miracle if the poet represents the lady's affection as rendering her inside into man. But he succeeds, with this mixture, in depositing with us the image of a very powerful affection.

From the strict point of view of literary criticism it must be insisted that the miraculism which produces the humblest conceit is the same miraculism which supplies to religions their substantive content. (This is said to assert the dignity not of the conceits but of the religions.) It is the poet and nobody else who gives to the God a nature, a form, faculties, and a history; to the God, most comprehensive of all terms, which, if there were no poetic impulse to actualize or "find" Him, would remain the driest and deadest among Platonic ideas, with all intension sacrificed to infinite extension. The myths are conceits, born of metaphors. Religions are periodically produced by poets and destroyed by naturalists. Religion depends for its ontological validity upon a literary understanding, and that is why it is frequently misunderstood. The metaphysical poets, perhaps like their spiritual fathers the mediæval Schoolmen, were under no illusions about this. They recognized myth, as they recognized the conceits, as a device of expression; its sanctity as the consequence of its public or social importance.

But whether the topics be Gods or amorous experiences, why do poets resort to miraculism? Hardly for the purpose of controverting natural fact or scientific theory. Religion pronounces about God only where science is silent and philosophy is negative; for a positive is wanted, that is, a God who has his being in the physical world as well as in the world of principles and abstractions. Likewise with the little secular enterprises of poetry. Not now are the poets so brave, not for a very long time have they been so brave, as to dispute the scientists on what they call their "truth"; though it is a pity that the statement cannot be turned round. Poets will concede that every act of science is legitimate, and has its efficacy. The metaphysical poets of the seventeenth century particularly admired the methodology of science, and in fact they copied it, and their phrasing is often technical, spare, and polysyllabic, though they are not repeating actual science but making those metaphorical substitutions that are so arresting.

The intention of Metaphysical Poetry is to complement science, and improve discourse. Naturalistic discourse is incomplete, for either of two reasons. It has the minimum of physical content and starves the sensibility, or it has the maximum, as if to avoid the appearance of evil, but is laborious and pointless. Platonic Poetry is too idealistic, but Physical Poetry is too realistic, and realism is tedious and does not maintain interest. The poets therefore introduce the psychological device of the miracle. The predication which it permits is clean and quick but it is not a scientific predication. For scientific predication concludes an act of attention but miraculism initiates one. It leaves us looking, marvelling, and revelling in the thick *dinglich* substance that has just received its strange representation.

Let me suggest as a last word, in deference to a common Puritan scruple, that the predication of Metaphysical Poetry is true enough. It is not true like history, but no poetry is true in that sense, and only a part of science. It is true in the pragmatic sense in which some of the generalizations of science are true: it accomplishes precisely the sort of representation that it means to. It suggests to us that the object is perceptually or physically remarkable, and we had better attend to it.

THE METAPHYSICAL POETS

(1921)

T. S. Eliot

By collecting these poems [1] from the work of a generation more often named than read, and more often read than profitably studied, Professor Grierson has rendered a service of some importance. Certainly the reader will meet with many poems already preserved in other anthologies, at the same time that he discovers poems such as those of Aurelian Townshend or Lord Herbert of Cherbury here included. But the function of such an anthology as this is neither that of Professor Saintsbury's admirable edition of Caroline poets nor that of the *Oxford Book of English Verse*. Mr. Grierson's book is in itself a piece of criticism and a provocation of criticism; and we think that he was right in including so many poems of Donne, elsewhere (though not in many editions) accessible, as documents in the case of "metaphysical poetry." The phrase has long done duty as a term of abuse or as the label of a quaint and pleasant taste. The question is to what extent the so-called metaphysicals formed a school (in our own time we should say a "movement"), and how far this so-called school or movement is a digression from the main current.

Not only is it extremely difficult to define metaphysical poetry, but difficult to decide what poets practice it and in which of their verses. The poetry of Donne (to whom Marvell and Bishop King are sometimes nearer than any of the other authors) is late Elizabethan, its feeling often very close to that of Chapman. The "courtly" poetry is derivative from Jonson, who borrowed liberally from the Latin; it expires in the next century with the sentiment and witticism of Prior. There is finally the devotional verse of Herbert, Vaughan, and Crashaw (echoed long after by Christina Rossetti and Francis Thompson); Crashaw, sometimes more profound and less sectarian than the others, has a quality which returns through the Elizabethan period to the early Italians. It is difficult to find any precise use of metaphor, simile, or other conceit, which is common to all the poets and at the same time important enough as an element of style to isolate these poets as a group. Donne, and often Cowley, employ a device which is sometimes considered characteristically "metaphysical"; the elaboration

[1] *Metaphysical Lyrics and Poems of the Seventeenth Century*: Donne to Butler. Selected and edited, with an Essay, by Herbert J. C. Grierson (Oxford: Clarendon Press. London: Milford). [*Author's note.*]

(contrasted with the condensation) of a figure of speech to the farthest stage to which ingenuity can carry it. Thus Cowley develops the commonplace comparison of the world to a chess-board through long stanzas (*To Destiny*), and Donne, with more grace, in *A Valediction,* the comparison of two lovers to a pair of compasses. But elsewhere we find, instead of the mere explication of the content of a comparison, a development by rapid association of thought which requires considerable agility on the part of the reader.

> On a round ball
> A workman that hath copies by, can lay
> An Europe, Afrique, and an Asia,
> And quickly make that, which was nothing, All,
> So doth each teare,
> Which thee doth weare,
> A globe, yea, world by that impression grow,
> Till thy tears mixt with mine doe overflow
> This world, by waters sent from thee, my heaven dissolved so.

Here we find at least two connections which are not implicit in the first figure, but are forced upon it by the poet: from the geographer's globe to the tear, and the tear to the deluge. On the other hand, some of Donne's most successful and characteristic effects are secured by brief words and sudden contrasts:

> A bracelet of bright hair about the bone,

where the most powerful effect is produced by the sudden contrast of associations of "bright hair" and of "bone." This telescoping of images and multiplied associations is characteristic of the phrase of some of the dramatists of the period which Donne knew: not to mention Shakespeare, it is frequent in Middleton, Webster, and Tourneur, and is one of the sources of the vitality of their language.

Johnson, who employed the term "metaphysical poets," apparently having Donne, Cleveland, and Cowley chiefly in mind, remarks of them that "the most heterogeneous ideas are yoked by violence together." The force of this impeachment lies in the failure of the conjunction, the fact that often the ideas are yoked but not united; and if we are to judge of styles of poetry by their abuse, enough examples may be found in Cleveland to justify Johnson's condemnation. But a degree of heterogeneity of material compelled into unity by the operation of the poet's mind is omnipresent in poetry. We need not select for illustration such a line as:

> Notre âme est un trois-mâts cherchant son Icarie;

we may find it in some of the best lines of Johnson himself (*The Vanity of Human Wishes*):

His fate was destined to a barren strand,
A petty fortress, and a dubious hand;
He left a name at which the world grew pale,
To point a moral, or adorn a tale—

where the effect is due to a contrast of ideas, different in degree but the same in principle, as that which Johnson mildly reprehended. And in one of the finest poems of the age (a poem which could not have been written in any other age), the *Exequy* of Bishop King, the extended comparison is used with perfect success: the idea and the simile become one, in the passage in which the Bishop illustrates his impatience to see his dead wife, under the figure of a journey:

Stay for me there; I will not faile
To meet thee in that hollow Vale.
And think not much of my delay;
I am already on the way,
And follow thee with all the speed
Desire can make, or sorrows breed.
Each minute is a short degree,
And ev'ry houre a step towards thee.
At night when I betake to rest,
Next morn I rise nearer my West
Of life, almost by eight houres sail,
Than when sleep breath'd his drowsy gale . . .
But heark! My Pulse, like a soft Drum
Beats my approach, tells Thee I come;
And slow howere my marches be,
I shall at last sit down by Thee.

(In the last few lines there is that effect of terror which is several times attained by one of Bishop King's admirers, Edgar Poe.) Again, we may justly take these quatrains from Lord Herbert's Ode, stanzas which would, we think, be immediately pronounced to be of the metaphysical school:

So when from hence we shall be gone,
And be no more, nor you, nor I,
As one another's mystery,
Each shall be both, yet both but one.

This said, in her up-lifted face,
Her eyes, which did that beauty crown,
Were like two starrs, that having faln down,
Look up again to find their place:

While such a moveless silent peace
Did seize on their becalmed sense,
One would have thought some influence
Their ravished spirits did possess.

There is nothing in these lines (with the possible exception of the stars, a simile not at once grasped, but lovely and justified) which fits Johnson's general observations on the metaphysical poets in his essay on Cowley. A good deal resides in the richness of association which is at the same time borrowed from and given to the word "becalmed"; but the meaning is clear, the language simple and elegant. It is to be observed that the language of these poets is as a rule simple and pure; in the verse of George Herbert this simplicity is carried as far as it can go—a simplicity emulated without success by numerous modern poets. The *structure* of the sentences, on the other hand, is sometimes far from simple, but this is not a vice; it is a fidelity to thought and feeling. The effect, at its best, is far less artificial than that of an ode by Gray. And as this fidelity induces variety of thought and feeling, so it induces variety of music. We doubt whether, in the eighteenth century, could be found two poems in nominally the same metre, so dissimilar as Marvell's *Coy Mistress* and Crashaw's *Saint Teresa;* the one producing an effect of great speed by the use of short syllables, and the other an ecclesiastical solemnity by the use of long ones:

> Love, thou art absolute sole lord
> Of life and death.

If so shrewd and sensitive (though so limited) a critic as Johnson failed to define metaphysical poetry by its faults, it is worth while to inquire whether we may not have more success by adopting the opposite method: by assuming that the poets of the seventeenth century (up to the Revolution) were the direct and normal development of the precedent age; and, without prejudicing their case by the adjective "metaphysical," consider whether their virtue was not something permanently valuable, which subsequently disappeared, but ought not to have disappeared. Johnson has hit, perhaps by accident, on one of their peculiarities, when he observes that "their attempts were always analytic"; he would not agree that, after the dissociation, they put the material together again in a new unity.

It is certain that the dramatic verse of the later Elizabethan and early Jacobean poets expresses a degree of development of sensibility which is not found in any of the prose, good as it often is. If we except Marlowe, a man of prodigious intelligence, these dramatists were directly or indirectly (it is at least a tenable theory) affected by Montaigne. Even if we except also Jonson and Chapman, these two were notably erudite, and were notably men who incorporated their erudition into their sensibility: their mode of feeling was directly and freshly altered by their reading and thought. In Chapman especially there is a direct sensuous apprehension of thought, or a re-creation of thought into feeling, which is exactly what we find in Donne:

> . . . in this one thing, all the discipline
> Of manners and of manhood is contained;

> A man to join himself with th' Universe
> In his main sway, and make in all things fit
> One with that All, and go on, round as it;
> Not plucking from the whole his wretched part,
> And into straits, or into nought revert,
> Wishing the complete Universe might be
> Subject to such a rag of it as he;
> But to consider great Necessity.

We compare this with some modern passage:

> No, when the fight begins within himself,
> A man's worth something. God stoops o'er his head,
> Satan looks up between his feet—both tug—
> He's left, himself, i' the middle; the soul wakes
> And grows. Prolong that battle through his life!

It is perhaps somewhat less fair, though very tempting (as both poets are concerned with the perpetuation of love by offspring), to compare with the stanzas already quoted from Lord Herbert's Ode the following from Tennyson:

> One walked between his wife and child,
> With measured footfall firm and mild,
> And now and then he gravely smiled.
> The prudent partner of his blood
> Leaned on him, faithful, gentle, good,
> Wearing the rose of womanhood.
> And in their double love secure,
> The little maiden walked demure,
> Pacing with downward eyelids pure.
> These three made unity so sweet,
> My frozen heart began to beat,
> Remembering its ancient heat.

The difference is not a simple difference of degree between poets. It is something which had happened to the mind of England between the time of Donne or Lord Herbert of Cherbury and the time of Tennyson and Browning; it is the difference between the intellectual poet and the reflective poet. Tennyson and Browning are poets, and they think; but they do not feel their thought as immediately as the odour of a rose. A thought to Donne was an experience; it modified his sensibility. When a poet's mind is perfectly equipped for its work, it is constantly amalgamating disparate experience; the ordinary man's experience is chaotic, irregular, fragmentary. The latter falls in love, or reads Spinoza, and these two experiences have nothing to do with each other, or with the noise of the typewriter or the smell of cooking; in the mind of the poet these experiences are always forming new wholes.

We may express the difference by the following theory: The poets of the seventeenth century, the successors of the dramatists of the sixteenth, possessed a mechanism of sensibility which could devour any kind of experience. They are simple, artificial, difficult, or fantastic, as their predecessors were; no less nor more than Dante, Guido Cavalcanti, Guinizelli, or Cino. In the seventeenth century a dissociation of sensibility [2] set in, from which we have never recovered; and this dissociation, as is natural, was aggravated by the influence of the two most powerful poets of the century, Milton and Dryden. Each of these men performed certain poetic functions so magnificently well that the magnitude of the effect concealed the absence of others. The language went on and in some respects improved; the best verse of Collins, Gray, Johnson, and even Goldsmith satisfies some of our fastidious demands better than that of Donne or Marvell or King. But while the language became more refined, the feeling became more crude. The feeling, the sensibility, expressed in the *Country Churchyard* (to say nothing of Tennyson and Browning) is cruder than that in the *Coy Mistress.*

The second effect of the influence of Milton and Dryden followed from the first, and was therefore slow in manifestation. The sentimental age began early in the eighteenth century, and continued. The poets revolted against the ratiocinative, the descriptive; they thought and felt by fits, unbalanced; they reflected. In one or two passages of Shelley's *Triumph of Life,* in the second *Hyperion,* there are traces of a struggle toward unification of sensibility. But Keats and Shelley died, and Tennyson and Browning ruminated.

After this brief exposition of a theory—too brief, perhaps, to carry conviction—we may ask, what would have been the fate of the "metaphysical" had the current of poetry descended in a direct line from them, as it descended in a direct line to them? They would not, certainly, by classified as metaphysical. The possible interests of a poet are unlimited; the more intelligent he is the better; the more intelligent he is the more likely that he will have interests: our only condition is that he turn them into poetry, and not merely meditate on them poetically. A philosophical theory which has entered into poetry is established, for its truth or falsity in one sense ceases to matter, and its truth in another sense is proved. The poets in question have, like other poets, various faults. But they were, at best, engaged in the task of trying to find the verbal equivalent for states of mind and feeling. And this means both that they are more mature, and that they wear better, than later poets of certainly not less literary ability.

It is not a permanent necessity that poets should be interested in philosophy, or in any other subject. We can only say that it appears likely that poets in our civilization, as it exists at present, must be *difficult.* Our civilization comprehends great variety and complexity,

[2] On the phrase "dissociation of sensibility," which Eliot coined in his essay on Dryden, see Eliot's latest qualifying comment in his "Milton," *Sewanee Review,* 56 (Spring, 1948), 193-194. [*Editor's note.*]

and this variety and complexity, playing upon a refined sensibility, must produce various and complex results. The poet must become more and more comprehensive, more allusive, more indirect, in order to force, to dislocate if necessary, language into his meaning. (A brilliant and extreme statement of this view, with which it is not requisite to associate oneself, is that of M. Jean Epstein, *La Poésie d'aujourd'hui.*) Hence we get something which looks very much like the conceit —we get, in fact, a method curiously similar to that of the "metaphysical poets," similar also in its use of obscure words and of simple phrasing.

> O géraniums diaphanes, guerroyeurs sortilèges,
> Sacrilèges monomanes!
> Emballages, dévergondages, douches! O pressoirs
> Des vendanges des grands soirs!
> Layettes aux abois,
> Thyrses au fond des bois!
> Transfusions, représailles,
> Relevailles, compresses et l'éternal potion,
> Angélus! n'en pouvoir plus
> De débâcles nuptiales! de débâcles nuptiales!

The same poet could write also simply:

> Elle est bien loin, elle pleure,
> Le grand vent se lamente aussi . . .

Jules Laforgue, and Tristan Corbière in many of his poems, are nearer to the "school of Donne" than any modern English poet. But poets more classical than they have the same essential quality of transmuting ideas into sensations, of transforming an observation into a state of mind.

> Pour l'enfant, amoureux de cartes et d'estampes,
> L'univers est égal à son vaste appétit.
> Ah, que le monde est grand à la clarté des lampes!
> Aux yeux du souvenir que le monde est petit!

In French literature the great master of the seventeenth century—Racine—and the great master of the nineteenth—Baudelaire—are in some ways more like each other than they are like any one else. The greatest two masters of diction are also the greatest two psychologists, the most curious explorers of the soul. It is interesting to speculate whether it is not a misfortune that two of the greatest masters of diction in our language, Milton and Dryden, triumph with a dazzling disregard of the soul. If we continued to produce Miltons and Drydens it might not so much matter, but as things are it is a pity that English poetry has remained so incomplete. Those who object to the "artificiality" of Milton or Dryden sometimes tell us to "look into our hearts and write." But that is not looking deep enough;

Racine or Donne looked into a good deal more than the heart. One must look into the cerebral cortex, the nervous system, and the digestive tracts.

May we not conclude, then, that Donne, Crashaw, Vaughan, Herbert and Lord Herbert, Marvell, King, Cowley at his best, are in the direct current of English poetry, and that their faults should be reprimanded by this standard rather than coddled by antiquarian affection? They have been enough praised in terms which are implicit limitations because they are "metaphysical" or "witty," "quaint" or "obscure," though at their best they have not these attributes more than other serious poets. On the other hand, we must not reject the criticism of Johnson (a dangerous person to disagree with) without having mastered it, without having assimilated the Johnsonian canons of taste. In reading the celebrated passage in his essay on Cowley we must remember that by wit he clearly means something more serious than we usually mean today; in his criticism of their versification we must remember in what a narrow discipline he was trained, but also how well trained; we must remember that Johnson tortures chiefly the chief offenders, Cowley and Cleveland. It would be a fruitful work, and one requiring a substantial book, to break up the classification of Johnson (for there has been none since) and exhibit these poets in all their difference of kind and of degree, from the massive music of Donne to the faint, pleasing tinkle of Aurelian Townshend—whose *Dialogue Between a Pilgrim and Time* is one of the few regrettable omissions from the excellent anthology of Professor Grierson.

TENSION IN POETRY

(1938)

ALLEN TATE

I

MANY POEMS that we ordinarily think of as good poetry—and some, besides, that we neglect—have certain common features that will allow us to invent, for their sharper apprehension, the name of a single quality. I shall call that quality tension. In abstract language, a poetic work has distinct quality as the ultimate effect of the whole, and that whole is the "result" of a configuration of meaning which it is the duty of the critic to examine and evaluate. In setting forth this duty as my present procedure I am trying to amplify a critical approach that I have used on other occasions, without wholly giving up the earlier method, which I should describe as the analysis of the general ideas implicit in the poetic work.

Towards the end of this essay I shall cite examples of "tension," but I shall not say that they exemplify tension only, or that other qualities must be ignored. There are all kinds of poetry, as many as there are good poets, as many even as there are good poems, for poets may be expected to write more than one kind of poetry; and no single critical insight may impute an exclusive validity to any one kind. In all ages there are schools demanding that one sort only be written—their sort: political poetry for the sake of the cause; picturesque poetry for the sake of the home town; didactic poetry for the sake of the parish; even a generalized personal poetry for the sake of the reassurance and safety of numbers. This last I suppose is the most common variety, the anonymous lyricism in which the common personality exhibits its commonness, its obscure and standard eccentricity, in a language that seems always to be deteriorating; so that today many poets are driven to inventing private languages, or very narrow ones, because public speech has become heavily tainted with mass feeling.

Mass language is the medium of "communication," and its users are less interested in bringing to formal order what is today called the "affective state" than in arousing that state.

Once you have said that everything is One it is obvious that literature is the same as propaganda; once you have said that no truth can be known apart from the immediate dialectical process of history it is obvious that all contemporary artists must prepare the same fashionplate. It is clear too that the One is limited in space as well as time, and the no less Hegelian Fascists are right in saying that all art is patriotic.

What Mr. William Empson calls patriotic poetry sings not merely in behalf of the State; you will find it equally in a lady-like lyric and in much of the political poetry of our time. It is the poetry of the mass language, very different from the "language of the people" which interested the late W. B. Yeats. For example:

> What from the splendid dead
> We have inherited—
> Furrows sweet to the grain, and the weed subdued—
> See now the slug and the mildew plunder.
> Evil does overwhelm
> The larkspur and the corn;
> We have seen them go under.

From this stanza by Miss Millay we infer that her splendid ancestors made the earth a good place that has somehow gone bad—and you get the reason from the title: *Justice Denied in Massachusetts.* How Massachusetts could cause a general dessication, why (as we are told in a footnote to the poem) the execution of Sacco and Vanzetti should have anything to do with the rotting of the crops, it is never made clear. These lines are mass language: they arouse an affective state in one set of terms, and suddenly an object quite unrelated to those terms gets the benefit of it; and this effect, which is usually achieved, as I think it is here, without conscious effort, is sentimentality. Miss Millay's poem was admired when it first appeared about ten years ago, and is no doubt still admired, by persons to whom it communicates certain feelings about social justice, by persons for whom the lines are the occasion of feelings shared by them and the poet. But if you do not share those feelings, as I happen not to share them in the images of dessicated nature, the lines and even the entire poem are impenetrably obscure.

I am attacking here the fallacy of communication in poetry. (I am not attacking social justice.) It is no less a fallacy in the writing of poetry than of critical theory. The critical doctrine fares ill the further back you apply it; I suppose one may say—if one wants a landmark—that it began to prosper after 1798; for on the whole nineteenth century English verse is a poetry of communication. The poets were trying to use verse to convey ideas and feelings that they secretly thought could be better conveyed by science (consult Shelley's *Defense),* or by what today we call, in a significantly bad poetic phrase, the Social Sciences. Yet possibly because the poets believed the scientists to be tough, and the poets joined the scientists in thinking the poets tender, the poets stuck to verse. It may hardly be said that we change this tradition of poetic futility by giving it a new name, Social Poetry. May a poet hope to deal more adequately with sociology than with physics? If he seizes upon either at the level of scientific procedure, has he not abdicated his position as poet?

At a level of lower historical awareness than that exhibited by Mr. Edmund Wilson's later heroes of the Symbolist school, we find the kind of verse that I have been quoting, verse long ago intimidated by the pseudo-rationalism of the Social Sciences. This sentimental intimidation has been so complete that, however easy the verse looked on the page, it gave up all claim to sense. (I assume here what I cannot now demonstrate, that Miss Millay's poem is obscure but that Donne's *Second Anniversarie* is not.) As another example of this brand of obscurity I have selected at random a nineteenth century lyric, *The Vine,* by James Thomson:

> The wine of love is music,
> And the feast of love is song:
> When love sits down to banquet,
> Love sits long:
>
> Sits long and rises drunken,
> But not with the feast and the wine;
> He reeleth with his own heart,
> That great rich Vine.

The language here appeals to an existing affective state; it has no coherent meaning either literally or in terms of ambiguity or implication; it may be wholly replaced by any of its several paraphrases, which are already latent in our minds. One of these is the confused image of a self-intoxicating man-about-town. Now good poetry can bear the closest literal examination of every phrase, and is its own safeguard against our irony. But the more closely we examine this lyric, the more obscure it becomes; the more we trace the implications of the imagery, the denser the confusion. The imagery adds nothing to the general idea that it tries to sustain; it even deprives that idea of the dignity it has won at the hands of a long succession of better poets going back, I suppose, to Guinizelli:

> Al cor gentil ripara sempre Amore
> Come alla selva augello in la verdura . . .

What I want to make clear is the particular kind of failure, not the degree, in a certain kind of poetry. Were we interested in degrees we might give comfort to the nineteenth century by citing lines from John Cleveland or Abraham Cowley, bad lyric verse no better than *The Vine,* written in an age that produced some of the greatest English poetry. Here are some lines from Cowley's *Hymn: to light,* a hundred-line inventory of some of the offices performed by the subject in a universe that still seems to be on the whole Ptolemaic; I should not care to guess the length the poem might have reached under the Copernican system. Here is one of the interesting duties of light:

> Nor amidst all these Triumphs does thou scorn
> The humble glow-worm to adorn,
> And with those living spangles gild,
> (O Greatness without Pride!) the Bushes of the Field.

Again:

> The Violet, springs little Infant, stands,
> Girt in thy purple Swadling-bands:
> On the fair Tulip thou dost dote;
> Thou cloath'st it in a gay and party-colour'd Coat.

This, doubtless, is metaphysical poetry; however bad the lines may be—they are pretty bad—they have no qualities, bad or good, in common with *The Vine.* Mr. Ransom has given us, in a remarkable essay, "Shakespeare at Sonnets" (*The World's Body,* 1938), an excellent description of this kind of poetry: "The impulse to metaphysical poetry . . . consists in committing the feelings in the case . . . to their determination within the elected figure." That is to say, in metaphysical poetry the logical order is explicit; it must be coherent; the imagery by which it is sensuously embodied must have at least the appearance of logical determinism: perhaps the appearance only, because the varieties of ambiguity and contradiction possible beneath the logical surface are endless, as Mr. Empson has demonstrated in his elucidation of Marvell's *The Garden.* Here it is enough to say that the development of imagery by extension, its logical determinants being an Ariadne's thread that the poet will not permit us to lose, is the leading feature of the poetry called metaphysical.

But to recognize it is not to evaluate it; and I take it that Mr. Ransom was giving us a true Aristotelian definition of a genus, in which the identification of a type does not compel us to discern the implied values. Logical extension of imagery is no doubt the key to the meaning of Donne's *Valediction: forbidding mourning;* it may equally initiate inquiry into the ludicrous failure of *Hymn: to light,* to which I will now return.

While *The Vine* and *Hymn: to light* seem to me equally bad poetry, Cowley's failure is somewhat to be preferred; its negative superiority lies in a firmer use of the language. There is no appeal to an affective state; the leading statement can be made perfectly explicit: God is light, and light is life. The poem is an analytical proposition exhibiting the properties inherent in the major term; that is, exhibiting as much of the universe as Cowley could get around to before he wearied of logical extension. But I think it is possible to infer that good poetry could have been written in Cowley's language; and we know that it was. Every term, even the verbs converted into nouns, denotes an object, and in the hands of a good poet would be amenable to controlled distortions of literal representation. But here the distortions are uncontrolled. Everything is in this language that a poet needs except the poetry, or the imagination, or what I shall presently illustrate under the idea of tension.

I have called *Hymn: to light* an analytical proposition. That is the form in which the theme must have appeared to Cowley's mind; that is to say, simple analysis of the term, *God*, gave him, as it gave everybody else in Christendom, the proposition: God is light. (Perhaps, under neo-Platonic influence, the prime Christian symbol, as Professor Fletcher and others have shown in reducing to their sources the powers of the Three Blessed Ladies of the *Divine Comedy*.) But in order to write his poem Cowley had to develop the symbol by synthetic accretion, by adding to light properties not inherent in its simple analysis:

> The Violet, springs little Infant, stands,
> Girt in thy purple Swadling-bands . . .

The image, such as it is, is an addition to the central figure of light, an assertion of a hitherto undetected relation among the objects, light, diapers, and violets—a miscellany that I recommend to the consideration of Mr. E. E. Cummings, who could get something out of it that Cowley did not intend us to get. If you will think again of *The Vine*, you will observe that Thomson permits, in the opposite direction, an equal license with the objects *de*noted by his imagery, with the unhappy results that we have already seen.

The Vine is a failure in denotation. *Hymn: to light* is a failure in connotation. The language of *The Vine* lacks objective content. Take "music" and "song" in the first two lines; the context does not allow us to apprehend the terms in extension; that is, there is no reference to objects that we may distinguish as "music" and "song"; the wine of love could have as well been song, its feast music. In *Hymn: to light*, a reduction to their connotations of the terms *violet, swadling-bands*, and *light* (the last being represented by the pronoun *thou*) yields a clutter of images that may be unified only if we forget the firm denotations of the terms. If we are going to receive as valid the infancy of the violet, we have to ignore the metaphor that conveys it, for the metaphor renders the violet absurd; by ignoring the diaper, and the two terms associated with it, we cease to read the passage, and begin for ourselves the building up of acceptable denotations for the terms of the metaphor.

Absurd: but on what final ground I call these poems absurd I cannot state as a principle. I appeal to the reader's experience, and invite him to form a judgment of his own. It is easy enough to say, as I shall say in detail in a moment, that good poetry is a unity of all the meanings from the furthest extremes of intension and extension. Yet our recognition of the action of this unified meaning is the gift of experience, of culture, of, if you will, our humanism. Our powers of discrimination are not deductive powers, though they may be aided by them; they wait rather upon the cultivation of our total human powers, and they represent a special application of those powers to a single medium of experience—poetry.

I have referred to a certain kind of poetry as the embodiment of the fallacy of communication: it is a poetry that communicates the affective state, which (in terms of language) results from the irresponsible denotations of words. There is a vague grasp of the "real" world. The history of this fallacy, which is as old as poetry but which towards the end of the eighteenth century began to dominate not only poetry, but other arts as well—its history would probably show that the poets gave up the language of denotation to the scientists, and kept for themselves a continually thinning flux of peripheral connotations. The companion fallacy, to which I can give only the literal name, the fallacy of mere denotation, I have also illustrated from Cowley: this is the poetry which contradicts our most developed human insights in so far as it fails to use and direct the rich connotation with which language has been informed by experience.

II

We return to the inquiry set for this discussion: to find out whether there is not a more central achievement in poetry than that represented by either of the extreme examples that we have been considering. I proposed as descriptive of that achievement, the term *tension*. I am using the term not as a general metaphor, but as a special one, derived from lopping the prefixes off the logical term *ex*tension and *in*tension. What I am saying, of course, is that the meaning of poetry is its "tension," the full organized body of all the extension and intension that we can find in it. The remotest figurative significance that we can derive does not invalidate the extensions of the literal statement. Or we may begin with the literal statement and by stages develop the complications of metaphor: at every stage we may pause to state the meaning so far apprehended, and at every stage the meaning will be coherent.

The meanings that we select at different points along the infinite line between extreme intension and extreme extension will vary with our personal "drive," or "interest," or "approach": the Platonist will tend to stay pretty close to the end of the line where extension, and simple abstraction of the object into a universal, is easiest, for he will be a fanatic in morals or some kind of works, and will insist upon the shortest way with what will ever appear to him the dissenting ambiguities at the intensive end of the scale. The Platonist (I do not say that his opponent is the Aristotelian) might decide that Marvell's

To His Coy Mistress recommends immoral behavior to the young men, in whose behalf he would try to suppress the poem. That, of course, would be one "true" meaning of *To His Coy Mistress*, but it is a meaning that the full tension of the poem will not allow us to entertain exclusively. For we are compelled, since it is there, to give equal weight to an intensive meaning so rich that, without contradicting the literal statement of the lover-mistress convention, it lifts that convention into an insight into one phase of the human predicament—the conflict of sensuality and asceticism.

I should like to quote now, not from Marvell, but a stanza from Donne that I hope will reinforce a little what I have just said and connect it with some earlier remarks.

> Our two soules therefore, which are one,
>   Though I must goe, endure not yet
> A breach, but an expansion,
>   Like gold to aiery thinnesse beate.

Here Donne brings together the developing imagery of twenty lines under the implicit proposition: the unity of two lovers' souls is a nonspatial entity, and is therefore indivisible. That, I believe, is what Mr. John Crowe Ransom would call the logic of the passage; it is the abstract form of its extensive meaning. Now the interesting feature here is the logical contradiction of embodying the unitary, nonspatial soul in a spatial image: the malleable gold is a plane whose surface can always be extended mathematically by one-half, towards infinity; the souls are this infinity. The finite image of the gold, in extension, logically contradicts the intensive meaning (infinity) which it conveys; but it does not invalidate that meaning. We have seen that Cowley compelled us to ignore the denoted diaper in order that we might take seriously the violet which it pretended to swathe. But in Donne's *Valediction: forbidding mourning* the clear denotation of the gold contains, by intension, the full meaning of the passage. If we reject the gold, we reject the meaning, for the meaning is wholly absorbed into the image of the gold. Intension and extension are here one, and they enrich each other.

Before I leave this beautiful object, I should like to notice two incidental features in further proof of Donne's mastery. "Expansion" —a term denoting an abstract property common to many objects, perhaps here one property of a gas: it expands visibly the quality of the beaten gold.

> . . . endure not yet
> a breach . . .

But if the lovers' souls are the formidable, inhuman entity that we have seen, are they not superior to the contingency of a breach? Yes and no: both answers are true answers; for by means of the sly "yet"

Donne subtly guards himself against our irony, which would otherwise be quick to scrutinize the extreme metaphor. The lovers have not endured a breach, but they are simple, miserable human beings, and they may quarrel tomorrow.[1]

Now all this meaning and more, and it is all one meaning, is embedded in that stanza: I say more because I have not exhausted the small fraction of significance that my limited powers have permitted me to see. For example, I have not discussed the rhythm, which is of the essential meaning; I have violently isolated four lines from the meaning of the whole poem. Yet, fine as it is, I do not think the poem the greatest poetry; perhaps only very little of Donne makes that grade, or of anybody else. Donne offers many examples of tension in imagery, easier for the expositor than greater passages in Shakespeare.

But convenience of elucidation is not a canon of criticism. I wish now to introduce other kinds of instance, and to let them stand for us as a sort of Arnoldish touchstones to the perfection that poetic statement has occasionally reached. I do not know what bearing my comment has had, or my touchstones may have, upon the larger effects of poetry or upon long poems. The long poem is partly a different problem. I have of necessity confined both commentary and illustration to the slighter effects that seemed to me commensurate with certain immediate qualities of language. For, in the long run, whatever the poet's "philosophy," however wide may be the extension of his meaning—like Milton's Ptolemaic universe in which he didn't believe—by his language shall you know him; the quality of his language is the valid limit of what he has to say.

I have not searched out the quotations that follow: they at once form the documentation and imply the personal bias from which this inquiry has grown. Only a few of the lines will be identified with the metaphysical technique, or, in Mr. Ransom's fine phrase, the metaphysical strategy. Strategy would here indicate the point on the intensive-extensive scale at which the poet deploys his resources of meaning. The metaphysical poet as a rationalist begins at or near the extensive or denoting end of the line; the romantic or Symbolist poet at the other, intensive end; and each by a straining feat of the imagination tries to push his meanings as far as he can towards the opposite end, so as to occupy the entire scale. I have offered one good and one bad example of the metaphysical strategy, but only defective examples of the Symbolist, which I cited as fallacies of mass language: Thomson was using language at its mass level, unhappily ignorant of the need to embody his connotations in a rational order of thought. (I allude here also, and in a quite literal sense, to Thomson's personal

[1] Mr. F. O. Matthiessen informs me that my interpretation here, which detaches the "yet" from the developing figure, is not the usual one. Mr. Matthiessen refers the phrase to the gold, for which in his view it prepares the way.

unhappiness, as well as to the excessive pessimism and excessive optimism of other poets of his time.) The great Symbolist poets, from Rimbaud to Yeats, have heeded this necessity of reason. It would be a hard task to choose between the two strategies, the Symbolist and the metaphysical; both at their best are great, and both are incomplete.

These touchstones, I believe, are not poetry of the extremes, but poetry of the center: poetry of tension, in which the "strategy" is diffused into the unitary effect.

Ask me no more whither doth hast
The Nightingale when May is past:
For in your sweet dividing throat
She winters, and keeps warm her note.

. . . . .

O thou Steeled Cognizance whose leap commits
The agile precincts of the lark's return . . .

. . . . .

That time of year thou mayst in me behold
When yellow leaves, or none, or few do hang
Upon those boughs which shake against the cold,
Bare ruined choirs where late the sweet birds sang.

. . . . .

Beauty is but a flower
Which wrinkles will devour;
Brightness falls from the air,
Queens have died young and fair,
Dust hath closed Helen's eye.
I am sick, I must die.
Lord, have mercy upon us!

. . . . .

And then may chance thee to repent
The time that thou hast lost and spent
To cause thy lovers sigh and swoon;
Then shalt thou know beauty but lent,
And wish and want as I have done.

. . . . .

We have lingered in the chambers of the sea
By seagirls wreathed with seaweed red and brown
Till human voices wake us and we drown.

. . . . .

I am of Ireland
And the Holy Land of Ireland
And time runs on, cried she.
Come out of charity
And dance with me in Ireland.

. . . . .

And my poor fool is hanged! No, no, no life!
Why should a dog, a horse, a rat, have life
And thou no breath at all? Thou'lt come no more,
Never, never, never, never, never!—
Pray you undo this button; thank you, sir.—
Do you see this? Look on her,—look,—her lips,—
Look there, look there!

. . . . .

'Tis madness to resist or blame
The force of angry heavens flame:
And, if we would speak true,
Much to the Man is due,
Who, from his private Gardens, where
He liv'd reserved and austere,
As if his highest plot
To plant the Bergamot,
Could by industrious Valour climbe
To ruin the great Work of Time,
And cast the Kingdome old
Into another Mold.

. . . . .

Cover her face; mine eyes dazzle; she died young.

III

There are three more lines that I wish to look at: a tercet from the *Divine Comedy*. I know little of either Dante or his language; yet I have chosen as my final instance of tension—the instance itself will relieve me of the responsibility of the term—I have chosen not a great and difficult passage, but only a slight and perfect one. It is from a scene that has always been the delight of the amateur reader of Dante; we can know more about it with less knowledge than about any other, perhaps, in the poem. The damned of the Second Circle are equivocally damned: Paolo and Francesca were illicit lovers but their crime was incontinence, neither adultery nor pandering, the two crimes of sex for which Dante seems to find any real theological reprobation, for they are committed with the intent of injury.

You will remember that when Dante first sees the lovers they are whirling in a high wind, the symbol here of lust. When Francesca's conversation with the poet begins, the wind dies down, and she tells him where she was born, in these lines:

Siede la terra dove nata fui
Sulla marina dove il Po discende
Per aver pace co' seguaci sui.

Mr. Courtney Landon renders the tercet:

> The town where I was born sits on the shore,
> Whither the Po descends to be at peace
> Together with the streams that follow him.

But it misses a good deal; it misses the force of *seguaci* by rendering it as a verb. Professor Grandgent translates the third line: "To have peace with its pursuers," and comments: "The tributaries are conceived as chasing the Po down to the sea." Precisely; for if the *seguaci* are merely followers, and not pursuers also, the wonderfully ordered density of this simple passage is sacrificed. For although Francesca has told Dante where she lives, in the most directly descriptive language possible, she has told him more than that. Without the least imposition of strain upon the firmly denoted natural setting, she fuses herself with the river Po near which she was born. By a subtle shift of focus we see the pursued river as Francesca in Hell: the pursuing tributaries are a new visual image for the pursuing winds of lust. A further glance yields even more: as the winds, so the tributaries at once pursue and become one with the pursued; that is to say, Francesca has completely absorbed the substance of her sin—she *is* the sin; as, I believe it is said, the damned of the *Inferno* are plenary incarnations of the sin that has put them there. The tributaries of the Po are not only the winds of lust by analogy of visual images; they become identified by means of sound:

> . . . di*sc*ende
> Per aver pa*ce* co' segua*ci* sui.

The sibilants dominate the line; they are the hissing of the wind. But in the last line of the preceding tercet Francesca has been grateful that the wind has subsided so that she can be heard—

> Mentre che il vento, come fa, si tace.

After the wind has abated, then, we hear in the silence, for the first time, its hiss, in the susurration of the descending Po. The river is thus both a visual and an auditory image, and since Francesca is her sin and her sin is embodied in this image, we are entitled to say that it is a sin that we can both hear and see.

THE LANGUAGE OF PARADOX

(1942)

CLEANTH BROOKS

FEW OF US are prepared to accept the statement that the language of poetry is the language of paradox. Paradox is the language of sophistry, hard, bright, witty; it is hardly the language of the soul. We are willing to allow that paradox is a permissible weapon which a Chesterton may on occasion exploit. We may permit it in epigram, a special subvariety of poetry; and in satire, which though useful, we are hardly willing to allow to be poetry at all. Our prejudices force us to regard paradox as intellectual rather than emotional, clever rather than profound, rational rather than divinely irrational.

Yet there is a sense in which paradox is the language appropriate and inevitable to poetry. It is the scientist whose truth requires a language purged of every trace of paradox; apparently the truth which the poet utters can be approached only in terms of paradox. I overstate the case, to be sure; it is possible that the title of this chapter is itself to be treated as merely a paradox. But there are reasons for thinking that the overstatement which I propose may light up some elements in the nature of poetry which tend to be overlooked.

The case of William Wordsworth, for instance, is instructive on this point. His poetry would not appear to promise many examples of the language of paradox. He usually prefers the direct attack. He insists on simplicity; he distrusts whatever seems sophistical. And yet the typical Wordsworth poem is based upon a paradoxical situation. Consider his celebrated

> It is a beauteous evening, calm and free,
> The holy time is quiet as a Nun
> Breathless with adoration. . . .

The poet is filled with worship, but the girl who walks beside him is not worshiping. The implication is that she should respond to the holy time, and become like the evening itself, nunlike; but she seems less worshipful than inanimate nature itself. Yet

> If thou appear untouched by solemn thought,
> Thy nature is not therefore less divine:

Thou liest in Abraham's bosom all the year;
And worship'st at the Temple's inner shrine,
God being with thee when we know it not.

The underlying paradox (of which the enthusiastic reader may well be unconscious) is nevertheless thoroughly necessary, even for that reader. Why does the innocent girl worship more deeply than the self-conscious poet who walks beside her? Because she is filled with an unconscious sympathy for *all* of nature, not merely the grandiose and solemn. One remembers the lines from Wordsworth's friend, Coleridge:

He prayeth best, who loveth best
All things both great and small.

Her unconscious sympathy is the unconscious worship. She is in communion with nature "all the year," and her devotion is continual whereas that of the poet is sporadic and momentary. But we have not done with the paradox yet. It not only underlies the poem, but something of the paradox informs the poem, though, since this is Wordsworth, rather timidly. The comparison of the evening to the nun actually has more than one dimension. The calm of the evening obviously means "worship," even to the dull-witted and insensitive. It corresponds to the trappings of the nun, visible to everyone. Thus, it suggests not merely holiness, but, in the total poem, even a hint of Pharisaical holiness, with which the girl's careless innocence, itself a symbol of her continual secret worship, stands in contrast.

Or consider Wordsworth's sonnet, *Composed upon Westminster Bridge*. I believe that most readers will agree that it is one of Wordsworth's most successful poems; yet most students have the greatest difficulty in accounting for its goodness. The attempt to account for it on the grounds of nobility of sentiment soon breaks down. On this level, the poem merely says: that the city in the morning light presents a picture which is majestic and touching to all but the most dull of souls; but the poem says very little more about the sight: the city is beautiful in the morning light and it is awfully still. The attempt to make a case for the poem in terms of the brilliance of its images also quickly breaks down: the student searches for graphic details in vain; there are next to no realistic touches. In fact, the poet simply huddles the details together:

. . . silent, bare,
Ships, towers, domes, theatres, and temples lie
Open unto the fields . . .

We get a blurred impression—points of roofs and pinnacles along the skyline, all twinkling in the morning light. More than that, the sonnet as a whole contains some very flat writing and some well-worn comparisons.

The reader may ask: Where, then, does the poem get its power? It gets it, it seems to me, from the paradoxical situation out of which the poem arises. The speaker is honestly surprised, and he manages to get some sense of awed surprise into the poem. It is odd to the poet that the city should be able to "wear the beauty of the morning" at all. Mount Snowden, Skiddaw, Mont Blanc—these wear it by natural right, but surely not grimy, feverish London. This is the point of the almost shocked exclamation:

> Never did sun more beautifully steep
> In his first splendour, *valley, rock,* or *hill*...

The "smokeless air" reveals a city which the poet did not know existed: man-made London is a part of nature too, is lighted by the sun of nature, and lighted to as beautiful effect.

> The river glideth at his own sweet will...

A river is the most "natural" thing that one can imagine; it has the elasticity, the curved line of nature itself. The poet had never been able to regard this one as a real river—now, uncluttered by barges, the river reveals itself as a natural thing, not at all disciplined into a rigid and mechanical pattern: it is like the daffodils, or the mountain brooks, artless, and whimsical, and "natural" as they. The poem closes, you will remember, as follows:

> Dear God! the very houses seem asleep;
> And all that mighty heart is lying still!

The city, in the poet's insight of the morning, has earned its right to be considered organic, not merely mechanical. That is why the stale metaphor of the sleeping houses is strangely renewed. The most exciting thing that the poet can say about the houses is that they are *asleep*. He has been in the habit of counting them dead—as just mechanical and inanimate; to say they are "asleep" is to say that they are alive, that they participate in the life of nature. In the same way, the tired old metaphor which sees a great city as a pulsating heart of empire becomes revivified. It is only when the poet sees the city under the semblance of death that he can see it as actually alive—quick with the only life which he can accept, the organic life of "nature."

It is not my intention to exaggerate Wordsworth's own consciousness of the paradox involved. In this poem, he prefers, as is usual with him, the frontal attack. But the situation is paradoxical here as in so many of his poems. In his preface to the second edition of the *Lyrical Ballads* Wordsworth stated that his general purpose was "to choose incidents and situations from common life" but so to treat them that "ordinary things should be presented to the mind in an unusual aspect." Coleridge was to state the purpose for him later, in terms which make even more evident Wordsworth's exploitation of the paradoxical: "Mr. Wordsworth . . . was to propose to himself as his object, to give the charm of novelty to things of every day, and to excite a feeling analogous to the supernatural, by awakening the mind's attention from the lethargy of custom, and directing it to the loveliness and the wonders of the world before us . . ." Wordsworth, in short, was consciously attempting to show his audience that the common was really uncommon, the prosaic was really poetic.

Coleridge's terms, "the charm of novelty to things of every day," "awakening the mind," suggest the Romantic preoccupation with wonder—the surprise, the revelation which puts the tarnished familiar world in a new light. This may well be the *raison d'être* of most Romantic paradoxes; and yet the neo-classic poets use paradox for much the same reason. Consider Pope's lines from *The Essay on Man:*

> In doubt his Mind or Body to prefer;
> Born but to die, and reas'ning but to err;
> Alike in ignorance, his Reason such,
> Whether he thinks too little, or too much . . .
>
> Created half to rise, and half to fall;
> Great Lord of all things, yet a Prey to all;
> Sole Judge of Truth, in endless Error hurl'd;
> The Glory, Jest, and Riddle of the world!

Here, it is true, the paradoxes insist on the irony, rather than the wonder. But Pope too might have claimed that he was treating the things of every day, man himself, and awakening his mind so that he would view himself in a new and blinding light. Thus, there is a certain awed wonder in Pope just as there is a certain trace of irony implicit in the Wordsworth sonnets. There is, of course, no reason why they should not occur together, and they do. Wonder and irony merge in many of the lyrics of Blake; they merge in Coleridge's *Ancient Mariner.* The variations in emphasis are numerous. Gray's *Elegy* uses a typical Wordsworth "situation" with the rural scene and with peasants contemplated in the light of their "betters." But in the *Elegy* the balance is heavily tilted in the direction of irony, the revelation an ironic rather than a startling one:

> Can storied urn or animated bust
> Back to its mansion call the fleeting breath?
> Can Honour's voice provoke the silent dust?
> Or Flatt'ry sooth the dull cold ear of Death?

But I am not here interested in enumerating the possible variations; I am interested rather in our seeing that the paradoxes spring from the very nature of the poet's language: it is a language in which the connotations play as great a part as the denotations. And I do not mean that the connotations are important as supplying some sort of frill or trimming, something external to the real matter in hand. I mean that the poet does not use a notation at all—as the scientist may properly be said to do so. The poet, within limits, has to make up his language as he goes.

T. S. Eliot has commented upon "that perpetual slight alteration of language, words perpetually juxtaposed in new and sudden combinations," which occurs in poetry. It *is* perpetual; it cannot be kept out of the poem; it can only be directed and controlled. The tendency of science is necessarily to stabilize terms, to freeze them into strict denotations; the poet's tendency is by contrast disruptive. The terms are continually modifying each other, and thus violating their dictionary meanings. To take a very simple example, consider the adjectives in the first lines of Wordsworth's evening sonnet: *beauteous, calm, free, holy, quiet, breathless.* The juxtapositions are hardly startling; and yet notice this: the evening is like a nun breathless with adoration. The adjective "breathless" suggests tremendous excitement; and yet the evening is not only quiet but *calm.* There is no final contradiction, to be sure: it is *that* kind of calm and *that* kind of excitement, and the two states may well occur together. But the poet has no one term. Even if he had a polysyllabic technical term, the term would not provide the solution for his problem. He must work by contradiction and qualification.

We may approach the problem in this way: the poet has to work by analogies. All of the subtler states of emotion, as I. A. Richards has pointed out, necessarily demand metaphor for their expression. The poet must work by analogies, but the metaphors do not lie in the same plane or fit neatly edge to edge. There is a continual tilting of the planes; necessary overlappings, discrepancies, contradictions. Even the most direct and simple poet is forced into paradoxes far more often than we think, if we are sufficiently alive to what he is doing.

But in dilating on the difficulties of the poet's task, I do not want to leave the impression that it is a task which necessarily defeats him, or even that with his method he may not win to a fine precision. To use Shakespeare's figure, he can

> . . . with assays of bias
> By indirections find directions out.

Shakespeare had in mind the game of lawnbowls in which the bowl is distorted, a distortion which allows the skillful player to bowl a curve. To elaborate the figure, science makes use of the perfect sphere and its attack can be direct. The method of art can, I believe, never be direct—is always indirect. But that does not mean that the master of the game cannot place the bowl where he wants it. The serious difficulties will only occur when he confuses his game with that of science and mistakes the nature of his appropriate instrument. Mr. Stuart Chase a few years ago, with a touching naïveté, urged us to take the distortion out of the bowl—to treat language like notation.

I have said that even the apparently simple and straightforward poet is forced into paradoxes by the nature of his instrument. Seeing this, we should not be surprised to find poets who consciously employ it to gain a compression and precision otherwise unobtainable. Such a method, like any other, carries with it its own perils. But the dangers are not overpowering; the poem is not predetermined to a shallow and glittering sophistry. The method is an extension of the normal language of poetry, not a perversion of it.

I should like to refer the reader to a concrete case. Donne's *Canonization* ought to provide a sufficiently extreme instance.[1] The basic metaphor which underlies the poem (and which is reflected in the title) involves a sort of paradox. For the poet daringly treats profane love as if it were divine love. The canonization is not that of a pair of holy anchorites who have renounced the world and the flesh. The hermitage of each is the other's body; but they do renounce the world, and so their title to sainthood is cunningly argued. The poem then is a parody of Christian sainthood; but it is an intensely serious parody of a sort that modern man, habituated as he is to an easy yes or no, can hardly understand. He refuses to accept the paradox as a serious rhetorical device; and since he is able to accept it only as a cheap trick, he is forced into this dilemma. Either: Donne does not take love seriously; here he is merely sharpening his wit as a sort of mechanical exercise. Or: Donne does not take sainthood seriously; here he is merely indulging in a cynical and bawdy parody.

Neither account is true; a reading of the poem will show that Donne takes both love and religion seriously; it will show, further, that the paradox is here his inevitable instrument. But to see this plainly will require a closer reading than most of us give to poetry.

The poem opens dramatically on a note of exasperation. The "you" whom the speaker addresses is not identified. We can imagine that it is a person, perhaps a friend, who is objecting to the speaker's love affair. At any rate, the person represents the practical world which regards love as a silly affectation. To use the metaphor on which the poem is built, the friend represents the secular world which the lovers have renounced.

Donne begins to suggest this metaphor in the first stanza by the contemptuous alternatives which he suggests to the friend:

> . . . chide my palsie, or my gout,
> My five gray haires, or ruin'd fortune flout. . . .

The implications are: (1) All right, consider my love as an infirmity, as a disease, if you will, but confine yourself to my other infirmities,

[1] The text of Donne's *Canonization* is provided in an appendix to this essay.

my palsy, my approaching old age, my ruined fortune. You stand a better chance of curing those; in chiding me for this one, you are simply wasting your time as well as mine. (2) Why don't you pay attention to your own welfare—go on and get wealth and honor for yourself. What should you care if I do give these up in pursuing my love.

The two main categories of secular success are neatly, and contemptuously epitomized in the line

> Or the Kings reall, or his stamped face...

Cultivate the court and gaze at the king's face there, or, if you prefer, get into business and look at his face stamped on coins. But let me alone.

This conflict between the "real" world and the lover absorbed in the world of love runs through the poem; it dominates the second stanza in which the torments of love, so vivid to the lover, affect the real world not at all—

> What merchants ships have my sighs drown'd?

It is touched on in the fourth stanza in the contrast between the word "Chronicle" which suggests secular history with its pomp and magnificence, the history of kings and princes, and the word "sonnets" with its suggestions of trivial and precious intricacy. The conflict appears again in the last stanza, only to be resolved when the unworldly lovers, love's saints who have given up the world, paradoxically achieve a more intense world. But here the paradox is still contained in, and supported by, the dominant metaphor: so does the holy anchorite win a better world by giving up this one.

But before going on to discuss this development of the theme, it is important to see what else the second stanza does. For it is in this second stanza and the third, that the poet shifts the tone of the poem, modulating from the note of irritation with which the poem opens into the quite different tone with which it closes.

Donne accomplishes the modulation of tone by what may be called an analysis of love-metaphor. Here, as in many of his poems, he shows that he is thoroughly self-conscious about what he is doing. This second stanza he fills with the conventionalized figures of the Petrarchan tradition: the wind of lovers' sighs, the floods of lovers' tears, etc.—extravagant figures with which the contemptuous secular friend might be expected to tease the lover. The implication is that the poet himself recognizes the absurdity of the Petrarchan love metaphors. But what of it? The very absurdity of the jargon which lovers are expected to talk makes for his argument: their love, however absurd it may appear to the world, does no harm to the world. The practical friend need have no fears: there will still be wars to fight and lawsuits to argue.

The opening of the third stanza suggests that this vein of irony is to be maintained. The poet points out to his friend the infinite fund of such absurdities which can be applied to lovers:

> Call her one, mee another flye,
> We'are Tapers too, and at our owne cost die. . . .

For that matter, the lovers can conjure up for themselves plenty of such fantastic comparisons: *they* know what the world thinks of them. But these figures of the third stanza are no longer the threadbare Petrarchan conventionalities; they have sharpness and bite. The last one, the likening of the lovers to the phoenix, is fully serious, and with it, the tone has shifted from ironic banter into a defiant but controlled tenderness.

The effect of the poet's implied awareness of the lovers' apparent madness is to cleanse and revivify metaphor; to indicate the sense in which the poet accepts it, and thus to prepare us for accepting seriously the fine and seriously intended metaphors which dominate the last two stanzas of the poem.

The opening line of the fourth stanza,

> Wee can dye by it, if not live by love,

achieves an effect of tenderness and deliberate resolution. The lovers are ready to die to the world; they are committed; they are not callow but confident. (The basic metaphor of the saint, one notices, is being carried on; the lovers, in their renunciation of the world, have something of the confident resolution of the saint. By the bye, the word "legend"—

> . . . if unfit for tombes and hearse
> Our legend bee—

in Donne's time meant "the life of a saint.") The lovers are willing to forego the ponderous and stately chronicle and to accept the trifling and insubstantial "sonnet" instead; but then if the urn be well wrought, it provides a finer memorial for one's ashes than does the pompous and grotesque monument. With the finely contemptuous, yet quiet phrase, "halfe-acre tombes," the world which the lovers reject expands into something gross and vulgar. But the figure works further; the pretty sonnets will not merely hold their ashes as a decent earthly memorial. Their legend, their story, will gain them canonization; and approved as love's saints, other lovers will invoke them.

In this last stanza, the theme receives a final complication. The lovers in rejecting life actually win to the most intense life. This paradox has been hinted at earlier in the phoenix metaphor. Here it receives a powerful dramatization. The lovers in becoming hermits, find that they have not lost the world, but have gained the world in each other, now a more intense, more meaningful world. Donne is not content to treat the lovers' discovery as something which comes to them passively, but rather as something which they actively achieve They are like the saint, God's athlete:

> Who did the whole worlds soule *contract,* and *drove*
> Into the glasses of your eyes....

The image is that of a violent squeezing as of a powerful hand. And what do the lovers "drive" into each other's eyes? The "Countries, Townes," and "Courts," which they renounced in the first stanza of the poem. The unworldly lovers thus become the most "worldly" of all.

The tone with which the poem closes is one of triumphant achievement, but the tone is a development contributed to by various earlier elements. One of the more important elements which works toward our acceptance of the final paradox is the figure of the phoenix, which will bear a little further analysis.

The comparison of the lovers to the phoenix is very skillfully related to the two earlier comparisons, that in which the lovers are like burning tapers, and that in which they are like the eagle and the dove. The phoenix comparison gathers up both: the phoenix is a bird, and like the tapers, it burns. We have a selected series of items: the phoenix figure seems to come in a natural stream of association. "Call us what you will," the lover says, and rattles off in his desperation the first comparisons that occur to him. The comparison to the phoenix seems thus merely another outlandish one, the most outrageous of all. But it is this most fantastic one, stumbled over apparently in his haste, that the poet goes on to develop. It really describes the lovers best and justifies their renunciation. For the phoenix is not two but one, "we two being one, are it"; and it burns, not like the taper at its own cost, but to live again. Its death is life: "Wee dye and rise the same . . ." The poet literally justifies the fantastic assertion. In the sixteenth and seventeenth centuries to "die" means to experience the consummation of the act of love. The lovers after the act are the same. Their love is not exhausted in mere lust. This is their title to canonization. Their love is like the phoenix.

I hope that I do not seem to juggle the meaning of *die.* The meaning that I have cited can be abundantly justified in the literature of the period; Shakespeare uses "die" in this sense; so does Dryden. Moreover, I do not think that I give it undue emphasis. The word is in a crucial position. On it is pivoted the transition to the next stanza,

> Wee can dye by it, if not live by love,
> And if unfit for tombes...

Most important of all, the sexual submeaning of "die" does not contradict the other meanings: the poet is saying: "Our death is really a more intense life"; "We can afford to trade life (the world) for death (love), for that death is the consummation of life"; "After all, one does not expect to live *by* love, one expects, and wants, to die *by* it." But in the total passage he is also saying: "Because our love is not mundane, we can give up the world"; "Because our love is not merely lust, we can give up the other lusts, the lust for wealth and power"; "because," and this is said with an inflection of irony as by one who knows the world too well, "because our love can outlast its consummation, we are a minor miracle, we are love's saints." This passage with its ironical tenderness and its realism feeds and supports the brilliant paradox with which the poem closes.

There is one more factor in developing and sustaining the final effect. The poem is an instance of the doctrine which it asserts; it is both the assertion and the realization of the assertion. The poet has actually before our eyes built within the song the "pretty room" with which he says the lovers can be content. The poem itself is the well-wrought urn which can hold the lovers' ashes and which will not suffer in comparison with the prince's "halfe-acre tomb."

And how necessary are the paradoxes? Donne might have said directly, "Love in a cottage is enough." *The Canonization* contains this admirable thesis, but it contains a great deal more. He might have been as forthright as a later lyricist who wrote, "We'll build a sweet little nest,/ Somewhere out in the West,/ And let the rest of the world go by." He might even have imitated that more metaphysical lyric, which maintains, "You're the cream in my coffee." *The Canonization* touches on all these observations, but it goes beyond them, not merely in dignity, but in precision.

I submit that the only way by which the poet could say what *The Canonization* says is by paradox. More direct methods may be tempting, but all of them enfeeble and distort what is to be said. This statement may seem the less surprising when we reflect on how many of the important things which the poet has to say have to be said by means of paradox: most of the language of lovers is such—*The Canonization* is a good example; so is most of the language of religion—"He who would save his life, must lose it"; "The last shall be first." Indeed, almost any insight important enough to warrant a great poem apparently has to be stated in such terms.[2] Deprived of the character of paradox with its twin concomitants of irony and wonder, the matter of Donne's poem unravels into "facts," biological, sociological, and economic. What happens to Donne's lovers if we consider them "scientifically," without benefit of the supernaturalism which the poet confers upon them? Well, what happens to Shakespeare's lovers, for

2 Brooks's formulation, as stated here and elsewhere in *The Well Wrought Urn*, is disputed by John Crowe Ransom in "Poetry: The Formal Analysis," *Kenyon Review*, 9 (Summer, 1947). See also R. S. Crane's critique of Brooks in *Modern Philology*, 45 (May, 1948), 226-245. [*Editor's note.*]

Shakespeare uses the basic metaphor of *The Canonization* in his *Romeo and Juliet?* In their first conversation, the lovers play with the analogy between the lover and the pilgrim to the Holy Land. Juliet says:

> For saints have hands that pilgrims' hands do touch
> And palm to palm is holy palmers' kiss.

Considered scientifically, the lovers become Mr. Aldous Huxley's animals, "quietly sweating, palm to palm."

For us today, Donne's imagination seems obsessed with the problem of unity; the sense in which the lovers become one—the sense in which the soul is united with God. Frequently, as we have seen, one type of union becomes a metaphor for the other. It may not be too far-fetched to see both as instances of, and metaphors for, the union which the creative imagination itself effects. For that fusion is not logical; it apparently violates science and common sense; it welds together the discordant and the contradictory. Coleridge has of course given us the classic description of its nature and power. It "reveals itself in the balance or reconcilement of opposite or discordant qualities: of sameness, with difference; of the general, with the concrete; the idea, with the image; the individual, with the representative; the sense of novelty and freshness, with old and familiar objects; a more than usual state of emotion, with more than usual order . . ." It is a great and illuminating statement, but is a series of paradoxes. Apparently Coleridge could describe the effect of the imagination in no other way.

Shakespeare, in one of his poems, has given a description that oddly parallels that of Coleridge.

> Reason in it selfe confounded,
> Saw Division grow together,
> To themselves yet either neither,
> Simple were so well compounded.

I do not know what his *The Phoenix and the Turtle* celebrates. Perhaps it *was* written to honor the marriage of Sir John Salisbury and Ursula Stanley; or perhaps the Phoenix is Lucy, Countess of Bedford; or perhaps the poem is merely an essay on Platonic love. But the scholars themselves are so uncertain, that I think we will do little violence to established habits of thinking, if we boldly pre-empt the poem for our own purposes. Certainly the poem is an instance of that magic power which Coleridge sought to describe. I propose that we take it for a moment as a poem about that power;

> So they loved as love in twaine,
> Had the essence but in one,
> Two distincts, Division none,
> Number there in love was slaine.

Hearts remote, yet not asunder;
Distance and no space was seene,
Twixt this *Turtle* and his Queene;
But in them it were a wonder....

Propertie was thus appalled,
That the selfe was not the same;
Single Natures double name,
Neither two nor one was called.

Precisely! The nature is single, one, unified. But the name is double, and today with our multiplication of sciences, it is multiple. If the poet is to be true to his poetry, he must call it neither two nor one: the paradox is his only solution. The difficulty has intensified since Shakespeare's day: the timid poet, when confronted with the problem of "Single Natures double name," has too often funked it. A history of poetry from Dryden's time to our own might bear as its subtitle "The Half-Hearted Phoenix."

In Shakespeare's poem, Reason is "in it selfe confounded" at the union of the Phoenix and the Turtle; but it recovers to admit its own bankruptcy:

Love hath Reason, Reason none,
If what parts, can so remaine....

and it is Reason which goes on to utter the beautiful threnos with which the poem concludes:

Beautie, Truth, and Raritie,
Grace in all simplicitie,
Here enclosde, in cinders lie.

Death is now the *Phoenix* nest,
And the *Turtles* loyall brest,
To eternitie doth rest....

Truth may seeme, but cannot be,
Beautie bragge, but tis not she,
Truth and Beautie buried be.

To this urne let those repaire,
That are either true or faire,
For these dead Birds, sigh a prayer.

Having pre-empted the poem for our own purposes, it may not be too outrageous to go on to make one further observation. The urn to which we are summoned, the urn which holds the ashes of the phoenix, is like the well-wrought urn of Donne's *Canonization* which holds the phoenix-lovers' ashes: it is the poem itself. One is reminded of still another urn, Keats's Grecian urn, which contained for Keats,

Truth and Beauty, as Shakespeare's urn encloses "Beautie, Truth, and Raritie." But there is a sense in which all such well-wrought urns contain the ashes of a phoenix. The urns are not meant for memorial purposes only, though that often seems to be their chief significance to the professors of literature. The phoenix rises from its ashes; or ought to rise; but it will not arise for all our mere sifting and measuring the ashes, or testing them for their chemical content. We must be prepared to accept the paradox of the imagination itself; else "Beautie, Truth, and Raritie" remain enclosed in their cinders and we shall end with essential cinders, for all our pains.

—

APPENDIX

'The Canonization'

For Godsake hold your tongue, and let me love,
Or chide my palsie, or my gout,
My five gray haires, or ruin'd fortune flout,
With wealth your state, your minde with Arts improve,
Take you a course, get you a place,
Observe his honour, or his grace,
Or the Kings reall, or his stamped face
Contemplate, what you will, approve,
So you will let me love.

Alas, alas, who's injur'd by my love?
What merchants ships have my sighs drown'd?
Who saies my teares have overflow'd his ground?
When did my colds a forward spring remove?
When did the heats which my veines fill
Adde one more to the plaguie Bill?
Soldiers finde warres, and Lawyers finde out still
Litigous men, which quarrels move,
Though she and I do love.

Call us what you will, wee are made such by love;
Call her one, mee another flye,
We'are Tapers too, and at our owne cost die,
And wee in us finde the'Eagle and the Dove.
The Phoenix ridle hath more wit
By us, we two being one, are it.
So to one neutrall thing both sexes fit,
We dye and rise the same, and prove
Mysterious by this love.

Wee can dye by it, if not live by love,
And if unfit for tombes and hearse
Our legend bee, it will be fit for verse;
And if no peece of Chronicle wee prove,
We'll build in sonnets pretty roomes;
As well a well wrought urne becomes
The greatest ashes, as half-acre tombes,
And by these hymnes, all shall approve
Us Canoniz'd for Love:

And thus invoke us; You whom reverend love
Made one anothers hermitage;
You, to whom love was peace, that now is rage;
Who did the whole worlds soule contract, and drove
Into the glasses of your eyes
(So made such mirrors, and such spies,
That they did all to you epitomize,)
Countries, Townes, Courts: Beg from above
A patterne of your love!

THE USE OF "NEGATIVE" EMOTIONS

(1925)

EDGELL RICKWORD

AN EFFECT of the triumph of the romantic movement in the last century has been to separate the poet from the subjects which abound in ordinary social life and particularly from those emotions engendered by the clash of personality and the hostility of circumstances. A distinct bias has been created against the expression of particular grievances, which are supposed to offend against the proper attitude to poetry. This convention is as dangerous as the distinction which the French classicists draw between noble and vulgar emotions, and has a similar reflection in its effect on the poet's vocabulary—the erection of a literary language. Certain words become sacrosanct and are repeatedly invited to contribute, not for themselves but for the prestige they bring with them. The same prejudice towards a definite poetic suitability accounts for the contemporary preponderance of "nature" themes and imagery drawn from the back-garden of the week-end cottage. Under the pressure of this romantic theory personality and, still more, personalities have been squeezed out of contemporary verse. This is partly caused, no doubt, by the extension of the audience. It is doubtful if subjective poetry (that is, poetry which is not communal like the epic, drama, or narrative) is, by its own nature, capable of being stretched over such a wide area as that covered by the modern publisher. In fact, it demands an audience homogeneous in culture, and to some extent in its attitude to life, otherwise the difficulties of communication cannot be overcome, and the poet must fall back on commonplace, coarse reactions, or invest his small genuine discovery with a theatrical grandeur in order to get it a hearing.

The modern poet is to his audience an author, not a man. It is interested in his more generalized emotions, not in his relations with the life and people round him. Yet to himself the poet should be in the first place a man, not an author. He should not be conscious of a distinction between the sensations he gets from his immediate contact with things and the sensations he uses as the material of his art. At present he is inhibited from expressing a set of emotions (those we call negative emotions) because of a prejudice against them which is based on a temporary social queasiness. With what consternation would the critics and the public receive from a reputable poet such furious but measured invective as that with which Churchill attacked the dying Hogarth! I shall not quote that passage on Hogarth's physical ruin, which begins:

> With all the symptoms of assur'd decay...

since it is fairly well known. An assault from another direction shows exactly the kind of subject from which the modern poet is cut off, though not because he is unfamiliar with it:

> Oft have I known Thee, Hogarth, weak and vain,
> Thyself the idol of thy awkward strain,
> Thro' the dull measure of a summer's day,
> In phrase most vile, prate long, long hours away,
> Whilst Friends with Friends all gaping sit and gaze
> To hear a Hogarth babble Hogarth's praise.

Churchill has little verbal delicacy and none of the fatal wit of Pope; he stuns his opponent under the cumulate blows of the obvious. But he is also capable of varying the tone of his anger, and the impression we receive from the whole of the Epistle to Hogarth is not that of a small dog snarling at a big one; it is really sensitive, and so poetic, indignation. Apart from the political issues involved such as Hogarth's antagonism to Churchill's hero, Wilkes, it is a poem of the repulsion one personality may exert on another, the expression of the emotion with which one sophisticated social being may regard another, and made more poignant by the exploitation of Hogarth's decrepitude. Such material is taboo to contemporary taste; the artist is unable to approach it with an unprejudiced mind, since a low sort of agreement to universal solicitude has been reached by the modern community. In this respect the world of the eighteenth century is almost as remote from us as that of the Satyricon. Could we tolerate the innocent opportunism of the Matron of Ephesus except in the licensed playground of the classics?

Churchill is not pre-eminently a satirist; he has not sufficient detachment. He is a poet of invective, passionately absorbed in his subject. He cannot forget the miserable condition of Hogarth, and the thought of the venom which this almost extinct monster had the audacity to breathe out, stirs him to fresh indignant eloquence:

> I dare thy worst, with scorn behold thy rage,
> But with an eye of pity view thy Age;
> Thy feeble Age, in which as in a glass,
> We see how Men to dissolution pass.
> Thou *wretched Being*, whom on Reason's plan,
> So changed, so lost, I cannot call a Man,
> What could persuade thee at this time of life
> To launch afresh into the sea of strife?

Better for thee, scarce crawling on the earth,
Almost as much a child as at thy birth,
To have resigned in peace thy parting breath,
And sunk unnoticed in the arms of death.

Verse like this, though not often so fine as this, formed a not negligible part of the reading matter of the eighteenth century; to-day it has no survivors, and by some canons of criticism it would seem that we are well rid of it. It would most commonly be censured as unpoetic, since the term "poetry" tends to be narrowed down to expressions of certain kinds of experiences. Blake, who is qualified as an authority here, drew without immediate discrimination on his mundane comprehensions as well as on his celestial apprehensions:

When Sir Joshua Reynolds died
All Nature was degraded;
The King dropped a tear into the Queen's ear,
And all his pictures faded.

There is no doubt that literature suffers from the absence of a socialized medium to carry off these reactions, explosions of the spleen or long-rumored fulminations, and bring about that relief and cleansing of the mind which is one of the functions of expression. Such "negative" responses, which religion has exiled in forms of demons, are essential components of any fully satisfying work. So long as they are ignored we may continue to have a poetry fit for adolescents, but not for men; and the judgment of the common person, that poetry is "sloppy," will be quite justified.

Emotion acts not unlike such a fluid as the early scientists invented to explain the effects of electricity; it has really one continuous circular movement, but to the subject it appears to have two, parallel and in opposite directions. That is to say, it has a positive and a negative pole; it can be orientated, at its extreme, in either of two ways: as delight in, or disgust with, an object. Romantic poetry is always the expression of one of these extremes, but, since reactions are rarely so pure as to be fit to be represented as ecstasy, or complete revulsion, a great deal of the poetry based on this convention fails to satisfy modern sophistication. We need a poetry in which the moods are more subtly balanced. But, the more discordant the elements of a poem and the more freely they are associated, the greater becomes the difficulty of creating an æsthetic entity to bring about the catharsis which is the function of a poem. In the romantic convention this is achieved by an assertion transcending the values of ordinary emotional experience, and very effective it may be, but, like all phantasmal satisfactions, in its continued employment it leads to impotence; the abused nerves are stretched beyond the limit of responsiveness.

The poetry of the negative emotions, of those arising from disgust with the object, provides the means for a whole series of responses in parts of the mind which have been lying fallow for nearly two hundred years. This contemporary value is greater than its absolute value, for it shares with the romantic lyric the paucity of the too-sharply differentiated response, the facile catharsis. Even, since delight is more valued socially than disgust, an aphrodisiac more than an anaphrodisiac, it is likely to be always under-estimated by criticism; but this natural prejudice should not be allowed to obscure, as it too frequently does, the perfection of expression the negative poem may achieve, as for instance in the concluding lines of the *Dunciad*.

Swift is a great master of this kind of poetry. His verse has no pleasure-value beyond that of its symmetry and concision, but it is the most intricate labyrinth of personality that any poet has built round himself, not excepting Donne. It is characteristic that the study of "negative" emotions in poetry should tend to centre particularly in the fact of personality. That Swift was morbid is a commonplace; his verse would supply a textbook of psychopathology with as much material as it could use. The interest for the literary critic lies in Swift's success in transforming this material into forms of art. As a preliminary, we may examine the conclusion of one of his most repugnant descriptions, *The Lady's Dressing Room:*

> When Celia all her glory shows,
> If Strephon would but stop his nose...
> He soon will learn to think like me
> And bless his ravished eyes to see
> Such order from confusion sprung,
> Such gaudy tulips raised from dung.

After the long and exhaustive inventory which precedes them, these lines produce an expansion which is of the nature of a catharsis. It is effected by the sudden breaking of the monotonous revulsion with the introduction of a mass of irony and the final completely satisfying plastic image. Without sacrificing the integrity of his disgust he draws up the blind on a landscape towards which the mind may leap with justified delight, since the idea of erecting order out of chaos is an absolutely valuable one, whatever the implication in this particular instance. After this momentary concession Swift brings down the shade again with the last word, rhyme-enforced, but the image floats on in the consciousness. A similar process of expression, more complex æsthetically, and with the positive bias uppermost, may be observed in such of Baudelaire's poems as the *Hymne à la Beauté* or in *L'Amour du Mensonge,* which concludes:

> Qu'importe ta bêtise ou ton indifférence?
> Masque ou décor, salut! J'adore ta beauté!

Catharsis is a term which should perhaps be limited to works in which the emotion is objectified in characters and action. Yet an analogous process is the essential of success in a poem. A poem must, at some point or another, release, enable to flow back to the level of active life, the emotions caught up from life and pent in the æsthetic reservoir. Otherwise the poem is an artifice, a wax effigy in a glass case, a curiosity. In a poem there may be several such points of release, or of partial release, and it seems necessary that the predominant release should take place sufficiently near the end of the poem to be held in the consciousness till the poem is concluded. It need not take place in the last lines of a poem, though in fact it often does, but this is an effect which becomes mechanical and may be tiresome to sophisticated readers. The final couplet of the Shakespearean sonnet imposes this localization on a poet; it is a demand which is sometimes disadvantageous to Shakespeare himself. All fully-evolved formalistic structures, like the heroic couplet and the ballade, are susceptible to this automatism; lacking the element of surprise, their effectiveness as agents of the release is quickly diminished.

It seems that an early step to be taken, if poetry is to be liberated so that it may become a natural form of expression in the modern world, is an examination of the kinds of effect which have been employed to bring about the essential release.

PURE AND IMPURE POETRY[1]

(1943)

ROBERT PENN WARREN

CRITICS ARE rarely faithful to their labels and their special strategies. Usually the critic will confess that no one strategy—the psychological, the moralistic, the formalistic, the historical—or combination of strategies, will quite work the defeat of the poem. For the poem is like the monstrous Orillo in Boiardo's *Orlando Innamorato*. When the sword lops off any member of the monster, that member is immediately rejoined to the body, and the monster is as formidable as ever. But the poem is even more formidable than the monster, for Orillo's adversary finally gained a victory by an astonishing feat of dexterity: he slashed off both the monster's arms and quick as a wink seized them and flung them into the river. The critic who vaingloriously trusts his method to account for the poem, to exhaust the poem, is trying to emulate this dexterity: he thinks that he, too, can win by throwing the lopped-off arms into the river. But he is doomed to failure. Neither fire nor water will suffice to prevent the rejoining of the mutilated members to the monstrous torso. There is only one way to conquer the monster: you must eat it, bones, blood, skin, pelt, and gristle. And even then the monster is not dead, for it lives in you, is assimilated into you, and you are different, and somewhat monstrous yourself, for having eaten it.

So the monster will always win, and the critic knows this. He does not want to win. He knows that he must always play stooge to the monster. All he wants to do is to give the monster a chance to exhibit again its miraculous power.

With this fable, I shall begin by observing that poetry wants to be pure. And it always succeeds in this ambition. In so far as we have poetry at all, it is always pure poetry; that is, it is not non-poetry. The poetry of Shakespeare, the poetry of Pope, the poetry of Herrick, is pure, in so far as it is poetry at all. We call the poetry "higher" or "lower," we say "more powerful" or "less powerful" about it, and we are, no doubt, quite right in doing so. The souls that form the great rose of Paradise are seated in banks and tiers of ascending blessedness, but they are all saved, they are all perfectly happy; they are all "pure," for they have all been purged of mortal taint. This is not to say, however, that if we get poetry from one source, such a single

[1] This essay was delivered as one of the Mesures Lectures at Princeton in 1942. [*Editor's note.*]

source, say Shakespeare, should suffice us in as much as we can always appeal to it, or that, since all poetry is equally pure, we engage in a superfluous labor in trying to explore or create new sources of poetry. No, for we can remember that every soul in the great rose is precious in the eyes of God. No soul is the substitute for another.

Poetry wants to be pure, but poems do not. At least, most of them do not want to be too pure. The poems want to give us poetry, which is pure, and the elements of a poem, in so far as it is a good poem, will work together toward that end, but many of the elements, taken in themselves, may actually seem to contradict that end, or be neutral toward the achieving of that end. Are we then to conclude that, because neutral or recalcitrant elements appear in poems, even in poems called great, these elements are simply an index to human frailty, that in a perfect world there would be no dross in poems which would, then, be perfectly pure? No, it does not seem to be merely the fault of our world, for the poems include, deliberately, more of the so-called dross than would appear necessary. They are not even as pure as they might be in this imperfect world. They mar themselves with cacophonies, jagged rhythms, ugly words and ugly thoughts, colloquialisms, clichés, sterile technical terms, head work and argument, self-contradictions, cleverness, irony, realism—all things which call us back to the world of prose and imperfection.

Sometimes a poet will reflect on this state of affairs, and grieve. He will decide that he, at least, will try to make one poem as pure as possible. So he writes:

> Now sleeps the crimson petal, now the white;
> Nor waves the cypress in the palace walk;
> Nor winks the gold fin in the porphyry font:
> The firefly wakens: waken thou with me.

We know the famous garden. We know how all nature conspires here to express the purity of the moment: how the milk-white peacock glimmers like a ghost, and how like a ghost the unnamed "she" glimmers on to her tryst; how earth lies "all Danaë to the stars," as the beloved's heart lies open to the lover; and how, in the end, the lily folds up her sweetness, "and slips into the bosom of the lake," as the lovers are lost in the sweet dissolution of love.

And we know another poet and another garden. Or perhaps it is the same garden, after all:

> I arise from dreams of thee
> In the first sweet sleep of night,
> When the winds are breathing low
> And the stars are shining bright.
> I arise from dreams of thee,
> And a spirit in my feet
> Hath led me — who knows how?
> To thy chamber window, Sweet!

We remember how, again, all nature conspires, how the wandering airs "faint," how the Champak's odors "pine," how the nightingale's complaint "dies upon her heart," as the lover will die upon the beloved's heart. Nature here strains out of nature, it wants to be called by another name, it wants to spiritualize itself by calling itself another name. How does the lover get to the chamber window? He refuses to say how, in his semi-somnambulistic daze, he got there. He blames, he says, "a spirit in my feet," and hastens to disavow any knowledge of how that spirit operates. In any case, he arrives at the chamber window. Subsequent events and the lover's reaction toward them are somewhat hazy. We only know that the lover, who faints and fails at the opening of the last stanza, and who asks to be lifted from the grass by a more enterprising beloved, is in a condition of delectable passivity, in which distinctions blur out in the "purity" of the moment.

Let us turn to another garden: the place, Verona; the time, a summer night, with full moon. The lover speaks:

> But soft! what light through yonder window breaks?
> It is the east . . . .

But we know the rest, and know that this garden, in which nature for the moment conspires again with the lover, is the most famous of them all, for the scene is justly admired for its purity of effect, for giving us the very essence of young, untarnished love. Nature conspires beneficently here, but we may chance to remember that beyond the garden wall strolls Mercutio, who can celebrate Queen Mab, but who is always aware that nature has other names as well as the names the pure poets and pure lovers put upon her. And we remember that Mercutio outside the wall, has just said:

> . . . 'twould anger him
> To raise a spirit in his mistress's circle
> Of some strange nature, letting it there stand
> Till she had laid it and conjured it down.

Mercutio has made a joke, a bawdy joke. That is bad enough, but worse, he has made his joke witty and, worst of all, intellectually complicated in its form. Realism, wit, intellectual complication—these are the enemies of the garden purity.

But the poet has not only let us see Mercutio outside the garden wall. Within the garden itself, when the lover invokes nature, when he spiritualizes and innocently trusts her, and says,

> Lady, by yonder blessed moon I swear,

the lady herself replies,

> O, swear not by the moon, the inconstant moon,
> That monthly changes in her circled orb.

The lady distrusts "pure" poems, nature spiritualized into forgetfulness. She has, as it were, a rigorous taste in metaphor, too; she brings a logical criticism to bear on the metaphor which is too easy; the metaphor must prove itself to her, must be willing to subject itself to scrutiny beyond the moment's enthusiasm. She injects the impurity of an intellectual style into the lover's pure poem.

And we must not forget the voice of the nurse, who calls from within, a voice which, we discover, is the voice of expediency, of half-measures, of the view that circumstances alter cases—the voice of prose and imperfection.

It is time to ask ourselves if the celebrated poetry of this scene, which as poetry is pure, exists despite the impurities of the total composition, if the effect would be more purely poetic were the nurse and Mercutio absent and the lady a more sympathetic critic of pure poems. I do not think so. The effect might even be more vulnerable poetically if the impurities were purged away. Mercutio, the lady, and the nurse are critics of the lover, who believes in pure poems, but perhaps they are necessary. Perhaps the lover can only be accepted in their context. The poet seems to say: "I know the worst that can be said on this subject, and I am giving fair warning. Read at your own risk." So the poetry arises from a recalcitrant and contradictory context; and finally involves that context.

Let us return to one of the other gardens, in which there is no Mercutio or nurse, and in which the lady is more sympathetic. Let us mar its purity by installing Mercutio in the shrubbery, from which the poet was so careful to banish him. You can hear his comment when the lover says:

> And a spirit in my feet
> Hath led me—who knows how?
> To thy chamber window, Sweet!

And we can guess what the wicked tongue would have to say in response to the last stanza.

It may be that the poet should have made his peace early with Mercutio, and have appealed to his better nature. For Mercutio seems to be glad to cooperate with a poet. But he must be invited; otherwise, he is apt to show a streak of merry vindictiveness about the finished product. Poems are vulnerable enough at best. Bright reason mocks them like sun from a wintry sky. They are easily left naked to laughter when leaves fall in the garden and the cold winds come. Therefore, they need all the friends they can get, and Mercutio, who is an ally of reason and who himself is given to mocking laughter, is a good friend for a poem to have.

On what terms does a poet make his peace with Mercutio? There are about as many sets of terms as there are good poets. I know that

I have loaded the answer with the word *good* here, that I have implied a scale of excellence based, in part at least, on degree of complication. I shall return to this question. For the moment, however, let us examine a poem whose apparent innocence and simple lyric cry should earn it a place in any anthology of "pure poetry."

> Western wind, when wilt thou blow
> That the small rain down can rain?
> Christ, that my love were in my arms
> And I in my bed again!

The lover, grieving for the absent beloved, cries out for relief. Several kinds of relief are involved in the appeal to the wind. First, there is the relief that would be had from the sympathetic manifestation of nature. The lover, in his perturbation of spirit, invokes the perturbations of nature. He exclaims,

> Western wind, when wilt thou blow

and Lear exclaims,

> Blow, winds, and crack your cheeks! rage! blow!

Second, there is the relief that would be had by the fulfillment of grief—the frost of grief, the drought of grief broken, the full anguish expressed, then the violence allayed in the peace of tears. Third, there is the relief that would be had in the excitement and fulfillment of love itself. There seems to be a contrast between the first two types of relief and the third type; speaking loosely, we may say that the first two types are romantic and general, the third type realistic and specific So much for the first two lines.

In the last two lines, the lover cries out for the specific solace of his case: reunion with his beloved. But there is a difference between the two lines. The first is general, and romantic. The phrase "in my arms" does not seem to mean exactly what it says. True, it has a literal meaning, if we can look close at the words, but it is hard to look close because of the romantic aura—the spiritualized mist about them.[2] But with the last line the perfectly literal meaning suddenly comes into sharp focus. The mist is rifted and we can look straight at the words, which, we discover with a slight shock of surprise, do mean exactly what they say. The last line is realistic and specific. It is not even content to say,

> And I in bed again!

[2] It may be objected here that I am reading the phrase "in my arms" as a twentieth century reader. I confess the fact. Certainly, several centuries have passed since the composition of the little poem, and those centuries have thickened the romantic mist about the words, but it is scarcely to be believed that the sixteenth century was the clear, literal Eden dawn of poetry when words walked without the fig leaf.

It is, rather, more scrupulously specific, and says,

And I in *my* bed again! [3]

All of this does not go to say that the realistic elements here are to be taken as cancelling, or negating, the romantic elements. There is no ironical leer. The poem is not a celebration of carnality. It is a faithful lover who speaks. He is faithful to the absent beloved, and he is also faithful to the full experience of love. That is, he does not abstract one aspect of the experience and call it the whole experience. He does not strain nature out of nature; he does not over-spiritualize nature. This nameless poet would never have said, in the happier days of his love, that he had been led to his Sweet's chamber window by "a spirit in my feet"; and he certainly would not have added the coy disavowal, "who knows how?" But because the nameless poet refused to over-spiritualize nature, we can accept the spirituality of the poem.

Another poem gives us another problem.

Ah, what avails the sceptered race,
  Ah, what the form divine!
What every virtue, every grace!
  Rose Aylmer, all were thine.

Rose Aylmer, whom these wakeful eyes
  May weep, but never see,
A night of memories and of sighs
  I consecrate to thee.

This is another poem about lost love: a "soft" subject. Now to one kind of poet the soft subject presents a sore temptation. Because it is soft in its natural state, he is inclined to feel that to get at its poetic essence he must make it softer still, that he must insist on its softness, that he must render it as "pure" as possible. At first glance, it may seem that Landor is trying to do just that. What he says seems to be emphatic, unqualified, and open. Not every power, grace, and virtue could avail to preserve his love. That statement insists on the pathetic contrast. And in the next stanza, wakefulness and tearfulness are mentioned quite unashamedly, along with memories and sighs. It is all blurted out, as pure as possible.

But only in the paraphrase is it "blurted." The actual quality of the first stanza is hard, not soft. It is a chiseled stanza, in which formality

[3] In connection with the word *my* in this line, we may also feel that it helps to set over the comfort and satisfaction there specified against the bad weather of the first two lines. We may also glance at the word *small* in the second line. It is the scrupulous word, the word that, realistically, makes us believe in the rain. But, too, it is broader in its function. The storm which the lover invokes will not rend the firmament, it will not end the world; it will simply bring down the "small" rain, a credible rain.

is insisted upon. We may observe the balance of the first and second lines; the balance of the first half with the second half of the third line, which recapitulates the structure of the first two lines; the balance of the two parts of the last line, though here the balance is merely a rhythmical and not a sense balance as in the preceding instances; the binders of discreet alliteration, repetition, and assonance. The stanza is built up, as it were, of units which are firmly defined and sharply separated, phrase by phrase, line by line. We have the formal control of the soft subject, ritual and not surrender.

But in the second stanza the rigor of this formality is somewhat abated, as the more general, speculative emphasis (why cannot pomp, virtue, and grace avail?) gives way to the personal emphasis, as though the repetition of the beloved's name had, momentarily, released the flood of feeling. The first line of the second stanza spills over into the second; the "wakeful eyes" as subject find their verb in the next line, "weep," and the *wake-weep* alliteration, along with the rest after *weep,* points up the disintegration of the line, just as it emphasizes the situation. Then with the phrase "but never see" falling away from the long thrust of the rhetorical structure to the pause after *weep,* the poem seems to go completely soft, the frame is broken. But, even as the poet insists on "memories and sighs," in the last two lines he restores the balance. Notice the understatement of "A night." It says: "I know that life is a fairly complicated affair, and that I am committed to it and to its complications. I intend to stand by my commitment, as a man of integrity, that is, to live despite the grief. Since life is complicated, I cannot, if I am to live, spare too much time for indulging grief. I can give *a* night, but not all nights." The lover, like the hero of Frost's poem *Stopping by Woods on a Winter Evening,* tears himself from the temptation of staring into the treacherous, delicious blackness, for he, too, has "promises to keep." Or he resembles the Homeric heroes who, after the perilous passage is made, after their energy has saved their lives, and after they have beached their craft and eaten their meal, can then set aside an hour before sleep to mourn the comrades lost by the way—the heroes who, as Aldous Huxley says, understand realistically a whole truth as contrasted with a half-truth.

Is this a denial of the depth and sincerity of the grief? The soft reader, who wants the poem pure, may be inclined to say so. But let us look at the last line to see what it gives us in answer to this question. The answer seems to lie in the word *consecrate.* The meter thrusts this word at us; we observe that two of the three metrical accents in the line fall on syllables of this word forcing it beyond its prose emphasis. The word is important and the importance is justified, for the word tells us that the single night is not merely a lapse into weakness, a trivial event to be forgotten when the weakness is overcome. It is, rather, an event of the most extreme and focal importance.

an event formally dedicated, "set apart for sacred uses," an event by which other events are to be measured. So the word *consecrate* formalizes, philosophizes, ritualizes the grief; it specifies what style in the first stanza has implied.

But here is another poem of grief, grief at the death of a child:

> There was such speed in her little body,
> And such lightness in her footfall,
> It is no wonder that her brown study
> Astonishes us all.
>
> Her wars were bruited in our high window.
> We looked among orchard trees and beyond
> Where she took arms against her shadow,
> Or harried unto the pond
>
> The lazy geese, like a snow cloud
> Dripping their snow on the green grass,
> Tricking and stopping, sleepy and proud,
> Who cried in goose, Alas,
>
> For the tireless heart within the little
> Lady with rod that made them rise
> From their noon apple dreams, and scuttle
> Goose-fashion under the skies!
>
> But now go the bells, and we are ready;
> In one house we are sternly stopped
> To say we are vexed at her brown study,
> Lying so primly propped.

Another soft subject, softer, if anything, than the subject of *Rose Aylmer,* and it presents the same problem. But the problem is solved in a different way.

The first stanza is based on two time-honored clichés: first, "Heaven, won't that child ever be still, she is driving me distracted"; and second, "She was such an active, healthy-looking child, would you've ever thought she would just up and die?" In fact, the whole poem develops these clichés, and exploits, in a backhand fashion, the ironies implicit in their inter-relation. And in this connection, we may note that the fact of the clichés, rather than more original or profound observations, at the root of the poem is important; there is in the poem the contrast between the staleness of the clichés and the shock of the reality. Further we may note that the second cliché is an answer, savagely ironical in itself, to the first: the child you wished would be still *is* still, despite all that activity which your adult occupations deplored.

But such a savage irony is not the game here. It is too desperate, too naked, in a word, too pure. And ultimately, it is, in a sense, a meaningless irony if left in its pure state, because it depends on a mechanical, accidental contrast in nature, void of moral content. The poem is concerned with modifications and modulations of this brute, basic irony, modulations and modifications contingent upon an attitude taken toward it by a responsible human being, the speaker of the poem. The savagery is masked, or ameliorated.

In this connection, we may observe, first, the phrase "brown study." It is not the "frosted flower," the "marmoreal immobility," or any one of a thousand such phrases which would aim for the pure effect. It is merely the brown study which astonishes—a phrase which denies, as it were, the finality of the situation, underplays the pathos, and merely reminds one of those moments of childish pensiveness into which the grown-up cannot penetrate. And the phrase itself is a cliché—the common now echoed in the uncommon.

Next, we may observe that stanzas two, three, and four simply document, with a busy yet wavering rhythm (one sentence runs through the three stanzas) the tireless naughtiness which was once the cause of rebuke, the naughtiness which disturbed the mature going-on in the room with the "high window." But the naughtiness has been transmuted, by events just transpired, into a kind of fanciful storybook dream-world, in which geese are whiter than nature, and the grass greener, in which geese speak in goose language, saying "Alas," and have apple dreams. It is a drowsy, delicious world, in which the geese are bigger than life, and more important. It is an unreal (now unreal because lost), stylized world. Notice how the phrase "the little lady with rod" works: the detached, grown-up primness of "little lady"; the formal, stiff effect gained by the omission of the article before *rod;* the slightly unnatural use of the word *rod* itself, which sets some distance between us and the scene (perhaps with the hint of the fairy story, a magic wand, or a magic rod—not a common, everyday stick). But the stanzas tie back into the premises of the poem in other ways. The little girl, in her naughtiness, warred against her shadow. Is it crowding matters too hard to surmise that the shadow here achieves a sort of covert symbolic significance? The little girl lost her war against her "shadow," which was always with her. Certainly the phrase "tireless heart" has some rich connotations. And the geese which say "Alas!" conspire with the family to deplore the excessive activity of the child. (They do not conspire to express the present grief, only the past vexation—an inversion of the method of the pastoral elegy, or of the method of the first two garden poems.)

The business of the three stanzas, then, may be said to be twofold. First, they make us believe more fully in the child and therefore in the fact of the grief itself. They "prove" the grief, and they show the deliciousness of the lost world which will never look the same from the high window. Second, and contrarywise, they "transcend" the grief, or at least give a hint of a means for transcending the immediate anguish: the lost world is, in one sense, redeemed out of time, it enters the pages of the picture book where geese speak, where the untrue is true, where the fleeting is fixed. What was had cannot, after all, be lost. (By way of comparison—a comparison which, because extreme, may be helpful—I cite the transcendence in *La Recherche du Temps Perdu.*) The three stanzas, then, to state it in another way, have validated the first stanza and have prepared for the last.

The three stanzas have made it possible for us to say, when the bell tolls, "we are ready." Some kind of terms, perhaps not the best terms possible but some kind, have been made with the savage underlying irony. But the terms arrived at do not prevent the occasion from being a "stern" one. The transcendence is not absolute, and in the end is possible only because of an exercise of will and self-control. Because we control ourselves, we can say "vexed" and not some big word. And the word itself picks up the first of the domestic clichés on which the poem is based—the outburst of impatience at the naughty child who, by dying, has performed her most serious piece of naughtiness. But now the word comes to us charged with the burden of the poem, and further, as re-echoed here by the phrase "brown study," charged by the sentence in which it occurs: we are gathered formally, ritualistically, sternly together to say the word *vexed.*[4] *Vexed* becomes the ritualistic, the summarizing word.

I have used the words *pure* and *impure* often in the foregoing pages, and I confess that I have used them rather loosely. But perhaps it has been evident that I have meant something like this: the pure poem tries to be pure by excluding, more or less rigidly, certain elements which might qualify or contradict its original impulse. In other words the pure poems want to be, and desperately, all of a piece. It has also been evident, no doubt, that the kinds of impurity which are admitted or excluded by the various little anthology pieces which have been analyzed, are different in the different poems. This is only to be expected, for there is not one doctrine of "pure poetry"—not one definition of what constitutes impurity in poems—but many. And not all of the doctrines are recent. When, for example, one cites Poe as the

[4] It might be profitable, in contrast with this poem, to analyze *After the Burial,* by James Russell Lowell, a poem which is identical in situation. But in Lowell's poem the savagery of the irony is unqualified. In fact, the whole poem insists, quite literally, that qualification is impossible: the scheme of the poem is to set up the brute fact of death against possible consolations. It insists on "tears," the "thin-worn locket," the "anguish of deathless hair," "the smallness of the child's grave," the "little shoe in the corner." It is a poem which, we might say, does not progress, but ends where it begins, resting in the savage irony from which it stems; or we might say that it is a poem without any "insides" for the hero of the poem is not attempting to do anything about the problem which confronts him—it is a poem without issue, without conflict, a poem of unconditional surrender. In other words, it tries to be a pure poem, pure grief, absolutely inconsolable. It is a strident poem, and strident in its rhythms. The fact that we know this poem to be an expression of a bereavement historically real makes it an embarrassing poem, as well. It is a naked poem.

father of *the* doctrine of pure poetry, one is in error; Poe simply fathered *a* particular doctrine of pure poetry. One can find other doctrines of purity long antedating Poe. When Sir Philip Sidney, for example, legislated against tragi-comedy, he was repeating a current doctrine of purity. When Ben Jonson told William Drummond that Donne, for not keeping of accent, deserved hanging, he was defending another kind of purity, and when Dryden spoke to save the ear of the fair sex from metaphysical perplexities in amorous poems, he was defending another kind of purity, just as he was defending another when he defined the nature of the heroic drama. The 18th Century had a doctrine of pure poetry, which may be summed up under the word *sublimity,* but which involved two corollary doctrines, one concerning diction and the other concerning imagery. But at the same time that this century, by means of these corollary doctrines, was tidying up and purifying, as Mr. Monk and Mr. Henn have indicated, the doctrine derived from Longinus, it was admitting into the drama certain impurities which the theorists of the heroic drama would not have admitted.[5]

But when we think of the modern doctrine of pure poetry, we usually think of Poe, as critic and poet, perhaps of Shelley, of the Symbolists, of the Abbé Brémond, perhaps of Pater, and certainly of George Moore and the Imagists. We know Poe's position: the long poem is "a flat contradiction in terms," because intense excitement, which is essential in poetry, cannot be long maintained; the moral sense and the intellect function more satisfactorily in prose than in poetry, and, in fact, "Truth" and the "Passions," which are for Poe associated with intellect and the moral sense, may actually be inimical to poetry; vagueness, suggestiveness, are central virtues, for poetry has for "its object an *indefinite* instead of a *definite* pleasure"; poetry is not supposed to undergo close inspection, only a cursory glance, for it, "above all things, is a beautiful painting whose tints, to minute inspection, are confusion worse confounded, but start out boldly to the cursory glance of the connoisseur"; poetry aspires toward music, since it is concerned with "indefinite sensations, to which music is an *essential,* since the comprehension of sweet sound is our most indefinite conception"; melancholy is the most poetical effect and enters into all the higher manifestations of beauty. We know, too, the Abbé Brémond's mystical interpretation, and the preface to George Moore's anthology, and the Imagist manifesto.

But these views are not identical. Shelley, for instance, delights in the imprecision praised and practiced by Poe, but he has an enormous appetite for "Truth" and the "Passions," which are, except for purposes of contrast, excluded by Poe. The Imagist manifesto, while excluding ideas, endorses precision rather than vagueness in render-

[5] Samuel Holt Monk: *The Sublime: a Study of Critical Theories in XVIII-Century England,* and T. R. Henn: *Longinus and English Criticism.*

ing the image, and admits diction and objects which would have seemed impure to Poe and to many poets of the nineteenth century, and does not take much stock in the importance of verbal music. George Moore emphasizes the objective aspect of his pure poetry, which he describes as "something which the poet creates outside his own personality," and this is opposed to the subjective emphasis in Poe and Shelley; but he shares with both an emphasis on verbal music, and with the former a distaste for ideas.

But more recently, the notion of poetic purity has emerged in other contexts, contexts which sometimes obscure the connection of the new theories with the older theories. For instance Max Eastman has a theory. "Pure poetry," he says in *The Literary Mind,* "is the pure effort to heighten consciousness." Mr. Eastman, we discover elsewhere in his book, would ban idea from poetry, but his motive is different from, say, the motive of Poe, and the difference is important: Poe would kick out the ideas because the ideas hurt the poetry, and Mr. Eastman would kick out the ideas because the poetry hurts the ideas. Only the scientist, he tells us, is entitled to have ideas on any subject, and the rest of the citizenry must wait to be told what attitude to take toward the ideas which they are not permitted to have except at second-hand. Literary truth, he says, is truth which is "uncertain or comparatively unimportant." But he assigns the poet a function—to heighten consciousness. But in the light of this context we would have to rewrite his original definition: pure poetry is the pure effort to heighten consciousness, but the consciousness which is heightened must not have any connection with ideas, must involve no attitude toward any ideas.

Furthermore, to assist the poet in fulfilling the assigned function, Mr. Eastman gives him a somewhat sketchy doctrine of "pure" poetic diction. For instance, the word *bloated* is not admissible into a poem because it is, as he testifies, "sacred to the memory of dead fish," and the word *tangy* is, though he knows not exactly how, "intrinsically poetic." The notion of a vocabulary which is intrinsically poetic seems, with Mr. Eastman, to mean a vocabulary which indicates agreeable or beautiful objects. So we might rewrite the original definition to read: pure poetry is the pure effort to heighten consciousness, but the consciousness which is heightened must be a consciousness exclusively of agreeable or beautiful objects—certainly not a consciousness of any ideas.

In a recent book, *The Idiom of Poetry,* Frederick Pottle has discussed the question of pure poetry. He distinguishes another type of pure poetry in addition to the types already mentioned. He calls it the "Elliptical," and would include in it symbolist and metaphysical poetry (old and new) and some work by poets such as Collins, Blake, and Browning. He observes—without any pejorative implication, for he is a critical relativist and scarcely permits himself the luxury of evaluative judgments—that the contemporary product differs from older examples of the elliptical type in that "the modern poet goes much further in employing private experiences or ideas than would formerly have been thought legitimate." To the common reader, he says, "the prime characteristic of this kind of poetry is not the nature of its imagery but its obscurity: its urgent suggestion that you add something to the poem without telling you what that something is." This omitted "something" he interprets as the prose "frame," to use his word, the statement of the occasion, the logical or narrative transitions, the generalized application derived from the poem, etc. In other words, this type of pure poetry contends that "the effect would be more powerful if we could somehow manage to feel the images fully and accurately without having the effect diluted by any words put in to give us a 'meaning'—that is, if we could expel all the talk *about* the imaginative realization and have the pure realization itself." [6]

For the moment I shall pass the question of the accuracy of Mr. Pottle's description of the impulse of Elliptical Poetry and present the question which ultimately concerns him. How pure does poetry need to be in practice? That is the question which Mr. Pottle asks. He answers by saying that a great degree of impurity *may* be admitted, and cites our famous didactic poems, *The Faerie Queene, The Essay on Man, The Vanity of Human Wishes, The Excursion.* That is the only answer which the relativist, and nominalist, can give. Then he turns to what he calls the hardest question in the theory of poetry: what kind of prosaism is acceptable and what is not? His answer, which he advances very modestly, is this:

> ... the element of prose is innocent and even salutary when it appears as—take your choice of three metaphors—a background on which the images are projected, or a frame in which they are shown, or a thread on which they are strung. In short, when it serves a *structural* purpose. Prose in a poem seems offensive to me when ... the prosaisms are sharp, obvious, individual, and ranked coordinately with the images.

At first glance this looks plausible, and the critic has used the sanctified word *structural.* But at second glance we may begin to wonder what the sanctified word means to the critic. It means some-

[6] F. W. Bateson, in *English Poetry and the English Language,* discusses the impulse in contemporary poetry. Tennyson, he points out in connection with *The Sailor Boy,* dilutes his poetry by telling a story as well as writing a poem, and "a shorter poem would have spoilt his story." The claims of prose conquer the claims of poetry. Of the Victorians in general: "The dramatic and narrative framework of their poems, by circumventing the disconcerting plunges into *medias res* which are the essence of poetry, brings it down to a level of prose. The reader knows where he is; it serves the purpose of introduction and note." Such introduction and notes in the body of the poem itself are exactly what Mr. Pottle says is missing in Elliptical Poetry. Mr. Bateson agrees with Poe in accepting intensity as the criterion of the poetic effect, and in accepting the corollary that a poem should be short. But he, contradicting Poe, seems to admire precise and complicated incidental effects.

thing rather mechanical—background, frame, thread. The structure is a showcase, say a jeweler's showcase, in which the little jewels of poetry are exhibited, the images. The showcase shouldn't be ornamental itself ("sharp, obvious, individual," Mr. Pottle says), for it would then distract us from the jewels; it should be chastely designed, and the jewels should repose on black velvet and not on flowered chintz. But Mr. Pottle doesn't ask what the relation among the bright jewels should be. Apparently, not only does the showcase bear no relation to the jewels, but the jewels bear no relation to each other. Each one is a shining little focus of heightened consciousness, or pure realization, existing for itself alone. Or perhaps he should desire that they be arranged in some mechanical pattern, such a pattern, perhaps, as would make it easier for the eye to travel from one little jewel to the next when the time comes to move on. Structure becomes here simply a device of salesmanship, a well arranged showcase.

It is all mechanical. And this means that Mr. Pottle, after all, is himself an exponent of pure poetry. He locates the poetry simply in the images, the nodes of "pure realization." This means that what he calls the "element of prose" includes definition of situation, movement of narrative, logical transition, factual description, generalization, ideas. Such things, for him, do not participate in the poetic effect of the poem; in fact, they work against the poetic effect, and so, though necessary as a frame, should be kept from being "sharp, obvious, individual." [7]

I have referred to *The Idiom of Poetry*, first, because it is such an admirable and provocative book, sane, lucid, generous-spirited, and second, because, to my mind, it illustrates the insidiousness with which a doctrine of pure poetry can penetrate into the theory of a critic who is suspicious of such a doctrine. Furthermore, I have felt that Mr. Pottle's analysis might help me to define the common denominator of the various doctrines of pure poetry.

That common denominator seems to be the belief that poetry is an essence that is to be located at some particular place in a poem, or in some particular element. The exponent of pure poetry persuades himself that he has determined the particular something in which the poetry inheres, and then proceeds to decree that poems shall be

[7] Several other difficulties concerning Mr. Pottle's statement may suggest themselves. First, since he seems to infer that the poetic essence resides in the image, what view would he take of meter and rhythm? His statement, strictly construed, would mean that these factors do not participate in the poetic effect, but are simply part of the frame. Second, what view of dramatic poetry is implied? It seems again that a strict interpretation would mean that the story and the images bear no essential relation to each other, that the story is simply part of the frame. That is, the story, characters, rhythms, and ideas, are on one level and the images, in which the poetry inheres, are on another. But Miss Spurgeon, Mr. Knight, and other critics have given us some reason for holding that the images do bear some relation to the business of the other items. In fact, all of the items, as M. Maritain has said, "feelings, ideas, representations, are for the artist merely materials and means, still symbols." That is, they are all elements in a single expressive structure.

composed, as nearly as possible, of that element and of nothing else. If we add up the things excluded by various critics and practitioners, we get a list about like this:

1. ideas, truths, generalizations, "meaning"
2. precise, complicated, "intellectual" images
3. unbeautiful, disagreeable, or neutral materials
4. situation, narrative, logical transition
5. realistic details, exact descriptions, realism in general
6. shifts in tone or mood
7. irony
8. metrical variation, dramatic adaptations of rhythm, cacophony, etc.
9. meter itself
10. subjective and personal elements

No one theory of pure poetry excludes all of these items, and, as a matter of fact, the items listed are not on the same level of importance. Nor do the items always bear the same interpretation. For example, if one item seems to be central to discussions of pure poetry, it is the first: "ideas," it is said, "are not involved in the poetic effect, and may even be inimical to it." But this view can be interpreted in a variety of ways. If it is interpreted as simply meaning that the paraphrase of a poem is not equivalent to the poem, that the poetic gist is not to be defined as the statement embodied in the poem with the sugar-coating as bait, then the view can be held by opponents as well as exponents of any theory of pure poetry. We might scale down from this interpretation to the other extreme interpretation that the poem should merely give the sharp image in isolation. But there are many complicated and confused variations possible between the two extremes. There is, for example, the interpretation that "ideas," though they are not involved in the poetic effect, must appear in poems to provide, as Mr. Pottle's prosaisms do, a kind of frame, or thread, for the poetry—a spine to support the poetic flesh or a Christmas tree on which the baubles of poetry are hung.[8] T. S. Eliot has said something of this sort:

> The chief use of the "meaning" of a poem, in the ordinary sense, may be (for here again I am speaking of some kinds of poetry and not all) to satisfy one habit of the reader, to keep his mind diverted and quiet, while the poem does its work upon him: much as the imaginary burglar is always provided with a bit of nice meat for the house-dog.

Here, it would seem, Mr. Eliot has simply inverted the old sugar-coated pill theory: the idea becomes the sugar-coating and the "poetry"

[8] Such an interpretation seems to find a parallel in E. M. Forster's treatment of plot in fiction. Plot in his theory becomes a mere spine and does not really participate, except in a narrow, formal sense, in the fictional effect. By his inversion of the Aristotelian principle, the plot becomes merely a necessary evil.

becomes the medicine. This seems to say that the idea in a poem does not participate in the poetic effect, and seems to commit Mr. Eliot to a theory of pure poetry. But to do justice to the quotation, we should first observe that the parenthesis indicates that the writer is referring to some sort of provisional and superficial distinction and not to a fundamental one, and second observe that the passage is out of its context. In the context, Mr. Eliot goes on to say that some poets "become impatient of this 'meaning' [explicit statement of ideas in logical order] which seems superfluous, and perceive possibilities of intensity through its elimination." This may mean either of two things. It may mean that ideas do not participate in the poetic effect, or it may mean, though they do participate in the poetic effect, they need not appear in the poem in an explicit and argued form. And this second reading would scarcely be a doctrine of pure poetry at all, for it would involve poetic casuistry and not poetic principle.

We might, however, illustrate the second interpretation by glancing at Marvell's *Horatian Ode* on Cromwell. Marvell does not give us narrative; he does not give us an account of the issues behind the Civil War; he does not state the two competing ideas which are dramatized in the poem, the idea of "sanction" and the idea of "efficiency." But the effect of the poem does involve these two factors; the special reserved, scarcely resolved, irony, which is realized in the historical situation, is an irony derived from unstated materials and ideas. It is, to use Mr. Pottle's term again, a pure poem in so far as it is elliptical in method, but it is anything but a pure poem if by purity we mean the exclusion of idea from participation in the poetic effect. And Mr. Eliot's own practice implies that he believes that ideas do participate in the poetic effect. Otherwise, why did he put the clues to his ideas in the notes at the end of the *Waste Land* after so carefully excluding any explicit statement of them from the body of the poem? If he is regarding those ideas as mere bait—the "bit of nice meat for the house-dog"—he has put the ideas in a peculiar place, in the back of the book—like giving the dog the meat on the way out of the house with the swag or giving the mouse the cheese after he is in the trap. All this would lead one to the speculation that Marvell and Mr. Eliot have purged away statement of ideas from their poems, not because they wanted the ideas to participate less in the poetry, but because they wanted them to participate more fully, intensely, and immediately. This impulse, then, would account for the characteristic types of image, types in which precision, complication, and complicated intellectual relation to the theme are exploited; in other words, they are trying—whatever may be their final success—to carry the movement of mind to the center of the process. On these grounds they are the exact opposite of poets who, presumably on grounds of purity, exclude the movement of mind from the center of the poetic process—from the internal structure of the poem—but pay their respect to it as a kind of footnote, or gloss, or application coming at the end. Marvell and Eliot, by their cutting away of frame, are trying to emphasize the participation of ideas in the poetic process. Then Elliptical Poetry is not, as Mr. Pottle says it is, a pure poetry at all if we regard intention; the elliptical poet is elliptical for purposes of inclusion, not exclusion.

But waiving the question of Elliptical Poetry, no one of the other theories does—or could—exclude all the items on the list above. And that fact may instruct us. If all of these items were excluded, we might not have any poem at all. For instance, we know how some critics have pointed out that even in the strictest imagist poetry idea creeps in—when the image leaves its natural habitat and enters a poem it begins to "mean" something. The attempt to read ideas out of the poetic party violates the unity of our being and the unity of our experience. "For this reason," as Santayana puts it, "philosophy, when a poet is not mindless, enters inevitably into his poetry, since it has entered into his life; or rather, the detail of things and the detail of ideas pass equally into his verse, when both alike lie in the path that has led him to his ideal. To object to theory in poetry would be like objecting to words there; for words, too, are symbols without the sensuous character of the things they stand for; and yet it is only by the net of new connections which words throw over things, in recalling them, that poetry arises at all. Poetry is an attenuation, a rehandling, an echo of crude experience; it is itself a theoretic vision of things at arm's length." Does this not lead us to the conclusion that poetry does not inhere in any particular element but depends upon the set of relationships, the structure, which we call the poem?

Then the question arises: what elements cannot be used in such a structure? I should answer that nothing that is available in human experience is to be legislated out of poetry. This does not mean that anything can be used in *any* poem, or that some materials or elements may not prove more recalcitrant than others, or that it might not be easy to have too much of some things. But it does mean that, granted certain contexts, any sort of material, a chemical formula for instance, might appear functionally in a poem. It also may mean that, other things being equal, the greatness of a poet depends upon the extent of the area of experience which he can master poetically.

Can we make any generalizations about the nature of the poetic structure? First, it involves resistances, at various levels. There is the tension between the rhythm of the poem and the rhythm of speech (a tension which is very low at the extreme of free verse and at the extreme of verse such as that of *Ulalume,* which verges toward a walloping doggerel); between the formality of the rhythm and the informality of the language; between the particular and the general, the concrete and the abstract; between the elements of even the simplest metaphor; between the beautiful and the ugly; between ideas (as in Marvell's poem); between the elements involved in irony (as in *Bells for John Whiteside's Daughter* or *Rose Aylmer*); between prosaisms and poeticisms (as in *Western Wind*). This list is not intended to be exhaustive; it is intended to be merely suggestive. But it may be taken to imply that the poet is like the jiujitsu expert; he wins by utilizing the resistance of his opponent—the materials of the poem. In other words, a poem, to be good, must earn itself. It is a motion toward a point of rest, but if it is not a resisted motion, it is motion of no consequence. For example, a poem which depends upon stock materials and stock responses is simply a toboggan slide, or a fall through space. And the good poem must, in some way, involve the resistances; it must carry something of the context of its own creation; it must come to terms with Mercutio. This is another way of saying that a good poem involves the participation of the reader; it must, as Coleridge puts it, make the reader into "an active creative being." Perhaps we can see this most readily in the case of tragedy: the definition of good or evil is not a "given" in tragedy, it is something to be earned in the process, and even the tragic villain must be "loved." We must kill him, as Brutus killed Caesar, not as butchers but as sacrificers. And all of this adds up to the fact that the structure is a dramatic structure, a movement through action toward rest, through complication toward simplicity of effect.

In the foregoing discussion, I have deliberately omitted reference to another type of pure poetry, a type which, in the context of the present war, may well become dominant. Perhaps the most sensible description of this type can be found in an essay by Herbert Muller:

> If it is not the primary business of the poet to be eloquent about these matters [faith and ideals], it still does not follow that he has more dignity or wisdom than those who are, or that he should have more sophistication. At any rate the fact is that almost all poets of the past did freely make large, simple statements, and not in their prosy or lax moments.

Mr. Muller then goes on to illustrate by quoting three famous large, simple statements:

> In la sua voluntade e nostra pace

and

> We are such stuff
> As dreams are made on; and our little lives
> Are rounded with a sleep.

and

> The mind is its own place, and in itself
> Can make a heaven of hell, a hell of heaven.

Mr. Muller is here attacking the critical emphasis on ironic tension in poetry. His attack really involves two lines of argument. First, the poet is not wiser than the statesman, philosopher, or saint, people who are eloquent about faith and ideals and who say what they mean, without benefit of irony. This Platonic (or pseudo-Platonic) line of argument is, I think, off the point in the present context. Second, the poets of the past have made large, simple affirmations, have said what they meant. This line of argument is very much on the point.

Poets *have* tried very hard, for thousands of years, to say what they mean. But they have not only tried to say what they mean, they have tried to prove what they mean. The saint proves his vision by stepping cheerfully into the fires. The poet, somewhat less spectacularly, proves his vision by submitting it to the fires of irony—to the drama of his structure—in the hope that the fires will refine it. In other words, the poet wishes to indicate that his vision has been earned, that it can survive reference to the complexities and contradictions of experience. And irony is one such device of reference.

In this connection let us look at the first of Mr. Muller's exhibits. The famous line occurs in Canto III of the *Paradiso*. It is spoken by Piccarda Donati, in answer to Dante's question as to why she does not desire to rise higher than her present sphere, the sphere of the moon. But it expresses, in unequivocal terms, a central theme of the *Commedia,* as of Christian experience. On the one hand, it may be a pious truism, fit for sampler work, and on the other hand, it may be a burning conviction, tested and earned. Dante, in his poem, sets out to show how it has been earned and tested. One set of ironic tensions, for instance, which centers about this theme concerns the opposition between the notion of human justice and the notion of divine justice. The story of Paolo and Francesca is so warm, appealing, and pathetic in its human terms and their punishment so savage and unrelenting, so incommensurable, it seems, with the fault, that Dante, torn by the conflict, falls down as a dead body falls. Or Farinata, the enemy of Dante's house, is presented by the poet in terms of his human grandeur, which now, in Hell, is transmuted into a superhuman grandeur,

> com' avesse l'inferno in gran dispitto.

Ulysses remains a hero, a hero who should draw special applause from Dante, who defined the temporal end of man as the conquest of knowledge. But Ulysses is damned, as the great Brutus is damned, who hangs from the jaws of the fiend in the lowest pit of traitors. So divine justice is set over against human pathos, human dignity, human grandeur, human intellect, human justice. And we recall how Virgil, more than once, reminds Dante that he must not apply human standards to the sights he sees. It is this long conflict, which appears in many forms, this ironic tension, which finally gives body to the simple eloquence of the line in question; the statement is meaningful, not for what it says, but for what has gone before. It is earned. It has been earned by the entire poem.

I do not want to misrepresent Mr. Muller. He does follow his quotations by the sentence: "If they are properly qualified in the work as a whole, they may still be taken straight, they *are* [he italicizes the word] taken so in recollection as in their immediate impact." But can this line be taken so in recollection, and was it taken so in its "immediate impact"? And if one does take it so, is he not violating, very definitely, the poet's meaning, for the poet means the *poem,* he doesn't mean the line.

It would be interesting to try to develop the contexts of the other passages which Mr. Muller quotes. But in any case, he was simply trying, in his essay, to guard against what he considered to be, rightly or wrongly, a too narrow description of poetry; he was not trying to legislate all poetry into the type of simple eloquence, the unqualified statement of "faith and ideas." But we have already witnessed certain, probably preliminary, attempts to legislate literature into becoming a simple, unqualified, "pure" statement of faith and ideal. We have seen the writers of the 1920's called the "irresponsibles." We have seen writers such as Proust, Eliot, Dreiser, and Faulkner, called writers of the "death drive." Why are these writers condemned? Because they have tried, within the limits of their gifts, to remain faithful to the complexities of the problems with which they were dealing, because they refused to take the easy statement as solution, because they tried to define the context in which, and the terms by which, faith and ideals could be earned. But this method will scarcely satisfy the mind which is hot for certainties; to that mind it will seem merely an index to lukewarmness, indecision, disunity, treason. The new theory of purity would purge out all complexities and all ironies and all self-criticism. And this theory will forget that the hand-me-down faith, the hand-me-down ideals, no matter what the professed content, is in the end not only meaningless but vicious. It is vicious because, as parody, it is the enemy of all faith.

THE SOCIAL FUNCTION OF POETRY

(1945)

T. S. ELIOT

I AM very glad that this title [1]—*le rôle social des poètes*— was suggested to me, because I want to make a slight change in it; for the change of title gives me a pretext for something I want to say. I shall call this talk "le rôle social de la poésie." What difference does this make? It makes no direct difference, but an indirect difference of some significance. I accept the term "poet" only as a convenient designation for this, that or the other person who has written one or more good poems. I have known a good many poets, including some very good ones: but I cannot think of anything in common between them all except the fact that they have all written poems. It is true that most of them also take an interest in poetry; but a good many other people, who do not write, are also interested in poetry. I have known young men whose aspiration was "to be a poet": this seems to me a dangerous ambition, for it easily becomes the desire to be admired by others, and to be able to admire oneself. A better ambition, I say, is to aspire simply to write a good poem, at the moment when there is a poem that one wants to write. And there is another, allied reason for my preference for the term "poetry." A poet, a particular individual, may have more social roles than one. He is not writing poetry all the time; and there is no reason why he should not have some other function and perform it quite well; on the other hand there is no reason why he should have another function, if he is not obliged to and does not want to. He is a citizen and may be a father: as such he has the same functions as other citizens and fathers. But as a poet his function is to write poetry: and it is therefore with the social role of poetry that we are concerned.

The shift of attention, from the poet to the poetry, also enables us to dismiss two special kinds of "social role" which might distract our attention. The first is the historical role which has been performed by particular *kinds* of poetry. There are primitive runes and chants, in metrical form and of poetic merit, which had very practical magical purposes: to avert the evil eye, to cure some disease, or to propitiate some divinity; and such forms of poem may be said to have had a

[1] *Le Rôle Social des Poètes.* This is the original text of an address delivered to an audience in Paris in May, 1945.

definite social role in primitive society. Poetry was early associated with religious ritual; and in the hymn, the sequence, the litany, we are still using poetry for a social purpose. Early forms of epic and saga transmitted what was held to be history: and, apart from its emotional effect upon the audience the assistance of a verse form to primitive story tellers in helping them to commit to memory immense quantities of matter, was very considerable. And in more advanced societies, such as that of ancient Greece, the recognised social functions of poetry are very conspicuous. The drama was part of a public celebration of religious origin; the Pindaric ode developed in relation to a particular kind of social occasion. We can still say that the *lyric*—the poem written to be sung to music, whether by a group of people together, or by one singer to an audience, and the poetic drama, are forms of poetry which have a peculiar social role, different from that of poetry which is primarily intended for the reading of one person in solitude.

Now, it should be obvious that with the *song* and with the *drama* we have to do with two *special* functions of poetry. In the former, you have a special kind of poetry combined with a special kind of music, and both the poet and the musician are working within certain limits. Poetry to be sung must be a very simplified poetry: and in the opera it can hardly afford to be more than competent verse. In any kind of verse to be sung the role of the poet is quite secondary to that of the composer. The situation in the writing of dramatic verse is rather different, because the poet can, at moments, take precedence over the dramatist, but chiefly because the poet and the dramatist, in a verse play, are the same person. But the poet who sets out to write a play must try to be, first and always, a dramatist. It is to dramatic laws that he owes obedience; and in so far as he succeeds in conforming to the necessities of drama, he will find himself writing a different kind of poetry. For it is poetry written not for his own voice, but for the voice of an unknown interpreter, and poetry which must make an immediate and collective effect upon a mixed group of listeners, none of whom may be assumed to have read the text before hearing it. In the song and in the drama we have two forms of poetry, each with an important social function: but with these, we have to do with a double role, the co-operation of poet and composer in a common function, or the subordination of the poet as poet to the poet as dramatist. Yet in both, our appreciation is enhanced by analytical study: a fine lyric, or a great poetic play, is better enjoyed if we have not only heard it performed in public, but read it in private: so that the function of the lyric or the play appears to be in part the same as that of any other kind of poetry. We cannot, that is, say that the social function of poetry, or the role of the poet, is exhibited only in poetry which has to be performed in public.

Let us next consider the role of the poet, and the function of poetry, in relation to the *purpose* of the poet himself. It very often happens that the poet wishes to propagate some doctrine, religious, philosophical, or social; to provoke his readers to some particular attitude or course of action; to inculcate some moral lesson; or even to convey information. These are by no means recent applications: in fact, it is the opposite view, that art should serve no end beyond itself, which is the more modern. It was indeed a commonplace amongst Renaissance critics that poetry should inspire men to moral virtue. And there is no question that some of the greatest poets have had very definite purposes. They have not dissimulated them; their poems would be meaningless without them. Here, I think, we must avoid being seduced into one or the other of two extreme opinions. The first is, that it is simply the value of the *ideas* expressed in a poem which gives the value of the poetry; or that it is the *truth* of his view of life—by which we ordinarily mean its congruity with our own view—that matters. The other is, that the ideas, the beliefs of the poet do not matter at all; that they are rather like some alloy, necessary for the poet in order to manipulate his true material, which is refined out of the poetry in the course of time. To arrive at what seems to me the more correct view, we may consider first, that when a poet has expressed successfully a philosophy we find that it is a philosophy which is already in existence, not one of his own invention; when he has made a successful poem which conveys information, the facts are not of his own discovery. As examples of the first, we may take Lucretius or Dante: they both drew their material from the work of philosophers who were not poets. As an example of the second, we may take Virgil in his *Georgics:* he was not aiming to popularise a wholly new and revolutionary theory of farming, but rather to preserve and unify the principles which had been practised by good farmers before his time. And this leads me to conclude, that these poems were not designed to persuade the readers to an intellectual assent, but to convey an emotional equivalent for the ideas. What Lucretius and Dante teach you, in fact, is *what it feels like* to hold certain beliefs; what Virgil teaches you, is to feel yourself inside the agrarian life. The poem may persuade some readers to accept the ideas, by the association of the idea with emotion which the reader enjoys experiencing. But the purpose of Dante, I should say, was not so much to persuade readers to give intellectual assent to the Christian cosmogony, as to make readers, who already accepted that cosmogony, or who at least were not prepared to deny it, *feel* it as a matter of personal experience.

I see no reason why future poets should not set themselves a similar task. But I believe it to be a condition of success, that the view of life which they attempt to express in poetry, should be one which is already accepted. I do not think you can make poetry out of ideas when they are too *original,* or too *new.* The poet himself must already have lived them, and lived them communally. For the business of a poet is to express the culture in which he lives, and to which he belongs, not to express aspiration towards one which is not yet incarnate.

This is not, of course, meant to imply that the poet has to approve the society in which he lives: to express an actual culture, and to approve a social situation, are two quite different things. This expression of his culture, indeed, may set the poet into violent opposition to a social situation which violates that culture.

I say that I think it is the business of the poet to express, and to criticise, the culture in which he lives and to which he belongs. But what it is the task of the poet to do, is always something more than, and can be something very different from his conscious purpose. That the purpose of a poet, what he sets out to do and what he thinks he is doing, is relevant to the understanding of his poetry I do not deny; nor do I deny that when he has a conscious purpose, it may be one which can be greatly to the advantage, or alternatively to the detriment of his poetry. I only say that the function of his poetry cannot be judged by his purpose. I can best make clear what I mean by this, by reference to a vast body of literature to which students of æsthetics and psychology might perhaps pay more attention: I mean *bad* poetry. Here, I must distinguish first between the *true* bad poet and the *false* bad poet. By the latter, I mean every person (and that is perhaps the majority of people who have received some rudiments of literary education) who is moved at some moment of adolescence to express himself in verse and who for a brief period cherishes the illusion that what he has written is poetry. The true bad poet is a person of perseverance and industry, who goes on writing after this adolescent crisis has been passed, to the end of his life. He devotes himself to writing bad poetry: it is his vocation. He is a person of some talent. But there are two types of true bad poet. This first is a lover of words; he has nothing to say that has not already been said, but he thinks that originality consists in expressing the commonplace sentiment in a slightly unusual syntax, metric, and vocabulary. I knew one such poet, a very intelligent and charming man, who made one great discovery: that by placing a comma, not at the end of the line, but at the beginning of the next line, he could achieve a certain appearance of originality. The other type of bad poet is not a virtuoso; he has found a serious purpose; he has a message to convey. This type of bad poet is apt to run to very long poems, even to the epic. He usually keeps to a well-tried vocabulary and long approved metre; he aims at the sublime rather than the eccentric. He has a religious, or a philosophical, or a political turn of mind; and his poetry is the vehicle of a message which he is sure is of importance to the world. He has a social purpose: and he has nothing else.

I find that, in reading the work of a *good* poet, I am apt to be struck by a certain ambiguity. At moments I feel that his language is merely the perfect instrument for what he has to say; at other moments I feel that he is simply making use of, even exploiting, his beliefs for the sake of the verbal beauty in which he can express them. He appears to be both inside and outside of his beliefs and interests. Where this doubt about the attitude of the poet cannot arise, one is tempted to suspect the poetry. If we can enjoy the form while indifferent to the content, that poetry is for us mere virtuosity; if we can attend to the ideas and be indifferent to the words in which they are expressed, what we are reading is for us merely bad prose.

It is necessary, certainly, that the poet should have other interests besides writing poetry. And he should be interested in other subjects for their own sake. Just as it is a mistake to seek for any kind of experience, for the purpose of making poetry out of it, so we should not pursue any subject of knowledge, scientific, historical, or philosophical, for the sake of having something to write about. We cannot simply *use* poetry to express our thought or feeling, and we cannot simply seek for knowledge or experience, for the sake of writing poetry. Those whom we call the great poets, have usually been men of wide interests; but the condition of their being poets at all, is that their learning and thought, as well as their experience of men and actions, should have been assimilated by their sensibility. And for this to happen, the experience must come on its own terms, the intellectual study must be pursued for its own sake.

If I am right, then a great deal more goes to the making of poetry than the conscious purpose of the poet; and, if this is so, the poet's social role also is more than, and other than, any conscious social purpose of his part. The poet may, or may not, have a deliberate intention to teach or to persuade. It is easy to see that Virgil had a particular attitude towards the Roman people, the Roman City, the Roman Empire, to communicate to his audience in the *Aeneid;* that Dante, and Milton in a different way, were aiming to teach a particular theology, in their more abstract passages, and to make this theology real to their readers, in their descriptions of scenes, events, and characters: and the effect of their poetry upon contemporary readers may be assumed to have been very close to their intentions. But with the passage of time, their poetry reveals new and different significance. And with other poets, also of the first rank, it is not always easy to see what their conscious purpose was, or whether they had any, or whether it matters. Even with the Greek dramatists, did the poet really hope or intend to benefit his audience by precept or example? And did Racine create Roxane in order to warn society against the dangers of uncontrolled passion; or did Shakespeare create Lear as a warning against the self-deceptions of senile vanity?

It is obvious that any attempt to define the function of poetry in terms of the purpose of the poet, is to involve ourselves in a labyrinth from which there is no extrication. All we can say is that when a poet has had a clear and distinct purpose, this purpose appears to have been a necessary condition of his writing the poetry: his purpose was useful to him. And when he has had such a purpose, we have to take account of it, whether we sympathise with it or not, in order fully to appreciate his poetry; and this is as true when his poem has to do with affairs two thousand years ago as when it deals with affairs contemporary with ourselves. The direct social value of poetry was much in the minds of critics and theorists of the Renaissance, for whom every notable man of antiquity was an example to be imitated or avoided, as the illustration of some virtue or vice described by Aristotle. Later moralists have been less naïve, but also more vague. And in recent times, a reason why we have become more cautious in accepting a poet's expressed intention as evidence of what he was really doing, is that we have all become more conscious of the role of the unconscious.

If we are to discover the social role of poetry, we must find out what it does everywhere, at all times and in all languages. We must avoid considering the various functions which some poetry has performed, at some times and in some places, and the different roles which particular poets have filled or tried to fill. We must also avoid imposing a new role upon poetry; we must not say, "this is what poetry *ought* to do" unless it is something which all good poetry has always done. So let us begin with its most obvious test of excellence. First of all, it must give pleasure. If anyone asks "what sort of pleasure?" I can only say "the sort of pleasure that good poetry can give"; and if anyone asks "to whom should it give pleasure?" I can only say "to those people who appreciate poetry." For any other answer would immediately take us into speculations about æsthetics, for which I have neither the competence nor the interest. Of course one may read poetry for other reasons, without enjoying it as poetry. You may read the work of a poet in order to gain an understanding of his period of history; but he would not be important enough to reward such investigation, unless a number of people had in his own time enjoyed reading his poetry. Even if you set yourself to read the work of bad poets of the past, it will probably be to find out why people ever thought them good poets. It is obvious that a poem which has never given any pleasure to anyone but the author, can have no social function at all.

This statement of the obvious raises the question, whether the social role of a poet is greater than another's if his work has given pleasure to more people. It sometimes happens that a poet has been read and enjoyed in his own generation by a vast number of people, and now has no readers at all; while another poet may have been read with enjoyment only by a few people at any time, but continues, throughout the centuries, to give pleasure to a few people in every generation. I do not think that we should say that the social role of the first was greater than that of the second. Shall we not say, that the second poet's work has *permanence,* and that the work of the former was a temporary fashion—and that the permanent has the greater social value? I think we do feel that a poem must continue to please readers in every generation, or at least must have the power of giving fresh pleasure after a period of neglect, so long as there are readers who can understand the language in which it is written.

With this qualification, it is nevertheless generally true that the greatest poets are those who have given the most pleasure to the largest number, and the greatest *variety,* of human beings, throughout the period of time since they wrote. And, in general, I am also taking account of a poet's public in foreign countries through translations of his work. There are, of course, several sorts of poetry for which translation is justified. There is poetry in which visual imagery dominates, and which therefore can convey some of its effect in any language. There may be the poetry of a poet whose temperament has an affinity with the spirit of some language not his own; conversely, there is poetry which finds a translator whose temperament has an affinity to that of the author. And lastly, there is the most *universal* poetry, which, however much it may lose in translation, retains much that can be read with pleasure and advantage in a foreign language. But even the greatest poets, the men of undoubted international or universal importance, are also local: indeed, they may be more profoundly local, for their own people and their own language, than smaller poets whose work can be only locally appreciated. Every poet has a significance for his own people that he cannot have for others; and a poet must be a great poet for his own people, if he is to be also a great European, or a great universal poet.

We observe that poetry differs from the other arts, in that it has a value for people of the poet's race, country and language, which it cannot have for others. It is true that music and painting have also local characters; and that a piece of music, or a painting, may communicate something to the artist's compatriots which a foreigner will miss. But, at least within the circle of European culture, a good critic can form a sound opinion of the merit of foreign works of art: there are at least common laws of construction, common standards of technical mastery. And of all the forms of art for which language is used—the theatre, the novel, the prose work of every kind—poetry is the most indissoluble from its language. With poetry alone, we can never feel *quite* certain of our judgement, without the support of critics who belong to the same country and the same language. And if the poet is more dependent upon his particular language than other artists, or even other writers, so I may be allowed to conclude that that language is more dependent upon the poet than upon men of any other profession. And this leads me at last to what I believe to be *the* social role of the poet. I think that it is important for every language, if that language is to be worth preserving, to have its own poetry—not simply for those who enjoy reading poetry, but for the sake of the people as a whole. I think that the existence of a national literature—and I rank poetry as the most indispensable part of literature—makes a difference, not only to those who enjoy poetry, but to everybody; even to those who hardly know the names of their greatest national poets; even, I might also say, to the wholly illiterate. So it is through his service to people who do *not* read his poetry, that I assign to the poet his greatest *social* role.

We observe that the impulse towards the literary use of the vernacular begins in poetry: it was in poetry that the modern languages of Europe first exercised themselves, while Latin was still the language of learning and prose. This appears to be inevitable, when we recognise that poetry, however intellectual, has to do with the expression of feeling and emotion; that feeling and emotion are experienced in the language of daily life; and that feeling and emotion are particular, while thought is general. It is easier to *think* in a foreign tongue than to *feel* in it. No art is more stubbornly national than poetry. A people may have its language taken away from it, suppressed in public use, and forbidden in its schools; but unless you teach that people may have its language, you have not eradicated the old one, and it will re-affirm itself first of all in poetry. And when I speak of *feeling* in another language, I mean something more radical than merely "expressing one's feelings in another language." A thought expressed in another language may be practically the same thought; but a feeling expressed in a different language cannot be quite the same feeling. For emotion, poetry is a more *precise* medium than prose. One of the reasons for trying to learn a foreign language is that it gives us a kind of supplementary personality: one of the reasons for not acquiring another language to use instead of our own is that hardly anybody really wants to become a different person. The extermination of a superior language is the extermination of a superior people.

Emotion and feeling, then, can only be fully expressed in the vernacular language which a particular people has fashioned for itself through many generations, and which, in its turn, has gone to fashion the mode of feeling of its people. It must be fundamentally the language of all classes of that people: the structure, the rhythms, the sounds, the idioms of a language express the personality of the race that speaks it. When I say that it is poetry rather than prose, which is concerned with the analysis and definition of emotion and feeling, I do not ignore, on the one hand, the intellectual content of poetry, or on the other, the emotional qualities of prose. Sensibility and intellect are not separable in the individual, nor are they in the language he speaks. I am merely stressing specific characteristics. And I do not admit that poetry, in order to have a social function, must limit itself to the expression of feelings which *everybody* can recognise and understand and share. We must not limit poetry to popular poetry. It is enough, in a healthy and homogeneous civilisation, that the feelings of the most refined and complex individuals have something in common with those of the crudest and least educated, which they do not share with persons of their own level of culture who speak another language. It is true, I believe, that in a healthy society, the really great poet should be understood in part, and responded to, by compatriots of the humblest, as well as by those of the highest level of culture. But his most *general* social role will be in relation, not to his readers, but to his language as spoken by everyone.

We may say, then, that just as the first duty of a man *qua* citizen is to his country, so his first duty *qua* poet is to the language of his country. First, he has the duty to *preserve* that language: his use of it must not weaken, coarsen, or degrade it. Second, he has the duty to *develop* that language, to bring it up to date, to investigate its unexplored possibilities. So far as he expresses, in his poetry, what other people feel, he is also affecting that feeling by making it more conscious: in giving people words for their feelings, he is teaching them something about themselves. But he is not merely more conscious than others; he is also different from them, and different from other poets, and can therefore give his readers knowledge of feelings which they have never experienced. That is the difference between the writer who is merely eccentric or grotesque, and the genuine poet: the former may have feelings which are unique, but which cannot be shared, or are not worth sharing, and which are therefore socially useless; while the genuine poet discovers new shades and variations of sensibility in which others can participate. And in expressing them, he is developing and enriching the language, for the ultimate advantage of a public far wider than his circle of readers.

I have said enough about the differences of feeling of different peoples as expressed by their several languages. But people experience life differently not only in different places and different languages: the same people experience it differently at different times. Our sensibility differs from that of the Chinese or the Hindu; but also, it is not the same as that of our ancestors of a few centuries ago. It is not even quite the same as that of our parents; indeed, we ourselves are not unchanged in the course of a lifetime. This is obvious; what is not quite so obvious is that this is the reason why no people can afford to *stop* producing poetry. Most men take a certain pride in the great authors of their language and country, though they may never have read them; they are proud of them as of any other distinction of their country. A few authors even become celebrated enough to be cited occasionally by political orators. But most people do not realise that this is not enough—to have great writers of the past; that, unless we can go on producing great authors, and especially great poets, our language will deteriorate. Our culture will deteriorate, and in the end may become so weakened that it will yield to an alien and stronger one. And, unless we have always a contemporary literature, we shall ourselves become more and more alien to the literature of our own past. That literature, if it has no living progeny, will become more and more remote from us, until it is hardly more than the literature of another and vanished race. Our language goes on changing whether we want it to or not; our way of life changes under the pressure of every sort of change in our environment. So to cope with these changes we need constantly new poets, men who combine an exceptional sensibility with an exceptional power over words: otherwise our own ability, the ability of a whole people, not merely to express, but even to feel, civilised emotions, will degenerate.

The changes and developments of language operated in every generation by a few authors—authors, perhaps, who in their own time have but a small number of readers—will work themselves into the language gradually, through their influence on other, more popular writers; and by the time their influence has been absorbed, a new advance will be called for. So, in the long run, it makes a difference to the speech, to the sensibility, to the lives of all the members of a society or community, to the whole people: even, as I have said, to those who do not know the names of their poets. The influence of poetry, at its furthest periphery, is of course very diffused, very indirect. To follow it is like following the flight of a bird or an aeroplane in a clear sky; if you have noticed it when it was quite near, and kept your eye on it, you can still see it at a great distance at which the eye of another person will be unable to detect it. So you can find the influence of poetry everywhere, in a healthy society: for in a healthy society there is a constant circulation of influence from each part to the others.

I should not like you to think that I am making an exorbitant claim for poetry, and that I suppose that the language we speak is determined by poets. It is equally true to say that the language of poets is determined by the language which they hear spoken around them. A poet must be dependent upon his language in the state in which he finds it, in his own time and in his own environment. If it is improving, so much the better for him; if it is deteriorating, he must make the best of it. Poetry can do something to preserve, and even restore, the health of a language; it can also help that language to develop, in order that it may be just as subtle, strong, and exact in the more complicated conditions and for the changing purposes of modern life, as it was in an earlier and simpler age. But in that baffling social personality which we call our "culture," the elements depend upon each other; and poetry, like everything else, depends upon a great many influences which are beyond its control.

My emphasis appears to have been upon the national and local functions of poetry. I do not wish this discussion to become confused with the political and economic issues which are suggested by the word *nationality,* or by the more controversial word *nationalism.* But I ought to make clear what I do believe in relation to my subject. I cannot accept the ideal of a general *uniformity* of culture among the several parts, large and small, of Europe; on the other hand, I do not believe that these parts of Europe can flourish in cultural isolation from each other. I should like each part to preserve its individuality. With the extent of political and economic independence necessary for the preservation of this individuality, I am not here concerned. Both unity and diversity are necessary. It seems difficult enough, in the future before us, to achieve any European unity; it seems difficult enough, on the other hand, for each nation to preserve its distinct and traditional culture: what we have to attempt seems more difficult than either, because it is *both.*

As an illustration, in closing: there is much to be said, for certain limited purposes, for the propagation of some universal *lingua franca,* a common "second language" of communication between peoples. But supposing that all communication between those who are foreigners to each other was carried on in an artificial language which was the language of no one in particular, this might be adequate for some purposes, but would be worse than useless for others. Poetry is a constant reminder of all the things which can only be said in one language. The spiritual communication between nation and nation cannot be carried on without the help of those individuals who study each other's languages perseveringly enough to be able to *feel* in a foreign language. The study of another people's poetry is particularly illuminating. When I was very young, before I was able to speak French at all, or even to understand it when spoken, I generally found that I did not understand a piece of prose until I understood it according to the standards of the schoolmaster: that is, I had to be sure of the meaning of every word, grasp the grammar, and then think it in English. But I also found that sometimes a piece of poetry, which I could not have translated, which contained many words unknown to me, and sentences which I could not construe, could yet convey to me something unique, something indefinably different from anything in English, which I could not explain yet which I felt I understood. It was not an illusion: on learning the language better, I found that what I had divined to be in the poetry was really there, as well as much more. So I should like to re-write the story of the Tower of Babel as follows: So long as the builders all spoke their several languages, with the assistance of *liaison* officers, all went fairly well. But, disapproving of the privileged position of these officers, and suspicious of their efficiency, they dismissed them. Then, being unable to communicate with each other at all, each group set to work independently, and the results were much less satisfactory. So they invented a new language which was not the language of anybody in particular, and finally the tower collapsed: because, although they were all using the same words, they all attached different meanings to them. Against this revised version of the Tower of Babel, I would set the story of Pentecost, which I do not desire to tamper with: for the various peoples there assembled heard the Apostles, not in Esperanto or Basic English, but each in his own tongue: and what they all heard was the same message.

PART II

CRITIQUES: HOW TO CRITICIZE THE WORK

INTRODUCTORY COMMENT

PART II illustrates critical procedure. Whereas in Part I the object of criticism is seen through theory, in Part II the object is seen through critical practice alone, apart from theory. Here the object is the play as well as the poem. The texts analyzed are three Shakespeare plays, the poetry of Shelley, and *The Four Quartets* of T. S. Eliot. *Macbeth, Coriolanus,* and *King Lear* are among the greatest of Shakespeare's plays; they ask for and reward our greatest critical scrutiny. Of *Coriolanus* it may be said, as similarly for *Hamlet* in relation to the nineteenth century, that it is the one Shakespeare work which has a special meaning for our time, inasmuch as it symbolizes the world-feeling of our age. In the essay on *Macbeth,* Knight introduces a new analytical method. By this spatial approach, the art-work is viewed as an area in space as well as a sequence in time, each segment possessing in its own right a new depth of meaning apart from the meaning it has as a link in the dramatic sequence or narrative structure. This spatial method, which here illuminates the play, is used by Joseph Frank in analyzing the novel (in Part III). "Spatial Form in Modern Literature" investigates the literary work in terms of its space-time logic, and it thereby opens a new method of interpreting not only the novel but also the poem.

The criticism practiced here is technical criticism. (Additional instances of technical criticism are located in Part III.) These critiques illustrate how to criticize a work. They are representative specimens of that kind of criticism by which modern critics have become identified—close textual analysis.

THE MILK OF CONCORD: AN ESSAY ON LIFE-THEMES IN MACBETH

(1931)

G. WILSON KNIGHT

> . . . *Thy will be done, in earth as it is in heaven; give us this day our daily bread, and forgive us our trespasses as we forgive them that trespass against us; and lead us not into temptation but deliver us from evil.*

THE OPPOSITION of life and death forces is strong in *Macbeth*. Here we find the dark and evil negation endued with a positive strength, successfully opposing things of health and life. Elsewhere I have discussed the evil: here I give a primary attention to the life-themes it opposes. They are: (i) Warrior-honour, (ii) Imperial magnificence, (iii) Sleep and Feasting, and (iv) Ideas of creation and nature's innocence. These are typical Shakesperian themes. In *Hamlet* we find the same opposition. There it is often baffling. Here life forces are vividly and very clearly contrasted with evil, with forces of death and ill-omen, darkness and disorder. Especially, creation is opposed by destruction.

Throughout the main action of *Macbeth* we are confronted by fear. The word occurs ubiquitously. Fear is at the heart of this play. Now, if we consider the beginning and ending too, we find a very clear rhythm of courage, fear and courage. The play ends on a note of courage. Macbeth is from the first a courageous soldier. His warrior-honour is emphasized. He is "brave Macbeth," "valour's minion," "Bellona's bridegroom," "noble Macbeth." Duncan exclaims:

> O valiant cousin! worthy gentleman! (I. ii. 24)

He is "a peerless kinsman"—the Duncan-Macbeth relationship is always stressed. Courage in war is a thing of "honour." So Macbeth is rewarded for his valour by a title, earnest of an even greater "honour." At the start Macbeth's honourable valour is firmly contrasted with the traitor's ignoble revolt. There is no honour in absolute courage: it must be a service, or it is worthless. Macbeth knows this. Duncan lavishes praises on him and he replies:

> The service and the loyalty I owe,
> In doing it, pays itself. Your Highness' part

> Is to receive our duties; and our duties
> Are to your throne and state, children and servants,
> Which do but what they should, by doing everything
> Safe toward your love and honour. (I. iv. 22)

"Honour" again: the word occurs throughout, strongly emphasized. Notice the "family" suggestion. Throughout, thoughts of the family (especially childhood), clan, or nation are associated here. All are units of peace, concord, life. All are twined with "honour." So the subject is bound to his lord by love and honour. The value of warriorship may not be dissociated from allegiance: it is one with the ideal of kingship and imperial power. But against this bond the evil is urging Macbeth. The evil in him hates to hear Duncan proclaiming princely honours on Malcolm, despite the promise of more distinctions for such as himself:

> Sons, kinsmen, thanes,
> And you whose places are the nearest, know
> We will establish our estate upon
> Our eldest, Malcolm, whom we name hereafter
> The Prince of Cumberland; which honour must
> Not unaccompanied invest him only,
> But signs of nobleness, like stars, shall shine
> On all deservers. (I. iv. 35)

Here we should observe the suggestion of harmony and order. Sons, kinsmen, thanes—all are bound close together. Scotland is a family, Duncan its head. A natural law binds all degrees in proper place and allegiance. Only in terms of this allegiance is courage an honourable ideal. Observe, too, how the king's "honours" are compared to "stars," the king's gentle rule of love thus blending with the universal lights. But the evil that grips Macbeth must hide from such things of brilliance and universal beauty:

> Stars, hide your fires;
> Let not light see my black and deep desires;
> The eye wink at the hand; yet let that be
> Which the eye fears, when it is done, to see.
> (I. iv. 50)

Throughout, the evil in Macbeth is opposed to such order, to all family and national peace, and is alien to sun, moon, or star, blotting their radiance from man (II. iv. 7; II. i. 2; II. i. 4-5). Now Macbeth, having accomplished so much, strikes next at the very roots of his own new-bright honour:

> We will proceed no further in this business.
> He hath honour'd me of late; and I have bought
> Golden opinions from all sorts of people,
> Which would be worn now in their newest gloss,
> Not cast aside so soon. (I. vii. 31)

By such a deed of dishonour no substantial honour may be won. The valour of such an act is itself shameful:

> Prithee, peace:
> I dare do all that may become a man;
> Who dares do more is none. (I. vii. 45)

Yet Lady Macbeth wins largely by appealing to Macbeth's "valour." If he now fails in courage, she will henceforth despise equally his courage and his love (I. vii. 39): warriorship and love being ever close in Shakespeare, either in contrast or association. And Macbeth really gives way all along from fear: from fear of fear. He has fought for the King, exulting wildly in absolute courage. Next there is an extreme reaction to absolute fear. Thus the evil finds the only thing he fears: dishonour. He suffers at his first temptation from abstract fear, which fixes itself to a ghastly act so that it may form some contact with the real. That act is one of essential dishonour. He has thus been terrified ever since the evil gripped him, ever since he muttered "present fears are less than horrible imaginings." The same contrast is expressed by him when fronting Banquo's ghost (III. iv. 99-107). He fears no hostile actuality, only the unreal evil, the abstract and absolute fear. This evil he dare not face from the start, so flies from it to actuality, expresses it there. He lacks spiritual courage to meet it on its own spiritual terms, and hence projects his disordered soul into action and murders Duncan. Undue horror and fear of the deed drive him to it: in the same way his fearful conscience will not let him rest there, and he commits more murders. He is all the time flying from evil instead of facing it. But at the end he emerges fearless. And this is not only a warrior's valour when opposed by Malcolm's army. By his murderous acts he has at last actually conquered his fear of evil, that is, his fear of fear:

> I have supp'd full with horrors;
> Direness, familiar to my slaughterous thoughts,
> Cannot once start me. (V. v. 13)

He sees himself a criminal: sees the evil in himself. Not daring to see his own potential criminality, he became a criminal. But now, seeing his own evil, he becomes fearless. From the beginning there was no possible antagonist for the supernatural evil but an equivalently supernatural good. The evil was never properly actualized: to fight it there must be a good also set beyond the actual. Hence the birth of our religions; hence, too, the constant opposition of "grace" and thoughts of divinity in *Macbeth* set against the things of dark and evil.[1] Macbeth at the last, by self-knowledge, attains grace. He knows that he must forfeit "honour" and all things of concord and life:

[1] This opposition of "grace" and "evil" I have already observed in *The Wheel of Fire*. It has also been recently stressed by Mgr. Kolbe, who notes that phrases or words suggestive of a "sin"-"grace" contrast occur more than four hundred times in *Macbeth*

> . . . that which should accompany old age,
> As honour, love, obedience, troops of friends,
> I must not look to have; but, in their stead,
> Curses, not loud but deep, mouth-honour, breath,
> Which the poor heart would fain deny, and dare not.
> (V. iii. 24)

These are the social realities he has desecrated by his fearsome rule A rule of fear. Fear is ever our dominant emotion. Not only Macbeth—all are paralysed by fear during the middle action. At the start, we saw courage, unity, honour, under the gracious rule of Duncan. But the valour of Scotland is temporarily smothered by evil. When at the end security and peace return, the contrast is marked by Siward's words on his son, who "has paid a soldier's debt," and died "like a man":

> SIWARD. Had he his hurts before?
> ROSS. Ay, on the front.
> SIWARD. Why then, God's soldier be he!
> Had I as many sons as I have hairs,
> I would not wish them to a fairer death.
> (V. viii. 46)

So we see courage desecrated by evil and fear, then at the end courage—in Macbeth or young Siward—victorious. This is how the Macbeth-negation hits into, destroys for a while, the positive ideals of honour and warriorship, so that not only Macbeth but Banquo, Macduff, Malcolm, Ross—all suffer fear, all for a while are powerless under the evil. The matter of young Siward's death marks the restoration of nobility and courage, accompanying Malcolm's restoration to his rightful kingship.

This warrior-theme is closely twined with our next positive value: imperial magnificence. On the ethical—as opposed to the metaphysical—plane, Macbeth fails through trying to advance from deserved honour as a noble thane to the higher kingly honour to which he has no rights. This kingship he attains, yet never really possesses it. He is never properly king: his regality is a mockery. Now, through the murk which envelops the action, there are yet glimpses of this sensuous glory which Macbeth desires but which ever eludes his grasp. Such suggestions stare out, dully glowing, solid things of world-power. This sensuous glory is always undermined, blurred, by the dark, the abysmal negation, the evil. The Macbeth-world is insubstantial, an emptiness, its bottom knocked out of it; a hideous nightmare falling, like Satan dropping in his flight through chaos. Solidity, reality, are grasped in vain by the falling soul. Macbeth and his wife reach out for power and glory: the sense-forms correspondent are crowns and sceptres. The glint of these burns sullenly through the murk.

Lady Macbeth would drive from her lord

> All that impedes thee from the golden round,
> Which fate and metaphysical aid doth seem
> To have thee crown'd withal. (I. v. 29)

The "golden round": solid, glorious gold to bind the brow with royalty. The same glinting solidity burns in the phraseology, especially the final word, of:

> Which shall to all our nights and days to come
> Give solely sovereign sway and masterdom. (I. v. 70)

These things are, as it were, the finest flower of world-honour, the sweetest prizes of life. They are glorious things of life. So she presses him on to win the "ornament of life," though Macbeth objects to this absurd grasping of additional royalty by a man royally honoured already. He would wear his "golden opinions" in "their newest gloss" rather than risk losing them so soon. So Macbeth sees clearly that the gold of evil desire will add nothing to his real honour: yet he cannot resist. Miss Spurgeon has observed that "dresses" and dress-metaphors occur frequently in *Macbeth*. Often, as in this passage, these may be considered to blend with our "crowns" and "sceptres" to build a vague background of royal splendour. But all are vague. Their solidity is rendered dubious, is blurred, by the evil, the dark, the insubstantiality. They are things of noble reality dreamed in hell; unenjoyed by the guilty soul, to whom nightmare is reality and all sense-splendour an unattainable dream. Outward royalty is, by itself, a nothing in comparison with nature's kingliness:

> Our fears in Banquo
> Stick deep; and in his royalty of nature
> Reigns that which would be fear'd . . . (III. i. 49)

So he fears, envies, hates Banquo who has the reality of honour whereas he has but a mockery, a ghoulish dream of royalty. He envies Banquo's posterity their royal destiny won in terms of nature, not in terms of crime; and is maddened at the insecure mockery of his own kingship:

> Upon my head they plac'd a fruitless crown,
> And put a barren sceptre in my gripe . . . (III. i. 61)

He has grasped these gold power-symbols to himself: and they are utterly "barren" in every sense; barren of joy and content, barren of posterity. So falsely has Macbeth made himself the centre and end of all things: a "fruitless" philosophy. To this the evil has tricked him. He and his wife are without "content." When he visits the Weird Sisters in their cavern he sees an apparition with a crown. Again, the glint of royal metal shines through the dark:

What is this
That rises like the issue of a king,
And wears upon his baby-brow the round
And top of sovereignty? (IV. i. 86)

Notice the vivid suggestion of babyhood: I return to it later. Again, in his vision of future Scottish kings, these same sense-forms are emphasized and their maddening effect on him redoubled:

Thou art too like the spirit of Banquo; down!
Thy crown does sear mine eyeballs. And thy hair,
Thou other gold-bound brow, is like the first.
A third is like the former . . . (IV. i. 112)

As though this were not enough sensuous blaze of kingship, there is the eighth figure with a glass reflecting more kings, with exaggerated symbols of glory and power:

. . . and some I see
That two-fold balls and treble sceptres carry:
Horrible sight! Now, I see, 't is true;
For the blood-bolter'd Banquo smiles upon me,
And points at them for his. (IV. i. 120)

Macbeth's agony is not properly understood till we realize his utter failure to receive any positive joy from the imperial magnificence to which he aspired. Hence his violent jealousy when he sees Banquo's crowned and sceptred posterity. He lives a life of death, in darkness, reft of all sense-grandeur and solid joy. He cannot conquer the evil in his soul and rest in the acclamations and honour of his land: rather he spreads his own spiritual darkness over Scotland. His robes are ridiculous on him:

Now does he feel his title
Hang loose about him, like a giant's robe
Upon a dwarfish thief. (V. ii. 20)

He is a "tyrant bloody-scepter'd" (IV. iii. 104). His life reads as an absurd lust for the impossible. Malcolm, in his pretence of Macbeth-villainy, stresses two vices: lust and avarice. Macbeth's crime, on this level, is almost an inverted, an introverted, lust or love; a self-desire, expressed by an action which aims at grasping glory-forms to itself. So Malcolm pretends he would

. . . cut off the nobles for their lands,
Desire his jewels and this other's house.
(IV. iii. 79)

Such riches-references are valuable. They serve to relate the utter negation of *Macbeth* with love-themes in Shakespeare. Macbeth's evil is a kind of lust, like Malcolm's supposed iniquity:

. . . your wives, your daughters,
Your matrons, and your maids, could not fill up
The cistern of my lust . . . (IV. iii. 61)

An introverted, selfish "lust." Malcolm's confession must be exactly related to Macbeth, suggestive of Macbeth's lust and avarice. Macbeth's awareness of "spirit" naked, divorced from the actual, is thus seen to take the shape of avarice, self-love, greed: an absolute introversion expressed in action. Though the evil itself is more ultimate than "ambition" or "greed," yet such ideas help us to understand the imaginative value of what sensuous splendour we find dully glowing in this insubstantial, insensible, world of negation. The "riches" thought is, moreover, vivid in Macduff's

I would not be the villain that thou think'st
For the whole space that's in the tyrant's grasp,
And the rich East to boot. (IV. iii. 35)

"The rich East"; and Malcolm mentioned "jewels." Both are frequent in Shakespeare's love-imagery. The gracious Duncan distributed "largesse" and a diamond to his hosts. Moreover, the nearest imaginative correspondence to *Macbeth* in all Shakespeare is to be found in *Lucrece*. There is the same abysmal evil, the same guilt-horror, the same darkness, the same fear. *Lucrece* is a valuable and necessary commentary on *Macbeth:* much that is implicit in *Macbeth* is explicitly and prolixly stressed there. So Macbeth compares himself to Tarquin. Macbeth's evil is a lust, like unruly love; a centring of reality in the self. A turning-inward of the mind and its purposes, an obsession with the solitary self unharmonized with wider considerations. So he sells his "eternal jewel" for the riches and glory of unrighteous kingship. "Jewels" may thus suggest spiritual or earthly riches here, as elsewhere in Shakespeare. That is why the gracious Duncan gives largesse and diamonds, why the Holy King of England heals "the Evil" with "a golden stamp, put on with holy prayers." Thus imperial magnificence is continually suggested, only to be blurred by the dark and evil effects. The evil is opposed to the supreme glory of kingship. In blood-imagery, the two curiously blend: sensuous glory with horror. The evil smear of dull red becomes twice a brilliant gold:

I'll gild the faces of the grooms withal;
For it must seem their guilt. (II. ii. 56)

and,

Here lay Duncan,
His silver skin lac'd with his golden blood,
And his gash'd stabs look'd like a breach in nature
For ruin's wasteful entrance. (II. iii. 117)

The gold-blood association is vivid again in "an untitled tyrant bloody-scepter'd," noted above.

So much for Macbeth's insecure tenure of imperial magnificence. Now I pass to the even more fundamental ideas of "sleep," "feasting," and "nature." Sleep and feasting are important. Peaceful sleep is often disturbed by nightmare; this I have observed elsewhere. Here we may observe how closely "sleep" is twined with "feasting." Both are creative, restorative, forces of nature. So Macbeth and his Queen are reft of both during the play's action. Feasting and sleep are twin life-givers:

> Methought I heard a voice cry, "Sleep no more!
> Macbeth does murder sleep,"—the innocent sleep,
> Sleep that knits up the ravell'd sleave of care,
> The death of each day's life, sore labour's bath,
> Balm of hurt minds, great nature's second course,
> Chief nourisher in life's feast,— (II. ii. 36)

The retributive suffering is apt. Macbeth murdered Duncan in sleep, after feasting him. It was a blow delivered at "innocent sleep"; sleep, like death in *Antony and Cleopatra,* the gentle nurse of life. Macbeth does more than murder a living being: he murders life itself. Because he murdered hospitality and sleep, therefore his punishment is a living death, without peaceful sleep or peaceful feeding:

> But let the frame of things disjoint, both the worlds suffer,
> Ere we will eat our meal in fear, and sleep
> In the affliction of these terrible dreams
> That shake us nightly . . . (III. ii. 16)

So Lennox prays for the time when Scotland

> . . . may again
> Give to our tables meat, sleep to our nights,
> Free from our feasts and banquets bloody knives,
> Do faithful homage and receive free honours . . .
> (III. vi. 33)

"Homage" and "honours." The thought is ever—as I have noted above—of a society, or family, built into a unity by mutual respect, place and degree, in which alone "honour" can exist: so Macbeth's crime is a kind of parricide—hence the suggestions of parricide in II. iv. and III. vi. Such suggestions, untrue to fact, hold yet an imaginative truth. And this society is a life-force blending with "sleep" and "feasts."

Now the evil-feasting opposition is powerful here. Duncan compares his joy in Macbeth's success to a banquet:

> True, worthy Banquo; he is full so valiant;
> And in his commendations I am fed;
> It is a banquet to me. (I. iv. 54)

Macbeth's honourable prowess is a life-bringing food to Duncan, to Scotland. Lady Macbeth's hospitality to Duncan is emphasized: she is his "honoured hostess," his "fair and noble hostess." She and Macbeth entertain him with a fine feast:

> *Hautboys and torches. Enter a* Sewer, *and divers* Servants *with dishes and service, and pass over the stage.* (I. vii)

Feasting and music: a usual grouping of effects, as in *Timon, Coriolanus,* and *Antony and Cleopatra.* Lady Macbeth plots murder whilst Duncan is feasting:

> He has almost supp'd: why have you left the chamber? (I. vii. 29)

Duncan, wearied by "his day's hard journey," goes to his chamber to sleep "soundly," after having distributed his bounty to his hosts: he is "in unusual pleasure" and "shut up in measureless content," the "content" that his murderers never achieve. So Lady Macbeth is again called "most kind hostess." Next "wine and wassail" is put to the dastardly use of drugging Duncan's grooms. They are made "the slaves of drink and thralls of sleep." Lady Macbeth steels herself by the same means. There is the grim irony of the bell which "invites" Macbeth to the murder:

> Go, bid thy mistress, when my drink is ready,
> She strike upon the bell. (II. i. 31)

The domestic and feminine note jars hideously with the horror beneath. "Drink" is often suggested. There is the porter whose drunken festivities are used to heighten our awareness that hellish evil is stalking the earth: here again, evil conquers the innocent festivity. Through all these effects we see the same opposition: feasting, a life-force, especially the hospitality wherewith the sacred Duncan is greeted by his "kinsman" and "subject"; and against this, the hideous murder. It is at once, as Macbeth observes a desecration of a "double trust": hospitality, social order, allegiance, life itself: "the wine of life" is drawn.

After the murder, feasting is again emphasized. It is shown how

> This even-handed justice
> Commends the ingredients of our poisoned chalice
> To our own lips. (I. vii. 10)

Macbeth finds he has "put rancours in the vessel of" his "peace." He may not feast with his lords in peace and harmony. Banquo's ghost breaks into the attempted festivity, disperses it, throws it into disorder. At the start, hospitality, conviviality, "welcome" and "degree" are emphasized: the very things Macbeth has so brutally desecrated.

MACBETH. You know your own degrees; sit down: at first
And last, the hearty welcome.
LORDS. Thanks to your majesty.
MACBETH. Ourself will mingle with society,
And play the humble host.
Our hostess keeps her state, but in best time
We will require her welcome.
LADY MACBETH. Pronounce it for me, sir, to all our friends;
For my heart speaks they are welcome.
MACBETH. See, they encounter thee with their hearts' thanks.
Both sides are even; here I'll sit i' th' midst.
Be large in mirth; anon we'll drink a measure
The table round. (III. iv. 1)

Hospitality is bounteous. Every phrase there is important. The murderer withdraws Macbeth's attention and Lady Macbeth again stresses the thought of welcome:

LADY MACBETH. My royal lord,
You do not give the cheer: the feast is sold
That is not often vouch'd, while 't is a-making,
'T is given with welcome. To feed were best at home;
From thence, the sauce to meat is ceremony;
Meeting were bare without it.
MACBETH. Sweet remembrancer!
Now, good digestion wait on appetite,
And health on both! (III. iv. 33)

"Digestion," "health," "sauce," "meat." Against this life-force of feasting, conviviality, social friendliness and order, comes a death, a ghost, smashing life-forms with phantasms of evil and guilt: an unreality, a "nothing," like the air-drawn dagger, creating chaos of order and reality, dispersing the social unit. It is the conquest of the real and the life-giving by the unreal and deathly. It corresponds to the murderous deed whose "hideous trumpet" waked the "downy sleep" of Macbeth's guests at Inverness, raising them to walk like "sprites" from death, like Hamlet's father, shattering at that dead hour all natural peace and rest. After the ghost's disappearance Macbeth recovers, again speaks words of "love," "health," and friendly communion:

Come, love and health to all;
Then I'll sit down. Give me some wine; fill full.
I drink to the general joy o' the whole table,
And to our dear friend Banquo, whom we miss;
Would he were here! to all, and him, we thirst,
And all to all. (III. iv. 87)

The ghost reappears. It is, like the phantasmal dagger, a "horrible shadow," an "unreal mockery," and it opposes the natural joys of feasting and "health," life-forms, life-forces, just as Macbeth's original "horrible imaginings," the "horrid image" of the proposed murder, unfixed his hair and made his heart beat wildly "against the use of nature," shook his "state of man" and smothered "function" in "surmise." So the evil makes of unity, "love," feasting and social order a chaos, dispersing and disintegrating the society. The disorder-thought is important, running throughout Shakespeare and vividly apparent here: order is the natural grouping of life-forms, disorder is evil—Macbeth's crime was essentially an act of disorder, a desecration of the ties of hospitality, blood-relationship, and allegiance.

> LADY MACBETH. You have displaced the mirth, broke the good meeting,
> With most admired disorder. (III. iv. 109)

The guests are to "stand not upon the order" of their "going"—a phrase contrasting vividly with Macbeth's opening words: "You know your own degrees." Macbeth and Lady Macbeth dwell in but "doubtful joy" after their act of "destruction." Death, destruction, chaos—these are the forms of evil opposed to the life-joys of feast and friendship, and all social concord.

The three outstanding scenes of the middle action all illustrate the evil-feasting opposition. First, there is Duncan's murder in sleep and after elaborate feasting by his host, kinsman, and subject: all concepts which stress Macbeth's ruthless desecration of social units of human life. Next, we find Banquo's ghost violently forbidding that Macbeth enjoy that hospitality and feasting which he has desecrated. Our third scene is that with the Weird Sisters in their cavern. The contrast with the banquet scene is vivid. Here we watch a devils'-banqueting, the Weird Women with their cauldron and its holocaust of hideous ingredients. The banquet-idea has been inverted. Instead of suggesting health, this one is brewed to cause "toil and trouble." The ingredients are absurd bits of life like those of Othello's ravings now jumbled together to "boil and bake" in the cauldron: "eye of newt," "toe of frog," a dog's tongue, a lizard's leg, and so on. (Mgr. Kolbe has well called them "chaotic incongruities.") But not only are there animal-pieces: we have a Jew's liver, a Turk's nose, a Tartar's lips, the "finger of birth-strangled babe." Though the bodies from which these are torn are often themselves, by association, evil, yet we must note the additional sense of chaos, bodily desecration, and irrationality in the use of these absurd derelict members, things like the "pilot's thumb" mentioned earlier. The ingredients suggest an absolute indigestibility. It is a parody of banqueting, a death-banquet, a "hell-broth." It is all quite meaningless, nameless, negative, utterly black:

> MACBETH. How now, you secret, black and midnight hags!
> What is 't you do?
> THE WEIRD WOMEN. A deed without a name. (IV. i. 48)

Formerly an "unreal mockery," a death-phantom, shattered a life-giving banquet. Here, by inversion, a death-banquet produces from its hideous "gruel" not bodily sustenance, but more phantoms. The one is a life reality disorganized by a spirit suggesting life that is past (Banquo's ghost); the other is a feast of death and essential disorder (because of the disjointed ingredients) giving birth to spirits suggesting life that is to come (the Apparitions and their prophecies). The evil disorder in the cauldron produces forms of futurity, futurity being essentially a disorder-force until it is bodied into the life-forms of the present. Thus the spirits, whether of life past or life to come, are equally inimical to Macbeth's peace. This hell-broth is a death-food, though it is not meant to be eaten: eating is good, in the cause of life. It brings forth spirits, that is evil, not earthly, things: spirit uninfused in bodies being, in the phraseology of my interpretations, purely evil. Equally evil are the correspondent bodies disorganized (bodies of nature, state, family, or man): for bodies disorganized are formless, and, if formless, soulless, "soul" and "form" being naturally equated. Therefore here and elsewhere, all disorder symbols may readily be equated with "naked spirit." So here the disordered ingredients produce correlevant spirits, apparitions rise from the deathly cauldron and its chaotic contents. Though in this sense, and in their effect, evil, these spirits yet accomplish their purpose by suggesting life-forces: the Bloody Child and the Child crowned with a Tree in his hand. But to Macbeth they bring evil. On them Macbeth's derelict soul feeds its fill, feeds on death-food—"I have supp'd full with horrors." He drinks down the ghostly future. He feeds his starved soul with hope, thinks that

> . . . our high-plac'd Macbeth
> Shall live the lease of nature, pay his breath
> To time and mortal custom. (IV. I. 98)

He is readily convinced by the Apparitions' assurances in terms of "nature"—Birnam Wood, childbirth. As I observe later, he fails to understand the real significance of these Apparitions. His spiritual sustenance feeds him with hope—not, as it pretends and he thinks, in terms of natural law, but only in terms of itself, that is, unreality, meaningless essences abstracted from the future; things which do not exist, and, when they do, will be different from their present blurred appearance as received by him. It is all a death-banquet and its spiritual food, to him, a poison. Hence it at once leads Macbeth to a deed of family destruction. He murders Lady Macduff, her children, Macduff's household, all that "trace him in his line"; again, a chaotic blow against a life-force, a family unit.

The Cauldron Scene, with its disjected members of animal and human bodies, and also its prophecies relating to "nature," suggests a yet wider view of the opposition active throughout *Macbeth*. The

Macbeth-evil attacks honour and imperial magnificence, life-forms of feeding, health, society: it also decisively attacks "nature." Nature in its purity is clearly another "life" theme, only one degree removed from "feasting." But nature is seldom apparent here in purity and grace: when it is, that appearance is important. Nature-references blend with human themes, especially in point of procreation and childhood. First, I will suggest images of nature's purity, many of them thus blending with thoughts of human birth. Birth and childhood are, indeed, our outstanding life-themes. Thence I shall pass to the more fantastical effects of unreality and supernature.

We do not find here quite the close human-nature association of *Lear*. But natural effects are, however, numerous. We are confronted usually by a nature-distortion, a reality essentially unnatural, all but unreal. Most of the nature here is therefore an impossible, an unnatural nature. There are, however, a few suggestions of nature in her native integrity and beauty. Like our numerous thoughts of divine "grace" and angels, these contrast with the evil. So the gracious Duncan regards Macbeth as a flower nurtured by himself:

> I have begun to plant thee, and will labour
> To make thee full of growing. (I. iv. 28)

His "plenteous joys" are "wanton in fulness" (I. iv. 33). Lady Macbeth counsels her lord to

> . . . look like th' innocent flower,
> But be the serpent under 't. (I. v. 66)

A characteristic Shakespearian thought of nature's "innocence," the only aspect of nature which is, curiously, truly "natural" to mankind. Nature's creative beauty is remarked by Banquo:

> DUNCAN. This castle hath a pleasant seat; the air
> Nimbly and sweetly recommends itself
> Unto our gentle senses.
> BANQUO. This guest of summer,
> The temple-haunting martlet, does approve,
> By his loved mansionry, that the heaven's breath
> Smells wooingly here; no jutty, frieze,
> Buttress, nor coign of vantage, but this bird
> Hath made his pendent bed and procreant cradle:
> Where they most breed and haunt, I have observ'd
> The air is delicate. (I. vi. 1)

Notice the strong emphasis on "senses," "wooing," and "delicate" air; and the "procreant cradle," the thought of "breeding": the passage has a vivid similarity to *Antony and Cleopatra*. Notice, too, the word "guest," and touches of divine suggestion, "temple," "heaven," which blend with other such throughout *Macbeth*. The dialogue gives us a perfect contrast in microcosm to the Macbeth-evil. Macbeth's crime is a blow against nature's unity and peace, a hideous desecration of all creative, family, and social duties, all union and concord: this is the bond he breaks, the "great bond" that keeps him "pale" (III. ii. 49). Now that "humane statute" has "purged the general weal," it is natural to mankind to live in peace and love. But Macbeth breaks all fetters of restraining humanity. He ruthlessly destroys Macduff's family. Lady Macduff thus compares her lord to a parent bird, in a passage which closely corresponds to the dialogue just quoted. Macduff, mysteriously conquered by the evil, or, rather, in order to oppose it (both are fundamentally the same) has deserted his family:

> He loves us not,
> He wants the natural touch; for the poor wren,
> The most diminutive of birds, will fight,
> Her young ones in her nest, against the owl.
> (IV. ii. 8)

She urges that Macduff's flight was dictated by "fear," not "love" or "wisdom." It is partly true: fear grips every one whilst the evil rages in Scotland. Macduff is forced to sacrifice the bond of family love—"those precious motives, the strong knots of love." He leaves them to their death:

> What, all my pretty chickens and their dam
> At one fell swoop? (IV. iii. 218)

An unnatural act, necessitated by the unnatural evil. All is chaos, turbulence, disorder—to be contrasted with family or national peace, humanity's natural concord.

Nature's food of "milk" is often mentioned in this connexion. Lady Macbeth fears her lord's "nature": he is "too full o' the milk of human kindness." She invokes spirits of evil to take her own "milk for gall." Then, boasting of her conquest over natural pity, she speaks the terrible lines:

> I have given suck, and know
> How tender 't is to love the babe that milks me;
> I would, while it was smiling in my face,
> Have pluck'd my nipple from his boneless gums,
> And dash'd the brains out, had I so sworn as you
> Have done to this. (I. vii. 54)

The child-thought is frequent. There is the unnatural horror of the "birth-strangled babe," and the matter of Macduff's mysterious birth. Again:

> And pity, like a naked new-born babe,
> Striding the blast, or heaven's cherubim, hors'd
> Upon the sightless couriers of the air . . .
> (I. vii. 21)

Unsullied nature's fresh innocence here blends with the angelic hosts—"heaven's cherubim"—of supernatural grace. Babyhood and "milk" are thus often suggested. There is another milk-reference. Malcolm, pretending to be another Macbeth, would

> Pour the sweet milk of concord into hell,
> Uproar the universal peace, confound
> All unity on earth. (IV. iii. 98)

Notice the close association of childhood's innocency ("milk") with "concord." This evil is antagonistic not only to man but the universe, a blow at all "unity," at nature, creation, and the "universal peace," so terrible that the sun is blackened and heaven's thunder reverberates the desolation of human families:

> . . . each new morn
> New widows howl, new orphans cry, new sorrows
> Strike heaven on the face, that it resounds
> As if it felt with Scotland, and yell'd out
> Like syllable of dolour. (IV. iii. 4)

Innocent nature is in agony. Twice Macbeth is contrasted with a lamb (IV. iii. 16—"a weak poor innocent lamb"; and IV. iii. 54). Evil fear is contrasted with "a summer's cloud" and "good men's lives" die like "flowers." So nature will rise to avenge Macduff whose slaughtered wife and children demand redress:

> . . . your eye in Scotland
> Would create soldiers, make our women fight,
> To doff their dire distresses. (IV. iii. 186)

Nature would "create" soldiers to avenge Macduff's children, make "women" fight to avenge his wife. "Creation" is an important idea in the play. Toward the close, nature's assistance is vividly apparent. Macbeth is "ripe for shaking." He himself knows it:

> I have liv'd long enough: my way of life
> Is fall'n into the sear, the yellow leaf . . .
> (V. iii. 22)

But the avenging forces are mostly young and fresh, to avenge the desecration of nature's childlike peace:

> . . . there is Siward's son,
> And many unrough youth that even now
> Protest their first of manhood. (V. ii. 9)

Malcolm himself is compared to a flower dew-sprinkled: the Scottish lords would "dew the sovereign flower and drown the weeds." So sweet a nature-image again suggests nature's assistance: which thought is even more clearly apparent in the matter of Birnam Wood. Not a human army only attacks Dunsinane. The very trees rise against Macbeth, league with his enemies. That is creative nature accusing, asserting her strength after her long torment of destruction. So Birnam Wood marches against Macbeth.

For nature is here tormented. I have observed some normal nature references. There are many more abnormal ones. Our vision here presents an experience of utter negation which wrenches all life-forms into distorted and ghoulish impossibilities. Many such images I have discussed elsewhere. But there are a few more points to observe. The Weird Sisters from the start are presented as in essence unnatural.[2] They "look not like the inhabitants o' the earth, and yet are on't." Banquo wonders whether they are "fantastical" or that which "outwardly" they "show," that is, whether they are real life-forms. Their otherness to all natural laws is emphasized by their power to vanish, to become what they are, a pure nothing, death-symbols:

> BANQUO. The earth hath bubbles, as the water has,
> And these are of them. Whither are they vanish'd?
> MACBETH. Into the air; and what seem'd corporal melted
> As breath into the wind. Would they had stay'd!
> BANQUO. Were such things here as we do speak about?
> Or have we eaten on the insane root
> That takes the reason prisoner? (I. iii. 79)

So vividly their unnaturalness and unreality are stressed. They are outside nature and the reflection of nature in the mind, "reason." They are things of insanity, related to that abortion of nature's vegetation—the "insane root." The Macbeth-evil is so clearly opposed to nature that Lady Macbeth, who fears her own as well as Macbeth's nature, prays to be "unsexed." She continues:

> . . . make thick my blood;
> Stop up th' access and passage to remorse,
> That no compunctious visitings of nature
> Shake my fell purpose, nor keep peace between
> Th' effect and it! Come to my woman's breasts,
> And take my milk for gall, you murd'ring ministers,
> Wherever in your sightless substances
> You wait on nature's mischief! (I. v. 44)

Twice here "nature" is stressed. This is a play of things outside nature, of "sightless substances." She goes on to pray that "thick night" and hell-smoke may hide her deed from the eye. That is our usual contrast: blackness, nothingness, and life-forms of nature, of sense. The evil torments nature. Its nightmare is a nature-distortion—"the cursed thoughts that nature gives way to in repose." In this world "nature

[2] I omit the Hecate scenes and speeches. They do not seem to me to blend with the whole play. Even so, they may be Shakespearian, added at some later date than the original composition: which would account for their inclusion in the Folio.

seems dead" and "wicked dreams" are active. So the "present horror" of deadest night must not be interrupted by any sense-forms of sight or sound. The deed of murder is one which must not be looked on—Miss Spurgeon has shown that this is often emphasized. Nor must it be heard:

> Thou sure and firm-set earth
> Hear not my steps, which way they walk, for fear
> Thy very stones prate of my whereabout,
> And take the present horror from the time,
> Which now suits with it. (II. i. 56)

Macduff's knocking aptly strikes avenging sounds after this act of silence and darkness. Death is, indeed, the exact opposite of nature and all natural effects:

> . . . death and nature do contend about them,
> Whether they live or die. (II. ii. 7)

Our whole world is unnatural, beyond physical laws, "metaphysical." All sense-forms and natural phenomena are attacked. There is a powerful sense-nothing opposition: in which *Macbeth* is directly analogous to *Timon*. Timon moves towards a death-philosophy and attains the "nothing" of death. It is exactly this "nothing," this death-negation, that is here projected into action and attacks our life-forms. And, in respect of this negation opposed to creation, we may note a similarity to *Othello*. There "values" are attacked: love, warriorship. Here not only values, but all life-forces and forms. This opposition is most vivid in the air-drawn dagger scene. "Sense" here contrasts with the "delicate senses" of the martlet passage. The dagger is a nothing, to be contrasted with ordinary sense-forms:

> Art thou not, fatal vision, sensible
> To feeling as to sight? or art thou but
> A dagger of the mind, a false creation,
> Proceeding from the heat-oppressed brain?
> (II. i. 36)

Again,

> Mine eyes are made the fools o' the other senses,
> Or else worth all the rest . . . (II. i. 44)

That incident is typical of the whole play: evil is opposed to all natural processes; that is, a pervading death opposes life. The Macbeth "nothing" pits its "fantastical" realities or unrealities against sense-forms and life-forces, against "nature": the weird behaviour of sun, tempest, falcon and owl, Duncan's horses—all is "unnatural, even like the deed that's done"; all has "turn'd wild in nature"; all is " 'gainst nature still." All this is one with a murder which gashed "a breach in nature," a murder against nature's outward form of life, the body, "nature's copy"; and against sleep, "great nature's second course," the "season of all natures." As Macbeth's course becomes more reckless, the evil forces him to imprecate wholesale tempest and disorder on the universe. He would have the "winds" untied, fighting against "churches," swallowing up "navigation," blowing down "corn" and "trees"; castles, palaces, pyramids, let all fall; he would let "the treasure of nature's germens tumble all together" till destruction itself "sicken." Notice here the suggestions of (i) the Macbeth "grace" (churches), (ii) imperial sway ("palaces" [3]), and (iii) nature: against all these the evil fights. So the torment goes on: essential disorder, essential destruction—Timon's curses put into violent action. Lady Macbeth's sleep-walking is "a great perturbation in nature," for

> Unnatural deeds
> Do breed unnatural troubles . . . (V. i. 79)

It is a fitting culmination to this theme of dark and nightmare, evil which is set beyond any natural law of sense-contact:

> DOCTOR. You see, her eyes are open.
> GENTLEWOMAN. Ay, but their sense is shut. (V. i. 28)

So she walks, her body present but her consciousness beyond the imaginable universe pacing the lonely corridors of agonized remembrance in the other world of sleep. The play's action has been all along a waking nightmare: here nightmare usurps the powers allowed to waking life. It is Death's supreme conquest over "nature." But the death-evil itself is outside nature, beyond it. This is suggested by the Doctor's words to Macbeth, who asks if he can minister to his wife's spiritual disease:

> Therein the patient
> Must minister to himself. (V. iii. 45)

Either that—or call in some supernatural "grace." The Doctor suggested as much before:

> More needs she the divine than the physician.
> God, God forgive us all! (V. i. 82)

The mighty forces of "grace" and "evil" must finally decide the issue for Macbeth. That is another profound opposition. An equivalent abstraction—one might almost say "unreality"—must be "solicited" to counter-act the abstraction and unreality which is evil. But, under the

[3] And, we might add, "pyramids." That these have imperial significance in Shakespeare is apparent from *Antony and Cleopatra*:

> . . . rather make
> My country's high pyramides my gibbet . . . (V. ii. 60)

So minute are the effects of *Macbeth*. It is the same with the Porter's speech: nature's "plenty," irrational action, equivocation, hell and heaven, thoughts of dress—all are typical Macbeth-ideas.

banner of divine grace ("the most pious Edward"), all our forces are embattled for Scotland's weal: imperial right (Malcolm); warrior-honour (Siward and his son); nature itself (Birnam Wood); and, finally, even disorder and deathly abnormality, turning against itself (Macduff, child of unnatural birth).

I have regarded the evil in relation to life-forces. These may be divided as follows: (i) Human values, Warrior-honour and Imperial sway; (ii) Human nature, sleep and feasting; (iii) Pure nature—animals, birds, winds, sun, and stars. Most important of all, we must observe the emergence of child-references. The negation here opposes all values, health, and nature: the creative process. Destruction is set against creation: hence our many references to mother's "milk," the martlet's and wren's nest and young, to "chickens," "lambs," the strange use of "egg" and "fry," and the child-themes: the phrase, "child of integrity," Lady Macbeth's baby at her breast, the baby-spirit of Pity astride the winds of heaven, the two child apparitions—the Bloody Child, and the Child whose "baby-brow" is crowned with gold: Banquo's descendants, Malcolm, Donalbain, Fleance, the scene of Macduff's son, his "babes," crying "orphans," the birth-strangled babe (IV. i. 30), young Siward, who "only lived but till he was a man," and the other "unrough youths." Subjects are "children" of the king, Scotland the "mother" of its people now turned to a "grave," a vivid birth-death contrast; Scotland's peace is those people's "birthdom," the throne Malcolm's "due of birth," the Queen that "bore" him a saintly mother. The "nothing" of death-atmosphere, here active and pervasive, silhouettes these "birth" and "child" themes which struggle to assert themselves, struggle to be born from death into life. At the end youth comes armed against Macbeth. Birth opposes death. "Issue" is an important word. Youth and babyhood oppose our evil. Macbeth murdered aged innocence and purity linked to the "great office" of kingship. Child innocence with all heaven, all imperial sovereignty, and all nature on its side, tree-sceptred, confronts the murderer:

> What is this
> That rises like the issue of a king,
> And wears upon his baby-brow the round
> And top of sovereignty? (IV. i. 86)

Macbeth, himself destruction, is destroyed: thus he is a symbol of time itself from its death-aspect. In so far as you see time as destruction, you see it itself continually destroyed: in so far as a man becomes destructive, he is himself destroyed. The time-concept is very clearly woven with Macbeth's tale, contrasting with the eternity of *Antony and Cleopatra*. The Weird Women first met Macbeth as voices of past, present, and future, with their prophecies about Glamis, Cawdor, and Kingship. They suggest absolute time. Macbeth's crime is, however, an attempt to dislocate time, to wrench the future into the present, just as it is a crime against order and degree, a wild vaulting ambition to attain unrightful "honour." He wants all time to be his, and so gets none of it. He would "ravin up" his "own life's means." He wrongs the majestic and unhurrying pace of time. What is time but a succession of deaths, minute by minute? And yet again it is a succession of births. Macbeth would expedite the death-aspect of time, and so catch the "future in the instant," would destroy the present, Duncan. But in the Cauldron Scene we see time as creation. There is a vivid destruction-birth sequence. The Armed Head recalling Macdonwald's head "fixed" on the "battlements," blends with the "chaos" and "disorder" thought throughout, the torn animal and human limbs that constitute the cauldron's ingredients, and moreover suggests both the iron force of evil and also its final destruction. This is followed by the Bloody Child and the "Child, crowned, with a Tree in his hand"; observe how the crown contrasts with the severed head, and how its victory is directly associated with nature. The order is important. Violent destruction, itself to be destroyed; the blood-agony of birth that travails to wrench into existence a force to right the sickening evil; the future birth splendid in crowned and accomplished royalty. It suggests the creative process in all its miraculous strength and power to pursue its purpose. Ironically, these apparitions give to Macbeth, who regards their words whilst remaining blind to themselves, not despair, but hope. He, who has placed his trust in chaos, hopes himself to "live the lease of nature." But this joy is short-lived. For we may note again how powerfully our positive, creative essences are next suggested by the "show of eight Kings." They are rich in imperial glory. But they are more. They, too, suggest, in a wide sense, the creative process itself, the process Macbeth would annihilate, would cut off at the present root. He too readily grasped his own future to himself: but would annihilate the future of others. He would have time disjointed to serve his ends. But Banquo is to have all the wealth of posterity, all that creative joy in which alone human happiness consists. Too late he learns that to get kings is more blessed than to be king, creation more blessed than possession. For possession divorced from creation melts in the grasping hand: like flowers "dying or ere they sicken." So here, a right kingly creation in all its inevitable splendour and future integrity passes before his eyes; in its imperial strength and unending glory, its line stretching even to "the crack of doom," it confronts his own brief-living destructive self, doomed to end, his "eternal jewel" lost, with the end of his own agony. This is shown him by the Weird Women, the "instruments of darkness" and evil; and they thus league against him, know and show the limitations imposed on evil, for Macbeth is childless, with a fruitless crown and barren sceptre, as evil is ever childless, unproductive. So he knows the process of life to hold no hope for him. It is merely a cruel catalogue of deaths strung together in time:

> To-morrow, and to-morrow, and to-morrow,
> Creeps in this petty pace from day to day
> To the last syllable of recorded time;
> And all our yesterdays have lighted fools
> The way to dusty death. Out, out, brief candle!
> Life's but a walking shadow, a poor player
> That struts and frets his hour upon the stage
> And then is heard no more. It is a tale
> Told by an idiot, full of sound and fury,
> Signifying nothing. (V. v. 19)

He sees all life from the death-aspect of time. And he is now himself reconciled to the "nothing," the negation of evil and death. He finds peace in the profundities of his own nihilistic death-experience: death and "nothing" are realities: life has no meaning. The evil has worked its way with him, and left him with no hope in life. Even so, there is yet death. Like the earlier Cawdor, he dies well.

The Weird Women, I have said, are not themselves from every aspect opposed to creation and life. They know evil to be futile, they know their own futility. They are unreal, and know it, know their existence and purposes to be self-contradictory. So, of their two main prophecies in the Cauldron Scene, those relating to Birnam Wood and Macduff's birth, the one is fulfilled in terms of natural law, the other in terms of an event itself so abnormal as to be all but unnatural:

> And let the angel whom thou still hast served
> Tell thee, Macduff was from his mother's womb
> Untimely ripp'd. (V. viii. 14)

If Macduff means that his mother died before his birth, the suggestion is pregnant to our interpretation: life born out of death. But, in whatever sense we take its meaning, we see that disorder itself turns on disorder. So, too, the death-concept ever contradicts itself and becomes life to any intense contemplation. Absolute disorder prohibits self-consistency: it helps to slay itself. Death gives birth to life. Not nature alone, but "both the worlds," natural and unnatural, life and death, come against Macbeth. And here we may observe an important effect in the Cauldron Scene. The three apparitions suggesting the conflict of death and birth rise from the hell-broth in the cauldron to "thunder." The Weird Sisters instinctively fear Macbeth's demand about Banquo's descendants—"Seek to know no more." Even the Apparitions, being reflections of human reality, were their "masters." Now, threatened by Macbeth's "eternal curse," they reluctantly expose their own impermanency, the eternal unreality of evil. The cauldron vanishes, and the line of future kings passes to the music of "hautboys" (IV. i. 106).

In a final judgment the whole play may be writ down as a wrestling of destruction with creation: with sickening shock the phantasmagoria of death and evil are violently loosed on earth, and for a while the agony endures, destructive; there is a wrenching of new birth, itself disorderly and unnatural in this disordered world, and then creation's more firm-set sequent concord replaces chaos. The baby-peace is crowned.

CORIOLANUS

(1937)

D. A. TRAVERSI

CORIOLANUS has never satisfied the critics. Most of them have felt that it stands in some way apart from the main body of Shakespeare's work; they find it frigid, and they even tell us that Shakespeare's interest in it flagged. On the other hand, an important minority—including Mr. Eliot—have been considerably attracted by the play, and have even found an important place for it in the development of their own experience. The only point upon which there seems to be agreement is that *Coriolanus* is difficult, and that its artistic quality is peculiar. Even sympathetic critics must account for the fact that the figure of the hero is harsh and, at times, grotesque, whilst Aufidius' behavior is puzzling and inconsistent. It is the task of a critical interpretation to show whether these contradictions are part of the stuff of the author's experience, or whether they are only the odds and ends left over by imperfect assimilation. On the common view it is quite clear that these facts cannot be accounted for, that they are a sign of serious failure. This paper proposes, by approaching the play through its verse and language, to show that these "difficulties" are part of Shakespeare's intention and result in an artistic success as assured as that of *Macbeth;* I shall also try to define the nature of that success, and to assess its value as a kind of tragedy more new and interesting than many have realized.

The mastery displayed in the verse of *Coriolanus* does not suggest declining powers or lack of interest. There is an interesting example of this in the very first verse speech of the play, when Menenius rebukes the citizens for their mutterings:

> For your wants,
> Your suffering in this dearth, you may as well
> Strike at the heaven with your staves as lift them
> Against the Roman state, whose course will on
> The way it takes, cracking ten thousand curbs
> Of more strong link asunder than can ever
> Appear in your impediment. For the dearth,
> The gods, not the patricians, make it, and
> Your knees to them, not arms, must help . . . (I. i. 67-76)

It is impossible not to feel that this is an example of the unique, free mastery of Shakespeare's later verse. We should be aware of the conciseness of the last sentence, of the way in which the "not arms" parenthesis enables us to grasp the essential contrast without the distraction that would result from a full statement of the alternatives; it is a telescoping of language that follows the movement of living thought. More important for our purpose is the way in which the rhythm of the earlier lines serves to develop a nervous power in the words, expressing the irresistible motion of tremendous and insentient force. The essential lines are:

> . . . whose course will on
> The way it takes, cracking ten thousand curbs
> Of more strong link asunder than can ever
> Appear in your impediment.

The force is, as usual, not only stated, but given concrete embodiment in the movement of the verse. The division of "cracking" and "asunder," both words which carry with them strong feelings of physical separation, serves to carry the reader over the intervening words so that his experience partakes of the irresistible movement of the Roman state. The emotional impetus thus created is then brought to a sudden curb by the ending of the sentence in the middle of the familiar blank verse unit of the line, an ending prepared for and emphasized by the strong, decisive Latin word "impediment." The movement of the verse, in fact, is that of a poet who is in complete mastery of his medium, which has become a pliant instrument to express the subtle movements of his consciousness. It is sufficient to suggest that *Coriolanus* is a great play.

I quoted the passage, however, less to establish Shakespeare's powers of versification in *Coriolanus,* than to introduce the issues with which it deals. The central feeling of the speech is clearly that suggested by the phrase, "strike at the heaven with your staves," and emphasized in the nervous strength of the passage we have discussed. To be certain of this, we may reinforce the impression of "staves" by referring to Menenius' talk of the citizens' "bats and clubs" just above, echoed once more by "stiff bats and clubs" in the course of the same argument. Mr. Wilson Knight, in *The Imperial Theme,* acutely pointed out that these phrases, together with others of the same kind, were sufficiently prominent to give a peculiar sensation of hardness and ruthless inpenetrability to the play. In other words, the sense of social stiffness and utter incompatibility is woven by Shakespeare into the emotional texture of his work, and gives a peculiar tone to the political and social study which underlies it. The "bats and clubs" of the contending parties strike at one another in a closed universe; "the heavens" with all their associations of light and "grace," remain rigid and impenetrable, so that we can almost hear the "stiff" weapons clang when raised against them. This sense of hardness and hostility is essential to *Coriolanus,* for, as we shall see, it is repeated in the play's attitude to war and in the character of the hero himself. For the present, we shall merely note the vividness of Shakespeare's political study of Roman conditions, the sense of a social order hardened into insentience on the one hand and unworthiness on the other, the patricians and the people utterly out of contact with one another, hard, hostile, exclusive in their attitude. The patricians have no contact with the people; Menenius' speech already quoted stresses their merciless lack of feeling and responsibility, and Coriolanus himself caricatures his warlike valour in the following speech:

> Would the nobility lay aside their ruth,
> And let me use my sword, I'd make a quarry
> With thousands of these quarter'd slaves, as high
> As I could pick my lance. (I. i. 201)

This perversion of the traditional speech of warlike heroes is a masterpiece of irony. On the other hand—and this everyone admits—the people are weak, worthless, and brutal, easily led astray by the scheming tribunes, and quite incapable of seeing beyond the selfish ends of the moment.

All this is more or less apparent. Much more important is the image under which Shakespeare develops this discord, and gives it significance. The theme is actually a variation of that of "degree," so prominent in *Troilus and Cressida,* but here less "metaphysically" and more socially conceived. It is worth noting, however, that the verse of *Troilus,* even that given to Ulysses, is not equal to that of *Coriolanus* in the precision which denotes mastery of experience; the comparative lack of organization which accompanies the extraordinary complexity of the language in the earlier play indicates a mind overwhelmed by a superabundance of new conceptions—conceptions which will need to be worked out in the developing pattern of the tragedies. As in *Troilus,* however, the essential image which Shakespeare chose to give point to his study is that of the functioning of the human body. As usual, it appears almost at once in order to set clearly the tone of the play. Menenius develops it fully in his fable to the citizens:

> There was a time when all the body's members
> Rebell'd against the belly: thus accus'd it:
> That only like a gulf it did remain
> I' the midst of the body, idle and unactive,
> Still cupboarding the viand, never bearing
> Like labour with the rest, where th' other instruments
> Did see and hear, devise, instruct, walk, feel,
> And mutually participate, did minister
> Unto the appetite and affection common
> Of the whole body . . . (I. i. 99)

Now this speech, and the discussion which follows, are based on North's Plutarch, but they are there stated in the abstract manner of the moralist, occupying only a few lines and in no way suggesting the individuality of Shakespeare's version. Upon this basis, the poet created a fundamental criticism of Roman society—fundamental, precisely because it was not merely political, like so many of the fashionable accounts of the contemporary situation by Left-minded writers, but based upon a sensation of fine living developed through the whole pattern of the tragedies. I nearly sub-titled this essay as "A study on Shakespearean politics," but was deterred by dangerous associations of which one can hardly fail to be aware. I do suggest, however, that my attempted analysis of this play is an effort to show in what way Shakespeare is not only "great," but urgent and relevant, a reminder that the most needed criticism to-day is one based on an awareness of the possibilities of living, which exist, however obscured they may be by our depression. Keeping this aside in view, we may return to Menenius, and study the way in which Shakespeare has invested a political commonplace with his own sense of poetic significance.

The first point to notice is one that precedes the formal development of the political situation; it concerns the quality of feeling which Shakespeare has introduced into his verse. The prevailing tone is one of idleness, of stagnation, of a general obstruction of everything that suggests life and activity. We note before everything the unhealthy heaviness of "idle and inactive," and the direct coarseness implied by the vernacular of "cupboarding." Then we find this contrasted with the very noticeable livening of the verse when we come to speak of "the other instruments," the sense and active parts of the body. This balance of two contrasted elements, the keenness of the senses carrying with it a related feeling of physical repulsion and sluggishness, is already evident in the earlier plays. Here, too, Shakespeare connects this intensity of feeling with the contrasted baseness and satiation of lust. The feeling of the speech is given another subtle turn by the reference to "the appetite and affection common"; "appetite" has behind it associations with "the universal wolf" of Ulysses' great speech, as well as with frequent Elizabethan references to incontinence; the latter, of course, are further strengthened by the word "common," so often used by Shakespeare's contemporaries to indicate promiscuity. We have, then, a feeling, very like that of Troilus, of a social organism in disorder and decay, an impression further strengthened by the prominence given to the idea of food and the process of digestion. Greed and satiety are the main images by which we are prepared for the tragedy of *Coriolanus.*

So far, in substance if not in every detail, we have most of the critics with us. It is generally recognized that there are elements of disorder and decay in the Rome of Coriolanus. But there is also a feeling that the author's sympathies were with the patricians. This view, however, immediately lands us in the perplexities already indicated, on the strength of which the play has so often been condemned as a failure. If Coriolanus is really the "hero," and the patricians on the whole an admirable class, why is his behaviour so inconsistent, not to say degrading? A moment's consideration of this same speech will show us that the subtlety of Shakespeare's political analysis is much beyond that of his critics. For the patricians are presented to us in the likeness of the "belly," with the result that there is an essential contrast between their stagnation and their indispensability. Menenius makes a just criticism of the failure of the populace to play a proper part in the social organism; but the figure he chooses to elaborate his point turns the argument against his own class. Though the belly was essential to the proper working of the body, it was also "idle and inactive" and self-satisfied; in this connection we should note that brilliant stroke:

> With a kind of smile,
> Which ne'er came from the lungs, but even thus . . .

with its fine balance between the comic and the complacent. Shakespeare even goes further. He gives to the First Citizen some of the most bitter and penetrating words in the whole discussion. There is no hiding the force with which the "cormorant belly" and "the sink o' the body" cut through the complacent assumption of superiority recorded by Menenius. Lastly, we should not pass over Shakespeare's ambiguous attitude to the belly as distributor of food to the whole body; if it gives life to the rest of the body, it is also the receptacle of the worthless bran.

The result of this speech, then, is a very subtle apprehension of the condition of a social organism, as revealed by the power of a living and penetrating sensibility. We are shown a populace incapable of discerning its own good, vicious and vulgar, and needing the leadership of a class superior to itself. On the other side, we are also shown a patrician class who have forfeited their right to superiority by showing a complete selfishness and lack of responsibility. They are, in fact, merely subsisting on a position gained in the more or less distant past. Both these factions are set in an iron social framework which permits no contact, no community of interests, nothing but repression on one side and animal discontent on the other. That is the full meaning of the inflexible quality of Menenius' first speech.

* * *

Having provided as a background such a subtle social study, Shakespeare was not likely to place in the foreground a hero whom he regarded as a simple and romantic warrior struck down by the worthless and ungrateful people. Even those who have tended to this view have always been baffled by the way in which Shakespeare stresses both Coriolanus' proud obstinacy and his unnatural lack of feeling for the whole setting of his past life. It is more hopeful to approach the hero through the feeling expressed in the war poetry of the play. The eulogy of him by Cominius at the Capitol gives us a suitable opportunity to do this:

His pupil age
Man-enter'd thus, he waxed like a sea;
And, in the brunt of seventeen battles since,
He lurch'd all swords of the garland . . .
. . . as weeds before
A vessel under sail, so men obey'd,
And fell below his stern: his sword, death's stamp,
Where it did mark, it took; from face to foot
He was a thing of blood, whose every motion
Was timed with dying cries. Alone he enter'd
The mortal gate of th' city, which he painted
With shunless destiny; aidless came off,
And with a sudden re-inforcement struck
Corioli like a planet; now all's his:
When, by and by, the din of war 'gan pierce
His ready sense, then straight his doubled spirit
Re-quicken'd what in flesh was fatigate,
And to the battle came he; where he did
Run reeking o'er the lives of men, as if
'T were a perpetual spoil; and till we call'd
Both field and city ours, he never stood
To ease his breast with panting. (II. ii. 102)

It is impossible not to feel at once, without any detailed discussion, that this is Shakespeare at his mature best; who else would have used that bold compression "man-enter'd," in which explicitness is waived in favour of speed and immediacy of expression? The verse moves with the utmost ease and freedom, a perfectly plastic medium for catching shifts of feeling; such a shift is recorded in the emphasized contrast between the splendour of "he waxed like a sea," reminiscent of *Antony and Cleopatra* in its suggestion of unbounded energy, and the leaden reality of "lurch'd" and "brunt." These things are conveyed easily to a reader who is prepared for them; the voice is carried irresistibly by rhythms which are always based on living speech to the proper emphasis, the delicately felt pause by which Shakespeare so often converts the statement of a fact into its apprehension by the act of a completely sensitive response. The line:

And with a sudden re-inforcement struck
Corioli . . .

with its telling isolation of "struck" at the end of the line, is an outstanding example; it produces the sense of weighty and fatal pressure which is so essential to the impression at which Shakespeare aimed.

So we come to the feeling of the speech. In it Shakespeare is using his unique capacity for compressing the complex feelings that underlie his exploration of a situation into the unity of a single speech, whose central images are conversely radiated out into the surrounding matter, of which they serve at once as a concentration and a point of departure. It is in this sense that the mature plays could be described as organic, the product of a sensibility whose life was not only diffused through a play, but was concentrated into every part of it. The speech gives us a peculiar impression of Coriolanus as a warrior. It stresses at once his vitality, his splendid and superabundant life, and his heaviness, his cruelty, almost his fantastic absurdity; and the two are part of the same man. The first of these qualities is expressed not only in the rich, splendid image we have already noticed—"he waxed like a sea"—but it is also given a definite living quality, a fine nervous delicacy in:

> . . . the din of war 'gan pierce
> His ready sense, then straight his doubled spirit
> Re-quicken'd what in flesh was fatigate . . .

This superb sensitive response to "the din of war" is not new in *Coriolanus*. We are carried at once back to Othello's reaction to "the spirit-stirring drum, the ear-piercing fife," which gives the same impression of the senses at work at the confines of their intensity. War gives rise here to a fine keenness of feeling that is only paralleled by Shakespeare's reaction to love in *Antony and Cleopatra*. It is, indeed, worth remembering that the two plays were written at the same period, for we shall see that there is some association between their respective treatments of war and love.

All this does not mean, of course, that Shakespeare was a crude and ignorant enthusiast for war. He had already, in his earlier period, made a complete study of the uncompromising, egoistic patriot in *Henry V*, and the greatness of this speech in *Coriolanus* depends upon the manner in which there is intertwined with the sense of superb vitality a dead heaviness, which culminates in an almost grotesque insentience. That is the reason why the munificence of "he waxed like a sea" is immediately qualified by the ponderous impact of "brunt" and "lurch'd." It should be seen, further, that these lines are dealing with Coriolanus' growth into manhood. They suggest perfectly the double process which Shakespeare saw and conveyed in his verse in the history of the great soldier. On the one hand, Coriolanus grew into the full development of his powers, the complete expression of his maturity. On the other hand, his new power converted itself more and more, with success, into heaviness and indifference to vitality, into an exclusion of the very qualities of life and sensitivity which maturity should have crowned. So we pass through the splendid and ruthless image of the "vessel under sail" to the description of the sword as "death's stamp," a description which gives it the destructive weight and inflexibility of a battering-ram. These things prepare us for the entry of a mechanical warrior, a man turned into an instrument of war, grotesquely unaware of the suffering he caused:

> . . . from face to foot
> He was a thing of blood, whose every motion
> Was timed with dying cries.

This impression is further reinforced by the suggestion of an irresistible impact behind "planet," which helps to make him, no longer a mere warrior, but an "instrument" (the word is significant, in view of what we have already said about the battering-ram) "of shunless destiny" against "the mortal gates of the city." In that word "mortal" is contained not only an expression of helplessness, but a protest on the part of down-trodden life against this insentient minister of fate. Then, to balance the argument, comes that remarkable quickening of the machine which we have already noted, a quickening followed, however, by the renewed grotesque callousness of:

> . . . he did
> Run reeking o'er the lives of men, as if
> 'T were a perpetual spoil,

and we are left with Coriolanus "panting" like a hot-blooded bull after his orgy of destruction. In this way, right through Cominius' eulogy, Shakespeare holds a balance which is essential to a proper reading of the play.

In case it be thought that too much stress has been laid upon a single passage (though the power and immediacy of the imagery is enough to dispose of such an objection) it can easily be shown how this balance is preserved throughout the play, and is, indeed, an integral part of its structure. There is the feeling of the iron, mechanical warrior in the earliest scenes, as when Titus Lartius speaks of:

> . . . thy grim looks and
> The thunder-like percussion of thy sounds;

and, at the end, when Coriolanus seems to be on the point of taking his revenge on Rome, we have a very remarkable prose passage from Menenius:

MENENIUS: The tartness of his face sours ripe grapes: when he walks, he moves like an engine, and the ground shrinks before his treading: he is able to pierce a corslet with his eye; talks like a knell, and his hum is a battery. He sits in his state, as a thing made for Alexander. What he bids to be done is finished with his bidding. He wants nothing of a god but eternity and a heaven to throne in.

SICINIUS: Yes, mercy, if you report him truly.

MENENIUS: I paint him in the character. Mark what mercy his mother shall bring from him; there is no more mercy in him than there is milk in a male tiger. (V. iv. 18)

This is a fine example of the prose of Shakespeare's late period, prose which is not content merely to develop the facts of a situation, but is informed with the same continual consciousness of the emotional unity of the play as that which informs the verse. Passing by that fine enlistment of the palate in the opening image, we come once more to a description of the human war-machine, this time absolutely explicit. The later part of the speech suggests not only the grotesque lack of human feeling in this machine, but also the futility of this artificial insentience. This comparison of Coriolanus' pretentions with a state of divinity was clearly Shakespeare's expression of a fundamental criticism, for he had already put it once into the mouth of the tribunes; Brutus had said:

You speak o' th' people,
As if you were a god to punish, not
A man of their infirmity. (III. i. 80)

On a great many accounts of this play, it would be very hard to explain the wisdom of these utterances, given to the otherwise detestable tribunes. But, as we have suggested, Shakespeare's insight was keener than that of his critics, and so the tribunes are allowed to throw the clearest light of all upon Coriolanus' futility. And this futility is brought home to us by a further stroke of irony, for we know, as Menenius does not, that this would-be implacable warrior has not only self-consciously paraded his firmness before Aufidius—

Shall I be temped to infringe my vow,
In the same time 't is made? I will not . . .

Aufidius, and you Volsces, mark; for we'll
Hear nought from Rome in private. Your request?
(V. iii. 20, 92)

—but has capitulated at the very moment of his posing. As Aufidius says, with a bitter cynicism which is part of the spirit of this play:

At a few drops of woman's rheum, which are
As cheap as lies, he sold the blood and honour
Of our great action . . . (V. vi. 46)

That, at least, is one aspect of Coriolanus' career as a warrior.

The other aspect, however, as we have already suggested in discussing Cominius' speech, is equally present. There is no question that this play connects the action of war with a sense of splendid and living ecstasy. The most obvious example is to be found in the scene where Coriolanus first meets Aufidius, after his exile, and the Volscian general addresses him in the following terms:

Let me twine
Mine arms about that body, where against
My grained ash an hundred times hath broke,
And scarr'd the moon with splinters. Here I clip
The anvil of my sword, and do contest
As hotly and as nobly with thy love
As ever in ambitious strength I did
Contend against thy valour. Know thou first,
I lov'd the maid I married: never man
Sigh'd truer breath; but that I see thee here,
Thou noble thing! more dances my rapt heart
Than when I first my wedded mistress saw
Bestride my threshold . . . (IV. v. 112)

The note of exultation reminds us once more of *Antony and Cleopatra.* Here too the life that expresses itself in war is communicated in terms of love. From Aufidius' behaviour in this play, we should not have expected him to express ecstasy (if, indeed, such a word were within the compass of his experience) in terms of his own emotions in love. But the justification, of course, is less in character than in the emotional make-up of the play. In character, the discrepancy between poetry and behaviour helps to emphasize the dual nature of Aufidius, poised oddly between heroism and treachery prompted by jealous selfishness, just as Coriolanus, in Cominius' speech, is poised between divinity and insentience. But these divergences of personal principle are only products of the disharmony we have found in the social analysis of the play, and this analysis is merely a projection of the original poetic mood. The martial exultation of Coriolanus and Aufidius is counterbalanced by their respective brutality and treachery, in the same way as the superior keenness and vividness of the senses in Menenius' opening parable is necessarily attached to the grossness of "the cormorant belly" from which they try in vain to escape.

A type of poetry which is identical in quality with that we have just discussed in Aufidius is also to be found in Coriolanus himself, as we shall see if we consider some of the speeches, which are among his finest, made when he returns to his family after his triumph at Corioli. Mr. Middleton Murry has pointed to the beauty of:

My gracious silence, hail!
Wouldst thou have laugh'd had I come coffin'd home,
That weep'st to see me triumph?

The experience with which the critic of *Coriolanus* has to establish contact is one that, whilst forming a single emotional whole, has to include the divergence between this and the warrior who "moves like an engine" over the corpses he has battered to death. That is the central contradiction, to which those in Aufidius' behaviour are merely subsidiary. There is a split at the heart of Shakespeare's experience, which introduces a division into the fabric of his play, both at Rome and at Corioli. That sensation of life as expressed in terms of passions, which Shakespeare worked out so triumphantly in Antony, is here studied, probably at almost the same period, in its relationship to war; and war is seen as a product of the same life, but one which tends to the death which is its opposite. *Coriolanus,* in fact, is the complement of *Antony and Cleopatra,* and its reversal. In the latter play, defeat in war was only the prelude to a triumph in the vitality of love, expressed above all in Cleopatra's death; in *Coriolanus,* victory in war was accompanied by a callous hardening of feeling, which only re-asserted itself to give an ironic note to the hero's fate.

It is worth while, at this point, to refer a little more fully to the irony of the play, because this gives it a note which is not easily squared with its usual definition as a tragedy; this fact helps, perhaps more than anything, to account for the prevalent critical uneasiness. This irony is a critical irony: that is, it springs out of a vigilant hostility to unsustained pretensions and unexamined enthusiasms. Perhaps its most successful expression is that exposure of the characters of Volumnia and Valeria (I. 3), which shows the lack of human feeling in Coriolanus to be rooted in the outlook of his family, and so, in turn, in the general social maladjustments we have already discussed. In this way, the scene has an important structural position, for it serves to connect the personal "tragedy" of *Coriolanus*—if we may use the word "tragedy" in the highly individual way demanded by this play—with the wider social study. The scene is an invention of Shakespeare; one cannot imagine that Plutarch would have thought of Valeria speaking of Coriolanus' son in this way:

> O' my word, the father's son; I'll swear, 't is a very pretty boy. O' my troth, I looked upon him o' Wednesday half an hour together; has such a confirmed countenance. I saw him run after a gilded butterfly; and when he caught it, he let it go again; and after it again; and over and over he comes, and up again; catched it again; or whether his fall enraged him, or how 't was, he did so set his teeth, and tear it; O, I warrant, how he mammocked it! (I. iii. 62)

The whole passage is a sufficient exposure of the deadly lack of feeling which surrounded Coriolanus, and of which he partook; indeed, it is emphasized that the boy is "his father's son." To complete the impression, we need only the crushing irony implicit in Valeria's next comment—"Indeed, la, 't is a noble child." The author of this scene was the same who had once written Falstaff's penetrating remarks on "honour" in the assured balance of a spirit that was not less artistic for being truly critical. Instead of Sir Walter Blunt's "grinning honour," we have Volumnia's ideal:

> . . . had I a dozen sons, . . . I had rather eleven die nobly for their country than one voluptuously surfeit out of action.

But in *Coriolanus,* the clear-sighted outlook of *Henry IV* is reinforced by the experience gained in the whole body of the tragedies, so that it becomes part of an emotional whole more complex than itself. A good deal in the study of the hero was taken from traditional sources; Plutarch, according to North, had already suggested that Coriolanus was "so cholericke and impacient, that he would yeeld to no living creature: which made him churlishe, unciuill, and altogether unfit for any man's conuersation." It is also true that there was a substantial precedent in traditional farce for the refusal to accept a great classical warrior at the most heroic estimate; Shakespeare had done this himself in *Troilus.* When the Roman soldiers refuse to follow Coriolanus into the gates of the besieged city, and when he scolds the people with most unheroic vituperation, his behaviour was not strange to an Elizabethan mind. Only the scholars might be shocked.

When we have accounted for all this, however, there remains the essence of Shakespeare's achievement to be accounted for. As we have suggested, the greatness and uniqueness of this play, which has so disconcerted many of its readers, are due to the fact that Shakespeare judged the political situation in Rome in the light of his own experience developed in the tragedies. The failure of Coriolanus, contrasted with the triumphant life of Antony, is a failure in sensitivity, a failure in living; and it represents a failure on the part of a whole society. The hero is shown always in relation to that society, and conditioned by it; it explains him, and his tragedy illuminates it. Perhaps the fundamental quality of the verse lies in the sense of a continual clash between a certain natural fineness of sensibility and an iron rigidity which accompanies and contrasts with it. Some of these contrasts are expressed in incidental comparisons that have a magnificent tactual immediacy; such are:

> When steel grows soft as the parasite's silk,

and:

> . . . nature,
> Not to be other than one thing, not moving
> From the casque to the cushion, but commanding peace
> Even with the same austerity and garb
> As he controll'd the war . . .

where the first gives an immediate impression of different and opposed textures in the closest contact, and where the second emphasizes the contrast between the casques and the cushion by the rigid strength given in "austerity and garb." Such passages indicate the quality of the play. In it we find a sensation of life expressed in terms of a transcendant passion, but continually chafing against the iron of an unnatural rigidity, which is an individual inflexibility, a stiffness in family relations, and a hardened social order. Coriolanus's great lyric passages are not continual and spontaneous, like those of Antony. They seem rather to burst out against a perpetual restraint, to be produced by a continual friction against the iron insentience which he inherited. Coriolanus is hopelessly divided between his unnatural discipline of "honour" and his natural humanity. That is the real source of the play's irony, and the reason why he never carries any course to its complete fulfilment. His "honour" is turned by his class and family into a willingness, if only temporary, to gain power at any price. There are few things in Shakespeare more ironic than the way he has to use his wounds to gain election to the consulship; but, having disgraced himself (be it noted), his natural pride intervenes, and he falls. But, precisely because he is divided, his reaction does not reinstate him as a heroic character, but expresses itself in petulant and ridiculous curses against the "common cry of curs," "the reek o' the rotten fens" the people whom he had just courted to gain power. The same essential contradiction is seen in his last exploits. Egoism always prompted him to his wars; we are told in the opening dialogue, that his prowess was due to his desire "to please his mother, and to be partly proud." It drove him to neglect all natural feeling and to return at the head of his old enemies to sack Rome. Such a change, after his sworn hatred of Aufidius, was itself ironic. But such an inhuman project could not overcome the other part of his nature—what should have been in a harmonious personality natural feeling, and was in his divided nature weakness—so that he gave up his idea in the very moment of success. Such division and paralysis could only end in his rather absurd and ironic death. Shakespeare makes him die indignant at being called "Boy!" by those he had once beaten, in a mixture of "scolding" (by his own confession) and an attempt to justify himself in the light of his past exploits. Such justification is felt to be the final proof of futility.

Coriolanus is a very great play. It suggests how valuable might be a sensitive artist's study of a social situation, what weight a fine experience could add to otherwise ephemeral political discussion. It provides, too, an unparalleled relation between tragedy and irony which has a certain relevance to the modern situation. A small part of Shakespeare's capacity for deep experience would have made impossible the weakness and inadequacy of a work like Auden's *Dog Beneath the Skin*. It would inevitably have broken into the pitifully facile development of the author's thesis, and exposed the device by which insubstantial characters are set up to be destroyed in the interests of a dogma that has never been enriched by a free and unconditioned response to life. But such a work of destruction could only be salutary, and the vitality which accomplished it later bear fruit in a play in which social analysis could play its part without frustration by moral and artistic poverty.

THE UNITY OF *KING LEAR*

(1948)

ROBERT B. HEILMAN

MARK VAN DOREN prescribes, as one of the duties laid upon the students in a great-books college of which he has written a brief account, the ability to state precisely the unity of *King Lear.* It may be added that when the students are able to pass this test, their understanding of at least one drama ought to satisfy a quite exacting preceptor. For the unity of *King Lear* lies very little on the surface; it can be described only partially in terms of plot relationships; indeed, as in all high art, it is a question of theme; and theme extends itself subtly into the ramifications of dramatic and imagistic constructs. This unity is not much discussed by the professorial gentlemen to whom Mr. Van Doren's young men might turn for dramaturgic clues; the various editors of the play, in fact, are intently and innocently questing for sources, and dates, and stage history; and in their busyness they have not much time left, as one of them candidly—and undisturbedly—puts it, for aesthetic criticism. But some of them do desire to show that the master, being the master, has not erred in his duplicity of plot; so Gloucester's family situation and experiences, we are told, heighten the effect produced by Lear's family situation and experiences; and again, the two plots come together in the dealings between Lear and Gloucester, and between Edmund and the two sisters who desire him; and again, in these interrelationships inhere some remarkable ironies which otherwise the play would be without. These points are soundly made, and they are necessary preliminaries. To them we might add, also, that the Gloucester plot is initiated after the Lear plot is firmly under way, and effectually ended while Lear has still much left to do—a kind of chronological discipline of the materials which betokens the author's tact. And in IV. vi, in which Lear's madness brings him to a climax of disillusioned insight, so that the gnomic Edgar can distill from this scene the paradox "Reason in madness," Lear weaves Gloucester into his brilliant synthesis of the world and of the play: ". . . Your eyes are in a heavy case, your purse in a light. You see how the world goes. . . . A man may see how the world goes with no eyes." Insofar as the subject of the play is Lear's mind, Gloucester has become a part of that subject.

But these considerations are relatively peripheral, and we still need to inquire in what way it is that the two stories of youth-and-age, of father-and-child, are not mere replicas, and what advantage in their coexistence transcends the rhetorical. What, in other words, is the meaning of the Lear plot, and the meaning of the Gloucester plot, and how are the meanings related? To define this fundamental kinship we must first examine the tragic flaws of the protagonists. The flaws may be described, I think, as errors of understanding, and *King Lear* may be read as a play about the ways of perceiving truth: it has a good deal to say about the ways in which the human reason may function, and about the imagination. Our problem then is to discover how this thematic substance receives necessarily different, rather than arbitrarily repetitious, formulations in the Lear plot and in the Gloucester plot.

Lear does not have the pride in reason of, say, Oedipus or Faustus, but he does undertake to reason about certain phenomena, and by reasoning faultily he inaugurates a series of tragic consequences. His very first error is typically rationalistic: the introduction of a mensurational standard where it is not applicable. He insists upon the untenable proposition that love can be measured, as if it were a material quantum of a certain size or shape. In his intellectual confusion he forgets that deeds rather than words are the symbols of love. The confusion may be described quite literally as a failure of imagination: love must be apprehended by images, and the images are richly available to him not in verbal shortcuts and formulae, but in the lives of daughters whom he has observed from infancy. Now this kind of evidence, when it is not abstracted by literary art from the full and resistant texture of experience, is vast and inchoate and difficult; Lear shirks a demanding task—the imaginative apprehension of symbols, we all know, is not easy—and seeks an easy rationalistic way out. His failure of understanding here is analogous to his failure to perceive that a king cannot be a king without a crown and cannot maintain his perquisites by a kind of oral recipe or contract, that is, a purely rationalized formulation of a status which involves responsibilities as well as rights. From his endeavor to bound a value by irrelevant standards of measurement, Lear goes on to still another error: his misinterpretation of those verbal measurements of love which his demands have brought forth: he is wholly taken in by the meaningless abstractions and hyperboles of Goneril and Regan and—in another striking failure of imagination—completely misses the import of Cordelia's precise metaphor, "I love your Majesty / According to my bond; no more nor less." Lear, then, invites tragedy by three errors of understanding—errors with regard to the nature of kingship, the nature of love, and the nature of language (the value of certain statements about love). Then: these errors are not the negligible slips of a mere observer who has time to check and prove and correct; they are the terrible mistakes of a man of action, of a man whose action is a public action. Lear *imposes* on his world his erroneous conclusions about children and court.

Gloucester accepts rather than imposes: his trouble is inaugurated by Edmund's spontaneously undertaking, without being offered such an opening as Lear gives to Goneril and Regan, to deceive his father. Both fathers, of course, are muddled; even while, ironically, they feel astute, they reason wrongly from the evidence. Like Lear, Gloucester might have consulted his non-rational, experiential awareness of his child's quality. Yet Gloucester is the object of manipulation; his error of understanding is that he too easily falls under the influence exerted upon him. We have other evidence, however, of the nature of his flaw. Edmund's illegitimacy we are never allowed to forget, and near the end Edgar specifically connects Gloucester's suffering with his adultery; he tells Edmund, "The dark and vicious place where thee he got/ Cost him his eyes." Then there is the even more obvious evidence of Gloucester's attitude to the new Goneril-Regan regime: Gloucester plainly has doubts about the way things are going, but that a principle is involved, a principle which insists that he make a stand, simply does not occur to him. He regrets Cornwall's stocking Lear's follower, Kent; but he himself contributes to the infuriation of Lear by his efforts to "fix it up" between him and Cornwall. "You know the fiery quality of the Duke," he tells Lear, and, more maddeningly for Lear, "I would have all well betwixt you." Gloucester has hopes that he can "do business with" Cornwall: despite his genuine discomfort, he is inclined to accept the status quo. Now, what a glance at his whole career tells us is that his conduct is all of a piece: Gloucester is the passive man who is too ready to fall in with whatever influences are brought to bear upon him. He is the man who falls into step with the world, especially when to be out of step would mean a stern quarrel both with the world and with a part of himself. In the liaison of which Edmund is the fruit he fell in with the worldliness that took sexual morality lightly; years later—even in Edmund's hearing, it seems—he refers jauntily to Edmund's origin. Then he falls in with Edmund's suggestions about the evil purposes of Edgar: he becomes the man of the world who knows a plot when he sees one and knows what to do about it, and who is incapable of opposing the immediate pressure by drawing, painstakingly, upon the knowledge which transcends the circumstances of the moment. Finally, as we have seen, he falls in with, does his best to get on with, the Goneril-Regan tyranny. A fine stroke in the management of this part of the play is the ambiguity of the lines in which Gloucester tells Edmund that he intends to aid Lear. His sympathies are unquestionably aroused; that is one part of the picture. But it is also true that he says, "These injuries the King now bears will be revenged home; there's part of a power already footed; we must incline to the King." He does pity Lear, but it is equally true that to be pro-Lear may be a good thing; and Gloucester is at least in part maneuvering toward the comfortable stream of things. Not until he suffers for it is his new commitment morally in the clear. His whole tendency toward conformity—toward "adjustment," as we say in these high times—has already been admirably summarized by his astrological habit of mind, which, we should observe, is shared by no one else in the play. It exactly suits Gloucester. If "These late eclipses in the sun and moon portend no good to us," what can he do about it? It is Gloucester's flaw never wholly to understand what is implied in the situations in which he finds himself, even though he feels worldlywise enough. Not that he voluntarily seeks what is evil: it is simply that he too easily yields to that in which he should see evil.

Lear, without questioning his own rightness, imposes his will upon others; Gloucester accepts the will of others without effectually questioning their rightness. Thus Lear and Gloucester are, in terms of structure, not duplicates, but complements: this is one key to the unity of *King Lear*. The completeness of the play, its cosmic inclusiveness, which we sense without being able to put our finger upon it, is in part attributable to this doublefocused presentation of the tragic error of understanding. We see its basic forms, action and inaction; one tragic character imposes error, the other accepts it. The roles continue consistently throughout the play—Lear as active, Gloucester as passive. Gloucester, it is clear, does at times *act*—enough to become more than an allegorical figure, than a worldlier Griselda. But things keep happening *to* him: whereas Lear combats his daughters furiously and dashes of his own will out into the night, Gloucester is betrayed, is captured, and is tortured. The master touch in the depiction of his career is that his giving in finally becomes giving up: he yields to despair (the Christian anachronisms are familiar to all commentators), suicide is to be his final adjustment. It is wholly right, for the worldly man is one who, by accepting the custom of the time, despairs of the good. But Lear is always a vigorous, aggressive figure; he fights his daughters to the bitter end; even in his madness he imposes his personality upon the others. At the time of his recovery he is contrastingly quiet for a brief while, but again at the end he becomes a commanding, dominating figure beside whom the others seem small. He kills "the slave that was a hanging thee" (V. iii. 274) and dies trying to establish that Cordelia is alive.

Lear and Gloucester are tragic heroes: they are essentially good men. We have seen the complementary errors of understanding to which the good man is liable, and thus two kinds of genesis of evil in the world. Now a part of the remarkable fullness of the play is that it shows us not only the release of evil but the subsequent course of evil. In Goneril and Regan, and in Edmund, we see the evil which originates in Lear and Gloucester set free in the world. The old men themselves come to insight through suffering, but they have loosed forces that do terrible damage before they destroy themselves. Yet other children of Lear and Gloucester not only combat the evil forces but also, by their very existence and by positive aid to their unjust parents, contribute to whatever of recovery the old men achieve. The children as a group, that is to say, represent the different elements which are in conflict in the fathers; hence, in a play with an unusually large number of main characters and a great complexity of actions, there is the tightest integration of their component elements. We see good and evil in conflict in the world, but by the structure of the play we are reminded that the conflict is an emanation of that in the individual soul. By the fact of relationship the outer and the inner evil become one, the two struggles are united. The children are not children for nothing; to be the father of Goneril is to create a symbol of the evil brought forth from oneself. The discerning reader of the play will hardly feel that he has done all his duty by hating Goneril.

Edmund's worldliness is an amplification and a positivizing of Gloucester's. Gloucester wants to do as the world does and be comfortable; Edmund wants to have what the world has—"have lands by wit," as he puts it—and "grow" and "prosper" in it. The shallow foxiness which Gloucester exhibits in his imagined detection of Edgar ripens into an effective wiliness in Edmund. Gloucester forgets morality; Edmund flouts it. Edmund is half of Gloucester, liberated from the other half, and matured in its own terms. Gloucester's gullibility—the ironic failure of his self-conscious worldliness—becomes the whole of Edgar as Edgar is seen at the beginning of the play; the emergent moral mastery of Gloucester is paralleled in the development of personal force in Edgar; the kindliness of Gloucester to Lear is the same love and loyalty which come to Gloucester himself from Edgar. Edgar's final defeat of Edmund, Edgar's reunion with his father, and his conquest of his father's despair may all be read as a symbolic version of the gaining of the upper hand, in Gloucester, of the portion of his moral being which had long been in eclipse. But this extension of inner conflicts into conflicting characters who in part objectify the warring subjective elements is most marked in Lear's family. From the start, of course, we discern in Cordelia the sharp insight into people and values of which Lear is capable and to which he is restored by the eventual, tardy revival of his imagination; in her is Lear's submerged tenderness, just as his tempestuousness is echoed in Kent; in the aid which both of them give him we see Lear's better side struggling for the mastery. Yet Cordelia is more complex than some critics have been willing to admit, for there is in her some admixture of what Coleridge called sullenness—of a recusancy, a stubborn antipathy to the disciplining, restricting action which involvement in the world makes inevitable. The unfettered personality may in some contexts be the right moral goal; but it may lead to a narrow protection of self;

it is not a moral absolute. Lear will not rule, and he will not understand the terms in which experience speaks; Cordelia will not accept the terms of speech imposed by experience. There is a clash of wills, each combatant bent on self-protection. Lear's withdrawal ironically evokes Cordelia's withdrawal; the daughter springs from the father. In this reading Cordelia becomes a part of the tragic substance rather than a mere innocent and pathetic victim of the forces clashing in the world.

The symbolism of kinship is subtlest and most important in the link between Lear and his elder daughters: here we find the central irony of the play and a fundamental statement of theme. Lear's tragic flaw is the whole being of Goncril and Regan. Lear makes a fatal error of understanding: then his essential method of thought is picked up by his daughters and made their way of life. In dividing the land, Lear introduces a principle which Goneril and Regan carry on to a logical extreme; they show what happens when an element in him is freed from the restraint imposed by the rest of the personality. In this play, personality is the equilibrium of conflicting forces; evil is ready at all times to break loose from the spiritual whole; autonomy is its end, and any disturbance of tensions may set it on its way. Lear, we have seen, forces the use of the principle of measurement where it is not applicable; he introduces a spirit of calculation; and he is ruthless in punishing what does not contribute to his proposed advantage. Thus Goneril and Regan come to power. And what comes to power with them is the spirit of calculation: in fact, throughout the rest of the play we see Shakespeare tracing the history of three people—Edmund's alliance with the sisters is morally right—in whom the cold calculation of advantage has almost totally excluded adherence to other values. Shelley said of his world that it had substituted calculation for imagination. That is precisely what has happened in the world of the play: Lear's imagination has failed—the value-preserving faculty—and so there have come into control the imagination-less calculators. One by one they dispose of, or plan to dispose of, their enemies. In the final irony they turn on and dispose of each other—a magnificent symbol of the self-destructiveness of their kind of world.

The play, of course, is full of ironic reversals. Of those relevant to the question of unity, the most remarkable is the coming to understanding of Gloucester and Lear. Gloucester gains full insight just as he is blinded; the man who accepts too easily is punished at his one moment of high affirmation—the assertion of the values of the old order against the up-to-date world. Lear's new insight is initially pounded into him in I. iv and II. iv, the scenes in which he is all but incredulous of the blows poured upon him by Goneril and Regan. These scenes demand our notice because it is they which establish the moral link between Lear and his elder daughters. For in these scenes the main business is the quarrel over the number of retainers Lear is to have: the quarrel takes the form of bargaining, even haggling. But this is not the first haggling in the play: the first dispute over amounts and prices, so to speak, is that brought about in I. i by Lear's demanding that his daughters measure their love for him. There, he insisted on an inappropriate calculation; here, he is the victim of an inappropriate calculation by the very daughters who had profited from his own misapplied arithmetic. The daughters' love required a different kind of estimate from that which Lear proposed; likewise his demand for a hundred retainers needs to be estimated by another standard than the rational one of necessity. The daughters apply Lear's own error—the seeking of a rationalistic shortcut through a difficult area of meaning which has to be traversed, in the long run, by extra-rational means. Love must be felt through its proper symbols; the retainers must be imaginatively understood as symbols of position. The utilitarian standard is absolutely irrelevant. So the whole issue is brilliantly summarized in the first line of Lear's last speech before the storm: "O, reason not the need" (II. iv. 267). But the reasoning of need in these scenes is a symptom of the new way of life that is to dominate Lear's kingdom. That way of life was prepared for by Lear himself. His daughters might have said to Lear, "We cannot reason our love." In effect Cordelia did say it: by using a metaphor rather than the neat logical statement Lear wanted.

King Lear suggests the reasons why it is right for tragedy to use characters "in high place" and intra-family complications—as it regularly did in Greek and Elizabethan practice. Rulers were public figures; their tragedies became representative; ennoblement through suffering was a general and meaningful, not a shut-off private experience by which many suffered but few were ennobled. Yet in the public plot melodrama is just around the corner: our view of public life always inclines to the melodramatic, for we look for heroes and villains whom we can understand simply. We tend to identify evil with certain figures or groups, and if we can injure or destroy them, we cause the good to triumph. We look for Gonerils and Regans and Edmunds and turn all our wrath upon them; we forget the Goneril and Regan and Edmund that are within us all. The public event may obscure the private reality, the private reality in terms of which the experience is universal. But the ultimate identity of public and private is exactly figured forth in the symbolism of kinship: the family mediates between the soul of man and the community to which he belongs. It is at once a public fact and a projection of the soul; through it the representatively public and the representatively private are seen to be one. By being the father of Goneril and of Cordelia, Lear includes both of them within himself; we cannot then idly hate Goneril as evil but we must recognize the genesis of evil and hence modify our sympathetic identification with Lear so that it includes a sensitiveness to the spiritual trouble within him. Thus we move from melodrama, which represents the externalized conflict as reality, to tragedy, in which the externalized conflict exactly corresponds to the war within the soul—whether the begetting is an affirmation and an imposition of error or a Gloucester-like acquiescence in worldly imperfections. Some such understanding of tragedy, and of the mode of its universality, follows from an examination of the remarkable unity of *King Lear*.

SHELLEY

(1935)

F. R. Leavis

If Shelley had not received some distinguished attention in recent years (and he has been differed over by the most eminent critics) there might, perhaps, have seemed little point in attempting a restatement of the essential critical observations—the essential observations, that is, in the reading and appreciation of Shelley's poetry. For they would seem to be obvious enough. Yet it is only one incitement out of many when a critic of peculiar authority, contemplating the common change from being "intoxicated by Shelley's poetry at the age of fifteen" to finding it now "almost unreadable," invokes for explanation the nature of Shelley's "ideas" and, in reference to them, that much-canvassed question of the day, "the question of belief or disbelief":

> It is not so much that thirty years ago I was able to read Shelley under an illusion which experience has dissipated, as that because the question of belief or disbelief did not arise I was in a much better position to enjoy the poetry. I can only regret that Shelley did not live to put his poetic gifts, which were certainly of the first order, at the service of more tenable beliefs—which need not have been, for my purposes, beliefs more acceptable to me.

This is, of course, a personal statement; but perhaps if one insists on the more obvious terms of literary criticism—more strictly critical terms—in which such a change might be explained, and suggests that the terms actually used might be found unfortunate in their effect, the impertinence will not be unpardonable. It does, in short, seem worth endeavouring to make finally plain that, when one dissents from persons who, sympathizing with Shelley's revolutionary doctrines and with his idealistic ardours and fervours—with his "beliefs," exalt him as a poet, it is strictly the "poetry" one is criticizing. There would also appear to be some reason for insisting that in finding Shelley almost unreadable one need not be committing oneself to a fashionably limited taste—an inability to appreciate unfashionable kinds of excellence or to understand a use of words that is unlike Hopkins's or Donne's.

It will be well to start, in fact, by examining the working of Shelley's poetry—his characteristic modes of expression—as exemplified in one of his best poems.

> Thou on whose stream, mid the steep sky's commotion,
> Loose clouds like earth's decaying leaves are shed,
> Shook from the tangled boughs of Heaven and Ocean,
>
> Angels of rain and lightning: there are spread
> On the blue surface of thine aëry surge,
> Like the bright hair uplifted from the head
>
> Of some fierce Maenad, even from the dim verge
> Of the horizon to the zenith's height,
> The locks of the approaching storm.

The sweeping movement of the verse, with the accompanying plangency, is so potent that, as many can testify, it is possible to have been for years familiar with the Ode—to know it by heart—without asking the obvious questions. In what respects are the "loose clouds" like "decaying leaves"? The correspondence is certainly not in shape, colour or way of moving. It is only the vague general sense of windy tumult that associates the clouds and the leaves; and, accordingly, the appropriateness of the metaphor "stream" in the first line is not that it suggests a surface on which, like leaves, the clouds might be "shed," but that it contributes to the general "streaming" effect in which the inappropriateness of "shed" passes unnoticed. What again, are those "tangled boughs of Heaven and Ocean"? They stand for nothing that Shelley could have pointed to in the scene before him; the "boughs," it is plain, have grown out of the "leaves" in the previous line, and we are not to ask what the tree is. Nor are we to scrutinize closely the "stream" metaphor as developed: that "blue surface" must be the concave of the sky, an oddly smooth surface for a "surge"—if we consider a moment. But in this poetic surge, while we let ourselves be swept along, there is no considering, the image doesn't challenge any inconvenient degree of realization, and the oddness is lost. Then again, in what ways does the approach of a storm ("loose clouds like earth's decaying leaves," "like ghosts from an enchanter fleeing") suggest streaming hair? The appropriateness of the Maenad, clearly, lies in the pervasive suggestion of frenzied onset, and we are not to ask whether her bright hair is to be seen as streaming out in front of her (as, there is no need to assure ourselves, it might be doing if she were running before a still swifter gale: in the kind of reading that got so far as proposing to itself this particular reassurance no general satisfaction could be exacted from Shelley's imagery).

Here, clearly, in these peculiarities of imagery and sense, peculiarities analysable locally in the mode of expression, we have the manifestation of essential characteristics—the Shelleyan characteristics as envisaged by the criticism that works on a philosophical plane and makes judgments of a moral order. In the growth of those "tangled boughs" out of the leaves, exemplifying as it does a general tendency of the images to forget the status of the metaphor or simile that introduced them and to assume an autonomy and a right to propagate, so that we lose in confused generations and perspectives the perception or thought that was the ostensible *raison d'être* of imagery, we have a recognized essential trait of Shelley: his weak grasp upon the actual. This weakness, of course, commonly has more or less creditable accounts given of it—idealism, Platonism, and so on; and even as unsentimental a judge as Mr. Santayana correlates Shelley's inability to learn from experience with his having been born a "nature preformed," a "spokesman of the *a priori*," "a dogmatic, inspired, perfect and incorrigible creature." [1] It seems to me that Mr. Santayana's essay, admirable as it is, rates the poetry too high. But for the moment it will be enough to recall limitations that are hardly disputed: Shelley was not gifted for drama or narrative. Having said this, I realize that I had forgotten the conventional standing of *The Cenci;* but controversy may be postponed: it is at any rate universally agreed that (to shift tactfully to positive terms) Shelley's genius was "essentially lyrical."

This predicate would, in common use, imply a special emotional intensity—a vague gloss, but it is difficult to go further without slipping into terms that are immediately privative and limiting. Thus there is certainly a sense in which Shelley's poetry is peculiarly emotional, and when we try to define this sense we find ourselves invoking an absence of something. The point may be best made, perhaps, by recalling the observation noted above, that one may have been long familiar with the *Ode to the West Wind* without ever having asked the obvious questions; questions that propose themselves at the first critical inspection. This poetry induces—depends for its success on inducing—a kind of attention that doesn't bring the critical intelligence into play: the imagery feels right, the associations work appropriately, if (as it takes conscious resistance not to do) one accepts the immediate feeling and doesn't slow down to think.

Shelley himself can hardly have asked the questions. Not that he didn't expend a great deal of critical labour upon his verse. "He composed rapidly and attained to perfection by intensive correction. He would sometimes write down a phrase with alterations and rejections time after time until it came within a measure of satisfying him. Words are frequently substituted for others and lines interpolated." The *Ode to the West Wind* itself, as is shown in the repository [2] of fragments the preface to which supplies these observations, profited by the process described, which must be allowed to have been in some sense critical. But the critical part of Shelley's creative labour was a matter of getting the verse to feel right, and feeling, for Shelley as a

[1] See the essay on Shelley in *Winds of Doctrine.*

[2] *Verse and Prose from the Manuscripts of Percy Bysshe Shelley.* Edited by Sir John C. E. Shelley-Rolls, Bart., and Roger Ingpen.

poet, had—as the insistent concern for "rightness," the typical final product being what it is, serves to emphasize—little to do with thinking (though Shelley was in some ways a very intelligent man).

We have here, if not sufficient justification for the predicate "essentially lyrical," certainly a large part of the reason for Shelley's being found essentially poetical by the succeeding age. He counted, in fact, for a great deal in what came to be the prevailing idea of "the poetical" —the idea that had its latest notable statement in Professor Housman's address, *The Name and Nature of Poetry.* The Romantic conceptions of genius and inspiration [3] developed (the French Revolution and its ideological background must, of course, be taken into account) in reaction against the Augustan insistence on the social and the rational. When Wordsworth says that "all good poetry is the spontaneous overflow of powerful feelings" he is of his period, though the intended force of this dictum, the force it has in its context and in relation to Wordsworth's own practice, is very different from that given it when Shelley assents, or when it is assimilated to Byron's "poetry is the lava of the imagination, whose eruption prevents an earthquake." [4] But Byron was for the young Tennyson (and the Ruskin parents) [5] the poet, and Shelley (Browning's "Sun-treader") was the idol of the undergraduate Tennyson and his fellow Apostles, and, since the poetry of "the age of Wordsworth" became canonical, the assent given to Wordsworth's dictum has commonly been Shelleyan.

The force of Shelley's insistence on spontaneity is simple and unequivocal. It will be enough to recall a representative passage or two from the *Defense of Poetry:*

> . . . for the mind in creation is as a fading coal, which some invisible influence, like an inconstant wind, awakes to transitory brightness; this power arises from within, like the colour of a flower which fades and changes as it is developed, and the conscious portions of our nature are unprophetic either of its approach or its departure.

"Inspiration" is not something to be tested, clarified, defined and developed in composition,

> . . . but when composition begins, inspiration is already on the decline, and the most glorious poetry that has ever been communicated to the world is probably a feeble shadow of the original conceptions of the poet. . . . The toil and delay recommended by critics can be justly interpreted to mean no more than a careful observation of the inspired

[3] See *Four Words* (now reprinted in *Words and Idioms*), by Logan Pearsall Smith.

[4] *Letters and Journals,* ed. R. E. Prothero, vol. iii, p. 405 (1900). (I am indebted for this quotation to Mr. F. W. Bateson's *English Poetry and the English Language.*)

[5] "His ideal of my future,—now entirely formed in conviction of my genius,—was that I should enter at college into the best society, take all the best prizes every year, and a double first to finish with; marry Lady Clara Vere de Vere; write poetry as good as Byron's, only pious; preach sermons as good as Bossuet's, only Protestant; be made, at forty, Bishop of Winchester, and at fifty, Primate of England." *Praeterita,* vol. i, p. 340 (1886).

> moments, and an artificial connexion of the spaces between their suggestions, by the intertexture of conventional expressions; a necessity only imposed by the limitedness of the poetical faculty itself....

The "poetical faculty," we are left no room for doubting, can, of its very nature, have nothing to do with any discipline, and can be associated with conscious effort only mechanically and externally, and when Shelley says that Poetry

> . . . is not subject to the control of the active powers of the mind, and that its birth and recurrence have no necessary connexion with consciousness or will . . .

he is not saying merely that the "active powers of the mind" are insufficient in themselves for creation—that poetry cannot be written merely by taking thought. The effect of Shelley's eloquence is to hand poetry over to a sensibility that has no more dealings with intelligence than it can help; to a "poetic faculty" that, for its duly responsive vibrating (though the poet must reverently make his pen as sensitive an instrument as possible to "observe"—in the scientific sense—the vibrations), demands that active intelligence shall be, as it were, switched off.

Shelley, of course, had ideas and ideals; he wrote philosophical essays, and it need not be irrelevant to refer, in discussing his poetry, to Plato, Godwin and other thinkers. But there is nothing grasped in the poetry—no object offered for contemplation, no realized presence to persuade or move us by what it is. A. C. Bradley, remarking that "Shelley's ideals of good, whether as a character or as a mode of life, resting as they do on abstraction from the mass of real existence, tend to lack body and individuality," adds: "But we must remember that Shelley's strength and weakness are closely allied, and it may be that the very abstractness of his ideal was a condition of that quivering intensity of aspiration towards it in which his poetry is unequalled." [6] That is the best that can be respectably said. Actually, that "quivering intensity," offered in itself apart from any substance, offered instead of any object, is what, though it may make Shelley intoxicating at fifteen makes him almost unreadable, except in very small quantities of his best, to the mature. Even when he is in his own way unmistakably a distinguished poet, as in *Prometheus Unbound,* it is impossible to go on reading him at any length with pleasure; the elusive imagery, the high-pitched emotions, the tone and movement, the ardours, ecstasies and despairs, are too much the same all through. The effect is of vanity and emptiness (Arnold was right) as well as monotony.

The force of the judgment that feeling in Shelley's poetry is divorced from thought needs examining further. Any suspicion that Donne is the implied criterion will, perhaps, be finally averted if for the illumi-

[6] *Oxford Lectures on Poetry,* p. 167.

nating contrast we go to Wordsworth. Wordsworth is another "Romantic" poet; he too is undramatic; and he too invites the criticism (Arnold, his devoted admirer, made it) that he lacks variety. "Thought" will hardly be found an assertive presence in his best poetry; in so far as the term suggests an overtly active energy it is decidedly inappropriate. "Emotion," his own word, is the word most readers would insist on, though they would probably judge Wordsworth's emotion to be less lyrical than Shelley's. The essential difference, however—and it is a very important one—seems, for present purposes, more relevantly stated in the terms I used in discussing Wordsworth's "recollection in tranquillity." The process covered by this phrase was one of emotional discipline, critical exploration of experience, pondered valuation and maturing reflection. As a result of it an organization is engaged in Wordsworth's poetry, and the activity and standards of critical intelligence are implicit.

An associated difference was noted in the sureness with which Wordsworth grasps the world of common perception. The illustration suggested was *The Simplon Pass* in comparison with Shelley's *Mont Blanc*. The element of Wordsworth in *Mont Blanc* (it is perceptible in these opening lines) serves only to enhance the contrast:

> The everlasting universe of things
> Flows through the mind, and rolls its rapid waves,
> Now dark—now glittering—now reflecting gloom—
> Now lending splendour, where from secret springs
> The source of human thought its tribute brings
> Of waters—with a sound but half its own,
> Such as a feeble brook will oft assume
> In the wild woods, among the mountains lone,
> Where waterfalls around it leap for ever,
> Where woods and winds contend, and a vast river
> Over its rocks ceaselessly bursts and raves.

The metaphorical and the actual, the real and the imagined, the inner and the outer, could hardly be more unsortably and indistinguishably confused. The setting, of course, provides special excuse for bewildered confusion; but Shelley takes eager advantage of the excuse and the confusion is characteristic—what might be found unusual in *Mont Blanc* is a certain compelling vividness. In any case, Wordsworth himself is explicitly offering a sense of sublime bewilderment, similarly inspired:

> Black drizzling crags that spake by the wayside
> As if a voice were in them, the sick sight
> And giddy prospect of the raving stream,
> The unfettered clouds and region of the heavens,
> Tumult and peace, the darkness and the light—
> Were all like workings of one mind, the features
> Of the same face . . .

He is, of course, recollecting in tranquillity; but the collectedness of those twenty lines (as against Shelley's one hundred and forty) does not belong merely to the record; it was present (or at least the movement towards it was) in the experience, as those images, "one mind," "the same face"—epitomizing, as they do, the contrast with Shelley's ecstatic dissipation—may fairly be taken to testify.

This comparison does not aim immediately at a judgment of relative value. *Mont Blanc* is very interesting as well as idiosyncratic, and is not obviously the product of the less rare gift. There are, nevertheless, critical judgments to be made—judgments concerning the emotional quality of Wordsworth's poetry and of Shelley's: something more than mere description of idiosyncrasy is in view. What should have come out in the comparison that started as a note on Wordsworth's grasp of the outer world is the unobtrusiveness with which that "outer" turns into "inner": the antithesis, clearly, is not altogether, for present purposes, a simple one to apply. What is characteristic of Wordsworth is to grasp surely (which, in the nature of the case, must be delicately and subtly) what he offers, whether this appears as belonging to the outer world—the world as perceived, or to inner experience. He seems always to be presenting an object (wherever this may belong) and the emotion seems to derive from what is presented. The point is very obviously and impressively exemplified in *A slumber did my spirit seal,* which shows Wordsworth at his supreme height. Here (compare it with the *Ode to the West Wind,* where we have Shelley's genius at its best; or, if something more obviously comparable is required, with Tennyson's *Break, break, break*) there is no emotional comment—nothing "emotional" in phrasing, movement or tone; the facts seem to be presented barely, and the emotional force to be generated by them in the reader's mind when he has taken them in—generated by the two juxtaposed stanzas, in the contrast between the situations or states they represent.

Shelley, at his best and worst, offers the emotion in itself, unattached, in the void. "In itself" "for itself"—it is an easy shift to the pejorative implications of "for its own sake"; just as, for a poet with the habit of sensibility and expression described, it was an easy shift to deserving them. For Shelley is obnoxious to the pejorative implications of "habit": being inspired was, for him, too apt to mean surrendering to a kind of hypnotic rote of favourite images, associations and words. "Inspiration," there not being an organization for it to engage (as in Wordsworth, whose sameness is of a different order from Shelley's, there was), had only poetical habits to fall back on. We have them in their most innocent aspect in those favourite words: *radiant, aërial, odorous, daedal, faint, sweet, bright, wingèd, -inwoven,* and the rest of the fondled vocabulary that any reader of Shelley could go on enumerating. They manifest themselves as decidedly deplorable in *The Cloud* and *To a Skylark,* which illustrate the dangers of fostering the kind of inspiration that works only when critical intelligence is switched off. These poems may be not unfairly described as the products of switching poetry on.[7] There has been in recent years some controversy about particular points in *To a Skylark,* and there are a score or more points inviting adverse criticism. But this need hardly be offered; it is, or should be, so plain that the poem is a mere tumbled out spate ("spontaneous overflow") of poeticalities, the place of each one of which Shelley could have filled with another without the least difficulty and without making any essential difference. They are held together by the pervasive "lyrical emotion," and that this should be capable of holding them together is comment enough on the nature of its strength.

Cheaper surrenders to inspiration may easily be found in the collected Shelley; there are, for instance, gross indulgences in the basest Regency album taste.[8] But criticism of Shelley has something more important to deal with than mere bad poetry; or, rather, there are badnesses inviting the criticism that involves moral judgments. It must have already appeared (it has virtually been said) that surrendering to inspiration cannot, for a poet of Shelley's emotional habits, have been very distinguishable from surrendering to temptation. The point comes out in an element of the favoured vocabulary not exemplified above: *charnel, corpse, phantom, liberticide, aghast, ghastly,* and so on. The wrong approach to emotion, the approach from the wrong side or end (so to speak), is apparent here; Shelley would clearly have done well not to have indulged these habits and these likings: the viciousness and corruption are immediately recognizable. But viciousness and corruption do not less attend upon likings for tender ("I love Love"),[9] sympathetic, exalted and ecstatic emotions, and may be especially expected to do so in a mind as little able to hold an object in front of it as Shelley's was.

The transition from the lighter concerns of literary criticism to the diagnosis of radical disabilities and perversions, such as call for moral comment, may be conveniently illustrated from a favourite anthology-piece, *When the lamp is shattered:*

> When the lamp is shattered
> The light in the dust lies dead—
> When the cloud is scattered
> The rainbow's glory is shed.

[7] Poesy's unfailing river
Which through Albion winds forever
Lashing with melodious wave
Many a sacred poet's grave...
Lines Written Among the Euganean Hills.

[8] See, for instance, the poem beginning, "That time is dead for ever, child."

[9] See the last stanza of *Rarely, rarely comest thou.*

When the lute is broken,
Sweet tones are remembered not;
When the lips have spoken,
Loved accents are soon forgot.

As music and splendour
Survive not the lamp and the lute,
The heart's echoes render
No song when the spirit is mute:—
No song but sad dirges,
Like the wind through a ruined cell;
Or the mournful surges
That ring the dead seaman's knell.

When hearts have once mingled
Love first leaves the well-built nest;
The weak one is singled
To endure what it once possessed.
O Love! who bewailest
The frailty of all things here,
Why choose you the frailest
For your cradle, your home, and your bier?

Its passions will rock thee
As the storms rock the ravens on high;
Bright reason will mock thee,
Like the sun from a wintry sky.
From thy nest every rafter
Will rot, and thine eagle home
Leave thee naked to laughter,
When leaves fall and cold winds come.

The first two stanzas call for no very close attention—to say so, indeed, is to make the main criticism, seeing that they offer a show of insistent argument. However, reading with an unsolicited closeness, one may stop at the second line and ask whether the effect got with "lies dead" is legitimate. Certainly, the emotional purpose of the poem is served, but the emotional purpose that went on being served in that way would be suspect. Leaving the question in suspense, perhaps, one passes to "shed"; "shed" as tears, petals and coats are shed, or as light is shed? The latter would be a rather more respectable use of the word in connexion with a rainbow's glory, but the context indicates the former. Only in the vaguest and slackest state of mind—of imagination and thought—could one so describe the fading of a rainbow; but for the right reader "shed" sounds right, the alliteration with "shattered" combining with the verse-movement to produce a kind of inevitability. And, of course, suggesting tears and the last rose of summer, it suits with the general emotional effect. The nature of this is by now so unmistakable that the complete nullity of the clinching "so," when it arrives—of the two lines that justify the ten preparatory lines of analogy—seems hardly worth stopping to note:

> The heart's echoes render
> No song when the spirit is mute.

Nor is it surprising that there should turn out to be a song after all, and a pretty powerful one—for those who like that sort of thing; the "sad dirges," the "ruined cell," the "mournful surges" and the "dead seaman's knell" being immediately recognizable as currency values. Those who take pleasure in recognizing and accepting them are not at the same time exacting about sense.

The critical interest up to this point has been to see Shelley, himself (when inspired) so unexacting about sense, giving himself so completely to sentimental banalities. With the next stanza it is much the same, though the emotional *clichés* take on a grosser unction and the required abeyance of thought (and imagination) becomes more remarkable. In what form are we to imagine Love leaving the well-built nest? For readers who get so far as asking, there can be no acceptable answer. It would be unpoetically literal to suggest that, since the weak one is singled, the truant must be the mate, and, besides, it would raise unnecessary difficulties. Perhaps the mate, the strong one, is what the weak one, deserted by Love, whose alliance made possession once possible, now has to endure? But the suggestion is frivolous; the sense is plain enough—enough, that is, for those who respond to the sentiment. Sufficient recognition of the sense depends neither on thinking, nor on realization of the metaphors, but on response to the sentimental commonplaces: it is only when intelligence and imagination insist on intruding that difficulties arise. So plain is this that there would be no point in contemplating the metaphorical complexity that would develop if we could take the tropes seriously and tried to realize Love making of the weak one, whom it (if we evade the problem of sex) leaves behind in the well-built nest, a cradle, a home and a bier.

The last stanza brings a notable change; it alone in the poem has any distinction, and its personal quality, characteristically Shelleyan, stands out against the sentimental conventionality of the rest. The result is to compel a more radical judgment on the poem than has yet been made. In "Its passions will rock thee" the "passions" must be those of Love, so that it can no longer be Love that is being apostrophized. Who, then, is "thee"? The "frailest"—the "weak one"—it would appear. But any notion one may have had that the "weak one," as the conventional sentiments imply, is the woman must be abandoned: the "eagle home," to which the "well-built nest" so incongruously turns, is the Poet's. The familiar timbre, the desolate intensity (note particularly the use of "bright" in "bright reason"), puts it beyond doubt that Shelley is, characteristically, addressing himself—the "pardlike Spirit beautiful and swift," the "Love in desolation masked," the "Power girt round with weakness."

Characteristically: that is, Shelley's characteristic pathos is self-regarding, directed upon an idealized self in the way suggested by the tags just quoted.[10] This is patently so in some of his best poetry; for instance, in the *Ode to the West Wind.* Even there, perhaps, one may find something too like an element of luxury in the poignancy (at any rate, one's limiting criticism of the Ode would move towards such a judgment); and that in general there must be dangers and weakness attending upon such a habit will hardly be denied. The poem just examined shows how gross may be, in Shelley, the corruptions that are incident. He can make self-pity a luxury at such a level that the conventional pathos of album poeticizing, not excluding the banalities about (it is plainly so in the third stanza) the sad lot of woman, can come in to gratify the appetite.

The abeyance of thought exhibited by the first three stanzas now takes on a more sinister aspect. The switching-off of intelligence that is necessary if the sentiments of the third stanza are to be accepted has now to be invoked in explanation of a graver matter—Shelley's ability to accept the grosser, the truly corrupt, gratifications that have just been indicated. The antipathy of his sensibility to any play of the critical mind, the uncongeniality of intelligence to inspiration, these clearly go in Shelley, not merely with a capacity for momentary self-deceptions and insincerities, but with a radical lack of self-knowledge. He could say of Wordsworth, implying the opposite of himself, that

> . . . he never could
> Fancy another situation
> From which to dart his contemplation
> Than that wherein he stood.

But, for all his altruistic fervours and his fancied capacity for projecting his sympathies, Shelley is habitually—it is no new observation—his own hero: Alastor, Laon, The Sensitive Plant

> (It loves, even like Love, its deep heart is full,
> It desires what it has not, the Beautiful)

and Prometheus. It is characteristic that he should say to the West Wind

10 *Cf.* Senseless is the breast, and cold,
Which relenting love would fold;
Bloodless are the veins and chill
Which the pulse of pain did fill;
Every little living nerve
That from bitter words did swerve
Round the tortured lips and brow,
Are like sapless leaflets now,
Frozen upon December's brow.
Lines Written Among the Euganean Hills.

> A heavy weight of hours has chained and bowed
> One too like thee: tameless, and swift, and proud,

and conclude:

> Be thou, Spirit fierce,
> My spirit! Be thou me, impetuous one!

About the love of such a nature there is likely at the best to be a certain innocent selfishness. And it is with fervour that Shelley says, as he is always saying implicitly, "I love Love." Mr. Santayana acutely observes: "In him, as in many people, too intense a need of loving excludes the capacity for intelligent sympathy." Perhaps love generally has less in it of intelligent sympathy than the lover supposes, and is less determined by the object of love; but Shelley, we have seen, was, while on the one hand conscious of ardent altruism, on the other peculiarly weak in his hold on objects—peculiarly unable to realize them as existing in their own natures and their own right. His need of loving (in a sense that was not, perhaps, in the full focus of Mr. Santayana's intention) comes out in the erotic element that, as already remarked in these pages, the texture of the poetry pervasively exhibits. There is hardly any need to illustrate here the tender, caressing, voluptuous effects and suggestions of the favourite vocabulary and imagery. The consequences of the need, or "love," of loving, combined, as it was, with a notable lack of self-knowledge and a capacity for ecstatic idealizing, are classically extant in *Epipsychidion*.

The love of loathing is, naturally, less conscious than the love of Love. It may fairly be said to involve a love of Hate, if not of hating: justification enough for putting it this way is provided by *The Cenci,* which exhibits a perverse luxury of insistence, not merely upon horror, but upon malignity. This work, of course, is commonly held to require noting as, in the general account of Shelley, a remarkable exception: his genius may be essentially lyrical, but he can, transcending limitations, write great drama. This estimate of *The Cenci* is certainly a remarkable instance of *vis inertiae*—of the power of conventional valuation to perpetuate itself, once established. For it takes no great discernment to see that *The Cenci* is very bad and that its badness is characteristic. Shelley, as usual, is the hero—here the heroine; his relation to Beatrice is of the same order as his relation to Alastor and Prometheus, and the usual vices should not be found more acceptable because of the show of drama.

Nor is this show the less significantly bad because Shelley doesn't know where it comes from—how he is contriving it. He says in his *Preface* that an idea suggested by Calderon is "the only plagiarism which I have intentionally committed in the whole piece." Actually, not only is the "whole piece" Shakespearian in inspiration (how peculiarly dubious an affair inspiration was apt to be for Shelley we have seen), it is full of particular echoes of Shakespeare—echoes protracted, confused and woolly; plagiarisms, that is, of the worst kind. This Shakespearianizing, general and particular is—and not the less so for its unconsciousness—quite damning. It means that Shelley's drama and tragedy do not grow out of any realized theme; there is nothing grasped at the core of the piece. Instead there is Beatrice-Shelley, in whose martyrdom the Count acts Jove—with more than Jovian gusto:

> I do not feel as if I were a man,
> But like a fiend appointed to chastise
> The offences of some unremembered world.
> My blood is running up and down my veins;
> A fearful pleasure makes it prick and tingle:
> I feel a giddy sickness of strange awe;
> My heart is beating with an expectation
> Of horrid joy. (IV. i. 160)

The pathos is of corresponding corruptness. The habits that enable Shelley to be unconscious about this kind of indulgence enable him at the same time to turn it into tragic drama by virtue of an unconscious effort to be Shakespeare.

There are, of course, touches of Webster: Beatrice in the trial scene is commonly recognized to have borrowed an effect or two from the White Devil. But the Shakespearian promptings are everywhere, in some places almost ludicrously assorted, obvious and thick. For instance, Act III, Sc. ii starts (stage direction: "Thunder and the sound of a storm") by being at line two obviously Lear. At line eight Othello comes in and carries on for ten lines; and he reasserts himself at line fifty. At line fifty-five Hamlet speaks. At line seventy-eight we get an effect from *Macbeth,* to be followed by many more in the next act, during which, after much borrowed suspense, the Count's murder is consummated.

The quality of the dramatic poetry and the relation between Shelley and Shakespeare must, for reasons of space, be represented—the example is a fair one—by a single brief passage (Act V, Sc. iv, l. 48):

> O
> My God! Can it be possible I have
> To die so suddenly? So young to go
> Under the obscure, cold, rotting, wormy ground!
> To be nailed down into a narrow place;
> To see no more sweet sunshine; hear no more
> Blithe voice of living thing; muse not again
> Upon familiar thoughts, sad, yet thus lost—
> How fearful! to be nothing! Or to be . . .
> What? Oh, where am I? Let me go not mad!
> Sweet Heaven, forgive weak thoughts! If there should be
> No God, no Heaven, no Earth in the void world;
> The wide, gray, lampless, deep, unpeopled world! . . .

This patently recalls Claudio's speech in *Measure for Measure* (Act III, Sc. i):

> Ay, but to die, and go we know not where;
> To lie in cold obstruction and to rot;
> This sensible warm motion to become
> A kneaded clod; and the delighted spirit
> To bathe in fiery floods, or to reside
> In thrilling region of thick-ribbed ice;
> To be imprison'd in the viewless winds,
> And blown with restless violence round about
> The pendent world; or to be worse than worst
> Of those that lawless and uncertain thoughts
> Imagine howling; 't is too horrible!
> The weariest and most loathed worldly life
> That age, ache, penury, and imprisonment
> Can lay on nature is a paradise
> To what we fear of death.

The juxtaposition is enough to expose the vague, generalizing externality of Shelley's rendering. Claudio's words spring from a vividly realized particular situation; from the imagined experience of a given mind in a given critical moment that is felt from the inside—that is lived—with sharp concrete particularity. Claudio's "Ay, but to die . . ." is not insistently and voluminously emotional like Beatrice's ("wildly")

> O
> My God! Can it be possible . . .

but it is incomparably more intense. That "cold obstruction" is not abstract; it gives rather the essence of the situation in which Claudio shrinkingly imagines himself—the sense of the warm body (given by "cold") struggling ("obstruction" takes an appropriate effort to pronounce) in vain with the suffocating earth. Sentience, warmth and motion, the essentials of being alive as epitomized in the next line, recoil from death, realized brutally in the concrete (the "clod" is a vehement protest, as "clay," which "kneaded" nevertheless brings appropriately in, would not have been). Sentience, in the "delighted spirit," plunges, not into the delightful coolness suggested by "bathe," but into the dreadful opposite, and warmth and motion shudder away from the icy prison ("reside" is analogous in working to "bathe"). The shudder is there in "thrilling," which also—such alliteration as that of "thrilling region" and "thick-ribbed" is not accidental in a Shakespearian passage of this quality—gives the sharp reverberating report of the ice as, in the intense cold, it is forced up into ridges or ribs (at which, owing to the cracks, the thickness of the ice can be seen).

But there is no need to go on. The point has been sufficiently enforced that, though this vivid concreteness of realization lodged the passage in Shelley's mind, to become at the due moment "inspiration," the passage inspired is nothing but wordy emotional generality. It does not grasp and present anything, but merely makes large gestures towards the kind of effect deemed appropriate. We are told emphatically what the emotion is that we are to feel; emphasis and insistence serving instead of realization and advertising its default. The intrusion of the tag from Lear brings out the vague generality of that unconscious set at being Shakespeare which Shelley took for dramatic inspiration.

Inspection of *The Cenci,* then, confirms all the worst in the account of Shelley. Further confirmation would not need much seeking; but, returning to the fact of his genius, it is pleasanter, and more profitable, to recall what may be said by way of explaining how he should have been capable of the worst. His upbringing was against him. As Mr. Santayana says: "Shelley seems hardly to have been brought up; he grew up in the nursery among his young sisters, at school among the rude boys, without any affectionate guidance, without imbibing any religious or social tradition." Driven in on himself, he nourished the inner life of adolescence on the trashy fantasies and cheap excitements of the Terror school. The phase of serious tradition in which, in incipient maturity, he began to practise poetry was, in a subtler way, as unfavourable: Shelley needed no encouragement to cultivate spontaneity of emotion and poetical abeyance of thought. Then the state of the world at the time must, in its effect on a spirit of Shelley's sensitive humanity and idealizing bent, be allowed to account for a great deal—as the sonnet *England in 1819* so curiously intimates:

> An old, mad, blind, despised, and dying king,—
> Princes, the dregs of their dull race, who flow
> Through public scorn,—mud from a muddy spring,—
> Rulers who neither see, nor feel, nor know,
> But leech-like to their fainting country cling,
> Till they drop, blind in blood, without a blow,—
> A people starved and stabbed in the untilled field,—
> An army, which liberticide and prey
> Makes as a two-edged sword to all who wield,—
> Golden and sanguine laws which tempt and slay;
> Religion Christless, Godless—a book sealed;
> A Senate,—Time's worst statute unrepealed,—
> Are graves, from which a glorious Phantom may
> Burst, to illumine our tempestuous day.

The contrast between the unusual strength (for Shelley) of the main body of the sonnet and the pathetic weakness of the final couplet is eloquent. Contemplation of the actual world being unendurable, Shelley devotes himself to the glorious Phantom that may (an oddly ironical stress results from the rime position) work a sudden miraculous change but is in any case as vague as Demogorgon and as unrelated to actuality—to which Shelley's Evil is correspondingly unrelated.

The strength of the sonnet, though unusual in kind for Shelley, is not of remarkably distinguished quality in itself; the kindred strength of *The Mask of Anarchy* is. Of this poem Professor Elton says: [11] "There is a likeness in it to Blake's [gift] which has often been noticed; the same kind of anvil-stroke, and the same use of an awkward simplicity for the purposes of epigram." The likeness to Blake is certainly there—much more of a likeness than would have seemed possible from the characteristic work. It lies, not in any assumed broadsheet naïveté or crudity such as the account cited might perhaps suggest, but in a rare emotional integrity and force, deriving from a clear, disinterested and mature vision.

> When one fled past, a maniac maid,
> And her name was Hope, she said:
> But she looked more like Despair,
> And she cried out in the air:
>
> 'My father Time is weak and gray
> With waiting for a better day;
> See how idiot-like he stands,
> Fumbling with his palsied hands!
>
> He has had child after child,
> And the dust of death is piled
> Over every one but me—
> Misery, oh, Misery!'
>
> Then she lay down in the street,
> Right before the horses' feet,
> Expecting, with a patient eye,
> Murder, Fraud, and Anarchy.

These stanzas do not represent all the virtue of the poem, but they show its unusual purity and strength. In spite of "Murder, Fraud, and Anarchy," there is nothing of the usual Shelleyan emotionalism—no suspicion of indulgence, insistence, corrupt will or improper approach. The emotion seems to inhere in the vision communicated, the situation grasped: Shelley sees what is in front of him too clearly, and with too pure a pity and indignation, to have any regard for his emotions as such; the emotional value of what is presented asserts itself, or rather, does not need asserting. Had he used and developed his genius in the spirit of *The Mask of Anarchy* he would have been a much greater, and a much more readable, poet.

[11] *Survey of English Literature, 1780-1830,* Vol. II, p. 202.

But *The Mask of Anarchy* is little more than a marginal throw-off, and gets perhaps too much stress in even so brief a distinguishing mention as this. The poetry in which Shelley's genius manifests itself characteristically, and for which he has his place in the English tradition, is much more closely related to his weaknesses. It would be perverse to end without recognizing that he achieved memorable things in modes of experience that were peculiarly congenial to the European mind in that phase of its history and are of permanent interest. The sensibility expressed in the *Ode to the West Wind* is much more disablingly limited than current valuation allows, but the consummate expression is rightly treasured. The Shelleyan confusion appears, perhaps, at its most poignant in *The Triumph of Life,* the late unfinished poem. This poem has been paralleled with the revised *Hyperion,* and it is certainly related by more than the *terza rima* to Dante. There is in it a profounder note of disenchantment than before, a new kind of desolation, and, in its questioning, a new and profoundly serious concern for reality:

> . . . their might
> Could not repress the mystery within,
> And for the morn of truth they feigned, deep night
> Caught them ere evening . . .
>
> For in the battle Life and they did wage,
> She remained conqueror . . .
>
> 'Whence camest thou? and whither goest thou?
> How did thy course begin?' I said, 'and why?
>
> Mine eyes are sick of this perpetual flow
> Of people, and my heart sick of one sad thought—
> Speak!'
>
> as one between desire and shame
> Suspended, I said—If, as it doth seem,
> Thou comest from the realm without a name
>
> Into this valley of perpetual dream,
> Show whence I came and where I am, and why—
> Pass not away upon the passing stream.

But in spite of the earnest struggle to grasp something real, the sincere revulsion from personal dreams and fantasies, the poem itself is a drifting phantasmagoria—bewildering and bewildered. Vision opens into vision, dream unfolds within dream, and the visionary perspectives, like those of the imagery in the passage of *Mont Blanc,* shift elusively and are lost; and the failure to place the various phases or levels of visionary drift with reference to any grasped reality is the more significant because of the palpable effort. Nevertheless, *The Triumph of Life* is among the few things one can still read and go back to in Shelley when he has become, generally, "almost unreadable."

Shelley's part in the later notion of "the poetical" has been sufficiently indicated. His handling of the medium assimilates him readily, as an influence, to the Spenserian-Miltonic line running through *Hyperion* to Tennyson. Milton is patently present in *Alastor,* the earliest truly Shelleyan poem; and *Adonais*—

> Afar the melancholy thunder moaned,
> Pale Ocean in unquiet slumber lay

—relates him as obviously to *Hyperion* as to *Lycidas.* Indeed, to compare the verse of *Hyperion,* where the Miltonic Grand Style is transmuted by the Spenserianizing Keats, with that of *Adonais* is to bring out the essential relation between the organ resonances of *Paradise Lost* and the pastoral melodizing [12] of *Lycidas.* Mellifluous mourning in *Adonais* is a more fervent luxury than in *Lycidas,* and more declamatory ("Life like a dome of many-coloured glass"—the famous imagery is happily conscious of being impressive, but the impressiveness is for the spell-bound, for those sharing the simple happiness of intoxication); and it is, in the voluptuous self-absorption with which the medium enjoys itself, rather nearer to Tennyson.

But, as was virtually said in the discussion of imagery from the *Ode to the West Wind,* the Victorian poet with whom Shelley has some peculiar affinities is Swinburne.

. . . . .

Swinburne, too, depends for his effects upon a suspension, in the reader, of the critical intelligence. If one says loosely that he is more verbal and literary than Shelley, that is to express one's sense that his imagery derives much less directly from sensory experience than Shelley's and is vaguer, and that his emotions (in his poetry) belong to a specialized poetic order, cultivated apart from ordinary living. His peculiarities are notorious and not difficult to analyse. It will be enough here to examine briefly the opening stanza of his best-known piece.

> When the hounds of spring are on winter's traces,
> The mother of months in meadow or plain
> Fills the shadows and windy places
> With lisp of leaves and ripple of rain;
> And the brown bright nightingale amorous
> Is half assuaged for Itylus,
> For the Thracian ships and the foreign faces,
> The tongueless vigil, and all the pain.

[12] O Golden tongued Romance, with serene lute!
Fair plumed Syren, Queen of far-away!
Leave melodizing on this wintry day,
Shut up thine olden pages, and be mute:
Keats. *Sonnet: on sitting down to read* King Lear *once again.*

The dependence upon the tripping onrush of the measure, which rushes us by all questions, and upon the general hypnotic effect (the alliteration playing an essential part in both) is plain. We are not to visualize the hounds of spring, or to ask in what form winter is to be seen or conceived as flying or whether the traces are footprints in the snow, or snow and frost on the grass: the general sense of triumphant chase is enough. "The mother of months," we feel vaguely, must be classical; whether she is the moon, the year, the spring, or Demeter—it doesn't matter. She's certainly right to be there; the alliteration makes her inevitable. As for

the brown bright nightingale amorous,

—one may have read the poem fifty times without asking, why "bright"? The bird's eye may be bright, and "bright" might possibly (by some one) be defended as a description of its song. But it is plain enough that "bright" comes there because it alliterates with "brown" and rimes with the first syllable of "nightingale." That it has no application to the nightingale escapes notice, for we have been made to give the poem a kind of reading that looks for no stricter organization of words than Swinburne offers: "bright" belongs to the general effect of gleam and dazzle, and so far as meaning is concerned, may be thrown in anywhere. We have here a further justification for calling Swinburne "verbal"; it is plain that, in his poetry, one word will bring in a train of others less because of meaning than because they begin with the same letter or chime with like sounds.

FOUR QUARTETS: A COMMENTARY
(1942, 1946)

HELEN L. GARDNER

THE PUBLICATION of the Quartets in one volume has made their interpretation easier in one way but more difficult in another. Read consecutively each illuminates the others, and the symbols employed become richer and more solid with repetition; but the cross-references between the poems are now seen to be so various, subtle and complex that formal interpretation seems more than ever clumsy and impertinent, and may even mislead readers, by appearing to impose a logical scheme on poems which continually escape from the logic of discourse into something nearer to the conditions of musical thought. But however difficult it may be to attempt an interpretation, and however unsatisfactory any interpretation is, it seems to be necessary with a poet so steeped in tradition as Mr. Eliot and with poems so original in their form and manner. It need hardly be said that any interpretation bears about as much resemblance to the poems as a map does to a landscape, and like a map exists to be discarded by a walker who really knows the country. But a map is useful to strangers, and even to others it may suggest unfamiliar routes and places that have been overlooked.

The best kind of interpretation is that supplied by an author's other works, and this is particularly true of Mr. Eliot, since he constantly repeats himself, as he himself owns—

> You say I am repeating
> Something I have said before. I shall say it again.
> Shall I say it again?

His poetry is extraordinarily self-consistent, and there is almost nothing he has published that does not form part of his poetic personality. One of the results of this integrity is that his later work interprets his earlier, as much as his earlier work does his later; so that criticism of *The Waste Land* to-day is modified by *Ash Wednesday,* and *Ash Wednesday* is easier to understand after reading the Quartets. Mr. Eliot's poetic career has shown to a high degree the quality that Keats called "negative capability," when a man is "capable of being in uncertainties, mysteries, doubts, without any irritable reaching after fact and reason"; he has never forced his poetic voice, but has been content with "hints and guesses." His readers must show the same patience. They must be ready to grow into knowledge of his poetry and to wait for Keats's moment when "several things dovetailed in my mind." This commentary will try to interpret the Quartets by the earlier works and by the reading that lies behind them, in order to help readers to that moment when they share with the poet the joy of apprehending significant relations.

The structure of the poems is seen very clearly when they are read together, and can be recognized as being essentially the same as the structure of *The Waste Land.* It is far more rigid than we should suspect from reading any one of the poems by itself. In fact, Mr. Eliot has invented for himself, as the word Quartets suggests, a kind of poetic equivalent of "sonata form," containing what are best described as five "movements," each with an inner necessary structure, and capable of the symphonic richness of *The Waste Land* or the chamber-music beauties of *Burnt Norton.*[1] The five movements suggest the five acts of a drama, and the poems are built on a dialectical basis, employing deliberate reversals and contrasts in matter and style. This form seems perfectly adapted to its creator's way of thinking and feeling: to his desire to submit to the poetic discipline of strict law, and to his desire to find a form which gives him the greatest possible liberty in the development of a flexible, dramatic verse, and the greatest freedom in "violently yoking together heterogeneous ideas." The combination of an extreme apparent freedom with a great inner strictness corresponds to the necessities of his temperament.

The first movement in each of the Quartets consists of statement and counter-statement in a free blank verse. This must not be pressed too hard, for in *East Coker* the first movement falls into four parts, the statement and its contradiction being repeated; in *The Dry Salvages* the metaphors of river and sea are more absolutely opposed than are the two paragraphs of *Burnt Norton,* while in *Little Gidding* the opposing statements of the first two paragraphs are blended in the third, the vivid particularity of the scene in "midwinter spring" and the assertion of unparticularity, the sameness of the experience, being summed up in the final phrase "England and nowhere. Never and always." But on the whole the opening movement is built on contradictions which the poem is to reconcile. The second movement shows the most striking similarities from poem to poem. It opens with a highly "poetical" lyric passage—octosyllabics rhyming irregularly in *Burnt Norton* and *East Coker,* a simplified sestina in *The Dry Salvages* and three lyric stanzas in *Little Gidding.* This is imme-

[1] *Cf. The Music of Poetry,* 1942. "I believe that the properties in which music concerns the poet most nearly, are the sense of rhythm and the sense of structure.... The use of recurrent themes is as natural to poetry as to music. There are possibilities for verse which bear some analogy to the development of a theme by different groups of instruments; there are possibilities of transitions in a poem comparable to the different movements of a symphony or a quartet; there are possibilities of contrapuntal arrangement of subject-matter."

diately followed by an extremely colloquial passage, in which the idea which had been treated in metaphor and symbol in the first half of the movement is expanded, and given personal application, in a conversational manner. In the first three poems this is done in free blank verse, but in *Little Gidding* the metre employed is a modification of *terza rima.* Though the metre is regular and the style has a greater dignity, it still has colloquial force and the dialogue has the same personal and topical reference as is found in the same section of the other poems. The third movement is the core of each poem, out of which reconciliation grows: it is an exploration, with a twist, of the ideas of the first two movements. In *Burnt Norton* the twilight world of the London Tube [2] "neither plenitude nor vacancy" fades into the world of perpetual solitude. In *East Coker* there is a sudden shift in the emotions aroused by the word *darkness,* which gives point to the whole poem. In *The Dry Salvages* the change is a change of temper, from the reflective to the hortatory, and in *Little Gidding* the turn is from the personal and individual to the historic. The fourth movement is a lyric in all four poems. The fifth is again in two parts, but the change in manner and metre is slighter than in the second movement and it is reversed. Here the colloquial passage comes first, and then, without a feeling of sharp break, the rhythm tightens and the manner becomes graver for a kind of falling close. The whole movement recapitulates the themes of the poem, with personal and topical applications,[3] and makes a resolution of the discords of the first.

The Waste Land, if one allows for its much wider scope, dramatic method, and hosts of characters, follows the same pattern. *The Burial of the Dead* contains far more than two statements, but formally it is a series of contrasts of feeling towards persons and experiences. *The Game of Chess* opens with the elaborate description, in ornate style, of the lady at her dressing table, which contrasts violently, though not in its theme, with the talk of the women in the public-house. *The Fire Sermon,* the poem's heart, with its suffocating intensity, has moments when the oppression lifts, and a feeling of release and purification floods in. This twist is given by the evocations of another world: "Et O ces voix d'enfants, chantant dans la coupole!", the "inexplicable splendour of Ionian white and gold," the "white towers," and the mingled emotions aroused by the word *burning,* for we remember not only St. Paul's use of it to express the torment of desire, but also the brand plucked out, and the fire of the *Purgatorio.* The reference to the Buddha, the "collocation of western and eastern asceticism," to which attention is drawn in the notes, anticipates the

[2] In the first three poems, at this point, the image of passengers in a train is introduced. The "place of disaffection" with "men and bits of paper, whirled by the cold wind" in *Burnt Norton* is surely the London Tube.

[3] With the exception of *The Dry Salvages* all the poems open the fifth movement with a consideration of the nature of words and poetry.

use of the *Bhagavad-gita* in *The Dry Salvages.* The fourth section is as always a brief lyric, and the fifth, while naturally being far more complex than the final movements of the later poems, fulfils the same function of resolution. Most people would agree to-day, in the light of Mr. Eliot's later work, that the original critics of *The Waste Land* misread it, not recognizing it as an *Inferno* which looked towards a *Purgatorio.* Finding in it "the disillusion of a generation," they failed to see in it what its treatment of history should have shown them, the disillusion of those in every generation, "qui se haïssent et qui cherchent un être véritablement aimable."

Burnt Norton, East Coker, The Dry Salvages and *Little Gidding* are poems on one theme, or rather on different aspects of the same theme, and they are closely linked with *The Family Reunion,* which is a dramatic treatment of the subject. The theme can be variously defined, since we are speaking of poetry, not of philosophy or theology. It might be called the relation of time to eternity, or the meaning of history, or the redemption of time and the world of man. *The Family Reunion* emphasizes the idea of redemption, for Harry is seeking salvation and release from his sense of guilt. As he flies from the pursuing Eumenides, he is a man fleeing from the eternal, turning his back upon it to immerse himself in futile movement; when he recognizes them and accepts their summons, they become "bright angels" and the ministers of his purgation. But this recognition springs out of his discovery of the past, his own and that of his family. As Agatha talks to him and tells him of his parents' unhappiness and sin, he at last understands the meaning of his own unhappy childhood and of his own marriage. He becomes then "the consciousness of his unhappy family" and so can make expiation.[4]

The close connection of *The Family Reunion* with these poems will become apparent in the course of the discussion, but the themes had appeared in Mr. Eliot's poetry before. They are made fully explicit in the choruses of *The Rock,* which contrast the determined and endless motion of the world of time with the stillness of eternity, and celebrate the union of time and eternity in

> a moment in time and of time,
> A moment not out of time, but in time, in what we call
> history: transecting, bisecting the world of time, a moment
> in time but not like a moment of time,
> A moment in time but time was made through that moment:
> for without the meaning there is no time, and that moment of time gave the meaning.

[4] It is probable that the close of the play owes something to Bazin's *Life of Charles de Foucauld.* It is impossible for anyone who has read this book not to be reminded of it when Harry speaks of

> The worship in the desert, the thirst and deprivation,
> A stony sanctuary and a primitive altar,
> The heat of the sun and the icy vigil,
> A care over lives of humble people.

The same preoccupation with time is present in *Ash Wednesday*. In the fourth section the cry is heard, "Redeem the time." It is a common sundial motto and is appropriate there in a garden poem, as the memory of the phrase is at the opening of *Burnt Norton*. The problem of history and the time-process is one of the great themes of *The Waste Land,* where it is mingled with the desire for cosmic and personal salvation. No poem has ever shown a greater sense of the pressure of the past upon the present and of its existence in the present.

The problem of the time-process and its meaning is handled in the Quartets under different natural images and metaphors. All four poems have place-names for titles, two of them connected with Mr. Eliot's family history. *Burnt Norton* differs from the others in having no field of reference, personal or historic. Its subject is a Cotswold manor house: merely a deserted house and garden which the poet has wandered into without knowing anything about the history of the house or who had lived in it. East Coker is a Somersetshire village from which in the seventeenth century Andrew Eliot set out for the New World. The Dry Salvages are a group of rocky islands off the coast of Massachusetts, part of the landscape of the poet's childhood, and part of the new experience of his ancestors after they had crossed the seas. Little Gidding is a village in Huntingdonshire to which in 1625 Nicholas Ferrar and his family retired in order to lead a common life of devotion. The starting point in all the poems is a landscape and the emotion and thought are bound up with a deeply felt sense of place.

Burnt Norton is a land-locked poem: its whole feeling is enclosed. It builds up, by suggestion, the picture of a house and formal garden. Its imagery is social and civilized, weighted with human history and culture. A formal garden is an admirable symbol for man's attempt to impose a pattern on his experience and to discipline nature. The picture gradually given here is of shrubbery and alley-walk, rose-garden, low box-borders and pools, sunflowers in the borders, clematis hanging from the wall and clipped yews. Within the house there are dried rose-leaves in a bowl, and there are references to a Chinese jar and to the music of the violin. All this is human and civilized, and the image used for reality is human too—the hidden laughter of children among the leaves of the garden.[5] This garden imagery of *Burnt Norton* is used at the climax of *The Family Reunion,* in the dialogue between Harry and Agatha in the second scene of Part II. Agatha speaks there of "looking through the little door, when the sun was shining on the rose-garden." It is a moment of

[5] It has been suggested to me that the setting of the poem and the image of the laughing children hidden among the leaves may have been caught from Rudyard Kipling's *They*. The children there are both "what might have been and what has been," appearing to those who have lost their children in the house of a blind woman who has never borne a child.

escape from the endless walking "down a concrete corridor," or "through the stone passages of an immense and empty hospital." This moment of release from the deadening feeling of meaningless sequence—"in and out, in an endless drift," "to and fro, dragging my feet"—into what is always present, the moment when, in Harry's phrase, "the chain breaks" is the subject of *Burnt Norton*. The experience in the poem is pure of the tragic emotions of the play; it is an experience of a moment when one suddenly feels at home, accepted, free from anxiety, "the practical desire." It is not a moment that can be held, though it can be remembered. It is a moment which happens unexpectedly, as a grace, without the mind's preparing itself, or making any effort. The laughter of the children is a lovely surprise; "sudden in a shaft of sunlight" comes "the moment in and out of time."

Burnt Norton does not suggest any dogma: its lyric movement, with its halting tentative rhythms, is purely natural in its theme and images. The subject of the poem is an experience for which theology provides an explanation and on which religion builds a discipline, the immediate apprehension of a timeless reality, felt in time and remembered in time, the sudden revelation of "the one end, which is always present." It is in the third section only that the poem suggests another way to the stillness at the heart of movement, by a deliberate descent into the world of perpetual solitude, the negative way. Christianity has found room in itself for both types of mystical experience, that which finds all nature a theophany, and that which feels the truth of Pascal's favourite text: "Vere tu es Deus absconditus." The way through the darkness is the subject of *East Coker*.

East Coker is much less confined in its setting; its background is a village and its environs, a landscape full of human history, but history of a ruder, less cultivated kind. It is set in a countryside where the sea is not far off, and the sea-wind can be felt. The first movement ends with a lightly touched reference to the sea; the sea provides an image of overwhelming desolation at the close of the second; and the final impulse of release and escape is given by the image of "the vast waters of the petrel and the porpoise." The village is seen in its setting of open fields and the manor house is felt as part of the village, not a place private and walled-in. There is reference to the rhythm of the seasons and the farm. The metaphors used for reality are mostly non-human—the winter lightning, the wild strawberry, the whisper of running streams: the images of desolation are the dark wood, brambles and rocks.

In *The Family Reunion,* when Harry has become fully aware of the sin he has to expiate, he feels a sense of happiness and exclaims, "This is like an end"; to which Agatha replies, "And a beginning." *East Coker* plays throughout with Mary Stuart's motto, "In my end is my beginning," inverting it to a statement of rigid determinism at the opening, breaking it, and exploiting the various meanings of the word *end*. The final use of the phrase holds more than one meaning: *end* can mean death or the purpose for which we were created. The opening statement of the poem is determinist, and establishes by powerful rhythm and repetition the cyclic view of life and history. The life of man and of mankind and of the works of man is shown to be on the pattern of the life of the earth: all are an endlessly recurring succession of birth, growth, decay, and death. Contrasted, within the first movement, with the two statements of life as rhythm, pattern and sequence, are two passages in which the idea of stillness and rest is given. There is first the picture of the village sleeping in the hot silence of a late summer afternoon, and, at the close, the delicate hint of the breathless stillness of the dawn of a hot day. The notion of pattern and repetition leads only to despair: "Feet rising and falling." (This was Agatha's image for the sensation of imprisonment in time.) "Eating and drinking. Dung and death."

The lyrical passage with which the second movement opens contradicts both the rigid order and the stillness of the first. The idea of pattern is rejected, but so is the idea of peace. The seasons are all disordered. Spring thunder peals in November: the flowers of high summer jostle those of spring and winter. There is war too among the constellations, ending with the apocalyptic vision of the end of the world, burnt out to an icy cinder. But this romantic vision of chaos the poet rejects, for a plain, almost prosaic statement of the same chaos in the life of the individual. There too we find no ordered sequence, pattern or development. The metaphor of autumnal serenity is false applied to man; experience does not bring wisdom, nor old age peace. The time when one knows never arrives, and the pattern is falsified by every new moment. We are always in the dark wood, in which Dante found himself in the middle of his life, the wood "where the straight way is lost." As we try to hold the past, it slips from us, engulfed in the darkness of the present.

> The houses are all gone under the sea.
> The dancers are all gone under the hill.

The third movement opens with this idea of darkness, with blind Samson's cry of anguish; but this anguish soon turns to a sombre triumph. The darkness, in which we are lost, swallows up and hides from us the base, the trivial and the ignoble, the meaningless pomps and vanities of the world. The poet rejoices in this victory of the dark in the same way as the writers of the early seventeenth century rejoiced in the levelling power of death. But this welcome to the darkness takes then another turn, and it is welcomed not only because it obliterates, but also because it reveals. Within the darkness is light; within the stillness, movement and dancing; within the silence, sound.

Mr. Eliot is here writing in the tradition of those mystics who followed the negative way. It is a tradition that goes back beyond Christianity to the Neo-Platonists, who turned what had been a method of knowing—the dialectical method of arriving at truth by negations of the false—into a method of arriving at experience of the One. This doctrine of the ascent or descent ("the way up is the way down") into union with reality, by successively discarding ideas which would limit the one idea of Being, found a natural metaphor in darkness and night. It was a double-edged metaphor, since night expressed both the obliteration of self and all created things, and also the uncharacterized Reality which was the object of contemplation. The anonymous English mystic who wrote in this tradition in the fourteenth century used for his symbol a cloud, and called his book *The Cloud of Unknowing*. He taught that the soul in this life must be always between two clouds, a cloud of forgetting beneath, which hides all creatures and works, and a cloud of unknowing above, upon which it must "smite with a sharp dart of longing love." "For all of other creatures and their works, yea, and of the works of God's self, may a man through grace have fullhead of knowing, and well he can think of them: but of God Himself can no man think. And therefore I would leave all that thing that I can think, and choose to my love that thing that I cannot think. For why: He may well be loved, but not thought. By love may He be gotten and holden; but by thought never."

The actual phrase "a cloud of unknowing" occurs in *The Family Reunion,* and a line in *Little Gidding* comes directly from the book, but in *East Coker* the great paradoxes of the negative way are taken from its most famous doctor, St. John of the Cross. The riddling paradoxical statements at the close of the third movement are an almost literal rendering of the maxims under the "figure" which stands as frontispiece to *The Ascent of Mount Carmel* and which appear in a slightly different form at the close of chapter 13 of the first book of that treatise.[6] From this deliberately unpoetical close there is an

6 In order to arrive at having pleasure in everything,
Desire to have pleasure in nothing.
In order to arrive at possessing everything,
Desire to possess nothing.
In order to arrive at knowing everything,
Desire to know nothing.
In order to arrive at that wherein thou hast no pleasure,
Thou must go by a way wherein thou hast no pleasure.
In order to arrive at that which thou knowest not,
Thou must go by a way that thou knowest not.
In order to arrive at that which thou possessest not,
Thou must go by a way that thou possessest not.
In order to arrive at that which thou art not,
Thou must go through that which thou art not.

The Complete Works of St. John of the Cross, translated by E. Allison Peers, Vol. I, p. 63.

abrupt transition to the fourth movement with its majestic firmness of rhythm and its powerful imagery.

The lyrical movement also unites despair and triumph, but now in the contemplation of human pain. If to know you must know nothing, then to live you must die. *East Coker* is far more concerned with the response made to experience than *Burnt Norton* is; and the experience to which response has to be made is a tragic one, of loss and deprivation and homelessness. The lyric, therefore, is a poem on the Passion, translated into the metaphor of a hospital, and possibly suggested by Sir Thomas Browne's phrase, "For this world, I count it not an Inn, but an Hospital; a place not to live, but to dye in." The Passion is thought of here not as a single historic event, but as an eternal act perpetually operative in time, and it is linked with the Eucharist. The grave heavy beat of the lines, the rigid stanza form, the mood, the paradoxes, the sense of tragic triumph, which the rhythm gives, make this lyric very like an early Passion hymn:

> Salve ara, salve victima,
> de passionis gloria,
> qua vita mortem pertulit
> et morte vitam reddidit.

In the final movement, the feeling that every moment is a new moment and a beginning, but that the past is alive in the present, modifying it and being modified by it also, is at first applied to the poet and the problems of expression and finally to the life of the individual. The poem ends with the injunction to be "still and still moving," that we may pass through the "dark cold and the empty desolation" to the open waters of the sea, which men have always regarded as a symbol of eternity. The close is typical of the whole poem, at once terrifying and exalting.

The Dry Salvages has for its landscape the sea-coast of New England; its dominant imagery is of rocks and the sea. This landscape of his childhood Mr. Eliot had used in the final section of *Ash Wednesday,* looking on it there with longing, as on a world hard to renounce. Of all three poems, *The Dry Salvages* is the most beautifully integrated and marries most absolutely metaphor and idea. The sea imagery runs through it with a freedom and a power hardly equalled in Mr. Eliot's other poetry. He seems to expatiate freely here and be at ease in nature.

The first movement is built on the contrast between two metaphors, the river of life and the sea of life. The river is an old metaphor for the life of man, and its flow from source to mouth is linked here with the flow of the seasons from spring to winter, and that of man's life from birth to death. The river is a reminder of what we should like to forget, our bondage to nature. Though it can for a time be ignored, it can assert its power by catastrophe as well as by its inevitable progress. "The river is within us"; we feel it in our pulses. The sea is time of another kind, the time of history, what Bacon meant when he spoke of "the vast seas of time." Individual man launches himself on this ocean of life and makes his short voyage, one of countless similar voyages. "The sea is all about us." This metaphor of the tossing seas of history denies both the cyclic view of history, the biological interpretation, which imposes on events the rhythm of a succession of rivers, each culture being first young and vigorous, then mature, and finally decayed and outworn, and also the doctrine of human progress, which finds in history an upward development. We have instead a meaningless, perpetual flux, a repetition without a pattern, to which each separate voyage adds nothing but itself. But through the apparently incoherent restlessness of the sea, there is carried to our ears the rhythm of the ground swell, different from the rhythm of the river, which we hear in our heartbeats, coming from the very depths of the ocean itself.

> And the ground swell, that is and was from the beginning,
> Clangs
> The bell.

The reminiscence of the doxology gives us the implication of the symbol of the ground swell, which makes itself felt in our hearts by the bell. The bell sounds a warning and a summons: it demands a response. Like the bell of the Angelus it is a call to prayer, and a commemoration of the mystery of the Incarnation; like the bell at the consecration it is a call to worship and announces the presence of Christ; like the tolling bell it reminds us of our death, and calls us to die daily.[7]

The sestina, with which the second movement opens, is a poem on these several annunciations. Under the metaphor of fishermen setting out on their perilous voyages, over "an ocean littered with wastage,"

[7] The image of the sea-bell and the figures of the Eumenides in *The Family Reunion* seem to me to hold the same meaning. Both are visitations of the divine, messengers from eternity, terrifying till accepted. The underlying meaning of both symbols is finely expressed by M. François Mauriac in a passage from *Dieu et Mammon*. M. Mauriac is also thinking of the Annunciation of history and the annunciations of our individual lives and he too is linking the summons with the sense of freedom in the soul. "Aussi souverainement que son Incarnation a partagé l'histoire humaine, Jésus-Christ cherche la seconde propice pour s'insérer dans ce destin, pour s'unir à ce flot de chaque destinée particulière, pour introduire sa volonté dans cette apparente fatalité, pour détruire enfin cette fatalité. Tentatives quelquefois cachées et comme détournées, renouvelées à longs intervalles, souvent directes, impérieuses, pressantes comme une occasion unique et solennelle, mais qui donnent toujours à l'homme le plus asservi le sentiment qu'il demeure maître du oui ou du non. Il a pu croire, à l'approche de la tentation trop connue, qu'aucune force au monde ne l'empêcherait d'y succomber, et que ce péché familier était vraiment l'acte qu'il ne dépendait pas de lui de ne pas commettre. Mais voici que devant l'insistance de cette force qui demande à absorber sa faiblesse, tout d'un coup, il se voit terriblement libre."

it pictures the lives of individual men, the sum of which makes history. It finds meaning in the process only in the union of the temporal with the eternal, in annunciations: the calamitous annunciation of terror and danger, the last annunciation of death, and the one Annunciation of history. The only *end* to the flux of history is man's response to the eternal. As in *The Waste Land,* it is "by the awful daring of a moment's surrender" that we exist, by praying

> the hardly, barely prayable
> Prayer of the one Annunciation.

The meaningless monotony and pointless waste of living finds its purpose in the Virgin's words, "Be it unto me according to Thy word."

As in the other poems, the idea of the lyrical passage, given in metaphor and symbol, is then translated into the experience and idioms of every day. The past does not die; the visitations, particularly the visitations of anguish, are a perpetual experience, always recurring, preserved in memory and time. The whole of this passage reads like a commentary on the scene in *The Family Reunion* in which Agatha explains the past to Harry. It might have been written of Harry that he

> had the experience but missed the meaning
> And approach to the meaning restored the experience.

The pattern of the past is not a mere sequence, neither is it a development: if it were we could disown it and look to the future. But we cannot disown our past nor the past of others, nor the past of the human race; it lives within us and in moments of illumination it is restored to us.

The third movement turns to the future. Mr. Eliot here introduces, as he had in *The Waste Land,* the scriptures of the East. He finds the same doctrine of response to what is always present in the *Bhagavad-gita.*[8] There Arjuna is concerned with the problem of the innate sinfulness of action, and Krishna replies to his doubts by insisting on the necessity for disinterestedness. Man must not look for

[8] It might be objected, and it is an objection I feel strongly myself, that to introduce Krishna at this point is an error and destroys the poem's imaginative harmony. There is an unbridgeable gap between a religion that despairs of the material world and a religion that is built upon faith in an event by which the material world was not condemned but saved. It is in their view of history and the time-process that Christianity and Hinduism are most irreconcilably opposed; the incarnations of Vishnu give no significance to history, as does the unique Incarnation of Christian belief. But I feel I may be misunderstanding the intention of the poet in making this objection, since Mr. Eliot himself in *After Strange Gods,* p. 40, makes rather this point in discussing modern cosmopolitanism. It is, perhaps, unkind to quote Mr. Eliot against himself, but he has owned that two years' study of Sanskrit and "a year in the mazes of Patanjali's metaphysics" left him "in a state of enlightened mystification." That is the feeling that this passage leaves with me.

the fruits of action; he must live as if there were no future, as if every moment were the moment of death. The New Testament teaches a similar carelessness for the morrow, which was echoed in the choruses of *The Rock*.

> Take no thought of the harvest, but only of proper sowing.

Here the future is at first thought as of something that already exists, as if it were already past, but not yet encountered, and the metaphor of the travellers, more lightly touched in the first two poems, is fully explored. First in the train, and then on the ocean, the travellers fare forward, bearing their past with them, and their future also, and yet in a real sense in a space between two lives. But to divide time harshly into past, present and future is to divide ourselves:

> You are not the same people who left that station
> Or who will arrive at any terminus.

Personality has meaning only in the present, in what we are. Our real destination is here; where we are going is where we are.[9]

The lyrical fourth movement is a prayer to Our Lady, and its tender gravity and perfect fitness springs from the union in the poem of idea and symbol. She is rightly prayed to in a poem of the sea, because she is *Stella Maris,* to whom the fishermen and their wives pray. She appears also, at the lyric climax, as the handmaid of the Lord, who made the great response to the message of the angel, and as the mother of Christ, whose birth gives meaning to time. She is also prayed to as *Mater Dolorosa,* for this is a poem of sorrows, and the whole lyric takes up the theme of the lovely melancholy sestina of the second movement; it recalls the dangerous voyages, the "ocean littered with wastage," and over all

> the sound of the sea-bell's
> Perpetual angelus.

The fifth movement opens with a topical passage on the themes of past and future, which men peer into for comfort and guidance, turning to astrologers and fortune tellers, for reassurance about the future

9 It is worth noting that the phrase

> this thing is sure,
> That time is no healer: the patient is no longer here,

echoes Pascal, while contradicting him: "Le temps guérit les douleurs et les querelles, parce qu'on change, on n'est plus la même personne. Ni l'offensant, ni l'offensé, ne sont plus eux-mêmes" (*Pensées,* II, 122). Earlier in the same section Pascal had asserted the persistence of personality: "Tout ce qui se perfectionne par progrès périt aussi par progrès, tout ce qui a été faible ne peut jamais être absolument fort. On a beau dire: *il est crû, il est changé*; il est aussi le même" (88). A reading of the *Pensées* would be a good general introduction to any study of Mr. Eliot.

which they dread, like the "anxious worried women" of the first movement, or turning to the past to explain the present.

> Men's curiosity searches past and future
> And clings to that dimension.

Opposed to this search into past and future is "the occupation of the saint," the attempt to apprehend "the point of intersection of the timeless with time." For the ordinary man, who is not a saint, there are moments of illumination, "hints and guesses" upon which he founds his life of "prayer, observance, discipline, thought and action." In these apprehensions of the eternal, preserved in memory, and fruitful beyond the moment in which they were first felt, we find freedom from the tyranny of past and future, and cease to feel ourselves the helpless victims of natural forces. Because of this inner freedom, we can accept our temporal destiny and our bond with nature, the "dung and death" to which "our temporal reversion" must return. In the "hint half guessed, the gift half understood," we find the meaning of our own lives and the purpose of history. By this, time is redeemed and is seen to be no enemy; for in time the world was made, in time God was and is manifested, and, as Blake asserted in his *Marriage of Heaven and Hell,* "Eternity is in love with the productions of time."

In contrast with *The Dry Salvages,* which is peopled by the anonymous, the fishermen "forever bailing, setting and hauling," the "anxious worried women lying awake," the passengers settling for a journey, *Little Gidding* is full of particular destinies. The setting of the poem has a historical not a personal significance, and place and time are exactly defined. It is "while the light fails on a winter's afternoon, in a secluded chapel"; and the poem is a record of a visit with a definite purpose: "You are here to kneel where prayer has been valid." We are not concerned with the "hints and guesses" of the earlier poems, but with the life of "prayer, observance, discipline, thought and action" of the last lines of *The Dry Salvages.* It is the actions of men, particularly their political actions, all that area of experience in which we are most aware of our freedom, which is the subject of meditation, things done rather than things suffered and endured. The thought of sin occurs here for the first time, not the sickness of the soul as in *East Coker,* but actual sin—"things ill done and done to others' harm."

Little Gidding is a place of dedication, to which people come with purpose. It was not the ancestral home of the Ferrars, but a house which old Mrs. Ferrar had bought the year before and to which the family went in the plague of 1624. In the next year Nicholas Ferrar "grew to a full Resolution and determination of that thing and course of life he had so often wished for and longingly desired. And that week before Whitsunday gave himself to a very private Retirement, both in his thoughts and in his person, and was observed to fast much, eate sparingly and sleep little and on Whitsun Eve he was up all night in his study." On Trinity Sunday he went with his tutor to see Laud, and was ordained deacon, refusing all his life to proceed to the priesthood, and returned to Little Gidding to share his goods with his family and to lead that life of ordered devotion and good works which made this remote Huntingdonshire village famous throughout England. An admirable picture of the life at Little Gidding can be found in Shorthouse's novel *John Inglesant*. It is a book of singular charm and refinement of feeling and all that is necessary for an understanding of what the name of the poem should suggest can be found in it. King Charles visited the community in 1633, and again during the troubled year of 1642, and legend says he came there for shelter by night, "a broken king," after the final defeat of Naseby, just before he went north to give himself up to the Scots. Little Gidding is then a place of defeat. The community was scattered in 1647 and the chapel left ruined, and though the chapel was restored for worship in the nineteenth century, Nicholas Ferrar's ideal of a religious community based on the Christian family was never revived in the Anglican Church. Little Gidding remains "a symbol perfected in death."

The first movement of the poem is in three parts, but the transitions are not abrupt, and the third part is a kind of recapitulation or development of the second, opening with the same phrase and coming round to a modification of the same conclusion. The first paragraph gives a vivid impression of the "midwinter spring," the season that is "not in time's covenant," a time of "frost and fire" and "blossom of snow." The second paragraph asserts that at any time or any season this is a place of destiny, while the third brings us to the particular purpose here, which is prayer, and to the thought of the dead whose communication is "tongued with fire beyond the language of the living."

The beautiful lyric on decay, disintegration and death which opens the second movement recalls the imagery of the earlier poems. The "burnt roses" and the "dust in the air suspended" are from *Burnt Norton,* the "wall, the wainscot and the mouse" from *East Coker,* the "dead water and dead sand" from *The Dry Salvages.* The symbolism of the four elements which runs throughout the Quartets here reaches its fullest expression. The effect of the lyric is cumulative; human emotion and passion depart into the air, human effort crumbles into dust, the monuments of the human spirit are rotted by the corrosion of water and fire. The disintegration into the four elements whose mysterious union makes life finds its most poignant symbol in the final image of the gutted and water-logged ruins of "sanctuary and choir."

This theme of the "death of hope and despair" and of the "vanity of toil" underlies the colloquy that follows. Whereas in the other poems this section is a meditation, here, in keeping with the historical subject, we have an episode, a particular moment in time described. It is at dawn, between the departure of the last bomber and the sounding of the All Clear, and the scene is the streets of London. Instead of the poet's own reflections we have the conversation with the "dead master," a communication from one whose "concern was speech," and who in his day had his own "thought and theory." The setting, the style and above all the metre at once suggest *The Divine Comedy.* The stranger has the "brown baked features" of Brunetto Latini (*Inferno xv*), and he ends his speech with the thought of the "refining fire" of the *Purgatorio,* while his melancholy sense of supersession—"last season's fruit is eaten"—recalls the words of Oderisi (*Purgatorio xi*). But although the *Comedy* is full of interviews such as this, and in spite of the Dantean imagery and reminiscences, we are not to identify this "familiar compound ghost" with Dante or with any other single poet. The ghost is "both one and many"; he is "intimate and unidentifiable"; he speaks of the experience of the poet in all ages and the fact that he adapts a line from Mallarmé and appears to recall a famous phrase of Virgil [10] seems to depersonalize him rather than to suggest any identification. But the tone of the speech and some of the phrases recall strongly one great English poet, and that is Milton, the Milton of the close of *Paradise Lost,* of *Paradise Regained* and of *Samson.* It is Milton's melancholy picture of old age that we remember when we hear the disclosure of the "gifts reserved for age."

> Thou must outlive
> Thy youth, thy strength, thy beauty, which will change
> To withered weak and gray; thy Senses then
> Obtuse, all taste of pleasure must forgoe,
> To what thou hast.

And the close of the speech has a haunting Miltonic echo. "I cannot praise a fugitive and cloistered virtue *unexercised* and unbreathed," wrote the confident Milton of 1644. The mood is very different and deeply troubled in *Paradise Regained* when political action is considered and in *Samson* where "patience is the *exercise* of saints." The weight of human suffering in Milton's later poetry, a touch of the scorn with which he cries "What is glory but the blaze of fame," and the patience of his spirit seem to be suggested in this conversation in

[10] The line, "To purify the dialect of the tribe," is a reminiscence of Mallarmé's "Donner un sens plus pur aux mots de la tribu" (*Le Tombeau d'Edgar Allen Poe*). The contexts are so different that the reference does not illuminate the passage in *Little Gidding.* It appears to be a lovely line accidentally remembered for the precision of its definition of the poet's function.

I take it that the line, "When I left my body on a distant shore," is a periphrasis for dying, the distant shore being the *ulterior ripa* of Virgil.

the disfigured streets of London, and indeed Milton, whom Mr. Eliot once found so antipathetic as a poet and a man, is very much in mind throughout the poem. The reference is explicit in the next section where along with Strafford, Laud and Charles who died on the scaffold, the poet remembers "one who died blind and quiet"; [11] and though the words are not Milton's the repeated "all shall be well" cannot but remind us of the conclusion of Milton's last poem, the final chorus of *Samson*.

> All is best, though we oft doubt,
> What th' unsearchable dispose
> Of highest wisdom brings about
> And ever best found in the close.

After the grave melancholy of the second movement the third opens with a tone of confidence and in a rhythm that is almost gay. The beautiful imagery of the first movement is recalled in the metaphor of the hedgerow and the change in human beings from attachment to detachment is thus felt to be something natural occurring in the proper course of things. Between these two states "unflowering" is the detachment of the Stoics or of the Gnostic *illuminati,* the sterile apparent freedom from desire of those who have never felt love. These general reflections on the pattern of our individual lives yield to the thought of the pattern of history, where we can feel a unity between men who in a "warlike various and tragical age" found themselves opposed. At the turn of the movement and again at its close and at the close of the whole poem, which is also the close of the series, Mr. Eliot has set the mysterious words of Julian of Norwich.[12] Dame Julian, whom some think the greatest of the medieval English mystics, received sixteen "shewings" in the year 1373, which she wrote down and amplified and explained fifteen years later. Her revelations were of the Passion and of words spoken to her from the Cross. In her thirteenth revelation she was much troubled by the thought of the origin of sin in a world created by infinite Goodness, but the voice which spoke to her said: "Sin is behovable, but all shall be well, and all shall be well, and all manner of things shall be well," and in her fourteenth revelation concerning prayer she heard the words: "I am Ground of thy Beseeching." For fifteen years, as she tells us, she

[11] "Hee dy'd," wrote Milton's nephew, John Phillips, "in a fitt of the Gout, but with so little pain or Emotion, that the time of his expiring was not perceiv'd by those in the room. And though hee had bin long troubl'd with that disease, insomuch that his Knuckles were all callous, yet was hee not ever observ'd to be very impatient."

[12] There is an appropriateness in Mr. Eliot's use of Dame Julian for the medieval English mystics were much loved in the seventeenth century, particularly, of course, by those "who died forgotten in other places abroad," the exiled Romanists. Dame Julian was printed in a modernized edition in 1670 by Serenus de Cressy, once fellow of Merton and Chaplain to Falkland, later a Benedictine at Douai. Cressy appears in *John Inglesant* at a moving moment in the story to urge on Inglesant the claims of the monastic life.

pondered on the meaning of what she had heard and seen, and she was at last answered: "Wouldst thou learn thy Lord's meaning in this thing? Learn it well: Love was His meaning. Who shewed it thee? Love. What shewed He thee? Love. Wherefore shewed it He? For Love. Hold thee therein and thou shalt learn and know more in the same. But thou shalt never know or learn therein other thing without end."

This Love is the theme of the lyric movement. The fires which have flamed and glowed throughout the poem here break out and declare their nature. Man cannot help loving; his choice is between the fire of self-love and the fire of the love of God. The "dark disordered fire of our soul," as William Law wrote, "can as well be made the foundation of Heaven as it is of Hell. For when the fire and strength of the soul is sprinkled with the blood of the Lamb, then its fire becomes a fire of light, and its strength is changed into a strength of triumphing love, and will be fitted to have a place among those flames of love that wait about the throne of God." As *East Coker* has at this point a lyric on the eternal Passion, *Little Gidding* celebrates the eternal Pentecost, the perpetual descent of the Dove in tongues of fire.

The assurance and serenity of the final movement crown the whole sequence. The line dividing its two paragraphs, which comes from the second chapter of *The Cloud of Unknowing,* makes explicit the meaning of the "moment in the rose-garden," the bell heard beneath the waves, and the "communication of the dead." History is the field of the operation of the Spirit; it is a "pattern of timeless moments"; the historic moment, the moment of choice is always here. We are back again at the close in the garden of *Burnt Norton,* passing through the first gate into our first world, and the children are there in the appletree. Effort and exploration are forgotten in the sense of the given; living is the discovery of the already known, and beginning and end are one. All shall be well, when all is gathered in love, and the rose, the symbol of natural beauty and natural love, is one with the fire, the love by which all things are made. *Little Gidding* is a poem of fire, the fire which is torment to the self-loving, purgation to the penitent, and ecstasy to the blessed, and it closes with mortal and immortal life united in the resurrection symbol of the rose of heaven. "And I saw full surely," wrote Dame Julian at the close of her book, "that ere God made us He loved us; which love was never slacked, nor ever shall be. And in this love He hath done all His works; and in this love He hath made all things profitable to us; and in this love is our life everlasting. In our making we had beginning; but the love wherein He made us was in Him without beginning: in which love we have our beginning. And all this shall we see in God, without end."

PART III

CRITICAL METHODS AND PROBLEMS

INTRODUCTORY COMMENT

PART III is a pooling of inquiries into the problems of methodology and evaluation. In the main, these essays represent that part of modern criticism which has not applied itself to technical analysis or made this its major preoccupation. The evidence, as Cleanth Brooks points out in his Foreword, does not support the rather widespread assumption that modern critics are exclusively technical critics. The greater part of this criticism has concerned itself with theoretical study.

For instance, Kenneth Burke establishes a system of categories, poetic and dramatic techniques, in his "Lexicon Rhetoricae"; in "An Outline of Poetic Theory," Elder Olson constructs a poetics of the lyric; W. K. Wimsatt, Jr. and M. C. Beardsley expose a psychological fallacy in poetic appreciation; and René Wellek queries the problem of the poem in relation to poet and reader.

These essays examine or illustrate the critical problems and concepts which have been the dominant issues throughout the whole body of modern criticism. They are the recurrent themes of the essays in this book. For instance, the problem of the Place and Function of Meaning, which is summed up by Warren in Part I, is scrutinized here by Winters, Wellek, Burke, Richards, Empson, and Frank. Form in Art is analyzed here by Burke, Olson, and Frank; in Part II the analyses of formal structures provide illustrations of achieved form. The problem of Poetic Belief, posed by Richards and used critically by Schwartz, Gardner, and Blackmur here in Part III, is again discussed by James in Part IV. The problem of the Personal Element, noted by Hulme and Rickword in Part I, is here introduced by Eliot in his essay on Tradition. His idea of the Objective Correlative, which is criticized by Vivas, reappears in scattered instances throughout this selection. The problem of Intentions is treated by Eliot in Part I and by Wellek here in Part III. Etc.

PRELIMINARY PROBLEMS

(1943)

Yvor Winters

FIRST PROBLEM

Is it possible to say that Poem A (one of Donne's *Holy Sonnets,* or one of the poems of Jonson or of Shakespeare) is better than Poem B (Collins' *Ode to Evening*) or vice versa?

If not, is it possible to say that either of these is better than Poem C (*The Cremation of Sam Magee,* or something comparable)?

If the answer is no in both cases, then any poem is as good as any other. If this is true, then all poetry is worthless; but this obviously is not true, for it is contrary to all our experience.

If the answer is yes in both cases, then there follows the question of whether the answer implies merely that one poem is better than another for the speaker, or whether it means that one poem is intrinsically better than another. If the former, then we are impressionists, which is to say relativists; and are either mystics of the type of Emerson, or hedonists of the type of Stevens and Ransom. If the latter, then we assume that constant principles govern the poetic experience, and that the poem (as likewise the judge) must be judged in relationship to those principles. It is important, therefore, to discover the consequences of assuming each of these positions.

If our answer to the first question is no and to the second yes, then we are asserting that we can distinguish between those poems which are of the canon and those which are not, but that within the canon all judgment is impossible. This view, if adopted, will require serious elucidation, for on the face of it, it appears inexplicable. On the other hand, one cannot deny that within the canon judgment will become more difficult, for the nearer two poems may be to the highest degrees of excellence, the harder it will be to choose between them. Two poems, in fact, might be so excellent that there would be small profit in endeavoring to say that one was better, but one could arrive at this conclusion only after a careful examination of both.

SECOND PROBLEM

If we accept the view that one poem can be regarded as better than another, the question then arises whether this judgment is a matter of inexplicable intuition, or whether it is a question of intuition that can be explained, and consequently guided and improved by rational elucidation.

If we accept the view that the judgment in question is inexplicable, then we are again forced to confess ourselves impressionists and relativists, unless we can show that the intuitions of all men agree at all times, or that the intuitions of one man are invariably right and those of all others wrong whenever they differ. We obviously can demonstrate neither of these propositions.

If we start, then, with the proposition that one poem may be intrinsically superior to another, we are forced to account for differences of opinion regarding it. If two critics differ, it is possible that one is right and the other wrong, more likely that both are partly right and partly wrong, but in different respects: neither the native gifts nor the education of any man have ever been wholly adequate to many of the critical problems he will encounter, and no two men are ever the same in these respects or in any others. On the other hand, although the critic should display reasonable humility and caution, it is only fair to add that few men possess either the talent or the education to justify their being taken very seriously, even those who are nominally professional students of these matters.

But if it is possible by rational elucidation to give a more or less clear account of what one finds in a poem and why one approves or disapproves, then communication between two critics, though no doubt imperfect, becomes possible, and it becomes possible that they may in some measure correct each other's errors and so come more near to a true judgment of the poem.

THIRD PROBLEM

If rational communication about poetry is to take place, it is necessary first to determine what we mean by a poem.

A poem is first of all a statement in words.

But it differs from all such statements of a purely philosophical or theoretical nature, in that it has by intention a controlled content of feeling. In this respect, it does not differ from many works written in prose, however.

A poem differs from a work written in prose by virtue of its being composed in verse. The rhythm of verse permits the expression of more powerful feeling than is possible in prose when such feeling is needed, and it permits at all times the expression of finer shades of feeling.

A poem, then, is a statement in words in which special pains are taken with the expression of feeling. This description is merely intended to distinguish the poem from other kinds of writing; it is not offered as a complete description

FOURTH PROBLEM

What, however, are words?

They are audible sounds, or their visual symbols, invented by man to communicate his thoughts and feelings. Each word has a conceptual content, however slight; each word, exclusive, perhaps, of the particles, communicates vague associations of feeling.

The word *fire* communicates a concept; it also connotes very vaguely certain feelings, depending on the context in which we happen to place it—depending, for example, on whether we happen to think of a fire on a hearth, in a furnace, or in a forest. These feelings may be rendered more and more precise as we render the context more and more precise; as we come more and more near to completing and perfecting our poem.

FIFTH PROBLEM

But if the poem, as compared to prose, pays especial attention to feeling, are we to assume that the rational content of the poem is unimportant to its success?

The rational content cannot be eliminated from words; consequently the rational content cannot be eliminated from poetry. It is there. If it is unsatisfactory in itself, a part of the poem is unsatisfactory; the poem is thus damaged beyond argument. If we deny this, we must surely explain ourselves very fully.

If we admit this, we are faced with another problem: is it conceivable that rational-content and feeling-content may both be perfect, and yet that they may be unrelated to each other, or imperfectly related? To me this is inconceivable, because the emotional content of words is generated by our experience with the conceptual content, so that a relationship is necessary.

This fact of the necessity of such relationship may fairly return us for a moment to the original question: whether imperfection of rational content damages the entire poem. If there is a necessary relationship between concept and feeling, and concept is unsatisfactory, then feeling must be damaged by way of the relationship.

SIXTH PROBLEM

If there is a relationship between concept and feeling, what is the nature of that relationship?

To answer this, let us return to the basic unit, the word. The concept represented by the word motivates the feeling which the word communicates. It is the concept of fire which generates the feelings communicated by the word, though the sound of the word may modify these feelings very subtly, as may other accidental qualities, especially if the word be used skillfully in a given context. The accidental qualities of a word, however, such as its literary history, for example, can only modify, cannot essentially change, for these will be governed ultimately by the concept; that is, *fire* will seldom be used to signify *plum-blossom,* and so will have few opportunities to gather connotations from the concept, *plum-blossom.* The relationship, in the poem, between rational statement and feeling, is thus seen to be that of motive to emotion.

SEVENTH PROBLEM

But has not this reasoning brought us back to the proposition that all poems are equally good? For if each word motivates its own feeling, because of its intrinsic nature, will not any rational statement, since it is composed of words, motivate the feeling exactly proper to it?

This is not true, for a good many reasons, of which I shall enumerate only a few of the more obvious. In making a rational statement, in purely theoretical prose, we find that our statement may be loose or exact, depending upon the relationships of the words to each other. The precision of a word depends to some extent upon its surroundings. This is true likewise with respect to the connotations of words. Two words, each of which has several usably close rational synonyms, may reinforce and clarify each other with respect to their connotations or they may not do so.

Let me illustrate with a simple example from Browning's *Serenade at the Villa:*

> So wore night; the East was gray,
> White the broad-faced hemlock flowers.

The lines are marred by a crowding of long syllables and difficult consonants, but they have great beauty in spite of the fault. What I wish to point out, for the sake of my argument, is the relationship between the words *wore* and *gray.* The verb *wore* means literally that the night passed, but it carries with it connotations of exhaustion and attrition which belong to the condition of the protagonist; and grayness is a color which we associate with such a condition. If we change the phrase to read: "Thus night passed," we shall have the same rational meaning, and a meter quite as respectable, but no trace of the power of the line: the connotation of *wore* will be lost, and the connotation of *gray* will remain merely in a state of ineffective potentiality. The protagonist in seeing his feeling mirrored in the landscape is not guilty of motivating his feeling falsely, for we know his general motive from the poem as a whole; he is expressing a portion of the feeling motivated by the total situation through a more or less common psychological phenomenon. If the poem were such, however, that we did not know why the night *wore* instead of *passed,* we should have just cause for complaint; in fact, most of the strength of the word would probably be lost. The second line contains other fine effects, immediately with reference to the first line, ultimately with reference to the theme; I leave the reader to analyze them for himself, but he will scarcely succeed without the whole poem before him.[1]

Concepts, as represented by particular words, are affected by connotations due to various and curious accidents. A word may gather connotations from its use in folk-poetry, in formal poetry, in vulgar speech, or in technical prose: a single concept might easily be represented by four words with these distinct histories; and any one of the words might prove to be proper in a given poetic context. Words gain connotation from etymological accidents. Something of this may be seen in the English word *outrage,* in which is commonly felt, in all likelihood, something associated with *rage,* although there is no rage whatever in the original word. Similarly the word *urchin,* in modern English, seldom connotes anything related to hedgehogs, or to the familiars of the witches, by whose intervention the word arrived at its modern meaning and feeling. Yet the connotation proper to any stage in the history of such a word might be resuscitated, or a blend of connotations effected, by skillful use. Further, the connotation of a word may be modified very strongly by its function in the metrical structure. . . .

This is enough to show that exact motivation of feeling by concept is not inherent in any rational statement. Any rational statement will govern the general possibilities of feeling derivable from it, but the task of the poet is to adjust feeling to motive precisely. He has to select words containing not only the right relationships within themselves, but the right relationships to each other. The task is very difficult; and this is, no doubt, the reason why the great poetry of a great poet is likely to be very small in bulk.

EIGHTH PROBLEM

Is it not possible, however, to escape from this relationship of motive to emotion by confining ourselves very largely to those words which denote emotion: love, envy, anger, and the like?

This is not possible; for these words, like others, represent concepts. If we should confine ourselves strictly to such a vocabulary, we should merely write didactic poetry: poetry about love in general, or about anger in general. The emotion communicated would result from our apprehension of the ideas in question. Such poetry is perfectly legitimate, but it is only one kind of poetry, and it is scarcely the kind which the Romantic theorist is endeavoring to define.

[1] For criticism of this paraphrase by Winters see Cleanth Brooks's *The Well Wrought Urn* (1947), pp. 183-184.

Such poetry has frequently been rendered particular by the use of allegory. The playful allegorizing of minor amoristic themes which one encounters in the Renaissance and which is possibly descended from certain neo-Platonic elements in medieval poetry may serve as illustration. Let us consider these and the subsequent lines by Thomas Lodge:

> Love in my bosom like a bee
> Doth suck his sweet;
> Now with his wings he plays with me,
> Now with his feet.

Love itself is a very general idea and might include many kinds of experience; the idea is limited by this allegory to the sentimental and sensual, but we still have an idea, the subdivision of the original idea, and the feeling must be appropriate to the concept. The concept is rendered concrete by the image of Cupid, whose actions, in turn, are rendered visible by comparison to the bee: it is these actions which make the poem a kind of anticipatory meditation on more or less sensual love, a meditation which by its mere tone of expression keeps the subject in its proper place as a very minor one. Sometimes the emphasis is on the mere description of the bee, sometimes on the description of Cupid, sometimes on the lover's feelings; but the feeling motivated in any passage is governed by this emphasis. The elements, once they are united in the poem, are never really separated, of course. In so far as the poet departs from his substantial theme in the direction of mere bees and flowers, he will achieve what Ransom calls irrelevance; but if there is much of this the poem will be weakened. Whether he so departs or not, the relation of motive to emotion must remain the same, within each passage. (I have discussed this problem in my essay on Ransom.)

A common romantic practice is to use words denoting emotions, but to use them loosely and violently, as if the very carelessness expressed emotion. Another is to make a general statement, but seem to refer it to a particular occasion, which, however, is never indicated: the poet thus seems to avoid the didactic, yet he is not forced to understand the particular motive. Both these faults may be seen in these lines from Shelley:

> Out of the day and night
> A joy has taken flight;
> Fresh spring, and summer, and winter hoar,
> Move my faint heart with grief, but with delight
> No more—oh, never more.

The poet's intention is so vague, however, that he achieves nothing but stereotypes of a very crude kind.

The Romantics often tried other devices. For example, it would be possible to write a poem on fear in general, but to avoid in some measure the effect of the purely didactic by illustrating the emotion along the way with various experiences which might motivate fear. There is a danger here, though it is merely a danger, that the general idea may not dominate the poem, and that the poem may thus fall apart into a group of poems on particular experiences. There is the alternative danger, that the particular quality of the experiences may be so subordinated to the illustrative function of the experiences, that within each illustration there is merely a stereotyped and not a real relationship of motive to feeling: this occurs in Collins' *Ode to Fear,* though a few lines in the Epode come surprisingly to life. But the methods which I have just described really offer no semblance of an escape from the theory of motivation which I am defending.

Another Romantic device, if it is conscious enough to be called a device, is to offer instead of a defensible motive a false one, usually culled from landscape. This kind of writing represents a tacit admission of the principle of motivation which I am defending, but a bad application of the principle. It results in the kind of writing which I have called pseudo-reference in my volume, *Primitivism and Decadence.* One cannot believe, for example, that Wordsworth's passions were charmed away by a look at the daffodils, or that Shelley's were aroused by the sight of the leaves blown about in the autumn wind. A motive is offered, and the poet wants us to accept it, but we recognize it as inadequate. In such a poem there may be fragments of good description, which motivate a feeling more or less purely appropriate to the objects described, and these fragments may sustain our liking for the poem: this happens in Collins' *Ode to Evening;* but one will find also an account of some kind of emotion essentially irrelevant to the objects described, along with the attempt, more or less explicit, to deduce the emotion from the object.

There remains the method of the Post-Romantics, whether French Symbolists or American Experimentalists: the method of trying to extinguish the rational content of language while retaining the content of association. (This method I have discussed in *Primitivism and Decadence.*)

NINTH PROBLEM

The relationship in the poem of rational meaning to feeling we have seen to be that of motive to emotion; and we have seen that this must be a satisfactory relationship. How do we determine whether such a relationship is satisfactory? We determine it by an act of moral judgment. The question then arises whether moral judgments can be made, whether the concept of morality is or is not an illusion.

If morality can be considered real, if a theory of morality can be said to derive from reality, it is because it guides us toward the greatest happiness which the accidents of life permit: that is, toward the fullest realization of our nature, in the Aristotelian or Thomistic sense. But is there such a thing, abstractly considered, as full realization of our nature?

To avoid discussion of too great length, let us consider the opposite question: is there such a thing as obviously unfulfilled human nature? Obviously there is. We need only turn to the feeble-minded, who cannot think and so cannot perceive or feel with any clarity; or to the insane, who sometimes perceive and feel with great intensity, but whose feelings and perceptions are so improperly motivated that they are classed as illusions. At slightly higher levels, the criminal, the dissolute, the unscrupulously selfish, and various types of neurotics are likely to arouse but little disagreement as examples.

Now if we are able to recognize the fact of insanity—if in fact we are forced to recognize it—that is, the fact of the obvious maladjustment of feeling to motive, we are forced to admit the possibility of more accurate adjustment, and, by necessary sequence, of absolutely accurate adjustment, even though we admit the likelihood that most people will attain to a final adjustment but very seldom indeed. We can guide ourselves toward such an adjustment in life, as in art, by means of theory and the critical examination of special instances; but the final act of judgment is in both life and art a unique act—it is a relationship between two elements, the rational understanding and the feeling, of which only one is classificatory and of which the other has infinite possibilities of variation.

TENTH PROBLEM

If the final act of adjustment is a unique act of judgment, can we say that it is more or less right, provided it is demonstrably within the general limits prescribed by the theory of morality which has led to it? The answer to this question is implicit in what has preceded; in fact the answer resembles exactly that reached at the end of the first problem examined. We can say that it is more or less nearly right. If extreme deviation from right judgment is obvious, then there is such a thing as right judgment. The mere fact that life may be conducted in a fairly satisfactory manner, by means of inaccurate judgment within certain limits, and that few people ever bother to refine their judgment beyond the stage which enables them to remain largely within those limits, does not mean that accurate judgment has no reality. Implicit in all that has preceded is the concept that in any moral situation, there is a right judgment as an ultimate possibility; that the human judge, or actor, will approximate it more or less nearly; that the closeness of his approximation will depend upon the accuracy of his rational understanding and of his intuition, and upon the accuracy of their interaction upon each other.

ELEVENTH PROBLEM

Nothing has thus far been said about human action, yet morality is supposed to guide human action. And if art is moral, there should be a relationship between art and human action.

The moral judgment, whether good, bad, or indifferent, is commonly the prelude and instigation to action. Hastily or carefully, intelligently or otherwise, one arrives at some kind of general idea of a situation calling for action, and one's idea motivates one's feeling: the act results. The part played by will, or the lack of it, between judgment and act, the possibility that action may be frustrated by some constitutional or habitual weakness or tendency, such as cowardice or a tendency to anger, in a person of a fine speculative or poetic judgment, are subjects for a treatise on ethics or psychology; a treatise on poetry stops with the consideration of the speculative judgment, which reaches its best form and expression in poetry. In the situations of daily life, one does not, as a rule, write a poem before acting: one makes a more rapid and simple judgment. But if the poem does not individually lead to a particular act, it does not prevent action. It gives us a better way of judging representative acts than we should otherwise have. It is thus a civilizing influence: it trains our power of judgment, and should, I imagine, affect the quality of daily judgments and actions.

TWELFTH PROBLEM

What, then, is the nature of the critical process?

It will consist (1) of the statement of such historical or biographical knowledge as may be necessary in order to understand the mind and method of the writer; (2) of such analysis of his literary theories as we may need to understand and evaluate what he is doing; (3) of a rational critique of the paraphraseable content (roughly, the motive) of the poem; (4) of a rational critique of the feeling motivated—that is, of the details of style, as seen in language and technique; and (5) of the final act of judgment, a unique act, the general nature of which can be indicated, but which cannot be communicated precisely, since it consists in receiving from the poet his own final and unique judgment of his matter and in judging that judgment. It should be noted that the purpose of the first four processes is to limit as narrowly as possible the region in which the final unique act is to occur.

In the actual writing of criticism, a given task may not require all of these processes, or may not require that all be given equal emphasis; or it may be that in connection with a certain writer, whether because of the nature of the writer or because of the way in which other critics have treated him previously, one or two of these processes must be given so much emphasis that others must be neglected for lack of space. These are practical matters to be settled as the occasions arise.

THE MODE OF EXISTENCE OF A LITERARY WORK OF ART

(1942)

René Wellek

THIS ABSTRUSE-SOUNDING TITLE [1] is the best name I can think of for a problem which is, in all sorts of disguises, widely discussed and of far-reaching importance both for critical theory and practice. What is meant by saying that a certain person does not understand the real poem? What is the real poem, where should we look for it, how does it exist? A correct answer to these questions must solve several critical problems and open a way to the proper analysis of a work of art. It, at least, will dispose of many pseudo-problems. We shall not, of course, find an answer to the question whether a given poem is good or bad, but we might find an answer which would tell us where to look for the genuine poem and how to avoid the pitfalls into which criticism has frequently fallen because of a lack of clarity on some of these fundamental semi-philosophical questions.

To the question what and where is a poem, or rather a literary work of art in general, several traditional answers have been given which must be criticized and eliminated before we can attempt an answer of our own. One of the most common and oldest answers is the view that a poem is an artifact, an object of the same nature as a piece of sculpture or a painting. Thus the work of art is considered identical with the black lines of ink on white paper or parchment or, if we think of a Babylonian poem, with the grooves in the brick. Obviously this answer is quite unsatisfactory. There is, first of all, the huge oral "literature" (a question-begging term in its etymology). There are poems or stories which have never been fixed in writing and still continue to exist. Thus the lines in black ink are merely a method of recording a poem which must be conceived as existing elsewhere. If we destroy the writing or even all copies of a printed book we still may not destroy the poem, as it might be preserved in oral tradition or in the memory of a man like Macaulay who boasted of knowing

[1] Part of this paper is an elaboration of a passage in my "Theory of Literary History" (in the *Travaux du Cercle Linguistique de Prague* VI, 1936, 173-191). There detailed acknowledgements are made to the linguistic theories of the Prague Linguistic Circle as well as to the logical theories of Edmund Husserl and his Polish pupil Roman Ingarden.

Paradise Lost and *Pilgrim's Progress* by heart. On the other hand, if we destroy a painting or a piece of sculpture or a building, we destroy it completely, though we may preserve descriptions or records in another medium and might even try to reconstruct what has been lost. But we shall always create a different work of art (however similar), while the mere destruction of the copy of a book or even of all its copies may not touch the work of art at all. That the writing on the paper is not the "real" poem can be demonstrated also by another argument. The printed page contains a great many elements which are extraneous to the poem: the size of the type, the sort of type used (roman, italic), the size of the page and many other factors. If we should take seriously the view that a poem is an artifact, we would have to come to the conclusion that every single copy is a different work of art. There would be no *a priori* reason why copies in different editions should be copies of the same book. Besides, not every printing is considered by us, the readers, a correct printing of a poem. The very fact that we are able to correct printer's errors in a text which we might not have read before or, in some rare cases, restore the genuine meaning of the text shows that we do not consider the printed lines as the genuine poem. In accepting, for instance, Theobald's emendation in the Hostess's story of Falstaff's death from "a table of green fields" to "a babbled of green fields" we do not give rein to our imagination nor do we correct and criticize the author as we should if we would change the color of a painting or chip off a piece of marble from a statue. We know that we have restored the genuine poem and that we have corrected a way of recording. Thus we have shown that the poem (or any literary work of art) can exist outside its printed version and that the printed artifact contains many elements which we all must consider as not included in the genuine poem.

Still, this negative conclusion should not blind us to the enormous practical importance, since the invention of writing and printing, of our methods of recording poetry. There is no doubt that much literature has been lost and thus completely destroyed because its written records have disappeared and the theoretically possible means of oral tradition have failed or have been interrupted. Writing and especially printing have made possible the continuity of literary tradition and must have done much to increase the unity and integrity of works of art. Besides, at least in certain periods of the history of poetry, the graphic picture has become a part of some finished works of art. I am thinking of such poems as the *Altar* or the *Church-floor* of George Herbert or of similar poems of the metaphysicals which can be paralleled on the Continent in Spanish Gongorism, Italian Marinism, in German Baroque poetry and elsewhere. Also modern poetry in America (E. E. Cummings), in Germany (Arno Holz), in France (Apollinaire) and elsewhere, has used graphic devices like unusual line arrangements or even beginnings at the bottom of the page, different colors of printing, etc. In the novel *Tristram Shandy,* Sterne used, as far back as the eighteenth century, blank and marbled pages. All such devices are integral parts of these particular works of art. Though we know that a majority of poetry is independent of them, they cannot and should not be ignored in those cases. Besides, the role of print in poetry is by no means confined to such comparatively rare extravaganzas; the line-ends of verses, the grouping into stanzas, the paragraphs of prose passages, eye-rhymes or puns which are comprehensible only through spelling and many similar devices must be considered integral factors of literary works of art. A purely oral theory tends to exclude all considerations of such devices, but they cannot be ignored in any complete analysis of many works of literary art. Their existence merely proves that print has become very important for the practice of poetry in modern times, that poetry is written for the eye as well as for the ear. Though the use of graphic devices is not indispensable, they are far more frequent in literature than in music, where the printed score is in a position similar to the printed page in poetry. In music such uses are rare, though by no means non-existent. There are many curious optical devices (colors, etc.) in Italian madrigal scores of the sixteenth century. The supposedly "pure" composer Handel wrote a chorus speaking of the Red Sea flood where the "water stood like a wall" and the notes on the printed page of music form firm rows of evenly spaced dots suggesting a phalanx or wall.

We have started with a theory which probably has not many serious adherents today. The second answer to our original question puts the essence of a literary work of art into the sequence of sounds uttered by a speaker or reader of poetry. This is a widely accepted solution favored especially by reciters. But the answer is equally unsatisfactory. Every reading aloud or reciting of a poem is merely a performance of a poem and not the poem itself. It is on exactly the same level as the performance of a piece of music by a musician. There is—to follow the line of our previous argument—a huge written literature which may never be sounded at all. To deny this, we have to subscribe to some such absurd theory as that of some behaviorists that all silent reading is accompanied by movements of the vocal cords. Actually, all experience shows that unless we are almost illiterate or are struggling with the reading of a foreign language or want to articulate the sound whisperingly on purpose we usually read "globally," that is, we grasp printed words as wholes without breaking them up into sequences of phonemes and thus do not pronounce them even silently. In reading quickly we have no time even to articulate the sounds with our vocal cords. To assume besides that a poem exists in the reading aloud leads to the absurd consequence that a poem is nonexistent when it is not sounded and that it is re-created afresh by every reading. Moreover, we could not show how a work like Homer's *Iliad,* or Tolstoy's *War and Peace,* exists as a unity as it can never be read aloud all in one sitting. But most importantly, every reading of a poem is more than the genuine poem: each performance contains elements which are extraneous to the poem and individual idiosyncrasies of pronunciation, pitch, tempo and distribution of stress—elements which are either determined by the personality of the speaker or are symptoms and means of his interpretation of the poem. Moreover, the reading of a poem not only adds individual elements but it always represents only a selection of factors implicit in the text of a poem: the pitch of the voice, the speed in which a passage is read, the distribution and intensity of the stresses, these may be either right or wrong, and even when right may still represent only one version of reading a poem. We must acknowledge the possibility of several readings of a poem: readings which we either consider wrong readings as we feel them as distortions of the true meaning of the poem or readings which we have to consider as correct and admissible, but still may not consider ideal. The reading of the poem is not the poem itself, as we can correct the performance mentally. Even if we hear a recitation which we acknowledge to be excellent or perfect we cannot preclude the possibility that somebody else, or even the same reciter at another time, may give a very different rendering which would bring out other elements of the poem equally well. The analogy to a musical performance is again helpful: the performance of a symphony even by Toscanini is not the symphony itself, as it is inevitably colored by the individuality of the performers and adds concrete details of tempo, rubato, timbre, etc. which may be changed in a next performance, though it would be impossible to deny that the same symphony has been performed for the second time. Thus we have shown that the poem can exist outside its sounded performance, and that the sounded performance contains many elements which we must consider as not included in the poem.

Still, in some literary works of art (especially in lyrical poetry) the vocal side of poetry may be an important factor of the general structure. Attention can be drawn to it by various means like meter, patterns of vowel or consonant sequences, alliteration, assonance, rhyme, etc. This fact explains—or rather helps to explain—the inadequacy of much translating of lyrical poetry, since these potential sound-patterns cannot be transferred into another linguistic system, though a skilful translator may approximate their general effect in his own language. There is, however, an enormous literature which is relatively independent of sound-patterns, as can be shown by the historical effects of many works in even pedestrian translations. But the importance of sound-patterns, in lyrical poetry, has also been frequently overrated for several reasons. One is the fact that most critics in speaking about the sound of poetry actually refer to effects induced by meaning. Apart from the associations aroused by the meaning most sound-structures are, purely as sound, indifferent. Mr. John Crowe Ransom has demonstrated amusingly how much the sound effect of Tennyson's verse depends on the meaning by suggesting a change from "the murmuring of innumerable bees" to "the murdering of innumerable beeves" which, though only slightly different as sound-pattern, completely alters the effect of the sound. Mr. I. A. Richards has made a similar experiment by taking a stanza from Milton's *Ode on Christ's Nativity* and rewriting it into nonsense words while keeping the meter and the vowel patterns as closely as possible. The poetic sound-effect has altogether disappeared. Another argument frequently quoted in support of the paramount importance of sound is the fact that we enjoy the sound of poetry read aloud in a foreign language, though we do not understand its meaning. Actually, in hearing foreign poetry recited we do not hear merely a sound-pattern, but the inflections of the voice, the changes of intonation; the gestures and physiognomy of the speaker convey much information on meaning. All this does not deny that sound may be an important factor in the structure of a poem, but the answer that a poem is a sequence of sounds is as unsatisfactory as the solution which puts faith in the print on the page.

The third, very common answer to our question says that a poem is the experience of the reader. A poem, it is argued, is nothing outside the mental processes of individual readers and is thus identical with the mental state or process which we experience in reading or listening to a poem. Again this "psychological" solution seems unsatisfactory. It is true, of course, that a poem can be known only through individual experiences, but it is not identical with such an individual experience. Every individual experience of a poem contains something idiosyncratic and purely individual. It is colored by our mood and our individual preparation. The education, the personality of every reader, the general cultural climate of a time, the religious or philosophical or purely technical preconceptions of every reader will add something instantaneous and extraneous to every reading of a poem. Two readings at different times by the same individual may vary considerably either because he has matured mentally or is weakened in his alertness by momentary circumstances such as fatigue, worry, or distraction. Every experience of a poem thus both leaves out something or adds something individual. The experience will never be commensurate with the poem: even a good reader will discover new details in poems which he had not experienced during previous readings and it is needless to point out how distorted or shallow may be the reading of a less trained or untrained reader. The view that the mental experience of a reader is the poem itself leads to the absurd conclusion that a poem is nonexistent unless experienced and that it is re-created in every experience. There thus would not be one *Divine Comedy,* but as many Divine Comedies as there are and were and will be readers. We end in complete scepticism and anarchy and arrive at the vicious maxim of *De gustibus non est disputandum*. If we should take this view seriously it would be impossible to explain why one experience of a poem by one reader should be better than the experience of any other reader and why it is possible to correct the interpretation of another reader. It would mean the definite end of all teaching of literature which aims at enhancing the understanding and appreciation of a text. The writings of Mr. I. A. Richards, especially his book on *Practical Criticism*, have shown how much can be done in analyzing the individual idiosyncrasies of readers and how much a good teacher can achieve in rectifying false approaches. Curiously enough, Mr. Richards, who constantly criticizes the experiences of his pupils, holds to an extreme psychological theory which is in flat contradiction to his excellent critical practice. The idea that poetry is supposed to order our impulses and the conclusion that the value of poetry is in some sort of psychical therapy leads him finally to the admission that this goal may be accomplished by a bad as well as a good poem, by a carpet as well as by a sonata. Thus the supposed pattern in our mind is not definitely related to the poem which caused it. The psychology of the reader, however interesting in itself or useful for pedagogical purposes, will always remain outside the object of literary study—the concrete work of art—and is unable to deal with the question of the structure and value of the work of art. Psychological theories must be theories of effect and may lead in extreme cases to such criteria of the value of poetry as that proposed by A. E. Housman in a lecture, *Name and Nature of Poetry* (1933), where he tells us (one hopes with his tongue in his cheek) that good poetry can be recognized by the thrill down our spine. This is on the same level as eighteenth-century theories which measured the quality of a tragedy by the amount of tears shed by the audience or the movie scout's conception of the quality of a comedy on the basis of the number of laughs he has counted in the audience. Thus anarchy, scepticism, a complete confusion of values, is the result of every psychological theory, as it must be unrelated either to the structure or the quality of a poem.

The psychological theory is only very slightly improved by Mr. I. A. Richards when he defines a poem as the "experience of the right kind of reader." Obviously the whole problem is shifted to the conception of the *right* reader—and the meaning of that adjective. But even assuming an ideal condition of mood in a reader of the finest background and the best training, the definition remains unsatisfactory as it is open to all criticism we have made of the psychological method. It puts the essence of the poem into a momentary experience which even the right kind of reader could not repeat unchanged. It will always fall short of the full meaning of a poem at any given instance and will always add the inevitable personal elements to the reading.

A fourth answer has been suggested to obviate this difficulty. The poem, we hear, is the experience of the author. Only in parenthesis, we may dismiss the view that the poem is the experience of the author at any time of his life after the creation of his work, when he rereads it. He then has obviously become simply a reader of his work and is liable to errors and misinterpretations of his own work almost as much as any other reader. Many instances of glaring misinterpretations by an author of his own work could be collected: the old anecdote about Browning professing not to understand his own poem has probably its element of truth. It happens to all of us that we misinterpret or do not fully understand what we have written some time ago. Thus the suggested answer must refer to the experience of the author during the time of creation. By experience of the author we might mean, however, two different things: the conscious experience, the intentions which the author wanted to embody in his work, or the total conscious and unconscious experience during the prolonged time of creation. The view that the genuine poem is to be found in the intentions of an author is widespread even though it is not always explicitly stated. It justifies much historical research and is at the bottom of many arguments in favor of specific interpretations. However, for most works of art we have no evidence to reconstruct the intentions of the author except the finished work itself. Even if we are in possession of contemporary evidence in the form of an explicit profession of intentions, such a profession need not be binding on a modern observer. "Intentions" of the author are always *a posteriori* rationalizations, commentaries which certainly must be taken into account but also must be criticized in the light of the finished work of art. The "intentions" of an author may go far beyond the finished work of art: they may be merely pronouncements of plans and ideals, while the performance may be either far below or far aside the mark. If we could have interviewed Shakespeare he probably would have expressed his intentions in writing *Hamlet* in a way which we should find most unsatisfactory. We would still quite rightly insist on finding meanings in *Hamlet* (and not merely inventing them) which were probably far from clearly formulated in Shakespeare's conscious mind.

Artists may be strongly influenced by a contemporary critical situation and by contemporary critical formulae while giving expression to their intentions, but the critical formulae themselves might be quite inadequate to characterize their actual artistic achievement. The baroque age is an obvious case in point, where a surprisingly new artistic practice found little expression either in the pronouncements of the artists or the comments of the critics. A sculptor such as Bernini could lecture to the Paris Academy expounding the view that his own practice was in strict conformity to that of the ancients, and Daniel

Adam Pöppelmann, the architect of that highly rococo building in Dresden called the Zwinger, wrote a whole pamphlet in order to demonstrate the strict agreement of his creation with the purest principles of Vitruvius. The metaphysical poets had only a few quite inadequate critical formulae (like "strong lines") which scarcely touch the actual novelty of their practice; and medieval artists frequently had purely religious or didactic "intentions" which do not even begin to give expression to the artistic principles of their practice. Divergence between conscious intention and actual performance is a common phenomenon in the history of literature. Zola sincerely believed in his scientific theory of the experimental novel, but actually produced highly melodramatic and symbolic novels. It is simply impossible to rely on the study of the intentions of an author, as they might not even represent a reliable commentary on his work, and at their best are not more than such a commentary.[2]

But also the alternative suggestion: that the genuine poem is in the total experience, conscious and unconscious, during the time of the creation, is very unsatisfactory. In practice this conclusion has the serious disadvantage of putting the problem into a completely inaccessible and purely hypothetical *x* which we have no means of reconstructing or even of exploring. Beyond this insurmountable practical difficulty, the solution is also unsatisfactory because it puts the existence of the poem into a subjective experience which already is a thing of the past. The experiences of the author during creation ceased precisely when the poem had begun to exist. If this conception were right, we should never be able to come into direct contact with the work of art itself, but have constantly to make the assumption that our experiences in reading the poem are in some way identical with the long past experiences of the author. Mr. E. M. Tillyard in his book on *Milton* has tried to use the idea that *Paradise Lost* is about the state of the author when he wrote it, and could not, in a long and frequently irrelevant exchange of arguments with C. S. Lewis, acknowledge that *Paradise Lost* is, first of all, about Satan and Adam and Eve and hundreds and thousands of different ideas, representations and concepts, rather than about Milton's state of mind during creation. That the whole content of a poem was once in contact with the conscious and subconscious mind of Milton is perfectly true, but this state of mind is inaccessible and might have been filled, in those particular moments, with millions of experiences of which we cannot find a trace in the poem itself. Taken literally, this whole solution

[2] There can be no objections against the study of "intention," if we mean by it merely a study of the integral work of art which would not ignore some elements and would be directed to the total meaning. But this use of the term "intention" is different and somewhat misleading. [*Author's note.*] See "The Intentional Fallacy," by W. K. Wimsatt, Jr. and M. C. Beardsley: *Sewanee Review,* 54 (Summer, 1946), 458-488. And "A Note on Intentions" by R. W. Stallman: *College English,* 10 (October, 1948), 40-41. [*Editor's note.*]

must lead to absurd speculations about the exact duration of the state of mind of the creator and its exact content which might include a toothache at the moment of creation.[3] The whole psychological approach through states of mind whether of the reader or the listener or the speaker or the author raises more problems than it can possibly solve.

A better way is obviously in the direction of defining the work of art in terms of social and collective experience. There are two possibilities of solution which, however, still fall short of solving our problem satisfactorily. We may say that the work of art is the sum of all past and possible experiences of the poem: a solution which leaves us with an infinity of irrelevant individual experiences, bad and false readings, perversions, etc. In short, it merely gives us the answer that the poem is in the state of mind of its reader, multiplied by infinity. The other answer I have seen suggested solves the question by stating that the genuine poem is the experience common to all the experiences of the poem. But this answer would obviously reduce the work of art to the common denominator of all these experiences. This denominator must be the *lowest* common denominator, the most shallow, most superficial and trivial experience. This solution, besides its practical difficulties, would completely impoverish the total meaning of a work of art.

II

An answer to our question in terms of individual or social psychology cannot, I am convinced, be found. A poem, we have to conclude, is not an individual experience or a sum of experiences, but only a potential cause of experiences. Definition in terms of states of mind fails because it cannot account for the normative character of the genuine poem, for the simple fact that it might be experienced correctly or incorrectly. In every individual experience only a small part can be considered as adequate to the true poem. Thus, the real poem must be conceived as a system of norms, realized only partially in the actual experience of its many readers. Every single experience (reading, reciting, and so forth) is only an attempt—more or less successful and complete—to grasp this set of norms or standards.

The term "norms" as used here should not, of course, be confused with norms which are either classical or romantic, ethical or political. The norms we have in mind are implicit norms which have to be extracted from every individual experience of a work of art and together make up the genuine work of art as a whole. It is true, that if we compare works of art among themselves, similarities or differences

[3] M. Pierre Audiat, who, in his well-known *Biographie de l'oeuvre littéraire* (1925), has argued that the work of art "represents a period in the life of the writer," actually becomes involved in such impossible and quite unnecessary dilemmas. [*Author's note.*]

between these norms will be ascertained, and from the similarities themselves it ought to be possible to proceed to a classification of works of art according to the type of norms they embody. We may finally arrive at theories of genres and ultimately at theories of literature in general. To deny this as it has been denied by those who, with some justification, stress the uniqueness of every work of art, seems to push the conception of individuality so far that every work of art would become completely isolated from tradition and thus finally both incommunicable and incomprehensible. Assuming that we have to start with the analysis of an individual work of art, we still can scarcely deny that there must be some links, some similarities, some common elements or factors which would approximate two or more given works of art and thus would open the door to a transition from the analysis of one individual work of art to a type such as Greek tragedy and hence to tragedy in general, to literature in general, and finally to some all-inclusive structure common to all arts.

But this is a further problem. We, however, have still to decide where and how these norms exist. A closer analysis of a work of art will show that it is best to think of it as not merely one system of norms, but rather a system which is made up of several strata, each implying its own subordinate group. There is a system of norms implied in the sound-structure of a literary work of art and this, in turn, implies units of meaning based on the sentence patterns, and these units in their turn construct a world of objects to which the meaning refers. It is useful to illustrate this conception by the parallel which can be drawn from linguistics. Linguists such as the Geneva school and the Prague Linguistic Circle carefully distinguish between *langue* and *parole,* the system of language and the individual speech-act; and this distinction corresponds to that between the individual experience of the poem and the poem as such. The system of language is a collection of conventions and norms whose workings and relations we can observe and describe as having a fundamental coherence and identity in spite of the very different, imperfect or incomplete pronouncements of individual speakers. In this respect at least, a literary work of art is in exactly the same position as a system of language. We as individuals shall never realize it completely as we shall never use our own language completely and perfectly. The very same situation is actually exhibited in every single act of cognition. We shall never know an object in all its qualities, but still we can scarcely deny the identity of objects even though we may see them from different perspectives. We always grasp some "structure of determination" in the object which makes the act of cognition not an act of arbitrary invention of subjective distinctions, but the recognition of some norms imposed on us by reality. Similarly the structure of a work of art has the character of a "duty which I have to realize." I shall always realize it imperfectly, but in spite of some incompleteness, a certain "structure of determination" remains, just as in any other object of knowledge.

. . . . .

Just as modern linguists have analyzed the potential sounds as phonemes, they can also analyze morphemes and syntagmas. The sentence, for instance, can be described not merely as an *ad hoc* utterance, but as a syntactic pattern. Outside of phonemics, modern functional linguistics is still comparatively undeveloped, but the problems, though difficult, are not insoluble or completely new: they are rather restatements of the morphological and syntactical questions as they were discussed in older grammars. The analysis of a literary work of art has to cope with parallel problems, with units of meaning and their specific organization towards aesthetic purposes. Such problems as those of poetic semantics and diction and imagery are reintroduced in a new and more careful restatement which avoids the pitfalls of the psychological and impressionist approaches. Units of meaning, sentences and sentence-structures refer to objects, construct imaginative realities such as landscapes, interiors, characters, actions, or ideas. These also can be analyzed in a way which does not confuse them with empirical reality and does not ignore the fact that they inhere in linguistic structures. A figure in a novel or play grows only out of the units of meaning, is made of the sentences either pronounced by the figure or pronounced about it. It has an indeterminate structure in comparison with a biological person who has his coherent past. Thus speculations about Hamlet's studies in Wittenberg or his father's influence on his youth, or the number of Lady Macbeth's children are shown as confusions between fiction and reality, of the same order as if a spectator should try to find the continuation of a picture under its frame. The advantage of all these distinctions of strata is that they supersede the age-old superficial and misleading distinction of content and form. The content will reappear in close contact with the linguistic substratum, in which it is implied and on which it is dependent.

But this conception of the literary work of art as a stratified system of norms still leaves undetermined the actual mode of existence of this system. To deal with this matter properly we should have to solve such questions as those of nominalism versus realism, mentalism versus behaviorism,—in short, all main problems of epistemology. For our purposes it will be, it seems, sufficient to steer clear of two opposite pitfalls, of the Charybdis of Platonism and the Scylla of extreme nominalism as it is advocated today by behaviorists and some positivists. There is no need to hypostatize or "reify" this system of norms, to make it a sort of Platonic idea floating in a timeless void of essences. The literary work of art is not of the same ontological status as the idea of a triangle, or of a number, or a quality like "redness." In difference from such "subsistences" the literary work of art is, first of all, created at a certain point in time, and secondly is subject to change and even complete destruction. In this respect it rather resembles the system of language, though the exact moment of creation or death is probably much less clearly definable in the case of language than with the literary work of art which is usually an individual creation. Also language, of course, is no Platonic essence, immutable and indestructible. On the other hand, one should recognize that an extreme nominalism which rejects the concept of a "system of language" and thus of a work of art in our sense, or admits it only as a useful fiction or a "scientific description," misses the whole problem and the point at issue. All these objections are founded on the extremely narrow preconception of behaviorism which declares anything to be "mystical" or "metaphysical" which does not conform to a very limited conception of empirical reality. To call the phoneme a "fiction" or the system of language merely a "scientific description of speech-acts" is to ignore the problem of truth. We recognize norms and deviations from norms and do not merely devise some purely verbal descriptions. The whole behaviorist point of view is, in this respect, based on a bad theory of abstraction. Numbers or norms are what they are whether we construct them or not. Certainly I perform the counting, I perform the reading, but number-presentation or recognition of a norm is not the same as the number or norm itself. The pronouncement of the sound *h* is not the phoneme *h*. We recognize some structure of norms within reality and do not simply invent verbal constructs. The objection that we have access to these norms only through individual acts of cognition and that we cannot get out of these acts or beyond them, is only apparently impressive. It is the objection which has been made to Kant's criticism of our cognition and can be refuted with the Kantian arguments. It is true we are ourselves liable to misunderstandings and lack of comprehension of these norms, but this does not mean that the critic assumes a superhuman role of criticizing our comprehension from the outside or that he pretends to grasp the perfect whole of the system of norms in some act of intellectual intuition. We criticize rather a part of our knowledge in the light of the higher standard set by another part. We are not supposed to put ourselves into the position of a man who, in order to test his vision, tries to look at his own eyes, but into the position of a man who compares the objects he sees clearly with those he sees only dimly, makes then generalizations as to the kinds of objects which fall into the two classes, and explains the difference by some theory of vision which takes account of distance, light, and so forth.

Analogously, we can distinguish between right and wrong readings of a poem, or between a recognition or a distortion of the norms implicit in a work of art by acts of comparison, by a study of different false or incomplete realizations. We can study the actual workings, relations, and combinations of these norms, just as the phoneme can be studied. The literary work of art is neither an empirical fact, in the sense of being a state of mind of any given individual or of any group of individuals, nor is it an ideal changeless object such as a triangle. The work of art may become an object of experience; it is, we admit, accessible only through individual experience, but it is not identical with any experience. It differs from ideal objects such as numbers precisely because it is accessible only through the empirical part of its structure, the sound-system, while a triangle or a number can, I presume, be intuited directly. It also differs from ideal objects in one important respect. It has something which can be called "Life." It arises at a certain point of time, changes in the course of history and may perish. A work of art is "timeless" only in the sense that, if preserved, it has some fundamental structure of identity since its creation, but it is "historical" too. It has a development which can be described. This development is nothing but the series of concretizations of a given work of art in the course of history which we may, to a certain extent, reconstruct from the reports of critics and readers about their experiences and judgments and the effect of a given work of art on other works. Our consciousness of earlier concretizations (readings, criticisms, misinterpretations) will affect our own experience: earlier readings may educate us to a deeper understanding or may cause a violent reaction against the prevalent interpretations of the past. All this shows the importance of the history of criticism, or in linguistics, of historical grammar, and leads to difficult questions about the nature and limits of individuality. How far can a work of art be said to be changed and still remain identical? The *Iliad* still "exists," that is, it can become again and again effective and is thus different from a historical phenomenon like the battle of Waterloo which is definitely past, though its course may be reconstructed and its effects may be felt even today. In what sense can we, however, speak of an identity between the *Iliad* as the contemporary Greeks heard or read it, and the *Iliad* we now read? Even assuming that we know the identical text, our actual experience must be very different. We cannot contrast its language with the everyday language of Greece, and cannot therefore feel the deviations from colloquial language on which much of the poetic effect must depend. We are unable to understand many verbal ambiguities which are an essential part of every poet's meaning. Obviously it requires in addition some imaginative effort, which can have only very partial success, to think ourselves back into the Greek belief in gods, or the Greek scale of moral values. Still, it could scarcely be denied that there is a substantial identity of structure which has remained the same throughout the ages. This structure, however, is dynamic: it changes throughout the process of history while passing through the minds of its readers, critics and fellow artists. Thus the system of norms is growing and changing and will remain, in some sense, always incompletely and imperfectly realized. But this dynamic conception does not mean mere subjectivism and relativism. All the different points of view are by no means equally right. It will always be possible to determine which point of view grasps the subject most thoroughly and deeply. A hierarchy of viewpoints, a criticism of the grasp of norms, is implied in the concept of the adequacy of interpretation. All relativism is ultimately defeated by the recognition that the Absolute is in the relative, though not finally and fully in it.

The work of art, then, appears as an object of knowledge *sui generis* which has a special ontological status. It is neither real (like a statue) nor mental (like the experience of light or pain) nor ideal (like a triangle). It is a system of norms of ideal concepts which are intersubjective. They must be assumed to exist in collective ideology, changing with it, accessible only through individual mental experiences, based on the sound-structure of its sentences.

Our interpretation of the literary work of art as a system of norms has served its purpose if it has suggested an argument against the insidious psychological relativism which must always end in scepticism and finally mental anarchy. It may also have demonstrated the truism —of which we cannot be reminded too frequently—that all problems, pursued far enough, even in such an apparently concrete and limited field as literary criticism, lead to ultimate questions and decisions about the nature of reality and truth, the processes of our cognition and the motives of our actions.

We have avoided the problem of value: no distinction could be made between a good and bad literary work of art in our context. But I am convinced that a profitable discussion of the problem of value and valuation has to begin with the recognition of the work of art as a system of norms.

PSYCHOLOGY AND FORM

(1925)

KENNETH BURKE

IT IS NOT, one will recall, until the fourth scene of the first act that Hamlet confronts the ghost of his father. As soon as the situation has been made clear, the audience has been, consciously or unconsciously, waiting for this ghost to appear, while in the fourth scene this moment has been definitely promised. For earlier in the play Hamlet had arranged to come to the platform at night with Horatio to meet the ghost, and it is now night, he is with Horatio and Marcellus, and they are standing on the platform. Hamlet asks Horatio the hour.

> HOR. I think it lacks of twelve
> MAR. No, it is struck.
> HOR. Indeed? I heard it not: then it draws near the season
> Wherein the spirit held his wont to walk.

Promptly hereafter there is a sound off-stage. "A flourish of trumpets, and ordnance shot off within." Hamlet's friends have established the hour as twelve. It is time for the ghost. Sounds off-stage, and of course it is not the ghost. It is, rather, the sound of the king's carousal, for the king "keeps wassail." A tricky, and effective detail. We have been waiting for a ghost, and get, startlingly, a blare of trumpets. And again, once the trumpets are silent, we feel all the more just how desolate are these three men waiting for a ghost, on a bare "platform," feel it by this sudden juxtaposition of an imagined scene of lights and merriment. But the trumpets announcing a carousal have suggested a subject of conversation. In the darkness Hamlet discusses the excessive drinking of his countrymen. He points out that it tends to harm their reputation abroad, since, he argues, this one showy vice makes their virtues "in the general censure take corruption." And for this reason, although he himself is a native of this place, he does not approve of the custom. Indeed, there in the gloom he is talking very intelligently on these matters, and Horatio answers, "Look, my Lord, it comes." All this time we had been waiting for a ghost, and it comes at the one moment which was not pointing towards it. This ghost, so assiduously prepared for, is yet a surprise. And now that the ghost has come, we are waiting for something further. Programme: a speech from Hamlet. Hamlet must confront the ghost. Here again Shakespeare can feed well upon the use of contrast for his effects. Hamlet has just been talking in a sober, rather argumentative manner—but now the flood-gates are unloosed:

> Angels and ministers of grace defend us!
> Be thou a spirit of health or goblin damn'd,
> Bring with thee airs from heaven or blasts from hell...

and the transition from the matter-of-fact to the grandiose, the full-throated and full-vowelled, is a second burst of trumpets, perhaps even more effective than the first, since it is the rich fulfilment of a promise. Yet this satisfaction in turn becomes an allurement, an itch for further developments. At first desiring solely to see Hamlet confront the ghost, we now want Hamlet to learn from the ghost the details—which are, however, with shrewdness and husbandry, reserved for "Scene V. —Another Part of the Platform."

I have gone into this scene at some length, since it illustrates so perfectly the relationship between psychology and form, and so aptly indicates how the one is to be defined in terms of the other. That is, the psychology here is not the psychology of the *hero,* but the psychology of the *audience.* And by that distinction, form would be the psychology of the audience. Or, seen from another angle, form is the creation of an appetite in the mind of the auditor, and the adequate satisfying of that appetite. This satisfaction—so complicated is the human mechanism—at times involves a temporary set of frustrations, but in the end these frustrations prove to be simply a more involved kind of satisfaction, and furthermore serve to make the satisfaction of fulfilment more intense. If, in a work of art, the poet says something, let us say, about a meeting, writes in such a way that we desire to observe that meeting, and then, if he places that meeting before us—that is form. While obviously, that is also the psychology of the audience, since it involves desires and their appeasements.

The seeming breach between form and subject-matter, between technique and psychology, which has taken place in the last century is the result, it seems to me, of scientific criteria being unconsciously introduced into matters of purely aesthetic judgment. The flourishing of science has been so vigorous that we have not yet had time to make a spiritual readjustment adequate to the changes in our resources of material and knowledge. There are disorders of the social system which are caused solely by our undigested wealth (the basic disorder being, perhaps, the phenomenon of overproduction: to remedy this, instead of having all workers employed on half time, we have half working full time and the other half idle, so that whereas overproduction could be the greatest reward of applied science, it has been, up to now, the most menacing condition our modern civilization has had to face). It would be absurd to suppose that such social disorders would not be paralleled by disorders of culture and taste, especially since science is so pronouncedly a spiritual factor. So that we are, owing to the sudden wealth science has thrown upon us, all *nouveaux-riches* in matters of culture, and most poignantly in that field where lack of native firmness is most readily exposed, in matters of aesthetic judgment.

One of the most striking derangements of taste which science has temporarily thrown upon us involves the understanding of psychology in art. Psychology has become a body of information (which is precisely what psychology in science should be, or must be). And similarly, in art, we tend to look for psychology as the purveying of information. Thus, a contemporary writer has objected to Joyce's *Ulysses* on the ground that there are more psychoanalytic data available in Freud. (How much more drastically he might, by the same system, have destroyed Homer's *Odyssey!*) To his objection it was answered that one might, similarly, denounce Cézanne's trees in favour of state forestry bulletins. Yet are not Cézanne's landscapes themselves tainted with the psychology of information? Has he not, by perception, *pointed out* how one object lies against another, *indicated* what takes place between two colours (which is the psychology of science, and is less successful in the medium of art than in that of science, since in art such processes are at best implicit, whereas in science they are so readily made explicit)? Is Cézanne not, to that extent, a state forestry bulletin, except that he tells what goes on in the eye instead of on the tree? And do not the true values of his work lie elsewhere—and precisely in what I distinguish as the psychology of form?

Thus, the great influx of information has led the artist also to lay his emphasis on the giving of information—with the result that art tends more and more to substitute the psychology of the hero (the subject) for the psychology of the audience. Under such an attitude, when form is preserved it is preserved as an annex, a luxury, or, as some feel, a downright affectation. It remains, though sluggish, like the human appendix, for occasional demands are still made upon it; but its true vigour is gone, since it is no longer organically required. Proposition: The hypertrophy of the psychology of information is accompanied by the corresponding atrophy of the psychology of form.

In information, the matter is intrinsically interesting, and by intrinsically interesting I do not necessarily mean intrinsically valuable, as to witness the intrinsic interest of backyard gossip or the most casual newspaper items. In art, at least the art of the great ages (Aeschylus, Shakespeare, Racine) the matter is interesting by means of an extrinsic use, a function. Consider, for instance, the speech of Mark Anthony, the "Brutus is an honourable man." Imagine in the same place a very intelligently developed thesis on human conduct, with statistics, intelligence tests, definitions; imagine it as the finest thing of the sort ever written, and as really being at the roots of an understanding of Brutus. Obviously, the play would simply stop until Anthony had finished. For in the case of Anthony's speech, the value lies in the fact that his words are shaping the future of the audience's desire, not the desires of the Roman populace, but the desires of the pit. This is the psychology of form as distinguished from the psychology of information.

The distinction is, of course, absolutely true only in its nonexistent extremes. Hamlet's advice to the players, for instance, has little of the quality which distinguishes Anthony's speech. It is, rather, intrinsically interesting, although one could very easily prove how the play would benefit by some such delay at this point, and that anything which made this delay possible without violating the consistency of the subject would have, in this, its formal justification. While it would, furthermore, be absurd to rule intrinsic interest out of literature, I wish simply to have it restored to its properly minor position, seen as merely one out of many possible elements of style. Goethe's prose, often poorly imagined, or neutral, in its line-for-line texture, especially in the treatment of romantic episode—perhaps he felt that the romantic episode in itself was enough?—is strengthened into a style possessing affirmative virtues by his rich use of aphorism. But this is, after all, but one of many possible facets of appeal. In some places, notably in *Wilhelm Meister's Lehrjahre* when Wilhelm's friends disclose the documents they have been collecting about his life unbeknown to him, the aphorisms are almost rousing in their efficacy, since they involve the story. But as a rule the appeal of aphorism is intrinsic: that is, it satisfies without being functionally related to the context.[1] . . . Also, to return to the matter of Hamlet, it must be observed that the style in this passage is no mere "information-giving" style; in its alacrity, its development, it really makes this one fragment into a kind of miniature plot.

One reason why music can stand repetition so much more sturdily than correspondingly good prose is because music, of all the arts, is by its nature least suited to the psychology of information, and has remained closer to the psychology of form. Here form cannot atrophy. Every dissonant chord cries for its solution, and whether the musician resolves or refuses to resolve this dissonance into the chord which the body cries for, he is dealing in human appetites. Correspondingly good prose, being more prone to the temptations of pure information, cannot so much bear repetition since the aesthetic value of information is lost once that information is imparted. If one returns to such a work again it is purely because, in the chaos of modern life, he has been caused to forget it. With a desire, on the other hand, its

[1] Similarly, the epigram of Racine is "pure art," because it usually serves to formulate or clarify some situation within the play itself. In Goethe the epigram is most often of independent validity, as in *Die Wahlverwandtschaften*, where the ideas of Ottilie's diary are obviously carried over boldly from the author's notebook. In Shakespeare we have the union of extrinsic and intrinsic epigram, the epigram growing out of its context and yet valuable independent of its context.

recovery is as agreeable as its discovery. One can memorize the dialogue between Hamlet and Guildenstern, where Hamlet gives Guildenstern the pipe to play on. For, once the speech is known, its repetition adds a new element to compensate for the loss of novelty. We cannot take a recurrent pleasure in the new (in information) but we can in the natural (in form). Already, at the moment when Hamlet is holding out the pipe to Guildenstern and asking him to play upon it, we "gloat over" Hamlet's triumphal descent upon Guildenstern, when, after Guildenstern has, under increasing embarrassment, protested three times that he cannot play the instrument, Hamlet launches the retort for which all this was preparation:

> Why, look you now, how unworthy a thing you make of me. You would play upon me, you would seem to know my stops; you would pluck out the heart of my mystery; you would sound me from my lowest note to the top of my compass; and there is much music, excellent voice, in this little organ, yet cannot you make it speak. 'Sblood, do you think I am easier to be played on than a pipe? Call me what instrument you will, though you can fret me, you cannot play upon me.[2]

In the opening lines we hear the promise of the close, and thus feel the emotional curve even more keenly than at first reading. Whereas in most modern art this element is underemphasized. It gives us the gossip of a plot, a plot which too often has for its value the mere fact that we do not know its outcome.[3]

Music, then, fitted less than any other art for imparting information, deals minutely in frustrations and fulfilments of desire,[4] and for that reason more often gives us those curves of emotion which, because they are natural, can bear repetition without loss. It is for this reason that music, like folk tales, is most capable of lulling us to sleep. A lullaby is a melody which comes quickly to rest, where the obstacles are easily overcome—and this is precisely the parallel to those waking dreams of struggle and conquest which (especially during childhood) we permit ourselves when falling asleep or when trying to induce sleep. Folk tales are just such waking dreams. Thus it is right that art should be called a "waking dream." The only difficulty with this definition (indicated by Charles Baudouin in his

[2] One might indicate still further appropriateness here. As Hamlet finishes his speech, Polonius enters, and Hamlet turns to him, "God bless you, sir!" Thus, the plot is continued (for Polonius is always the promise of action) and a full stop is avoided: the embarrassment laid upon Rosencrantz and Guildenstern is not laid upon the audience.

[3] Yet modern music has gone far in the attempt to renounce this aspect of itself. Its dissonances become static, demanding no particular resolution. And whereas an unfinished modulation by a classic musician occasions positive dissatisfaction, the refusal to resolve a dissonance in modern music does not dissatisfy us, but irritates or stimulates. Thus, "energy" takes the place of style.

[4] Suspense is the least complex kind of anticipation, as surprise is the least complex kind of fulfilment. [*Author's note.*] On suspense, see Elder Olson's diagnosis in his *Outline of Poetic Theory.* [*Editor's note.*]

Psychoanalysis and Aesthetics, a very valuable study of Verhaeren) is that to-day we understand it to mean art as a waking dream for the artist. Modern criticism, and psychoanalysis in particular, is too prone to define the essence of art in terms of the artist's weaknesses. It is, rather, the audience which dreams, while the artist oversees the conditions which determine this dream. He is the manipulator of blood, brains, heart, and bowels, which, while we sleep, dictate the mould of our desires. This is, of course, the real meaning of artistic felicity—an exaltation at the correctness of the procedure, so that we enjoy the steady march of doom in a Racinian tragedy with exactly the same equipment as that which produces our delight with Benedick's "Peace! I'll stop your mouth." (*Kisses her*), which terminates the imbroglio of *Much Ado About Nothing.*

The methods of maintaining interest which are most natural to the psychology of information (as it is applied to works of pure art) are surprise and suspense. The method most natural to the psychology of form is eloquence. For this reason the great ages of Aeschylus, Shakespeare, and Racine, dealing as they did with material which was more or less a matter of common knowledge so that the broad outlines of the plot were known in advance (while it is the broad outlines which are usually exploited to secure surprise and suspense) developed formal excellence, or eloquence, as the basis of appeal in their work.

Not that there is any difference in kind between the classic method and the method of cheapest contemporary melodrama. The drama, more than any other form, must never lose sight of its audience: here the failure to satisfy the proper requirements is most disastrous. And since certain contemporary work is successful, it follows that rudimentary laws of composition are being complied with. The distinction is one of intensity rather than of kind. The contemporary audience hears the lines of a play or novel with the same equipment as it brings to reading the lines of its daily paper. It is content to have facts placed before it in some more or less adequate sequence. Eloquence is the minimizing of this interest in fact, *per se,* so that the "more or less adequate sequence" of their presentation must be relied on to a much greater extent. Thus, those elements of surprise and suspense are subtilized, carried down into the writing of a line or a sentence, until in all its smallest details the work bristles with disclosures, contrasts, restatements with a difference, ellipses, images, aphorism, volume, sound-values, in short all that complex wealth of minutiae which in their line-for-line aspect we call style and in their broader outlines we call form.

As a striking instance of a modern play with potentialities in which the intensity of eloquence is missing, I might cite a recent success, Capek's *R. U. R.* Here, in a melodrama which was often astonishing in the rightness of its technical procedure, when the author was finished he had written nothing but the scenario for a play by Shakespeare. It was a play in which the author produced time and again the opportunity, the demand, for eloquence, only to move on. (At other times, the most successful moments, he utilized the modern discovery of silence, writing moments wherein words could not possibly serve but to detract from the effect: this we might call the "flowering" of information.) The Adam and Eve scene of the last act, a "commission" which the Shakespeare of the comedies would have loved to fill, was in the verbal barrenness of Capek's play something shameless to the point of blushing. The Robot, turned human, prompted by the dawn of love to see his first sunrise, or hear the first bird-call, and forced merely to say "Oh, see the sunrise," or "Hear the pretty birds"—here one could do nothing but wring his hands at the absence of that aesthetic mould which produced the overslung "speeches" of *Romeo and Juliet.*

Suspense is the concern over the possible outcome of some specific detail of plot rather than for general qualities. Thus, "Will A marry B or C?" is suspense. In *Macbeth,* the turn from the murder scene to the porter scene is a much less literal channel of development. Here the presence of one quality calls forth the demand for another, rather than one tangible incident of plot awaking an interest in some other possible tangible incident of plot. To illustrate more fully, if an author managed over a certain number of his pages to produce a feeling of sultriness, or oppression, in the reader, this would unconsciously awaken in the reader the desire for a cold, fresh northwind —and thus some aspect of a northwind would be effective if called forth by some aspect of stuffiness. A good example of this is to be found in a contemporary poem, T. S. Eliot's *The Waste Land,* where the vulgar, oppressively trivial conversation in the public house calls forth in the poet a memory of a line from Shakespeare. These slobs in a public house, after a desolately low-visioned conversation, are now forced by closing time to leave the saloon. They say good-night. And suddenly the poet, feeling his release, drops into another good-night, a good-night with *désinvolture,* a good-night out of what was, within the conditions of the poem at least, a graceful and irrecoverable past.

> "Well that Sunday Albert was home, they had a hot gammon,
> And they asked me in to dinner, to get the beauty of it hot"
> —[at this point the bartender interrupts: it is closing time]
> "Goonight Bill. Goonight Lou. Goonight May. Goonight.
> Ta ta. Goonight. Goonight.
> Good-night, ladies, good-night, sweet ladies, good-night, good-night."

There is much more to be said on these lines, which I have shortened somewhat in quotation to make my issue clearer. But I simply wish to point out here that this transition is a bold juxtaposition of one quality created by another, an association in ideas which, if not logical, is nevertheless emotionally natural. In the case of *Macbeth,* similarly, it would be absurd to say that the audience, after the murder scene, wants a porter scene. But the audience does want the quality which this porter particularizes. The dramatist might, conceivably, have introduced some entirely different character or event in this place, provided only that the event produced the same quality of relationship and contrast (grotesque seriousness followed by grotesque buffoonery). . . . One of the most beautiful and satisfactory "forms" of this sort is to be found in Baudelaire's *Femmes Damnées,* where the poet, after describing the business of a Lesbian seduction, turns to the full oratory of his apostrophe:

> Descendez, descendez, lamentables victimes,
> Descendez le chemin de l'enfer éternel . . .

while the stylistic efficacy of this transition contains a richness which transcends all moral (or unmoral) sophistication: the efficacy of appropriateness, of exactly the natural curve in treatment. Here is morality even for the godless, since it is a morality of art, being justified, if for no other reason, by its paralleling of that staleness, that disquieting loss of purpose, which must have followed the procedure of the two characters, the *femmes damnées* themselves, a remorse which, perhaps only physical in its origin, nevertheless becomes psychic.[5]

But to return, we have made three terms synonymous: form, psychology, and eloquence. And eloquence thereby becomes the essence of art, while pity, tragedy, sweetness, humour, in short all the emotions which we experience in life proper, as non-artists, are simply the material on which eloquence may feed. The arousing of pity, for instance, is not the central purpose of art, although it may be an adjunct of artistic effectiveness. One can feel pity much more keenly at the sight of some actual misfortune—and it would be a great mistake to see art merely as a weak representation of some actual experience.[6] That artists to-day are content to write under such an aesthetic accounts in part for the inferior position which art holds in the community. Art, at least in the great periods when it has flowered, was the conversion, or transcendence, of emotion into eloquence, and was thus a factor added to life. I am reminded of St. Augustine's caricature of the theatre: that whereas we do not dare to wish people unhappy, we

[5] As another aspect of the same subject, I could cite many examples from the fairy tale. Consider, for instance, when the hero is to spend the night in a bewitched castle. Obviously, as darkness descends, weird adventures must befall him. His bed rides him through the castle; two halves of a man challenge him to a game of nine-pins played with thigh bones and skulls. Or entirely different incidents may serve instead of these. The quality comes first, the particularization follows.

[6] Could not the Greek's public resistance to Euripides be accounted for in the fact that he, of the three great writers of Greek tragedy, betrayed his art, was guilty of aesthetic impiety, in that he paid more attention to the arousing of emotion *per se* than to the sublimation of emotion into eloquence?

do want to feel sorry for them, and therefore turn to plays so that we can feel sorry although no real misery is involved. One might apply the parallel interpretation to the modern delight in happy endings, and say that we turn to art to indulge our humanitarianism in a well-wishing which we do not permit ourselves towards our actual neighbours. Surely the catharsis of art is more complicated than this, and more reputable.

Eloquence itself, as I hope to have established in the instance from Hamlet which I have analysed, is no mere plaster added to a framework of more stable qualities. Eloquence is simply the end of art, and is thus its essence. Even the poorest art is eloquent, but in a sorry manner, with less intensity, until this aspect is obscured by others fattening upon its leanness. Eloquence is not showiness; it is, rather, the result of that desire in the artist to make a work perfect by adapting it in every minute detail to the racial appetites.

The distinction between the psychology of information and the psychology of form involves a definition of aesthetic truth. It is here precisely, to combat the deflection which the strength of science has caused to our tastes, that we must examine the essential breach between scientific and artistic truth. Truth in art is not the discovery of facts, not an addition to human knowledge in the scientific sense of the word.[7] It is, rather, the exercise of human propriety, the formulation of symbols which rigidify our sense of poise and rhythm. Artistic truth is the externalization of taste.[8] I sometimes wonder, for instance, whether the "artificial" speech of John Lyly might perhaps be "truer" than the revelations of Dostoevsky. Certainly at its best, in its feeling for a statement which returns upon itself, which attempts the systole to

[7] One of the most striking examples of the encroachment of scientific truth into art is the doctrine of "truth by distortion," whereby one aspect of an object is suppressed the better to emphasize some other aspect; this is, obviously, an attempt to *indicate* by art some fact of knowledge, to make some implicit aspect of an object as explicit as one can by means of the comparatively dumb method of art (dumb, that is, as compared to the perfect ease with which science can indicate its discoveries). Yet science has already made discoveries in the realm of this "factual truth," this "truth by distortion" which must put to shame any artist who relies on such matter for his effects. Consider, for instance, the motion-picture of a man vaulting. By photographing this process very rapidly, and running the reel very slowly, one has upon the screen the most striking set of factual truths to aid in our understanding of an athlete vaulting. Here, at our leisure, we can observe the contortions of four legs, a head, and a butt. This squirming thing we saw upon the screen showed us an infinity of factual truths anent the balances of an athlete vaulting. We can, from this, observe the marvellous system of balancing which the body provides for itself in the adjustments of moving. Yet, so far as the aesthetic truth is concerned, this on the screen was not an athlete, but a squirming thing, a horror, displaying every fact of vaulting except the exhilaration of the act itself.

[8] The procedure of science involves the elimination of taste, employing as a substitute the corrective norm of the pragmatic test, the empirical experiment, which is entirely intellectual. Those who oppose the "intellectualism" of critics like Matthew Arnold are involved in an hilarious blunder, for Arnold's entire approach to the appreciation of art is through delicacies of taste intensified to the extent almost of squeamishness.

a diastole, it *could* be much truer than Dostoevsky.[9] And if it is not, it fails not through a mistake of Lyly's aesthetic, but because Lyly was a man poor in character whereas Dostoevsky was rich and complex. When Swift, making the women of Brobdingnag enormous, deduces from this discrepancy between their size and Gulliver's that Gulliver could sit astride their nipples, he has written something which is aesthetically true, which is, if I may be pardoned, profoundly "proper," as correct in its Euclidean deduction as any corollary in geometry. Given the companions of Ulysses in the cave of Polyphemus, it is true that they would escape clinging to the bellies of the herd let out to pasture. St. Ambrose, detailing the habits of God's creatures, and drawing from them moral maxims for the good of mankind, St. Ambrose in his limping natural history rich in scientific inaccuracies that are at the very heart of emotional rightness, St. Ambrose writes "Of night-birds, especially of the nightingale which hatches her eggs by song; of the owl, the bat, and the cock at cock-crow; in what wise these may apply to the guidance of our habits," and in the sheer rightness of that programme there is the truth of art. In introducing this talk of night-birds, after many pages devoted to other of God's creatures, he says,

> What now! While we have been talking, you will notice how the birds of night have already started fluttering about you, and, in this same fact of warning us to leave off with our discussion, suggest thereby a further topic—

and this seems to me to contain the best wisdom of which the human frame is capable, an address, a discourse, which can make our material life seem blatant almost to the point of despair. And when the cock crows, and the thief abandons his traps, and the sun lights up, and we are in every way called back to God by the well-meaning admonition of this bird, here the very blindnesses of religion become the deepest truths of art.

[9] As for instance, the "conceit" of Endymion's awakening, when he forgets his own name, yet recalls that of his beloved.

LEXICON RHETORICAE

(1931)

KENNETH BURKE

THE PRESENT ESSAY attempts to define the principles underlying the appeal of literature. By literature we mean written or spoken words. Primarily we are concerned with literature as art, that is, literature designed for the express purpose of arousing emotions. But sometimes literature so designed fails to arouse emotions—and words said purely by way of explanation may have an unintended emotional effect of considerable magnitude. A discussion of effectiveness in literature should be able to include unintended effects as well as intended ones. Also, such a discussion will be diagnostic rather than hortatory: it will be more concerned with *how* effects are produced than with *what effects should be produced.*

As far as possible, we shall proceed simply by definition and example. We propose: to analyze the five aspects of form (The Nature of Form); to show how these forms are implicit in subject-matter (The Individuation of Forms); to discuss subject-matter and forms as combined in the Symbol (Patterns of Experience); to distinguish between the scientific formulation of experience and the poet's formulation of experience (Ritual); and to consider the problems of literary excellence (Permanence, Universality, Perfection).[1] Then, having completed our Lexicon, we propose to examine certain critical issues of the past and of the present, testing our terms as equipment for the discussion of these issues.

THE NATURE OF FORM

(1) *Form* in literature is an arousing and fulfilment of desires. A work has form in so far as one part of it leads a reader to anticipate another part, to be gratified by the sequence. The five aspects of form may be discussed as progressive form (subdivided into syllogistic and qualitative progression), repetitive form, conventional form, and minor or incidental forms.

[1] The present text is not the complete Lexicon. The last two sections are not included, and of the first three aspects of form only the section on The Nature of Form stands unabridged. [*Editor's note.*]

(2) *Syllogistic progression* is the form of a perfectly conducted argument, advancing step by step. It is the form of a mystery story, where everything falls together, as in a story of ratiocination by Poe. It is the form of a demonstration in Euclid. To go from A to E through stages B, C, and D is to obtain such form. We call it syllogistic because, given certain things, certain things must follow, the premises forcing the conclusion. In so far as the audience, from its acquaintance with the premises, feels the rightness of the conclusion, the work is formal. The arrows of our desires are turned in a certain direction, and the plot follows the direction of the arrows. The peripety, or reversal of the situation, discussed by Aristotle is obviously one of the keenest manifestations of syllogistic progression. In the course of a single scene, the poet reverses the audience's expectations—as in the third act of *Julius Caesar,* where Brutus's speech before the mob prepares us for his exoneration, but the speech of Antony immediately after prepares us for his downfall.

(3) *Qualitative progression,* the other aspect of progressive form, is subtler. Instead of one incident in the plot preparing us for some other possible incident of plot (as Macbeth's murder of Duncan prepares us for the dying of Macbeth), the presence of one quality prepares us for the introduction of another (the grotesque seriousness of the murder scene preparing us for the grotesque buffoonery of the porter scene). In T. S. Eliot's *The Waste Land,* the step from "Ta ta. Goonight. Goonight" to "Good night, ladies, good night, sweet ladies" is a qualitative progression. In Malcolm Cowley's sonnet *Mine No. 6* there is a similar kind of qualitative progression, as we turn from the octave's description of a dismal landscape ("the blackened stumps, the ulcerated hill") to the sestet's "Beauty, perfection, I have loved you fiercely." Such progressions are qualitative rather than syllogistic as they lack the pronounced anticipatory nature of the syllogistic progression. We are prepared less to demand a certain qualitative progression than to recognize its rightness after the event. We are put into a state of mind which another state of mind can appropriately follow.

(4) *Repetitive form* is the consistent maintaining of a principle under new guises. It is restatement of the same thing in different ways. Thus, in so far as each detail of Gulliver's life among the Lilliputians is a new exemplification of the discrepancy in size between Gulliver and the Lilliputians, Swift is using repetitive form. A succession of images, each of them regiving the same lyric mood; a character repeating his identity, his "number," under changing situations; the sustaining of an attitude, as in satire; the rhythmic regularity of blank verse; the rhyme scheme of *terza rima*—these are all aspects of repetitive form. By a varying number of details, the reader is led to feel more or less consciously the principle underlying them—he then requires that this principle be observed in the giving of further details. Repetitive

form, the restatement of a theme by new details, is basic to any work of art, or to any other kind of orientation, for that matter. It is our only method of "talking on the subject."

(5) *Conventional form* involves to some degree the appeal of form *as form*. Progressive, repetitive, and minor forms, may be effective even though the reader has no awareness of their formality. But when a form appeals as form, we designate it as conventional form. Any form can become conventional, and be sought for itself—whether it be as complex as the Greek tragedy or as compact as the sonnet. The invocation to the Muses; the theophany in a play of Euripides; the processional and recessional of the Episcopalian choir; the ensemble before the front drop at the close of a burlesque show; the exordium in Greek-Roman oratory; the Sapphic ode; the triolet—these are all examples of conventional forms having varying degrees of validity today. Perhaps even the Jew-and-the-Irishman of the Broadway stage is an instance of repetitive form grown into conventional form. Poets who write beginnings *as beginnings* and endings *as endings* show the appeal of conventional form. Thus, in Milton's *Lycidas* we start disstinctly with the sense of introduction ("Yet once more, O ye laurels, and once more . . .") and the poem is brought to its dextrous gliding close by the stanza, clearly an ending: "And now the sun had dropped behind the hills, And now had dropped into the western bay. . ." But *Mother Goose,* throwing formal appeal into relief through "nonsense," offers us the clearest instance of conventional form, a "pure" beginning and "pure" end:

> I'll tell you a story of Jack O'Norey
> And now my story's begun;
> I'll tell you another about his brother
> And now my story is done.

We might note, in conventional form, the element of "categorical expectancy." That is, whereas the anticipations and gratifications of progressive and repetitive form arise *during the process* of reading, the expectations of conventional form may be *anterior* to the reading. If one sets out to read a sonnet, regardless of what the sonnet is to say he makes certain formal demands to which the poem must acquiesce. And similarly, the final Beethoven rejoicing of a Beethoven finale becomes a "categorical expectation" of the symphony. The audience "awaits" it before the first bar of the music has been played. And one may, even before opening a novel, look forward to an opening passage which will proclaim itself an opening.

(6) *Minor or incidental forms.* When analyzing a work of any length, we may find it bristling with minor or incidental forms—such as metaphor, paradox, disclosure, reversal, contraction, expansion, bathos, apostrophe, series, chiasmus—which can be discussed as formal

events in themselves. Their effect partially depends upon their function in the whole, yet they manifest sufficient evidences of episodic distinctness to bear consideration apart from their context. Thus a paradox, by carrying an argument one step forward, may have its use as progressive form; and by its continuation of a certain theme may have its use as repetitive form—yet it may be so formally complete in itself that the reader will memorize it as an event valid apart from its setting. A monologue by Shakespeare can be detached from its context and recited with enjoyment because, however integrally it contributes to the whole of which it is a part, it is also an independent curve of plot enclosed by its own beginning and end. The incident of Hamlet's offering the pipes to Guildenstern is a perfect instance of minor form. Euripides, when bringing a messenger upon the stage, would write him a speech which, in its obedience to the rhetorical laws of the times, was a separate miniature form. Edmund Burke sought to give each paragraph a structure as a paragraph, making it a growth, yet so confining it to one aspect of his subject that the closing sentence of the paragraph could serve as the logical complement to the opening one. Frequently, in the novel, an individual chapter is distinguished by its progress as a chapter, and not solely by its function in the whole. The Elizabethan drama generally has a profusion of minor forms.

(7) *Interrelation of forms.* Progressive, repetitive, and conventional and minor forms necessarily overlap. A specific event in the plot will not be exclusively classifiable under one head—as it should not, since in so organic a thing as a work of art we could not expect to find any principle of functioning in isolation from the others. Should we call the aphoristic couplet of the age of Pope repetitive form or conventional form? A closing scene may be syllogistic in that its particular events mark the dramatic conclusion of the dramatic premises; qualitative in that it exemplifies some mood made desirable by the preceding matter; repetitive in that the characters once again proclaim their identity; conventional in that it has about it something categorically terminal, as a farewell or death; and minor or incidental in that it contains a speech displaying a structural rise, development, and fall independently of its context. Perhaps the lines in *Othello,* beginning "Soft you, a word or two before you go," and ending "Seized by the throat the uncircumcised dog and smote him thus (*stabs himself*)," well exemplify the vigorous presence of all five aspects of form, as this suicide is the logical outcome of his predicament (syllogistic progression); it fits the general mood of gloomy forebodings which has fallen upon us (qualitative progression); the speech has about it that impetuosity and picturesqueness we have learned to associate with *Othello* (repetitive form); it is very decidedly a conclusion (conventional form); and in its development it is a tiny plot in itself (minor

form). The close of the *Odyssey* strongly combines syllogistic and qualitative progression. Ulysses' vengeance upon the suitors is the logical outcome of their conduct during his absence—and by the time it occurs, the reader is so incensed with them that he exults vindictively in their destruction. In most cases, we can find some aspects of form predominant, with others tenuous to the point of imperceptibility. Keats's *Ode to a Nightingale* is a striking instance of repetitive form; its successive stanzas take up various aspects of the mood, the *status evanescentiae,* almost as schematically as a lawyer's brief; but of syllogistic form there is barely a trace. . . . As, in musical theory, one chord is capable of various analyses, so in literature the appeal of one event may be explained by various principles. The important thing is not to confine the explanation to one principle, but to formulate sufficient principles to make an explanation possible. However, though the five aspects of form can merge into one another, or can be present in varying degrees, no other terms should be required in an analysis of formal functionings.

(8) *Conflict of forms.* If the various formal principles can intermingle, they can also conflict. An artist may create a character who, by the logic of the fiction, should be destroyed; but he may also have made this character so appealing that the audience wholly desires the character's salvation. Here would be a conflict between syllogistic and qualitative progression. Or he may depict a wicked character who, if the plot is to work correctly, must suddenly "reform," thereby violating repetitive form in the interests of syllogistic progression. To give a maximum sense of reality he may, like Stendhal, attempt to make sentences totally imperceptible as sentences, attempt to make the reader slip over them with no other feeling than their continuity (major progression here involving the atrophy of minor forms). Or conventional form may interfere with repetitive form (as when the drama, in developing from feudal to bourgeois subjects, chose "humbler" themes and characters, yet long retained the ceremonial diction of the earlier dignified period); and conversely, if we today were to attempt regaining some of these earlier ceremonial effects, by writing a play entirely in a ceremonial style, we should be using the appeal of repetitive form, but we should risk violating a contemporary canon of conventional form, since the non-ceremonial, the "domestic" dialogue, is now categorically expected.

(9) *Rhythm, Rhyme.* Rhythm and rhyme being formal, their appeal is to be explained within the terms already given. Rhyme usually accentuates the repetitive principle of art (in so far as one rhyme determines our expectation of another, and in so far as the rhyme-scheme in one stanza determines our expectation of its continuance in another). Its appeal is the appeal of progressive form in so far as the poet gets his effects by first establishing, and then altering, a

rhyme-scheme. In the ballade, triolet, etc., it can appeal as conventional form.

That verse rhythm can be largely explained as repetitive form is obvious, blank verse for instance being the constant recurrence of iambs with changing vowel and consonantal combinations (it is repetitive form in that it very distinctly sets up and gratifies a constancy of expectations; the reader "comes to rely" upon the rhythmic design after sufficient "co-ordinates of direction" have been received by him; the regularity of the design establishes conditions of response in the body, and the continuance of the design becomes an "obedience" to these same conditions). Rhythm appeals as conventional form in so far as specific awareness of the rhythmic pattern is involved in our enjoyment (as when the Sapphic metre is used in English, or when we turn from a pentameter sonnet in English to a hexameter sonnet in French). It can sometimes be said to appeal by qualitative progression, as when the poet, having established a pronounced rhythmic pattern, introduces a variant. Such a variant appeals as qualitative progression to the extent that it provides a "relief from the monotony" of its regular surroundings, to the extent that its appeal depends upon the previous establishment of the constant out of which it arises. Rhythm can also appeal as minor form; a peculiarity of the rhythm, for instance, may strikingly reinforce an incidental image (as with the use of spondees when the poet is speaking of something heavy).

In the matter of prose rhythms, the nature of the expectancy is much vaguer. In general the rhythmic unit is larger and more complex than the individual metric foot, often being the group of "scrambled" syllables between two caesuras. Though the constants of prose rhythm permit a greater range of metric variation than verse rhythms (that is, though in prose much of the metric variability is felt as belonging to the *constant* rather than to the *variation*), a prose stylist does definitely restrict the rhythmic expectations of the reader, as anyone can readily observe by turning from a page of Sir Thomas Browne to a page of Carlyle. However, one must also recall Professor George Saintsbury's distinction: "As the essence of verse-metre is its identity (at least in equivalence) and recurrence, so the essence of prose-rhythm lies in variety and divergence," or again: "Variety of foot arrangement, without definite equivalence, appears to be as much the secret of prose rhythm as uniformity of value, with equivalence or without it, appears to be that of poetic metre." The only thing that seems lacking in this distinction between verse rhythms and prose rhythms is a statement of some principle by which the *variety* in prose rhythms is guided. Perhaps the principle is a principle of logic. . . . That is, by logically relating one part of a sentence to another part of the sentence, the prose writer is led to a formal differentiation of the two related parts (or sometimes, which is *au fond* the same thing, he is led to a pronounced parallelism in the treatment of the related parts).

The logical grouping of one part with another serves as the guide to the formal treatment of both (as "planful" differentiation can only arise out of a sense of correspondence). The logical groupings upon which the rhythmic differentiations are based will differ with the individual, not only as to the ways in which he conceives a sentence's relationships, but also as to their number—and much of the "individuality" in a particular prose style could be traced to the number and nature of the author's logical groupings. Some writers, who seek "conversational" rather than "written" effects, apparently conceive of the sentence as a totality; they ignore its internal relationships almost entirely, preferring to make each sentence as homogeneous as a piece of string. By such avoidance of logical grouping they do undeniably obtain a simple fluency which, if one can delight in it sufficiently, makes every page of Johnson a mass of absurdities—but their sentences are, as sentences, uneventful. The "written" effects of prose seem to stress the progressive rather than the repetitive principle of form, since one part of the sentence is differentiated on the basis of another part (the formal identity of one part awakens in us a response whereby we can be pleased by a formal alteration in another part). But "conversational" rhythm, which is generally experienced "in the lump," as a pervasive monotone rather than as a group of marked internal structures, is—like verse—more closely allied to the repetitive principle. The "conversational" is thus seen to fall half-way between verse-rhythm and prose-rhythm, sharing something of both but lacking the pronounced characteristics of either.

So much for prose rhythm regardless of its subject-matter. We must also recognize the "secondary" aspect of rhythms whereby they can often be explained "at one remove." Thus, a tumultuous character would constantly restate his identity by the use of tumultuous speech (repetitive form), and the rhythm, in so far as it became tumultuous out of sympathy with its subject, would share the repetitive form of the subject. Similarly, it may be discussed as conventional or minor form (as when the author marshals his more aggressive images to make an ending, and parallels this with a kindred increase in the aggression of his rhythms). In a remote way, all such rhythmic effects may be described as a kind of "onomatopoetic parallelism," since their rhythmic identity would be explainable by the formal nature of the theme to which they are accommodated.

(10) *"Significant form."* Though admitting the "onomatopoetic correspondence" between form and theme, we must question a quasi-mystical attempt to explain all formal quality as "onomatopoetic" (that is, as an adaptation of sound and rhythm to the peculiarities of the sense). In most cases we find formal designs or contrivances which impart emphasis regardless of their subject. Whatever the

theme may be, they add saliency to this theme, the same design serving to make dismalness more dismal or gladness gladder. Thus, if a poet is writing in a quick metre, he may stress one point in his imagery as well as another by the use of spondees; or he may gain emphasis by injecting a burst of tonal saliency, as the aggressive repetition of a certain vowel, into an otherwise harmonious context. In either case the emphasis is gained though there be no discernible onomatopoetic correspondence between the form and the theme (the formal saliency being merely a kind of subtler italics, a mechanism for placing emphasis wherever one chooses, or such "absolute" stressing as comes of pounding the table with one's fist to emphasize either this remark or that). To realize that there is such absolute stressing, one has but to consider the great variety of emotions which can be intensified by climactic arrangement, such arrangement thus being a mere "coefficient of power" which can heighten the saliency of the emotion regardless of what emotion it may be.

As illustration, let us trace one formal contrivance through a set of diverse effects, as it is used in Wilde, Wordsworth, and Racine, and as it appeared by chance in actual life. Beginning with the last, we may recall a conversation between two children, a boy and a girl. The boy's mind was on one subject, the girl's turned to many subjects, with the result that the two of them were talking at cross-purposes. Pointing to a field beyond the road, the boy asked: "Whose field is that?" The girl answered: "That is Mr. Murdock's field"—and went on to tell where Mr. Murdock lived, how many children he had, when she had last seen these children, which of them she preferred, but the boy interrupted: "What does he do with the field?" "He usually plants the field in rye," she explained; "why, only the other day he drove up with a wagon carrying a plough, one of his sons was with him, they left the wagon at the gate, the two of them unloaded the plough, they hitched the"—but the boy interrupted severely: "Does the field go all the way over to the brook?" The conversation continued in this vein, always at cross-purposes, and growing increasingly humorous to eavesdroppers as its formal principle was inexorably continued. Note in *Salome,* however, this mechanism serving to produce a very different effect:

> SALOME: (to Iokanaan) . . . Suffer me to kiss thy mouth.
> IOKANAAN: Never! Daughter of Babylon! Daughter of Sodom! Never!
> SALOME: I will kiss thy mouth, Iokanaan. . . .
> The Young Syrian: . . . Look not at this man, look not at him. I cannot endure it. . . . Princess, do not speak these things.
> SALOME: I will kiss thy mouth, Iokanaan.

And as the Young Syrian, in despair, slays himself and falls dead at her feet, she continues: "Suffer me to kiss thy mouth, Iokanaan."

Turning now to Wordsworth's *We Are Seven:*

"You said that two at Conway dwell,
And two are gone to sea,
Yet ye are seven. I pray you tell,
Sweet maid, how this may be."

Then did the little Maid reply,
"Seven boys and girls are we;
Two of us in the churchyard lie,
Beneath the churchyard tree."

The poet argues with her: there were seven in all, two are now dead—so it follows that there are only five. But when he has made his point,

"How many are you, then," said I,
"If they two are in heaven?"
Quick was the little Maid's reply,
"O Master! we are seven."

Humour, *sournoiserie,* sentiment—we may now turn to Racine, where we find this talking at cross-purposes employed to produce a very poignant tragic irony. Agamemnon has secretly arranged to sacrifice his daughter, Iphigenia, on the altar; he is telling her so, but haltingly and cryptically, confessing and concealing at once; she does not grasp the meaning of his words but feels their ominousness. She has heard, she says, that Calchas is planning a sacrifice to appease the gods. Agamemnon exclaims: Would that he could turn these gods from their outrageous demands (his words referring to the oracle which requires her death, as the audience knows, but Iphigenia does not). Will the offering take place soon? she asks.—Sooner than Agamemnon wishes.—Will she be allowed to be present?—Alas! says Agamemnon.—You say no more, says Iphigenia.—"You will be there, my daughter"—the conflict in meanings being heightened by the fact that each of Agamemnon's non-sequitur rejoinders rhymes with Iphigenia's questions:

IPHIGÉNIE: Périsse le Troyen auteur de nos alarmes!
AGAMEMNON: Sa perte à ses vainqueurs coûtera bien des larmes.
IPHIGÉNIE: Les dieux deignent surtout prendre soin de vos jours!
AGAMEMNON: Les dieux depuis un temps me sont cruels et sourds.
IPHIGÉNIE: Calchas, dit-on, prépare un pompeux sacrifice?
AGAMEMNON: Puissé-je auparavant fléchir leur injustice!
IPHIGÉNIE: L'offrira-t-on bientôt?
AGAMEMNON: Plus tôt que je ne veux.
IPHIGÉNIE: Me sera-t-il permis de me joindre à vos voeux?
Verra-t-on à l'autel votre heureuse famille?
AGAMEMNON: Hélas!
IPHIGÉNIE: Vous vous taisez!
AGAMEMNON: Vous y serez, ma fille.

Perhaps the line, "Hurry up please, it's time," in the public-house scene of *The Waste Land,* as it is repeated and unanswered, could illustrate the use of this formal contrivance for still another effect.

THE INDIVIDUATION OF FORMS

. . . . .

(11) *Appeal of forms.* Form, having to do with the creation and gratification of needs, is "correct" in so far as it gratifies the needs which it creates. The appeal of the form in this sense is obvious: form *is* the appeal. . . .

(12) *"Priority" of forms.* There are formal patterns which distinguish our experience. They apply in art, since they apply outside of art. The accelerated motion of a falling body, the cycle of a storm, the gradations of a sunrise, the stages of a cholera epidemic, the ripening of crops—in all such instances we find the material of progressive form. Repetitive form applies to all manner of orientation, for we can continue to discuss a subject only by taking up in turn various aspects of it. (Recalling the schoolmen's subdivisions of a topic: *quis, quid, ubi, quibus auxiliis, cur, quo modo, quando.*) One talks about a thing by talking about something else. We establish a direction by co-ordinates; we establish a curve by three points, and thereupon can so place other points that they will be intercepted by this curve. Thus, though forms need not be prior to experience, they are certainly prior to the work of art exemplifying them. Psychology and philosophy may decide whether they are innate or resultant; so far as the work of art is concerned they simply *are*: when one turns to the production or enjoyment of work of art, a formal equipment is already present, and the effects of art are involved in its utilization. Such ultimate minor forms as contrast, comparison, metaphor, series, bathos, chiasmus, are based upon our modes of understanding anything; they are implicit in the processes of abstraction and generalization by which we think. (When analyzed so closely, they manifest the principles of repetitive and progressive form so frailly that we might better speak of coexistent unity and diversity—"something" in relation to "something else"—which is probably the basic distinction of our earliest perceptions. The most rudimentary manifestation of such coexistent unity and diversity in art is perhaps observable in two rhyming monosyllables, room—doom, where diversity of sound in the initial consonants coexists with unity of sound in the vowels and final consonants, a relation describable either as repetitive or as progressive.)

Such basic forms may, for all that concerns us, be wholly conventional. The subject-predicate form of sentence, for instance, has sanction enough if we have learned to expect it. It may be "natural" only as a path worn across a field is natural. But if experience has worn a path, the path is there—and in using the path we are obeying the authority of a prior form.

An ability to function in a certain way implies gratification in so functioning. A capacity is not something which lies dormant until used—a capacity is a command to act in a certain way. Thus a pinioned bird, though it has learned that flight is impossible, must yet spread out its wings and go through the motions of flying: its muscles, being equipped for flight, require the process. Similarly, if a dog lacks a bone, he will gnaw at a block of wood; not that he is hungry—for he may have his fill of meat—but his teeth, in their fitness to endure the strain of gnawing, feel the need of enduring that strain. So the formal aspects of art appeal in that they exercise formal potentialities of the reader. They enable the mind to follow processes amenable to it. *Mother Goose* is little more than an exerciser of simple mental functions. It is almost wholly formal, with processes of comparing, contrasting, and arranging. Though the jingles may, in some instances, have originated as political lampoons, etc., the ideas as adapted in the nursery serve purely as gymnastics in the fundamental processes of form.

The forms of art, to summarize, are not exclusively "aesthetic." They can be said to have a prior existence in the experiences of the person hearing or reading the work of art. They parallel processes which characterize his experiences outside of art.

(13) *Individuation of forms.* Since there are no forms of art which are not forms of experience outside of art, we may—so far as form is concerned—discuss the single poem or drama as an individuation of formal principles. Each work re-embodies the formal principles in different subject-matter. A "metaphor" is a concept, an abstraction—but a specific metaphor, exemplified by specific images, is an "individuation." Its appeal as form resides in the fact that its particular subject-matter enables the mind to follow a metaphor-process. In this sense we would restore the Platonic relationship between form and matter. A form is a way of experiencing; and such a form is made available in art when, by the use of specific subject-matter, it enables us to experience in this way. The images of art change greatly with changes in the environment and the ethical systems out of which they arise; but the principles of art, as individuated in these changing images, will be found to recur in all art, where they are individuated in one subject-matter or another. Accordingly, the concept of the individuation of forms constitutes the bridge by which we move from a consideration of form to a consideration of subject-matter.

(14) *Form and information.* The necessity of embodying form in subject-matter gives rise to certain "diseases" of form. The subject-matter tends to take on an intrinsic interest, to appeal independently of its functional uses. Thus, whereas realism originated to meet formal

requirements (the introduction of life-like details to make outlandish plots plausible), it became an end in itself; whereas it arose in the attempt to make the unreal realistic, it ended by becoming a purpose in itself and making the real realistic. Similarly, description grows in assertiveness until novelists write descriptions, not for their use in the arousing and fulfilling of expectation, but because the novelists have something to describe which they consider interesting in itself (a volcano, a remarkable savage tribe, an unusual thicket). This tendency becomes frankly "scientific" in the thesis drama and the psychological novel, where the matter is offered for its value as the "exposure" of a burning issue. In the psychological novel, the reader may often follow the hero's mental processes as noteworthy facts, just as he would follow them in a scientific treatise on the human mind, except that in the novel the facts are less schematically arranged from the standpoint of scientific presentation. In so far as the details in a work are offered, not for their bearing upon the business of moulding and meeting the reader's expectations, but because these details are interesting in themselves, the appeal of form retreats behind the appeal of information. Atrophy of form follows hypertrophy of information.

There is, obviously, no "right" proportion of the two. A novelist, for instance, must give enough description for us to feel the conviction of his story's background. Description, to this extent, is necessary in the interests of form—and there is no clearly distinguishable point at which description for the purposes of the plot goes over into description for its own sake. Similarly, a certain amount of psychological data concerning the characters of a fiction helps the author to make the characters of moment to the reader, and thus has a formal function in the affecting of the reader's desires: yet the psychology can begin to make claims of its own, and at times the writer will analyse his hero not because analysis is formally needed at this point, but because the writer has some disclosures which he considers interesting in themselves.

The hypertrophy of information likewise tends to interfere with our enjoyment in the repetition of a work. For the presence of information as a factor in literature has enabled writers to rely greatly upon ignorance as a factor in appeal. Thus, they will relieve the reader's ignorance about a certain mountain of Tibet, but when they have done so they will have less to "tell" him at a second reading. Surprise and suspense are the major devices for the utilization of ignorance (the psychology of information), for when they are depended upon, the reader's interest in the work is based primarily upon his ignorance of its outcome. In the classic drama, where the psychology of form is emphasized, we have not surprise but disclosure (the surprise being a surprise not to the audience, but to the characters); and likewise suspense here is not based upon our ignorance of the forthcoming scenes. There is, perhaps, more formal suspense at a second reading than at a first in a scene such as Hamlet's giving of the pipes to Guildenstern. It is the suspense of certain forces gathering to produce a certain result. It is the suspense of a rubber band which we see being tautened. We know that it will be snapped—there is thus no ignorance of the outcome; our satisfaction arises from our participation in the process, from the fact that the beginnings of the dialogue lead us to feel the logic of its close.

Painting, architecture, music are probably more amenable to repetition without loss because the formal aspects are not so obscured by the subject-matter in which they are embodied. One can repeat with pleasure a jingle from *Mother Goose,* where the formality is obvious, yet one may have no interest whatsoever in memorizing a psychological analysis in a fiction. He may wish to remember the observations themselves, but his own words are as serviceable as the author's. And if he does choose to memorize the particular wording of the author, and recites it with pleasure, the passage will be found to have a formal, as well as an informational, validity.

(15) *Form and ideology.* The artist's manipulation of the reader's desires involves his use of what the reader considers desirable. If the reader believes in monogamistic marriage, and in the code of fidelity surrounding it, the poet can exploit this belief in writing an *Othello.* But the form of his drama is implicated in the reader's belief, and Othello's conduct would hardly seem "syllogistic" in polyandrous Tibet. Similarly, the conventional form which marks the close of Baudelaire's *Femmes Damnées,* as he turns from the dialogue of the two Lesbians to his eloquent apostrophe, "Descendez, descendez, lamentables victimes," is an effect built out of precisely that intermingling of church morality and profanation which Baudelaire always relies upon for his deepest effects. He writes for neither pure believers nor pure infidels, but for infidels whose infidelity greatly involves the surviving vocabulary of belief. In war times, the playwright who would depict a villain has only to designate his man as a foreign spy—at other times he must be more inventive to find something so exploitable in the ideology of his audience. A slight change in ideology, in fact, can totally reverse our judgments as to the form which it embodies. Thus, Euripides was accused of misusing the *deus ex machina.* In his *Iphigenia at Aulis,* for instance, his syllogistic progression leads the heroine inexorably to the sacrificial altar—whereupon a god descends and snatches her unharmed from her father's knife. Approached from the ideology of an Aristotle, this would constitute a violation of form, since the dramatic causality leads to one end and the poet gives us another. But we can consider the matter differently: the drama was a survival of a religious rite; as such, the god certainly had a place in it; Euripides frankly attempted to regain some of the earlier dramatic forms which Aeschylus and Sophocles had suppressed

and which brought out more clearly its religious affiliations; could we not, accordingly, look upon the appearance of the god as a part of Euripides' program? Euripides would, that is, write a play in which the details of the plot led the heroine so inexorably towards destruction that nothing could save her but the intervention of the gods. By this ideology, the closing theophany is formally correct: it is not a way of avoiding a bad ending (the "syllogistically" required death of an Iphigenia who has won the audience's sympathies); it is a syllogistic preparation for the god's appearance. As another instance of how the correctness of the form depends upon the ideology, we may consider a piece of juvenile fiction for Catholic boys. The hero will be consistently a hero: he will show bravery, honesty, kindness to the oppressed, strength in sports, gentleness to women—in every way; by the tenets of repetitive form, he will repeat the fact that he is a hero. And among these repetitions will be his converting of Indians to Catholicism. To a Catholic boy, this will be one more repetition of his identity as an ideal hero: but to the Protestant boy, approaching the work from a slightly different ideology, repetitive form will be endangered at this point.

The shifts in ideology being continuous, not only from age to age but from person to person, the individuation of universal forms through specific subject-matter can bring the formal principles themselves into jeopardy. . . .

. . . . .

(20) *The Symbol.* The Symbol is the verbal parallel to a pattern of experience. The poet, for instance, may pity himself for his undeserved neglect, and this self-pity may colour his day. It may be so forceful, and so frequently recurrent as to become selective, so that he finds ever new instances of his unappreciated worth. Self-pity assumes enough prominence in his case to become a pattern of experience. If he converts this pattern into a plot, The King and the Peasant (about a King who has but the trappings of kingliness and a Peasant who is, in the true sense, a King) he has produced a Symbol. He might have chosen other Symbols to verbalize the same pattern. In fact, if his pattern continues to obsess him, he undoubtedly will exemplify the same pattern in other Symbols: he will next produce The Man Against the Mob, or A Saint Dying in Neglect. Or he may be still more devious, and finding his own problems writ large in the life of some historic figure, he may give us a vigorous biography of the Little Corporal.

The Symbol is often quite obvious, as in *Childe Harold, Madame Bovary, Euphues, Don Quixote, Tom Sawyer, Wilhelm Meister, Hamlet.* In lyrics of mood it is not so readily summed up in a name. It is pervasive but not condensed. The Symbol of *The Tempest?* Perhaps it is more nearly condensed in the songs and doings of Ariel than elsewhere in the play, but essentially it is a complex attitude which pervades the setting, plot, and characters. The Symbol might be called a word invented by the artist to specify a particular grouping or pattern or emphasizing of experiences—and the work of art in which the Symbol figures might be called a definition of this word. The novel, *Madame Bovary,* is an elaborate definition of a new word in our vocabulary. In the lyric, in *The Tempest,* the Symbol is present as definition, though not as a word. The Symbol is a formula.

(21) *Appeal of the Symbol.* . . . A Symbol appeals:

As the interpretation of a situation. It can, by its function as name and definition, give simplicity and order to an otherwise unclarified complexity. It provides a terminology of thoughts, actions, emotions, attitudes, for codifying a pattern of experience. The artist, through experiencing intensively or extensively a certain pattern, becomes as it were an expert, a specialist, in this pattern. And his skill in articulation is expended upon the schematizing of his subject. The schematizing is done not by abstraction, as in science, but by idealization, by presenting in a "pure" or consistent manner some situation which, as it appears among the contingencies of real life, is less effectively coordinated; the idealization is the elimination of irrelevancies.

By enabling the acceptance of a situation. At times the situation revealed by the Symbol may not be particularly complex, but our minds have been closed to the situation through the exigencies of practical life. The Symbol can enable us to admit, for instance, the existence of a certain danger which we had emotionally denied. A humorous Symbol enables us to admit the situation by belittling it; a satirical Symbol enables us to admit the situation by permitting us to feel aloof from it; a tragic Symbol enables us to admit the situation by making us feel the dignity of being in such a situation; the comic Symbol enables us to admit the situation by making us feel our power to surmount it. A Symbol may also force us to admit a situation by sheer thoroughness of the Symbol, but if the situation is one which we had strong motives for denying, and if the Symbol is not presented by some such accompanying attitude as above noted, the admitting of the situation will probably be accompanied by a revulsion against the Symbol.

As the corrective of a situation. Life in the city arouses a compensatory interest in life on a farm, with the result that Symbols of farm life become appealing; or a dull life in the city arouses a compensatory interest in Symbols depicting a brilliant life in the city; etc. In such cases the actual situation to which the Symbol is adapted is left unformulated. Most stories of romantic love are probably in this class.

As the exerciser of "submerged" experience. A capacity to function in a certain way (as we have pointed out in the discussion of form) is not merely something which lies on a shelf until used—a capacity to function in a certain way is an obligation so to function. Even those "universal experiences" which the reader's particular patterns of experience happen to slight are in a sense "candidates"—they await with some aggression their chance of being brought into play. Thus though the artist's pattern may be different from the reader's, the Symbol by touching on submerged patterns in the reader may "stir remote depths." Symbols of cruelty, horror, and incest may often owe their appeal to such causes. . . .

(22) *The Symbol as generating principle.* When the poet has converted his pattern of experience into a Symbolic equivalent, the Symbol becomes a guiding principle in itself. Thus, once our poet suffering self-pity has hit upon the plot of The King and the Peasant, he finds himself with many problems remote from his self-pity. Besides showing his King as a weakling, he must show him as a King —whereupon accounts of court life. Similarly the treatment of the Peasant will entail harvest scenes, dances, descriptions of the Peasant's hut. There will be the Peasant's Wife and the Queen and a host of subsidiary characters. As the Symbol is ramified, Symbols within Symbols will arise, many of these secondary Symbols with no direct bearing upon the pattern of experience behind the key Symbol. These secondary or ramifying Symbols can be said to bear upon the underlying pattern of experience only in so far as they contribute to the workings of the key Symbol.

Again: Symbols will be subtilized in ways not contributory to the pattern. The weak King cannot be too weak, the manly Peasant cannot be too manly—thus we find the Poet "defending" to an extent the very character whom he would denigrate, and detracting from the character who is to triumph. Such considerations arise with the adoption of the Symbol, which is the conversion of an experiential pattern into a formula for affecting an audience.

The Symbol, in other words, brings up problems extrinsic to the pattern of experience behind it. The underlying pattern, that is, remains the same whether the poet writes The King and the Peasant, The Man Against the Mob, or A Saint Dying in Neglect. But in each case the Symbol is a generating principle which entails a selection of different subtilizations and ramifications. Thus, the difference between the selectivity of a dream and the selectivity of art is that the dream obeys no principle of selection but the underlying pattern, whereas art, which expands by the ramifying of the Symbol, has the Symbol as a principle of selection.

DOUBLE PLOTS:

HEROIC AND PASTORAL IN THE MAIN PLOT AND SUB-PLOT

(1935)

WILLIAM EMPSON

I

THE MODE of action of a double plot is the sort of thing critics are liable to neglect; it does not depend on being noticed for its operation, so is neither an easy nor an obviously useful thing to notice. Deciding which sub-plot to put with which main plot must be like deciding what order to put the turns in at a music hall, a form of creative work on which I know of no critical dissertation, but at which one may succeed or fail. As in the music hall, the parts may be by different hands, different in tone and subject matter, hardly connected by plot, and yet the result may be excellent; Middleton's *The Changeling* is the best example of this I can find. It is an easy-going device, often used simply to fill out a play, and has an obvious effect in the Elizabethans of making you feel the play deals with life as a whole, with any one who comes onto the street the scene so often represents; this may be why criticism has not taken it seriously when it deserved to be. Just because of this carelessness much can be put into it; to those who miss the connections the thing still seems sensible, and queer connections can be insinuated powerfully and unobtrusively; especially if they fit in with ideas the audience already has at the back of its mind. The old quarrel about tragi-comedy, which deals with part of the question, shows that the drama in England has always at its best had a certain looseness of structure; one might almost say that the English drama did not outlive the double plot. The matter is not only of theoretical interest; it seems likely that the double plot needs to be revived and must first be understood.

Probably the earliest form of double plot is the comic interlude, often in prose between serious verse scenes. Even here the relation between the two is neither obvious nor constant; the comic part relieves boredom and the strain of belief in the serious part, but this need not imply criticism of it. Falstaff may carry a half-secret doubt about the value of the kings and their quarrels, but the form derived from the Miracle Plays, and Mac's wife in the Nativity is doing something more peculiar. To hide a stolen sheep in the cradle and call it her newborn child is a very detailed parallel to the Paschal Lamb, hidden in the appearance of a newborn child, open to scandal because without a legal father, and kept among animals in the manger. The Logos enters humanity from above as this sheep does from below, or takes on the animal nature of man which is like a man becoming a sheep, or sustains all nature and its laws so that in one sense it is as truly present in the sheep as the man. The searchers think this a very peculiar child, a "natural" sent from the supernatural, and Mac's wife tries to quiet them by a powerful joke on the eating of Christ in the Sacrament:

> If ever I you beguiled
> May I eat this child,
> That lies in this cradle.

This parody must have had its effect on the many critics who have praised the scene, but I don't remember to have read one of them who mentioned it; I suppose those who were conscious of what was affecting them thought it obvious. The effect is hard to tape down; it seems a sort of test of the belief in the Incarnation strong enough to prove it to be massive and to make the humorous thieves into fundamental symbols of humanity.

Wyndham Lewis's excellent book, for one, points out that the Miracle Play tradition gave a hint of magic to Elizabethan drama; with nationalism and the disorder of religion the Renaissance Magnificent Man took the place of the patron saint, anyway on the stage; hence the tragic hero was a king on sacrificial as well as Aristotelian grounds; his death was somehow Christlike, somehow on his tribe's account, something like an atonement for his tribe that put it in harmony with God or nature. This seems a less wild notion if one remembers that a sixteenth-century critic would be interested in magical theories about kings; he would not be blankly surprised as at the psychoanalyst on Hamlet. In the obscure suggestions of the two plots one would expect to find this as a typical submerged concept, and in fact their fundamental use was to show the labour of the king or saint in the serious part and in the comic part the people, as "popular" as possible, for whom he laboured. This gave a sort of reality to the sentiments about the king or saint (*Marriage à la Mode* is an odd example—they needed giving reality there); even here the relation between the two parts is that of symbol and thing symbolised.

This in itself can hardly be kept from irony, and the comic part, once licensed, has an obvious subject for its jokes. Usually it provides a sort of parody or parallel in low life to the serious part; Faustus' servant, like his master, gets dangerously mixed up with the devils. This gives an impression of dealing with life completely, so that critics sometimes say that *Henry IV* deals with the whole of English life at some date, either Shakespeare's or Henry's; this is palpable nonsense, but what the device wants to make you feel. Also the play can thus anticipate the parody a hearer might have in mind without losing its dignity, which again has a sort of completeness. It is hard to feel that Mac's wife was meant to do this, but she is only the less conscious end of a scale, and perhaps no example occupies only one point of it. A remark by Middleton on clowns seems a comment on this process:

> There's nothing in a play to a clown, if he
> Have but the grace to hit on't; that's the thing indeed:
> The king shows well, but he sets off the king.

The ideas of *foil* to a jewel and *soil* from which a flower grows give the two different views of such a character, and with a long "s" the words are almost indistinguishable; it may be significant that the first edition of Tamburlane's Beauty speech reads *soil* for the accepted "foil," a variant I have never seen listed, but the line is at some distance from interpreting either word. A clear case of "foil" is given by the play of heroic swashbucklers which has a comic cowardly swashbuckler (Parolles), not at all to parody the heroes but to stop you from doing so: "If you want to laugh at this sort of thing laugh now and get it over." I believe the Soviet Government in its early days paid two clowns, Bim and Bom, to say as jokes the things everybody else would have been shot for saying.

An account of the double plot, then, is needed for a general view of pastoral because the interaction of the two plots give a particularly clear setting for, or machine for imposing, the social and metaphysical ideas on which pastoral depends. What is displayed on the tragicomic stage is a sort of marriage of the myths of heroic and pastoral, a thing felt as fundamental to both and necessary to the health of society. In a later part of this essay I shall take the hypostatised hero alone and try to show that his machinery is already like that of pastoral, and more will have to be said about the connections of heroic and pastoral in the essay on the *Beggar's Opera,* where the two halves of the stock double plot are written simultaneously. It will be clear, I hope, that the comic characters are in a sense figures of pastoral myth so far as they make profound remarks and do things with unexpectedly great effects, but I want now to look at some double plots in action without special attention to their clowns.

. . . . .

II

I shall add here some remarks about irony and dramatic ambiguity, arising out of the double plots, and only connected with pastoral so far as they describe a process of putting the complex into the simple. If the foregoing account of the double plots is at all true the process seems to leave room for critical theorising.

There are two elements in the type of joke made by Bim and Bom or Parolles. In part you treat the reader as an object of psychology and satisfy two of his impulses; in part you make him feel, as a rational being, that he can rely on your judgment because you know both sides of the case. But this is not in itself irony; you do not appeal to *his* judgment and he need not realise what you are doing. There is a good crude example in Tourneur's *The Atheist's Tragedy*. Castabella has been forced to marry the son of D'Amville, who has sent her lover Charlemont away; the son is dying, and too weak to consummate; she speaks of this as her only comfort in affliction. Levidulcia, in the next words of the play, tries to seduce Sebastian, and when he leaves her walks off with the servant Fresco, with the reflection

> Lust is a spirit, which whosoe'er doth raise
> The first man to encounter boldly, lays.

If you had been thinking this before, and feeling that Castabella's chastity was a little extravagant and heroical, then the contrast would show that the author knew it already; it is not that he is ignorant of human nature, but that Castabella really was very chaste. And again it is in part a less rational matter of satisfying impulses; after you have made an imaginative response of one kind to a situation you satisfy more of what is included in your own nature, you are more completely interested in the play, if the chief other response possible is called out too. The two may seem inextricable; at its crudest the device has something of the repose of wisdom as well as the ease of humour. But clearly Mac's Wife's parody was more "psychological" than rational.

Also the device sets your judgment free because you need not identify yourself firmly with any one of the characters (the drama of personality is liable to boil down to this); a situation is repeated for quite different characters, and this puts the main interest in the situation—not the characters. Thus the effect of having two old men with ungrateful children, of different sorts, is to make us generalise the theme of Lear and feel that whole classes of children have become unfaithful, all nature is breaking up, as in the storm. The situation is made something valuable in itself, perhaps for reasons hardly realised; it can work on you like a myth.

. . . . .

An irony has no point unless it is true, in some degree, in both senses; for it is imagined as part of an argument; what is said is made absurd, but it is what the opponent might say. There may be an obscure connection here with the reason why critics who agree about the degree of merit of the *Jew of Malta* can disagree about whether or not it is a joke, why so much of Handel can become funny without ceasing to be beautiful. It is not the joke that is fundamental but the conflict, and there is something like a conflict in the maintenance of a satisfying order.

> Would you keep your pearls from tramplers,
> Weigh the license, weigh the banns;
> Mark my song upon your samplers,
> Wear it on your knots and fans.

It is very hard to know what Smart himself felt about this excellent verse. There must be some sort of joke in the idea of the young lady flaunting a fan with "weigh the banns" on it, and striking terror through the ballroom, but the joke may be against *banns* or *fans*. (The advice was not too fantastic; the *Beggar's Opera* songs were put on fans.) The song is about a conflict between delight in the courageous trivialities of pleasure and terror of the forces a triviality may let loose; there is too little doubt of its force for a doubt about its "sincerity." Either a conscious overstatement was meant to add to the courage, and so the gaiety, of the pleasure, or the underlying terror of Smart's melancholia became too strong for the gaiety of the form; these are two sides of the same thing, and yet whichever you take there is an irony against the other. Any mutual comparison between people who would judge differently has a latent irony of this sort, if only because it is the material from which either irony could be made.

To do this on the stage might be regarded as combining the normal halves of the double plot into one. The quality Mr. Eliot described in Marlowe and Jonson seems to depend on it; Restoration heroic gives more obvious if more puzzling examples. The reason why the plays are satisfying though so unreal is that they are so close to their parodies; the mood of parody is hardly under the surface, only as it were officially ignored. Morat will not allow Nourmahal to kill Aurungzebe:

> NOURM. What am I, that you dare to bind my hand?
> So low, I've not a murder at command!

How bitter, how belittling, how destructive of the heroic attitude, this line might be in Pope; and yet the same feeling here somehow makes the reality of its dignity. The sentiment and the "pseudo-parody to disarm criticism," usually separated into the two plots, are combined in one.

Here the effect is, I suppose, known to be a clash, felt to be odd, by the author, but the same thing may be done without any suggestion of irony. Swinburne's *Before a Crucifix* gets all its beauty of metaphor from the Christian ideas it sets out to destroy, and its rhetoric is no less clear and strong when you have noticed the fact. The whole point of Housman's *Last Poems,* xxvii., is to deny the Pathetic Fallacy, to say that man is alone and has no sympathy from Nature; its method is to assume the Pathetic Fallacy as a matter of course.

> The diamond tears adorning
> Thy low mound on the lea,
> These are the tears of morning,
> That weeps, but not for thee.

It may weep for pains reassuringly similar to those of humanity, whether consciously or not, or actually for those of man though not of one individual. That the dew might not be tears at all the poetry cannot imagine, and this clash conveys with great pathos and force a sense that the position of man in the world is extraordinary, hard even to conceive. Dr. Richards in *Science and Poetry* said that this trick was played in order to hide facts the poet pretended to accept, and no doubt it often is, but I can see no weakness in its use here. That excellent story in Hugh Kingsmill's *Frank Harris* about the meeting with Professor Housman shows how misleading his irony can be,[1] and how excellent the poetry remains after you have been misled; it seems normal to this sort of "perfect" verse that, because so much has been polished away from the original feeling, it will satisfy a great variety of feelings, and because of its perfection of "form" will attract them.

The ironies I have quoted are clearly very different from that of *Jonathan Wild,* which appeals fiercely and singly to the readers' judgment, but I think they are only near the other end of a scale; and a scale on which no irony occupies only one point. It is a commonplace that irony is a dangerous weapon because two-edged, so that Defoe was arrested by his own party, and that there are usually partial ways of enjoying an irony, so that Gulliver makes a book for children. I shall take a comfortable example where one can see this at work.

> Fish say, they have their stream or pond,
> But is there anything beyond?
> This life cannot be all, they swear,
> For how unpleasant, if it were . . .
> Oh never fly conceals a hook,
> Fish say, in the eternal brook;
> But more than mundane weeds are there,
> And mud, celestially fair;
> Fat caterpillars drift around,
> And Paradisal grubs are found;
> Unfading moths, immortal flies,
> And the worm that never dies.

[1] Empson's comment here refers to Frank Harris' reading of irony in the poem *1887*, an intention which Housman denied. That the poem is not without irony, despite Housman's professed "intention," is the point of Brooks's interpretation of *1887* in *The Explicator,* 2 (March, 1944), 34. Charles C. Walcutt has an analysis of *1887* in *College English,* February 1944. For Brooks's summing up of Housman as poet and critic see *Kenyon Review,* Winter, 1941. [*Editor's note.*]

I take it many people like this playful thing by Rupert Brooke as making fish seem vain (touchingly absurd) but otherwise just like people (to try to imagine them as fish makes the universe seem inhuman, indifferent to people); they feel good from sympathising with fish, and agreeably superior to them because we are right about heaven and fish wrong. ("Anyway it is not true that fish talk like this, so the poem is not serious, and why should one read cynicism where there is so much tenderness?") A later stage would recognise the scepticism about human knowledge but take it as an essentially "poetical" mood, Poe's "tone of melancholy"; a false pretence of humility, like pastoral, designed only to give strength. This too does not find it a shock to theology; indeed finds in its readiness to conceive doubt something of the ease of certainty. I should say that both these pleasant interpretations were active in the author's mind and a source of the courage of the poem's gaiety; the tone of banter seems even to imply some sense of teasing his audience with the possible interpretations, or laughing at them for accepting the pleasant ones, like the fish. Not that the poem is unusually subtle; this sort of analysis would apply to quite crude work.

. . . . .

The fundamental impulse of irony is to score off both the arguments that have been puzzling you, both sets of sympathies in your mind, both sorts of fool who will hear you; a plague on both their houses. It is because of the strength given by this antagonism that it seems to get so safely outside the situation it assumes, to decide so easily about the doubt which it in fact accepts. This may seem a disagreeable pleasure in the ironist but he gives the same pleasure more or less secretly to his audience, and the process brings to mind the whole body of their difficulty with so much sharpness and freshness that it may give the strength to escape from it. It is when the ironist himself begins to doubt (late in Butler's *Fair Haven*) that the far-reaching ironies appear; and by then the thing is like a dramatic appeal to an audience, because both parties in the audience could swallow it. The essential is for the author to repeat the audience in himself, and he may safely seem to do nothing more. No doubt he has covertly, if it is a good irony, to reconcile the opposites into a larger unity, or suggest a balanced position by setting out two extreme views, or accept a lie (more or less consciously) to find energy to accept a truth, or something like that, but I am not concerned with these so much as with the machinery by which they are put across. I think it must be conceived as like a full-blown "dramatic ambiguity," in which different parts of the audience are meant to interpret the thing in different ways.

The two phrases "dramatic irony" and "ironical cheers," both concerned with an audience, take a wide view of irony as a matter of course. Dramatic irony, as the term is used, need only make some point (not a simple comparison) by reminding you of another part of the play. And the best ironical cheers do not mean "obviously you are wrong" but "obviously we can grant that; taking the larger view, your argument is in our favour." When Levidulcia brings out her couplet, those who take it as an irony against her hiss; those who feel it needed saying give an ironical cheer. The effect is like humour in its breadth, though like irony in its tension; humour need only say "it is cheering to watch her, she shows we are right by being so obviously wrong," whereas the cheer means "it is discreditable, but it is the other half of the truth." Language seems to agree with me here, that double irony is somehow natural to the stage.

The value of the state of mind which finds double irony natural is that it combines breadth of sympathy with energy of judgment; it can keep its balance among all the materials for judging. The word *sympathy* here is suspicious; it may range from "able to imagine what some one feels and so understand him" to "prepared to be sorry for him, because you are safe and superior"; indeed it may have shrunk towards the second. People say that Pope's satire has too little sympathy to be good, but sympathy in the first sense it certainly has. The Elizabethan feeling can be seen most clearly in the popular rogue pamphlets, which express warm sympathy for the villains while holding in mind both horror for their crimes as such and pity and terror for the consequences. Stories of successful cheats are "merry" because the reader imagines himself as the robber, so as to enjoy his courage, dexterity, etc., and as the robbed—he can stand up to this trick now that he has been told; a secret freedom kept the two from obstructing each other. This fulness in the audience clearly allowed of complex character-building; one need not put hero and villain in black and white; though not everybody in the audience understood such a character they did not object when they only understood partial conflicting interpretations of it. Probably one could make analyses of the possible ways of taking a Shakespeare "character" like my petty one of the ways of reading Brooke on fish; few people in the audience would get it in only one way, and few in all. And even the man who saw the full interpretation would still use the partial ones; both because he was in contact with the audience the play assumed and because he needed crude as well as delicate means of interpreting it quickly on the stage. This is obvious about surprise effects; the theatregoer has a quite different sequence of emotions in seeing the play a second time, and yet he has not lost the effects due to surprise, even as much as in re-reading a novel, because he can feel some one in the audience still being surprised. But to do this in more serious matters needs a special attitude. What is so impressive about the Elizabethans is that complexity of sympathy was somehow obvious to them; this same power,

I think, made them feel at home with dramatic ambiguity and with the vague suggestiveness of the double plot.

The supreme case of dramatic ambiguity is Verrall's interpretation of Euripides; the plays were to dramatise sacred myths for a popular religious festival, yet for some members of the audience they were to suggest criticism of the gods, for others to convey complete disbelief and actually rationalise the myths before their eyes. The whole point was to play off one part of the audience against the other, and yet this made a superb "complete play" for the critic who felt what was being felt in the whole audience. This total aesthetic effect would not be "in the play" if it was only a clever secret attack. But the plays are not addressed only to the few; the choruses are straightforward religious poetry; all shades of opinion were to be fused by the infection of the theatre into a unity of experience, under sufficiently different forms to avoid riots. On a smaller scale I think this is usual in the theatre. No doubt, as he said, it was painful to Shakespeare that his audiences were so crude, but any one who has seen Shaw acted in the provinces will know that a dramatist may actually depend on a variety of crudity; on a giggle here, and a clucking of the tongue there, and the power to make them change places. Any "solid" play, which can give the individual a rich satisfaction at one time, and therefore different satisfactions at different times from different "points of view," is likely to be a play that can satisfy different individuals; it can face an audience; the trouble with plays like Maeterlinck's is that they are only good from one "point of view." The Elizabethans had anyway to satisfy both groundlings and courtly critics; there had to be levels of interpretation, each of which made a presentable play. And yet, since the separation of ambiguity into different times for the reader or different persons for an audience is never complete, at each such level you would feel that there were others that made the play "solid"; so far as the audience is an inter-conscious unit they all work on it together.

The mind's ear catches a warning rumble from the psycho-analysts at this point, "far within, and in their own dimensions like themselves." Ernest Jones' essay on Hamlet, which may perhaps have caused Mr. Eliot to jettison the play in his later essay, brought out a very far-reaching use of double-plot methods and introduced at least one valuable technical term; in "decomposition" "one person of complex character is dissolved and replaced by several, each of whom possesses a different aspect of the character which in the simpler form of the myth is combined in one being." This is supposed always to be due to a regular repression, as by an Œdipus complex producing a tyrant and a loved father, but it obviously has a wider use—wherever a situation, conceived as a myth and repeated with variations, is the root material of the play. The trouble about this approach is its assumption that the only ideas with which an audience can be infected unconsciously are the fundamental Freudian ones. Freud's theory of the Group Mind assumes that once in a crowd the individual loses all the inhibitions of civilisation, and a theatre audience satisfies none of M'Dougall's five conditions without which a group cannot be other than infantile. (I should say this is less obviously untrue of a cinema audience, which can't let the actor know what it thinks of him and therefore makes less delicate exchanges of its opinions.) One might reply with a Freudian Opposite; the reason that a mob is the very cauldron of the inner depths is that an appeal to a circle of a man's equals is the fundamental escape into the fresh air of the mind. Mob thought may kill us all before our time, but the scientist's view of it should not be warped by horror, and the writer who isolates himself from all feeling for his audience acquires the faults of romanticism without its virtues. Probably an audience does to some extent let loose the hidden traditional ideas common to its members, which may be a valuable process, but it also forms a small "public opinion"; the mutual influence of its members' judgments, even though expressed by the most obscure means or only imagined from their presence, is so strong as to produce a sort of sensibility held in common, and from their variety it may be wider, more sensible, than that of any of its members. It is this fact that the theatre is more really public than the public of novelists which has made it so fruitful, and makes its failure or limitation to one class a social misfortune.

A reviewer of my book on ambiguity rightly said that I was confusing poetical with dramatic uses of it, which he said showed that I was treating poems as phenomena, not as things judged by a mind. Certainly to claim that one can slip from one view to the other is to assume a disorderly theory of aesthetics, a theory rather like the version of proletarian aesthetic I was attacking in the first chapter. It is clear that any theory has to deal with a puzzle here, and its main business is so to treat the puzzle as to keep it from doing harm. This is only Horace *v.* Longinus; a work of art is a thing judged by the artist and yet a thing inspired which may mean more than he knew—as may a mathematical formula for that matter; and a critic's judgment is only part of the effects of the play, which are what have to be judged. There is an old argument as to whether probability is a fundamental notion or one derived from statistics, and it seems possible that this is an insoluble puzzle because the two are mutually dependent, like the One and the Many. In the same way a poetical ambiguity depends on the reader's weighting the possible meanings according to their probability, while a dramatic ambiguity depends on the audience's having the possible reactions in the right proportions, but the distinction is only a practical one. Once you break into the godlike unity of the appreciator you find a microcosm of which the theatre is the macrocosm; the mind is complex and ill-connected like an audience, and it is as surprising in the one case as the other that a sort of unity can be produced by a play.

III

. . . . .

Mr. James Smith, in an excellent essay (*Scrutiny,* III, No. 2), said that the metaphysical conceit was always built out of the immediate realisation of a philosophical problem such as that of the One and the Many. I should agree with this, but I think it was nearly always arrived at in the way I am trying to describe. The supreme example of the problem of the One and the Many was given by the Logos who was an individual man. In all those conceits where the general is given a sort of sacred local habitation in a particular, so that this particular is made much more interesting than all similar particulars (absolutely more interesting, but with a rival suggestion of wit), and the others are all dependent on it, there is an implied comparison to the sacrificial cult-hero, to Christ as the Son of Man. To do this indeed was hardly more than to take personification seriously; it is incarnation already.

> If ever any beauty I did see,
> Which I desir'd, and got, 'twas but a dreame of thee.
>
> And therefore what thou wert, and who,
> I bid Love aske, and now
> That it *assume* thy body, I allow,
> And fixe itself in thy lip, eye, and brow.

This at once leads to the dependence of the world upon the person or thing treated as a personification: "This member of the class is the whole class, or its defining property: this man has a magical importance to all men." If you choose an important member the result is heroic; if you choose an unimportant one it is pastoral.

> Or if, when thou, the worlds soule, goest,
> It stay, tis but thy carcase then,
> The fairest woman, but thy ghost,
> But corrupt wormes, the worthyest men.
>
> O wrangling schooles, that search what fire
> Shall burne this world, had none the wit
> Unto this knowledge to aspire,
> That this her fever might be it?

All Donne's best poems, the *Canonization, Twickenham Garden, A Valediction of Weeping,* the *Nocturnal,* the *Funeral,* the *Relique,* are built out of this; it is forced into the *Exstasie* so violently as to make M. Legouis suspect the poem's sincerity:

> To our bodies turne wee then, that so
> Weake men on love reveal'd may looke;
> Loves mysteries in soules do grow,
> But yet the body is his booke.

The idea of arranging that everybody else can look, so as to do them good, ridiculous in itself, follows from the implied comparison to the universal Passion of Christ. This process of thought completed the usefulness of the globe-symbol: "we can rightly take our world (planet) as the world (universe), because to us it is that one of all the planets which has been made symbolic (in effect simply made real). The others are all like it, so need not be examined; the others are all dependent on it, so are controlled when it is."

But indeed this process of uniting particular and general is already involved in the idea of God. God cannot be prior to goodness, so that the good is simply his will, or he is a tyrant without morality; nor can goodness be prior to him, so that he is necessarily good, or he is not free. Though God is a person he and the good must be mutually dependent; it was because Milton refused to play the tricks of the metaphysical and made God merely one of the persons of his story that Satan had so strong a case. It is not an accidental product of a special theology that Christ once made God must be treated in this way. But in the devotional verse of the time the idea is stretched onto other individuals as easily as in the love poetry. Mary Magdalene is treated as a sort of rival Christ in Crashaw's *Weeper;* or perhaps she makes a second atonement, between Christ and the world. It is she now who underlies the order of nature.

> At these thy weeping gates,
> (Watching their watry motion)
> Each winged moment waits,
> Takes his Tear, and gets him gone.
> By thine Ey's tinct ennobled thus
> Time layes him up; he's pretious.

She is not merely a waterclock but *the* waterclock by which Nature measures time; if it were not for her sacrifice time would break up altogether. Since her tears are both the essential stars and the essential dew (and so on) they reconcile earth and heaven, they perform the function of the sacrificed god. "Portable and compendious oceans" has been thought an absurd phrase merely because it puts specially clearly what such critics would call the absurdity of the whole conception of the poem; her tears are the idea of water, all water, and make water do whatever it does. The Protestants were clearly right in calling this version of the invocation of saints heretical, because it destroys the uniqueness of Christ, but for literary purposes they continued to do it themselves. The idea is stated as clearly and is as central to the poem in a lovesong of Carew which seems to have got into the Oxford Book as an example of "careless ease."

> Ask me no more where Jove bestows
> When June is past, the fading rose;
> For in thy beauty's orient deep
> These flowers, as in their causes, sleep.

The trick was common but not as a rule forced on one's attention; there was another way of taking the thing to make it seem sensible, and you could take it that way alone. Queen Elizabeth and the person of importance chosen as a hero of tragedy had an obvious influence on public affairs; to the lover who was speaking the world would seem empty without the loved woman. Indeed if there was no other way of taking it the thing would be pointless. But Donne's use of it in the First Anniversary is peculiar because there is no obvious other way; it is an enormous picture of the complete decay of the universe, and this is caused by the death of a girl of no importance whom Donne had never seen. Ben Jonson said "if it had been written to the Virgin, it would have been something," but only Christ would be enough; only his removal from the world would explain the destruction foretold by astronomers. The only way to make the poem sensible is to accept Elizabeth Drury as the Logos. Of course this is not necessarily unchristian; those few persons who felt that life was empty after her death were supposed to find in their feelings about her the reality of the doctrines true about Christ. And Donne had very serious feelings about the break-up of the unified world of mediaeval thought with which to fill out his framework. But the frame is itself a symbol of the break-up. He could hardly have used it if he had not felt, with that secret largeness of outlook which is his fascination, that the ideas he handled did not necessarily belong to the one Jesus, that they might just as well, if the sorrowing parents would pay for it, be worked out for Elizabeth Drury.

Evidence as well as probability, then, lets one say that the position of the tragic hero was felt to be like that of Christ, and that elements were exchanged between them. Indeed, to call the Passion tragic, putting the thing the other way round, was a commonplace; of which Herrick provides a charming example:

> Not like a Thief, shalt Thou ascend the mount,
> But like a Person of some high Account;
> The Crosse shall be Thy Stage; and Thou shalt there
> The spacious field have for Thy Theater.
>
> And we (Thy Lovers) while we see Thee keep
> The Lawes of Action, will both sigh, and weep.

At the same time the two were very different, and the tragic idea, having a classical background, was by no means dependent on the Christian one. The famous passage in Chapman that uses the globe-metaphor, about the man that joins himself to the universe and goes on "round as it," shows how flatly the idea was derived from Roman Stoicism; the same metaphor for instance is in Marcus Aurelius (xi. 2). Mr. Eliot remarked about this that no man would join himself to the universe if he had anything better to join himself to, and certainly there is an element of revolt in the Elizabethan use of the idea. The reason that Donne's use of the globe is so much wittier and more solid than Chapman's is that he shows this; his globe is a way of shutting out the parsons as well as of completing himself. The idea that all men have a share in the fundamental and indivisible Reason was a stoical idea before it became a Christian one with the Logos, and in these uses is more comfortable in its pagan form. Indeed, the hero himself stood for a set of ideas covertly opposed to Christianity; that is why the mythological ideas about him remain in the background. He stood for "honour," pride rather than humility, self-realisation rather than self-denial, caste rather than democracy; he can become, as obviously in the comic hero Macheath, a sort of defense against Puritanism. The Elizabethans could use the separate systems of ideas together frankly and fully, but this was no longer possible after they had been fought over in the Civil War, and from then on one gets a more underground connection. Probably the most permanent element was this curious weight put covertly into metaphor or personification.

I shall list here a few examples which I am sorry to have let get crowded out. *Piers Plowman* is the most direct case of the pastoral figure who turns slowly into Christ and ruler. For device prior to irony, the tragic ballad with gay irrelevant refrain—"She leaned her back against a thorn (Fine flowers in the valley)." For one-in-many business, the *Lyke-Wake Dirge* and the *Dies Irae:*—

> This *ae* nighte, this ae nighte,
> *Every* nighte and alle
>
> Recordare, Jesu pie,
> Quod *sum* causa tuae viae,
> Ne *me* perdas illa die.

And *Wuthering Heights* is a good case of double plot in the novel, both for covert deification and telling the same story twice with the two possible endings.

AN OUTLINE OF POETIC THEORY

(1948)

Elder Olson [1]

I

When, in any field of learning, discussions of the subject are based upon different principles, employ different methods, and reach different conclusions, such differences tend to be interpreted, by expert and layman alike, as real disagreement. The differences are not of themselves dangerous to the subject; the tendency to interpret them as contradictions is. The dogmatist, however sound in his own method, usually regards them as signs of the chaos that must await any who depart from his position. The syncretist regards them as signs that all positions are at least partly false, and collects "truths," which frequently lose, in his synthesis, not only their supporting arguments but their original significance as well. The skeptic, finally, interprets such differences as implying the impossibility of philosophical knowledge in the field. All of these views are potentially harmful to learning in so far as in suppressing discussion they suppress some (and in the case of skepticim, all) of the problems, and because, consequently, they retard or even arrest progress within the subject. Skepticism, indeed, is most dangerous of all, for it does not arrest progress merely in certain respects, but arrests it wholly; and, once given head, does not pause until it has also cancelled whatever has been achieved in the past.

Criticism in our time is a sort of Tower of Babel. Moreover, it is not merely a linguistic but also a methodological Babel; yet, in the very pursuit of this analogy, it is well to remember that at Babel men did not begin to talk nonsense; they merely began to talk what *seemed* like nonsense to their fellows. A statement is not false, merely because it is unintelligible; though it will have to be made intelligible before we can say whether it is true. The extreme diversity of contemporary criticism is no more alarming than, and indeed it is connected with, the similar diversity of contemporary philosophy; and the chief import of both is of the need for some critique which shall examine radically how such diversity arises, by considering what aspects of a given subject

[1] This essay represents, in a very condensed form, an argument developed much more fully in a forthcoming book of mine on *General Criticism and the Shorter Forms of Poetry.*

are amenable to treatment, what problems they pose, and how these may be diversely formulated. For the diverse may be contradictory or not; theories of criticism which are not contradictory or incompatible may be translated into each other or brought to supplement each other, and a just decision may be given between those which are really contradictory, provided that we can isolate the differences of formulation from the differences of truths and falsities. True interpretation is impossible when one system is examined in terms of another, as is true refutation when the refutative arguments are systematically different from those against which they are directed. To propose such a critique is in effect to state the possibility of a fourth philosophic attitude: that of pluralism. Dogmatism holds the truth of a single position and the falsity, in some degree at least, of all others; syncretism holds the partial falsity of all; skepticism the total falsity of all. All these take into their consideration doctrines alone; pluralism, taking both doctrine and method into account, holds the possibility of a plurality of formulations of truth and of philosophic procedures —in short, a plurality of valid philosophies.

Such pluralism is possible both in philosophy and in criticism because criticism is a department of philosophy. A given comprehensive philosophy invariably develops a certain view of art; the critical theories of Plato, Aristotle, Hume, and Kant, for instance, are not any random views, but are generated and determined by their respective philosophies. And while a given criticism or theory of art may not originate in a comprehensive philosophy, and may resist reference to one already existent, it is not therefore really independent of a more comprehensive system, for the discussion of art must entail assumptions which involve more than art; it is merely part of a whole as yet undeveloped. In short, as criticism or the theory of art is part of philosophy, it has the same bases as philosophy, and is determinate or variable according to the same principles.

It is impossible within the scope of this essay to discuss all of the factors in the foundations of philosophies and criticisms; but perhaps a rough and partial statement may serve for illustration. I propose that the number of possible critical positions is relative to the number of possible philosophic positions; and that the latter is determined by two principal considerations: (1) the number of aspects of a subject which can be brought into discussion, as constituting its *subject-matter;* (2) the kinds of basic dialectic which may be exerted upon the subject-matter. I draw this distinction between the subject and the subject-matter: the subject is what is talked about; the subject-matter is that subject in so far as it is represented or implied in the discussion. Philosophers do not discuss *subjects themselves;* they can discuss only so much as the terms or materials of the discussion permit; and that is the subject-matter. We cannot discuss what we cannot first of all mention, or what we cannot bring to mind. In other words, any discussion of a "subject" is relative to its formulation. But, further, any discursive reasoning must employ some method of reasoning or inference; and since there are various possible systems of inference, we may say that a given discussion is a function of its subject-matter and of the dialectic, i.e., system of inference, exerted upon that subject-matter.

Whatever art in itself may be, as a *subject,* it is clear that criticism has employed certain aspects of it as subject-matters. Thus one aspect of art is its product; another, the instrumentality, active or passive, which produced the product; another, the product as relative to or determined by that instrumentality, and hence as a sign of the nature of that instrumentality, whether this last be viewed as actual or potential. Another is the relation of art to a certain subject or means, as a consequence, and hence as a sign, of these; still another aspect is its production of a certain effect, either of activity or passivity, upon those who are its spectators or auditors; and lastly, there is art viewed as instrumental to that effect. We may sum up all of this by saying that criticism has viewed art either as a product, or as an activity or passivity of the artist; or as certain faculties or as a certain character of the artist; or as a certain activity or passivity of the audience, or as certain faculties or as a certain character of the audience; or as an instrument; or as a sign, either of certain characteristics of the artist or his audience or of something else involved in art, e.g., its means, subject, etc.

The significances which the term "poem" assumes in critical discussions may illustrate this. In its most obvious meaning it refers to the product of the poetic art; but critics have often used it to refer to what they considered more important aspects of poetic art, or have differentiated it by reference to such aspects. Thus those who think that it is characterized by its instrumentality mean by "instrumentality" either the poet or the poetic powers; those who define poetry in terms of the poet see the poet as active craftsman or as the passive instrument of his inspiration, or as a mixture of the two, while those who define poetry in terms of poetic powers see the poet as possessed of faculties or qualities either of a certain kind or of a certain degree. With these differences, both consequently view the poem as a kind of behavior of the poet; and, for both, the literal poem, the product, becomes a sign of that behavior, which is in turn a sign of the poetic character or faculties. Others find the poem properly exists in the audience; the audience is the true poet, for without it the poem could never come to life; and the audience, like the poet, can be viewed as actualizing certain active or passive potentialities, or merely as possessing such potentialities. Hence the theories of "audience-participation" (the active view), of "art as experience" (the passive view), etc. Finally, "poem" may mean the end to which the product is instrumental, e.g., the psychological cure or ethical or political attitude or behavior.

These seem like "conflicting views"; hence they have been treated so in the history of criticism. If "conflicting" merely means "different," there is no quarrel, for these views are different enough. But if it means "contradictory" or "inconsistent," nothing could be more absurd. For, in the first place, all of these doctrines have different references, and it is impossible to have contradiction except in the same reference; and, secondly, where contradiction exists, one view must be false if the other is true, whereas all of these views are perfectly true in their proper senses, for all of them are founded upon perfectly obvious aspects of art, poetic or otherwise. Nor, if they are not contradictory, are they inconsistent, in the sense that they proceed from or result in contradiction; for, asserting the existence of certain aspects of art as they do, they are all true in some sense, and it is impossible for true propositions to be inconsistent. Indeed, nothing prevents certain philosophers, like Plato and Aristotle, from investigating all of these aspects of art.

Whatever aspect of art a critic may fix upon, he usually seeks to explain its nature, by reference to certain causes or reasons; thus those who are concerned with the product of art, for instance, have thought to explain the nature of the product by reference to its matter or medium, to the subject represented or depicted, to the depictive method of the artist or to some other productive cause, or to the end or effect of the product; and some have employed merely one of these causes or reasons, while others have used several or all. Aristotle, for instance, employs differentiations of object, means, manner, and effect to define tragedy, whereas a critic like Richard Hurd finds the nature of poetry adequately defined by its subject-matter.

I have remarked that the kind of dialectic exerted upon the subject-matter is the other determinant of a given mode of criticism. The variety of dialectics is an exceedingly complex question, but we may occupy ourselves here only with a single characteristic of dialectics—their concern with likeness or difference, or both. The integral or likeness-dialectic reaches solutions by combination of like with like; the differential or difference-dialectic, by the separation of dissimilars. Thus a criticism integral in its dialectic resolves its questions by referring poetry, for example, to some analogue of poetry, finding characteristics of poetry which are shared by the analogue; whereas a criticism differential in its dialectic resolves its questions by separating poetry from its analogues, finding characteristics which are peculiar to poetry.

Thus—to confine our illustrations to the various criticisms which deal with the product of art—we find criticisms differing as they center about either the subject-matter of art, or its medium, or its productive cause, or its end, or several of these, and as they proceed integrally or differentially. Subject-matter criticism of the integral kind resolves the subject-matter of the arts into something not peculiar to the arts, on the basis of likeness; and the principles of art, when so found, are always the principles of things other than art as well. Thus Plotinus finds the beautiful in art to consist in the imitation of the beautiful; but inquiry into that characteristic, for him, shows it to be common also to natural objects and to actions, and so upward to the Beauty which is almost indifferentiable from the Good; and the ultimate solution of artistic as well as of all problems lies, for him, in the contemplation of God. Differential criticism of this order, on the other hand, separates the kinds of subject-matter and argues on the basis of such separation, either to distinguish the arts from other faculties or activities, or to distinguish them *inter se*.

In pure subject-matter criticisms, once the subject-matter has been found, it determines all other questions, e.g., of artistic capacity or character, or of the techniques, forms, processes, criteria, and ends of art. For example, if the subject-matter in the raw, so to speak, is all-sufficient, the characteristics of the artist tend to appear as sharpness of observation and readiness of comprehension; if the subject-matter requires order and selection, correlative capacities for order and selection are constituents of the artistic character; and so on. A similar determination operates throughout all other problems: criteria, for instance, are produced from some correspondence or opposition, absolute or qualified, between the subject and the medium, or the artist, or the effect. Thus many of the theories of artistic realism have as their criterion the absolute correspondence of the effects of art with those of reality itself; art is thus copyistic and the work is a "slice of life," all formal criteria (such as order) being supplanted by attributes of the reality. Where the subject-matter of art is opposed to the reality, however—whether it requires an order and selection not found in reality, or differs from reality even more radically—such correspondence is qualified, or even negated, as in modern nonrepresentationalist theories.

Comparably, criticisms centering about the medium can be integral or differential, and solve their problems through reference to the medium. The integral criticism of this order is exemplified in the innumerable attempts to find general criteria for all literature, whether poetic, historical, philosophic, or personal, on the ground that all literature employs words; and the differential criticism is exemplified in the theories of men like I. A. Richards and Cleanth Brooks, who seek to differentiate poetry from prose by differentiation of the kind of diction employed in each, in order to discriminate appropriate criteria for each. The character of the artist varies as the character of the medium is stated; where the medium is viewed as indifferent to form, the capacities of the artist are at the maximum, and conversely, where the medium is viewed as tending toward form, the artist frequently appears as a kind of midwife to nature, assisting the bronze or the marble to a form which it implicitly contains. Criteria, again, can be found, by consideration of the degree to which a given work actualizes or fulfills the potentialities of the medium.

When the productive cause is central, the integral criticism establishes analogies between the artist or the artistic process and some more general cause, e.g., nature or natural process, or God and the divine creative process (Coleridge). Extreme criticisms of this order reduce the art-product almost to a by-product of the artistic character; Fracastoro and Carlyle, for example, refuse to limit the name of poet to those who actually write poems, since poetry is merely incidental to the possession of poetical character. Differential criticism of this kind, again, confines the conception of the artist to the unique maker of a certain product. When discussion centers on the natural elements of the artist, the artistic character lies outside the possibility of any deliberate achievement, as in Hazlitt; conversely, when the artistic character is defined in terms of acquired traits or disciplines (as in Reynolds), discussion of genius and inspiration is at a minimum, and the artistic character itself appears as amenable to art, and indeed often as the *chef d'oeuvre* of the artist.

When criticism turns on the ends of art, integral and differential dialectics are again possible; the ends of art can be analogized to other purposes of man, or to some natural or divine teleology, or conversely, differentiated from all else. And here, as above, the nature of the problems and of their solutions is determined by the choice of the ground-term.

All such criticisms may be called *partial,* for each attempts to resolve all problems by consideration only of a part. All fix upon a single *cause,* in Aristotle's sense of the word, and account for everything in terms of it, as if one were to account for a chair merely in terms of its wood, or merely in terms of its maker. None permits a full account, for the respects in which art is compared with or contrasted to other things are always only a part of its actual characteristics. This partiality remains even if several of these causal factors are combined, unless indeed all are involved.

As opposed to such partial criticisms there are comprehensive criticisms, such as those of Plato and Aristotle, the former being primarily integral, the latter primarily differential, although each includes both likeness and difference. These systems not only permit the discussion of all aspects of art, but a full causal account; for whereas Aristotle makes the maximum differentiation of causes, Platonic dialectic employs only a single cause, but one subsuming all. The difference—not in truth, or in cogency of argument, but in *adequacy*—between comprehensive and partial systems can be readily seen by comparing, say, Aristotle with the "Aristotelian" Scaliger: Aristotle can discuss any aspect of poetry, but Scaliger, basing all merely upon the medium, and viewing that only in its most general light—the universal power of language being to express fact or opinion—thereby confines himself to the treatment of poetry only as the instrument of instruction.

Recognition of methodological differences between systems of criticism, and of their consequent respective powers and limitations, quickly establishes the fact that twenty-five centuries of inquiry have not been spent in vain. On the contrary, the partial systems of criticism correct and supplement each other, the comprehensive intertranslate, to form a vast body of poetic knowledge; and contemporary theorists, instead of constantly seeking new bases for criticism, would do better to examine the bases of such criticisms as we have, and so avail themselves of that knowledge. Many a modern theory of criticism would have died a-borning, had its author done a little more reading as he thought, or thinking as he read. Critical knowledge, like all knowledge, must be constantly extended; but no one is very likely to extend it who is not fully aware of what has already been accomplished, or of what consequences follow from such accomplishments.

If a plurality of valid and true kinds of criticism is possible, choice must still be exercised, for it is impossible to employ all methods simultaneously, and the selection of method is by no means a matter of indifference. Choice is determined by the questions one wishes to ask and the form of answer one requires, and by the relative adequacy of given systems. The discovery of properties peculiar to a given kind of poetry demands a differential method, as that of properties which poetry holds in common with other things requires an integral method. If one wishes to know the nature of a given kind of poetry, as a certain *synolon* or composite, a whole and its parts specified with the maximum differentiation possible without the destruction of the universals upon which science depends, an Aristotelian criticism is requisite; if one proposes to view poetry in terms of principles of maximum community, a Platonic criticism is demanded. Every philosophy is addressed only to certain questions, and can answer them only in certain forms.

II

In the method of Aristotle, which underlies the following sketch, poetics is a science concerned with the differentiation and analysis of poetic forms or species in terms of all the causes which converge to produce their respective emotional effects. Scientific knowledge falls into three classes: theoretical, practical, and productive. The end of the first class, comprising metaphysics, mathematics, and the natural sciences, is knowledge; that of the second, comprising ethics and politics, is action; that of the third, comprising the fine and the useful arts, is some product over and above the actions which produce. Only the theoretical sciences are exact; the productive sciences, or arts, are less exact than the practical, since they involve a greater number of principles, and principles derived from many other sciences.

The poetics of a given species takes as its starting-point the definition of the product, i.e., a statement of the nature of the whole composite produced by an art, and thence proceeds by hypothetical reasoning to treat of the questions specific to that whole and its parts. Such analysis does not exhaust all aspects of the art; but any which it excludes are referred to other sciences. Thus the consideration of art as a skill falls under ethics, that of art as a political and social instrument under politics, and that of art as a mode of being under metaphysics, in accordance with the general Aristotelian practice of assigning questions to their appropriate sciences. A given special poetics, therefore, does not treat centrally of the faculties requisite for production, or of the effects to be produced by art, but of the special product, viewed as a differentiable synthesis of differentiable parts, and as such having the capacity or power (*dynamis*) of producing certain peculiar effects.

Before we can consider the various special arts of poetry, however, we must discuss the significance of certain concepts of a more general nature. Unity, beauty, and imitation, for instance, relate to things other than poetry, but are not therefore less important to poetic discussion. The term "imitation" is used coextensively with "artificial"; it differentiates art from nature. Natural things have an internal principle of motion and rest, whereas artificial things—a chair or table—have, *qua* products of art, no such principle; they change through propensities not of their form but of their matter. Natural and artificial things alike are composites of form and matter; but art imposes a form upon a matter which is not naturally disposed to assume, of itself, such a form. The acorn of itself grows into the oak; the stone does not of itself become a statue, or tend to become a statue rather than a column. Art may be said to imitate nature either in the sense that the form of the product derives from natural form (e.g., the human form in the painting resembles the natural human form) or in the sense that the artistic process resembles the natural (e.g., artificial fever in the art of medicine does what fever does naturally). The useful and the fine arts are both imitative; but the latter have as their end the imitation itself, as a form possessed of beauty. Since every imitation has some form imposed somehow upon some matter for some end, specification of all of these factors results in a definition of a given species of art; e.g., by specifying *what* is imitated in tragedy (object of imitation) *in what* (means of imitation) *how* (manner of imitation) to what effect, we construct the definition of tragedy. Such definitions are the principles from which reasoning proceeds in the arts; if a certain product or whole is to be produced, it will have a certain number of parts of a certain nature ordered in a certain way, etc.

A poem has unity in the sense in which anything which has continuity is unified; but, more than that, it is one in that it has a single form and is an ordered and complete whole. A piece of wire is one because it is continuous, and if you break the continuity you have two pieces; but some things are totals rather than wholes—a cord of wood, for instance, because the parts need merely be present, and not in any particular arrangement—and others are wholes proper, because they are not only complete and have all their parts, but also have them in the proper arrangement, i.e., the least important ordered to its superior part, and so on till the principal part is reached. Parts of a shoe stitched together anyhow are one in the sense of continuity, but not one in the sense of assemblage into a certain single form, the shoe; a poem is similarly an ordered and complete whole.

Moreover, it is not only a whole, but one of a certain nature; it is an imitation in a certain means; hence, since a given means can imitate only certain objects (color and line cannot imitate the course of thought, nor musical tones a face), poetry must imitate action, character, or thought, for a given means can be used to imitate only something having the same characteristics as it, or something of whose characteristics its own characteristics are signs, and speech (the medium of poetry) is either action or the sign of action, character, and passion. (For example, painting can represent color directly, but the third dimension only by signs, such as perspective diminution, faintness, etc., of objects.) Media are not such things as certain pigments or stones, but such as line, color, mass, musical tones, rhythms, and words. The object imitated, therefore, must be some form which these can take or which they can imply by signs. Hence, inference plays a large role in all the arts.

Inference and perception serve to institute opinions and mental images concerning the object, and opinions and mental images produce emotion. We see or infer the object to be such and such, and according to our opinion of what it is we react emotionally in a certain specific way. If we have the opinion, we react, whether the thing in fact is so or not, and if we do not have it, we do not react, whether the thing is so or not. The opinion that a disaster is imminent produces fear, and the opinion that the victim suffers undeservedly produces pity; and so on.

Emotions are mental pains (e.g. pity), pleasures (e.g. joy), or impulses (e.g. anger) instigated by opinion. The basis of our emotions toward art may be explained as follows. We feel some emotion, some form of pleasure or pain, because our desires are frustrated or satisfied; we feel the desires because we are friendly or hostile to, or favor or do not favor, the characters set before us, and because we approve or disapprove the events; and we are friendly or hostile to the characters because of their ethical character; in brief, we side with the good against the bad, or, in the absence of such marked moral difference, with the oppressed against the oppressor, with the weak against the strong, etc., our judgment now being primarily of the action rather than of the agents.

Since the object of imitation, as we opine it to be, determines the emotions which we feel, and since moral differentiation lies at the basis of our conception of the object, the possible objects of imitation in poetry, drama, and fiction may be schematized in terms of extremes, as follows. The serious, i.e., what we take seriously, comprises characters conspicuously better or worse than we are or at any rate such as are like ourselves and such as we can strongly sympathize with, in states of marked pleasure or pain, or in fortunes markedly good or bad. The comic, i.e., the ridiculous, comprises characters as involved in embarrassment or discomfiture to whom we are neither friendly nor hostile, of an inferiority not painful to us. We love or hate or sympathize profoundly with the serious characters; we favor or do not favor or condescend to the comic. Serious and comic both divide into two parallel classes: the former into the tragic kind, in which the character is better than we, and the punitive, in which the character is worse; the latter into what may be called lout-comic, in which the character, though good natured or good, is mad, eccentric, imprudent, or stupid, and the rogue-comic, in which the character is clever but morally deficient. These kinds are illustrated in drama by *Hamlet, The Duchess of Malfi, She Stoops to Conquer* and *The Alchemist;* the protagonists in these are, respectively, a man better than we, wicked men (the brothers of the Duchess), a good man with a ridiculous foible, and rogues. Between these extremes of the serious and the comic lie what I have called the "sympathetic" or the antipathetic; i.e., forms in which the morality of the characters does not function in the production of emotional effect so much as does our judgment of the events as, e.g., just or unjust; the man is indifferent, but the suffering is greater than even a criminal should undergo, etc. The emotions produced by the contrary objects are themselves contrary; for instance, the pity and fear of tragedy are opposed by the moral vindictiveness and the confidence of retribution in the punitive kinds. Again, the emotions are contrary as the events are contrary; that is, the spectacle of a good man going from good fortune to misfortune, or from a pleasant to a painful state, effects emotions contrary to those evoked by the spectacle of a good man going from misfortune to fortune, or from pain to pleasure. Again, comic "catastrophe" is mere embarrassment or discomfiture, and effects emotions contrary to those produced by catastrophe in the serious forms.

In short, the emotions we feel in poetry are, generally speaking, states of pleasure and pain induced by mental images of the actions, fortunes, and conditions of characters to whom we are well or ill disposed, in a greater or lesser degree, because of our opinions of their moral character, or, such failing, because of our natural sympathy or antipathy; or, in other words, our emotions are determined by the object of imitation, and vary with it. Emotion in art results, thus, not because we believe the thing "real," but because we vividly contemplate it, i.e., are induced by the work of art to make mental images of it. Compare such expressions as "He was horrified at the mere thought of it," "The very notion filled him with ecstasy," etc.

Pleasure in general is a settling of the soul into its natural condition; pleasure in poetry results primarily from the imitation of the object, and secondarily from such embellishments as rhythm, ornamental language, and generally any such development of the parts as is naturally pleasing. Where the object of imitation is itself pleasant, and vividly depicted, pleasure is direct; when the object is unpleasant, pleasure results from the catharsis or purgation of the painful emotions aroused in us, as in tragedy. Pleasure is commensurate, in other words, with the beauty of the poetic form; and distinctive forms, as they have peculiar beauties, evoke peculiar pleasures.

By "beauty" I mean the excellence of perceptible form in a composite continuum which is a whole; and by "excellence of perceptible form" I mean the possession of perceptible magnitude in accordance with a mean determined by the whole as a whole of such-and-such quality, composed of such-and-such parts. Assuming that parts of the number and quality required for the whole have been provided and ordered hierarchically to the principal part, the whole will be beautiful if that prime part is beautiful; and that part, as a continuity, must have magnitude and be composed of parts (e.g., plot, the prime part of tragedy, has magnitude and has parts); since it has magnitude, it admits of the more and the less, and hence of excess and deficiency, and consequently of a definite and proper mean between them, which constitutes its beauty. Specifically, in terms of the form itself, this mean is a proportion between whole and part, and consequently is relative to the different wholes and parts; in reference to perception, we may call it a mean between such minuteness of the parts and such extension of the whole as would interfere with the perception of the parts, as of their proper qualities, and as in interrelation with each other and the whole. Thus in tragedy the mean of plot-magnitude lies between the length required for the necessary or probable connection of the incidents and the limit imposed by the tragic change of fortunes. The constituents of beauty are, therefore, definiteness, order, and symmetry; the last being such commensurability of the parts as renders a thing self-determined, a measure to itself, as it were; for example, plot is symmetrical when complication and denouement are commensurate. As a thing departs from its proper magnitude, it either is spoiled (i.e., retains its nature but loses its beauty) or is destroyed (i.e., loses even its nature). Compare a drawing of a beautiful head; alter its definitive magnitude to a degree, and the beauty is lost; alter it further, and it is no longer recognizable as a head.

III

These questions are not peculiarly poetic ones but rather matters belonging to metaphysics, psychology, and ethics. The problems we now approach, however, are poetic, and may be divided into two kinds, general questions, common to all of the poetic arts, and special questions, peculiar to a given poetic art. Biology offers a parallel; for some attributes are common to all forms of life, others are peculiar. Similarly with poetics; some questions come about merely because the imitation is of action, like Aristotle's discussion of plot prior to Chapter xiii of the *Poetics,* others because of something specific, like his discussion of the tragic plot, imitating a certain kind of action. I shall here deal with both kinds, though illustratively only, and take up first the question of the definition of forms.

All the arts, as I have said, begin with definitions of their specific products as wholes, which they utilize as the principle or starting-point of their reasoning. These definitions, far from being arbitrary resolutions, must be collected from a conspectus of the historical growth of the species to which they relate; a kind of art, to be known and defined, must first actually exist. Not every aspect of the growth of artistic species, however, is relevant to their artistic character; hence their historical development must be examined in terms of their character as imitations. No single line of differentiation suffices for the separation of species: most broadly, the arts are distinguished in terms of their media, for, since nothing can be made actual which is not potentially in the medium, the potentialities of the medium, as matter, determine all else; yet the means even when fully differentiated, singly and in combination, is insufficient for specific distinction, for arts which have the same means may imitate opposite objects, as do comedy and tragedy. In turn, objects may be differentiated, but even such further differentiation is not definitive, for imitations may still differ in manner, although the possibilities of manner are now broadly determined. With the distinction of modes or manners of imitation, the account of the parts of imitation *qua* imitation is complete, and the historical survey of the rise of the arts—the synthesis of these differentiated parts into distinct wholes—is now possible. Such history begins as the causes emerge. The poetic, like the other fine arts, originate in instinct, some matter being given a form not natural to it, by an external efficiency, for the sake of the pleasure produced. Yet, though imitation is natural to man, instinct is insufficient to account for the further development of art; for art ramifies, rather than remains constant, as the universal cause of instinct would suggest; and its ramifications are determined by the character of the artist: the noble-minded imitate the noble, the low-minded the low. Even so the tale is not complete: for art develops further until a form is achieved, and valued for its own sake. Art passes, thus, through three stages, the instinctive, the ethical or practical, and the artistic, the first two of which are determined by the nature and character of the artist, and the last by the form. The achievement of form is signalized by a revolution in the ordering and constitution of the parts: once the specifically pleasurable effect has luckily been produced, the part which is primarily effective becomes principal, develops its proper extension and qualities, and all other parts readjust to it, in their proper artistic order. A distinctive synthesis—a species of art—has now formed, and its poetics may begin, for the formulation of the distinctive means, object, manner, and effect of the synthesis gives all four of the causes which are collectively but not singly peculiar to it, and a definition results.

Aristotle has frequently been defended on the ground that all poetic species reduce to those which he has enumerated, and more frequently attacked on the ground that they do not. Both defense and attack are mistaken; the former because it makes poetics predictive, the latter because it assumes that since Aristotle did not define certain species, his theory could not afford a basis for their definition. In fact, as the above account has shown, the poetics of a given species must always develop after the species has come into actual being, the definition being formed by induction; but, on the other hand, the poetic arts in their development do not leave their bases; they do not cease to have means, objects, and manners, or even the differentiations of these mentioned by Aristotle; they merely differentiate these further and produce new syntheses. The distinction between narrative and dramatic manner, for instance, has not been rendered obsolete, although it affords no significant distinction, in itself, between Homer and Henry James; yet to distinguish them we must begin with the different possibilities of telling, as opposed to impersonating, and discriminate the various complexities of narrative device.

Once object, means, manner, and effect have been specified to the emerging species, the definition of the artistic whole which so results permits an analysis into parts; and when the principal part has been identified and the order of importance of the remaining parts established, the proper construction of the principal part must be ascertained. That part is itself a whole composed of parts, and these parts—its beginning, middle, and end—must be determined, and the character of their conjunction—necessity and probability—must be shown. But the whole is not only a whole, but a whole of some magnitude; and since it is moreover to be a beautiful whole, it must be a whole of some definite magnitude. As I have remarked, this definite magnitude lies in a mean between excess of the part and excess of the whole, the former producing such vast extension that the whole cannot be comprehended, the latter such minuteness that the parts cannot be apprehended. This formula, however, is general, and must be specified to the species of art involved. Relatively to perception, it must always be determined in the temporal arts by the limits of memory, since in these arts the parts are not coexistent but successive, and consequently must be remembered if the whole is to be comprehended; but even this is relative to the species, differences of the parts and wholes of which impose different burdens upon the memory. (A lyric might be too long to be remembered, while a tragedy might not.) The wholeness, completeness, and unity of the principal part once established, the part can be divided into its species; hence, for example, Aristotle divides plots into simple and complex, which are different wholes, since the complex plot consists of differentiable parts (peripety and discovery) according to the efficient cause of the change of fortunes with which tragedy is concerned.

"Aristotelian" criticism has frequently centered merely upon this much, to produce mere *Formalismus,* but Aristotle himself goes farther. The principal part is only materially a whole, complete, one, etc.· formally, it has an effect or power of a certain specific order; tragic action, for instance, is not merely action, nor even serious action, but action differentiated by a certain act, the tragic deed committed in a certain way by the tragic hero, and Aristotle, investigating the possibilities of character and action, determines which of these result in the tragic effect, for that effect—the "working or power" of tragedy—is the form. Comparably, the poetics of any species must be addressed to the differentiation of its principal part, since it is this that primarily determines the emotional effect.

Once the principal part has been treated, the subordinate parts can be dealt with in the order of their importance, and according to their causes; the final cause of each being to serve its superior part, the formal cause being the beauty of the part itself. The whole analysis, thus, not merely indicates the possibilities of poetic construction, but discriminates among them as better or worse, to exhibit the construction of a synthesis beautiful as a whole, composed of parts of the maximum beauty consistent with that whole, and productive of its proper emotional effect to a maximum degree.

The method—one of multiple differentiation and systematic resolution of maximal composites into their least parts—may obviously be extended to poetic species which have emerged since Aristotle. Aristotle distinguishes broadly and between extremes; later theorists in his method must follow the basic lines and go further. For example, his poetics, as we have it, deals only with such poetry as has plot, i.e., such as imitates a *system* of actions. These are maximal forms; there are, that is, no "larger" poetic forms, nor any which have more parts than these; smaller forms, such as the species of lyric, can be treated by carrying such systems back to their elements.

Four kinds of action or behavior can thus be distinguished, without regard to seriousness or comicality, etc.: (1) a single character acting in a single closed situation. By "closed situation" I mean one in which the character's activity, however it may have been initiated, or however it may be terminated, is *uncomplicated* by any other agency. Most of what we call lyric poetry belongs here: any poem in which the character commits some verbal act (threatening, persuading, beseeching) upon someone existing only as the object of his action (Marvell's *To His Coy Mistress*), or deliberates or muses (Keats's *Ode to a Nightingale*), or is moved by passion (Landor's "Mother, I cannot mind my wheel"). (2) Two or more characters in a single closed situation. "Closed situation" here means "uncomplicated by any other agency than the characters originally present and remaining so throughout." This parallels the notion of "scene" in French classical drama; here belong all the *real* colloquies of persons acting upon and reacting to each other (Browning's *The Bishop Orders His Tomb*), although not the metaphorical colloquies such as dialogues between Body and Soul, etc. (3) A collection of such "scenes" as I have just mentioned about some central incident, to constitute an "episode" (Arnold's *Sohrab and Rustum*). (4) A system of such episodes, constituting the grand plot of tragedy, comedy, and epic which is treated by Aristotle.

These are whole and complete "actions"; hence the first differs from a speech in a play, the second from a dramatic scene, the third from a fragment of a tragedy; nevertheless, it is clear that, *in a sense,* the combination of speeches produces a scene, that of scenes an episode, that of episodes a plot. These classifications must not be confused with species; they are not poetic species, but lines of differentiation of the object of imitation which must be taken into account in defining species. Similar analysis of means and manner would extend Aristotle's system to include all poetic forms.

So much for Aristotle's general method and his apparatus for the definition of forms; I shall presently return to such questions again, in order to sketch a special poetics, but for the moment I wish to deal with three more problems of general poetics: those of unexpectedness, suspense, and representation, although we can do little more here than to touch on general points.

All emotions are greater if produced from their contraries—for example, fear in one who has been confident—and the unexpected effects just this. Like suspense, it is common to all temporal arts, the parts as well as the wholes, for whatever involves temporal succession may involve anticipation, and wherever we have anticipation we may have the unexpected. Expectation is the active entertainment of the opinion that something is necessary or probable at a given time, place, in certain relations, etc. The audience must infer, and infer incorrectly; they have the premisses, so to speak, for otherwise what happens would be improbable; but they cannot connect them to infer correctly, for otherwise what happens would be expected. Since they do not infer the probable, and do infer the improbable, two things must be noted: the causes of wrong inference, and the causes of failure to infer rightly. Since the premisses must be considered together for inference, and since the audience will reason only from premisses which they actively entertain and take to be true, failure to infer will be due to (1) forming no opinion, or forming a contradictory one, so that one or both of the premisses will not be used; (2) failure to collect the premisses although both are entertained; (3) failure to infer correctly, although both are entertained and collected. All of these can be developed to show what the poet may possibly do: for instance, opinion can be prevented by the use of remote signs (i.e., such as involve many inferences), or many and apparently contradictory signs, ambiguity of words or acts; acceptance as true can be prevented by the use of unusual consequents, by contrariety to general belief, by dependence upon the words of an apparently untrustworthy character, or by contradiction of an apparently trustworthy one; and so on.

All these things lead to non-expectation; but the truly unexpected comes about when the thing is not only not expected, but contrary to expectation. This will happen if the poet provides premisses which seem to prove the contrary. It is best when failure to infer the right thing and the faulty inference are brought about by the same premisses. This is effected by the use of qualification. For example, if A happens, B usually follows, except in circumstance C, but if that circumstance happens, the opposite of B results; now if C is bound to happen, but people do not know that, they will expect B after A, whereas the opposite results. Surprise will vary in degree with expectation of the contrary; consequently the audience will be most surprised when they are most convinced that B will happen. The less important, apparently, the reversing circumstance, the more surprise. Again, since the all-but-completed process makes its end most probable, expectation will be highest here; hence reversal just before the end will be most surprising. This underlies many "hair's-breadth escapes." Most surprising of all is the double unexpected, which occurs when from A comes the unexpected result B, which leads to the previously expected result C, which is now unexpected as the result of B. This is exemplified in Sophocles' *Oedipus,* where the inquiry into blood-guilt leads to the question of parentage, which seems at some remove; but the question of parentage resolves unexpectedly the question of blood-guilt.

Suspense is anxiety caused by extended anticipation; hence (1) by the uncertainty of what we wish to know, and (2) by delay of what we wish to have happen, although we know it already. (Gossips are in the first state before they have been told the scandal, in the second until they impart it.) The first results whenever we want to know either the event or the circumstances of the event, whether in past, present, or future time; hence the poet must avoid the necessary, the impossible, or the completely probable, or that which is unimportant either way, for we are never in suspense about these; instead he must choose the equally probable, or else that which is probable with a chance of its not happening, and something which is of a markedly pleasant, painful, good, evil, or marvellous nature. Suspense of the second order is produced by unexpected frustration, by having the thing seem just about to happen, and then probably averting it. The anticipated thing must have importance exceeding the suspense; otherwise irritation and indifference result.

Representation—what parts of the action are told or shown, and how, and what is left to inference—is a question of manner of imitation. Obviously poets sometimes exhibit more than the action (e.g., tragic poets exhibit events which are not part of the plot), sometimes less, leaving the rest to inference; sometimes follow the plot-order, sometimes convert it (e.g., using flashbacks); exhibit some things on a large and others on a small scale; and there are many other possibilities as well. It is impossible here to do more than suggest; in general, representation is determined by necessity and probability, emotional effect, and ornament, i.e., these are the main reasons for representing something. The poet must represent things which by their omission or their being left to inference would make the action improbable; hence, if an event is generally improbable but probable in a given circumstance, it must be represented in that circumstance (e.g., Antony's speech in *Julius Caesar*). Again, he must omit whatever would contradict the specific emotional effect (hence disgusting scenes such as the cooking of Thyestes' children are omitted, since disgust counteracts pity) or include what would augment the effect (hence scenes of lamentation and suffering in tragedy, since these make us poignantly aware of the anguish of the hero). Masques, pageants, progresses, etc., are ornaments. Representation, whether narrative or dramatic, always makes things more vivid, and the latter is more vivid than the former; and it affords the audience knowledge, whether directly or through inference by signs. In any poetic work the audience must at certain times know some things and not know others; generally the denouement discloses all, except in works which have wonder as their prime effect. Unless the audience knows somewhat, emotion is impossible, for emotion depends upon opinion; and unless it is ignorant of certain things, unexpectedness and some kinds of suspense are impossible. Hence in any work something is withheld till the end: either how the action began, or continued, or how it ends; the audience is ignorant of one or several of the following circumstances: agent, instrument, act, object, manner, purpose, result, time, place, concomitants. What must be concealed is the primary question; the next is the order in which things must be disclosed; and theory can make available to the poet a calculus of the frame of mind of the audience, of the nature of emotions, etc., to determine the order of representation which will produce the maximum emotional effect.

All of these questions can be developed to afford a vast body of working suggestions for the poet and of criteria for the critic; I shall be happy if I have suggested, even faintly, the character of the problems and the method of their treatment.

IV

We have seen that in any special poetics—whether that of tragedy or of epic of some kind of lyric or novel—reasoning proceeds from the distinctive whole which is the product of the art to determine what parts must be assembled if such a whole, beautiful of its kind, is to result, and that such terms as whole, part, beauty, etc., must be specified to the given art, because, for example, the beauty of a tragedy is not the same as the beauty of a lyric, any more than the distinctive beauty of a horse is the same as that of a man. Indeed, lyrics and tragedies even have some different parts; for instance, a lyric does not have plot, but plot is in fact the principal part of tragedy.

We may illustrate the nature of a special poetics a little further by outlining briefly that of the species to which Yeats's *Sailing to Byzantium* belongs.[2] It is a species which imitates a serious action of the first order mentioned above, i.e., one involving a single character in a closed situation, and the character is not simply in passion, nor is he acting upon another character, but has performed an act actualizing and instancing his moral character, that is, has made a moral choice. It is dramatic in manner—the character speaks in his own person; and the means is words embellished by rhythm and rhyme. Its effect is something that, in the absence of a comprehensive analysis of the emotions, we can only call a kind of noble joy or exaltation.

There are four parts of this poetic composite: choice, character, thought, and diction. For choice is the activity, and thought and character are the causes of the activity; and diction is the means. The choice, or deliberative activity of choosing, is the principal part, for reasons analogous to those which make plot the principal part of tragedy. Next in importance comes character; next thought; and last, diction.[3]

[2] See the Appendix to this essay for a detailed "grammatical" analysis.

[3] Nowadays when the nature of poetry has become so uncertain that everyone is trying to define it, definitions usually begin: "Poetry is words which, or language which, or discourse which," and so forth. As a matter of fact, it is nothing of the kind. Just as we should not define a chair as wood which has such and such characteristics—for a chair is not a kind of wood but a kind of furniture—so we ought not to define poetry as a kind of language. The chair is not wood but wooden; poetry is not words but verbal. In one sense, of course, the words are of the utmost importance; if we do not grasp them, we do not grasp the poem. In another sense, they are the least important element in the poem, for they do not determine the character of anything else in the poem; on the contrary, they are determined by everything else. They are the only things we see or hear; yet they are governed by imperceptible things which are inferred from them. And when we are moved by poetry, we are not moved by the words, except in so far as sound and rhythm move us; we are moved by the things that the words stand for.

The "activity" of the character is thought or deliberation producing choice determined by rational principles; it is thus, as I once remarked, a kind of argument or arguing. But there is a difference between logical proof and such poetic argument as we have here; in logical proof the conclusion is determined by the premisses; here it is of course mediated by the character of the man arguing, just as argument in a novel or a play is not supposed to be consistent with the premisses, but with the character. The limits of the activity are the limits of the deliberation; the parts of the activity are the phases of that deliberation, and they are conjoined by necessity and probability.

This species of poem, then, if it is to be beautiful, must have a certain definite magnitude as determined by the specific whole and its parts; and the proper magnitude will be the fullest extension possible, not exceeding the limits mentioned above, and accomplished by phases connected necessarily or probably. This is, it will be noted, different from the magnitude proper to comedy or tragedy, and even different from the magnitude proper to a speech exhibiting choice in any of these; for example, tragedy does not aim at making its constituent speeches or actions as full and perfectly rounded as possible absolutely, but only qualifiedly, in so far as that is compatible with the plot. Hence in properly made drama there are few if any "complete" speeches, let alone speeches developed to what would be their best proportions independently of the whole; this is true even in declamatory drama, where the speeches are of more importance than in the better kinds.

The activity, however, is not merely to be complete and whole, with its parts probably interrelated; it must effect certain serious emotions in us by exhibiting the happiness or misery of certain characters whom we take seriously. Hence the character must be better than we, but not so completely noble as to be beyond all suffering; for such people are god-like and can awaken only our admiration, for they are in a sense removed from such misfortunes as can excite dolorous emotions. Moreover, the choice imitated cannot be any choice, even of a moral order, but one which makes all the difference between happiness and misery; and since it is choice, it must be accomplished with full knowledge, and in accordance with rational principle, and as the man of rational prudence would determine it. Again, it must be choice not contingent upon the actions or natures of others, but as determined by the agent. And there must be no mistake (*hamartia*) here as in tragedy; for, since this is a single incident, *hamartia* is not requisite to make probable future consequences.

We could proceed indefinitely here, as on all of these points; my intention, I repeat, is the merest illustration.

V

Thus far we have proceeded on the supposition that the poetic arts have as their ends certain pleasures, produced through their play upon our emotions. Certainly these are ends of art, and such as any consideration of art must embrace; but to suppose that art has no further effects, and that it may have no further ends relative to these, is vastly to underestimate the powers of art. It exercises, for example, a compelling influence upon human action, individual, social, or political; for among the causes of the misdirection of human action are the failure to conceive vividly and the failure to conceive apart from self-interest; and these are failures which art above all other things is potent to avert, since it vivifies, and since in art we must view man on his merits and not in relation to our private interests. It is not that art teaches by precept, as older generations thought, nor that it moves to action; but clearly it inculcates moral attitudes; it determines our feelings toward characters of a certain kind for no other reason than that they are such characters. The ethical function of art, therefore, is never in opposition to the purely artistic end; on the contrary, it is best achieved when the artistic end has been best accomplished, for it is only a further consequence of the powers of art. The same thing is true of any political or social ends of art, providing that the state be a good state, or the society a moral society. To reflect on these things is to realize the importance and value of art, which, excellent in itself, becomes ever more excellent as we view it in ever more general relations.

Yet these relations can scarcely be recognized unless we first recognize the distinctive powers of each form of poetic art; these relations are possible, indeed, because art has first of all certain powers. And it is to these powers, in all their variety and force, that the poetic method of Aristotle is directed. Indeed, the most distinctive characteristic of Aristotle as critic seems to be that he founds his poetic science upon the emotional effects peculiar to the various species of art and reasons thence to the works which must be constructed to achieve them.

APPENDIX

"Sailing to Byzantium" by William Butler Yeats [1]

I

That is no country for old men. The young
In one another's arms, birds in the trees,
—Those dying generations—at their song,
The salmon-falls, the mackerel-crowded seas,
Fish, flesh, or fowl, commend all summer long
Whatever is begotten, born, and dies.
Caught in that sensual music all neglect
Monuments of unageing intellect.

II

An aged man is but a paltry thing,
A tattered coat upon a stick, unless
Soul clap its hands and sing, and louder sing
For every tatter in its mortal dress,
Nor is there singing school but studying
Monuments of its own magnificence;
And therefore I have sailed the seas and come
To the holy city of Byzantium.

III

O sages standing in God's holy fire
As in the gold mosaic of a wall,
Come from the holy fire, perne in a gyre,
And be the singing-masters of my soul.
Consume my heart away; sick with desire
And fastened to a dying animal
It knows not what it is; and gather me
Into the artifice of eternity.

IV

Once out of nature I shall never take
My bodily form from any natural thing,
But such a form as Grecian goldsmiths make
Of hammered gold and gold enamelling
To keep a drowsy Emperor awake;
Or set upon a golden bough to sing
To lords and ladies of Byzantium
Of what is past, or passing, or to come.

In *Sailing to Byzantium* an old man faces the problem of old age, of death, and of regeneration, and gives his decision. Old age, he tells us, excludes a man from the sensual joys of youth; the world appears to belong completely

[1] A portion of an essay published in the *University Review*, 8 (Spring, 1942). Reprinted with permission.

to the young, it is no place for the old; indeed, an old man is scarcely a man at all—he is an empty artifice, an effigy merely, of a man; he is a tattered coat upon a stick. This would be very bad, except that the young also are excluded from something; rapt in their sensuality, they are ignorant utterly of the world of the spirit. Hence if old age frees a man from sensual passion, he may rejoice in the liberation of the soul; he is admitted into the realm of the spirit; and his rejoicing will increase according as he realizes the magnificence of the soul. But the soul can best learn its own greatness from the great works of art; hence he turns to those great works, but in turning to them, he finds that these are by no means mere effigies, or monuments, but things which have souls also; these live in the noblest element of God's fire, free from all corruption; hence he prays for death, for release from his mortal body; and since the insouled monuments exhibit the possibility of the soul's existence in some other matter than flesh, he wishes reincarnation, not now in a mortal body, but in the immortal and changeless embodiment of art.

There are thus the following terms, one might say, from which the poem suspends: the condition of the young, who are spiritually passive although sensually active; the condition of the merely old, who are spiritually and physically impotent; the condition of the old, who, although physically impotent, are capable of spiritual activity; the condition of art considered as inanimate—i. e., the condition of things which are merely monuments; and finally the condition of art considered as animate—as of such things as artificial birds which have a human soul. The second term, impotent and unspiritual old age, is a privative, a repugnant state which causes the progression through the other various alternative terms, until its contrary is encountered. The first and third terms are clearly contraries of each other; taken together as animate nature they are further contrary to the fourth term, inanimate art. None of these terms represents a wholly desirable mode of existence; but the fifth term, which represents such a mode, amalgamates the positive elements and eliminates the negative elements of both nature and art, and effects thus a resolution of the whole, for now the soul is present, as it would not be in art, nor is it passive, as it would be in the young and sensual mortal body, nor is it lodged in a "dying animal," as it would be in the body of the aged man; the soul is now free to act in its own supremacy and in full cognizance of its own excellence, and its embodiment is now incorruptible and secure from all the ills of flesh.

About these several oppositions the poem forms. The whole turns on the old man's realization, now that he is in the presence of the images of Byzantium, that these images have souls; there are consequently two major divisions which divide the poem precisely in half, the first two stanzas presenting art as inanimate, the second two, as animate; and that this is the case can be seen from such signs as that in the first half of the poem the images are stated as passive objects—they are twice called "monuments," they are merely objects of contemplation, they may be neglected or studied, visited or not visited, whereas in stanzas III and IV they are treated as gods which can be prayed to for life or death, as beings capable of motion from sphere to sphere, as instructors of the soul, as sages possessed of wisdom; and the curious shift in the manner of consideration is signalized by the subtle phrasing of the first two lines of stanza III: "O sages standing in God's holy fire/ As in the gold mosaic of a wall." According to the first part, the images at Byzantium were images, and one should have expected at most some figurative apostrophe to them: "O images set in the gold mosaic of a wall, much as the sages stand in God's holy fire": but here the similitude is reversed, and lest there should be any error, the sages are besought to come from the holy fire and begin the tuition of the soul, the destruction of the flesh.

Within these two halves of the poem, further divisions may be found, coincident with the stanzaic divisions. Stanza I presents a rejection of passion, stanza II an acceptance of intellection; then, turning on the realization that art is insouled, stanza III presents a rejection of the corruptible embodiment, and stanza IV, an acceptance of the incorruptible. There is an alternation, thus, of negative and affirmative: out of passion into intellection, out of corruption into permanence, in clear balance, the proportion being I : II :: III : IV; and what orders these sections is their dialectical sequence. That is, passion must be condemned before the intellect can be esteemed; the intellect must operate before the images can be known to be insouled; the realization that the images are insouled precedes the realization that the body may be dispensed with; and the reincarnation of the soul in some changeless medium can be recognized as a possibility only through the prior recognition that the flesh is not the necessary matter of the soul. The parallel opposition of contraries constitutes a sharp demarcation; in stanza I a mortal bird of nature amid natural trees sings a brief song of sensual joy in praise of mortal things, of "whatever is begotten, born, and dies"; in stanza IV an immortal and artificial bird set in an artificial tree sings an eternal song of spiritual joy in praise of eternal things, of "what is past, or passing, or to come"; and similarly, in stanza II a living thing is found to be an inanimate artifice, "a tattered coat upon a stick," incapable of motion, speech, sense or knowledge whereas in Stanza III what had appeared to be inanimate artifice is found to possess a soul, and hence to be capable of all these. A certain artificial symmetry in the argument serves to distinguish these parts even further: stanzas I and IV begin with the conclusions of their respective arguments, whereas II and III end with their proper conclusions, and I is dependent upon II for the substantiation of its premisses, as IV is dependent upon III.

This much indication of the principal organization of the work permits the explication, in terms of this, of the more elementary proportions. The first line of stanza I presents immediately, in its most simple statement, the condition which is the genesis of the whole structure: "That is no country for old men"; old men are shut out from something, and the remainder of the first six lines indicates precisely what it is from which they are excluded. The young are given over to sensual delight, in which old men can no longer participate. But a wall, if it shuts out, also shuts in; if the old are excluded from something, so are the young; lines 7 and 8, consequently, exhibit a second sense in which "That is no country for old men," for the young neglect all intellectual things. Further, the use of "that" implies a possible "this"; that is, there is a country for the old as for the young; and, again, the use of "that" implies that the separation from the country of the young is already complete. The occupation of the young is shrewdly stated: at first sight the human lovers "in one another's arms" have, like the birds at their song, apparently a romantic and sentimental aura; but the curious interpolation of "Those dying generations" in the description of the birds foreshadows the significance they are soon to have; and the phrases immediately following remove all sentimentality: "the salmon-falls, the mackerel-crowded seas" intend the ascent of salmon to the headwaters, the descent of mackerel to the deep seas in the spawning season, and the ironic intention is clear: all—the human lovers, the birds, the fish, do but spawn, but copulate, and this is their whole being; and if the parallel statement does not make this sufficiently evident, the summation of all in terms merely of animal genera—"fish, flesh, or fowl"—is unmistakable. The country of the young, then, is in its air, in its waters, and on its earth, from headwaters to ocean, wholly given over to sensuality; its inhabitants "commend all summer long" anything whatsoever, so long as it be mortal and animal—they commend "whatever is begotten, born, and dies"; and while they "commend" because they have great joy, that which they praise, they who praise, and their praise itself are ephemeral, for these mortals praise the things of mortality, and their commendation, like their joy, lasts but a summer, a mating season. The concluding lines of the stanza remove all ambiguity, and cancel all possibility of a return to such a country; even if the old man could, he would not return to a land where "caught in that sensual music, all neglect / Monuments of unageing intellect." The young are "caught," they are really passive and incapable of free action; and they neglect those things which are unageing.

Merely to end here, however, with a condemnation of youthful sensuality would be unsatisfactory; as the second stanza expounds, old age itself is no solution; the old man cannot justly say, like Sophocles when he was asked whether he regretted the loss of youth and love, "Peace; most gladly have I escaped the thing of which you speak; I feel as if I had escaped from a mad and furious master"; for merely to be old is merely to be in a state of privation, it is to be "a paltry thing / A tattered coat upon a stick," it is to be the merest scarecrow, the merest fiction and semblance of a man, an inanimate rag upon a dead stick. A man merely old, then, is worse off than youth; if the souls of the young are captive, the old have, in this sense at least, no souls at all. Something positive must be added; and if the soul can wax and grow strong as the body wanes, then every step in the dissolution of the body—"every tatter in its mortal dress"—is cause for a further augmentation of joy. But this can occur only if the soul can rejoice in its own power and magnificence; this rejoicing is possible only if the soul knows of its own magnificence, and this knowledge is possible only through the contemplation of monuments which recall that magnificence. The soul of the aged must be strong to seek that which youth neglects. Hence the old must seek Byzantium; that is the country of the old; it is reached by sailing the seas, by breaking utterly with the country of the young; all passion must be left behind, the soul must be free to study the emblems of unchanging things.

Here the soul should be filled with joy; it should, by merely "studying," commend changeless things with song, as youth commends the changing with song; it would seem that the problem has been resolved, and the poem hence must end; but the contemplation of the monuments teaches first of all that these are no mere monuments but living things, and that the soul cannot grow into likeness with these beings of immortal embodiment unless it cast off its mortal body utterly. Nor is joy possible until the body be dissolved; the heart is still sick with the impossible desires of the flesh, it is still ignorant of its circumstances, and no song is possible to the soul while even a remnant of passion remains. Hence the old man prays to the sages who really stand in God's holy fire and have merely the semblance of images in gold mosaic; let them descend, "perning in a gyre," that is, moving in the circular motion which alone is possible to eternal things, let them consume with holy fire the heart which is the last seat of passion and ignorance, let them instruct the soul, let them gather it into the artifice of eternity and make the old man like themselves; even Byzantium, so long as the flesh be present, is no country for old men.

What it is to be like these, the soul, as yet uninstructed, can only conjecture; at any rate, with the destruction of the flesh it will be free of its ills; and if, as in Plato's myth of Er, the soul after death is free to choose some new embodiment, it will never again elect the flesh which is so quickly corruptible and which enslaves it to passion; it will choose some such form of art as that of the artificial birds in Theophilus' garden [2] it will be of incorruptible and passionless gold; and it will dwell among leaves and boughs which are also of incorruptible and passionless metal. And now all sources of conflict are resolved in this last: the old has become the ageless; impotency has been exchanged for a higher power; the soul is free of passion and free for its joy, and it sings as youth once sang, but now of "What is past, and passing, and to come"—of the divisions of Eternity—rather than of "Whatever is begotten, born, and dies"—of the divisions of mortal time. And it has here its country, its proper and permanent habitation.

[2] In his note to the poem (*Collected Poems,* New York, 1933, p. 450) Yeats remarks: "I have read somewhere that in the Emperor's palace at Byzantium was a tree made of gold and silver, and artificial birds that sang." Undoubtedly the Emperor was Theophilus (829-842), and the birds conform to the descriptions of certain automata constructed for him by Leo Mathematicus and John Hylilas. Cf. *Hist. Byzan. Script. post Theoph.,* Anon. Cont. Theoph., 107; Constantini Manassis, *Brev. Hist.,* 107; and Michaeli Glycae, *Annales,* 292. See also Gibbon, *Decline and Fall,* Chapter LIII, and George Finlay, *History of the Byzantine Empire* (London, 1906), pp. 140, 148, where further references are given.

THE BRIDLE OF PEGASUS

(1934)

I. A. Richards

> Be not as the horse, or the mule, who have no understanding; whose mouth must be held in with bit and bridle, lest they come near unto thee.—*Psalm* xxxii.

> This same stede shal bere you ever-more
> With-outen harm, til ye be ther yow leste.
> . . . . .
> Of sondry doutes thus they jangle and trete
> As lewed peple demeth comunly
> Of thinges that ben maad more subtilly
> Than they can in her lewedness comprehende;
> They demen gladly to the badder ende.
> *The Squieres Tale.*

May I invite attention to a few paragraphs from a representative present-day critic on Wordsworth's doctrine and practice of the interpretation of Nature? They will show us where much current opinion is, in this matter. And they provide a convenient specimen for the study of reading ability.

> What claim, for instance, is Wordsworth making for his feelings in these lines, from the *Excursion*?
>
> Far and wide the clouds were touched
> And in their silent faces could he read
> Unutterable love. Sound needed none
> Nor any voice of joy: his spirit drank
> The spectacle: sensation, soul, and form,
> All melted into him; they swallowed up
> His animal being; in them did he live
> And by them did he live; they were his life.
> In such access of mind, in such high hour
> Of visitation from the living God,
> Thought was not; in enjoyment it expired.
> No thanks he breathed, he proffered no request:
> Rapt into still communion that transcends
> The imperfect offices of prayer and praise. . . .
>
> These last are daring words and more definite perhaps than any others in Wordsworth, in what they claim. He is not merely equalling,

but transcending the offices of prayer and praise. Wordsworth is presumably asking us to take him seriously; and if we take him seriously we cannot let such phrases slip by, all merged in one gush of emotion. And once we are asked to consider a theological issue some elementary questions arise.

First, why is this different from pantheism? Does Wordsworth by any denial of his poetic art or of his joy in things suggest that he is communing with a personal God, entirely distinct from his joy in the clouds: or is God, like the poet Donne, merely preaching to him 'from a cloud, but in none'? Herbert tells us that God is not to be found in stars or clouds or any aspect of nature, but in 'the sweet original joy sprung from Thine eye.'

Again, how are we to know that Wordsworth really felt these very emotions when he looked at the cloud, and that some of them did not rather arrive later when he wrote the poem? And if we pass over this difficulty, it is possible, of course, that the presence, which Wordsworth felt was in the cloud, existed only in his own mind as a result of looking at the cloud. If so, God is an attribute of Wordsworth's brain or exists somewhere in the relation between Wordsworth's brain and the cloud. And even if a higher reality, beyond the usual grasp of the human brain, is in truth communicating to Wordsworth from the cloud, this might still have been some biological harmony having no spiritual significance at all.

But suppose we say that this is all cavilling; suppose we say that Wordsworth's emotion is so sublime and impressive that we accept his use of the word God in this passage, what does it mean? Why the living God? What could God be if not merely 'alive,' but eternal? The epithet suggests that Wordsworth must be referring to some deity other than the one personal God of the Christian Gospels, a kind of deity who could be either dead or alive. If so, what God? We are not told. And if Wordsworth is really referring to the personal God of Christianity, whom Herbert worshipped, we arrived at his meaning in spite of rather than because of his words. And if this is his meaning, how does the contemplation of a cloud transcend the offices of prayer? Can Wordsworth, then, only communicate with God under certain meteorological conditions?

This passage is taken from a recent number of *The Criterion* (Oct., 1932). I may remark to begin with that it is uncomfortably *not* surprising that this new Defender of the Faith, writing on Nicholas Ferrar and George Herbert, in a periodical known for its Anglo-Catholic tendency, should show himself ignorant of the language of the Book of Common Prayer. "Why the living God?" Because Wordsworth knew his Psalms:

> Like as the hart desireth the water-brooks,
> So longeth my soul after thee, O God.
> My soul is athirst for God, yea even for the living God;
> When shall I come to appear before the presence of God?
>
> (Psalm 42, *Quemadmodum*,
> The Evening of the 8th Day.)

In the First Prayer Book of Edward VI this psalm was part of the order for the burial of the dead.[1] And is Matthew xvi. 16 too recondite a reference?

We may note now, first, that Wordsworth's poem does not claim to transcend prayer and praise. An experience is described in it as doing so—that is all. As to whether Wordsworth "really felt these very emotions" and when: is the distinction between a poem and an autobiographical note, or an *affidavit*, really so difficult as this? And, as to the next set of difficulties: what is there about Wordsworth's lines which specially invites them? These are "elementary questions" indeed, so elementary that any human utterance of any kind brings them up. Nothing in Herbert or Donne, or any other poet, is a whit more immune from them. They must be reflected on by anyone who would read any poetry with sincerity. But to use them as missiles in this fashion is merely to show lack of acquaintance with them *as questions*, as "preliminary steps of the Methodical scale, at the top of which sits the author, and at the bottom the critic" (*Treatise on Method*, Snyder, 32).

However, this writer has been making some attempts to find out about these things. He continues on a later page:

> Emotion in itself has no religious significance: an emotion is merely a reaction of feeling in the mental plane, as spontaneous as feelings of the physical senses. The *Encyclopaedia of Religion and Ethics*, in summing up the view of emotion so far given by moral philosophy, says that emotion cannot in itself be moral or immoral, religious or irreligious: it only is the manner in which the intellect judges and the will controls the emotions, that can have a place among religious values. In another place in the *Prelude*, Wordsworth does attempt to give some such comment on the emotions, with the following result. He is describing a child listening to a singing shell:
>
> ... and his countenance soon
> Brightened with joy; for from within were heard
> Murmurings, whereby the monitor expressed
> Mysterious union with its native sea.
> Even such a shell the universe itself
> Is to the ear of Faith: and there are times
> I doubt not, when to you it doth import
> Authentic tidings of invisible things;
> Of ebb and flow, and ever during power;
> And central peace, subsisting at the heart
> Of endless agitation.
>
> But what is it in fact that a child hears, or you hear, when a shell is put to the ear? Not murmurings by which the monitor expresses mysterious union with the sea, but in actual fact murmurings which are

[1] It remains, in Latin, in the Roman Catholic Office for the Dead. The phrase may also be found in the Canon of the Mass.

the blood circulation in the listener's *own* head. To apply Wordsworth's illustration, as he asks us to apply it, what then are these 'authentic tidings' that he draws from nature? Something, for which a buzzing in his own head is his own chosen simile.

Had Wordsworth paused to reflect and to judge, instead of being swept away by emotions, he could never have misapplied this elementary fact at this crucial moment. Had he reflected and judged, he would have rather written with Hopkins:

> Elected Silence, sing to me
> And beat upon my whorlèd ear . . .

And once the mind appreciates the collapse of meaning, it can only turn from this passage and from all the other passages that it represents, with something of sense of failure and frustration, and even a loss of pleasure in the poetry itself.

The "collapse of meaning" however, is not in Wordsworth but in this critic's reading of him. The passage cited is, of course, Coleridge's Wind Harp theme again, an allegorical presentation of the central problem of philosophy. The reader has missed Wordsworth's deep self-critical humour, and so laughs *at* the lines when he should smile with them. To suggest that Wordsworth did not "pause to reflect and judge" shows an odd ignorance of this poet's habits in composition.

It is amusing to observe that he gives, "by way of comparison," as an example of "exact and careful reflection," this image, which refers to Herbert's own power of thought:

> Mark how the fire in flints doth quiet lie,
> Content and warm to itself alone.
> But when it would appear to other's eye
> Without a knock it never shone.

If Wordsworth had written this, how easily would the reader have pointed out that the fire is not in the flint but in the detached particle!

I have lingered with this example partly because it shows the kind of comment which Coleridge's doctrine, in my interpretation of it, must expect, but chiefly because it illustrates both erratic reading and lack of reflection upon the problems of symbolisation. There is a connection between these to-day which perhaps did not hold in former times. The capacity to read intelligently seems undoubtedly to have been greater among educated men in Coleridge's time than it is to-day. Three reasons at least may be suggested for this. More rigorous translation exercises in the schools; less shoddy reading material in our daily intake of printed matter; a greater homogeneity in the intellectual tradition. Only this last concerns us here. Intellectual tradition tells us, among other things, *how literally* to read a passage. It guides us in our metaphorical, allegorical, symbolical modes of interpretation. The hierarchy of these modes is elaborate and variable; and to read aright we need to shift with an at present indescribable adroitness and celerity from one mode to another. Our sixteenth- and seventeenth-century literature, supported by practice in listening to sermons and by conventions in speech and letter-writing which made "direct" statement rare to a point which seems to us unnatural, gave an extraordinary training [2] in this skill. But it was skill merely; it was not followed up by theory. With the eighteenth century, the variety of the modes of metaphor in speech and in writing rapidly declined. Dr. Johnson, for example, can show, at times, strange obtuseness in distinguishing between degrees of metaphor. It was this which made Donne seem artificial, absurd, unimpassioned and bewildering to him. But at the same time it is Johnson perhaps who shows us best the first steps of that reflective analytical scrutiny and comparison of the structures of meanings in poetry which is later to take a vast stride in Coleridge. For example, on these lines of Denham,

> O could I flow like thee, and make thy stream
> My great example as it is my theme!
> Though deep, yet clear; though gentle, yet not dull;
> Strong without rage, without o'erflowing full.

he remarks, "The lines are in themselves not perfect; for most of the words thus artfully opposed, are to be understood simply on one side of the comparison, and metaphorically on the other; and, if there be any language which does not express intellectual operations by material images, into that language they cannot be translated." There is, of course, no such language; but that Johnson should be applying such reflections to the analysis of poetry is instructive. A more persistent examination would have shown him that the transferences here were sometimes primary, sometimes secondary, sometimes went from the river to the mind, sometimes from the mind to the river. And, with that, the assumptions behind his first remark would have been broken down. Naturally enough an age which, partly through false theory, partly through social causes, is losing its skill in interpretation, begins the reflective inquiry which may lead to a theory by which the skill may be regained—this time as a less vulnerable and more deeply grounded, because more consciously recognized, endowment.

[2] As Coleridge was among the first to point out, "Shakespeare's time, when the English Court was still foster-mother of the State and the Muses; and when, in consequence, the courtiers and men of rank and fashion affected a display of wit, point, and sententious observation, that would be deemed intolerable at present—but in which a hundred years of controversy, involving every great political, and every dear domestic interest, had trained all but the lowest classes to participate. Add to this the very style of the sermons of the time, and the eagerness of the Protestants to distinguish themselves by long and frequent preaching, and it will be found that, from the reign of Henry VIII to the abdication of James II, no country ever received such a national education as England." (Raysor, I, 93.)

With Coleridge's generation came a recovery of skill, both in readers and writers. It was maintained—for modes of meaning close in structure to those in Wordsworth, Shelley or Keats—until towards the end of the nineteenth century. Then came a sudden decline in performance. Twentieth-century criticism has been marked not so much by an enlightening reaction against the biassed preferences of the nineteenth century, as by the betrayal of general inability to read anything with safety on the part of most of those who have anything to say. Scholars and textual critics escape this generalization; but then professional students rarely have much to say. "The true atheist is he whose hands are cauterized with holy things." Their work is probably better in quality than any in the past—but we must recall that, like men of science, they have a cumulative advantage in technique, and they are also in closer contact with the records of tradition. Unluckily they have usually so much the less touch with its new shoots. And they rarely have voices that can be heard—a fact which may be a gain to the world. For if one asks, "What can a lifetime of literary studies do towards judgment of the new?" the answer must, I fear, be a grim one. Thus the criticism that shapes public taste, and that may indirectly here and there influence original writing, is written by men of letters who are not primarily scholars. And it is this criticism that shows, I think demonstrably—though I decline the invidious task of demonstration—an alarming general drop in the capacity to construe the poetry which it discusses. Our "Neo-Classic" age is repeating those feats of its predecessor which we least applaud. It is showing a fascinating versatility in travesty. And the poets of the "Romantic" period provide for it what Shakespeare, Milton and Donne were to the early eighteenth-century grammarians and emendators—effigies to be shot at because what they represent is no longer understood. So the Chinese student bicycles to-day gaily and ribaldly round on the Altar of Heaven.

My point, however, is more general than these graceless and querulous remarks would suggest. It is that a great diversity in our current intellectual tradition, sharp opposition between its different branches, discontinuity in the process by which readers find themselves living in and with one or other of them, quick changes between them, insufficiently realized as they occur—in short, a general heterogeneity in our recent growth has disordered the conduct of reading. This shows itself most clearly, I think, in the frequency with which new and old-fashioned critics alike now pretend that their own inability to understand a poem is a sound argument against it. The conservatives use this plea against the new-fanglers quite as naïvely as do these against Shelley, Keats or Wordsworth. Both, of course, claim to be thereby upholding tradition. And both, to an onlooker, add sanction to Coleridge's adage, "Until you understand a writer's ignorance, presume yourself ignorant of his understanding."

The explanation of this embarrassing situation is not, I believe, in any fundamental difference in outlook between, say, Mr. T. S. Eliot and Mr. F. L. Lucas. No such gap separates them as divided Shelley from Dr. Johnson. Yet something impenetrably shrouds Mr. Eliot's constant preoccupation with the sources of nobility from Mr. Lucas' eye; and something has at times hidden from Mr. Eliot even those purposes of some romantic poetry which most resembled his own. I am tempted to connect these obstructions, to trace them to a common origin in divergent attitudes to language, to different ways in which words are used, and in which they are assumed to work.

Contemporary poetry (and very much of the poetry of other times in which contemporary readers are most interested) is generally supposed to be difficult. It will be fitting to conclude this examination of Coleridge's critical theories by considering what light they can throw upon this "difficulty." For it seems probable that in a large measure it derives from differences between the *actual* structures of the meanings of the poetry and the structures which, in various ways, are *supposed* to be natural and necessary to poetry, the structures which from habit and implicit theory are expected in its meanings.

But we must not confuse changes in the structures of poetic meanings with changes in the theories historically connected with them. Most theorizing upon meanings only very distantly reflects them. And this is our difficulty—with which Coleridge may help us. The technique of comparing the structures of meanings is still embryonic and much impeded by immature theories, due to the poets and others, as to what different kinds of poetry try to do and how they try to do it. In almost all familiar formulations, unreal problems of the *what* and of the *how* are distressingly entangled.

It is with deceptive ease, indeed, that the inquiry divides into questions about the *what* and the *how*. Or into questions about the *methods* a poet uses and the *feats* he thereby achieves. Or into questions about his *means* and his *ends*. Or about the *way* of his work and the *whither*. This ease is deceptive because, although for some purposes the division is necessary and for others convenient, in an examination of poetic structure the distinction prevents all advance by destroying the specimens we would examine.

How it does so may be best shown, perhaps, by taking the last of these formulations—between the *way* and the *whither* of a poem—and making the metaphor in it as explicit as possible, undeterred by any charges of "intoxication by the obvious" that may be occasioned.

The metaphor is that of a path leading to some destination, or of a missile (arrow or boomerang) going to some mark; but let us exercise a trifling ingenuity in inventing journeys without destinations—movements of the earth, the pigeons' flight, the tacking of a boat, an ant's tour of the spokes of a wheel—or in considering the different trajectories which an arrow will take in shifting winds, or that most illuminating instance here, the rocket; and we shall see clearly how unnecessary, as applying to poems, the assumptions behind any division between a *way* and a *whither* may be. However widely we generalize it (as means and ends) the division is here an impeding product of abstraction. From the *total meaning* of the poem, we have singled out some component to be treated as its *whither* and to be set over against the rest as its *way*. We have chosen something to be, in a narrower sense, its "meaning" and left the rest to be either the vehicle of this meaning or our further response to it. And until and unless we are explicitly aware of these processess of singling out partial meanings we can make no progress in comparative studies of poetic structures.

Traditionally or conventionally the *whither* of a poem has often been taken to be "what it says": and this, when thus singled out, has as often, in recent times, been regarded as of minor importance. As Professor Housman put it in his Leslie Stephen Lecture (*The Name and Nature of Poetry,* p. 37), "Poetry is not the thing said but a way of saying it." But this "thing said," if we try with most poetry to separate it from the "way of saying it," shows itself to be a most arbitrary thing. Unless we are unreasonably stern with it (or hold indefensible views on synonymity) we have to admit that even very slight changes in a way of saying anything *in poetry* change the thing said-and usually in evident and analysable respects. Only in abstracter matters than poetry ever touches is "the same thought" able to be uttered with different words. But by taking "the same thought" in a loose indefinite sense—as thoughts linked by a mere resemblance of topic—we can sometimes deceive ourselves and make the division between "the thing said" and the "way of saying it" seem useful and applicable.

" 'But no man may deliver his brother, nor make agreement unto God for him,' that," said Mr. Housman, "is to me poetry so moving that I can hardly keep my voice steady in reading it. And that this is the effect of language I can ascertain by experiment: the same thought in the Bible version, 'None of them can by any means redeem his brother, nor give to God a ransom for him,' I can read without emotion" (p. 37). That this is the effect of language we may grant without misgiving, but in what sense of *thought* that could be relevant do they utter the same thought? *Deliver—redeem; make agreement unto—give a ransom for:* the dominant metaphors are changed, and a defined explicit transaction has taken the place of a crowd of various or conflicting possibilities. It is surprising that so severe a textual critic and so rigorous an upholder of precision in literary studies as Mr. Housman should permit himself such an opinion. The ambiguity of *thought* and its power to mislead even the most wary could not be better shown.

This "thing said" is an abstraction from the whole meaning, and we may abstract it in various ways, taking a smaller or larger part of the whole meaning to be thus set over against the rest, and to be labelled, if we like, the poem's "thought" or "prose-sense." Mr. Housman calls it sometimes the "intellectual content," sometimes simply the "meaning." Whatever the name, it is clear both that different readers will, with the same poem, separate different parts of the total meaning as this prose-sense; and that different poems invite different kinds of division in this respect. Sometimes the prose-sense seems to be the source, sometime a tributary, sometimes a mere bank or dyke for the rest. These variations, from poem to poem, in the place and functions of the prose-sense, thought or "meaning"—are by far the most accessible and examinable aspects of poetic structure. Yet to these differences the difficulty of "understanding" poetry seems chiefly due. To understand a poem, in this sense, would be to permit the varied components of its total meaning to take their rightful places within it.

The besetting vice of all criticism is thus described by Coleridge—perhaps more clearly than by any other writer:

> We call, for we see and feel, the swan and the dove both transcendently beautiful. As absurd as it would be to institute a comparison between their separate claims to beauty from any abstract rule common to both, without reference to the life and being of the animals themselves—say rather if, having first seen the dove, we abstracted its outlines, gave them a false generalization, called them principle or ideal of bird-beauty and then proceeded to criticize the swan or the eagle—not less absurd is it to pass judgement on the works of a poet on the mere ground that they have been called by the same class-name with the works of other poets of other times and circumstances, or any ground indeed save that of their inappropriateness to their own end and being, their want of significance, as symbol and physiognomy (Raysor, I, 196).

The next step is to explore further the physiology, as it were, of poetry. In what we are apt to regard as the normal standard case, the prose-sense appears to be the source of the rest of our response.

> The Curfew tolls the knell of parting day,
> The lowing herd wind slowly o'er the lea,
> The plowman homeward plods his weary way,
> And leaves the world to darkness and to me.

Here everything which we need to think of is named by the words and described by the syntax, and any inferences we may add—that the poet is not weary as the ploughman is, or that the death of the day is to be compared with the end of their day of life for those lying in the churchyard—are fully prepared by this prose-sense. And, though it is, of course, merely by a figure of speech that we say that any one kind of component in a total meaning comes *before* another, it is clear that almost all the rest can be properly regarded as dependent from and controlled by the prose-sense here.

Now let us take a different case, Blake's song:

> Memory, hither come,
> And tune your merry notes:
> And, while upon the wind
> Your music floats,
> I'll pore upon the stream,
> Where sighing lovers dream,
> And fish for fancies as they pass
> Within the watery glass.

It is not hard to see that this has in some way a different structure. What is hard—but still must be attempted—is to say without exaggeration how its structure differs.

Some differences may be shown by these observations: that, if we abstract a plain sense from it, what we get is something very unlike, if separately considered, anything we are distinctly aware of in reading the words as poetry; secondly, that what prose-sense we obtain will be to some degree optional, will depend upon how we choose to interpret certain of the words in it. For example, *tune* may be read as "sing, utter" or as "accord, bring into order"; *the stream* may be the "mere river" or "the stream of life, or time," or desire; and *glass* may show merely the translucency of the water or turn it into an image-making reflection of things, as with a crystal we gaze into. But still, whatever we get from the poem as its *Sense*—whether, at one extreme, we make it merely an announcement of an intended revery, or, at the other, we load it with symbolic interpretations and make it a commentary on the theme, "The Temporal the All"—what we get still stands over against the actual whole poetic meaning which any good reader knows as he reads it. The sense, however elaborated, remains something which does not *explain* the poetic meaning as the sense in the lines from the *Elegy* does explain their poetic meaning.

There is another fashion, of course, in which the sense may "explain" the meaning. If we were asked, for example, "How did Napoleon do all he did?" and replied, "Because he was a great man!" our answer would not be an explanation in the stricter sense. But it might be an "explanation" in the sense of being another way of saying how what he did strikes us as remarkable. Most explanations of poems are perhaps to be regarded as parallel to this; they are comments upon, not accounts of, the total meaning.[3]

Observing this inadequacy or seeming irrelevance of the prose-sense, we shall perhaps be tempted to say that the poem has no sense, no meaning, no intellectual content. The strength of the temptation is shown by the fact that so strict a reader as Mr. Housman—for I have taken this example from him—did very nearly say this. He said (p. 43):

[3] See Cleanth Brooks's chapter "The Heresy of Paraphrase" in *The Well Wrought Urn* (1947). [*Editor's note.*]

> That answers to nothing real; memory's merry notes and the rest are empty phrases, not things to be imagined: the stanza does but entangle the reader in a net of thoughtless delight.

But are there really any "empty phrases" in it; and is the delight so "thoughtless" after all? For, granting that no prose-sense we can extract from it is an adequate reflection of it, it is undeniable that all the main words in it have sense. And that their senses are directly relevant to the total meaning is shown by this: that if we change in the least their susceptibility to take certain senses the whole poem collapses. Though experience shows that such experiments are highly resented by some (but any temporary damage to the poem is slight and evanescent in healthy minds), let us try replacing *stream* by *steam*. Or let us read *watery glass* in a sense consonant rather with Bass than with a rivulet. Who will doubt, after such trials, that these words *in the poem* have very definite senses in delicate interaction with those of the other words? But this is not to say that the whole poem derives simply from the articulation of these senses (as was almost the case with Gray); that would be to go too far in the opposite direction. The senses of the words here come to them as much from their feelings (to use this term as a convenient abbreviation for "the rest of their powers upon us") as their feelings come from their senses. The interchange here seems nearly equal. But even in a case where feeling wholly dominates sense, it would not be true to say that the words, if they did receive some sense from feeling, were empty phrases. And cases where no sense, by whatever means, is given to the words, are extremely rare if indeed they occur at all. Of course, to use a sense in our reading is not the same thing as to be aware in reflection that we are doing so.

Not until we have set aside these two opposite misconceptions: that the whole meaning of a poem is or should be always simply derivative from its articulated prose-sense (if it has one); and that it can consist (for any length) of "empty phrases"; can we examine poetic structures with any hope of discovering what may be happening.

Of the two errors the second is, at present, by far the most probable. It derives from that ambiguity of the word "meaning" which leads us to suppose that if a poem has no articulated prose-sense (or none of independent importance) it has no meaning—confusing this narrower use with a wider use of "meaning." In the wider sense there are no meaningless poems, as, in the narrower sense, there are few meaningless words, even in the least articulated poems.

Blake's song, more perhaps even than most songs, is *dramatic.* That is, someone other than the poet is speaking (or the poet as other than the man). To take a long shot in a field to which guesses only are admitted, the melancholy Jacques is speaking. For is not this song a quintessence of *As You Like It,* as *The Mad Song* is of the Storm Scene of *King Lear,* or Mr. de la Mare's *Mad Prince's Song* is of

Hamlet? However this may be, some poems are obviously more dramatic than others. By some we are invited to identify their voices with their authors'; others lend a character to or take one from other spokesmen; yet others, transcending personality, seem utterable only by

Miracle, bird or golden handiwork.

Behind these large and apparent differences hosts of contributory and derivative microscopic changes of structure may well be suspected. For example, so abstruse a poem as Mr. Yeats's magnificent *Byzantium* [4] might, if we were to take Mr. Yeats to be speaking—and if the poem had not passed "into the artifice of eternity"—challenge us to request explanations. But since the Superhuman, the Death-in-Life and Life-in-Death, is speaking, if we cannot "understand" it, there will be no help for us from lesser authorities. The impersonality should there protect us from the impertinences and pedantries of our lesser selves.

All poetry (as all utterances) *can* of course be looked on as dramatic; but some poems more invite such reading than others and when so read are best understood. For example, Hopkins is most often non-dramatic, he speaks for himself. Mr. Eliot's poems, on the other hand, are almost always dramatic. It is evident that if we simply and uniformly identify with the poet all poetry not plainly labelled "Dramatic" we shall perpetrate much misreading—especially with modern poets. This is so patent that I am almost ashamed to write it, and I sympathize with my reader if it irks him; but such points cannot be taken for granted when critics of repute complain, for example, that Mr. Eliot is far too young a man to compare himself with an "aged eagle" (*Ash Wednesday*), or that he actually wishes to be a live lobster,[5] or that, since he is self-confessed a Hollow Man, "headpiece stuffed with straw," no one should pay attention to him. And if these points of structure are so misconceived it will not be surprising if over-simple views prevail on finer points.

Many such critical preconceptions can be traced to mistaken endeavours to exalt poetry. "It should come from the heart," *i.e.*, the poet is unpacking his heart in words. Or "The more mysterious its action, the finer it probably is," *i.e.*, explanation is belittling.[6] This last seems often to favour the neglect of the prose-sense of poetry even when it is perfectly plain and evidently active in the meaning. A curious, but not uncommon, case is when the evident sense is ac-

[4] I agree with Mr. Eliot, *The Use of Poetry,* p. 140, that in *Science and Poetry* I did not properly appreciate Mr. Yeats's later work. I can plead that I wrote before *The Tower* was published.

[5] *Prufrock:*

I should have been a pair of ragged claws
Scuttling across the floors of silent seas

—it should be a crab, I think, for crabs go sideways, which is the point.

[6] See the essay by Wimsatt and Beardsley on "The Affective Fallacy." [*Editor's note.*]

cepted in the poetic reading but denied in the account afterwards given of it. I choose my example from Mr. Housman (*The Name and Nature of Poetry,* p. 46.).

> In these six simple words of Milton:
>
> Nymphs and shepherds, dance no more—
>
> What is it that can draw tears, as I know it can, to the eyes of more readers than one? What in the world is there to cry about? Why have the mere words the physical effect of pathos when the sense of the passage is blithe and gay? I can only say, because they are poetry, and find their way to something in man which is obscure and latent, something older than the present organization of his nature, like the patches of fen which still linger here and there in the drained lands of Cambridgeshire.

Surely there is much more to say than this? Are these words really inexplicable in their effect or even at all hard to explain? And is "the sense of the passage" really "blithe and gay"? To say so, seems to me to overlook all the force of the words "no more." Lear's "Thou'lt come no more" is the supreme instance. As Shenstone remarked (in 1761): "the words 'no more' have a singular pathos reminding us at once of past pleasure and the future exclusion of it." And the Nymphs and Shepherds that Milton pretends are going now to dance in England—we know, as he knew, that it is a pretence, that they have vanished; all that is over; and the dances in his *Masque* are no substitutes. Is the line lessened if we notice this? Is it not better to recognize that words work in intelligible (if intricate) ways than to appeal to a modern taste for primitiveness? And yet this very appeal has here taken a form which inversely reflects the very sense Milton put into his line.

While I am at this point, let me demur to one other implication in Mr. Housman's treatment. Of Blake's

> Hear the voice of the Bard!

he says, "that mysterious grandeur would be less grand if it were less mysterious; if the embryo ideas which are all that it contains should endue form and outline, and suggestion condense itself into thought."

"Embryo ideas" would be undeveloped ideas. There is a slighting implication in this description of them, whether or no we recall Milton's list of the destined contents of Limbo:

> Embryos, and Idiots, Eremits and Friers
> White, Black and Grey, with all their trumperie.

An embryo is at least a piteous and helpless thing, and commonly a parasite. And it is not certain at all here that the thought is dependent. Is it not equally likely that the ideas from which this poem derives its mysterious grandeur are not less but more fully developed as we receive them in the poem? I would suggest seriously that in the greater poems of great poets the ideas there brought into being in the mind are completer, not less complete; and that the process which extricates them by abstraction denatures them rather than develops them. The extracted abstract doctrine (if we arrive at any such) is a skeleton of the living knowledge, deformed and schematized for the legitimate purposes of comparison (as well as for the irrelevant purposes of argument). In the poem they are autonomous, sanctioned by their acceptability to the whole being of the reader. Out of the poem, they are doctrine merely, and a temptation to dispute.

But this perhaps is not so different as it seems from something Mr. Housman may have been implying. I have wished only to protest, on Blake's behalf, against an arrogant "intellectualist" assumption that the word "embryo" *may* introduce. Blake knew what he was doing when he wrote about these things in verse, not prose. But we do not know what he was doing if we think he was not speaking—for and to the whole man, not the abstractive analytic intellect only—about the most important things in the world,

> Of what is past, or passing, or to come.

To return to the division of the *way* and the *whither;* however we divide them, whether we make thoughts the way to the rest of the poem, or the rest of it the way to the thought—we shall, if we put the value of the poem either in the way or the whither, for most poems, misconceive it. We may *read* them aright but we shall describe them wrongly. No great matter in itself perhaps; but, as we may see, these errors are small-scale models for enormous evils. As we habitually mistake our lesser myths, so we warp our world-picture by attempting amiss to "understand" it, or by denying it all intelligibility, all meaning, because it lacks a certain sub-variety of meaning in the place in which we crave it. And, as with poetry, so with every mode of the mythopoeic activity by which we live, shape universes to live in, reshape, inquire, in a thousand varying ways, seek

> patiently to bend
> Our mind to sifting reason, and clear light
> That strangely figured in our soul doth wend,
> Shifting its forms, still playing in our sight
> Till something it present that we shall take for right.[7]

We wrong it and thus ourselves if we take, as its "point," some singled-out component only and disregard the rest. Yet having done this, by tradition, so long, we must now by conscious reflection compare the structures of different kinds of experience as of different kinds of poetry. Tradition, never really very successful in this, can no longer

7 Henry More, *Song of the Soul.*

teach us even what it could—now that we live in a confluence of so many and such different streams. Our remedy, if we are not increasingly to misunderstand one another (thus misunderstanding ourselves), is the dangerous one of analysis; but it is dangerous only when we take the divisions we make as established insurmountably in the order of things, and not as introduced to assist us to compare.

What I have been urging as to the opposition of the "thing said" and the "way of saying it" holds good, I think, of every other division we may make in comparing the structure of poems. They are useful if we do not then segregate the value of the poem into some compartment thus created. To do so is like saying that the point of an elephant is his strength (See Coleridge's remarks about the dove and the swan, cited above.) Apart from some forms of applied poetry—some satires or some devotional poems for example—poetry has no whither as opposed to a way. As Coleridge said in his description of a "just poem" (*B.L.*, II, 11):

> The reader should be carried forward, not merely or chiefly by the mechanical impulse of curiosity, or a restless desire to arrive at the final solution; but by the pleasurable activity of mind excited by the attractions of the journey itself.

With the best poetry there is nowhere to arrive, no final solution. The poem is no ticket to the Fortunate Isles, or even to Purgatory, or even to Moscow. The journey is its own end, and it will not, by having no destination, any less assist the world to become what Moscow should be.

Poems which have a destination, a final solution—whether it be the enunciation of a supposed truth, or suasion to a policy, or the attainment of an end-state of consciousness, or some temporary or permanent exclusive attitude to the world, to society, or to the self, have only a subordinate value. Instead of establishing, as the best poetry does, the norms of value, they have to be judged by standards more inclusive than themselves—a consideration very relevant to the supposed "difficulty" of much good poetry where this difficulty is conceived as an objection to it. As Coleridge put it:

> The elder languages were fitter for poetry because they expressed only prominent ideas with clearness, the others but darkly. . . . Poetry gives most pleasure when only generally and not perfectly understood. It was so by me with Gray's *Bard* and Collins' Odes. The *Bard* once intoxicated me, and now I read it without pleasure. From this cause it is that what I call metaphysical poetry gives me so much delight (*Anima Poetae*, p. 5).

"The elder languages" I take, perhaps arbitrarily, to be "Elizabethan" English, for example; and "prominent ideas" are not necessarily the most important.

It would be extremely interesting to know just what Coleridge included in "What I call metaphysical poetry" here. It was not what

Johnson and others have called by that name, Cowley being excluded but not Donne, and much of Wordsworth, almost undoubtedly, being added. "Only generally and not perfectly understood" is a phrase full of dangers, of course. Shift the sense of "understood" only a little and it is an excuse for every vague, undisciplined and erratic type of reading, for the merest misty indulgence is unformed "sentimental" revery. But no one who knows his Coleridge will suppose that he meant this. What he is pointing to is the superiority of the characteristic Shakespearian structure of meaning over the characteristic later eighteenth-century structures, or of Blake's over Southey's. And we may equally take him as pointing to the superiority of the poetic structures used by Mr. Yeats in his recent poetry, in the best poetry by Mr. Eliot, by Mr. Auden or Mr. Empson at their best, or by Hopkins—very different though these structures are—their superiority to, let us say, the characteristic structures used by Rupert Brooke or the chief representatives of "Georgian Poetry." The point of contrast can be put shortly by saying that Rupert Brooke's verse, in comparison with Mr. Eliot's, has no *inside*. Its ideas and other components, however varied, are all expressed with prominence; lovely though the display may be, it is a display; the reader is visiting an Exhibition of Poetic Products.

An idea which is expressed "but darkly" need be neither a dim nor a vague one—but it will be one which we have to look for. It is sometimes thought that this very process of "looking into" a poem is destructive of the poetic virtue. But whether this is so of course depends upon how we "look in"—upon what sort of a process this is. Certainly the detective intelligence, or the Cross-Word Puzzler's technique, is not a proper method in reading poetry. Something resembling them was, perhaps, a suitable mode of preparation for reading some of Mr. Eliot's earlier poems, *Burbank* or *A Cooking Egg* or some parts of *The Waste Land* for example. Those who went through it, however, found that what they thus discovered—though its discovery may have been necessary for them—was no essential part of the poetry when this came to life. That it can nearly all be forgotten without loss to the poetry, shows perhaps that it was scaffolding for the poet, as well as for the reader. But apart altogether from this play of extrinsic explicit conjecture, there is another way of "looking into" abstruse poetry—a receptive submission, which will perhaps *be reflected* in conjectures but into which inferences among these conjectures do not enter. For example, the differences between the opening lines of the first and last sections of Mr. Eliot's *Ash Wednesday:*

> Because I do not hope to turn again

and

> Although I do not hope to turn again

in their joint context and their coterminous subcontexts, will come into full being for very few readers without movements of exploration and resultant ponderings that I should not care to attempt to reflect in even the most distant prose translation. And yet these very movements—untrackable as they perhaps are, and uninducible as they almost certainly are by any other words—are the very life of the poem. In these searchings for meanings of a certain sort its being consists. The poem is a quest, and its virtue is not in anything said by it, or in the way in which it is said, or in a meaning which is found, or even in what is passed by in the search. For in this poem—to quote two lines from Coleridge's *Constancy to an Ideal Object* which is a meditation on the same theme—as in so much of the later poetry of Mr. Yeats,

> like strangers sheltering from a storm
> Hope and Despair meet in the porch of Death.

And though from their encounter comes

> strength beyond hope or despair
> Climbing the third stair

there is no account, in other terms than those of poetry, to be given of how it comes. Again the resemblance to the symbolism of Mr. Yeats' *The Winding Stair* is of more than slight or accidental interest. Is it not remarkable that not only Mr. Yeats, in his later poetry, and Mr. Eliot in his public penances for the sins of every generation,

> Now at this birth season of decease

but Mr. Auden also,

> O watcher in the dark, you wake
> Our dream of waking,

Mr. Empson, with his

> So Semele desired her Deity

and D. H. Lawrence, in all his last poetry,

> Turning to death as I turn to beauty

should be "thus devoted, concentrated in purpose"?

When Mr. Eliot discusses, in prose, the place of meanings in poetry and the bearing of false expectations about them on this alleged "difficulty" of modern poetry, what he says, though very helpful, needs to be read with a lively awareness of the ambiguities of the word *meaning* and a clear understanding of the narrowed sense in which he is using it. I will quote the whole passage in which he discusses these points:

> The difficulty of poetry (and modern poetry is supposed to be difficult) may be due to one of several reasons. First, there may be personal

causes which make it impossible for a poet to express himself in any but an obscure way; while this may be regrettable, we should be glad, I think, that the man has been able to express himself at all. Or difficulty may be due just to novelty: we know the ridicule accorded in turn to Wordsworth, Shelley and Keats, Tennyson and Browning—but must remark that Browning was the first to be *called* difficult; hostile critics of the earlier poets found them difficult, but called them silly. Or difficulty may be caused by the reader's having been told, or having suggested to himself, that the poem is going to prove difficult. The ordinary reader, when warned against the obscurity of a poem, is apt to be thrown into a state of consternation very unfavourable to poetic receptivity. Instead of beginning, as he should, in a state of sensitivity, he obfuscates his senses by the desire to be clever and to look very hard for something, he doesn't know what—or else by the desire not to be taken in. There is such a thing as stage fright, but what such readers have is pit or gallery fright. The more seasoned reader, he who has reached, in these matters, a state of greater *purity,* does not bother about understanding; not, at least, at first. I know that some of the poetry to which I am most devoted is poetry which I did not understand at first reading; some is poetry which I am not sure I understand yet: for instance, Shakespeare's. And finally, there is the difficulty caused by the author's having left out something which the reader is used to finding; so that the reader, bewildered, gropes about for what is absent, and puzzles his head for a kind of 'meaning' which is not there, and is not meant to be there.

The chief use of the 'meaning' of a poem, in the ordinary sense, may be (for here again I am speaking of some kinds of poetry and not all) to satisfy one habit of the reader, to keep his mind diverted and quiet, while the poem does its work upon him: much as the imaginary burglar is always provided with a bit of nice meat for the house-dog. This is a normal situation of which I approve. But the minds of all poets do not work that way; some of them, assuming that there are other minds like their own, become impatient of this 'meaning' which seems superfluous, and perceive possibilities of intensity through its elimination.

The "state of consternation," it may be remarked, wears off quickly for most readers—for those readers at least who would be likely, if not handicapped by it, to "understand" the poem in the end. And the *purer* reader, if he does not, in one sense, "bother about understanding" is still, in another sense, occupied with nothing else. But the modes of understanding are as many and as varied as the structures of meanings.

If we turn now from the mere recognition that no prepossessions that we can form can *prescribe* a structure for the meanings in poetry —and yet every poem is a fabric of meaning—a recognition to which Coleridge's account of Imagination inevitably leads us; and from the speculative analysis of the possibilities of diverse poetic structures—a task for the criticism of the future—to speculations upon the causes of changes in the structures most employed by poets of successive generations and from these to an attempt to divine the general direction of these changes, we shall find further reasons for thinking that Coleridge's "philosophic" approach to criticism is helpful.

That there has been a general drift in human interests in the West through the last four centuries—in the modes of our current mythology and in the functions of its parts—is hardly to be doubted. It shows itself in innumerable ways: in the growth of Science and History, in our changing attitudes to Authority in all its forms, to the Bible, to Tradition (as a body of truth to be received because of its source), to custom (to be accepted because established), to parental opinion. . . . It shows itself conspicuously in the philosophic movement from Descartes to Kant and on again to modern pragmatism and dialectic materialism; less conspicuously perhaps in the change from Locke's psychology to Freud's; less conspicuously still in the widespread increase in the aptitude of the average mind for self-dissolving introspection, the generally heightened awareness of the goings on of our own minds, merely *as goings on,* not as transitions from one well-known and linguistically recognized moral or intellectual condition to another. And together with this last (it is an aspect of the same change) it shows itself in the startling enhancement of our interest in the *sensory* detail and *nuance* of the visible scene as opposed to the practically useful information about things which these perceptions can give us.

In these last modifications of consciousness we may see more clearly and less debatably than with the others what has been happening. They witness to a change in the focus of what Coleridge called "the primary imagination . . . the living Power and prime Agent of all human Perception" (*B.L.,* I, 202) and are clearly enough reflected in those activities of character-drawing and description which are so large a part of the work of the "secondary imagination" of the Novelist. I have in view a very obvious contrast between the modes of depicting both character and the landscape practised by the best seventeenth- and eighteenth-century writers and the best modern novelists. George Moore somewhere in *Avowals,* wishing to say something derogatory of *Tom Jones,* described it, if memory serves me, as "an empty book without a glimpse of the world without or a hint of the world within." The remark is perfectly true. There is neither an outer nor an inner world in *Tom Jones* as these are to be found in the work of modern novelists. We can hunt through it in vain to find either a scene described primarily in terms of its appearance, or however short a stretch of the "stream of consciousness" given with the sensuous detail that any of a dozen modern writers could give it for us. And what is true of Fielding is true, with very rare exceptions, of all the greater seventeenth- and eighteenth-century writers. Defoe, for example, though he has plenty of descriptions, is never interested in the appearances of things for the sake of the appearances themselves or the reverberations of their *sensory* qualities in the percipient's mind. He is interested in the things and their condition, the help or hindrance they can be to man. To turn from his accounts of Crusoe's seashore to Mr. Joyce's description of Sandymount strand is to realize how great a change in man's interests (and perhaps in his perceptions themselves) has occurred. And to turn from Crusoe's moralizing self-examinations to those of Stephen Dedalus is to notice the same change. As Crusoe's eyes, looking outwards, see things there Stephen's see symbols of his own moods; so, when he looks into his own heart he finds a clear-cut world of hopes and fears, doubts and faiths—complex indeed but as well defined in their interrelations as chessmen. There is no uncertainty as to which movements belong to which side. But Stephen's inner world is as phantasmagoric as his outer, being composed of images which shift and flow and merge with an intricacy beyond the survey of any moral principles and too subtle to be described in the terms of any hitherto conceived psychology. The nomenclature of the faculties, of the virtues and the vices, of the passions, of the moods, the whole machinery through which self-examination with a view to increased order could be conducted by Defoe, has lapsed.

We may suspect, with Coleridge, that for some time it has been no such loss as it may appear; and that some dissolution of it must precede a reconstruction:

> The "King And No King" too, is extremely spirited in all its Characters; Arbaces holds up a Mirror to all Men of Virtuous Principles but violent Passions: hence he is, as it were, at once Magnanimity and Pride, Patience and Fury, Gentleness and Rigor, Chastity and Incest, and is one of the finest Mixtures of Virtues and Vices that any Poet has drawn, &c. (*Preface to Seward's Edition of Beaumont and Fletcher,* 1750.)

"These," Coleridge comments, "are among the endless instances of the abject state to which psychology had sunk from the reign of Charles I to the middle of the present reign of George III; and even now it is but just awaking." As chief awakener, he can speak with authority. Since his time the dissolution has gone further. The old vocabulary, from being a framework indispensable, but not necessarily sufficient, for orientation, has become a mere supply of words which, because of their past history, can be used as tinctures in the composition of states of mind to which none of them applies.

We are apt to regard this change as a great new conquest of literature over the unexplored land of ordinary human consciousness, overlooking perhaps the other possibility that ordinary human consciousness may not, until recently, have had a form which could be thus represented. And we are ready to acclaim the descriptions of the visible scene which Katherine Mansfield, Stella Benson or Virginia Woolf can give us as showing a subtlety in the observation of its sensory aspects and their emotional significance which is disappointingly absent in earlier writers. On one interpretation of the change, they have improved the descriptive technique of prose, have caught something always present which writers in the past could not (or did not wish to) catch; on another interpretation something new in the modes of perception has come into being for them to describe. The two accounts are not perhaps so opposed as they may seem, and I have no desire to decide between them. On either account man's interest in his own consciousness, whether of things without him or of the movements of his own mind, has changed, and with it the mode of an important part of his mythology.

That this change should show itself most clearly in prose is to be expected. For such prose as Mr. Joyce's or Mrs. Woolf's is a dilution (or better, an expansion, "like gold to ayery thinnesse beate") of a use of words that has in most ages been within the range of poetry. What is new is the composition of whole books with meanings of a structure which in poetry is found only in phrases or single lines supported by quite other structures. And these other structures are strengthened by just those other components which George Moore overlooked in reading *Tom Jones*. Empty though it is of "glimpses of the world without or hints of the world within" it contains judgment, a moral order, and action, with all that these entail. It contains *ideas,* not as stimulants to revery and whimsy, but as assured forms of mental activity with which coherent purpose may be maintained. And though, as we have seen with the ideas (or doctrines) that may be extracted from Coleridge's Wind Harp image, we must not identify the abstracted idea with the idea *in* the poem, yet ideas in the completeness they have in poetry are commonly main components in its structure. *Tom Jones,* of course, is not a poem; but the components which enter into its prose-fabric and give it its power are of kinds which do not enter into *Jacob's Room* or *Ulysses;* and, otherwise disposed and interrelated, they are more essential parts of the structure of great poetry than those which do. For these are, as Coleridge would say, only "the rudiments of imagination's power."

The dissolution of consciousness exhibited in such prose, at its best as much as in merely imitative writing, forces the task of reconstituting a less relaxed, a less adventitious order for the mind upon contemporary poetry. There can be no question of a return to any mythologic structures prevailing before the seventeenth century. The depth of the changes that then took place (they are described with admirable detachment and clarity in Mr. Basil Willey's *The Seventeenth Century Background*) prevents return. Poetry can no more go back on its past than a man can.

But the waning of any one mode of order—a traditional morality, or a religious sanction or symbolization for it—is not the loss of all possibilities of order. The traditional schemas by which man gave an account of himself and the world in which he lived were made by him, and though they have lost their power to help him as they formerly helped him, he has not lost his power to make new ones. It is easy to represent what has been occurring as a course of error, as due to the pernicious influence of arrogant science, or of Cartesianism or of Rousseau; as an infection of the mind by "heresies," or as departure from a norm to which, if man is to become again a noble animal, he must return. Dramas in which the proper balance of our faculties has been destroyed by exorbitant claims from one or other of them, in which science displaces religious belief, or sentiment ousts reason, or dreams cloud Reality,

> What will be forever
> What was from of old,

—by corruption from which disasters we now wander, a lost generation, in a wrecked universe—are not hard to invent.

> It was man did it, man
> Who imagined imagination;
> And he did what man can,
> He uncreated creation

as Mr. R. G. Eberhart exclaimed. But these dramatic pictures of our predicament are utterances of distress. Though they may sometimes pretend to be diagnoses, they are myths reflecting our unease. What they profess to describe is too vast a matter to be handled by that other system of myths (those of Science and History) to which diagnoses belong, and in which verification is possible. And as philosophic myths they are not of the kind which contribute directly to a new order. For the concepts they use belong to the order which has passed, and they are disqualified by the movement they describe. It is better, as an alternative philosophic myth, to suppose that the great drift is not due merely to internal conflicts between sub-orders of our mythology but rather to an inevitable growth of human awareness—inevitable because time goes on and man retains, in recent centuries, increasing touch with his past.

To put the burden of constituting an order for our minds on the poet may seem unfair. It is not the philosopher, however, or the moralist who puts it on him, but birth. And it is only another aspect of the drift by which knowledge in all its varieties—scientific, moral, religious—has come to seem a vast mythology with its sub-orders divided according to their different pragmatic sanctions, that the poet should thus seem to increase so inordinately in importance. (There is a figure of speech here, of course, for the burden is not on individual poets but upon the poetic function. With Homer, Dante and Shakespeare in mind, however, the importance of the single poet is not to be underestimated.) For while any part of the world-picture is regarded as not of mythopoeic origin, poetry—earlier recognized as mythopoeic—could not but be given a second place. If philosophic contemplation, or religious experience, or science gave us Reality, then poetry gave us something of less consequence, at best some sort of shadow. If we grant that all is myth, poetry as the myth-making which most brings "the whole soul of man into activity" (*B.L.*, II, 12), and as working with words, "parts and germinations of the plant" and, through them, in "the medium by which spirits communicate with one another" (*B.L.*, I, 168) becomes the necessary channel for the reconstitution of order.

But this last phrase is tainted also with a picturesque mock-desperate dramatization of our situation. The mind has never been in order. There is no vanished perfection of balance to be restored. The great ages of poetry have mostly been times torn by savage and stupid dissension, intolerant, unreasonable, and confused in other aspects of human endeavour.

> Allas, allas! now may men wepe and crye!
> For in our dayes nis but covetyse
> And doublenesse, and tresoun and envye,
> Poysoun, manslauhtre, and mordre in sondry wyse.

In all this our own age may be preparing to emulate them; but that is no more a reason to anticipate a new great age for poetry than the new possibility of a material paradise now offered by science is a reason for thinking that the day of poetry is over. Eras that produced no poetry that is remembered have been as disordered as ours. There are better reasons, in the work of modern poets, to hope that a creative movement is beginning and that poetry, freed from a mistaken conception of its limitations and read more discerningly than heretofore, will remake our minds and with them our world. Such an estimate of the power of poetry may seem extravagant; but it was Milton's no less than Shelley's, Blake's or Wordsworth's. It has been the opinion of many with whom we need not be ashamed to agree: "The study of poetry (if we will trust Aristotle) offers to mankind a certain rule, and pattern, of living well and happily; disposing us to all civil offices of society. If we will believe Tully, it nourisheth and instructeth our youth; delights our age; adorns our prosperity; comforts our adversity; entertains us at home . . . insomuch as the wisest and best learned have thought her the absolute mistress of manners, and nearest of kin to virtue." Ben Jonson here may merely be repeating commonplaces from antiquity; he may be writing a set piece without concern for what he is saying—but this is unlikely; he may not have been aware of the reasons for such opinions; they were left for Coleridge to display; but he was certainly well placed to judge whether they were creditable opinions or not. Neither the authorities he cites, nor "this robust, surly, and observing dramatist" himself, may be thought insufficiently acquainted with ordinary lives, or with the forces that may amend them.

Poetry may have these powers and yet, for removable and preventable causes, the study of poetry be of no great use to us. A candid witness must declare, I fear, that its benefits are often unobtrusive where we would most expect them. But the study of poetry, for those born in this age, is more arduous than we suppose. It is therefore rare. Many other things pass by its name and are encouraged to its detriment.

To free it from distracting trivialities, from literary chit-chat, from discussion of form which does not ask what has the form, from flattening rationalization, from the clouds of unchecked sensibility and unexamined interpretations is a minor duty of criticism. But there is a more positive task: to recall that poetry is the supreme use of language, man's chief co-ordinating instrument, in the service of the most integral purposes of life; and to explore, with thoroughness, the intricacies of the modes of language as working modes of the mind.

The sage may teach a doctrine without words; but, if so, it is a doctrine about another world than ours and for another life. Our world and our life have grown and taken what order they have for us through separated meanings which we can only hold together or keep apart through words. The sage may avoid words because our power of controlling certain kinds of meaning through them is too slight; but without the use of words in the past he would have had no doctrine to teach. The meanings sufficient for the dumb creatures are not enough for man.

Because all objects which we can name or otherwise single out—the simplest objects of the senses and the most recondite entities that speculation can conjecture, the most abstract constructions of the intellect and the most concrete aims of passion alike—are projections of man's interests; because the Universe as it is known to us is a fabric whose forms, as we can alone know them, have arisen in and through reflection; and because that reflection, whether made by the intellect in science or by "the whole soul of man" in poetry, has developed through language—and, apart from language, can neither be continued nor maintained—the study of the modes of language becomes, as it attempts to be thorough, the most fundamental and extensive of all inquiries. It is no preliminary or preparation for other profounder studies, which though they use language more or less trustfully, may be supposed to be autonomous, uninfluenced by verbal processes. The very formation of the objects which these studies propose to examine takes place through the processes (of which imagination and fancy are modes) by which the words they use acquire their meanings.

Criticism is the science of these meanings and the meanings which larger groups of words may carry. It is no mere account of what men have written or how they have written it, taken as questions to be asked without inquiry into the little that we can yet surmise about the growth of the mind and therewith the expansion of our outlook on the world.

Thus the more traditional subjects of criticism, Coleridge's differentiation of imagination from fancy, and his still abstruser ponderings on objectification and the living word, unite with the analysis of the ambiguities and confusions that are overt or latent in all cases of metaphor, transference or projection to form one study. It is embryonic still, through which its possibilities are the less restricted. It offers little intellectual rest or satisfaction; but should we look for satisfaction here where all the problems meet? What it does offer is an immense opportunity for improving our technique of understanding.

With Coleridge we step across the threshold of a general theoretical study of language capable of opening to us new powers over our minds comparable to those which systematic physical inquiries are giving us over our environment. The step across was of the same type as that which took Galileo into the modern world. It requires the shift from a preoccupation with the What and Why to the How of language. The problems of Poetry became for Coleridge, sometimes, interesting as problems with a structure of their own. They ceased to be mere voids waiting to be filled. The interest shifted from the answers to the questions; and, with that, a new era of criticism began. Beyond the old tasks of reaffirming ancient conclusions and defending them from foolish interpretations, an illimitable field of work has become accessible.

The change would have been delayed if Coleridge had not been a philosopher as well as a critic. And it has this consequence, that critics in the future must have a theoretical equipment of a kind which has not been felt to be necessary in the past. (So physicists may at times sigh for the days in which less mathematics was required by them.) But the critical equipment will not be *primarily* philosophical. It will be rather a command of the methods of general linguistic analysis. As the theory of Poetry develops, what is needed will be disengaged from philosophy much as the methodology of physics has been disengaged.

I have tried here to further this development by presenting Coleridge's Theory of Imagination [8] for more detailed consideration than

[8] See also D. G. James's *Scepticism and Poetry: An Essay on the Poetic Imagination* (1937), which is represented here by his essay on I. A. Richards. [*Editor's note.*]

it has hitherto received, and by adding suggestions towards extensions of his method of analysis. These must perhaps await fuller exposition before they become effective. But, with the history of opinions on Coleridge before us, it seemed but just that an account of his work should be attempted before new derivations from it again obscure our debt.

SPATIAL FORM IN MODERN LITERATURE
(1945)

JOSEPH FRANK

LESSING'S *Laokoon,* André Gide once remarked, is one of those books it is good to reiterate or contradict every thirty years. Despite this excellent advice, neither of these attitudes toward *Laokoon* has been adopted by modern writers.[1] Lessing's attempt to define the limits of literature and the plastic arts has become, at least to English and American critics, a dead issue—one to which respectful reference is occasionally made, but which no longer has any fecundating influence on esthetic thinking. One can understand how this came about in the nineteenth century, with its passion for historicism, but it is not so easy to understand at present when so many writers on esthetic problems are occupied with questions of form. To a historian of literature or the plastic arts, Lessing's effort to define the unalterable laws of these mediums may well have seemed quixotic; but modern critics, no longer overawed by the bugbear of historical method, have begun to take up again the problems he tried to solve.

Lessing's own solution to these problems seems, at first glance, to have little relation to modern esthetic thinking. The arguments of *Laokoon* were directed against the pictorial poetry of his time, which has long since ceased to interest the modern sensibility; and many of its conclusions about the plastic arts grew out of a now-antiquated archeology, which, to make matters worse, Lessing knew mainly at second-hand. But it was precisely his quixotic attempt to rise above history, to define the unalterable laws of esthetic perception rather than to attack or defend any particular school, which gives his work the perennial freshness to which André Gide alluded. Since the validity of his central thesis does not depend on its relationship to the literary movements of his time, or on the extent of his first-hand acquaintanceship with the artworks of antiquity, it may be taken up apart from these circumstances and used in the analysis of later developments.

[1] Irving Babbitt, in 1910, wrote *The New Laokoon* with the intention of doing for modern art what Lessing had done for the art of his own day. Briefly, Babbitt's thesis was that, just as the confusion of genres in Lessing's time could be traced to a false theory of imitation, so the artistic aberrations of our own time could be traced to a false theory of spontaneity. Babbitt's thesis, however, has nothing to do with Lessing's theories. The discussion of Lessing in the first half of the book merely reinforces the analogy between Lessing's purpose and Babbitt's own.

In *Laokoon,* Lessing fuses two currents of thought of great importance in the cultural history of his time. The archeological researches of Winckelmann, his contemporary, had stimulated a passionate interest in Greek culture among the Germans. Lessing went back to Homer, Aristotle and the Greek tragedians, using his first-hand knowledge to attack the distorted critical theories, supposedly based on classical authority, which had filtered into France through Italian commentators and then taken hold in Germany. At the same time, as Wilhelm Dilthey points out in his famous essay on Lessing, Locke and the empirical school of English philosophy had given a new impulse to esthetic speculation. Locke tried to solve the problem of knowledge by breaking down complex ideas into simple elements of sensation, and then examining the operations of the mind to see how these sensations were combined to form ideas. This method was soon taken over by estheticians who, instead of laying down rules for beauty, began to analyze esthetic perception. Writers like Shaftesbury, Hogarth, Hutcheson and Burke, to mention only a few, concerned themselves with the precise character and combination of impressions that gave esthetic pleasure to the sensibility. Lessing's friend and critical ally, Mendelssohn, popularized this method of dealing with esthetic problems in Germany; Lessing himself was a close student of these works and many others in the same general spirit. *Laokoon,* as a result, stands at the confluence of these intellectual currents: Lessing analyzes the laws of esthetic perception, shows how they prescribe necessary limitations to literature and the plastic arts, and then demonstrates how Greek writers and painters, especially Homer, created masterpieces by obeying these laws.

His argument starts from the simple observation that literature and the plastic arts, working through different sensuous mediums, must therefore differ in the fundamental laws governing their creation. "If it is true," Lessing wrote, "that painting and poetry in their imitations make use of entirely different means or symbols—the first, namely, of form and color in space, the second of articulated sounds in time—if these symbols indisputably require a suitable relation to the thing symbolized, then it is clear that symbols arranged in juxtaposition can only express subjects of which the wholes or parts exist in juxtaposition; while consecutive symbols can only express subjects of which the wholes or parts are themselves consecutive." Lessing, of course, did not originate this distinction, which has been traced as far back as classical antiquity. His contribution was to raise it from an isolated insight into a universal critical principle, in this way carrying to their logical conclusion the efforts of French classical critics to define the immutable laws of art as laid down by *la raison.*

Form in the plastic arts, according to Lessing, is necessarily spatial, because the visible aspect of objects can best be presented juxtaposed in an instant of time. Literature, on the other hand, makes use of language, composed of a succession of words proceeding through time; and it follows that literary form, to harmonize with the essential quality of its medium, must be based primarily on some form of narrative sequence. Lessing used this argument to attack two artistic genres highly popular in his day: pictorial poetry, and allegorical painting. The pictorial poet tried to paint with words, the allegorical painter to tell a story in visible images; both were doomed to fail because their aims contradicted the fundamental properties of their mediums. No matter how accurate and vivid a verbal description might be, Lessing argued, it could not give the unified impression of a visible object; no matter how skillfully figures might be chosen and arranged, a painting or piece of sculpture could not successfully set forth the various stages of an action.

Lessing develops his argument by attempting to prove that the Greeks, with an unfailing sense of esthetic propriety, respected the limits imposed on different art mediums by the conditions of human perception. The importance of Lessing's distinction, however, does not depend on these ramifications of his argument, nor even on his specific judgment of individual writers. Various critics have quarreled with one or another of these judgments, thinking that in doing so they were in some way undermining Lessing's position; but such a belief is based on a misunderstanding of *Laokoon's* importance in the history of esthetic theory. Lessing's insight may be used solely as instruments of analysis, without proceeding to judge the value of individual works by how closely they adhered to the norms he laid down; and unless this is done, as a matter of fact, the real meaning of *Laokoon* cannot be understood. For what Lessing offered was not a new set of opinions but a new conception of esthetic form.

The conception of esthetic form inherited by the eighteenth century from the Renaissance was a purely external one. Classical literature—or what was known of it—was presumed to have reached perfection, and later writers could do little better than imitate its example. A horde of commentators and critics had deduced certain rules from the classical masterpieces—rules like the Aristotelian unities, of which Aristotle had never heard—and modern writers were warned to obey these rules if they wished to appeal to a cultivated public. Gradually, these rules hardened to an external mold into which the material of a literary work had to be poured: the form of a work was nothing but the technical arrangement dictated by the rules. Such a mechanical notion of esthetic form, however, led to serious perversions of taste—Shakespeare was considered a barbarian even by so sophisticated a writer as Voltaire, and Pope found it necessary in translating Homer to do a good deal of editing. Lessing's point of view, breaking sharply with this external conception of form, marks out the road for esthetic speculation to follow in the future.

For Lessing, as we have seen, esthetic form is not an external arrangement provided by a set of traditional rules: it is the relation between the sensuous nature of the art medium and the conditions of human perception. Just as the natural man of the eighteenth century was not to be bound by traditional political forms, but was to create them in accordance with his own nature, so art was to create its own forms out of itself rather than accepting them ready-made from the practice of the past. Criticism was not to prescribe rules for art, but was to explore the necessary laws by which art governs itself. No longer was esthetic form confused with mere externals of technique—it was not a straitjacket into which the artist, willy-nilly, had to force his creative ideas, but issued spontaneously from the organization of the art work as it presented itself to perception. Time and space were the two extremes defining the limits of literature and the plastic arts in their relation to sensuous perception; and it is possible, following Lessing's example, to trace the evolution of art forms by their oscillations between these two poles.[2]

The purpose of the present essay is to apply Lessing's method to modern literature—to trace the evolution of form in modern poetry and, more particularly, in the novel. The first two sections will try to show that modern literature, exemplified by such writers as T. S. Eliot, Ezra Pound, Marcel Proust and James Joyce, is moving in the direction of spatial form. This means that the reader is intended to apprehend their work spatially, in a moment of time, rather than as a sequence. So far as the novel is concerned, this tendency reaches its culmination in Djuna Barnes's remarkable book *Nightwood,* which has never received the critical attention it deserves. The third section will deal with *Nightwood* in detail, analyzing its form and explaining its meaning. Finally, since changes in esthetic form always involve major changes in the sensibility of a particular cultural period, an effort will be made to outline the spiritual attitudes that have led to the predominance of spatial form.[3]

[2] German art criticism in the last few decades has experienced a veritable renaissance along the lines marked out by Lessing. Following the lead of Alois Riegl, the immediate predecessor of those later writers who occupied themselves with tracing the history of form in the plastic arts, the German scholars traced the changing apprehensions of space which they saw at the root of changes in esthetic form. The next step was to connect the change in the apprehension of space with broader changes in the history of culture. Finally, the inquiry was broadened to take in not only the plastic arts but also literature and music (thus bringing in the category of time) and even the varying conceptions of space and time in philosophical thought. The most extensive attempt at such a synthesis has been made by Dagobert Frey in his brilliant and suggestive book, *Gotik und Renaissance,* published in 1929. An excellent brief account of this whole critical movement may be found in *Die Philosophie der Kunstgeschichte in der Gegenwart,* by Walter Passarge.

Mention should also be made at this point of Edwin Muir's *Structure of the Novel,* the only work in English, so far as is known to the present writer, that attempts to discuss form in literature in terms of space and time.

[3] Readers interested in the last two sections of this essay are referred to the *Sewanee Review:* Summer & Autumn, 1945. [*Editor's note.*]

I

Modern Anglo-American poetry received its initial impetus from the Imagist movement of the years directly preceding and following the first World War. Imagism was important not for any actual poetry written by Imagist poets—no one knew quite what an Imagist poet was —but rather because it opened the way for later developments by its clean break with sentimental Victorian verbiage. The critical writings of Ezra Pound, the leading theoretician of Imagism, are an astonishing farrago of keen esthetic perceptions thrown in among a series of boyishly naughty remarks, whose chief purpose, it would seem, is to *épater le bourgeois*—to startle the stuffed shirts. But Pound's definition of the image, perhaps the keenest of his perceptions, is of fundamental importance for any discussion of modern literary form. "An image," Pound wrote, "is that which presents an intellectual and emotional complex in an instant of time." The implications of his definition should be noted—an image is not defined as a pictorial reproduction, but as the unification of disparate ideas and emotions into a complex presented spatially in an instant of time. Such a complex is not to proceed discursively, according to the laws of language, but is rather to strike the reader's sensibility with an instantaneous impact. Pound stresses this aspect by adding, in a later passage, that only the instantaneous presentation of such complexes gives "that sense of sudden liberation; that sense of freedom from time limits and space limits; that sense of sudden growth, which we experience in the presence of the greatest works of art."

At the very outset, therefore, modern poetry championed a poetic method in direct contradiction to the way in which, according to Lessing, language had to be perceived. By comparing Pound's definition of the image with Eliot's well-known description of the psychology of the poetic process, we can see how profoundly this conception has influenced our modern idea of the nature of poetry. For Eliot, the distinctive quality of a poetic sensibility is its capacity to form new wholes, to fuse seemingly disparate experiences into an organic unity. The ordinary man, Eliot writes, "falls in love, or reads Spinoza, and these two experiences have nothing to do with each other, or with the noise of the typewriter or the smell of cooking; in the mind of the poet these experiences are always forming new wholes." Pound, to be sure, had attempted to define the image in terms of its esthetic attributes, while Eliot, in this passage, is describing its psychological origin; but the result in a poem was likely to be the same.

This view of the nature of poetry immediately gave rise to numerous problems. How was more than one image to be included in a poem? If the chief value of an image was its capacity to present an intellectual and emotional complex simultaneously, to link up images in a sequence would clearly destroy most of their efficacy. Or was the poem itself one vast image, whose individual components were to be apprehended as a unity? But then it would be necessary to overcome the inherent consecutiveness of language, frustrating the reader's normal expectation of a sequence and forcing him to perceive the elements of the poem as juxtaposed in space rather than unrolling in time.

This is precisely what Eliot and Pound attempted in their major works. Both poets, in their earlier work, still retained some elements of conventional structure. Their poems were looked upon as daring and revolutionary chiefly because of technical matters, like the loosening of metrical pattern and the handling of subjects ordinarily considered non-poetic. Perhaps this is less true of Eliot than of Pound, especially the Eliot of the more complex early works like *Prufrock, Gerontion* and *Portrait of a Lady;* but even here, although the sections of the poem are not governed by syntactical logic, the skeleton of an implied narrative structure is always present. The reader of *Prufrock* is swept up in a narrative movement from the very first lines:

> Let us go then, you and I,
> When the evening...

And the reader, accompanying Prufrock, finally arrives at their mutual destination:

> In the room the women come and go
> Talking of Michelangelo.

At this point the poem becomes a series of more or less isolated fragments, each stating some aspect of Prufrock's emotional dilemma; but the fragments are now localized and focused on a specific set of circumstances: the reader can organize them by referring to the implied situation. The same method is employed in *Portrait of a Lady,* while in *Gerontion* the reader is specifically told that he has been reading the "thoughts of a dry brain in a dry season"—the stream-of-consciousness of "an old man in a dry month, being read to by a boy, waiting for the rain." In both cases there is a perceptible framework around which the seemingly disconnected passage of the poem can be organized. This was one reason why Pound's *Mauberly* and Eliot's early work were first regarded, not as forerunners of a new poetic form, but as latter-day *vers de société*—witty, disillusioned, with a somewhat brittle charm, but lacking that quality of "high seriousness" which Matthew Arnold considered the touchstone of poetic excellence. These poems were considered unusual mainly because *vers de société* had long fallen out of fashion: there was little difficulty in accepting them as an entertaining departure from the grand style of the nineteenth century. In the *Cantos* and *The Waste Land,* however, it should have been clear that a radical transformation was taking place in esthetic structure; but this transformation has been touched on only peripherally by modern critics. R. P. Blackmur comes closest to the central problem while analyzing what he calls Pound's "anecdotal" method. The special form of the *Cantos,* Blackmur explains, "is that of the anecdote begun in one place, taken up in one or more other places, and finished, if at all, in still another. This deliberate disconnectedness, this art of a thing continually alluding to itself, continually breaking off short, is the method by which the *Cantos* tie themselves together. So soon as the reader's mind is concerted with the material of the poem, Mr. Pound deliberately disconcerts it, either by introducing fresh and disjunct material or by reverting to old and, apparently, equally disjunct material." Blackmur's remarks apply equally well to *The Waste Land,* where syntactical sequence is given up for a structure depending on the perception of relationships between disconnected word-groups. To be properly understood, these word-groups must be juxtaposed with one another and perceived simultaneously; only when this is done can they be adequately understood; for while they follow one another in time, their meaning does not depend on this temporal relationship. The one difficulty of these poems, which no amount of textual exegesis can wholly overcome, is the internal conflict between the time-logic of language and the space-logic implicit in the modern conception of the nature of poetry.

Esthetic form in modern poetry, then, is based on a space-logic that demands a complete re-orientation in the reader's attitude towards language. Since the primary reference of any word-group is to something inside the poem itself, language in modern poetry is really reflexive: the meaning-relationship is completed only by the simultaneous perception in space of word-groups which, when read consecutively in time, have no comprehensible relation to each other. Instead of the instinctive and immediate reference of words and word-groups to the objects or events they symbolize, and the construction of meaning from the sequence of these references, modern poetry asks its readers to suspend the process of individual reference temporarily until the entire pattern of internal references can be apprehended as a unity. This explanation is, of course, the extreme statement of an ideal condition rather than of an actually existing state of affairs; but the conception of poetic form that runs through Mallarmé to Pound and Eliot, and which has left its traces on a whole generation of modern poets, can be formulated only in terms of the principle of reflexive reference. And this principle is the link connecting the esthetic development of modern poetry with similar experiments in the modern novel.

II

For a study of esthetic form in the modern novel, Flaubert's famous county fair scene in *Madame Bovary* is a convenient point of departure. This scene has been justly praised for its mordant caricature of bourgeois pomposity, its portrayal—unusually sympathetic for Flaubert—of the bewildered old servant, and its burlesque of the pseudo-romantic rhetoric by which Rodolphe woos the sentimental Emma. At present, it is enough to notice the method by which Flaubert handles the scene—a method we might as well call cinematographic, since this analogy comes immediately to mind. As Flaubert sets the scene, there is action going on simultaneously at three levels, and the physical position of each level is a fair index to its spiritual significance. On the lowest plane, there is the surging, jostling mob in the street, mingling with the livestock brought to the exhibition; raised slightly above the street by a platform are the speech-making officials, bombastically reeling off platitudes to the attentive multitudes; and on the highest level of all, from a window overlooking the spectacle, Rodolphe and Emma are watching the proceedings and carrying on their amorous conversation, in phrases as stilted as those regaling the crowds. Albert Thibaudet has compared this scene to the medieval mystery play, in which various related actions occur simultaneously on different stage levels; but this acute comparison refers to Flaubert's intention rather than to his method. "Everything should sound simultaneously," Flaubert later wrote, in commenting on this scene; "one should hear the bellowing of the cattle, the whisperings of the lovers and the rhetoric of the officials all at the same time."

But since language proceeds in time, it is impossible to approach this simultaneity of perception except by breaking up temporal sequence. And this is exactly what Flaubert does: he dissolves sequence by cutting back and forth between the various levels of action in a slowly-rising crescendo until—at the climax of the scene—Rodolphe's Chateaubriandesque phrases are read at almost the same moment as the names of prize winners for raising the best pigs. Flaubert takes care to underline this satiric similarity by description, as well as by juxtaposition, as if afraid the reflexive relations of the two actions would not be grasped: "From magnetism, by slow degrees, Rodolphe had arrived at affinities, and while M. le Président was citing Cincinnatus at his plow, Diocletian planting his cabbages and the emperors of China ushering in the new year with sowing-festivals, the young man was explaining to the young woman that these irresistible attractions sprang from some anterior existence."

This scene illustrates, on a small scale, what we mean by the spatialization of form in a novel. For the duration of the scene, at least, the time-flow of the narrative is halted: attention is fixed on the interplay of relationships within the limited time-area. These relationships are juxtaposed independently of the progress of the narrative; and the full significance of the scene is given only by the reflexive relations among the units of meaning. In Flaubert's scene, however, the unit of meaning is not, as in modern poetry, a word-group or a fragment of an anecdote, but the totality of each level of action taken as an integer; the unit is so large that the scene can be read with an illusion of complete understanding, yet with a total unawareness of the "dialectic of platitude" (Thibaudet) interweaving all levels, and finally linking them together with devastating irony. In other words, the struggle towards spatial form in Pound and Eliot resulted in the disappearance of coherent sequence after a few lines; but the novel, with its larger unit of meaning, can preserve coherent sequence within the unit of meaning and break up only the time-flow of narrative. (Because of this difference, readers of modern poetry are practically forced to read reflexively to get any literal sense, while readers of a novel like *Nightwood,* for example, are led to expect narrative sequence by the deceptive normality of language sequence within the unit of meaning.) But this does not affect the parallel between esthetic form in modern poetry and the form of Flaubert's scene: both can be properly understood only when their units of meaning are apprehended reflexively, in an instant of time.

Flaubert's scene, although interesting in itself, is of minor importance to his novel as a whole, and is skillfully blended back into the main narrative structure after fulfilling its satiric function. But Flaubert's method was taken over by James Joyce, and applied on a gigantic scale in the composition of *Ulysses.* Joyce composed his novel of an infinite number of references and cross-references which relate to one another independently of the time-sequence of the narrative; before the book fits together into any meaningful pattern, these references must be connected by the reader and viewed as a whole. Ultimately, if we are to believe Stuart Gilbert, the systems of reference form a complete picture of practically everything under the sun, from the stages of man's life and the organs of the human body to the colors of the spectrum; but these structures are far more important for Joyce, as Harry Levin has remarked, than they could ever possibly be for the reader. Students of Joyce, fascinated by his erudition, have usually applied themselves to exegetical problems that, unfortunately, have little to do with the perceptual form of Joyce's novel.

Joyce's most obvious intention in *Ulysses* is to give the reader a picture of Dublin seen as a whole—to re-create the sights and sounds, the people and places, of a typical Dublin day, much as Flaubert had re-created his provincial county fair. And, like Flaubert, Joyce wanted his depiction to have the same unified impact, the same sense of simultaneous activity occurring in different places. Joyce, as a matter of fact, frequently makes use of the same method as Flaubert—cutting back and forth between different actions occurring at the same time—and usually does so to obtain the same ironic effect. But Joyce had the problem of creating this impression of simultaneity for the life of a whole teeming city, and of maintaining it—or rather of strengthening it—through hundreds of pages that must be read as a sequence. To meet this problem, Joyce was forced to go far beyond what Flaubert had done. For while Flaubert had maintained a clear-cut narrative line, except in the county-fair scene, Joyce breaks up his narrative and transforms the very structure of his novel into an instrument of his esthetic intention.

Joyce conceived *Ulysses* as a modern epic, a form in which, as Stephen Dedalus tells us in *The Portrait of the Artist as a Young Man,* "the personality of the artist, at first sight a cry or a cadence and then a fluid and lambent narrative, finally refines itself out of existence, impersonalizes itself, so to speak . . . the artist, like the God of creation, remains within or beyond or above his handiwork, invisible, refined out of existence, indifferent, paring his fingernails." The epic is thus synonymous for Joyce with the complete self-effacement of the author; and with his usual uncompromising rigor, Joyce carries this implication further than anyone had dared before. He assumes—what is obviously not true—that his readers are Dubliners, intimately acquainted with Dublin life and the personal history of his characters. This allows him to refrain from giving any direct information about his characters, for such information would immediately have betrayed the presence of an omniscient author. What Joyce does, instead, is to present the elements of his narrative—the relations between Stephen and his family, between Bloom and his wife, between Stephen and Bloom and the Dedalus family—in fragments, as they are thrown out unexplained in the course of casual conversation, or as they lie embedded in the various strata of symbolic reference; and the same is true of all the allusions to Dublin life, history, and the external events of the twenty-four hours during which the novel takes place. In other words, all the factual background—so conveniently summarized for the reader in an ordinary novel—must be reconstructed from fragments, sometimes hundreds of pages apart, scattered through the book. As a result, the reader is forced to read *Ulysses* in exactly the same manner as he reads modern poetry—continually fitting fragments together and keeping allusions in mind until, by reflexive reference, he can link them to their complements.

Joyce intended, in this way, to build up in the reader's mind a sense of Dublin as a totality, including all the relations of the characters to one another and all the events which enter their consciousness. As the reader progresses through the novel, connecting allusions and references spatially, gradually becoming aware of the pattern of relationships, this sense was to be imperceptibly acquired; at the conclusion of the novel, it might almost be said, Joyce literally wanted the reader to become a Dubliner. For this is what Joyce demands: that the reader have at hand the same instinctive knowledge of Dublin life, the same sense of Dublin as a huge, surrounding organism, which the Dubliner possesses as a birthright. It is such knowledge which, at any one moment of time, gives him a knowledge of Dublin's past and present as a whole; it is only such knowledge that can enable the reader, like the characters, to place all the references in their proper context. This, it should be realized, is practically the equivalent of saying that Joyce cannot be read—he can only be re-read. A knowledge of the whole is essential to an understanding of any part; but unless one is a Dubliner, such knowledge can be obtained only after the book has been read and all the references fitted into their proper place and grasped as a unity. Although the burdens placed on the reader by this method of composition may seem insuperable, the fact remains that Joyce, in his unbelievably laborious fragmentation of narrative structure, proceeded on the assumption that a unified spatial apprehension of his work would ultimately be possible.

In a far more subtle manner than with Joyce and Flaubert, the same principle of composition is at work in Marcel Proust. Since Proust himself tells us that, before all else, his novel will have imprinted on it "a form which usually remains invisible, the form of Time," it may seem strange to speak of Proust in connection with spatial form. Almost without exception, he has been considered the novelist of time *par excellence,* the literary interpreter of that Bergsonian "real time" which, when intuited by the sensibility, places us in contact with ultimate reality. To stop at this point, however, is to miss what Proust himself considered the deepest significance of his work. Obsessed with the ineluctability of time, Proust was suddenly visited by certain mystical experiences that he describes in detail in *Le temps retrouvé,* the last volume of his great work. These experiences, by providing him with a technique for transcending time, seemed to free him from time's domination; and in writing a novel, in which he would translate the extra-temporal qualities of these experiences into esthetic form, he hoped to reveal their nature to the world. Not only did he wish to explain them conceptually, but, like a true artist, he wanted the world to feel the exact emotional impact he had felt himself.

To define the method by which this is accomplished, one must first understand clearly the precise nature of the Proustian revelation. Each such experience, Proust tells us, is marked by a feeling that "the permanent essence of things, usually concealed, is set free and our true self, which had long seemed dead but was not dead in other ways, awakes, takes on fresh life as it receives the celestial nourishment brought to it." This celestial nourishment consists of some sound, or odor, or other sensory stimulus, "sensed anew, simultaneously in the present and the past." But why should these moments seem so overwhelmingly valuable that Proust calls them celestial? Because, Proust observes, his imagination could only operate on the past; the material presented to his imagination, therefore, lacked any sensuous immediacy. But at certain moments, the physical sensations of the past came flooding back to fuse with the present; and in these moments, Proust believed, he grasped a reality "real without being of the present moment, ideal but not abstract." Only in these moments did he attain his most cherished ambition—"to seize, isolate, immobilize for the duration of a lightning flash" what otherwise he could not apprehend, "namely: a fragment of time in its pure state." For a person experiencing this moment, Proust adds, the word "death" no longer has meaning. "Situated outside the scope of time, what could he fear from the future?"

The significance of this experience, though obscurely hinted at throughout the book, is made explicit only in the concluding pages describing the final appearance of the narrator at the reception of the Princesse de Guermantes. The narrator decides to dedicate the remainder of his life to re-creating these experiences in a work of art; this work will differ essentially from all others because, at its foundation, will be a vision of reality that has been refracted through an extra-temporal perspective. Many critics, viewing Proust as the last and most debilitated of a long line of neurasthenic esthetes, have found in this decision to create a work of art merely the final step in his flight from the burdens of reality. Edmund Wilson links up this view with Proust's ambition to conquer time, assuming that Proust hoped to oppose time by establishing something—a work of art—impervious to its flux; but this interpretation scarcely does justice to Proust's own conviction, expressed with special intensity in the last volume of his work, that he was fulfilling a prophetic mission. It was not the work of art *qua* work of art that Proust cared about (his contempt for the horde of faddish scribblers was unbounded) but a work of art that should stand as a monument to his personal conquest of time. His own work could do this, however, not simply because it was a work of art, and like all works of art presumably timeless, but because it was a work that communicated the Proustian vision by a method which preserved its full emotional significance.

The prototype of this method, like the analysis of the revelatory moment, occurs during the reception at the Princesse de Guermantes. After spending years in a sanatorium, losing touch almost completely with the fashionable world of the earlier volumes, the narrator comes out of seclusion to attend the reception. His first reaction is one of bewilderment at the changes in social position and the even more striking changes in character and personality among his former friends. In the opinion of some socially-minded critics, Proust's intention in this scene was to paint the invasion of French aristocratic society by the upper bourgeoisie, and the gradual breakdown of all social and moral standards caused by the first World War. No doubt this process is incidentally described at some length; but as the narrator takes great pains to tell us, it is far from being the most important meaning of the scene for him. What strikes the narrator, almost with the force of a blow, is this: in trying to recognize old friends under the masks which, as he feels, the years have welded to them, he is jolted for the first time into a consciousness of the passage of time. When a young man addresses the narrator respectfully instead of familiarly, as if he were an elderly gentleman, the narrator realizes suddenly that he has *become* an elderly gentleman; but for him the passage of time had gone unperceived up until that moment. To become conscious of time, the narrator begins to understand, it had first been necessary to remove himself from his accustomed environment—or, what amounts to the same thing, from the stream of time acting on that environment—and then to plunge back into the stream after a lapse of years. In so doing, the narrator found himself presented with two images—the world as he had formerly known it, and the world, transformed by time, that he now saw before him; when these two images are juxtaposed, the narrator discovers, the passage of time is suddenly experienced through its visible effects. Habit, that universal soporific, ordinarily conceals the passage of time from those who have gone their accustomed ways: at any one moment of time the changes are so minute as to be imperceptible. "Other people," Proust writes, "never cease to change places in relation to ourselves. In the imperceptible, but eternal march of the world, we regard them as motionless in a moment of vision, too short for us to perceive the motion that is sweeping them on. But we have only to select in our memory two pictures taken of them at different moments, close enough together however for them not to have altered in themselves—perceptibly, that is to say—and the difference between the two pictures is a measure of the displacement that they have undergone in relation to us." By comparing these two images in a moment of time, the passage of time can be experienced concretely through the impact of its visible effects on the sensibility, rather than as a mere gap counted off in numbers. This discovery provides the narrator with a method which, in T. S. Eliot's phrase, is an "objective correlative" to the visionary apprehension of the fragment of "pure time" intuited in the revelatory moment.

When the narrator discovers this method of communicating his experience of the revelatory moment, he decides, we have already said, to incorporate it in a novel. But the novel the narrator decides to write has just been finished by the reader; and its form is controlled by the method that the narrator has outlined in its concluding pages. The reader, in other words, is substituted for the narrator, and is placed by the author throughout the book in the same position as the narrator occupies before his own experience at the reception of the Princesse de Guermantes. This is done by the discontinuous presentation of character—a simple device which, nevertheless, is the clue to the form of Proust's vast structure. Every reader soon notices that Proust does not follow any of his characters through the whole course of his novel: they appear and re-appear, in various stages of their lives, but hundreds of pages sometimes go by between the time they are last seen and the time they re-appear; and when they do turn up again, the passage of time has invariably changed them in some decisive way. Instead of being submerged in the stream of time—which, for Proust, would be the equivalent of presenting a character progressively, in a continuous line of development—the reader is confronted with various snapshots of the characters "motionless in a moment of vision," taken at different stages in their lives; and the reader, in juxtaposing these images, experiences the effects of the passage of time exactly as the narrator had done. As he had promised, therefore, Proust stamps his novel indelibly with the form of time; but we are now in a position to understand exactly what he meant by the promise.

To experience the passage of time, Proust learned, it was necessary to rise above it, and to grasp both past and present simultaneously in a moment of what he called "pure time." But "pure time," obviously, is not time at all—it is perception in a moment of time, that is, space. And by the discontinuous presentation of character, Proust forces the readers to juxtapose disparate images of his characters spatially, in a moment of time, so that the experience of time's passage will be fully communicated to their sensibility. There is a striking analogy here between Proust's method and that of his beloved Impressionist painters —an analogy that goes far deeper than the usual comments about the "impressionism" of Proust's style. The Impressionist painters juxtaposed pure tones on the canvas, instead of mixing them on the palette, in order to leave the blending of colors to the eye of the spectator. Similarly, Proust gives us what might be called pure views of his characters—views of them "motionless in a moment of vision" in various phases of their lives—and allows the sensibility of the reader to fuse these views into a unity. Proust's purpose is only achieved when these units of meaning are referred to each other reflexively in a moment of time. This is no doubt what Ramon Fernandez had in mind when, in a striking footnote to an essay on Proust, he threw out this observation: "In general, [Proust's] manner of making contact with his 'durée' is quite Bergsonian (see the episode of the madeleine), but the reactions of his intelligence on his sensibility, which determine the curve of his work, would orient him rather towards a *spatialisation* of time and of memory." (Italics in text.) As with Joyce and the modern poets, then, we see that spatial form is also the structural scaffolding of Proust's labyrinthine masterpiece.

POETRY AND BELIEFS

(1926)

I. A. RICHARDS

THE BUSINESS of the poet, as we have seen, is to give order and coherence, and so freedom, to a body of experience. To do so through words which act as its skeleton, as a structure by which the impulses which make up the experience are adjusted to one another and act together. The means by which words do this are many and varied. To work them out is a problem for psychology. A beginning has been indicated above, but only a beginning. What little can be done shows already that most critical dogmas of the past are either false or nonsense. A little knowledge is not here a danger, but clears the air in a remarkable way.

Roughly and inadequately, even in the light of our present knowledge, we can say that words work in the poem in two main fashions. As sensory stimuli and as (in the *widest* sense) symbols. We must refrain from considering the sensory side of the poem, remarking only that it is *not* in the least independent of the other side, and that it has for definite reasons prior importance in most poetry. We must confine ourselves to the other function of words in the poem, or rather, omitting much that is of secondary relevance, to one form of that function, let me call it *pseudo-statement.*

It will be admitted—by those who distinguish between scientific statement, where truth is ultimately a matter of verification as this is understood in the laboratory, and emotive utterance, where "truth" is primarily acceptability *by* some attitude, and more remotely is the acceptability *of* this attitude itself—that it is *not* the poet's business to make true statements. Yet poetry has constantly the air of making statements, and important ones; which is one reason why some mathematicians cannot read it. They find the alleged statements to be *false.* It will be agreed that their approach to poetry and their expectations from it are mistaken. But what exactly is the other, the right, the poetic, approach and how does it differ from the mathematical?

The poetic approach evidently limits the framework of possible consequences into which the pseudo-statement is taken. For the scientific approach this framework is unlimited. Any and every consequence is relevant. If any of the consequences of a statement conflicts with acknowledged fact, then so much the worse for the statement.

Not so with the pseudo-statement when poetically approached. The problem is—just how does the limitation work? The usual account is in terms of a supposed universe of discourse, a world of make-believe, of imagination, of recognised fictions common to the poet and his readers. A pseudo-statement which fits into this system of assumptions would be regarded as "poetically true"; one which does not, as "poetically false." This attempt to treat "poetic truth" on the model of general "coherence theories" is very natural for certain schools of logicians; but is inadequate, on the wrong lines from the outset. To mention two objections out of many: there is no means of discovering what the "universe of discourse" is on any occasion, and the kind of coherence which must hold within it, supposing it to be discoverable, is not an affair of logical relations. Attempt to define the system of propositions into which

O Rose, thou art sick!

must fit, and the logical relations which must hold between them if it is to be "poetically true"; the absurdity of the theory becomes evident.

We must look further. In the poetic approach the relevant consequences are not logical or to be arrived at by a partial relaxation of logic. Except occasionally and by accident logic does not enter at all. They are the consequences which arise through our emotional organisation. The acceptance which a pseudo-statement receives is entirely governed by its effects upon our feelings and attitudes. Logic only comes in, if at all, in subordination, as a servant to our emotional response. It is an unruly servant, however, as poets and readers are constantly discovering. A pseudo-statement is "true" if it suits and serves some attitude or links together attitudes which on other grounds are desirable. This kind of truth is so opposed to scientific truth that it is a pity to use so similar a word, but at present it is difficult to avoid the malpractice.[1]

This brief analysis may be sufficient to indicate the fundamental disparity and opposition between pseudo-statements as they occur in poetry and statements as they occur in science. A pseudo-statement is a form of words which is justified entirely by its effect in releasing or organising our impulses and attitudes (due regard being had for the better or worse organisations of these *inter se*); a statement, on the other hand, is justified by its truth, *i.e.*, its correspondence, in a highly technical sense, with the fact to which it points.

Statements true and false alike do of course constantly touch off attitudes and action. Our daily practical existence is largely guided by them. On the whole true statements are of more service to us than false ones. None the less we do not and, at present, cannot order our

[1] For an account of the various senses of truth and of the ways in which they may be distinguished in discussion *cf. The Meaning of Meaning* by C. K. Ogden and the author, Chs. 7 and 10.

emotions and attitudes by true statements alone. Nor is there any probability that we ever shall contrive to do so. This is one of the great new dangers to which civilisation is exposed. Countless pseudo-statements—about God, about the universe, about human nature, the relations of mind to mind, about the soul, its rank and destiny—pseudo-statements which are pivotal points in the organisation of the mind, vital to its well-being, have suddenly become, for sincere, honest and informal minds, impossible to believe. For centuries they have been believed; now they are gone, irrecoverably; and the knowledge which has killed them is not of a kind upon which an equally fine organisation of the mind can be based.

This is the contemporary situation. The remedy, since there is no prospect of our gaining adequate knowledge, and since indeed it is fairly clear that genuine knowledge cannot serve us here and can only increase our practical control of Nature, is to cut our pseudo-statements free from belief, and yet retain them, in this released state, as the main instruments by which we order our attitudes to one another and to the world. Not so desperate a remedy as may appear, for poetry conclusively shows that even the most important among our attitudes can be aroused and maintained without any belief entering in at all. Those of Tragedy, for example. We need no beliefs, and indeed we must have none, if we are to read *King Lear*. Pseudo-statements to which we attach no belief and statements proper such as science provides cannot conflict. It is only when we introduce illicit beliefs into poetry that danger arises. To do so is from this point of view a profanation of poetry.

Yet an important branch of criticism which has attracted the best talents from prehistoric times until to-day consists of the endeavour to persuade men that the functions of science and poetry are identical, or that the one is a "higher form" of the other, or that they conflict and we must choose between them.

The root of this persistent endeavour has still to be mentioned; it is the same as that from which the Magical View of the world arose. If we give to a pseudo-statement the kind of unqualified acceptance which belongs by right only to certified scientific statements, if we can contrive to do this, the impulses and attitudes with which we respond to it gain a notable stability and vigour. Briefly, if we can contrive to believe poetry, then the world *seems,* while we do so, to be transfigured. It used to be comparatively easy to do this, and the habit has become well established. With the extension of science and the neutralisation of nature it has become difficult as well as dangerous. Yet it is still alluring; it has many analogies with drug-taking. Hence the endeavours of the critics referred to. Various subterfuges have been devised along the lines of regarding Poetic Truth as figurative, symbolic; or as more immediate, as a truth of Intuition, not of reason; or as a higher form of the same truth as reason yields. Such attempts to use poetry as a denial or as a corrective of science are very common. One point can be made against them all; they are never worked out in detail. There is no equivalent to Mill's *Logic* expounding any such view. The language in which they are framed is usually a blend of obsolete psychology and emotive exclamations.

The long-established and much-encouraged habit of giving to emotive utterances—whether pseudo-statements simple, or looser and larger wholes taken as saying something figuratively—the kind of assent which we give to established facts, has for most people debilitated a wide range of their responses. A few scientists, caught young and brought up in the laboratory, are free from it; but then, as a rule, they pay no *serious* attention to poetry. For most men the recognition of the neutrality of nature brings about—through this habit—a divorce from poetry. They are so used to having their responses propped up by beliefs, however vague, that when these shadowy supports are removed they are no longer able to respond. Their attitudes to so many things have been forced in the past, over-encouraged. And when the world-picture ceases to assist there is a collapse. Over whole tracts of natural emotional response we are to-day like a bed of dahlias whose sticks have been removed. And this effect of the neutralisation of nature is only in its beginnings. Consider the probable effects upon love-poetry in the near future of the kind of enquiry into basic human constitution exemplified by psycho-analysis.

A sense of desolation, of uncertainty, of futility, of the groundlessness of aspirations, of the vanity of endeavour, and a thirst for a life-giving water which seems suddenly to have failed, are the signs in consciousness of this necessary reorganisation of our lives.[2] Our attitudes and impulses are being compelled to become self-supporting; they are being driven back upon their biological justification, made once again sufficient to themselves. And the only impulses which seem strong enough to continue unflagging are commonly so crude that, to more finely developed individuals, they hardly seem worth having. Such people cannot live by warmth, food, fighting, drink, and sex alone. Those who are least affected by the change are those who are emotionally least removed from the animals. As we shall see at the close of this essay, even a considerable poet may attempt to find relief by a reversion to primitive mentality.

It is important to diagnose the disease correctly and to put the blame in the right quarter. Usually it is some alleged "materialism"

[2] To those familiar with Mr. Eliot's *The Waste Land,* my indebtedness to it at this point will be evident. He seems to me by this poem, to have performed two considerable services for this generation. He has given a perfect emotive description of a state of mind which is probably inevitable for a while to all meditative people. Secondly, by effecting a complete severance between his poetry and *all* beliefs, and this without any weakening of the poetry, he has realised what might otherwise have remained largely a speculative possibility, and has shown the way to the only solution of these difficulties. "In the destructive element immerse. That is the way." [*Author's note.*] Eliot comments on this footnote in his essay on Dante, in *Selected Essays.* See the "Note to Section II," pp. 229-231. [*Editor's note.*]

of science which is denounced. This mistake is due partly to clumsy thinking, but chiefly to relics of the Magical View. For even if the Universe were "spiritual" all through (whatever that assertion might mean; all such assertions are probably nonsense), that would not make it any more accordant to human attitudes. It is not what the universe is made of but how it works, the law it follows, which makes knowledge of it incapable of spurring on our emotional responses, and further the nature of knowledge itself makes it inadequate. The contact with things which we therein establish is too sketchy and indirect to help us. We are beginning to know too much about the bond which unites the mind to its object in knowledge for that old dream of a perfect knowledge which would guarantee perfect life to retain its sanction. What was thought to be pure knowledge, we see now to have been shot through with hope and desire, with fear and wonder, and these intrusive elements indeed gave it all its power to support our lives. In knowledge, in the "How?" of events, we can find hints by which to take advantage of circumstances in our favour and avoid mischances. But we cannot get from it a *raison d'être* or a justification of more than a relatively lowly kind of life.

The justification, or the reverse, of any attitude lies, not in the object, but in itself, in its serviceableness to the whole personality. Upon its place in the whole system of attitudes, which is the personality, all its worth depends. This is true equally for the subtle, finely compounded attitudes of the civilized individual as for the simpler attitudes of the child.

In brief, experience is its own justification; and this fact must be faced, although sometimes—by a lover, for example—it may be very difficult to accept. Once it is faced, it is apparent that all the attitudes to other human beings and to the world in all its aspects, which have been serviceable to humanity, remain as they were, as valuable as ever. Hesitation felt in admitting this is a measure of the strength of the evil habit we have described. But many of these attitudes, valuable as ever, are now that they are being set free, more difficult to maintain, because we still hunger after a basis in belief.[3]

[3] For criticism of Richards' notion of pseudo-statement and of his theory of Poetic Belief see Allen Tate: "The Revolt Against Literature," *New Republic*, 44 (Feb. 9, 1927): T. S. Eliot: "Literature, Science and Dogma," *Dial*, 82 (Mar., 1927); James Burnham: "On Defining Poetry," *Symposium*, 1 (Apr., 1930); John Middleton Murry: "Beauty Is Truth," *Symposium*, 1 (Oct., 1930); T. S. Eliot: "Dante," *Selected Essays* (1932); pp. 229-231; Alick West: *Crisis and Criticism* (1937); D. G. James: *Scepticism and Poetry* (1937); Cleanth Brooks: *Modern Poetry and the Tradition* (1939); Philip Wheelwright: "On the Semantics of Poetry," *Kenyon Review*, 2 (Summer, 1940), 271-275; and Yvor Winters: *In Defense of Reason* (1947), pp. 475-476. Quotations from these and other articles on the problem of Poetic Belief are incorporated in a chapter of *The Critics' Notebook*, ed. by R. W. Stallman (1949).

D. G. James's essay, "I. A. Richards," should be read with the two selections from Richards' works which are here presented in *Critiques*. Richards' views on Poetic Belief are criticized in sections vi, vii, and viii of James's critique of Richards. [*Editor's note.*]

POETRY AND BELIEF IN THOMAS HARDY

(1940)

DELMORE SCHWARTZ

I

IT IS NATURAL that beliefs should be involved in poetry in a variety of ways. Hardy is a rich example of this variety. For that reason, it would be well to distinguish some of the important ways in which belief inhabits poetry.

Some poetry is written in order to state beliefs. The purpose of the versification is to make the doctrine plain. Lucretius is the obvious and much-used example, and Dante is probably another, although there is some dramatic justification for most passages of philosophical statement and discussion in the *Paradiso.*

Some poetry employs beliefs merely as an aspect of the thoughts and emotions of the human characters with which it is concerned. Almost every dramatic poet will serve as an example of this tendency. Human beings are full of beliefs, a fact which even the naturalistic novelist cannot wholly forget; and since their beliefs are very important motives in their lives, no serious poet can forget about beliefs all the time. One doubts that any serious poet would want to do so.

It is not difficult to distinguish the two poetic uses of belief from each other. The first kind is generally marked by the forms of direct statement, the second kind by a narrative or dramatic context. And when there is a shift in purpose, when the dramatic poet begins to use his characters merely as mouthpieces to state beliefs, the shift shows immediately in the surface of the poetry. The poet's use of his medium and his attitude toward his subject are always reflected strikingly in the looking glass of form.

Between these two extremes, there exist intermediate stages of which Hardy provides a number of examples. It is commonplace, in addition, that a poet may begin with the intention of stating a belief—or perhaps merely some observation which interests him—and conclude by modifying belief and observation to suit the necessities of versification, the suggestion of a rhyme or the implication of a metaphor.

But there is a prior way in which beliefs enter into a poem. It is prior in that it is inevitable in the very act of writing poetry, while the previous two ways may conceivably be avoided. The poet's beliefs operate within his poem whether he knows it or not, and apart from any effort to use them. This fundamental operation of belief can be seen when we consider a Christian poet's observations of Nature, and then compare them to similar observations on the part of a Romantic poet, such as Wordsworth or Keats. The comparison can be made more extreme with ease, if we substitute a Russian or a Chinese poet, using descriptive passages. It should be evident that poets with different beliefs when confronted with what is nominally the same object do not make the same observations. The same shift because of belief occurs in the slightest detail of language; such common words as *pain, animal, night, rock, hope, death,* and *sky* must of necessity have different powers of association and implication for the Christian poet and one whose beliefs are different. It is a simple fact that our beliefs not only make us see certain things, but also prevent us from seeing other things; and in addition, or perhaps one should say at the same time, our understanding of the language we use is changed.

In Hardy's poetry these three functions of belief all have an important part. Another and equally important factor is at work also. With the tone, the attitude implied by the tone, and often with the explicit statement of his poem, Hardy says with the greatest emphasis: "You see: this is what Life is." And more than that, he says very often: "You see: your old conception of what Life is has been shown to be wrong and foolish by this example."

One hesitates to make a simple synopsis of Hardy's beliefs. It is not that there is anything inherently obscure in them, but that they exist in his poetry so close to the attitudes, feelings, tones, and observations which make them different from their abstract formulation. For the purpose of lucidity, however, it is worth while saying that Hardy believed, in the most literal sense, that the fundamental factor in the nature of things was a "First or Fundamental Energy," as he calls it in the foreword to *The Dynasts.* This Energy operated without consciousness or order throughout the universe and produced the motions of the stars and the long development of the forms of life upon our own planet. Hardy did not hold this view simply, though on occasion he stated it thus. Stated thus, his writing would be an example of philosophical poetry. But this view is only one moment of his whole state of mind and does not by any means exist by itself. It is a view which Hardy affirms in active opposition, first of all, to the view that an intelligent and omnipotent Being rules the universe; second of all, in active opposition to what he knew of the nature of human life as something lived by human beings who in their conscious striving blandly disregarded the fact that they were merely products of the First or Fundamental Energy. Thus Hardy's state of mind is one example of the conflict between the new scientific view of Life which the nineteenth century produced and the whole attitude toward Life which had been traditional to Western culture. Hardy is a partisan of the new view, but acutely conscious always of the old view.

He holds the two in a dialectical tension. Indeed there are moments when it seems that Hardy is merely taking the Christian idea of God and the world, and placing a negative prefix to each of God's attributes. The genuine atheist, by contrast, is never so concerned with the view which he has rejected. Or if he is so concerned, he is, like Hardy, a being who is fundamentally religious and essentially possessed by a state of mind in which an old view of Life and a new one contest without conclusion.

There are certain poems in which this conflict is stated explicitly. In the lyric called *A Plaint to Man,* the false God of Christianity is personified and given a voice, and with that voice he addresses mankind, resuming the doctrine of evolution:

> When you slowly emerged from the den of Time,
> And gained percipience as you grew,
> And fleshed you fair out of shapeless slime,
>
> Wherefore, O Man, did there come to you
> The unhappy need of creating me—
> A form like your own—for praying to?

This false God, being told that mankind had need of some agency of hope and mercy, tells mankind that he, God, dwindles day by day "beneath the deicide eyes of seers," "and tomorrow the whole of me disappears," so that "the truth should be told, and the fact be faced"—the fact that if mankind is to have mercy, justice, and love, the human heart itself would have to provide it.

In another poem, *God's Funeral,* the ambiguity of Hardy's attitude becomes increasingly evident. The God of Christianity is being escorted to his grave by a long train of mourners who are described in Dantesque lines and who have thoughts which are overheard by the protagonist of the poem and which rehearse the history of monotheism from the standpoint of a higher criticism of the Bible. Among the funeral throng, however, the protagonist sees many who refuse to believe that God has died:

> Some in the background then I saw,
> Sweet women, youths, men, all incredulous,
> Who chimed: "This is a counterfeit of straw,
> This requiem mockery! Still he lives to us!"
>
> I could not buoy their faith: and yet
> Many I had known: with all I sympathized;
> And though struck speechless, I did not forget
> That what was mourned for, I, too, long had prized.

This confession that Hardy, too, had prized what he was so concerned to deny must be remembered for the light it gives us upon Hardy's poetry as a whole. In other poems, the wish to believe in the dying God is frankly declared. *The Oxen,* a poem which will require detailed attention, tells of an old Christmas story that the oxen kneel at the hour of Christ's nativity, and the poet declares in the most moving terms that if he should be asked at Christmas to come to the pen at midnight to see the oxen kneel, he would go "in the gloom," "Hoping it might be so"! In *The Dynasts,* this desire is given the most peculiar and pathetic form of all. The hope is stated at the very end that the Fundamental Energy which rules the nature of things will continue to evolve until It takes upon Itself the attribute of consciousness—"Consciousness the Will informing till It fashions all things fair!"—and thus, or such is the implication, becomes like the God of Christianity, a God of love, mercy, and justice.

At the same time, there is a decisive moment of Hardy's state of mind which is directly opposed to this one. Hardy works without end to manipulate the events in the lives of his characters so that it will be plain that human life is at the mercy of chance and the most arbitrary circumstances. Hardy not only makes his Immanent Will of the universe an active power of evil, but he engages his characters in the most incredible conjunctions of unfortunate accidents. There is such an intensity of interest in seeing chance thwart and annihilate human life that the tendency of mind seems pathological until one remembers that chance and coincidence have become for Hardy one of the primary motions of the universe. It is Providence, which is functioning in reverse; the poet has attempted to state a definite view of life in the very working out of his plot.

And at the same time also, the older and stronger view of Life inhabited the poet's mind at a level on which it was not opposed. Hardy inherited a substratum of sensibility of a definite character and formed by definite beliefs which denied the scientific view his intellect accepted. He inherited this sensibility from his fathers, just as he inherited the lineaments of his face, and he could as soon have changed one as the other. Hardy was convinced that the new scientific view was the correct one; he was convinced intellectually, that is to say, that Darwin, Huxley, Schopenhauer, Hartmann, and Nietzsche had attained to the truth about Life. But at the same time, he could not help seeing Nature and human life in the light which was as habitual as walking on one's feet and not on one's hands. He could not work as a poet without his profound sense of history and sense of the past, his feeling for the many generations who had lived and died in his countryside before him; and his mind, like theirs, naturally and inevitably recognized human choice, responsibility, and freedom, the irreparable character of human acts and the undeniable necessity of seeing life from the inside of the human psyche rather than from the astronomical-biological perspective of nineteenth-century science. But more than that, he could not work as a poet without such entities as "spectres, mysterious voices, intuitions, omens and haunted places," the operations of the supernatural in which he could not believe.

II

The cosmology of nineteenth-century science which affected Hardy so much has had a long and interesting history in the culture of the last forty years. Its effects are to be seen in the novels of Theodore Dreiser, in the plays of Bernard Shaw, the early philosophical writing of Bertrand Russell, the early poetry of Archibald MacLeish, and the poetry of Robinson Jeffers. A prime American example is Joseph Wood Krutch's *The Modern Temper,* where it is explicitly announced that such things as love and tragedy and all other specifically human values are not possible to modern man. The example of Bertrand Russell suggests that of I. A. Richards, whose sincerity ritual to test the genuineness of a poem works at least in part by envisaging the "meaninglessness" of the universe which follows or seemed to follow from the scientific view; and the example of Krutch suggests some of the best poems of Mark Van Doren, where the emptiness of the sky, the departure of the old picture of the world, is the literal theme. This array of examples, and the many others which might be added, should not only suggest how modern a poet Hardy is; they should also suggest how variously the scientific view may enter into the poet's whole being, what different attitudes it may engender, and how differently the poet's sensibility may attempt to handle it.

It is nothing if not fitting that I. A. Richards should look to Hardy for his perfect example in *Science and Poetry,* the book he has devoted to precisely this question, the effect of the scientific view upon the modern poet. Mr. Richards is at once very illuminating, I think, and very wrong in what he says of Hardy. It would not be possible for anyone to improve upon the appreciation of Hardy's virtues implicit in the three pages Mr. Richards devotes to him; but it would be equally difficult to invert the truth about Hardy as completely as Mr. Richards does in the interests of his general thesis. He quotes a remark about Hardy made by J. Middleton Murry: "His reaction to an episode has behind it and within it a reaction to the universe." And then his comment is: "This is not as I should put it were I making a statement; but read as a pseudo-statement, emotively, it is excellent; it makes us remember how we felt. Actually it describes just what Hardy, at his best, does not do. He makes no reaction to the universe, recognizing it as something to which no reaction is more relevant than another."

On the contrary, Hardy is almost always bringing his reaction to the universe into his poems. It is true that he sees the universe as something to which no reaction is more relevant than another; but it is just that view of the neutral universe which prepossesses Hardy almost always and gives much of the power to the most minute details of his poems. Perhaps one ought to say not Hardy's beliefs, but Hardy's disbeliefs; whichever term is exact, the fact is that his beliefs or disbeliefs make possible the great strength of his verse. We can see that this is so if we examine some of the poems in which Hardy's beliefs play a direct part.

THE OXEN

Christmas Eve, and twelve of the clock.
  "Now they are all on their knees,"
An elder said as we sat in a flock
  By the embers in hearthside ease.

We pictured the meek mild creatures where
  They dwelt in their strawy pen,
Nor did it occur to one of us there
  To doubt they were kneeling then.

So fair a fancy few would weave
  In these years! Yet, I feel,
If someone said on Christmas Eve,
  "Come; see the oxen kneel,

"In the lonely barton by yonder coomb
  Our childhood used to know,"
I should go with him in the gloom,
  Hoping it might be so.

The belief in this poem is of course a disbelief in the truth of Christianity. The emotion is the wish that it were true. But it must be emphasized that this emotion, which obviously motivates the whole poem, depends upon a very full sense of what the belief in Christianity amounted to; and this sense also functions to provide the poet with the details of the Christmas story which serves as the example of Christianity. It is Hardy's sensibility as the son of his fathers which makes possible his realization of the specific scene and story; this sensibility itself was the product of definite beliefs, to refer back to the point made at the beginning that we see what we do see because of our beliefs. But for the whole poem to be written, it was necessary that what Hardy's sensibility made him conscious of should be held against the scientific view which his intellect accepted. Both must enter into the poem. This is the sense in which a reaction to the universe, if one must use Mr. Murry's terms, is involved in Hardy's reaction to the Christmas story. Hardy, remembering the Christmas story of childhood, cannot help keeping in mind the immense universe of nineteenth-century science, which not only makes such a story seem untrue, but increases one's reasons for wishing that it were true. His sensibility's grasp of the meaning of Christmas and Christianity makes such a choice of detail as calling the oxen "meek mild creatures" likely, perfectly exact, and implicit with the Christian quality of humility. His intellectual awareness of the new world-picture engenders the fullness of meaning involved in the phrase, which is deliberately emphasized by the overflow, "In these years!" A reaction to the universe is involved in this phrase and in addition a reaction to a definite period in Western culture.

If we take a negative example, one in which Hardy's beliefs have operated to produce a poor poem, this function of belief will be seen with further definition. The following poem is as typical of Hardy's failures as *The Oxen* is of the elements which produced his successes:

THE MASKED FACE

I found me in a great surging space,
  At either end a door,
And I said: "What is this giddying place,
  With no firm-fixéd floor,
  That I knew not of before?"
  "It is Life," said a mask-clad face.

I asked: "But how do I come here,
  Who never wished to come;
Can the light and air be made more clear,
  The floor more quietsome,
  And the door set wide? They numb
  Fast-locked, and fill with fear."

The mask put on a bleak smile then,
  And said, "O vassal-wight,
There once complained a goosequill pen
  To the scribe of the Infinite
  Of the words it had to write
  Because they were past its ken."

Here too Hardy's picture of the universe is at work and Hardy is intent upon declaring his belief that Life is beyond human understanding. But there is a plain incongruity between the vaguely cosmological scene which is declared to be Life in the first stanza and the stenographic metaphor for human life in the last stanza, which, apart from this relationship, is grotesque enough in itself. There is no adequate reason in the poem why a giddying place with no firm-fixéd floor should be beyond understanding, and it is not made so by being entitled: Life. It reminds one rather of the barrel-rolls at amusement parks and by no means of the revolutions of day and night which

Hardy presumably had in mind. The masked face is probably intended to designate the Immanent Will; but here again, there is a gulf between what Hardy meant by that Will and any speaking face, and the gulf cannot be annulled merely by the device of personification. Moreover, it is difficult enough to see the human being as a goosequill pen; when the pen complains, the poem collapses because too great a weight of meaning has been put upon a figure which was inadequate at the start.

In poems such as these, and they are not few, Hardy has been merely attempting to versify his beliefs about the universe, and neither his mastery of language nor his skill at versification can provide him with all that he needs. He needs his sensibility; but his sensibility works only when the objects proper to it are in view. When it is required to function on a cosmological scene, it can only produce weak and incommensurate figures. It is possible for a poet to make poetry by the direct statement of his beliefs, but it is not possible for such a poet as Hardy. The true philosophical poet is characterized by an understanding of ideas and an interest in them which absorbs his whole being. Hardy was interested in ideas, too; but predominantly in their bearing upon human life. No better characterization could be formulated than the one Hardy wrote for his novel *Two on a Tower:* "This slightly-built romance was the outcome of a wish to set the emotional history of two infinitesimal lives against the stupendous background of the stellar universe, and to impart to readers the sentiment that of these contrasting magnitudes the smaller might be the greater to them as men."

III

Hardy failed when he tried to make a direct statement of his beliefs; he succeeded when he used his beliefs to make significant the observations which concerned him. This contrast should suggest that something essential to the nature of poetry may very well be in question. It is a long time since the statement was first made that poetry is more philosophical than history; the example of Hardy provides another instance of how useful and how illuminating the doctrine is. The minute particulars of Hardy's experience might have made a diary, history, or biography; what made them poetry was the functioning of Hardy's beliefs. The function of belief was to generalize his experience into something neither merely particular, which is the historian's concern; nor merely general, which is the philosopher's; but into symbols which possess the qualitative richness, as Mr. Ransom might say, of any particular thing and yet have that generality which makes them significant beyond their moment of existence, or the passing context in which they are located. And here again an examination of a particular poem will make the discussion specific:

A DRIZZLING EASTER MORNING

And he is risen? Well, be it so. . . .
And still the pensive lands complain,
And dead men wait as long ago,
As if, much doubting, they would know
What they are ransomed from, before
They pass again their sheltering door.

I stand amid them in the rain,
While blusters vex the yew and vane;
And on the road the weary wain
Plods forward, laden heavily;
And toilers with their aches are fain
For endless rest—though risen is he.

It is the belief and disbelief in Christ's resurrection which not only make this poem possible, but make its details so moving. They are not only moving; the weary wain which plods forward heavily and the dead men in the graveyard are envisaged fully as particular things and yet become significant of the whole experience of suffering and evil just because the belief exists for Hardy and provides a light which makes these particular things symbols. *Without the belief, it is only another rainy morning in March or April.* In passing, it should be noted that both belief and disbelief are necessary; the belief is necessary to the disbelief. And both are responsible here as elsewhere for that quality of language which is Hardy's greatest strength. The mere use of such words as *men, doubting, door, rain,* has a richness of implication, a sense of generations of human experience behind it; this richness is created immediately by the modifying words in the context, *pensive, weary, plod, vex, heavily,* and other workings of the words upon each other; but fundamentally by Hardy's ability to see particulars as significant of Life in general. He would not have had that ability without his beliefs and disbeliefs, though it is true that other poets get that ability by other means and other beliefs.

IV

Once we remember that good poems have been produced by the use of different and contradictory beliefs, we are confronted by the problem of belief in the modern sense.

There are good reasons for supposing that this is not, in itself, a poetic problem. But at any rate, it is true enough that many readers are profoundly disturbed by poems which contain beliefs which they do not accept or beliefs which are in direct contradiction to their own. Hardy's beliefs, as presented explicitly in his poems, offended and still offend his readers in this way.

In turn, the poet is wounded to hear that his poems are not enjoyed because his beliefs are untrue. Throughout his long career, both as poet and as novelist, Hardy was intensely disturbed by criticism on such a basis.

In the "Apology" to *Late Lyrics and Earlier,* Hardy spoke out with the tiredness and anger of an author who has suffered from reviewers for fifty years. His answer is curious and defective, however. He points out that the case against him is "neatly summarized in a stern pronouncement . . . 'This view of life is not mine.' " But instead of defending himself by pointing to all the great poetry which would be eliminated if it were judged merely on the basis of its agreement with the reader's beliefs, Hardy concedes the basic issue to his critics by claiming that his beliefs are better than they have been painted. He defends himself by saying that he is not a pessimist, but "an evolutionary meliorist." No one but another evolutionary meliorist could be persuaded by this kind of argument.

On another occasion, in the introduction to *The Dynasts,* Hardy attempts to solve the problem by requiring Coleridge's temporary "suspension of disbelief which constitutes poetic faith." But this formula would seem to provide for no more than the convention of theatrical or fictive illusion. When the curtain rises, we must suspend disbelief as to whether we see before us Elsinore, a platform before the castle. If we do not, then there can be no play. The case seems more difficult, at least on the surface, when we are asked to accept alien beliefs.

Now there are two ways in which we tend to handle alien beliefs. One of them is to reject those poems which contain beliefs we regard as false. This is an example of judging poetry in terms of its subject, considered in abstraction; and the difficulties are obviously numerous. For one thing, as has been said, we would have to reject most great poetry. Certainly we would have to do without Homer, and without Dante or Shakespeare.

The other alternative, which is in any case preferable to the first, is to judge poetry wholly in terms of its formal character. But this is an act of unjustifiable abstraction also. For it is evident that we enjoy more in a poem, or at least the poem presents more to us, than a refined use of language.

What we need, and what we actually have, I think, is a criterion for the beliefs in a poem which is genuinely a poetic criterion. In reading Hardy when he is successful, in *A Drizzling Easter Morning,* we find that the belief and disbelief operate upon the particular *datum* of the poem to give it a metaphorical significance it would not otherwise have. To repeat, without both belief and disbelief it is only another rainy morning in the spring. Conversely, in *The Masked Face,* the asserted belief, instead of generalizing the particulars of the poem, merely interferes with them and fails to give them the significance they are intended to have.

In both instances, we are faced with a relationship between the belief in the poem and its other particulars. This is a relationship *internal* to the poem, so to speak. It is not a question of the relationship of the poet's beliefs to the reader's. In *The Masked Face,* for example, the inadequacy proceeds from the relationship between the belief that Life is beyond human understanding, and the goose-quill pen which is required to represent the human mind.

It might be objected that this internal relationship between the belief and the rest of the poem is in turn good, or not good, in terms of what the given reader himself believes. Thus it might seem that for a reader who shares Hardy's beliefs, the goose-quill pen was an adequate figure for the human mind. Actually this cannot be so, unless the reader is not interested in poetry but merely in hearing his beliefs stated. If the reader is interested in poetry, the poem itself cannot give him the poetic experience of Life as beyond human understanding, which is its intention. The details of the poem, as presented in the context which the belief and the versification provide, do not do the work in the reader's mind which is done by such an element in *A Drizzling Easter Morning,* as the weary wain, which plods forward, laden heavily. And one reason why they lack that energy is their relationship, within the poem, to the belief the poem asserts. Whether or not the reader shares Hardy's beliefs, even if he shares them completely, the goose-quill pen is an inadequate figure for what it is intended to signify in the context. The belief in the poem fails to make it adequate, and this is a poetic failure, just as, in *The Oxen,* the kneeling animals are a poetic success because of the disbelief, whether the reader himself disbelieves in Christianity or not.

And again, it might be objected that only valid beliefs, in the end, can operate successfully upon the other elements of any poem. Once more we must refer back first to the fact that poets have written good poetry based upon opposed beliefs, and then to the point made at the start, that there is a basic way in which beliefs have much to do with the whole character of a poet's sensibility, with what he sees and does not see. The subject of poetry is experience, not truth—even when the poet is writing about ideas. When the poet can get the whole experience of his sensibility into his poem, then there will be an adequate relationship between the details of his poem and the beliefs he asserts, whether they are true or not. For then he is getting the actuality of his experience into his poem, and it does not matter whether that actuality is illusory or not; just as the earth may be seen as flat. The functioning of his sensibility guarantees his asserted beliefs; it guarantees them as aspects of experience, though not as statements of truth. The philosophical poet, as well as any other kind, must meet this test. The details of his poem are neither dramatic, nor lyrical, but there is the same question of the relationship between his asserted ideas and the language, tone, attitude, and figures which constitute the rest of the poem.

At any rate, by adopting this point of view, we avoid the two extremes, the two kinds of abstraction, which violate the poem as a concrete whole. And it is especially necessary to do this in Hardy's case, for it is unlikely that many readers will hold Hardy's beliefs as he held them. In the future we are likely to believe less or more; but we will not be in the same kind of intellectual situation as Hardy was.

The important thing is to keep Hardy's poetry, to keep as much of it as we can, and to enjoy it for what it is in its utmost concreteness. And if this is to be accomplished, it is necessary that we keep Hardy's beliefs *in* his poetry, and our own beliefs outside.

THE RELIGIOUS PROBLEM IN G. M. HOPKINS

(1937)

W. H. Gardner

The chief problem presented by the poetry of Hopkins derives from the repressed conflict between two sets of values—those of the poet and those of the priest; between the psychic individuality, or what I shall for convenience call the *personality* on the one hand, and the *character,* as determined by a strict regulative principle (the Jesuit discipline) on the other. Hence the central problem to be discussed may be stated as follows: How far and in what manner was the personality of Hopkins the poet stultified, or assisted, by the character of Father Hopkins, S.J.?

It is by now common knowledge that Hopkins, on becoming a Jesuit, burnt most of his early poems and resolved to write no more except by the wish of his superiors. Fortunately that sanction was not withheld; but the creative Hopkins was at all times, from 1868 till his death in 1889, profoundly influenced or even dominated by the devotional text-book of the Society of Jesus—the *Spiritual Exercises* of St. Ignatius. The basis of this "manual of election" is Self-abnegation, or rather (for the principle is really positive), the complete dedication of the Self to God and salvation, to a life of poverty, chastity and obedience. Right "election" in all crises of the soul entailed the renunciation of all attachments and pleasures which were not contributory to God's service and the soul's weal: "Take, O Lord, and receive my liberty, my memory, my understanding, and all my will." Hopkins acquiesced; yet how idiosyncratic his gesture of renunciation could be we hear in

> O feel-of-primrose hands, O feet
> That want the yield of plushy sward . . .

and in

> What life half lifts the latch of,
> What hell stalks towards the snatch of
> Your offering, with dispatch, of!

By a rigorous method of daily self-scrutiny called "the particular examen," the priest searched his conscience for the impure motive, the intrusive Self; it is therefore not surprising that a man so devout as Hopkins should carry the same moral scrupulosity into his poetry. We proceed to observe how the regulative principle affects the imagination, the highest conscious function of the personality.

Hopkins is continually examining the claims of what Keats called "the principle of Beauty in all things." To Keats, Beauty was single and good—it was Truth: to Hopkins it was two-fold—"mortal beauty" and immortal (or supernatural) beauty, and its influence or "instress" was equivocal; for Hopkins saw that beauty could be both an insidious lure to the lower levels of being and a constant admonition to the higher. It all depended upon the state of the receptive mind, the character. On the analogy of the sensitive soul's response to the transient beauty of this world, the Christian, by a definite motion of the will towards "the highest spiritual poverty," aspires to the immortal beauty of the supernatural world, union with God in the Beatific Vision. The necessary check put upon sensibility by the disciplined will is first stated in *The Habit of Perfection.* The enjoyment of beauty is a sacrament, and the implied obligation is an act of sacrifice:

Give beauty back . . . back to God.[1]

In a later poem, *To what serves Mortal Beauty?* Hopkins faces the danger of over-indulgence, and asks:

What do then? how meet beauty?

and the answer is an attempt to bridge the gap between the transient and the permanent, to reconcile the poet with his impulse of acceptance and the priest with his doctrine of "detachment":

Merely meet it; own,
Home-at-heart, heaven's sweet gift; then leave, let that alone.
Yea, wish that though, wish all, God's better beauty, grace.

Recognition of this fundamental belief helps us to understand those poems in which direct sensuous enjoyment of natural beauty leads up to a doctrinal, dogmatic, or quasi-mystical consummation—the spiritual exegesis of nature's parable: I mean the early nature sonnets, *God's Grandeur, The Starlight Night, Spring,* etc. On the other hand, failure to grasp or to sympathize with the poet's metaphysic leads to misconceptions like the following:

> The sensuous insistency with which, in these sonnets, earth and air are claimed for Christ is to my sense taut and artificial, suggesting a profound emotional dislocation, with the ensuing desolation of *Carrion Comfort* as its inevitable counterpart.[2]

The last part is merely a euphemistic way of saying that Hopkins was

[1] *The Golden Echo.*
[2] Basil de Sélincourt: *The Observer,* Jan. 20th, 1935.

a victim of self-deception, that the poet dragged in the name of Christ simply to mollify the conscience of the priest. To anyone who has no use for Christian Theism the Christ-symbol will almost certainly appear "taut and artificial"; yet that is no reason for saying that the frequency of this symbol betokens a "profound emotional dislocation" in a sincere believer like Hopkins. (Unless the *Letters* and *Notebooks* are grossly disingenuous, it is difficult to maintain now that Hopkins seriously questioned his faith.) To a fellow-Theist, the Christ-symbol indicates rather a profound and spontaneous unification of the intellect and the senses, that mystical fusion of the Many and the One which is at the root of all great conversions to the religious attitude and mode of life. As we know from his remarks on Keats and Whitman, Hopkins was not satisfied with a poetry which rested in the senses and the emotions alone; he desired intellectual satisfaction as well—what another Jesuit describes as "the unity and order and ultimate satisfaction of the intellect" which for him "the grandeur of theism"[3] could alone provide. Theism dressed not only his "days" but his thoughts about man and the universe "to a dexterous and starlight order"; and the nature sonnets are evidence not of "emotional dislocation" but of his discovery of a philosophy about which he could say, with confidence and joy, "On this principle hang the heavens and the earth."

To Hopkins nature was (in Milman's phrase) "a sublime theophany." In his own words:

> God's utterance of Himself in Himself is God the Word, outside Himself is this world. This world then is word, expression, news, of God.

Then follows a statement which is vital to a complete understanding of Hopkins's mind and poetry: "Therefore its end, its purpose, its purport, its meaning, is God, and its life or work to name and praise Him."[4] When he writes:

> I walk, I lift up, I lift up heart, eyes
> Down all that glory in the heavens to glean our Saviour.

we hear not a suggestion of emotional dislocation but rather of peace and certainty—that ecstasy which Dr. Richards once said Hopkins failed to reach. To most people, it is true, Christ stands for an ideal (or Utopian) code of morals, and they would see no connection between a code of morals and a mystical vision of external nature: to them such an arbitrary connection might well be a token of self-deception, a symptom of neurosis. But the phenomenon cannot be explained away so easily; for even in the earlier Wordsworth we find something like it. Speaking of the "tranquil restoration" of remembered, assimilated beauty, he says:

[3] M. C. D'Arcy, S.J.: *Mirage and Truth,* p. 89.
[4] Quoted by G. F. Lahey, S.J.: *Life of G.M.H.,* p. 124.

> feelings too
> Of unremembered pleasure: such perhaps
> As have no slight or trivial influence
> On that best portion of a good man's life,
> His little, nameless, unremembered acts
> Of kindness and of love.[5]

From this it is but a step to Hopkins's comment on a bluebell: "By its beauty I know the beauty of Our Lord." [6]

No one will deny that a profound emotional dislocation informs the later sonnets of despair; but before dealing with this question we will examine a poem which, although variously interpreted by agnostics and Roman Catholics, evinces in its final effect a perfect fusion of the poetic personality and the religious character: I mean *The Windhover*. The fact that Hopkins dedicated the sonnet "To Christ our Lord" suggests, first, that he saw in the kestrel, as in the bluebell and all things of beauty, a symbol of Christ or of some ethical principle; and secondly that he found a deep relief and self-justification in the writing of the poem.

The whole of the octave may be read with little difficulty as a vigorous and colourful piece of nature-poetry, a description of the kestrel in action. We have, indeed, met intelligent people who have read the whole sonnet as a direct tribute to the beauty of the bird and God's glory—"without *underthought* or *afterthought*," as Hopkins would say. Such a reading, however, is like playing the *Appassionata* with one finger: it robs the poem of depth and variety, to say nothing of its ontological and biographical significance.

One phrase, in line 7 of the octave, has provoked some speculation among critics:

> My *heart in hiding*
> Stirred for a bird,—

Because of this sonnet's unique dedication even a reader who knew nothing of Hopkins could have no doubt about the religious and specifically Christian connotation of "heart" in this passage. The poet's emotions—sympathy, admiration, love—were ever aroused by all natural or "mortal" beauty, but principally by the supreme pattern of "immortal" beauty—the character of Christ. For this ideal, the priest had renounced worldly ambition, the fullest life of the senses; hence his heart was "in hiding" with Christ, wholly dedicated to His love, praise and service.

"My heart in hiding" is the first giving out of the essential moral theme of the poem. The whole poem, it must be remembered, is addressed not to the bird, or to the reader, or to the poet himself,

[5] *Lines Written Above Tintern Abbey.*
[6] *Note-books and Papers,* Etc. (Oxford), p. 134.

but primarily and deliberately to Christ. Certain critics,[7] by slurring over this fact, have made the admittedly difficult sestet seem unwarrantably vague, ambiguous and pathological: neglecting the meaning as determined by the poet's *will,* they have exhausted their ingenuity in probing the arcana of his unconscious mind, attributing to him in the process motives which he himself would have rejected as incompatible with his purpose, beliefs and vocation. Such probings have their value, but only when assessed in relation to the poet's conscious purpose. The truth is that in this sestet Hopkins holds up to a passionate but critical judgment two conflicting sets of values, one represented by the "kingdom of daylight's dauphin"—the windhover, the other by the Kingdom of Heaven's "chevalier"—Christ. As the psychological critics have shown, and as the poet himself was aware, the sonnet embodies a spiritual conflict. The poet's decision is, moreover, cathartic: he finds relief in his reconciliation of opposite, discordant tendencies in the active personality and the consciously controlled character.

The reconciliation is between the claims of this life and the claims of the next; [8] between the value and the danger of "mortal beauty"; [9] between the desire for freedom of expression—the natural function "wild and self-instressed"—and the will to suffer, to subject oneself to the ascetic rule, to dedicate all one's powers to Christ's employment. The resolution of the conflict depends upon recognition of the fact that "mastery" and "achieve" in those mental and physical acts which excite the admiration of onlookers (activities of personality) may be sublimated—assimilated by the character and revealed with greater merit in the supreme act of sacrifice, which is derived from, due to, and rewarded by, Christ.

So the sestet begins:

> Brute beauty and valour and act, oh, air, pride, plume here
> Buckle!

The verb is imperative, making the whole a plea to Christ. The adverb "here," though ambiguous, means primarily "in this world, this life; in *my* particular being even as it happened in *Your* being when You became Man." The wild beauty and instinctive self-discipline of the kestrel are symbols of the controlled beauty given "back to God" and the military self-discipline of the Ignatian ideal. As the bird coordinates all its faculties in graceful flight and dangerous swoop, so the poet asks Christ's help in buckling or enclosing within the belt

[7] Principally Dr. I. A. Richards in *The Dial,* 81 (Sept. 19, 1926), and Mr. William Empson in *Seven Types of Ambiguity.* [*Author's note.*] The text of *The Windhover* is given in an appendix to this essay. [*Editor's note.*]

[8] *Cf.* "I am a eunuch—but it is for the kingdom of heaven's sake." (*Letters to Robert Bridges,* p. 270.)

[9] Cf. *To what serves Mortal Beauty?* (*Poems,* 2nd ed., No. 38.)

of the Jesuit rule all his own rich faculties.[10] The likeness between the bird and the partly repressed personality of the poet is obvious, so that the mind is capable of holding, in one act of comprehension, another relevant meaning of "buckle"—to bend, crumple up under weight or strain.

External evidence that Hopkins had this idea in mind is to be found in a letter and a sermon:

> Christ our Lord... was doomed to succeed by failure; his plans were baffled, his hopes dashed, and his work was done by being broken off undone.[11]

Having dwelt upon traditional accounts of Christ's physical beauty, he concludes:

> In his Passion all this strength was spent, this lissomness crippled, this beauty wrecked, this majesty beaten down.[12]

And there is another striking piece of evidence in one of Shakespeare's plays.[13]

For Hopkins, then, the example of Christ's life linked together three relevant and complementary meanings of "Buckle!"—buckle within (discipline), buckle to (labour), buckle under (sacrifice). Moreover, the story, implicit throughout the *Letters,*[14] of the poet's own "imitation of Christ," is epitomized in the sestet of this sonnet.

The rest of the tercet states the immediate outcome of this discipline which entails suffering and sacrifice:

> ... AND the fire that breaks from thee then a billion
> Times told lovelier, more dangerous, O my chevalier!

In a direct or straightforward reading, all this could be addressed to the kestrel, the "chevalier" of the air; but if, as I have decided, the stress is on "my," it is certainly intended for the listening Christ, the perfect example of *spiritual* activity as the bird is a perfect example of *physical* activity. By the same token, the glamour of "chevalier" is reflected back on to the poet himself, who resembles, in opposite ways,

[10] *Cf.* Shakespeare's use of "buckle" in

> He cannot buckle his distempered cause
> Within the belt of rule. (*Macbeth,* V. ii. 15-16.)

[11] *Correspondence of G. M. Hopkins and R. W. Dixon,* pp. 137-138.

[12] *Note-books and Papers,* Etc., pp. 262-263.

[13] 2 *Henry IV,* I. i. 140-142:

> And as the wretch whose fever-weaken'd joints
> Like strengthless hinges *buckle under life,*
> Impatient of his fit, *breaks* like a *fire*
> Out of his keeper's arms...

Hopkins, too, in the same line as *Buckle!* uses *fire* and *breaks.* It is also significant that in the next scene of the play Falstaff says: "He that *buckles* him *in* my belt cannot live in less." (Oxford Shakespeare, l. 160.)

[14] See especially *Letters to R.B.,* p. 175.

both the bird and the Master. By an act of will, the poet has turned from the ruthless freedom and joy of the kestrel to the compassionate servitude of Christ ("O my chevalier!"). Hopkins himself, when free to act, was the curvetting and caracoling knight-errant of poetry; but the King he chose to serve was He who once rode, slowly and humbly, upon an ass. The mental transition from "chevalier" to *chivalry,* and thence to *soldier of Christ* (the Jesuit priest) makes the next symbol of humble, useful toil—the plough [15]—both natural and moving. The sequence is: "The windhover flashes a trail of beauty across the morning sky; but the beauty in action, the inspiration, the glory of *Christ* (and in a lesser degree of the plodding, inhibited poet-priest) is far, far lovelier. The taut, swooping windhover is the terror of the air; but the disciplined life of the spirit is much more dangerous, because it is menaced by, and must itself attack and overcome, a far greater foe—the powers of evil." And "no wonder!" the poet cries, in his certainty and somewhat pained ardour—

> No wonder of it: shéer plód makes plough down sillion
> Shine . . .

The price, however, must be paid. How unlike the swoop of a hawk is the following symbol of "a man of sorrows," the jaded drudge, the gradual cooling off of youthful vigour and zeal—"blue-bleak embers"! It is a martyrdom, but the consolation is there too:

> . . . and blue-bleak embers, ah my dear,
> Fall, gall themselves, and gash gold-vermilion.

As Mr. Empson points out, these images suggest the Crucifixion, the martyr's blood and the crown of gold. As at the end of *That Nature is a Heraclitean Fire,* the collapse in defeat, agony and death is a reward, a sudden change as from ash to immortal diamond. The words "ah my dear," borrowed from George Herbert,[16] have a double significance: they express sympathy with Christ for his anguish and martyrdom [17] and at the same time a tender reproach that He should give His devout but frail servant such a heavy cross to bear.

No doubt *The Windhover* expresses more of the poet's "unconscious" than he was himself aware. It is a poem of tragic intensity though not necessarily of tragic import. To the Christian reader, the sense of loss is diminished by the compensatory sense of moral gain, of the Self over-mastered. But the final impression for any

[15] This image may be a reminiscence of Donne's lines to Mr. Tilman, who had taken orders:

> Thou, whose diviner soul hath caused thee now
> To put thy hand unto the holy plough, . . .

[16] See his *Love:*

> I, the unkind, ungrateful? Ah, my dear,
> I cannot look on Thee.

[17] . . . but that God should be crucified fascinates—with the interest of awe, of pity, of shame, of every harrowing feeling. (*Letters to R.B.,* p. 188.)

reader must be one of catharsis, "that sense of relief, of repose in the midst of stress, of balance and composure, given by Tragedy; for there is no other way in which such impulses, once awakened, can be set at rest without suppression."[18]

The appeasement and resignation expressed in *The Windhover* were not absolutely decisive. Yet up to 1885, when *Carrion Comfort* was "written in blood," Hopkins's work cannot as a whole be called unhappy. Many of these poems—*Henry Purcell, Brothers, The Blessed Virgin,* etc., are as much the consummation of pure joy as any in the language. In *Spelt from Sibyl's Leaves,* however, we hear harsh repercussions of the particular examen:

> Lét life, wáned, ah lét life wind
> Off hér once skéined stained véined varíety upon, áll on twó spools...
> ... black, white: right, wrong...

There, no doubt, is the dislocation which Dr. Richards and Mr. de Sélincourt have deplored—that the rich variety of such a poet's intellect, imagination and potential experience should be levelled down to this stern "dichotomy of right and wrong." Yet if we discount the moral aspect and consider only the poetry, can it truthfully be said that his cry "O our tale, our oraclé" is justified?—that the poet's dapple is really at an end?—that his valuable personality is quite steeped, pashed and dismembered in the larger unit of the Jesuit discipline? The answer is in the poem itself: diction, rhythm, imagery, organization of experience—all are new, individual.

An interesting pendant to *The Windhover* is the sonnet *In honour of St. Alphonsus Rodriguez* (1888). Despite its objective theme, it is, one feels, strongly subjective, and goes to prove that Hopkins's loyalty to the regulative principle had moulted no essential feather up to the year before his death. Like *The Windhover,* the poem deals with the "unseen war within the heroic breast" of the humble, plodding servant of Christ: and the note of triumph is unmistakable:

> Yet God that hews mountain and continent...
> *Could crowd career with conquest* while there went
> Those years and years by of world without event
> That in Majorca Alfonso watched the door.[19]

As with King Lear, this projection of the self into another was a kind of relief. The hurtle of the poet's own "fiercest fray" we hear in the sonnets Nos. 40, 41 and 45. Yet commentators on the so-called tragedy of Hopkins's whole life (Dr. Richards, for example) are so anxious to give full weight to these utterances that they ignore the psychological significance of first-rate poems of quite a different outlook. *Harry Ploughman* (1887) and the incomplete *Epithalamion* (1888)

[18] I. A. Richards: *Principles of Literary Criticism,* Ch. 32, p. 246.
[19] The italics are mine.

are both joyous products of the unimpeded personality. (There is no need to discover a pathological symptom in the violent physical action of the former or in the missing nuptial exegesis of the latter.) Moreover to anyone who can entertain even only the smallest wistful hope of Immortality, *That Nature is a Heraclitean Fire* must surely present as perfect a collaboration of priest and poet as *The Windhover*.[20]

How far the ill-health and depression so frequently mentioned in the *Letters* were due to thwarted physical impulses would be a dangerous matter for speculation by one who is not a trained neuropathologist. It is certain however that many of the later sonnets are concerned with the poet's struggle to live in accordance with the Ignatian rule. "One step," says a commentator on the *Exercises*, "is patience and meekness under affronts." Touching the former virtue Hopkins laments:

> Patience, hard thing! the hard thing but to pray,
> But bid for, Patience is!

And that his "elected silence," whether as patriot, priest, poet or plain man could at times prove almost unbearably irksome we learn from No. 44. In this he may be uttering a repressed desire to write an ode to England, a political pamphlet, or perhaps merely to speak his mind freely to those about him. But to some ears the sestet vibrates with a deeper, more tragic note, which hints at something more personal and essential than a sporadic patriotism or what Dr. Richards somewhat curiously calls "self-consciousness":

> Only what word
> Wisest my heart breeds dark heaven's baffling ban
> Bars or hell's spell thwarts. This to hoard unheard,
> Heard unheeded, leaves me a lonely began.

No doubt Hopkins suffered greatly; yet he had been prepared for periods of dejection and disillusion by the *Spiritual Exercises*, in which moods of desolation are minutely described and dogmatically accounted for. In the words of Father Keating, S.J.:

> Whatever experiences are reflected in the four or five "terrible sonnets," so full of spiritual "desolation," so expressive of "the dark night of the soul," that those close to Christ are at times privileged to pass through, they cannot have been due to a mere sense of failure and frustration, still less to doubt as to whether he had chosen aright.[21]

We may cite in corroboration Hopkins's own words: "I have never wavered in my vocation, but I have not lived up to it." [22] And as for

[20] *Cf.* "Hopkins's best poem for me is 48 (the *Heraclitean Fire*); this has the fusion required by a 'metaphysical' mind which had to work in harmony on two planes at once." (Louis MacNeice: *New Verse*, April, 1935.)

[21] *The Month*, July, 1935.

[22] Letter to Dixon: *Correspondence*, p. 88.

suffering, he had explicitly stated, in 1869, that suffering, nobly endured, was a mark of special grace:

> What suffering she had! ... But sufferings falling on such a person as your sister was are to be looked on as the marks of God's particular love, and this is truer the more exceptional they are.[23]

Yet those who maintain that much of his trouble was due to unsatisfied creative impulses have no mean evidence to go on. There is first the significant passage in a letter of 1885, where he regrets his inability to carry out his literary projects—"it kills me to be time's eunuch and never to beget"; [24] and frustration could hardly be more articulate than in No. 50, from its cry

> Why do sinners' ways prosper? and why must
> Disappointment all I endeavour end?

to the poignant repetition of

> ... birds build—but not I build; no, but strain,
> Time's eunuch, and not breed one work that wakes.

The mortification expressed here and in No. 44 is intensified in the acute anhedonia and spiritual dyspepsia of No. 45:

> I am gall, I am heartburn. God's most deep decree
> Bitter would have me taste: My taste was me; ...
> Selfyeast of spirit a dull dough sours ...

The active personality has not been perfectly assimilated by the passive religious character. "Selfyeast of spirit" suggests the individual vital principle, the psychic individuality, rather than the immortal soul of the Christian, which strives to annihilate the Self either in works of charity or in a perfect union with its Creator. The souring of the personality and the consequent loss of inspiration is a foretaste of perdition:

> I see
> The lost are like this, and their scourge to be
> As I am mine, their sweating selves; but worse.

—the mere husks of men, without vision or hope. Contrast this with the Scotist ecstasy of No. 34—"Selves, goes itself; *myself* it speaks and spells." [25] Now "What I do is me" seems to have become "What I cannot do is what I want to be." The last two words of the poem, placed in emphatic isolation, must not be misread: they safeguard the

[23] *Letters to Robert Bridges*, p. 25. The same idea is expressed in *The Wreck of the Deutschland* (1875), stanza 22.

[24] *Letters to R.B.*, p. 222.

[25] *Cf.* also: "Nothing else in nature comes near this unspeakable stress of pitch, distinctiveness, selving, this selfbeing of my own." (*Note-books and Papers of G.M.H.*, p. 309.)

priest's sincerity, for with a sudden twist the poet diverts our attention from himself to what without some saving grace he would become. As in *Carrion Comfort,* having groaned "I can no more" he immediately cries "I can." Yet when he remonstrates with God, or attributes the bitter taste of himself to "God's most deep decree" ("baffling ban"), he seems to confess that the mortification he endures is very much more than the voluntary mortification of the patient ascetic. The complaint we hear seems to come from a personality which is prevented by ill-health, overwork, or inhibition from reaching its full stature.

I think it probable that Father Keating has underestimated the agonies of failure and frustration which creative genius, without any religious complications, can undergo, and has ignored the neuroses which may be caused when powerful instincts and impulses are repressed or imperfectly satisfied. But this qualification does not, to my mind, altogether invalidate his belief in the supernatural origin and purpose of Hopkins's desolations. Such experiences have been regarded by many serious thinkers as a phenomenon worthy of consideration in any complete study of man. Admit the possibility and it follows that God's purpose with the spirit, as with the body, might well work itself out in ways which are clearly explainable in the light of psychology and physiology.

To sum up, whether the cry of anguish in the later sonnets was due to mutilation or to probation, the gain to poetry, on the whole, seems to me to outweigh the loss. Had Hopkins been physically stronger, less devout, less sensitive, less neurotic, we should have had more poems but not the ones we now treasure. His output was restricted but at the same time intensified—allotropized from graphite to diamond (Dixon's "terrible crystal") in the stringency of his "bleak asceticism." Being one of those described by William James as needing "some austerity, wintry negativity, roughness and danger to be mixed in to produce the sense of an existence with character, texture and power," [26] his moral fastidiousness, in union with his ritualistic sensualism, had valuable repercussions in the rigours and splendours of his poetic style. On the other hand, the religious life probably fostered that unsophisticated, intuitive approach to nature, life and language which, as Vico says, is an essential condition of the true "original" poet. So far from "whirling dizzily in a spiritual vacuum," [27] the personality of Hopkins found in its delimited experience a medium of considerable resistance through which it could at times beat up to heights unattempted before in English poetry.

26 *Varieties of Religious Experience,* p. 298.
27 Mr. Middleton Murry: *Aspects of Literature.*

APPENDIX

The Windhover:

To Christ Our Lord

I caught this morning morning's minion, king-
    dom of daylight's dauphin, dapple-dawn-drawn Falcon,
        in his riding
    Of the rolling level underneath him steady air, and striding
High there, how he rung upon the rein of a wimpling wing
In his ecstasy! then off, off forth on swing,
    As a skate's heel sweeps smooth on a bow-bend: the hurl and
        gliding
    Rebuffed the big wind. My heart in hiding
Stirred for a bird,—the achieve of, the mastery of the thing!

Brute beauty and valor and act, oh, air, pride, plume, here
    Buckle! AND the fire that breaks from thee then, a billion
Times told lovelier, more dangerous, O my chevalier!

    No wonder of it: shéer plód makes plow down sillion
Shine, and blue-bleak embers, ah my dear,
    Fall, gall themselves, and gash gold-vermilion.

THE LATER POETRY OF W. B. YEATS

(1940)

R. P. Blackmur

The later poetry of William Butler Yeats is certainly great enough in its kind, and varied enough within its kind, to warrant a special approach, deliberately not the only approach, and deliberately not a complete approach. A body of great poetry will awaken and exemplify different interests on different occasions, or even on the same occasions, as we may see in the contrasting and often contesting literatures about Dante and Shakespeare: even a relation to the poetry is not common to them all. I propose here to examine Yeats's later poetry with a special regard to his own approach to the making of it; and to explore a little what I conceive to be the dominant mode of his insight, the relations between it and the printed poems, and—a different thing—the relations between it and the readers of his poems.

The major facts I hope to illustrate are these: that Yeats has, if you accept his mode, a consistent extraordinary grasp of the reality of emotion, character, and aspiration; and that his chief resort and weapon for the grasping of that reality is magic; and that if we would make use of that reality for ourselves we must also make some use of the magic that inspirits it. What is important is that the nexus of reality and magic is not by paradox or sleight of hand, but is logical and represents, for Yeats in his poetry, a full use of intelligence. Magic performs for Yeats the same fructifying function that Christianity does for Eliot, or that ironic fatalism did for Thomas Hardy; it makes a connection between the poem and its subject matter and provides an adequate mechanics of meaning and value. If it happens that we discard more of Hardy than we do of Yeats and more of Yeats than we do of Eliot, it is not because Christianity provides better machinery for the movement of poetry than fatalism or magic, but simply because Eliot is a more cautious craftsman. Besides, Eliot's poetry has not even comparatively worn long enough to show what parts are permanent and what merely temporary. The point here is that fatalism, Christianity, and magic are none of them disciplines to which many minds can consciously appeal today, as Hardy, Eliot, and Yeats do, for emotional strength and moral authority. The supernatural is simply not part of our mental furniture, and when we meet it in our reading we say: Here is débris to be swept away. But if we sweep it away without first making sure what it is, we are likely to lose the poetry as well as the débris. It is the very purpose of a supernaturally derived discipline, as used in poetry, to set the substance of natural life apart, to give it a form, a meaning, and a value which cannot be evaded. What is excessive and unwarranted in the discipline we indeed ought to dismiss; but that can be determined only when what is integrating and illuminating is known first. The discipline will in the end turn out to have had only a secondary importance for the reader; but its effect will remain active even when he no longer considers it. That is because for the poet the discipline, far from seeming secondary, had an extraordinary structural, seminal, and substantial importance to the degree that without it he could hardly have written at all.

Poetry does not flow from thin air but requires always either a literal faith, an imaginative faith, or, as in Shakespeare, a mind full of many provisional faiths. The life we all live is not alone enough of a subject for the serious artist; it must be life with a leaning, life with a tendency to shape itself only in certain forms, to afford its most lucid revelations only in certain lights. If our final interest, either as poets or as readers, is in the reality declared when the forms have been removed and the lights taken away, yet we can never come to the reality at all without the first advantage of the form and lights. Without them we should *see* nothing but only glimpse something unstable. We glimpse the fleeting but do not see what it is that fleets.

So it was with Yeats; his early poems are fleeting, some of them beautiful and some that sicken, as you read them, to their own extinction. But as he acquired for himself a discipline, however unacceptable to the bulk of his readers, his poetry obtained an access to reality. So it is with most of our serious poets. It is almost the mark of the poet of genuine merit in our time—the poet who writes serious works with an intellectual aspect which are nonetheless poetry—that he performs his work in the light of an insight, a group of ideas, and a faith, with the discipline that flows from them, which taken together form a view of life most readers cannot share, and which, furthermore, most readers feel as repugnant, or sterile, or simply inconsequential.

All this is to say generally—and we shall say it particularly for Yeats later—that our culture is incomplete with regard to poetry; and the poet has to provide for himself in that quarter where authority and value are derived. It may be that no poet ever found a culture complete for his purpose; it was a welcome and arduous part of his business to make it so. Dante, we may say, completed for poetry the Christian culture of his time, which was itself the completion of centuries. But there was at hand for Dante, and as a rule in the great ages of poetry, a fundamental agreement or convention between the poet and his audience about the validity of the view of life of which the poet deepened the reality and spread the scope. There is no such agreement today. We find poets either using the small conventions of the individual life as if they were great conventions, or attempting to resurrect some great convention of the past, or, finally, attempting to discover the great convention that must lie, willy-nilly, hidden in the life about them. This is a labor, whichever form it takes, which leads as often to subterfuge, substitution, confusion, and failure, as to success; and it puts the abnormal burden upon the reader of determining what the beliefs of the poet are and how much to credit them before he can satisfy himself of the reality which those beliefs envisage. The alternative is to put poetry at a discount—which is what has happened.

This the poet cannot do who is aware of the possibilities of his trade: the possibilities of arresting, enacting, and committing to the language through his poems the expressed value of the life otherwise only lived or evaded. The poet so aware knows, in the phrasing of that prose-addict Henry James, both the sacred rage of writing and the muffled majesty of authorship; and knows, as Eliot knows, that once to have been visited by the muses is ever afterwards to be haunted. These are qualities that once apprehended may not be discounted without complete surrender, when the poet is no more than a haunt haunted. Yeats has never put his poetry at a discount. But he has made it easy for his readers to do so—as Eliot has in his way—because the price he has paid for it, the expense he has himself been to in getting it on paper, have been a price most readers simply do not know how to pay and an expense, in time and labor and willingness to understand, beyond any initial notion of adequate reward.

The price is the price of a fundamental and deliberate surrender to magic as the ultimate mode for the apprehension of reality. The expense is the double expense of, on the one hand, implementing magic with a consistent symbolism, and on the other hand, the greatly multiplied expense of restoring, through the *craft* of poetry, both the reality and its symbols to that plane where alone their experience becomes actual—the plane of the quickened senses and the concrete emotions. That is to say, the poet (and, as always, the reader) has to combine, to fuse inextricably into something like an organic unity the constructed or derived symbolism of his special insight with the symbolism animating the language itself. It is, on the poet's plane, the labor of bringing the representative forms of knowledge home to the experience which stirred them: the labor of keeping in mind *what* our knowledge is of: the labor of craft. With the poetry of Yeats this labor is, as I say, doubly hard, because the forms of knowledge, being magical, do not fit naturally with the forms of knowledge that ordinarily preoccupy us. But it is possible, and I hope to show it, that the difficulty is, in a sense, superficial and may be overcome with familiarity, and that the mode of magic itself, once familiar, will even seem rational for the purposes of poetry—although it will not thereby seem inevitable. Judged by its works in the representation of emotional reality—and that is all that can be asked in our context—magic and its burden of symbols may be a major tool of the imagination. A tool has often a double function; it performs feats for which it was designed, and it is heuristic, it discovers and performs new feats which could not have been anticipated without it, which it indeed seems to instigate for itself and in the most unlikely quarters. It is with magic as a tool in its heuristic aspect—as an agent for discovery—that I wish here directly to be concerned.

One of the finest, because one of the most appropriate to our time and place, of all Yeats's poems, is his *The Second Coming*.

> Turning and turning in the widening gyre
> The falcon cannot hear the falconer;
> Things fall apart; the centre cannot hold;
> Mere anarchy is loosed upon the world,
> The blood-dimmed tide is loosed, and everywhere
> The ceremony of innocence is drowned;
> The best lack all conviction, while the worst
> Are full of passionate intensity.
>
> Surely some revelation is at hand;
> Surely the Second Coming is at hand.
> The Second Coming! Hardly are those words out
> When a vast image out of *Spiritus Mundi*
> Troubles my sight: somewhere in sands of the desert
> A shape with lion body and the head of a man,
> A gaze blank and pitiless as the sun,
> Is moving its slow thighs, while all about it
> Reel shadows of the indignant desert birds.
> The darkness drops again; but now I know
> That twenty centuries of stony sleep
> Were vexed to nightmare by a rocking cradle,
> And what rough beast, its hour come round at last,
> Slouches towards Bethlehem to be born?

There is about it, to any slowed reading, the immediate conviction of pertinent emotion; the lines are stirring, separately and in their smaller groups, and there is a sensible life in them that makes them seem to combine in the form of an emotion. We may say at once then, for what it is worth, that in writing his poem Yeats was able to choose words which to an appreciable extent were the right ones to reveal or represent the emotion which was its purpose. The words deliver the meaning which was put into them by the craft with which they were arranged, and that meaning is their own, not to be segregated or given another arrangement without diminution. Ultimately, something of this sort is all that can be said of this or any poem, and when it is said, the poem is known to be good in its own terms or bad because not in its own terms. But the reader seldom reaches an ultimate position about a poem; most poems fail, through craft or conception, to reach an ultimate or absolute position: parts of the craft remain machinery and parts of the conception remain in limbo. Or, as in this poem, close inspection will show something questionable about it. It is true that it can be read as it is, isolated from the rest of Yeats's work and isolated from the intellectual material which it expresses, and a good deal gotten out of it, too, merely by submitting to it. That is because the words are mainly common, both in their emotional and intellectual senses; and if we do not know precisely what the familiar words drag after them into the poem, still we know vaguely what the weight of it feels like; and that seems enough to make a poem at one level of response. Yet if an attempt is made at a more complete response, if we wish to discover the precise emotion which the words mount up to, we come into trouble and uncertainty at once. There is an air of explicitness to each of the separate fragments of the poem. Is it, in this line or that, serious? Has it a reference?—or is it a rhetorical effect, a result only of the persuasive overtones of words?—or is it a combination, a mixture of reference and rhetoric?

Possibly the troubled attention will fasten first upon the italicized phrase in the twelfth line: *Spiritus Mundi;* and the question is whether the general, the readily available senses of the words are adequate to supply the specific sense wanted by the poem. Put another way, can the poet's own arbitrary meaning be made, merely by discovering it, to participate in and enrich what the "normal" meanings of the words in their limiting context provide? The critic can only supply the facts; the poem will in the end provide its own answer. Here there are certain facts that may be extracted from Yeats's prose writings which suggest something of what the words symbolize for him. In one of the notes to the limited edition of *Michael Robartes and the Dancer,* Yeats observes that his mind, like another's, has been from time to time obsessed by images which had no discoverable origin in his waking experience. Speculating as to their origin, he came to deny both the conscious and the unconscious memory as their probable seat, and finally invented a doctrine which traced the images to sources of supernatural character. I quote only that sentence which is relevant to the phrase in question "Those [images] that come in sleep are (1) from the state immediately preceding our birth; (2) from the *Spiritus Mundi*—that is to say, from a general storehouse of images which have ceased to be a property of any personality or spirit." It apparently follows, for Yeats, that images so derived have both an absolute meaning of their own and an operative force in determining meaning and predicting events in this world. In another place (the Introduction to *The Resurrection* in *Wheels and Butterflies*) he describes the image used in this poem, which he had seen many times, "always at my left side just out of the range of sight, a brazen winged beast that I associated with laughing, ecstatic destruction." Ecstasy, it should be added, comes for Yeats just before death, and at death comes the moment of revelation, when the soul is shown its kindred dead and it is possible to see the future.

Here we come directly upon that central part of Yeats' magical beliefs which it is one purpose of this poem emotionally to represent: the belief in what is called variously *Magnus Annus,* The Great Year, The Platonic Year, and sometimes in a slightly different symbolism, The Great Wheel. This belief, with respect to the history of epochs, is associated with the precession of the equinoxes, which bring, roughly every two thousand years, a Great Year of death and rebirth, and this belief, with respect to individuals, seems to be associated with the phases of the moon; although individuals may be influenced by the equinoxes and there may be a lunar interpretation of history. These beliefs have a scaffold of geometrical figures, gyres, cones, circles, etc., by the application of which exact interpretation is secured. Thus it is possible to predict, both in biography and history, and in time, both forwards and backwards the character, climax, collapse, and rebirth in antithetical form of human types and cultures. There is a subordinate but helpful belief that signs, warnings, even direct messages, are always given, from *Spiritus Mundi* or elsewhere, which the poet and the philosopher have only to see and hear. As it happens, the Christian era, being nearly two thousand years old, is due for extinction and replacement, in short for the Second Coming, which this poem heralds. In his note to its first publication (in *Michael Robartes and the Dancer*) Yeats expresses his belief as follows:

> At the present moment the life gyre is sweeping outward, unlike that before the birth of Christ which was narrowing, and has almost reached its greatest expansion. The revelation which approaches will however take its character from the contrary movement of the interior gyre. All our scientific, democratic, fact-accumulating, heterogeneous civilisation belongs to the outward gyre and prepares not the continuance of itself but the revelation as in a lightning flash, though in a flash that will not strike only in one place, and will for a time be constantly repeated, of the civilisation that must slowly take its place.

So much for a major gloss upon the poem. Yeats combined, in the best verse he could manage, the beliefs which obsessed him with the image which he took to be a specific illustration of the beliefs. Minor and buttressing glosses are possible for many of the single words and phrases in the poem, some flowing from private doctrine and some from Yeats's direct sense of the world about him, and some from both at once. For example: The "ceremony of innocence" represents for Yeats one of the qualities that made life valuable under the dying aristocratic social tradition; and the meaning of the phrase in the poem requires no magic for completion but only a reading of other poems. The "falcon and the falconer" in the second line has, besides its obvious symbolism, a doctrinal reference. A falcon is a hawk, and a hawk is symbolic of the active or intellectual mind; the falconer is perhaps the soul itself or its uniting principle. There is also the apposition which Yeats has made several times that "Wisdom is a butterfly/ And not a gloomy bird of prey." Whether the special symbolism has actually been incorporated in the poem, and in which form, or whether it is private débris merely, will take a generation of readers to decide. In the meantime it must be taken provisionally for whatever its ambiguity may seem to be worth. Literature is full of falcons, some that fly and some that lack immediacy and sit, archaic, on the poet's wrist; and it is not always illuminating to determine which is which. But when we come on such lines as

> The best lack all conviction, while the worst
> Are full of passionate intensity,

we stop short, first to realize the aptness of the statement to every plane of life in the world about us, and then to connect them with the remote body of the poem they illuminate. There is a dilemma of which the branches grow from one trunk but which cannot be solved; for these lines have, not two meanings, but two sources for the same meaning. There is the meaning that comes from the summary observation that this is how men are—and especially men of power—in the world we live in; it is knowledge that comes from knowledge of the "fury and the mire in human veins"; a meaning the contemplation of which has lately (April, 1934) led Yeats to offer himself to any government or party that, using force and marching men, will "promise not this or that measure but a discipline, a way of life." And there is in effect the same meaning, at least at the time the poem was written, which comes from a different source and should have, one would think, very different consequences in prospective party loyalties. Here the meaning has its source in the doctrines of the Great Year and the Phases of the Moon; whereby, to cut exegesis short, it is predicted as necessary that, at the time we have reached, the best minds, being subjective, should have lost all faith though desiring it, and the worst minds, being so nearly objective, have no need of faith and may be full of "passionate intensity" without the control of any faith or wisdom. Thus we have on the one side the mirror of observation and on the other side an imperative, magically derived, which comes to the conclusion of form in identical words.

The question is, to repeat, whether the fact of this double control and source of meaning at a critical point defeats or strengthens the unity of the poem; and it is a question which forms itself again and again in the later poems, sometimes obviously but more often only by suggestion. If we take another poem on the same theme, written some years earlier, and before his wife's mediumship gave him the detail of his philosophy, we will find the question no easier to answer in its suggested than in its conspicuous form. There is an element in the poem called *The Magi* which we can feel the weight of but cannot altogether name, and of which we can only guess at the efficacy.

> Now as at all times I can see in the mind's eye,
> In their stiff, painted clothes, the pale unsatisfied ones
> Appear and disappear in the blue depths of the sky
> With all their ancient faces like rain-beaten stones,
> And all their helms of silver hovering side by side,
> And all their eyes still fixed, hoping to find once more,
> Being by Calvary's turbulence unsatisfied,
> The uncontrollable mystery on the bestial floor.

I mean the element which, were Yeats a Christian, we could accept as a species of Christian blasphemy or advanced heresy, but which since he is not a Christian we find it hard to accept at all: the element of emotional conviction springing from intellectual matters without rational source or structure. We ought to be able, for the poem's sake, to accept the conviction as an emotional possibility, much as we accept *Lear* or Dostoevsky's *Idiot* as valid, because projected from represented experience. But Yeats's experience is not represented consistently on any one plane. He constantly indicates a supernatural validity for his images of which the authority cannot be reached. If we come nearer to accepting *The Magi* than *The Second Coming* it is partly because the familiar Christian paradigm is more clearly used, and in the last two lines what Yeats constructs upon it is given a more immediate emotional form, and partly because, *per contra,* there is less demand made upon arbitrary intellectual belief. There is, too, the matter of scope; if we reduce the scope of *The Second Coming* to that of *The Magi* we shall find it much easier to accept; but we shall have lost much of the poem.

We ought now to have enough material to name the two radical defects of magic as a tool for poetry. One defect, which we have just been illustrating, is that it has no available edifice of reason reared upon it conventionally independent of its inspiration. There is little that the uninspired reader can naturally refer to for authority outside the poem, and if he does make a natural reference he is likely to turn out to be at least partly wrong. The poet is thus in the opposite predicament; he is under the constant necessity of erecting his beliefs into doctrines at the same time that he represents their emotional or dramatic equivalents. He is, in fact, in much the same position that Dante would have been had he had to construct his Christian doctrine while he was composing *The Divine Comedy:* an impossible labor, The Christian supernaturalism, the Christian magic (no less magical than that of Yeats), had the great advantage for Dante, and imaginatively for ourselves, of centuries of reason and criticism and elaboration: It was within reason a consistent whole; and its supernatural element had grown so consistent with experience as to seem supremely *natural*—as indeed it may again. Christianity has an objective form, whatever the mysteries at its heart and its termini, in which all the phenomena of human life may find place and meaning. Magic is none of these things for any large fraction of contemporary society. Magic has a tradition, but it is secret, not public. It has not only central and terminal mysteries but has also peripheral mysteries, which require not only the priest to celebrate but also the adept to manipulate. Magic has never been made "natural." The practical knowledge and power which its beliefs lead to can neither be generally shared nor overtly rationalized. It is in fact held to be dangerous to reveal openly the details of magical experience: they may be revealed, if at all, only in arbitrary symbols and equivocal statements. Thus we find Yeats, in his early and innocuous essay on magic, believing his life to have been imperiled for revealing too much. Again, the spirits or voices through whom magical knowledge is gained are often themselves equivocal and are sometimes deliberately confusing. Yeats was told to remember, "We will deceive you if we can," and on another occasion was forbidden to record anything that was said, only to be scolded later because he had failed to record every word. In short, it is of the essence of magical faith that the supernatural cannot be brought into the natural world except through symbol. The distinction between natural and supernatural is held to be substantial instead of verbal. Hence magic may neither be criticized nor institutionalized; nor can it ever reach a full expression of its own intention. This is perhaps the justification of Stephen Spender's remark that there is more magic in Eliot's *The Hollow Men* than in any poem of Yeats; because of Eliot's Christianity, his magic has a rational base as well as a supernatural source: it is the magic of an orthodox, authoritative faith. The dogmas of magic, we may say, are all heresies which cannot be expounded except each on its own authority as a fragmentary insight; and its unity can be only the momentary unity of association. Put another way, magic is in one respect in the state of Byzantine Christianity, when miracles were quotidian and the universal frame of experience, when life itself was held to be supernatural and reason was mainly a kind of willful sophistication.

Neither Yeats nor ourselves dwell in Byzantium. At a certain level, though not at all levels, we conceive life, and even its nonrational features, in rational terms. Certainly there is a rational bias and a rational structure in the poetry we mainly agree to hold great—though the content may be what it will; and it is the irrational bias and the confused structure that we are mainly concerned to disavow, to apologize or allow for. It was just to provide himself with the equivalent of a rational religious insight and a predictable rational structure for the rational imagination that in his book, *A Vision* (published, in 1925, in a limited edition only, and then withdrawn), he attempted to convert his magical experience into a systematic philosophy. "I wished," he writes in the Dedication to that work, "for a system of thought that would leave my imagination free to create as it chose and yet make all that it created, or could create, part of the one history, and that the soul's." That is, Yeats hoped for systematizing it to escape from the burden of confusion and abstraction which his magical experience had imposed upon him. "I can now," he declares in this same Dedication, "if I have the energy, find the simplicity I have sought in vain. I need no longer write poems like 'The Phases of the Moon' nor 'Ego Dominus Tuus,' nor spend barren years, as I have done three or four times, striving with abstractions that substitute themselves for the play that I had planned."

"Having inherited," as he says in one of his poems, "a vigorous mind," he could not help seeing, once he had got it all down, that his system was something to disgorge if he could. Its truth as experience would be all the stronger if its abstractions could be expunged. But it could not be disgorged; its thirty-five years of growth was an intimate part of his own growth, and its abstractions were all of a piece with his most objective experience. And perhaps we, as readers, can see that better from outside than Yeats could from within. I suspect that no amount of will could have rid him of his magical conception of the soul; it was by magic that he knew the soul; and the conception had been too closely associated with his profound sense of his race and personal ancestry. He has never been able to retract his system, only to take up different attitudes towards it. He has alternated between granting his speculations only the validity of poetic myth and planning to announce a new deity. In his vacillation—there is a poem by that title—the rational defect remains, and the reader must deal with it sometimes as an intrusion upon the poetry of indeterminate value and sometimes as itself the subject of dramatic reverie or lyric statement. At least once he tried to force the issue home, and in a section of *A Packet for Ezra Pound* called *Introduction to the Great Wheel* he meets the issue by transforming it, for the moment, into wholly poetic terms. Because it reveals a fundamental honesty and clarity of purpose in the midst of confusion and uncertainty the section is quoted entire.

> Some will ask if I believe all that this book contains, and I will not know how to answer. Does the word belief, as they will use it, belong to our age, can I think of the world as there and I here judging it? I will never think any thoughts but these, or some modification or extension of these; when I write prose or verse they must be somewhere present though it may not be in the words; they must affect my judgment of friends and events; but then there are many symbolisms and none exactly resembles mine. What Leopardi in Ezra Pound's translation calls that 'concord' wherein 'the arcane spirit of the whole mankind turns hardy pilot'—how much better it would be without that word 'hardy' which slackens speed and adds nothing—persuades me that he has best imagined reality who has best imagined justice.

The rational defect, then, remains; the thought is not always in the words; and we must do with it as we can. There is another defect of Yeats's magical system which is especially apparent to the reader but which may not be apparent at all to Yeats. Magic promises precisely matters which it cannot perform—at least in poetry. It promises, as in *The Second Coming,* exact prediction of events in the natural world; and it promises again and again, in different poems, exact revelations of the supernatural, and of this we have an example in what has to many seemed a great poem, *All Souls' Night,* which had its first publication as an epilogue to *A Vision.* Near the beginning of the poem we have the explicit declaration: "I have a marvelous thing to say"; and near the end another: "I have mummy truths to tell." "Mummy truths" is an admirable phrase, suggestive as it is of the truths in which the dead are wrapped, ancient truths as old as Egypt perhaps, whence mummies commonly come, and truths, too, that may be unwound. But there, with the suggestion, the truths stop short; there is, for the reader, no unwinding, no revelation of the dead. What Yeats actually does is to summon into the poem various of his dead friends as "characters"—and this is the greatness, and only this, of the poem: the summary, excited, even exalted presentation of character. Perhaps the rhetoric is the marvel and the evasion the truth. We get an impact as from behind, from the speed and weight of the words, and are left with an ominous or terrified frame of mind, the revelation still to come. The revelation, the magic, was in Yeats's mind; hence the exaltation in his language; but it was not and could not be given in the words of the poem.

It may be that for Yeats there was a similar exaltation and a similar self-deceit in certain other poems, but as the promise of revelation was not made, the reader feels no failure of fulfillment. Such poems as *Easter, 1916, In Memory of Major Robert Gregory,* and *Upon a Dying Lady* may have buried in them a conviction of invocation and revelation; but if so it is no concern of ours: we are concerned only, as the case may be, with the dramatic presentations of the Irish patriots and poets, Yeats's personal friends, and Aubrey Beardsley's dying sister, and with, in addition, for minor pleasure, the technical means—the spare and delicate language, the lucid images, and quickening rhymes —whereby the characters are presented as intensely felt. There is no problem in such poems but the problem of reaching, through a gradual access of intimacy, full appreciation; here the magic and everything else are in the words. It is the same, for bare emotion apart from character, in such poems as *A Deep-Sworn Vow,* where the words accumulate by the simplest means an intolerable excitement, where the words are, called as they may be from whatever source, in an ultimate sense their own meaning.

> Others because you did not keep
> That deep-sworn vow have been friends of mine;

Yet always when I look death in the face,
When I clamber to the heights of sleep,
Or when I grow excited with wine,
Suddenly I meet your face.

Possibly all poetry should be read as this poem is read, and no poetry greatly valued that cannot be so read. Such is one ideal towards which reading tends; but to apply it as a standard of judgment we should first have to assume for the poetic intelligence absolute autonomy and self-perfection for all its works. Actually, autonomy and self-perfection are relative and depend upon a series of agreements or conventions between the poet and his readers, which alter continually, as to what must be represented by the fundamental power of language (itself a relatively stable convention) and what, on the other hand, may be adequately represented by mere reference, sign, symbol, or blue print indication. Poetry is so little autonomous from the technical point of view that the greater part of a given work must be conceived as the manipulation of conventions that the reader will, or will not, take for granted; these being crowned, or animated, emotionally transformed, by what the poet actually represents, original or not, through his mastery of poetic language. Success is provisional, seldom complete and never permanently complete. The vitality or letter of a convention may perish although the form persists. *Romeo and Juliet* is less successful today than when produced because the conventions of honor, family authority, and blood-feud no longer animate and justify the action; and if the play survives it is partly because certain other conventions of human character do remain vital, but more because Shakespeare is the supreme master of representation through the reality of language alone. Similarly with Dante; with the cumulative disintegration, even for Catholics, of mediaeval Christianity as the ultimate convention of human life, the success of *The Divine Comedy* comes more and more to depend on the exhibition of character and the virtue of language alone—which may make it a greater, not a lesser poem. On the other hand, it often happens that a poet's ambition is such that, in order to get his work done at all, he must needs set up new conventions or radically modify old ones which fatally lack that benefit of form which can be conferred only by public recognition. The form which made his poems available was only gradually conferred upon the convention of evil in Baudelaire and, as we may see in translations with contrasting emphases, its limits are still subject to debate; in his case the more so because the life of his language depended more than usual on the viability of the convention.

Let us apply these notions, which ought so far to be commonplace, to the later work of Yeats, relating them especially to the predominant magical convention therein. When Yeats came of poetic age he found himself, as Blake had before him, and even Wordsworth, but to a worse extent, in a society whose conventions extended neither intellectual nor moral authority to poetry; he found himself in a rational but deliberately incomplete, because progressive, society. The *emotion* of thought, for poetry, was gone, along with the emotion of religion and the emotion of race—the three sources and the three aims of the great poetry of the past. Tyndall and Huxley are the villains, Yeats records in his *Autobiographies,* as Blake recorded Newton; there were other causes, but no matter, these names may serve as symbols. And the dominant aesthetics of the time were as rootless in the realm of poetic import and authority as the dominant conventions. Art for Art's sake was the cry, the Ivory Tower the retreat, and Walter Pater's luminous languor and weak Platonism the exposition. One could say anything but it would mean nothing. The poets and society both, for opposite reasons, expected the poet to produce either exotic and ornamental mysteries or lyrics of mood; the real world and its significance were reserved mainly to the newer sciences, though the novelists and the playwrights might poach if they could. For a time Yeats succumbed, as may be seen in his early work, even while he attempted to escape; and of his poetic generation he was the only one to survive and grow in stature. He came under the influence of the French Symbolists, who gave him the clue and the hint of an external structure but nothing much to put in it. He read, with a dictionary, Villiers de L'Isle-Adam's *Axel,* and so came to be included in Edmund Wilson's book of that name—although not, as Wilson himself shows, altogether correctly. For he began in the late 'nineties, as it were upon his own account, to quench his thirst for reality by creating authority and significance and reference in the three fields where they were lacking. He worked into his poetry the substance of Irish mythology and Irish politics and gave them a symbolism, and he developed his experiences with Theosophy and Rosicrucianism into a body of conventions adequate, for him, to animate the concrete poetry of the soul that he wished to write. He did not do these things separately; the mythology, the politics, and the magic are conceived, through the personalities that reflected them, with an increasing unity of apprehension. Thus more than any poet of our time he has restored to poetry the actual emotions of race and religion and what we call abstract thought. Whether we follow him in any particular or not, the general poetic energy which he liberated is ours to use if we can. If the edifice that he constructed seems personal, it is because he had largely to build it for himself, and that makes it difficult to understand in detail except in reference to the peculiar unity which comes from their mere association in his life and work. Some of the mythology and much of the politics, being dramatized and turned into emotion, are part of our common possessions. But where the emphasis has been magical, whether successfully or not, the poems have been misunderstood, ignored, and the actual emotion in them which is relevant to us all decried and underestimated, merely because the magical mode of thinking is foreign to our own and when known at all is largely associated with quackery and fraud.

We do not make that mistake—which is the mistake of unwillingness—with Dante or the later Eliot, because, although the substance of their modes of thinking is equally foreign and magical, it has the advantage of a rational superstructure that persists and which we can convert to our own modes if we will. Yeats lacks, as we have said, the historical advantage and with it much else; and the conclusion cannot be avoided that this lack prevents his poetry from reaching the first magnitude. But there are two remedies we may apply, which will make up, not for the defect of magnitude, but for the defect of structure. We can read the magical philosophy in his verse *as if* it were converted into the contemporary psychology with which its doctrines have so much in common. We find little difficulty in seeing Freud's preconscious as a fertile myth and none at all in the general myth of extroverted and introverted personality; and these may be compared with, respectively, Yeats's myth of *Spiritus Mundi* and the Phases of the Moon: the intention and the scope of the meaning are identical. So much for a secular conversion. The other readily available remedy is this: to accept Yeats's magic literally as a machinery of meaning, to search out the prose parallels and reconstruct the symbols he uses on their own terms in order to come on the emotional reality, if it is there, actually in the poems—when the machinery may be dispensed with. This method has the prime advantage over secular conversion of keeping judgment in poetic terms, with the corresponding disadvantage that it requires more time and patience, more "willing suspension of disbelief," and a stiffer intellectual exercise all around. But exegesis is to be preferred to conversion on still another ground, which may seem repellent: that magic, in the sense that we all experience it, is nearer the represented emotions that concern us in poetry than psychology, as a generalized science, can ever be. We are all, without conscience, magicians in the dark.

But even the poems of darkness are read in the light. I cannot, of course, make a sure prognosis; because in applying either remedy the reader is, really, doctoring himself as much as Yeats. Only this much is sure: that the reader will come to see the substantial unity of Yeats's work, that it is the same mind stirring behind the poems on Crazy Jane and the Bishop, on Cuchulain, on Swift, the political poems, the biographical and the doctrinal—a mind that sees the fury and the mire and the passion of the dawn as contrary aspects of the real world. It is to be expected that many poems will fail in part and some entirely, and if the chief number, magic will not be the only cause of failure. The source of a vision puts limits upon its expression which the poet cannot well help overpassing. "The limitation of his view," Yeats wrote of Blake, "was from the very intensity of his vision; he was a too-literal realist of imagination, as others are of nature"; and the remark applies to himself. But there will be enough left to make the labor of culling worth all its patience and time. Before concluding, I propose to spur the reader, or inadvertently dismay him, by presenting briefly a few examples of the sort of reconstructive labor he will have to do and the sort of imaginative assent he may have to attempt in order to enter or dismiss the body of the poems.

As this is a mere essay in emphasis, let us bear the emphasis in, by repeating, on different poems, the sort of commentary laid out above on *The Second Coming* and *The Magi,* using this time *Byzantium* and *Sailing to Byzantium.*[1] Byzantium is for Yeats, so to speak, the heaven of man's mind; there the mind or soul dwells in eternal or miraculous form; there all things are possible because all things are known to the soul. Byzantium has both a historical and an ideal form, and the historical is the exemplar, the dramatic witness, of the ideal. Byzantium represents both a dated epoch and a recurrent state of insight, when nature is magical, that is, at the beck of mind, and magic is natural—a practical rather than a theoretic art. If with these notions in mind we compare the two poems named we see that the first, called simply *Byzantium,* is like certain cantos in the *Paradiso* the poetry of an intense and condensed declaration of doctrine; not emotion put into doctrine from outside, but doctrine presented as emotion. I quote the second stanza.

> Before me floats an image, man or shade,
> Shade more than man, more image than a shade;
> For Hades' bobbin bound in mummy-cloth
> May unwind the winding path;
> A mouth that has no moisture and no breath
> Breathless mouths may summon;
> I hail the superhuman;
> I call it death-in-life and life-in-death.

The second poem, *Sailing to Byzantium,* rests upon the doctrine but is not a declaration of it. It is, rather, the doctrine in action, the doctrine actualized in a personal emotion resembling that of specific prayer. This is the emotion of the flesh where the other was the emotion of the bones. The distinction should not be too sharply drawn. It is not the bones of doctrine but the emotion of it that we should be aware of in reading the more dramatic poem: and the nearer they come to seeming two reflections of the same thing the better both poems will be. What must be avoided is a return to the poem of doctrine with a wrong estimation of its value gained by confusion of the two poems. Both poems are serious in their own kind, and the reality of each must be finally in its own words whatever clues the one supplies to the other. I quote the third stanza.

[1] *Sailing to Byzantium* is analyzed by Elder Olson in the appendix to his essay "An Outline of Poetic Theory." [*Editor's note.*]

> O sages standing in God's holy fire
> As in the gold mosaic of a wall,
> Come from the holy fire, perne in a gyre,
> And be the singing-masters of my soul.
> Consume my heart away; sick with desire
> And fastened to a dying animal
> It knows not what it is; and gather me
> Into the artifice of eternity.

We must not, for example, accept "perne in a gyre" in this poem merely because it is part of the doctrine upon which the poem rests. Its magical reference may be too explicit for the poem to digest. It may be merely part of the poem's intellectual machinery, something that will *become* a dead commonplace once its peculiarity has worn out. Its meaning, that is, may turn out not to participate in the emotion of the poem: which is an emotion of aspiration. Similarly a note of aspiration would have been injurious to the stanza quoted from *Byzantium* above.

Looking at other poems as examples, the whole problem of exegesis may be put another way; which consists in joining two facts and observing their product. There is the fact that again and again in Yeats's prose, both in that which accompanies the poems and that which is independent of them, poems and fragments of poems are introduced at strategic points, now to finish off or clinch an argument by giving it as proved, and again merely to balance argument with witness from another plane. *A Vision* is punctuated by five poems. And there is the complementary fact that, when one has read the various autobiographies, introductions, and doctrinal notes and essays, one continually finds echoes, phrases, and developments from the prose in the poems. We have, as Wallace Stevens says, the prose that wears the poem's guise at last; and we have, too, the poems turning backwards, reilluminating or justifying the prose from the material of which they sprang. We have, to import the dichotomy which T. S. Eliot made for his own work, the prose writings discovering and buttressing the ideal, and we have the poems which express as much as can be actualized—given as concrete emotion—of what the prose discovered or envisaged. The dichotomy is not so sharp in Yeats as in Eliot. Yeats cannot, such is the unity of his apprehension, divide his interests. There is one mind employing two approaches in the labor of representation. The prose approach lets in much that the poetic approach excludes; it lets in the questionable, the uncertain, the hypothetic, and sometimes the incredible. The poetic approach, using the same material, retains, when it is successful, only what is manifest, the emotion that can be made actual in a form of words that need only to be understood, not argued. If props of argument and vestiges of idealization remain, they must be felt as qualifying, not arguing, the emotion. It should only be remembered and repeated that the poet invariably requires more machinery to secure *his* effects—the machinery of his whole life and thought—than the reader requires to secure what he takes as the *poem's* effects; and that, as readers differ, the poet cannot calculate what is necessary to the poem and what is not. There is always the débris to be cut away.

In such a fine poem as *A Prayer for My Son,* for example, Yeats cut away most of the débris himself, and it is perhaps an injury to judgment provisionally to restore it. Yet to this reader at least the poem seems to richen when it is known from what special circumstance the poem was freed. As it stands we can accept the symbols which it conspicuously contains—the strong ghost, the devilish things, and the holy writings—as drawn from the general stock of literary conventions available to express the evil predicament in which children and all innocent beings obviously find themselves. Taken so, it is a poem of natural piety. But for Yeats the conventions were not merely literary but were practical expressions of the actual terms of the predicament, and his poem is a prayer of dread and supernatural piety. The experience which led to the poem is recounted in *A Packet for Ezra Pound.* When his son was still an infant Yeats was told through the mediumship of his wife that the Frustrators or evil spirits would henceforth "attack my health and that of my children, and one afternoon, knowing from the smell of burnt feathers that one of my children would be ill within three hours, I felt before I could recover self-control the mediaeval helpless horror of witchcraft." The child *was* ill. It is from this experience that the poem seems to have sprung, and the poem preserves all that was actual behind the private magical conventions Yeats used for himself. The point is that the reader has a richer poem if he can substitute the manipulative force of Yeats's specific conventions for the general literary conventions. Belief or imaginative assent is no more difficult for either set. It is the emotion that counts.

That is one extreme to which the poems run—the extreme convention of personal thought. Another extreme is that exemplified in *A Prayer for My Daughter,* where the animating conventions *are* literary and the piety *is* natural, and in the consideration of which it would be misleading to introduce the magical convention as more than a foil. As a foil it is nevertheless present; his magical philosophy, all the struggle and warfare of the intellect, is precisely what Yeats in this poem *puts out of mind,* in order to imagine his daughter living in innocence and beauty, custom and ceremony.

A third extreme is that found in the sonnet *Leda and the Swan,* where there is an extraordinary sensual immediacy—the words meet and move like speaking lips—and a profound combination of the generally available or literary symbol and the hidden, magical symbol of the intellectual, philosophical, impersonal order. Certain longer poems and groups of poems, especially the series called *A Woman*

Young and Old, exhibit the extreme of combination as well or better; but I want the text on the page.

A sudden blow: the great wings beating still
Above the staggering girl, her thighs caressed
By the dark webs, her nape caught in his bill,
He holds her helpless breast upon his breast.

How can those terrified vague fingers push
The feathered glory from her loosening thighs?
And how can body, laid in that white rush,
But feel the strange heart beating where it lies?

A shudder in the loins engenders there
The broken wall, the burning roof and tower
And Agamemnon dead.

Being so caught up,
So mastered by the brute blood of the air,
Did she put on his knowledge with his power
Before the indifferent beak could let her drop?

It should be observed that in recent years new images, some from the life of Swift, and some from the Greek mythology, have been spreading through Yeats's poems; and of Greek images he has used especially those of Œdipus and Leda, of Homer and Sophocles. But they are not used as we think the Greeks used them, nor as mere drama, but deliberately, after the magical tradition, both to represent and hide the myths Yeats has come on in his own mind. Thus *Leda and the Swan* can be read on at least three distinct levels of significance, none of which interferes with the others: the levels of dramatic fiction, of condensed insight into Greek mythology, and a third level of fiction and insight combined, as we said, to represent and hide a magical insight. This third level is our present concern. At this level the poem presents in interfusion among the normal terms of the poem two of Yeats's fundamental magical doctrines in emotional form. The doctrines are put by Yeats in the following form in his essay on magic: "That the borders of our mind are ever shifting, and that many minds can flow into one another, as it were, and create or reveal a single mind, a single energy. . . . That this great mind can be evoked by symbols." Copulation is the obvious nexus for spiritual as well as physical seed. There is also present I think some sense of Yeats's doctrine of Annunciation and the Great Year, the Annunciation, in this case, that produced Greek culture. It is a neat question for the reader, so far as this poem is concerned, whether the poetic emotion springs from the doctrine and seizes the myth for a safe home and hiding, or whether the doctrine is correlative to the emotion of the myth. In neither case does the magic matter as such; it has become poetry, and of extreme excellence in its order. To repeat the interrogatory formula with which we began the commentary on *The Second Coming,* is the magical material in these poems incorporated in them by something like organic reference or is its presence merely rhetorical? The reader will answer one way or the other, as, to his rational imagination, to all the imaginative understanding he can bring to bear, it either seems to clutter the emotion and deaden the reality, or seems rather, as I believe, to heighten the emotional reality and thereby extend its reference to what we call the real world. Once the decision is made, the magic no longer exists; we have the poetry.

Other approaches to Yeats's poetry would have produced different emphases, and this approach, which has emphasized little but the magical structure of Yeats's poetic emotions, and has made that emphasis with an ulterior purpose: to show that magic may be a feature of a rational imagination. This approach should be combined with others, or should have others combined with it, for perspective and reduction. No feature of a body of poetry can be as important as it seems in discussion. Above all, then, this approach through the magical emphasis should be combined with the approach of plain reading—which is long reading and hard reading—plain reading of the words, that they may sink in and do as much of their own work as they can. One more thing: When we call man a rational animal we mean that reason is his great myth. Reason is plastic and takes to any form provided. The rational imagination in poetry, as elsewhere, can absorb magic as a provisional method of evocative and heuristic thinking, but it cannot be based upon it. In poetry, and largely elsewhere, imagination is based upon the reality of words and the emotion of their joining. Yeats's magic, then, like every other feature of his experience, is rational as it reaches words; otherwise it is his privation, and ours, because it was the rational defect of our society that drove him to it.

TRADITION AND THE INDIVIDUAL TALENT

(1919)

T. S. Eliot

In English writing we seldom speak of tradition, though we occasionally apply its name in deploring its absence. We cannot refer to "the tradition" or to "a tradition"; at most, we employ the adjective in saying that the poetry of So-and-so is "traditional" or even "too traditional." Seldom, perhaps, does the word appear except in a phrase of censure. If otherwise, it is vaguely approbative, with the implication, as to the work approved, of some pleasing archæological reconstruction. You can hardly make the word agreeable to English ears without this comfortable reference to the reassuring science of archæology.

Certainly the word is not likely to appear in our appreciations of living or dead writers. Every nation, every race, has not only its own creative, but its own critical turn of mind; and is even more oblivious of the shortcomings and limitations of its critical habits than of those of its creative genius. We know, or think we know, from the enormous mass of critical writing that has appeared in the French language the critical method or habit of the French; we only conclude (we are such unconscious people) that the French are "more critical" than we, and sometimes even plume ourselves a little with the fact, as if the French were the less spontaneous. Perhaps they are; but we might remind ourselves that criticism is as inevitable as breathing, and that we should be none the worse for articulating what passes in our minds when we read a book and feel an emotion about it, for criticizing our own minds in their work of criticism. One of the facts that might come to light in this process is our tendency to insist, when we praise a poet, upon those aspects of his work in which he least resembles anyone else. In these aspects or parts of his work we pretend to find what is individual, what is the peculiar essence of the man. We dwell with satisfaction upon the poet's difference from his predecessors, especially his immediate predecessors; we endeavour to find something that can be isolated in order to be enjoyed. Whereas if we approach a poet without this prejudice we shall often find that not only the best, but the most individual parts of his work may be those in which the dead poets, his ancestors, assert their immortality most vigorously. And I do not mean the impressionable period of adolescence, but the period of full maturity.

Yet if the only form of tradition, of handing down, consisted in following the ways of the immediate generation before us in a blind or timid adherence to its successes, "tradition" should positively be discouraged. We have seen many such simple currents soon lost in the sand; and novelty is better than repetition. Tradition is a matter of much wider significance. It cannot be inherited, and if you want it you must obtain it by great labour. It involves, in the first place, the historical sense, which we may call nearly indispensable to anyone who would continue to be a poet beyond his twenty-fifth year; and the historical sense involves a perception, not only of the pastness of the past, but of its presence; the historical sense compels a man to write not merely with his own generation in his bones, but with a feeling that the whole of the literature of Europe from Homer and within it the whole of the literature of his own country has a simultaneous existence and composes a simultaneous order. This historical sense, which is a sense of the timeless as well as of the temporal and of the timeless and of the temporal together, is what makes a writer traditional. And it is at the same time what makes a writer most acutely conscious of his place in time, of his contemporaneity.

No poet, no artist of any art, has his complete meaning alone. His significance, his appreciation is the appreciation of his relation to the dead poets and artists. You cannot value him alone; you must set him, for contrast and comparison, among the dead. I mean this as a principle of æsthetic, not merely historical, criticism. The necessity that he shall conform, that he shall cohere, is not one-sided; what happens when a new work of art is created is something that happens simultaneously to all the works of art which preceded it. The existing monuments form an ideal order among themselves, which is modified by the introduction of the new (the really new) work of art among them. The existing order is complete before the new work arrives; for order to persist after the supervention of novelty, the *whole* existing order must be, if ever so slightly, altered; and so the relations, proportions, values of each work of art toward the whole are readjusted; and this is conformity between the old and the new. Whoever has approved this idea of order, of the form of European, of English literature, will not find it preposterous that the past should be altered by the present as much as the present is directed by the past. And the poet who is aware of this will be aware of great difficulties and responsibilities.

In a peculiar sense he will be aware also that he must inevitably be judged by the standards of the past. I say judged, not amputated, by them; not judged to be as good as, or worse or better than, the dead; and certainly not judged by the canons of dead critics. It is a judgment, a comparison, in which two things are measured by each other. To conform merely would be for the new work not really to conform at all; it would not be new, and would therefore not be a work of art. And we do not quite say that the new is more valuable because it fits in; but its fitting in is a test of its value—a test, it is true, which can only be slowly and cautiously applied, for we are none of us infallible judges of conformity. We say: it appears to conform, and is perhaps individual, or it appears individual, and may conform; but we are hardly likely to find that it is one and not the other.

To proceed to a more intelligible exposition of the relation of the poet to the past: he can neither take the past as a lump, an indiscriminate bolus, nor can he form himself wholly on one or two private admirations, nor can he form himself wholly upon one preferred period. The first course is inadmissible, the second is an important experience of youth, and the third is a pleasant and highly desirable supplement. The poet must be very conscious of the main current, which does not at all flow invariably through the most distinguished reputations. He must be quite aware of the obvious fact that art never improves, but that the material of art is never quite the same. He must be aware that the mind of Europe—the mind of his own country—a mind which he learns in time to be much more important than his own private mind—is a mind which changes, and that this change is a development which abandons nothing *en route,* which does not superannuate either Shakespeare, or Homer, or the rock drawing of the Magdalenian draughtsmen. That this development, refinement perhaps, complication certainly, is not, from the point of view of the artist, any improvement. Perhaps not even an improvement from the point of view of the psychologists or not to the extent which we imagine, perhaps only in the end based upon a complication in economics and machinery. But the difference between the present and the past is that the conscious present is an awareness of the past in a way and to an extent which the past's awareness of itself cannot show.

Some one said: "The dead writers are remote from us because we *know* so much more than they did." Precisely, and they are that which we know.

I am alive to a usual objection to what is clearly part of my programme for the *métier* of poetry. The objection is that the doctrine requires a ridiculous amount of erudition (pedantry), a claim which can be rejected by appeal to the lives of poets in any pantheon. It will even be affirmed that much learning deadens or perverts poetic sensibility. While, however, we persist in believing that a poet ought to know as much as will not encroach upon his necessary receptivity and necessary laziness, it is not desirable to confine knowledge to whatever can be put into a useful shape for examinations, drawing-rooms, or the still more pretentious modes of publicity. Some can absorb knowledge, the more tardy must sweat for it. Shakespeare acquired more essential history from Plutarch than most men could from the whole British Museum. What is to be insisted upon is that the poet must develop or procure the consciousness of the past and that he should continue to develop this consciousness throughout his career.

What happens is a continual surrender of himself as he is at the moment to something which is more valuable. The progress of an artist is a continual self-sacrifice, a continual extinction of personality.

There remains to define this process of depersonalization and its relation to the sense of tradition. It is in this depersonalization that art may be said to approach the condition of science. I shall, therefore, invite you to consider, as a suggestive analogy, the action which takes place when a bit of finely filiated platinum is introduced into a chamber containing oxygen and sulphur dioxide.

II

Honest criticism and sensitive appreciation are directed not upon the poet but upon the poetry. If we attend to the confused cries of the newspaper critics and the *susurrus* of popular repetition that follows, we shall hear the names of poets in great numbers; if we seek not Blue-book knowledge but the enjoyment of poetry, and ask for a poem, we shall seldom find it. In the last article I tried to point out the importance of the relation of the poem to other poems by other authors, and suggested the conception of poetry as a living whole of all the poetry that has ever been written. The other aspect of this Impersonal theory of poetry is the relation of the poem to its author. And I hinted, by an analogy, that the mind of the mature poet differs from that of the immature one not precisely in any valuation of "personality," not by being necessarily more interesting, or having "more to say," but rather by being a more finely perfected medium in which special, or very varied, feelings are at liberty to enter into new combinations.

The analogy was that of the catalyst. When the two gases previously mentioned are mixed in the presence of a filament of platinum, they form sulphurous acid. This combination takes place only if the platinum is present; nevertheless the newly formed acid contains no trace of platinum, and the platinum itself is apparently unaffected; has remained inert, neutral, and unchanged. The mind of the poet is the shred of platinum. It may partly or exclusively operate upon the experience of the man himself; but, the more perfect the artist, the more completely separate in him will be the man who suffers and the mind which creates; the more perfectly will the mind digest and transmute the passions which are its material.

The experience, you will notice, the elements which enter the presence of the transforming catalyst, are of two kinds: emotions and feelings. The effect of a work of art upon the person who enjoys it is an experience different in kind from any experience not of art. It may be formed out of one emotion, or may be a combination of several; and various feelings, inhering for the writer in particular words or phrases or images, may be added to compose the final result. Or great poetry may be made without the direct use of any emotion whatever: composed out of feelings solely. Canto XV of the *Inferno* (Brunetto Latini) is a working up of the emotion evident in the situation; but the effect, though single as that of any work of art, is obtained by considerable complexity of detail. The last quatrain gives an image, a feeling attaching to an image, which "came," which did not develop simply out of what precedes, but which was probably in suspension in the poet's mind until the proper combination arrived for it to add itself to. The poet's mind is in fact a receptacle for seizing and storing up numberless feelings, phrases, images, which remain there until all the particles which can unite to form a new compound are present together.

If you compare several representative passages of the greatest poetry you see how great is the variety of types of combination, and also how completely any semi-ethical criterion of "sublimity" misses the mark. For it is not the "greatness," the intensity, of the emotions, the components, but the intensity of the artistic process, the pressure, so to speak, under which the fusion takes place, that counts. The episode of Paolo and Francesca employs a definite emotion, but the intensity of the poetry is something quite different from whatever intensity in the supposed experience it may give the impression of. It is no more intense, furthermore, than Canto XXVI, the voyage of Ulysses, which has not the direct dependence upon an emotion. Great variety is possible in the process of transmution of emotion: the murder of Agamemnon, or the agony of Othello, gives an artistic effect apparently closer to a possible original than the scenes from Dante. In the *Agamemnon*, the artistic emotion approximates to the emotion of an actual spectator; in *Othello* to the emotion of the protagonist himself. But the difference between art and the event is always absolute; the combination which is the murder of Agamemnon is probably as complex as that which is the voyage of Ulysses. In either case there has been a fusion of elements. The ode of Keats contains a number of feelings which have nothing particular to do with the nightingale, but which the nightingale, partly, perhaps, because of its attractive name, and partly because of its reputation, served to bring together.

The point of view which I am struggling to attack is perhaps related to the metaphysical theory of the substantial unity of the soul: for my meaning is, that the poet has, not a "personality" to express, but a particular medium, which is only a medium and not a personality, in which impressions and experiences combine in peculiar and unexpected ways. Impressions and experiences which are important for the man may take no place in the poetry, and those which become important in the poetry may play quite a negligible part in the man, the personality.

I will quote a passage which is unfamiliar enough to be regarded with fresh attention in the light—or darkness—of these observations:

> And now methinks I could e'en chide myself
> For doating on her beauty, though her death
> Shall be revenged after no common action.
> Does the silkworm expend her yellow labours
> For thee? For thee does she undo herself?
> Are lordships sold to maintain ladyships
> For the poor benefit of a bewildering minute?
> Why does yon fellow falsify highways,
> And put his life between the judge's lips,
> To refine such a thing—keeps horse and men
> To beat their valours for her? . . .

In this passage (as is evident if it is taken in its context) there is a combination of positive and negative emotions: an intensely strong attraction toward beauty and an equally intense fascination by the ugliness which is contrasted with it and which destroys it. This balance of contrasted emotion is in the dramatic situation to which the speech is pertinent, but that situation alone is inadequate to it. This is, so to speak, the structural emotion, provided by the drama. But the whole effect, the dominant tone, is due to the fact that a number of floating feelings, having an affinity to this emotion by no means superficially evident, have combined with it to give us a new art emotion.

It is not in his personal emotions, the emotions provoked by particular events in his life, that the poet is in any way remarkable or interesting. His particular emotions may be simple, or crude, or flat. The emotion in his poetry will be a very complex thing, but not with the complexity of the emotions of people who have very complex or unusual emotions in life. One error, in fact, of eccentricity in poetry is to seek for new human emotions to express; and in this search for novelty in the wrong place it discovers the perverse. The business of the poet is not to find new emotions, but to use the ordinary ones and, in working them up into poetry, to express feelings which are not in actual emotions at all. And emotions which he has never experienced will serve his turn as well as those familiar to him. Consequently, we must believe that "emotion recollected in tranquillity" is an inexact formula. For it is neither emotion, nor recollection, nor, without distortion of meaning, tranquillity. It is a concentration, and a new thing resulting from the concentration, of a very great number of experiences which to the practical and active person would not seem to be experiences at all; it is a concentration which does not happen consciously or of deliberation. These experiences are not "recollected," and they finally unite in an atmosphere which is "tranquil" only in that it is a passive attending upon the event. Of course this is not quite the whole story. There is a great deal, in the writing of poetry, which must be conscious and deliberate. In fact, the bad poet is usually unconscious where he ought to be conscious, and conscious where he ought to be unconscious. Both errors tend to make him "personal." Poetry is not a turning loose of emotion, but an escape from emotion; it is not the expression of personality, but an escape from personality. But, of course, only those who have personality and emotions know what it means to want to escape from these things.

III

ὁ δὲ νοῦς ἴσως θειότερόν τι καὶ ἀπαθές ἐστιν

This essay proposes to halt at the frontier of metaphysics or mysticism, and confine itself to such practical conclusions as can be applied by the responsible person interested in poetry. To divert interest from the poet to the poetry is a laudable aim: for it would conduce to a juster estimation of actual poetry, good and bad. There are many people who appreciate the expression of sincere emotion in verse, and there is a smaller number of people who can appreciate technical excellence. But very few know when there is expression of *significant* emotion, emotion which has its life in the poem and not in the history of the poet. The emotion of art is impersonal. And the poet cannot reach this impersonality without surrendering himself wholly to the work to be done. And he is not likely to know what is to be done unless he lives in what is not merely the present, but the present moment of the past, unless he is conscious, not of what is dead, but of what is already living.

HAMLET AND HIS PROBLEMS

(1919)

T. S. Eliot

Few critics have even admitted that *Hamlet* the play is the primary problem, and Hamlet the character only secondary. And Hamlet the character has had an especial temptation for that most dangerous type of critic: the critic with a mind which is naturally of the creative order, but which through some weakness in creative power exercises itself in criticism instead. These minds often find in Hamlet a vicarious existence for their own artistic realization. Such a mind had Goethe, who made of Hamlet a Werther; and such had Coleridge, who made of Hamlet a Coleridge; and probably neither of these men in writing about Hamlet remembered that his first business was to study a work of art. The kind of criticism that Goethe and Coleridge produced, in writing of Hamlet, is the most misleading kind possible. For they both possessed unquestionable critical insight, and both make their critical aberrations the more plausible by the substitution—of their own Hamlet for Shakespeare's—which their creative gift effects. We should be thankful that Walter Pater did not fix his attention on this play.

Two writers of our own time, Mr. J. M. Robertson and Professor Stoll of the University of Minnesota, have issued small books which can be praised for moving in the other direction. Mr. Stoll performs a service in recalling to our attention the labours of the critics of the seventeenth and eighteenth centuries,[1] observing that

> they knew less about psychology than more recent Hamlet critics, but they were nearer in spirit to Shakespeare's art; and as they insisted on the importance of the effect of the whole rather than on the importance of the leading character, they were nearer, in their old-fashioned way, to the secret of dramatic art in general.

Qua work of art, the work of art cannot be interpreted; there is nothing to interpret; we can only criticise it according to standards, in comparison to other works of art; and for "interpretation" the chief task is the presentation of relevant historical facts which the reader is not assumed to know. Mr. Robertson points out, very pertinently,

[1] I have never, by the way, seen a cogent refutation of Thomas Rymer's objections to *Othello*.

how critics have failed in their "interpretation" of *Hamlet* by ignoring what ought be very obvious; that *Hamlet* is a stratification, that it represents the efforts of a series of men, each making what he could out of the work of his predecessors. The *Hamlet* of Shakespeare will appear to us very differently if, instead of treating the whole action of the play as due to Shakespeare's design, we perceive his Hamlet to be superposed upon much cruder material which persists even in the final form.

We know that there was an older play by Thomas Kyd, that extraordinary dramatic (if not poetic) genius who was in all probability the author of two plays so dissimilar as *The Spanish Tragedy* and *Arden of Feversham*; and what this play was like we can guess from three clues: from *The Spanish Tragedy* itself, from the tale of Belleforest upon which Kyd's *Hamlet* must have been based, and from a version acted in Germany in Shakespeare's lifetime which bears strong evidence of having been adapted from the earlier, not from the later, play. From these three sources it is clear that in the earlier play the motive was a revenge-motive simply; that the action or delay is caused, as in *The Spanish Tragedy,* solely by the difficulty of assassinating a monarch surrounded by guards; and that the "madness" of Hamlet was feigned in order to escape suspicion, and successfully. In the final play of Shakespeare, on the other hand, there is a motive which is more important that that of revenge, and which explicitly "blunts" the latter; the delay in revenge is unexplained on grounds of necessity or expediency; and the effect of the "madness" is not to lull but to arouse the king's suspicion. The alteration is not complete enough, however, to be convincing. Furthermore, there are verbal parallels so close to *The Spanish Tragedy* as to leave no doubt that in places Shakespeare was merely revising the text of Kyd. And finally there are unexplained scenes—the Polonius-Laertes and the Polonius-Reynaldo scenes—for which there is little excuse; these scenes are not in the verse style of Kyd, and not beyond doubt in the style of Shakespeare. These Mr. Robertson believes to be scenes in the original play of Kyd reworked by a third hand, perhaps Chapman, before Shakespeare touched the play. And he concludes, with very strong show of reason, that the original play of Kyd was, like certain other revenge plays, in two parts of five acts each. The upshot of Mr. Robertson's examination is, we believe, irrefragable: that Shakespeare's *Hamlet,* so far as it is Shakespeare's, is a play dealing with the effect of a mother's guilt upon her son, and that Shakespeare was unable to impose this motive successfully upon the "intractable" material of the old play.

Of the intractability there can be no doubt. So far from being Shakespeare's masterpiece, the play is most certainly an artistic failure. In several ways the play is puzzling, and disquieting as is none of the others. Of all the plays it is the longest and is possibly the one on which Shakespeare spent most pains; and yet he has left in it superfluous and inconsistent scenes which even hasty revision should have noticed. The versification is variable. Lines like

> Look, the morn, in russet mantle clad,
> Walks o'er the dew of yon high eastern hill,

are of the Shakespeare of *Romeo and Juliet*. The lines in Act V, sc. ii,

> Sir, in my heart there was a kind of fighting
> That would not let me sleep...
> Up from my cabin,
> My sea-gown scarf'd about me, in the dark
> Grop'd I to find out them: had my desire;
> Finger'd their packet;

are of his mature period. Both workmanship and thought are in an unstable position. We are surely justified in attributing the play, with that other profoundly interesting play of "intractable" material and astonishing versification, *Measure for Measure,* to a period of crisis, after which follow the tragic successes which culminate in *Coriolanus*. *Coriolanus* may be not as "interesting" as *Hamlet,* but it is, with *Antony and Cleopatra,* Shakespeare's most assured artistic success.[2] And probably more people have thought *Hamlet* a work of art because they found it interesting, than have found it interesting because it is a work of art. It is the "Mona Lisa" of literature.

The grounds of *Hamlet's* failure are not immediately obvious. Mr. Robertson is undoubtedly correct in concluding that the essential emotion of the play is the feeling of a son towards a guilty mother:

> [Hamlet's] tone is that of one who has suffered tortures on the score of his mother's degradation.... The guilt of a mother is an almost intolerable motive for drama, but it had to be maintained and emphasized to supply a psychological solution, or rather a hint of one.

This, however, is by no means the whole story. It is not merely the "guilt of a mother" that cannot be handled as Shakespeare handled the suspicion of Othello, the infatuation of Antony, or the pride of Coriolanus. The subject might conceivably have expanded into a tragedy like these, intelligible, self-complete, in the sunlight. *Hamlet,* like the sonnets, is full of some stuff that the writer could not drag to light, contemplate, or manipulate into art. And when we search for this feeling, we find it, as in the sonnets, very difficult to localize. You cannot point to it in the speeches; indeed, if you examine the two famous soliloquies you see the versification of Shakespeare, but a content which might be claimed by another, perhaps by the author of the *Revenge of Bussy d'Ambois,* Act V, sc. i. We find Shakespeare's Hamlet not in the action, not in any quotations that we might select,

[2] *Coriolanus* is analyzed by D. A. Traversi. See Part II. [*Editor's note.*]

so much as in an unmistakable tone which is unmistakably not in the earlier play.

The only way of expressing emotion in the form of art is by finding an "objective correlative"; in other words, a set of objects, a situation, a chain of events which shall be the formula of that *particular* emotion; such that when the external facts, which must terminate in sensory experience, are given, the emotion is immediately evoked. If you examine any of Shakespeare's more successful tragedies, you will find this exact equivalence; you will find that the state of mind of Lady Macbeth walking in her sleep has been communicated to you by a skilful accumulation of imagined sensory impressions; the words of Macbeth on hearing of his wife's death strike us as if, given the sequence of events, these words were automatically released by the last event in the series. The artistic "inevitability" lies in this complete adequacy of the external to the emotion; and this is precisely what is deficient in *Hamlet*. Hamlet (the man) is dominated by an emotion which is inexpressible, because it is in excess of the facts as they appear. And the supposed identity of Hamlet with his author is genuine to this point: that Hamlet's bafflement at the absence of objective equivalent to his feelings is a prolongation of the bafflement of his creator in the face of his artistic problem. Hamlet is up against the difficulty that his disgust is occasioned by his mother, but that his mother is not an adequate equivalent for it; his disgust envelops and exceeds her. It is thus a feeling which he cannot understand; he cannot objectify it, and it therefore remains to poison life and obstruct action. None of the possible actions can satisfy it; and nothing that Shakespeare can do with the plot can express Hamlet for him. And it must be noticed that the very nature of the *données* of the problem precludes objective equivalence. To have heightened the criminality of Gertrude would have been to provide the formula for a totally different emotion in Hamlet; it is just because her character is so negative and insignificant that she arouses in Hamlet the feeling which she is incapable of representing.

The "madness" of Hamlet lay to Shakespeare's hand; in the earlier play a simple ruse, and to the end, we may presume, understood as a ruse by the audience. For Shakespeare it is less than madness and more than feigned. The levity of Hamlet, his repetition of phrase, his puns, are not part of a deliberate plan of dissimulation, but a form of emotional relief. In the character Hamlet it is the buffoonery of an emotion which can find no outlet in action; in the dramatist it is the buffoonery of an emotion which he cannot express in art. The intense feeling, ecstatic or terrible, without an object or exceeding its object, is something which every person of sensibility has known; it is doubtless a subject of study for pathologists. It often occurs in adolescence: the ordinary person puts these feelings to sleep, or trims down his feelings to fit the business world; the artist keeps them alive by his ability to intensify the world to his emotions. The Hamlet of Laforgue is an adolescent; the Hamlet of Shakespeare is not, he has not that explanation and excuse. We must simply admit that here Shakespeare tackled a problem which proved too much for him. Why he attempted it at all is an insoluble puzzle; under compulsion of what experience he attempted to express the inexpressibly horrible, we cannot ever know. We need a great many facts in his biography; and we should like to know whether, and when, and after or at the same time as what personal experience, he read Montaigne, II. xii, *Apologie de Raimond Sebond*. We should have, finally, to know something which is by hypothesis unknowable, for we assume it to be an experience which, in the manner indicated, exceeded the facts. We should have to understand things which Shakespeare did not understand himself.

THE OBJECTIVE CORRELATIVE OF T. S. ELIOT

(1944)

ELISEO VIVAS

IN HIS STUDY of T. S. Eliot in *The New Criticism,* John Crowe Ransom has pointed out that though Eliot is endowed with "an immediate critical sense which is expert and infallible," his judgments are not guided by a body of well elaborated principles, and the result is that many of his generalizations are at best half-truths.[1] Ransom supports this observation in an unanswerable way by means of a detailed analysis of Eliot's critical essays. Yet I hope that in spite of the fact that the conclusion at which I shall arrive in this paper agrees with one of his, there is still room for the following remarks on the notion of the objective correlative, on which Ransom's study touched from a different point of view.

On the surface the notion of the objective correlative seems clear enough. Devised to explain how the poem expresses the poet's emotion, it also asserts that the poet organizes his sensibility through the act of expression. The poet expresses his emotion by "finding . . . a set of objects, a situation, a chain of events which shall be the formula of that *particular* emotion" which he wishes to express, "such that when the external facts . . . are given, the emotion is immediately evoked."[2] The fact that Eliot holds this doctrine shows that, in spite of his avowed classicism, he accepts with the vast majority of his contemporaries the modern dogma that the artist is primarily concerned with emotion. There are other places in which Eliot indicates his belief that the poet's concern with objects is only instrumental, only a means of objectifying the emotion which he seeks to express. But the act of expression is not an end in itself for Eliot, but is in turn instrumental to the organization of sensibility which expression somehow accomplishes in the poem, and which is said to correspond (or lead) to a similar organization in the artist's own psyche. We are not told why or how expression organizes sensibility, but we are clearly told that it does, and that unless emotion is objectified it "remains to poison life and obstruct action." These words refer to Hamlet, but "the supposed

[1] John Crowe Ransom, *The New Criticism,* p. 145.

[2] T. S. Eliot, *Selected Essays,* pp. 124-125. See p. 387 in this volume. [*Editor's note.*]

identity of Hamlet with his author" is asserted to be "genuine at this point," and Eliot tells us that "Hamlet's bafflement at the absence of an objective equivalent to his feelings is a prolongation of the bafflement of his creator in the face of his artistic problem." [3] Eliot grafts a somewhat revamped doctrine of catharsis on to the popular theory of expression, and uses the product to justify poetry therapeutically. Poetry is on this theory a psychic antitoxin and makes action possible. This is a convenient way of chasing with the hounds of modernism while running with the hares of classicism. For in accepting the modern doctrine of expression Eliot is also able to hold that art is not useless, not an end in itself, as the modern theory of expression is so often taken to imply, but instead serves a medical purpose.

It is therefore a great pity that Eliot's theory cannot stand up under close scrutiny, as the analysis which follows will, I believe, demonstrate. For the sake of specificity, I have chosen for comment a single passage of Eliot's, in which the notion of the objective correlative receives as full a treatment as in any that I know of among his critical essays. I refer to the third paragraph of Part II of his famous *Tradition and the Individual Talent*.[4] But while my comments are addressed to this passage specifically, the ambiguities and confusions which are charged against it appear wherever Eliot, implicitly or explicitly, has used his notion of the objective correlative.

In the two paragraphs preceding the one I am about to quote Eliot tells us that the mind of the poet is like a catalytic agent by means of which the "passions which are its material" are "digested." And in the third paragraph he continues:

> The experience, you will notice, the elements which enter the presence of the transforming catalyst, are of two kinds: emotions and feelings. The effect of a work of art upon the person who enjoys it is an experience different in kind from any experience not of art. It may be formed out of one emotion, or may be a combination of several; and various feelings, inhering for the writer in particular words or phrases or images, may be added to compose the final result. Or great poetry may be made without the direct use of any emotion whatever: composed out of feelings solely. Canto XV of the *Inferno* (Brunetto Latini) is a working up of the emotion evident in the situation; but the effect, though single as that of any work of art, is obtained by considerable complexity of detail. The last quatrain [sic!] gives an image, a feeling attaching to an image, which 'came,' which did not develop simply out of what precedes, but which was probably in suspension in the poet's mind until the proper combination arrived for it to add itself to. The poet's mind is in fact a receptacle for seizing and storing up

[3] *Loc. cit.*

[4] *The Sacred Wood: Essays on Poetry and Criticism,* pp. 47-59; and *Selected Essays,* pp. 3-12; The long passage quoted in the following paragraph is found on p. 54 and p. 8 respectively, and is the same commented on by Ransom (*op. cit.,* p. 153). [*Author's note.*] See pp. 380-381 in this volume. [*Editor's note.*]

numberless feelings, phrases, images, which remain there until all the particles which can unite to form a new compound are present together.

We must first notice that Eliot distinguishes between emotions and feelings, and that the distinction seems to be an important one; but how he intends it to be taken cannot be gathered from the content. Though psychologists often use the terms "emotion" and "feeling" in different senses, they are not at all agreed as to their import. I have decided therefore not to introduce the distinction into the following discussion, first because I do not know how to take it, and second because it does not appear in other places where the notion of the objective correlative is used, and our interest centers solely on those aspects of the above paragraph that are representative and not on those that are idiosyncratic. We must notice next that according to Eliot's opening sentence, the stuff which makes up the poem consists of emotions and feelings. This statement can hardly be taken as a mere slip on Eliot's part, and yet it is hard to believe that he actually means what he says, for he, of all people, must know that ideational materials of all sorts regarding objective situations are also part of the poet's material. I rather suspect that historical inquiry will show that the dichotomy on which Eliot is here operating lines him up with the traditions in poetry which his criticism has taught us to disparage. But let us pass by this and let us rather notice that in the first few lines of the quotation, up to the reference to Canto XV, Eliot speaks both of the poet and of the feelings and emotions inhering for him in words and images on the one hand, and on the other of the reader. Seemingly he is not aware of the difficulties which the shift brings with it. And this is the source of a serious confusion. For it would seem as if the feelings which inhere for the poet in the phrase or image which he chooses also inhere in it for the reader. Yet we are not told whether for the latter the inherence consists in the fact that the image arouses the same feeling in him as it aroused in the poet; or whether the feeling is perceived as an objective quality of the image, which may be grasped as inhering in the phrase or image, though it need not be subjectively aroused in the reader for him to grasp it objectively.[5] Now it is perfectly possible that a phrase or image may arouse emotion or feeling and very likely it often happens, even in the case of readers who are more interested in poetry than they are in emotional experiences. But it also happens that a poem or any other object of art seems to possess among its objective characters emotion or feeling values, which "inhere" in it irrespective of our reactions to it. Whether

[5] This important distinction is frequently overlooked, though attention has often been called to it. See for instance "A Definition of The Aesthetic Experience" in *The Journal of Philosophy*, November 11, 1937, pp. 628 ff.; S. C. Pepper: *Aesthetic Quality*, Ch. 4, and *Dictionary of World Literature*, edited by J. T. Shipley, p. 410, article "Objective Correlative." Shipley's criticism of Eliot's notion, though succinct, is essentially the same as I am making here.

Eliot means one or the other alternative or both is not clear, though the difference is radical. On the latter alternative, exactly what may be meant by a feeling "inhering" in a phrase or image is anything but self-evident, and is precisely what requires explanation. But this is not the only difficulty that we encounter in this passage, for in the sentences following his reference to Canto XV he seems to distinguish between the emotion worked up in the Canto and the effect on the reader obtained by the complexity of the detail that Dante put into the Canto. But the statement that an emotion can be worked up in a Canto is, as it stands, unintelligible, since it cannot be taken literally. You just do not work up emotion into poetry the way a cabinet maker works up a few boards into a table.

The statements following the reference to the last "quatrain" pack a bewildering puzzle. Feelings stored up in the poet's mind, which is in fact a storage receptacle; words for which feelings wait in order to attach themselves at the time of composition; the pre-established harmony that must be assumed to exist between the waiting feeling and its verbal garment; the very assumption that a feeling can exist by itself in the mind and wait without symbolic expression of any kind whatever—all this is very dubious psychology. But let it be for the moment. Now let us rather note that Eliot says that the "quatrain" gives an image and a feeling attaching to an image. We have to ask once more whether he means that the "quatrain" *expresses* or that it *arouses* a feeling. And exactly how can feelings, something subjective, attach to images, something quite objective? This is precisely what requires explanation. Eliot is not the first writer to defend the expression theory. Numerous aestheticians before him have also tried to defend it. But whenever the effort has been seriously made to explain just how emotions or feelings happen to "attach" themselves to phrases, or "inhere" in them, the doctrine of expression has usually run into difficulty, and *has ended up by offering us as an explanation the fact to be explained.*[6] This is just what the doctrine of the objective correlative does.

It should now be clear that Eliot hesitates between the following two propositions—or perhaps it were better to say that he has not considered the important differences that exist between them: I) Poetry arouses emotion in the reader; II) The poem expresses emotion. The first proposition needs qualification, but does not require an ex-

[6] As evidence I should like to cite only two eminent writers on aesthetics, representing different philosophic points of view. In his *The Aesthetic Judgment* (1929) D. W. Prall, a realist, argues, in section 5 of Chapter X and in the following chapters, that the arts express feelings and emotions precisely. But when he tries to tell us *how* the expression takes place, all I am able to find is his eloquent asseveration that they do. The same thing is true of Th. M. Greene, in whose idealistic treatise, *The Arts and The Art of Criticism* (1940) will be found an excellent discussion of our problem, in pp. 113-115, and in Chs. 15 and 19. But Mr. Greene does not tell us *by what means, or how,* does an art express feeling. This is what aestheticians have not yet made clear.

planation; the second, however, does. We must therefore take up these propositions and see in what sense each can be held.

I) There is no question that poetry can and often indeed does make us sad, or compassionate, or angry, or fires us with patriotic fervor. It may even evoke or arouse specific but very complex emotions that prose is too crude to denote adequately. But in the light of the facts uncovered by psychological investigations in the last fifty years about the diversity of aesthetic responses I doubt whether we can maintain that art always arouses emotion in every spectator. It depends on the art and on the spectator, and on his attention. Not all spectators are dionysian or want to be.[7] But even if poetry always did arouse emotion, we would still have to ask whether poetry *should* seek to arouse emotion—for we cannot confuse the merely descriptive with the normative question. And it would also be a question whether, if we did hold that poetry *should* arouse emotion, we would not make it entirely impossible to draw the distinction between art and something else—between the aesthetic transaction and some other mode of experience. For the aesthetic would now be defined functionally by the presence of emotion, but the emotion aroused could be only ordinary emotion, since psychology does not recognize *sui generis* aesthetic emotions. Should we hold that poetry ought to arouse emotion, we also run up against a statement of Eliot's in an essay entitled *The Perfect Critic* [8] in which he tells us that "the end of the enjoyment of poetry is a pure contemplation from which all the accidents of personal emotion are removed." And yet, that the arousal of the emotion in the reader seems to be the way in which at least at times Eliot conceives the expression of emotion is to be gathered from the first statement of Eliot's quoted above, and which Matthiessen considers a *locus classicus* of contemporary criticism,[9] for in this passage we are told that when the objective correlative is presented "the emotion is immediately evoked." Eliot may answer that there is no contradiction between these two statements. For what he is opposed to is the indulgence of *personal* emotion, which is precisely what a correlative that is truly objective controls. But if there is one fact for which we have ample evidence in aesthetics today it is the fact that no artist, however skillful, can possibly control the subjective affective responses of his readers, and this is all the truer to the extent to which the culture to which either poet or reader belongs (or both of course) is complex and in a state of flux, and where therefore to accidental personal idiosyncracies must be

[7] The evidence is to be found conveniently summarized in A. R. Chandler: *Beauty and Human Nature,* Chs. 6 and 12, pp. 230-236. See also Vernon Lee: *Music and Its Lovers,* Chs. 1 and 2. See also, by the writer: "A Definition of the Aesthetic Experience" cited in note 5 and "A Note on the Emotion in Mr. Dewey's Theory of Art," *The Philosophical Review,* Sept. 1938, and "A Natural History of the Aesthetic Transaction" in *Naturalism and the Human Spirit,* edited by Yervant Krikorian (Columbia University Press, 1944), pp. 111 ff.

[8] *The Sacred Wood,* p. 14.

[9] F. O. Matthiessen: *The Achievement of T. S. Eliot* (1935), p. 57.

added the differences caused by heterogeneity of social determinants.[10]

II) Poetry may legitimately be said to "express" emotion in two senses, but the first of these is trivial.

a) In a dramatic scene, you know that the actor is feeling a certain emotion. And you are able to say, "What an intense scene!" Whether or not the actor really does feel the emotion he is expressing through representation is a question we need not ask here. It would seem that some actors need to feel what they are acting, while others act poorly when they are the victims of the emotion they must represent. In any case, all that an actor needs to do to be faithful to the exigencies of the drama is to simulate the emotion. Consider, let us say, Giotto's *Pieta.* The figures represented clearly express by their gesture the intense emotions that they are supposed to be feeling. This sense neither furthers nor delays critical analysis of art.

b) Poetry may also express emotion in another way. The poem may be about a situation or an object which socially is connected or invariably associated—whether naturally or conventionally—with an emotion. This is perhaps the only legitimate and unambiguous meaning that we can give the term "objective correlative." But in this case all the term means is that poetry refers denotatively to emotions, not by means of direct verbal reference, but through the whole poem itself—and how this takes place is precisely what calls for explanation and what the term "objective correlative" perhaps labels but otherwise leaves us in the dark about. Somehow, because of a complex connection which has not yet been adequately explained, the poem presents itself as a composite symbol, but not as a neutral, merely semantic, one; rather, as one which refers reflexibly to a fully qualitied, self-consistent whole, more heavily loaded with value than things of ordinary life usually are. These values, not without some reason, *may be called* emotions, though they are objective characters of the value-freighted reality present for the experiencer, since they seem to be the factors in the object that account for the rapturous quality of the experience. But to suppose that they alone function in this manner seems to me utterly erroneous, since the poem and its parts function as a whole whose form and content cannot be separated from each other. It is however in this sense that the poem denotes a specific and unique complex of emotions. But semantically (not psychologically) the relationship of denotation between poem and emotion is the same as that which exists between the word "cat" or "unicorn" and the animal to which it refers, whether one has had a direct experience of it or not. But just as words may be meaningful for us though we may not now experience or may never have experienced their semantic referents, so poetic symbols may denote emotions clearly and distinctly, though we may never have experienced them ourselves, and though we do not experience them as we read the poem. Indeed the educational and

?

[10] See note 7.

moral value of imaginative letters in general consists chiefly in their ability to widen imaginatively the horizon of our parochial experience. This is not to deny that in so far as we have ourselves experienced emotions similar to those denoted by a poem, our experience with that poem will have psychological connotations that it would otherwise lack. But it is to assert that adequate communication is possible though the areas of subjective experience may differ considerably as between poet and reader. And unless we insist that the function of poetry is to arouse emotion, we must grant that it does not fail simply because it may refer to an emotion which it does not happen to arouse in the reader. In any case poetry may legitimately be said to express emotion for any member of a group for whom a connection exists—conventionally or naturally—between the situation or object used by the poet and an emotion; and it expresses it whether it arouses it or not.

In order to make this clear, let us take a poem in which the emotion is strong and the connection between situation and emotion obvious. Garcia Lorca's *Llanto por Ignacio Sanchez Mejias* has been translated into English and, I take it, has been widely read and discussed in this country in the last few years.[11] It is an Elegy on the death of a bullfighter called Ignacio Sanchez Mejias. I translate literally the opening lines:

> Five o'clock in the afternoon,
> It was five sharp in the afternoon.
> A boy brought a white shroud
> At five in the afternoon.

One need not read the poem too closely to realize that the man who wrote it is lamenting the death of a bullfighter and that he feels very strongly about that death. One cannot name the emotion he feels by any precise term; and for a good reason, since its full complex specific expression is achieved only through the total poem; but one may loosely refer to it as a desolate sense of loss, a deep and anguishing loss at the death of a great bullfighter whom Garcia Lorca admired greatly. (*Que gran torero en la plaza!* What a great fighter in the ring!) This is the last stanza—again I translate literally:

> It will take a long time to be born, if one is born
> As famous an Andaluzian, one as rich in adventure.
> I sing his elegance with weeping words,
> And remember a sad breeze through the olive-grove.

Only occasionally does the poet speak directly of his own feelings, as he does for instance when, referring to the blood on the sand he exclaims:

[11] A translation of the *Llanto* by Lloyd Mallan appeared in *The Southern Review:* Winter, 1941. A study of Lorca by Edwin Honig has been published by *New Directions,* 1945.

But I don't want to see it.
Tell the moon to come,
For I don't want to see the blood
Of Ignacio on the sand.

More often than not, the poem refers to objects and situations directly involved in the death or somehow in the poet's mind connected with it. The expression of the emotion or emotions—for there is of course a whole complex of them referred to throughout the poem—is achieved through the presentation of these objects and situations; these are the objective correlatives. And the reader, whether he reads with interest or with indifference, knows by means of these objective correlatives how Garcia Lorca feels about the death of Ignacio. Note however that the emotions that each reader grasps through the objective correlative are for reasons similar to those mentioned above in connection with the discussion of the arousal of emotion, only partially within the control of the poet. Thus to a reader with strong moral objections against bullfighting, Garcia Lorca's poem will undoubtedly communicate or express different emotions from those it does to Hemingway or to the writer of these notes. But in so far as all of the readers share to some extent certain attitudes towards courage, skill and death, to that degree do they glean a somewhat similar objective emotional meaning.

All this should be more or less obvious, though it does not seem to be for Eliot. What may not be so readily accepted is that the emotion expressed through the objective correlative cannot be the same emotion which was originally felt by Garcia Lorca when he heard the news of Ignacio's death or saw the accident at the ring which he worked into the *Llanto*. To establish this contention adequately would take us far afield, and therefore I must state the reasons that support it briefly and dogmatically. The emotion originally felt by Garcia Lorca, assuming for the moment that he was actually writing of a historical bullfighter, was transmuted into something quite different as he began to produce the poem and began to concern himself with the problem of poetic composition. What Garcia Lorca felt before the poem began to shape itself in his mind is something he couldn't tell us except in the most inexact and inadequate fashion. Of course, being a poet, his ordinary conversation must have shown flashes of his poetical skill. But before he wrote the poem he could not have told us much more about his grief than you or I could have told had we been in his place—all he could have said was that he felt very bad, felt perhaps broken up over the death of Ignacio. What he really felt could only be expressed precisely through the poem, which is to say that he had to discover it through the act of composition. But the poem expresses more than a complex of emotions of which the original grief is only a part. And this more is at least as important as the emotions it expresses. For it exhibits for attention a story or incident or object, and does so, if it is an English poem, by means of meter, imagery, often rhyme, a subtle and complex musical quality, and a distinct tone. Taken together—and aesthetic apprehension is not analytic but naturally takes all these integrated factors together—they make up the internally consistent unit which is the poem, and which, if successful, has the power of compelling intense and intransitive attention on itself. In the case of the *Llanto* the original grief experienced by Garcia Lorca may have been the occasion of the composition of the poem; if there was such a grief it surely entered into the poem, in the sense that what the poet chose to include in his poem had to be psychologically congruous with his grief. But as the poem got itself written this original grief itself suffered a change, spending itself in the process of composition and sharing the poet's attention with his technical interests, whose stubborn exigencies had to be satisfied. The result, in our example, was an objective whole, the *Llanto,* in which the problems of versification which Garcia Lorca encountered somehow were solved satisfactorily to his interest as poet and congruously not only with the feelings, but also with the opinions and ideas, which he had of his friend and which demanded expression when he heard the news of his death.

Between interest in form and interest in content there is always a tension which for the artist, I take it, defines itself as a problem of sincerity or of integrity. We all have felt sometimes that the administration of justice is mocked by the forms and conventions of the law, and that there is a vast difference between justice and legality—if we could only wipe off all convention and precedent, all technique and all artificial court procedure, how much closer we would get to the justice we all crave! And so the artist in regard to his original emotion: how outrageously do the demands of form violate it, how deeply do they transmute it! For no form really suits it, no public means through which it can be expressed brings it utterly out of the shadow of its own ineffability. But isn't this the tragic fact which philosophy since Descartes has made its central problem, without succeeding in resolving it—the mind's need to reach beyond itself and its failure adequately to satisfy that need? In any case, neither can justice be administered, nor can emotion be expressed, without some means, and the means exact their price and violate the pristine integrity of that which they administer or express.

Why a poet feels that one object rather than another can serve him as an "objective correlative" is an important question, but one in regard to which we seem to be very much in the dark. Association was suggested above as the reason, but that was done merely to avoid raising at that point the difficulty which now we must face. Miss Langer may be right and there may be a correspondence between the "dynamic patterns of human experience," the "forms" of emotion, and the objective characters chosen by the artist to express it.[12] But this explanation

[12] Susanne K. Langer: *Philosophy in a New Key,* Ch. 8.

does no more than assert the fact and explains absolutely nothing until it is able to make adequately clear what is meant by the key phrase "dynamic pattern of experience" or "form of an emotion." In any case, association will not explain the process of choice, since the poet is not really choosing one image as against another because the former happens to correspond to a pre-existing feeling; what he is doing is creating imagery and conceiving novel situations; and association cannot explain the pat congruity that exists from the very first moment of conception between our symbol and the feelings or emotions which, outside of their symbolic embodiment, the artist neither understood nor could define. Be this as it may, as the creative activity proceeds, the original inchoate emotion which our poet felt for his gored friend gradually changed; it spent, perhaps, its original force; the dumb anguish subsided or became transmuted into interests of the most heterogeneous sorts, which were, nevertheless, fused together and seemed to possess an enveloping homogeneous tone.

The discussion has proceeded on two assumptions that it is now necessary to investigate more closely. We have assumed first that Garcia Lorca's emotion, before the poem was written, was itself something clear and definite. This is indeed what Eliot assumed in the passage already quoted, when he spoke of the feelings waiting in the poet's mind, which he said was a receptacle for storing them. Now in one sense, what I. A. Richards has called "the availability of the poet's experience" is an indubitable fact, however we explain it or even if we cannot explain it all.[13] But Eliot's explanation is utterly inadequate. For feelings certainly do not wait in the mind like tobacco in a pouch, till they can be used. We are more likely to remain close to the facts if we assume that before writing his poem Garcia Lorca experienced a heavy oppressive feeling or emotion, dumb and confused, inwardly disrupting, perhaps extremely painful, but hardly to be compared with the emotion he expressed through his poem, since it approached a confused physiological chaos, which the creative activity, in bringing to clarity through expression, relieved. The emotion the poem expresses, however, is not merely a clarified development from this inchoate affective mass. It is a more complex affair, since it has been informed by the poet in his poem through devices—meter, rhyme, imagery, etc.—that are themselves expressive, thus transforming the original inchoate affection into what it now is, an objectively significant, because communicable, piece of art.

But is it necessary to assume that Garcia Lorca felt genuine sorrow at the death of a real bullfighter whom he admired and that the poem was occasioned by the tragic death of Ignacio one afternoon in the ring? The whole episode, name and all, may have been imagined. Ignacio was indeed an historical figure whom Garcia Lorca knew and whose taurine art and courage he admired, but he need not have been.

[13] I. A. Richards: *Principles of Literary Criticism,* Ch. 22.

Had Garcia Lorca lived in a different period he might have written the poem as a commission from a prince. Consider Bach writing concertos for an insomniac patron, or any court poet celebrating to order the birth of a royal heir. It is not necessary to assume that the actual emotion that is worked up by the poet into the poem is the actual occasion of the creative act.

What then does a poem express? I incline to the belief that the aesthetic of expression is a useless and confusing muddle that mystifies far more than it explains. To this conclusion a great many writers have helped me, but chiefly, I believe, John Crowe Ransom, with his salutary insistence on the ontological interest of the poet.[14] What has been said above about how raw experience is transformed, or better *transubstantiated* by the creative process, indicates the direction along which I would seek for a full explanation as to what it is that the artist exhibits for contemplation. But many other fundamental points would have to be broached before the answer could be fully elucidated.[15] Here let it suffice to say that the object of aesthetic apprehension is a self-consistent structure, involving an ordered complex of values of a sensuous, formal, and of an immanently meaningful nature, which satisfies the alert mind turned towards it, and it does for two reasons: First, because its values are, in the isolation of the aesthetic experience, final values, inherently interesting for their own sake and not as means. And second, because beyond them we perceive an authentic vision of the structure of reality. This structure we sometimes catch a glimpse of in our daily world, when we peer beyond the chaos of our moral relations and beyond the onrush of natural events. But in art, as in philosophy, and I imagine in orison, the desire is gratified and the mind, rapt in its full and luminous possession, finds in it consummatory satisfaction. This ordered structure is ideal, in that its apprehension is rare, and that when we succeed in grasping it, it brings with it rewards of a noble kind: peace, serenity, release from the sting of passion and freedom from the indignity of living. That is why Schopenhauer valued it so highly. It is also ideal in that it can be grasped only by a mind fully alert. Yet it is real or natural, since the poet is no sorcerer, and has no means of going for his vision of the order he presents to us for our contemplation, to a metempirical realm where we unpoetical folk cannot follow him, but finds it in the same world in which we find our potatoes or our beans. Yet it is not merely in a pickwickian sense that we call poetry ideal, for poetry has about it a flush and a luster which do seem to lift us into a higher or a more intensely "real" world than the tarnished stuff of our daily experience. "Seem," for whether it does in truth or not is, as my people

[14] The help has sometimes been negative: See for instance "A Note on the Emotion in Mr. Dewey's Theory of Art," *The Philosophical Review*, Sept. 1938, pp. 527 ff.

[15] For instance, the problem of the freedom and spontaneity of the mind in the creative process.

say, flour from a different bag. Be that as it may, a poem expresses all that which the poet presents objectively in it for apprehension; true, among the elements making up the object there are some that we find easier to denote when we wish to refer to them verbally, through the terms which we use to denote emotions. But I see no reason to assume that all else in the poem is put there merely to arouse an emotion in us or to bring about its objective denotation. Surface, formal, and ideational elements are all in their own right of intrinsic interest. And while the emotion expressed is also of interest, it is not, and it should not be, of chief or exclusive interest to the reader.

It is too much to expect that a theory so popular as the expression theory shall be abandoned on account of its ultimate unintelligibility. But because it will continue to be used, it is of the uttermost importance for criticism to realize that the emotion expressed through the objective correlative is not that which the poet felt before the poem was written. The emotion as well as the correlative, are *found* through the process of *creation*. But if the term "creation" is taken seriously, the consequences for Eliot's critical approach are devastating. For it means that once finished no one can go behind the poem, not even the artist himself. Otherwise put, the emotion itself, naked and unexpressed, cannot be had for comparison with its expression through its objective correlative. And the assumption therefore that we can criticize the play *Hamlet* by comparing the emotion expressed in the play with Shakespeare's emotions, or that through the play we can discover the emotions that went into it, is a confusing illusion. The vocabulary of the emotions is thus confusing, if not indeed irrelevant, to literary criticism; and if it were dropped, and the critic confined himself only to the objects and situations and values communicated by the poem, there would ensue an enormous clarification in the practice of criticism.

THE AFFECTIVE FALLACY

(1948)

W. K. WIMSATT, JR. AND M. C. BEARDSLEY

We might as well study the properties of wine by getting drunk.
—Eduard Hanslick, *The Beautiful in Music.*

WE BELIEVE ourselves to be exploring two roads which have seemed to offer convenient detours around the acknowledged and usually feared obstacles to objective criticism, both of which, however, have actually led away from criticism and from poetry. The Intentional Fallacy is a confusion between the poem and its origins, a special case of what is known to philosophers as the Genetic Fallacy. It begins by trying to derive the standard of criticism from the psychological *causes* of the poem and ends in biography and relativism.[1] The Affective Fallacy is a confusion between the poem and its *results* (what it *is* and what it *does*), a special case of epistemological skepticism, though usually advanced as if it had far stronger claims than the over-all forms of skepticism. It begins by trying to derive the standard of criticism from the psychological effects of the poem and ends in impressionism and relativism. The result of either Fallacy, the Intentional or the Affective, is that the poem itself, as an object of specifically critical judgment, tends to disappear.

I

Plato's feeding and watering of the passions [2] was an early example of affective theory, and Aristotle's counter-theory of catharsis was another (with modern intentionalistic analogues in theories of "relief" and "sublimation"). There was also the "transport" of the audience in the *Peri Hupsous* (matching the great soul of the poet), and this had echoes of passion or enthusiasm among eighteenth-century Lon-

[1] See the authors' essay on "The Intentional Fallacy" in the *Sewanee Review,* 54 (Summer, 1946), 458-488. The first section of the essay "The Affective Fallacy," in which the authors make a semantic analysis of the subject, is here omitted; the sections are renumbered accordingly. [*Editor's note.*]

[2] Strictly, a theory not of poetry, but of morals, as, to take a curious modern instance, Lucie Guillet's *La Poéticothérapie, Efficacités du Fluide Poétique,* Paris, 1946, is a theory not of poetry but of healing. Aristotle's catharsis is a true theory of poetry, i.e., part of a definition of poetry.

ginians. We have had more recently the contagion theory of Tolstoy (with its intentionalistic analogue in the emotive expressionism of Veron), the *Einfühlung* or empathy of Lipps and related pleasure theories, either more or less tending to the "objectification" of Santayana: "Beauty is pleasure regarded as the quality of a thing." An affinity for these theories is seen in certain theories of the comic during the same era, the relaxation theory of Penjon, the laughter theory of Mr. Max Eastman. In their *Foundations of Aesthetics* Messrs. Ogden, Richards, and Wood listed sixteen types of aesthetic theory, of which at least seven may be described as affective. Among these the theory of Synaesthesis (Beauty is what produces an equilibrium of appetencies) was the one they themselves espoused. This was developed at length by Mr. Richards in his *Principles of Literary Criticism.*

The theories just mentioned may be considered as belonging to one branch of affective criticism, and that the main one, the emotive—unless the theory of empathy, with its transport of the self into the object, its vital meaning and enrichment of experience, belongs rather with a parallel and equally ancient affective theory, the imaginative. This is represented by the figure of vividness so often mentioned in the rhetorics—*efficacia, enargeia,* or the *phantasiai* in Chapter XV of *Peri Hupsous.* This if we mistake not is the imagination the "Pleasures" of which are celebrated by Addison in his series of *Spectators.* It is an imagination implicit in the theories of Leibniz and Baumgarten, that beauty lies in clear but confused, or sensuous, ideas; in the statement of Warton in his *Essay on Pope* that the selection of "lively pictures . . . chiefly constitutes true poetry." In our time, as the emotive form of psychologistic or affective theory has found its most impressive champion in Mr. I. A. Richards, so the imaginative form has, in Mr. Max Eastman, whose *Literary Mind* and *Enjoyment of Poetry* have much to say about vivid realizations or heightened consciousness.

But an important distinction can be made between those who have coolly investigated what poetry does to others and those who have testified what it does to themselves. The theory of intention or author-psychology, as we noted in our earlier essay, has been the intense conviction of poets themselves, Wordsworth, Keats, Housman, and since the romantic era, of young persons interested in poetry, the introspective amateurs and soul-cultivators. In a parallel way, affective theory has often been less a scientific view of literature than a prerogative—that of the soul adventuring among masterpieces, the contagious teacher, the poetic radiator—a magnetic rhapsode Ion, a Saintsbury, a Quiller-Couch, a William Lyon Phelps. Criticism on this theory has approximated the tone of the Buchmanite confession, the revival meeting. "To be quite frank," says Anatole France, "the critic ought to say: 'Gentleman, I am going to speak about myself apropos of

Shakespeare, apropos of Racine. . . .' "[3] The sincerity of the critic becomes an issue, as for the intentionalist the sincerity of the poet.

"The mysterious entity called the Grand Style," says Saintsbury. . . . "My definition . . . [of it] would . . . come nearer to the Longinian Sublime."

> Whenever this perfection of expression acquires such force that it transmutes the subject and transports the hearer or reader, then and there the Grand Style exists, for so long, and in such degree, as the transmutation of the one and the transportation of the other lasts.

And if we follow him further in his three essays on the subject (the Grand Style in Shakespeare, in Milton, in Dante), we discover that "It is nearly as impossible to describe, meticulously, the constituents of its grandeur as to describe that of the majesty of the sun itself."

> The fact is . . . that this Grand Style is not easily tracked or discovered by observation, unless you give yourself up primarily to the *feeling* of it.

With Dante, "It is pure magic: the white magic of style and of grand style." This is the grand style, the emotive style, of nineteenth century affective criticism. A somewhat less resonant style which has been heard in our columns of Saturday and Sunday reviewing and from our literary explorers is more closely connected with imagism and the kind of vividness sponsored by Mr. Eastman. In the *Book-of-the-Month Club News* Dorothy Canfield testifies to the power of a new novel: "To read this book is like living through an experience rather than just reading about it."[4] "And so a poem," says Hans Zinsser,

> means nothing to me unless it can carry me away with the gentle or passionate pace of its emotion, over obstacles of reality into meadows and covers of illusion. . . . The sole criterion for me is whether it can sweep me with it into emotion or illusion of beauty, terror, tranquillity, or even disgust.[5]

It is but a short step to what we may call the physiological form of affective criticism. Beauty, said Burke in the eighteenth century, is small and curved and smooth, clean and fair and mild; it "acts by relaxing the solids of the whole system." More recently, on the side of personal testimony, we have the oft-quoted goose-flesh experience in a letter of Emily Dickinson, and the top of her head taken off; the bristling of the skin while Housman was shaving, the "shiver down the spine," the sensation in "the pit of the stomach." And if poetry has

[3] *On Life and Letters,* First Series, trans. A. W. Evans (London, 1911), Preface, p. viii.

[4] *New York Times Book Review,* April 13, 1947, p. 29.

[5] *As I Remember Him,* quoted by J. Donald Adams, "Speaking of Books," *New York Times Book Review,* April 20, 1947, p. 2. Mr. Adams' weekly department is a happy hunting ground for such specimens.

been discerned by these tests, truth also. "All scientists," said D. H. Lawrence to Aldous Huxley, "are liars. . . . I don't care about evidence. Evidence doesn't mean anything to me. I don't feel it *here*." And, reports Huxley:

> he pressed his two hands on his solar plexus.[6]

An even more advanced grade of affective theory, that of hallucination, would seem to have played some part in the neo-classic conviction about the unities of time and place, was given a modified continuation of existence in phrases of Coleridge about a "willing suspension of disbelief" and a "temporary half faith," and may be found today in some textbooks. The hypnotic hypothesis of E. D. Snyder might doubtless be invoked in its support. As this form of affective theory is the least theoretical in detail, has the least content, and makes the least real claim on critical intelligence, so it is in its most concrete instances not a theory but a fiction or a fact of no critical significance. In the eighteenth century Fielding conveys a right view of the hallucinative power of drama in his comic description of Partridge seeing Garrick act the ghost scene in Hamlet. "O la! sir. . . . If I was frightened, I am not the only person. . . . You may call me coward if you will; but if that little man there upon the stage is not frightened, I never saw any man frightened in my life." Partridge is today found perhaps less often among the sophisticates at the theatre than among the myriad audience of movie and radio. It is said, and no doubt reliably, that during the war Stefan Schnabel played Nazi roles in radio dramas so convincingly that he received numerous letters of complaint, and in particular one from a lady who said that she had reported him to General MacArthur.[7]

II

As the systematic affective critic professes to deal not merely, if at all, with his own experiences, but with those of persons in general, his most resolute search for evidence will lead him into the dreary and antiseptic laboratory, to testing with Fechner the effects of triangles and rectangles, to inquiring what kinds of colors are suggested by a line of Keats, or to measuring the motor discharges attendant upon reading it.[8] If animals could read poetry, the affective critic might make discoveries analogous to those of W. B. Cannon about *Bodily Changes in Pain, Hunger, Fear and Rage*—the increased libera-

[6] *The Olive Tree* (New York, 1937), p. 212.

[7] *The New Yorker,* 19 (Dec. 11, 1943), 28.

[8] "The final averages showed that the combined finger movements for the Byron experiments were eighteen metres longer than they were for Keats." R. C. Givler: *The Psycho-Physiological Effect of the Elements of Speech in Relation to Poetry* (Princeton, 1915), p. 62, quoted by Thomas C. Pollock: *The Nature of Literature* (Princeton, 1942), p. 110.

tion of sugar from the liver, the secretion of adrenin from the adrenal gland. The affective critic is today actually able, if he wishes, to measure the "psychogalvanic reflex" of persons subjected to a given moving picture.[9] But, as a recent writer on *Science and Criticism* points out: "Students have sincerely reported an 'emotion' at the mention of the word 'mother,' although a galvanometer indicated no bodily change whatever. They have also reported no emotion at the mention of 'prostitute,' although the galvanometer gave a definite kick." [10] Thomas Mann and a friend came out of a movie weeping copiously—but Mann narrates the incident in support of his view that movies are not Art. "Art is a *cold* sphere." [11] The gap between various levels of physiological experience and the perception of value remains wide, whether in the laboratory or not.

In a similar way, general affective theory at the literary level has, by the very implications of its program, produced very little actual criticism. The author of the ancient *Peri Hupsous* is weakest at the points where he explains that passion and sublimity are the palliatives or excuses (*alexipharmaka*) of bold metaphors, and that passions which verge on transport are the lenitives or remedies (*panakeia*) of such audacities in speech as hyperbole. The literature of catharsis has dealt with the historical and theoretical question whether Aristotle meant a medical or a lustratory metaphor, whether the genitive which follows *katharsis* is of the thing purged or of the object purified. Even the early critical practice of Mr. I. A. Richards had little to do with his theory of synaesthesis. His *Practical Criticism* depended mainly on two important constructive principles of criticism which Mr. Richards has realized and insisted upon—(1) that rhythm (the vague, if direct, expression of emotion) and poetic form in general are intimately connected with and interpreted by other and more precise parts of poetic meaning, (2) that poetic meaning is inclusive or multiple and hence sophisticated. The latter quality of poetry may perhaps be the objective correlative of the affective state synaesthesis, but in applied criticism there would seem to be not much room for synaesthesis or for the touchy little attitudes of which it is composed.

The report of some readers, on the other hand, that a poem or story induces in them vivid images, intense feelings, or heightened consciousness, is neither anything which can be refuted nor anything which it is possible for the objective critic to take into account. The purely affective report is either too physiological or it is too vague. Feelings, as Hegel has conveniently put it, "remain purely subjective affections of myself, in which the concrete matter vanishes, as though narrowed into a circle of the utmost abstraction." And the only con-

[9] Wendell S. Dysinger and Christian A. Ruckmick: *The Emotional Responses of Children to the Motion Picture Situation* (New York, 1933).

[10] Herbert J. Muller: *Science and Criticism* (New Haven, 1943), p. 137.

[11] "Ueber den Film," in *Die Forderung des Tages* (Berlin, 1930), p. 387.

stant or predictable thing about the vivid images which more eidetic readers experience is precisely their vividness—as may be seen by requiring a class of average pupils to draw illustrations of a short story or by consulting the newest Christmas edition of a childhood classic which one knew with the illustrations of Howard Pyle or N. C. Wyeth. Vividness is not the thing in the work by which the work may be identified, but the result of a cognitive structure, which *is* the thing. "The story is good," as the student so often says in his papers, "because it leaves so much to the imagination." The opaque accumulation of physical detail in some realistic novels has been an absurd reduction of plastic or graphic theory aptly dubbed by Mr. Middleton Murry "the pictorial fallacy."

Certain theorists, notably Mr. Richards, have anticipated some difficulties of affective criticism by saying that it is not intensity of emotion that characterizes poetry (murder, robbery, fornication, horse-racing, war—perhaps even chess—take care of that better), but the subtle quality of patterned emotions which play at the subdued level of disposition or attitude. We have psychological theories of aesthetic distance, detachment, or disinterestedness. A criticism on these principles has already taken important steps toward objectivity. If Mr. Eastman's theory of imaginative vividness appears today chiefly in the excited puffs of the newspaper Book Sections, the campaign of the semanticists and the balanced emotions of Mr. Richards, instead of producing their own school of affective criticism, have contributed much to recent schools of cognitive analysis, of paradox, ambiguity, irony, and symbol. It is not always true that the emotive and cognitive forms of criticism will sound far different. If the affective critic (avoiding both the physiological and the abstractly psychological form of report) ventures to state with any precision what a line of poetry *does* —as "it fills us with a mixture of melancholy and reverence for antiquity"—either the statement will be patently abnormal or false, or it will be a description of what the meaning of the line *is:* "the spectacle of massive antiquity in ruins." Tennyson's *Tears, idle tears,* as it deals with an emotion which the speaker at first seems not to understand, might be thought to be a specially emotive poem. "The last stanza," says Mr. Brooks in his recent analysis, "evokes an intense emotional response from the reader." But this statement is not really a part of Mr. Brooks's criticism of the poem—rather a witness of his fondness for it. "The second stanza,"—Mr. Brooks might have said at an earlier point in his analysis—"gives us a momentary vivid realization of past happy experiences, then makes us sad at their loss." But he says actually: "The conjunction of the qualities of sadness and freshness is reinforced by the fact that the same basic symbol—the light on the sails of a ship hull down—has been employed to suggest both qualities." The distinction between these formulations may seem trivial, and in the first example which we furnished may be practically unimportant. Yet the difference between such translatable emotive formulas and those more physiological and psychologically vague ones which are cognitively untranslatable is theoretically of the greatest import. The distinction even when it is a very faint one is at the dividing point between paths which lead to polar opposites in criticism, to classical objectivity and to romantic reader psychology. The critic whose formulations lean to the emotive and the critic whose formulations lean to the cognitive will in the long run produce vastly different sorts of criticism.

The more specific the account of the emotion induced by a poem, the more nearly it will be an account of the reasons for emotion, the poem itself, and the more reliable it will be as an account of what the poem is likely to induce in other—sufficiently informed—readers. It will in fact supply the kind of information which will enable readers to respond to the poem. It will talk not of tears, prickles, or other physiological symptoms, of feeling angry, joyful, hot, cold, or intense, or of vaguer states of emotional disturbance, but of shades of distinction and relation between objects of emotion. It is precisely here that the discerning literary critic has his insuperable advantage over the subject of the laboratory experiment and over the tabulator of the subject's responses. The critic is not a contributor to statistically countable reports about the poem, but a teacher or explicator of meanings. His readers, if they are alert, will not be content to take what he says as testimony, but will scrutinize it as teaching. The critic's report will speak of emotions which are not only complex and dependent upon a precise object but also, and for these reasons, stable. This paradox, if it is one, is the analogue in emotive terms of the antique formula of the metaphysical critic, that poetry is both individual and universal—a concrete universal. It may well be that the contemplation of this object, or pattern of emotive knowledge, which is the poem, is the ground for some ultimate emotional state which may be termed the aesthetic (some empathy, some synaesthesis, some objectified feeling of pleasure). It may well be. The belief is attractive; it may exalt our view of poetry. But it is no concern of criticism, no part of criteria.

III

Poetry, as Matthew Arnold believed, "attaches the emotion to the idea; the idea *is* the fact." The objective critic, however, must admit that it is not easy to explain how this is done, how poetry makes ideas thick and complicated enough to attach emotions. In his essay on *Hamlet and His Problems* Mr. T. S. Eliot finds Hamlet's state of emotion unsatisfactory because it lacks an "objective correlative," a "chain of events" which are the "formula of that *particular* emotion." The emotion is "in *excess* of the facts as they appear." It is "inexpressible." Yet Hamlet's emotion must be expressible, we submit, and actually expressed too (by something) in the play; otherwise Mr. Eliot would not know it is there—in excess of the facts. That Hamlet himself or Shakespeare may be baffled by the emotion is beside the point. The second chapter of Mr. Ivor Winters' *Primitivism and Decadence* has gone much further in clarifying a distinction adumbrated by Mr. Eliot. Without embracing the extreme doctrine of Mr. Winters, that if a poem cannot be paraphrased it is a poor poem, we may yet with profit reiterate his main thesis: that there is a difference between the motive, as he calls it, or logic of an emotion, and the surface or texture of a poem constructed to describe the emotion, and that both are important to a poem. Mr. Winters has shown, we think, how there can be in effect "fine poems" about nothing. There is rational progression and there is "qualitative progression,"[12] the latter with several subtly related modes, a characteristic of decadent poetry. Qualitative progression is the succession, the dream float, of images, not substantiated by a plot. "Moister than an oyster in its clammy cloister, I'm bluer than a wooer who has slipped in a sewer," says Mr. Morris Bishop in a recent comic poem:

> Chiller than a killer in a cinema thriller,
> Queerer than a leerer at his leer in a mirror,
> Madder than an adder with a stone in the bladder.
> If you want to know why, I cannot but reply:
> It is really no affair of yours.[13]

The term "pseudo-statement" was for Mr. Richards a patronizing term by which he indicated the attractive nullity of poems. For Mr. Winters, the kindred term "pseudo-reference" is a name for the more disguised kinds of qualitative progression and is a term of reproach. It seems to us highly significant that for another psychological critic, Mr. Max Eastman, so important a part of poetry as metaphor is in effect too pseudo-statement. The vivid realization of metaphor comes from its being in some way an obstruction to practical knowledge (like a torn coat sleeve to the act of dressing). Metaphor operates by being abnormal or inept, the wrong way of saying something.[14] Without pressing the point, we should say that an uncomfortable resemblance to this doctrine appears in Mr. Ransom's logical structure and local texture of irrelevance.

What Mr. Winters has said seems basic. To venture both a slight elaboration of this and a return to the problem of emotive semantics

[12] The term, as Mr. Winters indicates, is borrowed from Mr. Kenneth Burke's *Counter-Statement*. [*Author's note.*] See p. 235 in this volume. [*Editor's note.*]

[13] *The New Yorker,* 23 (May 31, 1947), 33.

[14] On pp. 183-184 of his *Literary Mind,* Mr. Eastman notices the possibility of inept metaphor and seems about to explain why this would not be, on his hypothesis, even better than apt metaphor. But he never does. On p. 188 "Poetic metaphor is the employment of words to suggest impractical identifications." On p. 185 he alludes to the value of synecdoche as a focussing attention on qualities of objects. It would seem to escape his attention that metaphor does the same.

surveyed in our first section: it is a well-known but nonetheless important truth that there are two kinds of real objects which have emotive quality, the objects which are the literal reasons for human emotion, and those which by some kind of association suggest either the reasons or the resulting emotion—the thief, the enemy, or the insult that makes us angry, and the hornet that sounds and stings somewhat like ourselves when angry; the murderer or felon, and the crow that kills small birds and animals or feeds on carrion and is black like the night when crimes are committed by men. The arrangement by which these two kinds of emotive meaning are brought together in a juncture characteristic of poetry is, roughly speaking, the simile, the metaphor, and the various less clearly defined forms of association. We offer the following crude example as a kind of skeleton figure to which we believe all the issues can be attached.

1. X feels as angry as a hornet.
2. X whose lunch has been stolen feels as angry as a hornet.

No. 1 is, we take it, the qualitative poem, the vehicle of a metaphor, an objective correlative—for nothing. No. 2 adds the tenor of the metaphor, the motive for feeling angry, and hence makes the feeling itself more specific. The total statement has a more complex and testable structure. The element of aptitude, or ineptitude, is more susceptible of discussion. "Light thickens and the crow makes wing to the rooky wood" might be a line from a poem about nothing, but initially owed much of its power, and we daresay still does, to the fact that it is spoken by a tormented murderer who, as night draws on, has sent his agents out to perform a further "deed of dreadful note."

These distinctions bear a close relation to the difference between historical statement which may be a reason for emotion because it is believed (Macbeth has killed the king) and fictitious or poetic statement, where a large component of suggestion (and hence metaphor) has usually appeared. The first of course seldom occurs pure, at least not for the public eye. The coroner or the intelligence officer may content himself with it. Not the chronicler, the bard, or the newspaper man. To these we owe more or less direct words of value and emotion (the murder, the atrocity, the wholesale butchery) and all the repertoire of suggestive meanings which here and there in history—with somewhat to start upon—an Achilles, a Beowulf, a Macbeth—have created out of a mere case of factual reason for intense emotion a specified, figuratively fortified, and permanent object of less intense but far richer emotion. With the decline of heroes and of faith in objects as important, we have had within the last century a great flowering of poetry which has tried the utmost to do without any hero or action or fiction of these—the qualitative poetry of Mr. Winters' analysis. It is true that any hero and action when they become fictitious take the first step toward the simply qualitative, and all poetry, so far as separate from history, tends to be formula of emotion. The hero and action are taken as symbolic. A graded series from fact to quality might include: (1) the historic Macbeth, (2) Macbeth as Renaissance tragic protagonist, (3) a *Macbeth* written by Mr. Eliot, (4) a *Macbeth* written by Mr. Pound. As Mr. Winters has explained, "the prince is briefly introduced in the footnotes" of *The Waste Land;* "it is to be doubted that Mr. Pound could manage such an introduction." Yet in no one of these four stages has anything like a pure emotive poetry been produced. Even in the last stages a poetry of pure emotion is an illusion. What we have is a poetry where kings are only symbols or even a poetry of hornets and crows, rather than of human deeds. Yet a poetry about things. How these things are joined in patterns and with what names of emotion, remains always the critical question. "*The Romance of the Rose* could not, without loss," observes Mr. Lewis, "be rewritten as the *Romance of the Onion.*"

Poetry is characteristically a discourse about both emotions and objects, or about the emotive quality of objects, and this through its preoccupation with symbol and metaphor. An emotion felt for one object is identified by reference to its analogue felt for another—a fact which is the basis for the expressionist doctrine of "objectification" or the giving to emotion a solid and outside objectivity of its own. The emotions correlative to the objects of poetry become a part of the matter dealt with—not communicated to the reader like an infection or disease, not inflicted mechanically like a bullet or knife wound, not administered like a poison, not simply expressed as by expletives or grimaces or rhythms, but presented in their objects and contemplated as a pattern of knowledge. Poetry is thus a way of fixing or making emotions more permanently perceptible when objects have undergone a functional change from culture to culture, or when as simple facts of history they have lost emotive value with loss of immediacy. Though the reasons for emotion in poetry may not be so simple as Ruskin's "noble grounds for the noble emotions," yet a great deal of constancy for poetic objects of emotion—if we will look for constancy—may be traced through the drift of human history. The murder of Duncan by Macbeth, whether as history of the eleventh century or chronicle of the sixteenth, has not tended to become the subject of a Christmas carol. In Shakespeare's play it is an act difficult to duplicate in all its immediate adjuncts of treachery, deliberation, and horror of conscience. Set in its galaxy of symbols—the hoarse raven, the thickening light, and the crow making wing, the babe plucked from the breast, the dagger in the air, the ghost, the bloody hands—this ancient murder has become an object of strongly fixed emotive value. The corpse of Polyneices, a far more ancient object and partially concealed from us by the difficulties of the Greek, shows a similar pertinacity in remaining among the understandable motives of higher duty. Funeral customs have changed, but not the web of issues, religious, political, and private, woven about the corpse "unburied, unhonoured, all unhallowed." Again, certain objects partly obscured in one age wax into appreciation in another, and partly through the efforts of the poet. It is not true that they suddenly arrive out of nothing. The pathos of Shylock, for example, is not a creation of our time, though a smugly modern humanitarianism, because it has slogans, may suppose that this was not felt by Shakespeare or Southampton—and may not perceive its own debt to Shakespeare. "Poets," says Shelley, "are the unacknowledged legislators of the world." And it may be granted at least that poets have been leading expositors of the laws of feeling.[15]

To the relativist historian of literature falls the uncomfortable task of establishing as discrete cultural moments the past when the poem was written and first appreciated, and the present into which the poem with its clear and nicely interrelated meanings, its completeness, balance, and tension has survived. A structure of emotive objects so complex and so reliable as to have been taken for great poetry by any past age will never, it seems safe to say, so wane with the waning of human culture as not to be recoverable at least by a willing student. And on the same grounds a confidence seems indicated for the objective discrimination of all future poetic phenomena, though the premises or materials of which such poems will be constructed cannot be prescribed or foreseen. If the exegesis of some poems depends upon the understanding of obsolete or exotic customs, the poems themselves are the most precise emotive evaluation of the customs. In the poet's finely contrived objects of emotion and in other works of art the historian finds his most reliable evidence about the emotions of antiquity—and the anthropologist, about those of contemporary primitivism. To appreciate courtly love we turn to Chrétien de Troyes and Marie de France. Certain attitudes of late fourteenth century England, toward knighthood, toward monasticism, toward the bourgeoisie, are nowhere more precisely illustrated than in the prologue to *The Canterbury Tales.* The field worker among the Zunis or the Navahos finds no informant so informative as the poet or the member of the tribe who can quote its myths.[16]

[15] *Cf.* Paulhan: *The Laws of Feeling,* pp. 105, 110.

[16] See, for example, Clyde Kluckhohn and Dorothea Leighton: *The Navaho* (Cambridge, 1946), pp. 134-138; Ruth Benedict: *Zuni Mythology* (New York, 1935), Introduction. The emphasis of Bronislaw Malinowski's *Myth in Primitive Psychology* (New York, 1926) is upon the need of cultural context to interpret myth. Nevertheless the myth is the main point of the book. "The anthropologist," says Malinowski, "has the myth-maker at his elbow" (p. 17).

THE ENABLING ACT OF CRITICISM

(1941)

R. P. Blackmur

There is a kind of resolute candor necessary to a full approach to literature which is impossible to any particular approach. The best that the individual can do positively is to insist that his particular work aims in the general direction of that candor, and the least that he can do negatively is not only to admit but to insist that other particular approaches also aim in that direction. Failure to make either insistence leads to irrelevance and arrogance of judgment, and if persisted in at the level of practice—whether in book-reviewing or in major criticism—tends to complete the separation of the literary critic from his proper subject-matter. Instead of practicing literary criticism he will find himself practicing self-expression or casual philosophy, practices which will be deceptive in the degree that they were not candidly undertaken. Thus when the critic takes Criticism itself as his subject—when he faces his own practice, when he confronts other critics with their own practice—he must concern himself sooner or later with the relative stage of candor or deception, which that practice discloses. And the sooner he does this the better, because for the life of me, I cannot see how the critic judging of Criticism can do much more. Further, if he takes his job seriously, I cannot see how he can content himself with attempting less. Surely it is a tenable view that criticism must in the end come back to the task of saying what its objects are in terms of themselves; as surely, then, it is of first importance to distinguish in the work of a critic what is criticism from what is something else.

To put the matter quite practically, on the level where we actually use criticism, which is to say in our efforts towards a better understanding of literature, let us set up a series of questions designed to show the distinctions we want. We have a critic before us. What, when he is all done, does he tell us about the works he says he is examining? Is what he tells us everywhere subordinated to what we may call the interests of the works themselves: precisely, what it is within the work that interests us or defeats its own interest? Or, on the contrary, is what he tells us subordinated to some interest, no doubt worthy in itself, independent of the work in hand? If so, which interest predominates? And, if the extra-literary interest does predominate, can it yet be said that it nevertheless enlightens the literary interest, by situating it, say, among all the interests that go to make up a culture? This last, if we rephrase it, makes up the crucial question; for does it not ask, really, whether we can accept or reject a literary work by the application of literary standards alone? That is, to make one more rephrasing, do we in fact ever understand literature only by literary means?

If we can answer these questions as it were backwards, it is possible that we may come out somewhere near right in the end. At least we should have a beginning not merely provisional or wayward but with an end already and firmly in view: namely, a focus for literary experience, and a vantage for looking. We can think of the whole backward process as the enabling act of criticism.

Well, then, it is plain that we never do in fact understand literature solely by literary means any more than we understand water solely by drinking it, solely by chemical analysis, solely by looking at it, or solely by damming it up. It is the unified mind and sensibility that is engaged in the act of understanding; the act is imaginative; and to try to compartmentalize the act so as to emphasize one faculty over another is to invalidate the imagination and abort the act. Looked at in this way, the question of the final understanding of literature becomes either an artificial or an irrelevant question. If we do not use the whole mind we shall understand nothing; if we do use it, we do so as it were inarticulately, as the product of our whole culture: that is, we take it for granted.

But what is taken for granted must be attended just the same, like breathing; and in this case especially; for the unified, imaginative character of the understanding was not brought up here for nothing but indifferent acceptance. It was brought up in order to emphasize the fact that at the other end of the rod from criticism—in the act of the composition of literature itself—the process is the same. Serious writing is done under the full tolerable weight of mind and sensibility. Imagination is in that sense absolute. All that can be made to bear, bears. That is why the critic must bring his full tolerable imagination to bear before judgment is possible.

In the word *tolerable* we introduce a consideration which brings us to the next question in our backwards moving series, the question whether, really, we can accept or reject a literary work by the application of literary standards alone. Here the answer is double; partly yes and partly no, only good sense—the taste of practice—determining which. T. S. Eliot's remark is initially in order, that while we can only tell that a work is literature by literary standards, we cannot tell whether it is great literature except by other than literary standards. A first qualifying reflection is that there is not very much great literature; and a second is that, even when a critic is concerned with great literature, most of the problems he handles will not directly affect his estimate of its greatness. Greatness is come up to, felt, discovered; not handled. A critic who tried to handle merely the greatness of Shakespeare or Dante would see it disappear before his eyes. And a critic who attempted to establish the greatness of Joyce or Eliot or Yeats would be largely wasting his time; for greatness is established by custom, by time, by the apprehension in the minds of many men of inexhaustibility, and even so greatness is transitory and variable. Milton is not so great today as a century ago. Dante is greater. And I use the copulative deliberately, for greatness is an act of estimation not an assertion of fact, and hence may be expected to vary, but not, once estimated, ever to disappear irrecoverably. It would be intolerable as well as impossible for us today to look at Milton either with our own full mind and sensibility or with those of his own generation, or with those of the eighteenth century. We use of our own what will bear, of the others only what will elucidate—and then only putatively. On the other hand—and this is the aspect of critical activity to which we shall return—it would be intolerable if we did not bring the full force of our literary standards to bear in order to determine what of Milton is literature and what is not. Equally, the other way round, we should bring as much as possible of Milton's literary achievement to bear on the products of our own time; and the extent to which this can be done will constitute a literary judgment on both Milton and our own time. Those other, extra-literary standards, the standards of the convictions of our whole culture, will thus tend to disappear or be transformed into the literary standards.

A very different thing happens—at this time; though it may not be at another—in the example of Dante, whose greatness has grown so in our estimation that the force of his work seems almost a quality of the air that poets must breathe to invigorate their own verse. Dante, said Yeats, was the chief imagination of Christendom; and I think it may be hazarded that his greatness lies in the fact that he showed the highest and fullest unity the Christian order ever reached actually at work in light and air and earth. As Eliot says, the *Divine Comedy* is a vast ordering of actual human feelings and emotions; which are our own feelings and emotions, and as we apprehend them expose us, as little in our own poetry is able to do, to the conviction of our own fate. This is to say, perhaps, that no matter how much of our extra-literary standards we bring to bear on Dante, it is not enough; it is rather that Dante's standards enlighten ours; so that, as far as actually accepting or rejecting Dante goes, we have only our literary standards to resort to. (I suggest that it is not our Christianity that brings us to Dante, but our desperate lack of it.) If this statement of present affairs is provisionally correct it constitutes a profound judgment of defect in our culture, established, in the fact, by literary means alone. Thus, in effect, we witness literary standards operating the Christian order as a "mere" principle of composition. This is not offered with approval or disapproval, but hazarded as a possible mode of approaching the problem of judging literature; namely, by the transformation of literary standards to the level of general conviction. It should be added that there does not seem to be any other poet—certainly not Shakespeare, who dramatized inertia rather than order—where such a possibility shows itself. Dante is alone in achievement.

You would not think so from a quick rereading of the principal literary critics since the middle of the nineteenth century—since, that is, the specific decay of the Christian order began to be felt as a shifting towards disorder, towards dismay, towards corruption, in the general order of culture. In Taine and Sainte-Beuve; in Arnold and Pater; in Babbitt and More; in the psychologists, the aestheticians, and the Marxists; in the critics associated with the *Action Française,* and in the secular neo-Thomists as well; indeed almost everywhere that men have taken literature seriously, you will find the tendency prevalent, at varying intensities, to estimate the value of writers in the degree that their *literary* standards did or did not operate in the place of other standards. Writers have been generally judged, along the lines of the critic's particular interest, as to whether or not they were able to effect deliberately such a transformation of standards as we have just been suggesting that Dante effected as it were inadvertently. There is not a writer of the last century of any stature who has not been condemned, or at least run down, for his failure in this direction by one or more of these our most eminent and best trained critics.

Now it may be that these critics are right in their preoccupation. It may be that the vast task of ordering human feelings and emotions has been imposed upon the arts and especially upon literature by the present lack of any authority otherwise derived. It may be that we are committed—I will not say condemned—to a wholly secular culture. Faced with the immediate alternatives in the wave, as Mrs. Lindbergh calls it, of fascist and soviet culture, we may even hope for a secular culture. But if assent is given to that idea, it does not follow that the literary critic in emphasizing the Dantesque aspect of literature can escape his obligation to explore and to master the primary aspect of literature: that aspect in which it represents the experience of the actual which is beneath and beyond merely moral experience, and which alone grounds or situates moral experience. Eliot's remark holds true that as morals are only a primary consideration for the saint, so they are only a secondary consideration for the artist.

This brings us up sharp on our next question, as to whether the extra-literary interest, if it predominates in the critic's mind, enlightens the literary interest. With regard to the general mass of critics to whom we referred above, the answer is plainly negative, and may be drawn from two approximate facts about their work. They seem, in the mass, seldom to have enjoyed literature, and they seem as individuals, and especially when concerned with the literature of their own times, to have been concerned with what a given work did not do to the virtual exclusion of what it did do. In short, and this is what makes one most suspicious of their candor, they not only made their criticism autonomous, which is a sin of pride, but they also made criticism appear to do the work of literature, which is the sin of putting God in second place. They defiled their literary knowledge to the point where it hardly seems recognisable as knowledge of literature at all; with the curious but natural result that their morals or politics or sociology or theology seemed second-rate, vitiated by isolation from the actual world which lay before them in the literature which was their declared subject-matter. That the literature has survived in spite of its criticism and continues to arouse the same sort of attention suggests that it was not that the intent of the critics was mistaken but that their method was inefficient and their attention inadequate.

It is not the business of this paper to decide to what uses literature may be put, and it is not the predilection of this writer to see literature made into a kind of Pandora's box of panaceas, or even into the source of a merely moral order; but if there is a demand for that sort of thing, and there is, then it had better be done along lines that admit the possibility of success at the beginning. Those lines exist, are available, and may be taught; they are indicated in the frame of questions around which these paragraphs have been laid down. Assuming that literature, being imaginative, is understood if at all by the whole imagination before it is understood or used in any other way, acknowledging that many interests not literary but moral, political, spiritual, are nevertheless imaginatively present in literature, and even insisting that it is in the light of those interests that literature shows its stature (thereby adding to our own) and must be judged, it remains necessary to approach those other interests through the interests of the works themselves; through what is told, shown, expressed. It is there, in the interest of the actual, shaped and composed by what Santayana calls the enormous burden of perception—all that the intellect ignores or merely schematises—it is there, straight in front of you, in the words and the motions of the words, that the artist has focussed, or failed to focus, those interests you want. It could not be otherwise.

If you think otherwise, there is a primary defect in your contact with literature such as you would not permit yourself, say, in your contact with philosophy where it is a commonplace that the words are important and often difficult: where a universe is heaped in a phrase. If you think it is so but easy, you are rash and inexperienced. In the very degree that the work of literature does focus the interests you want it will be difficult—indeed an inexhaustible labor—to grasp the text. And until you have grasped the text you cannot paraphrase it; and to paraphrase in intellectual terms an imaginative experience is I suppose a generalized description of what you mean to do. But if you can grasp the text the rest will either come naturally, though arduously, or will seem irrelevant or superfluous. You will have either the labor of articulating your judgment of interest, or you will see that, so far as literature is concerned, it does not count.

The real difficulty lies further back, and is double in character. It consists, first, in being willing to concentrate your maximum attention upon the work which the words and the motions of the words—and by motions I mean all the technical devices of literature—perform upon each other. Secondly, it consists in submitting, at least provisionally, to whatever authority your attention brings to light in the words. In doing this you will be following in pretty close parallel the procedure which the writer followed. Whether your submission is permanent or must be withdrawn will be determined by the judgment of all the standards and all the interests you can bring to bear. These will differ with the work in hand. But the act of submission must be made before you can tell; it is an act of imagination, not of will; and it is the enabling act of criticism. If it does not provide you with another Dante, it will at least provide you with an interest in literature and without that you would not know a Dante if he appeared.*

* See for further discussion of critical problems and methods *The Critics' Notebook,* edited by R. W. Stallman, with a Foreword by Robert Penn Warren, to be published by the University of Minnesota Press and Oxford University Press, 1949. *The Critics' Notebook* orders into a sequence quotations from modern criticism under such categories as: the Nature and Function of Criticism, Life and Art, Form, Meaning. the Objective Correlative, the Personal Element, the Problem of Poetic Belief, the Problem of Intentions. [*Editor's note.*]

PART IV

KINDS OF CRITICS AND CRITICISM

INTRODUCTORY COMMENT

PART IV provides a revised perspective of the critical background, Saint -Evremond to Tate. As Martin Turnell's study of the French tradition indicates, the main current of aestheticism has been through French rather than through English literature.

These essays elucidate and criticize, or place in a synthesis, a wide variety of critical positions and kinds of criticism. (See also Olson's essay in Part III.) They take into account the formalist or technical kind (as represented by the Southern critics), the aesthetic (Baudelaire), the impressionistic (Remy de Gourmont), the historical-sociological (Taine, Sainte-Beuve, Van Wyck Brooks), the psychological (I. A. Richards), etc. The critical outlook of a Marxist critic is represented by Edmund Wilson, who explains and evaluates the historical-sociological approach. The psychological-sociological approach is seen at its best in the criticism of Van Wyck Brooks; his position is ably summed up by F. W. Dupee. (The question of the boundaries of criticism, whether the different critical approaches and kinds of criticism are mutually exclusive of each other, is answered, in Part III, by R. P. Blackmur in "The Enabling Act of Criticism.")

From the viewpoint of traditional critics who regard literature as literature and not as a document illustrating social history, the psychological-sociological and historical critics do not write criticism at all. The results of this kind of criticism have not measured up to the promise, and this failure has been pointed out by its own practitioners. As W. H. Auden says: "The results of a sociological approach to literary criticism have so far been, on the whole, disappointing. Demanding, as such a method does, a rare combination of historical scholarship and esthetic judgment, the good historians and the good critics have been too conscious of their deficiencies in the one domain or the other to attempt it, while, on the other hand, it has appealed only too strongly to the lazy-minded who are content with empty generalizations and the ax-grinders who have drawn their conclusions in advance." * That art should serve no end beyond itself is the modern view, as Eliot says in "The Social Function of Poetry." (See Part I.)

* W. H. Auden in *The New York Times Book Review,* December 14, 1947, p. 4.

LITERARY CRITICISM IN FRANCE–I

(1939)

MARTIN TURNELL

I. INTRODUCTORY

"IT WILL BE our criticism, perhaps, that will most fittingly last longest," wrote M. Charles Maurras in a characteristic pronouncement. "A Sainte-Beuve and a Renan will have a good chance of making posterity one day forget the Flauberts, the Leconte de Lisles and perhaps even the Hugos." [1] Frenchmen are sometimes extremely modest about their poets, but they are seldom modest about their critics. They have long regarded themselves as the great critics of the modern world and until lately no one has ventured to challenge their supremacy.

There is of course a good deal of evidence to support the French claims. In France literature is, as it has long been, a *métier* and criticism is regarded as a part of the profession. It seldom occurs to a French critic to preface his first book with an essay explaining and justifying the function of criticism. He would scarcely think of describing his art as "a charming parasite" or as "books about books." When he does discuss the value of criticism it is usually because he is hard up for a subject for his weekly *chronique* or he does it casually in an aside. Thus Remy de Gourmont concludes a discussion of the respective functions of novelist and critic by declaring categorically: "They must both be creators of Values" and leaves it at that.

The Frenchman's confidence, which appears so attractive and reassuring when compared with the doubt and uncertainty which beset English critics, has undoubtedly influenced the output of criticism in France. We may have doubts about the greatness of French criticism, but we can have none about its bulk or its seriousness. No one who glances over the shelves of a big library can help being impressed by the number of volumes of criticism by men whose names are household words in Europe or who like Brunetière and Faguet were reputed to be great critics in their day, though we think very differently of them now.

Although the fame of French criticism rests mainly on the work of the distinguished writers of the last century, the origins of the French

[1] *Prologue d'un essai sur la critique* (Paris, 1932), p. 21.

supremacy must be sought in an earlier age and it is interesting to compare passages from two representative seventeenth century critics who were exactly contemporary—Saint -Evremond and Dryden:

> Il est certain que personne n'a mieux entendu la nature que Corneille; mais il l'a expliquée différemment, selon ses temps différents. Étant jeune, il en exprimait les mouvements; étant vieux, il nous endécouvre les ressorts. Autrefois il donnait tout au sentiment; il donne plus aujourd'hui à la connaissance; il ouvre le coeur avec tout son secret; il le produisait avec tout son trouble...[2]

> Corneille a cru que ce n'était pas assez de les [3] faire agir; il est allé au fond de leur âme chercher le principe de leurs actions; il est descendu dans leur coeur pour y voir former les passions et y découvrir ce qu'il y a de plus caché dans leurs mouvements.[4]

> If Shakespeare were stripped of all the bombasts in his passions, and dressed in the most vulgar words, we should find the beauties of his thoughts remaining; if his embroideries were burnt down, there would still be silver in the melting pot. For what remains the excellency of that poet was, as I have said, in the manly passions; Fletcher's in the softer: Shakespeare writ better between man and man: Fletcher, between man and woman: consequently the one described friendship better; the other love; yet Shakespeare taught Fletcher to write love; and Juliet and Desdemona are originals... Shakespeare had an universal mind, which comprehended all characters and all passions...[5]

It can be seen that the extracts from Saint -Evremond are something that we recognize at once as *literary* criticism. The balance and maturity of his writing and the sureness with which he handles the language of criticism make Dryden's criticism of Shakespeare sound like an extract from a respectable essay by a sixth form boy. Dryden's thought is commonplace and, compared with Saint -Evremond's, his sensibility seems crude.

With these passages in front of us, it can scarcely be denied that the critical intelligence reached maturity far sooner in France than in England. Saint -Evremond's best work is the product of a society whose sensibility and powers of analysis were already highly developed.

[2] "It is certain that no one has understood nature better than Corneille; but he has interpreted it differently at different times. When he was young, he expressed its animation; old now, he reveals its springs. Formerly he was concerned wholly with feeling; today his work is more largely informed with knowledge; he opens the heart with all its secret; he exposes it in all its disorder..." *Oeuvres complètes,* ed. Planhol (Paris, 1927), I, pp. 218-219.

All quotations in Part I of Mr. Turnell's essay have been translated from the French by Professor Dorothy Van Ghent. [*Editor's note.*]

[3] Corneille's characters.

[4] "Corneille believed that it was not enough to make [his characters] act; he has gone to the depths of their souls to find the principle of their actions; he has descended into their hearts to watch the passions form there and to discover what is most hidden in their behavior." *Op. cit.,* I, p. 194.

[5] Preface to *Troilus and Cressida* (1679).

Nor must we overlook the work of another writer who was considered the greatest critic of his time. It is a little difficult to understand Boileau's contemporary reputation, but his judgments on French poets of the fifteenth and sixteenth centuries have almost all been endorsed by posterity. Although there is a danger of using single passages and isolated examples to prove too much, the fact that the seventeenth century had already made up its mind where the great French writers "came" points to the existence of an intellectual élite whose criticism had an immense influence on the work of the great writers of the period.

This does not mean that the seventeenth century possessed an abundance of good *written* criticism. The maturity of the French intelligence is more apparent in the moralists of the period than in its literary critics. Indeed, a society which produced the sort of philosophical and psychological analysis that we find in different ways in the *Traité des passions de l'âme,* in the *Caractères* of La Bruyère and the *Maximes* of La Rochefoucauld appears to have possessed in such a high degree the gifts which are necessary for good criticism that we may feel inclined to wonder why the bulk of the written criticism of the period was disappointing, why Boileau is crude in comparison to La Bruyère.

"The history of seventeenth-century society," replies the historian, "is a study of imperatives." [6] It is true that the tendency of the century was to reduce poetry to "the rules," conduct to an intricate code and human life to a series of neat formulas; and though this tendency was partly responsible for the discipline and economy of the great masters, its influence on lesser men was disastrous. It was the first stage in the conflict between natural good taste and subservience to a narrow dogmatism which runs through the whole of modern French criticism and which for all its boasted enlightenment dominates the nineteenth century when the dogmatism of Aristotle was exchanged for the dogmatism of the scientific philosophies.

It is significant that the French Academy began as a series of informal meetings between men who wished to discuss poetry; but almost at once the State, in the person of Richelieu, stepped in and transformed that informal literary society into an official body. There is no doubt that the Academy corresponded to the needs of the age or that it was from the first a symbol of the natural desire of the Frenchman for an authority which would tell him whether he was "right" in admiring a particular author. The symbol was one thing, but the reality was quite another. Once an external authority has been set up it easily turns into the Leviathan which crushes and represses. In the seventeenth century in spite of the disastrous attack on the *Cid,* the intellectual élite succeeded to a great extent in holding the balance between tradition and experiment and curbed the dogmatism of the

[6] Hugon: *Social France in the Seventeenth Century* (London, 1911), p. 17.

Academy; but when the élite had disappeared, dogmatism carried all before it.

The greatness of French literature in the seventeenth century lies partly in the balance between intellect and the senses. The skill with which the intellect analyses emotion without the least distortion gives the literature of the seventeenth century its extraordinary order and clarity. In the next century this correspondence between intellect and senses disappears. On the one hand, we have the impression that the senses are lagging behind the intellect; there is no growth of sensibility; feelings become conventional and criticism is full of counters like "sublime" which do not correspond to any living reality. On the other hand, we get a literature of revolt against dogmatism which produces the undisciplined growth of feeling that we find in Rousseau.

It is, however, the dogmatic principle which is reflected in eighteenth century criticism. Its intrinsic value is not great. Whatever his merits as a thinker, Vauvenargues' criticism is decidedly inferior to Sainte-Evremond's and it is clear from his chapter on Corneille and Racine that he had much less *direct* sensibility than his seventeenth century predecessor. The interest of Voltaire and La Harpe is mainly historical; and in spite of his revolutionary social theories, Voltaire appears in his literary criticism as a die-hard conservative. Diderot, it is true, belongs to a different order. Although the problems discussed in the *Paradoxe sur le comédien* no longer seem of immediate importance, the dialogue remains a masterpiece of dialectic and is still worth reading for the author's admirable handling of the language of criticism.

Voltaire and Diderot, however, were the men who marked the beginning of a new phase of French culture. In the eighteenth century the great gifts developed in the France of Louis XIV were turned against the civilization that produced them and were largely responsible for its ruin. The result was that at the beginning of the nineteenth century not only the intellectual élite, but also the sanctions behind seventeenth century civilization had vanished. The great task of the nineteenth century critics was therefore to find a philosophy on which to base their criticism, to find a justification not simply for criticism but for art. For though the desire for absolute authority remained, the philosophical basis of that authority seemed to the nineteenth century to have been swept away.

II. TAINE [7]

There is an interesting passage in Gourmont's paper on *L'idéalisme* which deserves attention from anyone who wishes to understand nineteenth century criticism in France:

> L'idéalisme signifie libre et personnel développement de l'individu intellectuel dans la série intellectuelle; le Symbolisme pourra (et même

[7] I have departed for my own purposes from the strict chronological order of the critics discussed in the three following sections.

devra) être considéré par nous comme le libre et personnel développement de l'individu esthétique dans la série esthétique; et les symboles qu'il imaginera ou qu'il expliquera seront imaginés ou expliqués selon la conception spéciale du monde morphologiquement possible à chaque cerveau symbolisateur.[8]

The striking thing about this passage is that the critic formulates his standards in terms of a *technical* philosophy. Where Arnold proposes as a test of poetry its "high seriousness" or its value as "a criticism of life," Gourmont uses terms like *"libre et personnel développement de l'individu intellectuel dans la série intellectuelle"* and *"monde morphologiquement possible à chaque cerveau symbolisateur."* These differences are not fortuitous; they are not disposed of by saying that Arnold was a product of Liberal Protestantism and Gourmont the product of nineteenth century scepticism. They are, I think, almost entirely due to the fact that technical philosophy is still part of the normal curriculum in French secondary schools, whereas scarcely any Englishmen study the subject at all.

I make no excuse for underlining this point because the influence of philosophy on nineteenth century criticism was decisive. French critics were looking for something to replace "the rules" and, had they but known it, the wisdom of the seventeenth century. It is hardly surprising that they selected one or other of the fashionable philosophical systems of the day. The confidence of the nineteenth century in science was unshakeable. Critics like Taine believed that they had at last found in the scientific philosophies a certain basis for literary judgment which would dispose of the vicissitudes of taste and the caprice of the individual, and the age was rich not only in philosophical, but also in critical systems.

Taine's distinction between "system" and "method" in criticism does not appear as important to the English mind as it does to the French, and even in France it has probably lost some of its importance with the passing of time. But the preface to the *Essais de critique et d'histoire* and the Introduction to the *History of English Literature* are of great value in understanding Taine's own approach to literature and French critical method in general during the last century. Taine regarded criticism as a natural history of the human mind, and no one can help noticing the frequency with which he borrows from the vocabulary of natural history and physiology.

. . . . .

[8] "Idealism means the free personal development of the intellectual individual in the intellectual series; Symbolism might (and even must) be considered by us as the free personal development of the aesthetic individual in the aesthetic series; and the symbols he will imagine or interpret will be imagined or interpreted according to the special conception of the world morphologically possible to each symbol-making brain.' Reprinted in *Le chemin de velours* (Paris, 1902), pp. 209-210.

. . . . Taine's theory of the relation between literature and society was not as obvious in 1866 as it is to-day; but neither was the danger of his theory. We all know that a knowledge of the contemporary background can help us to understand the literature of a period, that a grasp of the doctrinal differences in the seventeenth century and of the conflict between Jesuit and Jansenist will enable us to appreciate some of the differences between Corneille and Racine; but we also know that this knowledge can never be a substitute for literary judgment. It is not so much the theoretical side of Taine's system that is open to criticism, but his application of it to concrete cases. Although he insisted on the importance of the individual, he assumed in practice that once we know the *race,* the *moment* and the *milieu,* we can deduce the final term—the writer—from the first three. This approach sometimes prevented him from seeing the individual at all. The subject of most of his literary studies is not an individual writer, but a composite figure—*l'homme idéal et général*—a colourless abstraction deduced from the tendencies of his age in which the essential characteristics are lacking. This is strikingly illustrated by the study of Racine. Commenting on the line

Dans le fond des forêts votre image me suit

Taine remarks: *"Quand Hippolyte parle des forêts où il vit, entendez les grandes allées de Versailles."* [9] It seems to me, as I have said in another place, that the force of the line depends on the fact that *fond* suggests infinite extension which has no limit and no term; and by implication it comes to suggest the unexplored depths of the human mind or, as Taine more spectacularly puts it in another place, *"les gouffres où tout peut s'engloutir."* It is clear that Taine's arbitrary association of "forests" with Versailles ruins the meaning not only of this one line, but also of one of the greatest scenes in *Phèdre.* His Racine is a seventeenth century courtier and no more, who would have been incapable of the astonishing analysis of emotion which we find in the plays or the extraordinary power of evocation which makes his poetry unique.

The best way of testing Taine's merits as a critic, however, is to study the paper on Balzac in the *Nouveaux essais.* The first time that we read it, it is difficult not to be impressed. Taine possessed a good sensibility, and the essay is concrete and extremely well documented. The vigour of the writing, the wealth of images and the apparent critical intensity make us feel that here at last is genuine literary criticism. The novelist's style is carefully analysed, its main characteristics are illustrated, praised or blamed as the case demands, and then labelled and put away. But as we get into the essay we become uneasy. Can this really be *literary* criticism, one wonders, or is Taine

[9] *Nouveaux essais de critique et d'histoire,* 3rd ed. (1880), p. 188.

simply using his author to demonstrate the excellence of his own point of view. When Taine remarks of some of Balzac's characters:

> Les tirades de Mme. de Montsauf sont presque aussi désagréables que les concetti de Shakespeare. La comtesse Honorine, qui meurt par excès de pudeur, écrit en mourant la lettre la plus indécente. Mme Claës, au lit de mort, laisse échapper des allusions physiologiques et des axiomes métaphysiques dont heureusement elle était incapable. (p. 75).[10]

—it is clear that he is not concerned with Balzac's faults *as a writer* or with the *invraisemblance* of his characters; he dislikes them because their conduct shocks the susceptibilities of a mid-nineteenth century gentleman whose women friends do not indulge in *axiomes métaphysiques* and who even on their death-beds observe the *convenances*. Taine concludes from the behaviour of Balzac's characters that

> La vraie noblesse lui manque, les choses délicates lui échappent, ses mains d'anatomiste souillent les créatures pudiques, il enlaidit la laideur. (p. 97).[11]

When he writes, in an extremely revealing sentence, of *Eugénie Grandet*

> On a peur ici de la nature humaine; on sent qu'elle renferme des gouffres où tout peut s'engloutir, tout-à-l'heure la religion, à présent la paternité.[12]

—there is no longer any pretence of applying literary standards at all. The novelist has shown us something that was undreamed of in the philosophy of naturalism and Taine is incapable of dealing with these findings as a literary critic. The only way in which he can account for them is by attributing them to the novelist's ignorance of history:

> D'ailleurs cette amère philosophie manque chez lui de son contre poids, l'histoire, qu'il savait mal; il oubliait que si l'homme aujourd'hui offre beaucoup de vices et de manières, l'homme autrefois en offrait bien davantage, que l'expérience agrandie a diminué la folie de l'imagination, l'aveuglement de la superstition, la brutalité des moeurs, l'âpreté des souffrances, et que, chaque siècle, on voit s'accroître notre science et notre puissance, notre modération et notre sécurité. Pour philosopher sur l'homme, ce n'est pas assez d'une observation exacte, il faut une observation complète; et la peinture du présent n'est point vrai sans le souvenir du passé. (p. 129).[13]

[10] "The tirades of Mme. de Montsauf are almost as disagreeable as Shakespeare's puns. The Countess Honorine, dying from excess of modesty, writes the most obscene letter. Mme. Claës, on her death-bed, delivers herself of physiological allusions and metaphysical axioms of which, fortunately, she was incapable."

[11] "He is lacking in true nobility, delicate things escape him, his anatomist's hands soil modest creatures, he makes ugliness more ugly."

[12] "One is afraid here of human nature; one feels that it conceals gulfs where everything may be swallowed up, religion a moment ago, and now fatherhood."

[13] "Moreover this harsh philosophy of his lacks its counterpoise, history, which he understood badly; he forgot that if man today has many affectations and vices,

The most curious thing about these passages is the conception of literature which emerges from them. There are many grounds on which Balzac's work can be criticized, but it is noticeable that Taine never at any point asks the question that a literary critic must ask—whether the *Comédie humaine* is, or is not, a valid criticism of the contemporary situation. He either argues that Balzac's work conflicts with the philosophy of naturalism, or with his own complacent belief that every day and in every way humanity was getting better and better; or where he cannot deny the truth of the findings, he condemns them because they offend his sense of propriety. The underlying assumption is that literature should only interpret life as long as it does not shock or disturb, so that it becomes in the last resort a narcotic.

Taine keeps his parting shot for the last sentence of his essay:

> Avec Shakespeare et Saint-Simon, Balzac est le plus grand magazin de documents que nous ayons sur la nature humaine.[14]

Although this conclusion is thrown out with an air of playfulness, it is not a *boutade* but a perfectly serious statement of principle which informs the whole of Taine's criticism. In the Introduction to the *History of English Literature* he praises Stendhal because "he treated feelings as they ought to be treated, that is to say, as a naturalist and a physician, by measuring and classifying them." Ultimately, literature is valuable not as an experience, but as a document which tells us more clearly than any other how previous generations lived. "It resembles," he says, "those admirable apparatuses with their extraordinary sensitivity which physicians use to detect the intimate and delicate changes which take place in our bodies."

If Taine's approach had been due merely to the peculiarities of his age, there would be no point in dwelling on it. This curious performance, however, is by no means exceptional; it is the expression of a habit of mind which can be clearly discerned in a great deal of modern French criticism. Thus we find M. Ramon Fernandez writing in *Messages:*

> L'immense, l'incalculable intérêt de l'oeuvre stendhalienne réside moins dans sa valeur intrinsèque que dans les renseignements qu'elle nous livre sur les caractères respectifs de l'autobiographie et le roman, sur les vicissitudes d'un esprit qui, avec un sens admirable des valeurs spécifiques, a su mener jusqu'au bout une oeuvre autobiographique et

---

man in former times had many more, that increased experience has diminished the excesses of imagination, the blindness of superstition, the brutality of manners, the severity of suffering, and that, with each century, one can observe the growth of our knowledge and our power, our moderation and our security. In order to philosophize about mankind, exact observation is not enough, complete observation is necessary; and a truthful description of the present requires the memory of the past."

[14] "Together with Shakespeare and Saint-Simon, Balzac is our greatest storehouse of documents on human nature."

une oeuvre romanesque sans jamais perdre de vue leur différence irréductible ni les mêler l'une à l'autre. (p. 94).[15]

"The immense, the incalculable importance of the gas-cooker," you might as well say, "lies less in its intrinsic value than in the fact that it enables us to distinguish between the respective functions of the saucepan and the frying pan and allows the cook, with his admirable sense of the specific values of the different vitamins, to turn out a suet pudding and a pancake without ever losing sight of their irreducible difference or mixing one with the other." For it is unfortunately true that French critics are inclined to waste their admirable gifts in attaching futile and often misleading labels, in making petty distinctions between the "autobiography" and the "novel" or in trying to measure the number of psychological *aperçus* we get from a great novelist's work, while the true function of criticism is miserably disregarded.

III. SAINTE-BEUVE

Sainte-Beuve's reputation as a critic is something of a problem. As long as the supremacy of French criticism was unchallenged, he was fêted as the great European critic. It is hardly surprising that he has suffered severely from changing conceptions of the function of literary criticism. The danger of violent reactions is that they sometimes lead to injustice, and it would be a pity to let Sainte-Beuve's shortcomings as a critic blind us to his genuine achievement as a literary historian and as a propagandist for literature—as the apostle of culture to the new middle classes.

It is a curious fact that Sainte-Beuve's critics are seldom lukewarm. They either regard him like Amiel as "the prince of French critics" or they deny that he is, properly speaking, a literary critic at all. For those of us who are disposed to take the second view, it is a salutary exercise to read Remy de Gourmont's paper on *Sainte-Beuve créateur de valeurs* in the first volume of the *Promenades philosophiques,* which is probably the ablest defence of Sainte-Beuve that has ever been written. "The critic like the philosopher," said Gourmont, "creates values. The work of art is not a conclusion. Where there is a conclusion there is always criticism." (p. 33) According to Gourmont, the critic is primarily a judge and his function is to establish literary values, to decide where an author comes and whether we are right in admiring him. Until this is done the work of art remains incomplete. He goes on to say that Sainte-Beuve was responsible for fixing French literary values from Ronsard to Hugo—that he was, in fact, the person

15 "The immense, the incalculable importance of Stendhal's work lies less in its intrinsic value than in the information it gives us on the respective functions of the autobiography and the novel, and on the experiences of a writer who, with an admirable sense of specific values, was able to produce a work of either kind without ever losing sight of their irreducible difference or mixing one with the other."

who "created" the "value" of French Renaissance literature, of Port-Royal and Chateaubriand.

This view of Sainte-Beuve's influence is generally accepted and it would hardly become a foreigner to dispute it. There is, however, another and more general ground on which the validity of Gourmont's defence can be impugned. Although the "placing" of writers is an important part of the critic's function, it is not the whole of criticism. From the great critic we expect something more than this.[16]

"Sound literary judgment," wrote Gourmont in the same paper, "is not purely intellectual; feeling plays an important part in it. Now, feeling diminishes with age, or at any rate, the faculty of sympathy cannot be indefinitely extended and the moment comes when new arrivals, even if they still interest us, no longer excite us." (p. 38) Sainte-Beuve's later criticism possesses merits which are not to be found in the earlier, but in the first essays he is much more of the literary critic than he was later on. Some of his best criticism was written between the ages of twenty-five and thirty before his "method" had become hardened and dogmatic. The judgment is as sound, the mind freer and the sensibility more lively. His criticism of Racine in the three studies collected in the first volume of the *Portraits littéraires* still merits serious consideration; it is persuasive and the case is stated with a moderation that was sometimes wanting in the later work. The dissatisfaction that we feel with the essays as a whole lies, I think, in the contrast between the critic's air of knowing exactly where the writer "comes" and what he ought to say about him, which has contributed so much to Sainte-Beuve's immense authority, and the comparative poverty of his detailed criticism.

> Le style de Racine se présente, dès l'abord, sous une teinte assez uniforme d'élégance et de poésie; rien ne s'y détache particulièrement. Le procédé est d'ordinaire analytique et abstrait; chaque personnage principal, au lieu de répandre sa passion au dehors en ne faisant qu'un avec elle, regarde le plus souvent cette passion au dedans de lui-même, et la raconte par ses paroles telle qu'il la voit au sein de ce monde intérieur, au sein de ce *moi,* comme disent les philosophes: de là une manière générale d'exposition et de récit qui suppose toujours dans chaque héros ou chaque héroine un certain loisir pour s'examiner préalablement; de là encore un ordre d'images délicates, et un tendre coloris de demi-jour, emprunté à une savante métaphysique du coeur; mais peu ou point de réalité, et aucun de ces détails qui nous ramènent à l'aspect humain de cette vie. La poésie de Racine élude les détails, les dédaigne, et quand elle voudrait y atteindre, elle semble impuissante à les saisir. (p. 106).[17]

[16] It is perhaps the weakness of Gourmont's position that he was obliged to describe Boileau as "a great creator of values," though we know that he had a very low opinion of the intrinsic worth of his poetry.

[17] "Racine's style presents, from the first, a fairly uniform appearance of poetic elegance; nothing stands out conspicuously. The manner is usually analytical and abstract; each principal character, instead of showing what he feels by identifying

It is impossible not to be impressed by Sainte-Beuve's smooth accomplishment, by the skill and assurance with which he goes about his work. But the more we study the passage, the more doubtful we become whether it has anything to do with Racine or whether there is any correspondence between the critic's sensibility and the counters which he manipulates with such consummate ease. *"Rien,"* he says, *"ne s'y détache particulièrement."* Now the aim of the critic is to prevent anything from sticking out too sharply, to "create" the neat and accomplished craftsman whom Sainte-Beuve's contemporaries called Racine.[18] Thus the whole passage is a verbal construction in which every resource of style is devoted to evoking the genteel, the "tender" Racine of the nineteenth century myth. The emphasis therefore falls on the words *"élégance," "abstrait," "loisir," "délicates"* and *"tendre coloris de demi-jour."* The *"savante métaphysique du coeur"* (whatever that may be) is a neat way of evading the question of Racine's psychological acumen; and, as though to make sure that the phrase shall be phrase and no more, Sainte-Beuve goes on to add *"peu ou point de réalité"!* That the emotions of Racine's characters were the result of artificial contrivance and were not dictated by "inspiration" was of course a common criticism in the last century. It clearly suited Sainte-Beuve's purpose to assume that the criticism was just instead of testing its truth by a detailed examination of representative passages. The method of nineteenth century criticism, as we have already seen, was to start from a general conception of an age and to deduce the individual writer from it. It was therefore necessary for Racine to be transformed into a "courtier" and the discussion of his poetry, instead of being literary criticism in the true sense, is mainly an avoidance of criticism. Sainte-Beuve speaks of his style as though it were a separate entity and "elegance" and "poetry" simply ingredients. He points out, it is true, that the "elegance" was a product of *"le commerce paisible de cette société où une femme écrivait La Princesse de Clèves,"* but its true social validity is not discussed. It does not occur to him, for example, that Racine's elegance, like the elegance of the society in which he lived, was a surface elegance which intensified the ferocity of the passions beneath and the crumbling of the whole social order.

---

himself with the feeling, more often inspects that feeling within himself and describes it by telling what it looks like in the bosom of his interior world, in the recesses of his ego, as the philosophers say: hence a general manner of exposition and report which always presumes in each hero or heroine a certain amount of leisure for making a preliminary examination; hence also a delicate kind of imagery and a tender twilit coloring, deriving from a learned metaphysics of the heart; but with little bearing on reality, and with none of those details which call us back to the human aspect of life. The poetry of Racine evades such details, disdains them, and seems powerless to grasp them even when it would."

[18] In view of Gourmont's judgment on Sainte-Beuve, the whole passage should be compared with the reference to Racine in the *Problème du style,* pp. 50-51, quoted in Part II of this paper.

Although Sainte-Beuve criticized Taine shrewdly for trying to discover the writer from a study of his milieu, in many ways the theory formulated in his later work is not unlike Taine's. He, too, believed that criticism should be "a natural history of minds"; and for Taine's study of the milieu, he substituted a study of the "literary group." It was not, he thought, sufficient to study the man; the critic must investigate his family history and "the first group of friends and contemporaries in which he was living at the moment at which his talent manifested itself, entered into possession of itself and became mature." [19]

As this theory developed it led the critic almost inevitably further and further from his texts; but it was not without its compensations. Sainte-Beuve's later criticism is less "literary" than his early work, but it is, perhaps, of more lasting value. Its great value lies in the skill with which he describes backgrounds and tendencies which is more illuminating than anything he wrote about "style." It is interesting to compare his discussion of the background of *Polyeucte* in *Port-Royal* with a passage on Corneille's style in the *Portraits littéraires*.[20]

> Le *Polyeucte* de Corneille n'est pas plus beau à tous égards que cette circonstance réelle ("la journée du guichet") produite durant le bas âge du poète, et il n'émane pas d'une inspiration différente. C'est le même combat, c'est le même triomphe; si *Polyeucte* émeut et transporte, c'est que quelque chose de tel était et demeure possible encore à la nature humaine secourue. Je dis plus: si *Polyeucte* a été possible en son temps au génie de Corneille, c'est que quelque chose existait encore à l'entour (que Corneille le sût ou non) qui égalait et reproduisait les mêmes miracles. [21]

> La touche du poète est rude, sévère et vigoureuse. Je le comparerais volontiers à un statuaire qui, travaillaint sur l'argile pour y exprimer d'héroïques portraits, n'emploie d'autre instrument que le pouce, et qui, pétrissant ainsi son oeuvre, lui donne un suprême caractère de vie avec mille accidents heurtés qui l'accompagnent et l'achèvent; mais cela est incorrect, cela n'est pas lisse ni *propre*, comme on dit. Il y a peu de peinture et de couleur dans le style de Corneille; il est chaud plutôt qu'éclatant; il tourne volontiers à l'abstrait, et l'imagination y cède à la pensée et au raisonnement. Il doit plaire surtout aux hommes d'état,

[19] For a good summary of Sainte-Beuve's critical position see *Nouveaux lundis*, III, pp. 15-33.

[20] Most of the essays in the first volume of the *Portraits littéraires* were written before *Port-Royal* and collected later. But a footnote makes it clear that they were intended by the critic to be read in conjunction with his later pronouncements and presumably still represented his view of the authors concerned.

[21] "Corneille's *Polyeucte* is no more beautiful in every respect than that actual circumstance (known as '*la journée du guichet*') which occurred during the infancy of the poet, and its inspiration is the same. There is the same conflict, the same triumph; if *Polyeucte* is still deeply moving, it is because something of the same sort was and remains, by divine grace, yet possible in human nature. I say further· if the genius of Corneille could conceive *Polyeucte* in his time, it is because there still existed something in his surroundings (whether Corneille knew it or not) which equaled and reproduced the same miracles." *Port-Royal*, II, p. 115.

aux géomètres, aux militaires, á ceux qui goûtent les styles de Démosthène, de Pascal et de César.[22]

The first passage is a penetrating account of the relations between Corneille and contemporary society. It possesses the intuition which is essential to good history no less than to good criticism. But the second passage strikes me as commonplace and unfair. It seems impossible that the situation described in the first passage could have produced the work described in the second; and if it did, then the relation between Corneille and his milieu must have been different from Sainte-Beuve's description of it. For the description of Corneille's style is little more than a reiteration of the conventional criticisms which are very ably disposed of in the eulogy of *Polyeucte*. The most interesting thing in the passage is the image of the sculptor used to define Corneille's style. The great objection to Sainte-Beuve's imagery is that instead of illuminating his authors, it is at bottom a *substitute* for the critical distinction that one has a right to expect. There is no progress of thought; one thing is described in terms of another for the purpose of artful denigration. In this respect his use of imagery reminds me of that of a journalist like Hazlitt rather that of a genuine critic like Mrs. Woolf at her best.

The reasons for Sainte-Beuve's failings as a critic are not difficult to discover. "We judge a work of art," said Lawrence, "by its effect on our sincere and vital emotion and nothing else. . . . A critic must be able to *feel* the impact of a work of art in all its complexity and all its force." [23] No one knew better than Sainte-Beuve that a poem is a highly complex phenomenon, but he seldom managed to grasp it as a whole, seldom makes us feel that his criticism has behind it the whole force of his personality. In his discussion of a poem, there seems to be no continuity between the historian, the critic and the man who remain separate and distinct. It thus happens that though his writings contain interesting observations about language or the "content" of a work of art [24] he rarely gives us the "feel" of a poem. His response to his

[22] "The touch of the poet is rough, severe, and vigorous. I should like to compare him to a sculptor who, trying to express heroic likenesses in clay, uses only his thumb as an instrument, and who, moulding his work in this fashion, gives it a supremely living character along with the thousand accidental bruises that accompany the achievement; but that is not correct, that is not neat and tidy, as they say. There is little portraiture or color in the style of Corneille; it is fervid rather than brilliant; it inclines voluntarily to the abstract, and the imagination gives way to thoughtfulness and reason. It should be pleasing, above all, to statesmen, to geometricians, to military men, to those who enjoy the styles of Demosthenes, Pascal, and Caesar." *Portraits littéraires,* I, p. 48.

[23] *Phoenix,* p. 539. It is only fair to add that the same page contains a remarkable tribute to Sainte-Beuve as a critic! For more favourable estimates of his critical ability see M. André Thérive's Introduction to a volume of selections published in a collection called *Choisir* (Desclée de Brouwer, 1936) and the review of it in the *Criterion,* July, 1937, pp. 716-721.

[24] Of *Phèdre* he wrote: "La faiblesse et l'entraînement de notre misérable nature humaine n'ont jamais été plus mis à nu." (*Port-Royal,* VI, p. 131).

text is in general somewhat faint; and when he does succeed in communicating the impact of a work on his own personality it will be found that the emotion is seldom or never generated by the work alone; it is derived from some personal source that is only indirectly connected with it. In spite of his enthusiasm for scientific method, Sainte-Beuve was much less of a scientist or a philosopher than Taine. There was, indeed, a strange rootlessness—an absence of centre—in Sainte-Beuve as a man; and though this was a serious defect in the critic, it enabled him to experience to the full all the extraordinary spiritual vicissitudes of the first half of the nineteenth century which makes him a figure of capital importance in understanding the atmosphere of his age.

I have lingered over Taine and Sainte-Beuve because they seem to me to be peculiarly representative of French critical method and because it is on their work that the fame of French criticism largely depends. They were both products of the French love of systems, of a completely realized conception of man and his place in the universe; and they were both men who were passionately interested not perhaps in literature, but in culture and ideas. The work of both shows how a love of speculation spoilt that sensibility without which genuine literary criticism is impossible and how a natural love of authority, which may be a virtue, has a peculiarly disabling effect when the wrong authority is chosen. Neither curiosity about life nor mental agility is of much help alone in the education of public taste which is, perhaps, the first task of criticism. They both knew that literature was important, but Sainte-Beuve was unable to tell his public why it was important, and Taine's efforts to do so led him to turn it into a minor branch of history and psychology.

LITERARY CRITICISM IN FRANCE—II
(1939)

MARTIN TURNELL

I. BAUDELAIRE

THE MORE we study the criticism of the past, the more obvious it becomes that critics can be divided broadly into two main groups—those whose interest is purely "historical," and those whose work remains "actual" and can still help to form taste. Many of the critics in the first group have been men of outstanding ability; their work is still good reading; it provides us with useful information about the development of critical theory and the condition of taste at a particular period; but there its utility ends. The first group includes Dryden and Johnson in England, Boileau and Voltaire in France, and it is coming more and more to include Sainte-Beuve and Taine. The second group includes Coleridge and Arnold as well as Baudelaire and Gourmont.

What is not perhaps so obvious is that, though the life of a critic is necessarily shorter than that of an imaginative writer, the time factor is not decisive. Boileau's interest is purely historical, but parts of Saint -Evremond's work can still be read with profit; and though they were contemporaries, Baudelaire's criticism is more actual than Taine's. Nor is it simply a matter of being "right" about an author. Dryden was right in his placing of Shakespeare and Boileau in his placing of Villon; but though this was of great importance at the time, it has not prolonged the life of their criticism. A critic's value depends in the last resort on the quality of his sensibility and on his ability to stand aloof from the more ephemeral theories of his time.

These are some of the reasons why Baudelaire's importance as a critic remains great while that of his contemporaries diminishes. He was potentially the greatest French critic of the century and he possessed in a high degree all the essential attributes of criticism. There is no doubt that his output would have been still more impressive had he been able to work in more congenial circumstances. We know from his *Letters,* however, that many of his critical studies were written because he needed the money to pay his debts. He could not always choose his own subjects and he was not always free to express his true opinions. The result was that he expended his great gifts on minor writers and minor painters whose names only survive in his criticism. We may wonder, too, whether the long and flattering tributes to Hugo and Gautier would have been written if Baudelaire had felt able to dispense with their patronage.

It needs a real effort to read through *L'art romantique* and the *Curiosités esthétiques,* but Baudelaire's criticism is so fragmentary and scattered that the effort is a necessary one. There is a good deal that is not of great value; the excursions into aesthetic theory are not particularly helpful; and some of the theories like the theory of *correspondances* have not worn well. But the effort is well repaid. Baudelaire's best criticism is a valuable guide to his own practice, and his comments on contemporary schools and writers illuminate the intricacies of the French literary scene as no other criticism of the time does. Finally, it is possible to extract a small body of criticism which is of permanent value and a model of how good criticism should be written.

"Criticism," said Baudelaire, "should be partial, passionate and political, that is to say, written from an exclusive point of view, but from the point of view which opens up the widest horizons." His great merit as a critic lies, I think, in the fact that he possessed a genuinely philosophic mind and an extremely acute sensibility—two gifts which instead of destroying completed one another. He had an extraordinary faculty of going straight to the heart of a matter, in perceiving the importance of an artist or a movement in relation to "the present time." It is interesting to compare an extract from Sainte-Beuve's address on *Tradition in Literature,* which was delivered in 1858, with some passages on the same subject from Baudelaire's *Des écoles et des ouvriers* in the 1846 Salon. This is Sainte-Beuve:

> Mais l'atticisme, mais l'urbanité, mais le principe de sens et de raison qui s'y mêle à la grâce, ne nous en séparons pas. Le sentiment d'un certain beau conforme à notre race, à notre éducation, à notre civilisation, voilà ce dont il ne faut jamais se départir . . .
>
> Pour maintenir la tradition, il ne suffit point toutefois de la bien rattacher à ses monuments les plus élevés et les plus augustes; il convient de la vérifier, de la contrôler sans cesse sur les points les plus rapprochés, de la rajeunir même, et de la tenir dans un rapport perpétuel avec ce qui est vivant. Ici nous touchons à une question assez délicate; car il ne s'agit pas de venir introduire dans l'enseignement des noms trop nouveaux, de juger hors de propos des ouvrages du jour, de confondre les fonctions et les rôles.[1]

[1] "But let us not separate Atticism, urbanity, the principle of sense and reason, from the grace with which it is there blended. We must never depart from the feeling for a particular beauty which is in conformity with our race, our education, our civilization . . .

"To maintain the tradition, it is not enough always to adhere closely to its most elevated and august monuments; it is proper to verify it, to check it unceasingly at the most questionable points, even to renovate it, and to keep it in constant touch with the living. Here we touch upon a very delicate matter; for there is no question of wishing to introduce into the schools writers too recent, of judging works of the present day inopportunely, of confusing functions and rôles."

This quotation and the quotations which follow are here translated from the French by Professor Monroe K. Spears. [*Editor's note.*]

Comparing the order of the great tradition with the chaos and confusion of his own times, Baudelaire writes:

> Dans l'un, turbulence, tohu-bohu de styles et de couleurs, cacophonie de tons, trivialités énormes, prosaisme de gestes et d'attitudes, noblesse de convention, *poncifs* de toutes sortes, et tout cela visible et clair, non-seulement dans les tableaux juxtaposés, mais encore dans le même tableau, bref,—absence complète d'unité, dont le résultat est une fatigue effroyable pour l'esprit et pour les yeux.
>
> Dans l'autre, ce respect qui fait ôter leurs chapeaux aux enfants, et vous saisit l'âme, comme la poussière des tombes et des caveaux saisit la gorge, est l'effet, non point du vernis jaune et de la crasse du temps, mais de l'unité, de l'unité profonde . . .
>
> Là des écoles, et ici des ouvriers émancipés.
>
> Il y avait encore des écoles sous Louis XV, il y en avait une sous l'Empire,—une école, c'est-à-dire une foi, c'est-à-dire l'impossibilité du doute. Il y avait des élèves unis par des principes communs, obéissant à la règle d'un chef puissant, et l'aidant dans tous ses travaux.[2]

It is impossible not to be struck by the contrast between Sainte-Beuve's highflown rhetoric, which gets no nearer the concrete than *"un certain beau conforme à notre race,"* and the intense feeling behind *"ce respect qui . . . vous saisit l'âme, comme la poussière . . . saisit la gorge"* or, in another place, the ironic reference to *"quelques excentriques, sublimes et souffrants"* Tradition in literature, whatever else it means, must mean continuity of feeling. Now it is clear that Sainte-Beuve's address is lip-service to an abstraction. He was like most Frenchmen aware of tradition in a general way, but his attitude is historical and has nothing of the extraordinary actuality of Baudelaire's criticism. It was a closed circle and the only modern master who was not a Frenchman for whom he found a place was Shakespeare. He saw that modern writers must be incorporated in the ancient framework, but the process was to be a purely mechanical one. He did not *feel* the relation between the modern writer and masters of the past; his attitude, as expressed in the last three lines, was simply that of the selection

[2] "In one, turbulence, hurly-burly of styles and colors, cacaphony of tones, enormous trivialities, prosaic gestures and attitudes, nobility purely conventional, stereotypes of all sorts, and all this clearly apparent, not only in juxtaposed pictures, but even within the same picture. In short, a complete lack of unity, resulting in frightful fatigue for the mind and for the eyes.

"In the other, this respect which makes children take off their hats, and which catches you in the soul, as the dust of tombs and caverns catches you in the throat, is the effect not of the yellow varnish and grime of age, but of unity, of profound unity . . .

"There schools, and here emancipated craftsmen.

"There were still schools under Louis XV; there was one under the Empire,—one school, which is to say one faith, which is to say the impossibility of doubt. There were students united by common principles, obeying the discipline of a powerful master, and aiding him in all his work." *Curiosités esthétiques,* ed. Crépet, pp. 192-193.

committee of some public gallery. Baudelaire's criticism, on the other hand, is a perfect example of his combination of sensibility and wide powers of generalization. He feels the unity of the old order and the chaos of the new; his *"vaste population de médiocrités . . . qui cherchent à se faire un caractère par un système d'emprunts contradictoires"* is an admirably concrete statement of dilemma which is complacently ignored by Sainte-Beuve; and when he finds the source of the trouble in an absence of "faith" we can have no doubt about the correctness of his diagnosis.

Baudelaire was less of a technical philosopher than Taine or Gourmont and his mind was more flexible than theirs. Indeed, it is evident from his insistence on Original Sin both in his criticism and in the letters and diaries that his point of view was primarily theological.

. . . . .

Baudelaire shows the same sureness of touch, the same faculty for going straight to the root of the matter, when he passes judgment—an admirably generous and impartial judgment—on the Romantic Movement:

> Certainement il y aurait injustice à nier les services qu'a rendus l'école dite romantique. Elle nous rappela à vérité de l'image, elle détruisit les poncifs académiques, et même, au point de vue supérieur de la linguistique, elle ne mérite pas les dédains dont l'ont iniquement couverte certains pédants impuissants. Mais par son principe même, l'insurrection romantique était condamnée à une vue courte. La puérile utopie de l'école de *l'art pour l'art,* en excluant la morale, et souvent même la passion, était nécessairement stérile. Elle se mettait en flagrante contravention avec le génie de l'humanité. Au nom des principes supérieurs qui constituent la vie universelle, nous avons le droit de la déclarer coupable d'hétérodoxie . . .[3]

This passage is interesting because it shows that in making a critical judgment Baudelaire uses a definite body of principles as a point of reference. It is by this standard that he condemns the excesses of Romanticism, and the statement that it excludes morality is a philosophical way of pointing out its fundamental immaturity.

His extraordinary critical sensibility is still more evident in particular judgments. What could be fairer or more discriminating than

[3] "Certainly it would be unjust to deny the services rendered by the school called 'romantic.' It recalled us to the truth of the image, it destroyed academic stereotypes, and it does not, even from the higher point of view of linguistics, deserve the disdain which certain impotent pedants have heaped upon it. But the romantic rebellion was condemned, by its very principle, to short-sightedness. The puerile utopia of the 'art for art's sake' school, in excluding morality, and often passion too, was necessarily sterile. It set itself in flagrant opposition to the essential nature of humanity. In the name of the higher principles which are the basis of all life, we have the right to declare it guilty of heterodoxy . . ." *L'art romantique,* ed. Crépet, p. 177.

his opinion of Hugo—Hugo who at that time was universally regarded as "the great poet"?

> M. Victor Hugo, dont je ne veux certainement pas diminuer la noblesse et la majesté, est un ouvrier beaucoup plus adroit qu'inventif, un travailleur bien plus correct que créateur. Delacroix est quelquefois maladroit, mais essentiellement créateur. M. Victor Hugo laisse voir dans tous ses tableaux, lyriques et dramatiques, un système d'alignement et de contrastes uniformes. L'excentricité elle-même prend chez lui des formes symétriques. Il possède à fond et emploie froidement tous les tons de la rime, toutes les ressources de l'antithèse, toutes les tricheries de l'apposition. C'est un compositeur de décadence ou de transition, qui se sert de ses outils avec une dextérité véritablement admirable et curieuse. M. Hugo était naturellement académicien avant que de naître, et si nous étions encore au temps des merveilles fabuleuses, je croirais volontiers que les lions verts de l'Institut, quand il passait devant le sanctuaire courroucé, lui ont souvent murmuré d'une voix prophétique: "Tu seras de l'Académie!" [4]

. . . . .

Criticism is not so rich in colour that we can afford to overlook the following passage from the fine essay on Constantin Guys:

> La Turquie a fourni aussi à notre cher G. d'admirables motifs de compositions: les fêtes du Baïram, splendeurs profondes et ruisselantes, au fond desquelles apparaît, comme un soleil pâle, l'ennui permanent du sultan défunt.[5]

No one excels Baudelaire in "placing" a bad writer or a bad painter. He observes of a bad painter:

> Je hais cet homme parce que ses tableaux ne sont point de la peinture, mais une masturbation agile et fréquente, une irritation de l'épiderme français.[6]

Finally, one should look at the criticism of Balzac which is buried like hidden treasure in the dreary wastes of the essay on Gautier:

[4] "M. Victor Hugo, from whose nobility and majesty I certainly do not wish to detract, is a craftsman much more skilled than inventive, a workman much more correct than creative. Delacroix is sometimes awkward, but essentially creative. M. Victor Hugo reveals in all his pictures, lyric and dramatic, a system of alignment and of uniform contrasts. Eccentricity itself takes symmetrical forms in his work. He is complete master of, and employs coolly, all the tones of rhyme, all the resources of antithesis, all the trickeries of apposition. He is a composer of a decadent or transitional period, who uses his tools with a dexterity truly admirable and interesting. M. Hugo was by nature an academician before he was born, and if we were still in the age of fabulous wonders, I would willingly believe that the green lions of the Institute, when he passed before the haughty sanctuary, often murmured to him with prophetic voice: 'You will belong to the Academy.'" *Curiosités esthétiques*, p. 104.

[5] "Turkey has also furnished our dear G. with admirable motifs for compositions: the feasts of Baïram, profound and flowing splendors, through which appears, like a pallid sun, the permanent boredom of the dead sultan." *L'art romantique*, p. 80.

[6] "I hate this man because his canvases are not painting, but agile and repeated masturbation, an irritation of the French epidermis."

> Balzac, grand, terrible, complexe aussi, figure le monstre d'une civilisation, et toutes ses luttes, ses ambitions et ses fureurs... J'ai mainte fois été étonné que la grande gloire de Balzac fût de passer pour un observateur; il m'avait toujours semblé que son principal mérite était d'être visionnaire, et visionnaire passionné. Tous ses personnages sont doués de l'ardeur vitale dont il était animé lui-même. Toutes ses fictions sont aussi profondément colorées que les rêves. Depuis le sommet de l'aristocratie jusqu'aux bas-fonds de la plèbe, tous les acteurs de sa *Comédie* sont plus âpres à la vie, plus actifs et rusés dans la lutte, plus patients dans le malheur, plus goulus dans la jouissance, plus angéliques dans le dévouement, que la comédie du vrai monde ne nous les montre. Bref, chacun, chez Balzac, même les portières, a du génie. Toutes les âmes sont des armes chargées de volonté jusqu'à la gueule. C'est bien Balzac lui-même. Et comme tous les êtres du monde extérieur s'offraient à l'oeil de son esprit avec un relief puissant et une grimace saisissante, il a fait se convulser ses figures; il a noirci leurs ombres et illuminé leurs lumières. Son goût prodigieux du détail, qui tient à une ambition immodérée de tout voir, de tout faire voir, de tout deviner, de tout faire deviner, l'obligeait d'ailleurs à marquer avec plus de force les lignes principales, pour sauver la perspective de l'ensemble.[7]

There is, perhaps, more genuine criticism in this passage of Baudelaire than in the ninety pages of Taine's essay.

II. REMY DE GOURMONT

"As I have already explained on several occasions," wrote Remy de Gourmont, "contrary to the opinion generally held, criticism is perhaps the most subjective of all literary forms. It is a perpetual confession on the part of the critic. He may think that he is analysing the works of other people, but it is himself that he is revealing and exposing to the public. This necessity explains very well why criticism is as a rule so mediocre and why the critic seldom manages to hold our attention even when he is dealing with questions in which we are

[7] "Balzac, great, terrible, and complex, represents the freak of a civilization, and all his struggles, his ambitions and his furies... I have often been astonished that the great fame of Balzac was as an observer; it had always seemed to me that his chief merit was that he was a visionary, and an impassioned visionary. All his characters are endowed with the vital ardor by which he himself was animated. All his fictions are as deeply colored as dreams. From the height of the aristocracy to the bottom of the proletariat, all the actors of the *Comédie* are more avid for life, more active and crafty in the struggle, more patient in misfortune, greedier in enjoyment, more angelic in devotion, than the comedy of the real world ever reveals them to us. In short, everyone in Balzac, even the porters, has genius. Every soul is a gun loaded to the muzzle with Will. Indeed, each is Balzac himself. And as all the beings of the exterior world present themselves to the eye of his mind in strong relief and with a striking expression, he has made his figures move convulsively; he has darkened their shadows and heightened their lights. His prodigious love of detail, together with an immoderate ambition to see everything, to make the reader see everything, to divine everything, to make the reader divine everything, obliged him, besides, to draw the principal lines more heavily, in order to preserve the perspective of the whole." *L'art romantique,* p. 168.

most keenly interested. In order to be a good critic, indeed, one must possess a strong personality. The critic must impose himself on the reader and to this end he must rely not on the choice of subject, but on the quality of his own mind. The subject is of small importance in art, or at any rate it is only one part of art; it is of no more importance in criticism where it is never more than a pretext." [8]

This is not a complete definition of the function of criticism, nor, as we shall see from Gourmont's own work, is it wholly sound; but it draws attention to three points which are seen to be of particular importance when we remember the weaknesses of Sainte-Beuve and Taine. In the first place, it insists on the personal factor in criticism and is therefore a corrective to the attempts of nineteenth century critics to reduce criticism to an exact science. In the second place, although there can be no substitute for personal sensibility, this alone is not enough. Criticism must have behind it the whole force of the critic's personality, the whole force of his powerful, independent mind. In the third place, and perhaps the most important of all, we find a distinguished critic asserting for the first time that criticism is valuable for its own sake and is not (as Taine tried to make it) a branch of some other science.[9]

It was the clarity with which Gourmont grasped this third point that helped to make him one of the most distinguished critics of his time. The *Problème du style* has had, directly and indirectly, a considerable influence on contemporary English criticism. It is one of the finest works of general criticism that has appeared during the past fifty years and though it deals almost exclusively with French writers, it is essentially a European work and should be almost as valuable to the English as to the French specialist. The papers collected in the seven volumes of the *Promenades littéraires* have lost none of their freshness with the passing of time. When they first appeared these brief and eminently readable *chroniques* were something new in literary journalism. They took the place of Sainte-Beuve's elaborate *causeries* with their vast parade of erudition. Gourmont was not only more stimulating, more of a critic than Sainte-Beuve, but in the best of the *Promenades littéraires*–notably in the studies of Renan, Brunetière and Lemaître–he contrived in the space of nine or ten pages to say the essential about his authors. No one who works on the same authors can afford to overlook what Gourmont has said about them; and it is difficult to think of any collection of literary essays to which one returns more often or more profitably.

[8] *Promenades littéraires,* I, p. 14.

[9] As far as I am aware it is not until 1921 that we find an English critic making a similar declaration. In that year, Mr. Middleton Murry wrote in an article called *A Critical Credo* (reprinted in *Countries of the Mind,* I): "The function of criticism is, therefore, primarily the function of literature itself, to provide a means of expression for the critic."

In spite of his great merits, however, Gourmont's criticism leaves the reader with an ill-defined sense of dissatisfaction. I have sometimes thought that this impression may be due to the economy imposed by the *chronique,* to the fact that it may appear thin when compared with the weighty studies of Gourmont's immediate predecessors; but constant re-reading suggests that Gourmont's particular faults are inseparably connected with his particular virtues and the two can only be discussed together.

"La seule recherche féconde," he wrote in the Preface to the *Problème du style, "est la recherche du non-vrai."* It is a concise statement not only of his own method, but also of the temper which informed the whole of his writings. He was a sceptic and an amateur of physiology, possibly because physiology seemed to provide the only certain foothold in an age of crumbling systems. His scepticism was complete, but it was a genial scepticism. His criticism is singularly free from the faults which make critics of the same period who wrote in English seem crude and provincial. The fact that he was a Frenchman and his background Catholic enabled him to appreciate the issues better than an Englishman and preserved him from the Nonconformist conscience which has always been one of the greatest enemies of clear thinking. Although he remarked bluntly in his paper on Renan *"Je n'aime guère le style des écrivains dont je déteste la pensée,"* his treatment of writers whose beliefs he did not share was often remarkable for its justice and impartiality. His description of Verlaine as "one of France's greatest Catholic poets" errs, perhaps, on the side of generosity; but in the *Problème du style* he said admirably of Bossuet (whose "thought" can hardly have been sympathetic to him);

> Bossuet écrit pour édifier ou pour convaincre, mais sa sensibilité générale est si riche, sa vitalité si profonde, son énergie si violente, qu'il peut se dédoubler, et rester un écrivain en ne voulant être qu'un apôtre. (p. 94.) [10]

His criticism of the *Vie de Jésus,* which one might have expected him to find more sympathetic than Bossuet, is particularly interesting:

> Le plus contestable, pour le fond, des ouvrages de Renan, la *Vie de Jésus,* est précisément celui qui est le moins bien écrit. L'incertitude de l'idée a fait vaciller le style; cela tremblote comme une lampe d'église, une nuit que le vent souffle par un vitrail brisé. Dans beaucoup d'autres écrits de Renan, la souplesse solide de son écriture s'enroule merveilleusement à la solidité flexible de sa pensée. M. Brunetière parle de la "souveraine clarté" de sa langue, mais comment peut-il admirer une transparence, alors fâcheuse, qui n'a d'autre résultat que de faire mieux voir le trouble ou le néant du fond? Mais comment même peut-il se

[10] "Boussuet writes to edify or to convince, but his general sensibility is so rich, his vitality so deep, his energy so violent, that he can divide himself in two, and remain a writer while wishing only to be an apostle."

faire que l'eau soit pure et transparente quand le fond est bourbeux? Les ondes ne sont claires que si elles s'appuient sur la fermeté d'un fond de roche.[11]

This marks the end of the method, practised by Sainte-Beuve and Taine, of treating a writer's "style" and his "thought" as though they were in some way separable. Gourmont was preeminently a literary critic and in this passage he uses the methods of literary criticism to expose the fundamental weaknesses of Renan's work as a whole.

In spite of limitations of which I shall have something to say later, the sceptical approach is impressive in its astringency and up to a point it constitutes a genuine intellectual discipline. Gourmont was one of the first writers who systematically attacked vague romantic appreciation and tried to make criticism not a science, but scientific in a wide sense which was not Taine's sense; and his declaration that "style is a specialisation of sensibility" is a landmark in the history of criticism. The most valuable parts of the *Problème du style* are, indeed, those in which Gourmont sets out to define sensibility. In the well-known passage on Flaubert he wrote:

> Flaubert incorporait toute sa sensibilité à ses oeuvres; et par sensibilité, j'entends, ici comme partout, le pouvoir général de sentir tel qu'il est inégalement développé en chaque être humain. La sensibilité comprend la raison elle-même, qui n'est que de la sensibilité cristallisée. Hors de ses livres, où il se transvasait goutte à goutte, jusqu'à la lie, Flaubert est fort peu intéressant; il n'est plus que lie: son intelligence se trouble, s'exaspère en une fantaisie incohérente . . . Loin que son oeuvre soit impersonnelle, les rôles sont ici renversés: c'est l'homme qui est vague et tissé d'incohérences; c'est l'oeuvre qui vit, respire, souffre et sourit noblement. (p. 117.)[12]

For Gourmont the great writer is the writer whose work is his life, and the bad writer is the writer who is divided between writing and action. Thus he observes acutely of the solitaries of Port-Royal:

[11] "The most debatable, really, of Renan's works, the *Life of Jesus*, is precisely the one which is least well written. The uncertainty of the conception has made the style waver; it trembles like a church lamp on a night when the wind blows through a broken window. In many others of Renan's works, the solid suppleness of his writing marvelously surrounds the flexible solidity of his thought. M. Brunetière speaks of the 'sovereign clarity' of his language, but how can one admire a transparence which is unfortunate, which has no other result than to permit one to see better the disorder or the emptiness at bottom? But how can the water be pure and transparent when the bottom is muddy? Streams are clear only when they rest upon the strength of a rock bottom." *Promenades littéraires*, I, pp. 17-18.

[12] "Flaubert incorporated his whole sensibility in his works; and by sensibility I mean, here as everywhere, the general power of feeling, as it is unequally developed in each human being. Sensibility comprehends reason itself, which is only crystallized feeling. Outside of his books, into which he decanted himself drop by drop to the dregs, Flaubert is of very little interest; he is nothing but dregs; his intellect disturbs itself, exasperates itself in an incoherent fantasy. . . . Far from his work being impersonal, the rôles here are reversed: it is the man who is vague and woven of incoherences; it is the work which lives, breathes, suffers and smiles nobly."

> Ils écrivaient d'un style tout extérieur, où ils n'incorporaient presque aucune parcelle de leur sensibilité, la gardant toute pour leur vie, pour leur activité religieuse. (p. 48.) [13]

The definition of sensibility is undeniably impressive, but when we find Gourmont writing

> Racine, dont le style est si rarement plastique, garde pour ses maîtresses d'abord, pour Dieu ensuite, presque toute sa sensibilité. Le sentiment profond de l'amour, qui était en lui, n'a pas passé dans les actes de ses personnages; ils expriment des passions extrêmes en un style abstrait, glacé, et diplomatique. (pp. 50-51.) [14]

it is impossible not to feel disconcerted. There are, I think, two explanations. One is that the definition of sensibility is not as conclusive as it sounds. The other is that like most French critics, Gourmont was more impressive when making general statements of principle than when elucidating a text. They are both worth discussion.

Flaubert was a great novelist, but we may doubt whether he was the perfect writer for which Gourmont took him. Indeed, his admiration appears to be one of the symptoms of the peculiar limitations of his own critical sensibility. His emphasis on the physiological element in sensibility was timely and important, but when he observes

> Le style est un produit physiologique et l'un des plus constants, quoique dans la dépendance des diverses fonctions vitales. (*Ibid.*, p. 19.) [15]

we may suspect that in practice the definition was narrower than one would expect from the passage on Flaubert given above, that it was reduced to a physiological function in the interests of an inadequate metaphysic. It explains, for example, why Gourmont should admire Flaubert's style, which is rich in the expression of physical sensations, and find Racine's *"abstrait, glacé, et diplomatique."* The criticism of the style of the *Solitairies* is just, but when Gourmont goes on to assert

> L'art est incompatible avec une préoccupation morale ou religieuse; le beau ne porte ni à la piété, ni à la contrition, et la gloire de Dieu éclate principalement en des ouvrages de la mentalité la plus humble et de la rhétorique la plus médiocre. (p. 48) [16]

[13] "They wrote in a style wholly external, into which they incorporated hardly a particle of their sensibility, saving it all for their life, for their religious activity."

[14] "Racine, whose style is so seldom plastic, saves almost all his sensibilities first for his mistresses, then for God. The profound feeling for love which was in him did not enter into the actions of his characters; they express intense passions in an abstract, frigid, and diplomatic style."

[15] "Style is a physiological product, and one of the most constant, though dependent upon various vital functions."

[16] "Art is incompatible with a moral or religious preoccupation; beauty leads neither to piety nor to contrition, and the glory of God shines chiefly in works of the humblest intelligence and most mediocre rhetoric."

he imposes a drastic theoretical limitation which he would hardly tolerate in the concrete study of a poet.[17] This view is confirmed by his asides on the nature and value of artistic experience. When he tries to explain why it is valuable, he falls back on generalities:

> L'art est ce qui donne une sensation de beau et de nouveau à la fois, de beau inédit; on ne peut bien comprendre et cependant être ému.[18]

Poetry is transformed into a mystery which appears to call not for comprehension, but for adoration. It is a mystery to which only an élite are admitted. *"Car je crois,"* writes Gourmont, *"que l'art est, par essence, absolument inintelligible au peuple."*

The language that he uses to describe his favourite writers is not less instructive. He speaks enthusiastically of Mallarmé's *"sonnets les plus délicieusement obscurs"* and of *"l'art délicat et ingénieux d'aujourd'hui."* It is to his credit that he was the indefatigable champion of the "advanced" writers of his own time, but Mr. Eliot's description of him as "the critical consciousness of a generation" points to a serious limitation in his criticism. His intense preoccupation with the theories of the Symbolist Movement—a preoccupation that is apparent in his novels and his poetry as well as in his criticism—seems to have turned him into a dilettante who gloried in anything that was recondite and in "novel" and "deliciously obscure" sensations partly because they were inaccessible to other people. The terms that he used to describe poetic experience suggest that his sensibility was distinctly limited. His admiration for *le beau inédit* impaired his appreciation of Racine and his emphasis on "the delicate and ingenious art of to-day" accounts, perhaps, for his failure with Rimbaud whom he significantly called *"un crapaud congrument pustuleux."* For an adequate reading of that poet would have needed a range of feeling of which Gourmont was incapable.

It is one of the disadvantages of Gourmont's sceptical approach that he was more effective as a destructive critic and one of the finest papers in the whole of the *Promenades littéraires* is the brilliant attack on Brunetière. But it is symptomatic that his destructive work was limited to academic writers like Brunetière and the unhappy M. Abalat. His attempt to make poetry something for an élite is a sign of the negative attitude he adopted to one of the most pressing problems of his generation, as it is one of the most pressing problems of our own. He does not escape the charge of being the critic of the Ivory Tower whose aim is to take refuge from the barbarism of the outside world.

I have said that Gourmont was more impressive when making general statements of principle than when elucidating a text. It is not

[17] He was, in fact, obliged to qualify it on the next page when he made his admirable comment on Bossuet quoted above.

[18] "Art is that which produces a sensation of beauty and of novelty at the same time, of new beauty; one cannot understand entirely and still be moved."

without significance that he wrote better about the work of other critics than about poetry. Although he was the official critic of the Symbolist Movement, he never wrote a searching or substantial book about the *poetry* of the Movement; and compared with his able account of the philosophy of Symbolism in the paper on *Idealism,* his studies of individual writers like Corbière and Laforgue, Verlaine and Mallarmé, are fragmentary and disappointing. For in the last resort he was true to the French approach; he was more interested in the movement of ideas behind the poetry than in the poetry itself. His limitations as a critic sometimes made his discussion of ideas less impressive than it should have been. In his paper on Brunetière he quotes a passage from that critic's book on Balzac:

> "It is not only not true that everything appears differently to different people according to personal idiosyncracies . . . but reality is the same for all intelligences. There is only one point of view from which it is true and 'in conformity with its object,' just as in science there is only one formula that is truly scientific."
>
> With this principle [retorts Gourmont], one ends by denying the legitimacy of all individual activity. Art disappears altogether. . . . Every object, every fact, only permits of one valid representation, which is true; and ideas are necessarily divided into two classes—the true and the false . . .
>
> Let us remain true to the principles of subjective idealism which are impregnable. The world is my representation of it. It is the only creative principle, the only one which allows the full development and ordering of intelligence and sensibility.[19]

As a criticism of Brunetière this is final; as a statement of the philosophy inherent in the poetry of the period, it is undoubtedly true. But Gourmont was so impressed by idealism as a philosophy, so in love with freedom and individualism, that it did not occur to him to ask whether the influence of this philosophy on poetry was as advantageous as he chose to think. It did not strike him that an extreme individualism was actually having an unfortunate influence on language which was losing its ancient power of translating sensations into words and was already showing signs of developing into the *jeu de mots* which we now know as Surrealism; and the sort of criticism which Rivière made in his fine essay *Reconnaissance à Dada,* was beyond the scope of his method.

. . . . .

Gourmont was a very stimulating and, up to a point, a very able critic; but he seems to me to fall short of greatness. He was endowed in a high degree with the Frenchman's mental alertness and his curiosity about life; but it was precisely an undisciplined curiosity coupled with a fundamental dilettantism which led him into un-

[19] *Promenades littéraires,* III, pp. 32-33.

profitable ways and detracted from the critical intensity of his work. His scepticism, which was valuable as a critical approach in his time, had in the long run a disabling effect on his writing and it is impossible not to be struck over and over again with the fundamental poverty of his outlook.

III. CONCLUSION

It is time to draw some tentative conclusions of a more general nature, to decide how far the French critics of the last century fulfilled the function of criticism. "The aim of criticism," said Eliot, "is the elucidation of works of art and the correction of taste." The words must be understood in their widest sense. It is not enough for criticism to sharpen our appreciation of a writer's "style" or to interpret the "meaning" of his work; good criticism must provide the reader with an education, must establish a relation between literature and our ordinary everyday life. It is clear that these aims can only be accomplished if the critic possesses great sensibility and a philosophical outlook or, as Mrs. Q. D. Leavis once called it, a certain "wisdom." The main criticism which has to be made of French writers is that they try to make philosophy do the work of analysis and that they also use it as a substitute for that more general wisdom which we expect of a good critic.

The philosophical training which forms part of French education accounts for the apparent balance and maturity of French critics and the ease with which they handle a technical vocabulary. It stimulates the Frenchman's intellectual alertness and his curiosity about life which are the two greatest virtues of French criticism, and it certainly helps to give it an air of slick professionalism which sometimes makes English criticism look amateurish by comparison. The French mind is better endowed for speculative thought than the English, but it is on the whole less sensitive and less concrete. It is one of the consequences of a training in philosophy that it encourages the Frenchman's natural tendency to abstraction, to manipulate counters like *pensée* and *être moral* which instead of illuminating the work under discussion have precisely the opposite effect; they take the critic's mind off his text and carry him into a realm of abstract theorising for which the work of art is merely a pretext. The result is that the French critic is more concerned with his own system than with the intrinsic merits of his author, more interested in determining the "group" or "school" to which he belongs than in the excellence of his poetry.

A work of art may have important implications in the sphere of morality, but the discovery of these implications presupposes the full and unfettered response of the critic to the work before him for which no system of philosophy, whatever its intrinsic excellence, can ever be a substitute. It is tempting to make a theoretic distinction between the two "moments" of the critical act—the critic's response to his text and the philosophical analysis of that response, though we may doubt whether in practice there can be complete separation between the two. It remains true, however, that some critics are capable of excellent detailed analysis but are unable to perceive the general implications of the work that they criticize, while others are prevented by the excellence of their philosophical equipment from making that full and unfettered response to the work of art which is the basis of all criticism. This is undoubtedly true of many of the most eminent French critics. It thus happens that though French criticism in the nineteenth century was full of stimulating theories and curious speculations, it suffered from a pronounced defect of sensibility, and the standard of "practical criticism" was, with the exception of Baudelaire, Gourmont and Paul Bourget—a greatly underrated critic whom I have not been able to deal with—extremely low.

It has been suggested that French critics have substituted philosophy for the more general wisdom which is essential to good criticism. It is a notable fact that the French critic attaches more importance to the external order and coherence of his system than to its flexibility or its completeness. The result is that his work often turns out to be inferior to that of English writers whose philosophical equipment appears at first to be less impressive. For this reason it seems to me that men like Sainte-Beuve and Taine are in the last analysis inferior to the representatives of the great humanist tradition in England—to Coleridge and to Arnold.

HISTORICAL CRITICISM [1]

(1941)

EDMUND WILSON

I WANT to talk about the historical interpretation of literature—that is, about the interpretation of literature in its social, economic and political aspects.

To begin with, it will be worth while to say something about the kind of criticism which seems to be furthest removed from this. There is a kind of comparative criticism which tends to be non-historical. The essays of T. S. Eliot, which have had such an immense influence in our time, are, for example, fundamentally non-historical. Eliot sees, or tries to see, the whole of literature, so far as he is acquainted with it, spread out before him under the aspect of eternity. He then compares the work of different periods and countries, and tries to draw from it general conclusions about what literature ought to be. He understands, of course, that our point of view in connection with literature changes, and he has what seems to me a very sound conception of the whole body of writing of the past as something to which new works are continually being added, and which is not thereby merely increased in bulk but modified as a whole—so that Sophocles is no longer precisely what he was for Aristotle, or Shakespeare what he was for Ben Jonson or for Dryden or for Dr. Johnson, on account of all the later literature that has intervened between them and us. Yet at every point of this continual accretion, the whole field may be surveyed, as it were, spread out before the critic. The critic tries to see it as God might; he calls the books to a Day of Judgment. And, looking at things in this way, he may arrive at interesting and valuable conclusions which could hardly be reached by approaching them in any other way. Eliot was able to see, for example—what I believe had never been noticed before—that the French Symbolist poetry of the nineteenth century had certain fundamental resemblances to the English poetry of the age of Donne. Another kind of critic would draw certain historical conclusions from these purely aesthetic findings, as the Russian D. S. Mirsky did; but Eliot does not draw them.

Another example of this kind of non-historical criticism, in a somewhat different way and on a somewhat different plane, is the work

[1] A lecture delivered at Princeton University, October 23, 1940.

of the late George Saintsbury. Saintsbury was a connoisseur of wines; he wrote an entertaining book on the subject. And his attitude toward literature, too, was that of the connoisseur. He tastes the authors and tells you about the vintages; he distinguishes the qualities of the various wines. His palate was as fine as could be, and he possessed the great qualification that he knew how to take each book on its own terms without expecting it to be some other book and was thus in a position to appreciate a great variety of kinds of writing. He was a man of strong social prejudices and peculiarly intransigent political views, but, so far as it is humanly possible, he kept them out of his literary criticism. The result is one of the most agreeable and most comprehensive commentaries on literature that has ever been written in English. Most scholars who have read as much as Saintsbury don't have Saintsbury's discriminating taste. Here is a critic who has covered the whole ground like any academic historian, yet whose account of it is not merely a chronology but a record of fastidious enjoyment. Since enjoyment is the only thing he is looking for, he does not need to know the causes of things, and the historical background of literature does not interest him very much.

There is, however, another tradition of criticism which dates from the beginning of the eighteenth century. In the year 1725, the Neapolitan philosopher Vico published *La Scienza Nuova,* a revolutionary work on the philosophy of history, in which he asserted for the first time that the social world was certainly the work of man, and attempted what is, so far as I know, the first social interpretation of a work of literature. This is what Vico says about Homer: "Homer composed the *Iliad* when Greece was young and consequently burning with sublime passions such as pride, anger and vengeance—passions which cannot allow dissimulation and which consort with generosity; so that she then admired Achilles, the hero of force. But, grown old, he composed the *Odyssey,* at a time when the passions of Greece were already somewhat cooled by reflection, which is the mother of prudence—so that she now admired Ulysses, the hero of wisdom. Thus also, in Homer's youth, the Greek people liked cruelty, abuse, savagery, fierceness, ferocity; whereas, when Homer was old, they were already enjoying the luxuries of Alcinoüs, the delights of Calypso, the pleasures of Circe, the songs of the sirens and the pastimes of the suitors, who went no further in aggression and combat than laying siege to the chaste Penelope—all of which practices would appear incompatible with the spirit of the earlier time. The divine Plato is so struck by this difficulty that, in order to solve it, he tells us that Homer had foreseen in inspired vision these dissolute, sickly and disgusting customs. But in this way he makes Homer out to have been but a foolish instructor for Greek civilization, since, however much he may condemn them he is displaying for imitation these corrupt and decadent habits which were not to be adopted till long after the foundation of the nations of Greece, and accelerating the natural course which human events would take by spurring the Greeks on to corruption. Thus it is plain that the Homer of the *Iliad* must have preceded by many years the Homer who wrote the *Odyssey;* and it is plain that the former must belong to the northeastern part of Greece, since he celebrates the Trojan War, which took place in his part of the country, whereas the latter belongs to the southeastern part, since he celebrates Ulysses, who reigned there."

You see that Vico has here explained Homer in terms both of historical period and of geographical origin. The idea that human arts and institutions were to be studied and elucidated as the products of the geographical and climatic conditions in which the people who created them lived, and of the phase of their social development through which they were passing at the moment, made great progress during the eighteenth century. There are traces of it even in Dr. Johnson, that most orthodox and classical of critics—as, for example, when he accounts for certain characteristics of Shakespeare by the relative barbarity of the age in which he lived, pointing out, just as Vico had done, that "nations, like individuals, have their infancy." And by the eighties of the eighteenth century Herder, in his *Ideas on the Philosophy of History,* was writing of poetry that it was a kind of "Proteus among the people, which is always changing its form in response to the languages, manners, and habits, to the temperaments and climates, nay even to the accents of different nations." He said—what could still seem startling even so late as that—that "language was not a divine communication, but something men had produced themselves." In the lectures on the philosophy of history that Hegel delivered in Berlin in 1822-1823, he discussed the national literatures as expressions of the societies which had produced them—societies which he conceived as great organisms continually transforming themselves under the influence of a succession of dominant ideas.

In the field of literary criticism, this historical point of view came to its first complete flower in the work of the French critic Taine, in the middle of the nineteenth century. The whole school of historian-critics to which Taine belonged—Michelet, Renan, Sainte-Beuve—had been occupied in interpreting books in terms of their historical origins. But Taine was the first of these to attempt to apply these principles systematically and on a large scale to a work devoted exclusively to literature. In the Introduction to his *History of English Literature,* published in 1863, he made his famous pronouncement that works of literature were to be understood as the upshot of three interfusing factors: *the moment, the race and the milieu.* Taine thought he was a scientist and a mechanist, who was examining works of literature from the same point of view as the chemist in experimenting with chemical compounds. But the difference between the critic and the chemist is that the critic cannot first combine his elements and then watch to see what they will do: he can only examine phenomena which have already taken place. The procedure that Taine actually follows is to pretend to set the stage for the experiment by describing the moment, the race and the milieu, and then to say: "Such a situation demands such and such a kind of writer." He now goes on to describe the kind of writer that the situation demands, and the reader finds himself at the end confronted with Shakespeare or Milton or Byron, or whoever the great figure is—who turns out to prove the accuracy of Taine's prognosis by precisely fitting the description.

There is thus a certain element of imposture in Taine; but it is a very good thing that there is. If he had really been the mechanist that he thought he was, his work on literature would have had little value. The truth was that Taine loved literature for its own sake—he was at his best himself a brilliant artist—and he had very strong moral convictions which give his writing emotional power. His mind, to be sure, was an analytic one, and his analysis, though terribly oversimplified, does have an explanatory value. Yet his work was what we call creative. Whatever he may say about chemical experiments, it is evident when he writes of a great writer that the moment, the race and the milieu have combined, like the three sounds of the chord in Browning's poem about Abt Vogler, to produce not a fourth sound but a star.

To Taine's set of elements was added, dating from the middle of the century, a new element, the economic, which was introduced into the discussion of historical phenomena mainly by Marx and Engels. The non-Marxist critics themselves were at the time already taking into account the influence of the social classes. In his chapters on the Norman conquest of England, Taine shows that the difference between the literatures produced respectively by the Normans and by the Saxons was partly the difference between a ruling class, on the one hand, and a vanquished and oppressed class, on the other. And Michelet in his volume on the Regency, which was finished the same year that the *History of English Literature* appeared, studies the *Manon Lescaut* of the Abbé Prévost as a document representing the point of view of the small gentry before the French Revolution. But Marx and Engels derived the social classes from the way that people made or got their livings—from what they called the *methods of production;* and they tended to regard these economic processes as fundamental to civilization.

The Dialectical Materialism of Marx and Engels was not really so materialistic as it sounds. There was in it a large element of the Hegelian idealism that Marx and Engels thought they had got rid of. At no time did these two famous materialists take so mechanistic a view of things as Taine began by professing; and their theory of the relation of works of literature to what they called the *economic base* was a good deal less simple than Taine's theory of the moment, the race and the milieu. They thought that art, politics, religion, philosophy and literature belonged to what they called the *superstructure* of human activity; but they saw that the practitioners of these various departments tended also to constitute social groups, and that they were always pulling away from the kind of solidarity based on economic classes in order to establish a professional solidarity of their own. Furthermore, the activities of the superstructure could influence one another, and they could influence the economic base. It may be said of Marx and Engels in general that, contrary to the popular impression, they were tentative, confused and modest when it came down to fundamentals, where a materialist like Taine was cocksure. Marx once made an attempt to explain why the poems of Homer were so good when the society that produced them was from his point of view—that is, from the industrial point of view—so primitive; and this gave him a good deal of trouble. If we compare his discussion of this problem with Vico's discussion of Homer, we see that the explanation of literature in terms of a philosophy of social history is becoming, instead of simpler and easier, more difficult and more complex.

Marx and Engels were deeply imbued, moreover, with the German admiration for literature, which they had learned from the age of Goethe. It would never have occurred to either of them that *der Dichter* was not one of the noblest and most beneficent of humankind. When Engels writes about Goethe, he presents him as a man equipped for "practical life," whose career was frustrated by the "misery" of the historical situation in Germany in his time, and reproaches him for allowing himself to lapse into the "cautious, smug and narrow" Philistinism of the class from which he came; but Engels regrets this, because it interfered with the development of the "mocking, defiant, world-despising genius," *"der geniale Dichter," "der gewaltige Poet,"* of whom Engels would not even, he says, have asked that he should have been a political liberal if Goethe had not sacrificed to his bourgeois shrinkings his truer aesthetic sense. And the great critics who were trained on Marx—Franz Mehring and Bernard Shaw—had all this reverence for the priesthood of literature. Shaw deplores the absence of political philosophy and what he regards as the middle-class snobbery in Shakespeare; but he celebrates Shakespeare's poetry and his dramatic imagination almost as enthusiastically as Swinburne did, describing even those potboiling comedies—*Twelfth Night* and *As You Like It*—the themes of which seem to him most contemptible—as "the Crown Jewels of English dramatic poetry." Such a critic may do more for a writer by showing him as a real man dealing with a real world at a definite moment of time than the impressionist critic of Swinburne's type who flourished in the same period of the late nineteenth century. The purely impressionist critic approaches the whole of literature as an exhibit of belletristic jewels, and he can only write a rhapsodic catalogue. But when Shaw turned his spotlight on Shakespeare as a figure in the Shavian drama of history, he invested him with a new interest as no other English critic had done.

The insistence that the man of letters should play a political role, the disparagement of works of art in comparison with political action, were thus originally no part of Marxism. They only became associated with it later. This happened by way of Russia, and it was due to special tendencies in that country that date from long before the Revolution or the promulgation of Marxism itself. In Russia there have been very good reasons why the political implications of literature should particularly occupy the critics. The art of Pushkin itself, with its marvelous power of implication, had certainly been partly created by the censorship of Nicholas I, and Pushkin set the tradition for most of the great Russian writers who followed him. Every play, every poem, every story, must be a parable of which the moral is *implied*. If it were stated, the censor would suppress the book as he tried to do with Pushkin's *Bronze Horseman,* where it was merely a question of the packed implications protruding a little too plainly. Right down through the writings of Chekhov and up almost to the Revolution, the imaginative literature of Russia presents the peculiar paradox of an art that is technically objective and yet charged with social messages. In Russia under the Tsar, it was inevitable that social criticism should lead to political conclusions, because the most urgent need from the point of view of any kind of improvement was to get rid of the tsarist regime. Even the neo-Christian moralist Tolstoy, who pretends to be non-political, is as political in his implications as any, because his preaching will inevitably embroil him with the Church, and the Church is an integral part of the tsardom. Tolstoy's pamphlet called *What Is Art,* in which he throws overboard Shakespeare and a large part of modern literature, including his own novels, in the interest of his intransigent morality, is the example which is most familiar to us of the moralizing Russian criticism; but it was only the most sensational expression of a kind of approach which had been prevalent since Belinsky and Chernyshevsky in the early part of the century. The critics, who were usually journalists writing in exile or for a contraband press, were always tending to demand of the imaginative writers that they should dramatize bolder morals.

Even after the Revolution had destroyed the tsarist government, this situation did not change. The old habits of censorship persisted in the new socialist society of the Soviets, which was necessarily made up of people who had been stamped by the die of the despotism. We find the peculiar phenomenon of a series of literary groups attempting one after the other to obtain official recognition or to make themselves sufficiently powerful to establish themselves as arbiters of literature. Lenin and Trotsky and Lunacharsky had the sense to oppose these attempts: the comrade-dictators of Proletcult or Lev or Rapp would certainly have been just as bad as the Count Benckendorff who made Pushkin miserable, and when the Stalin bureaucracy, after the death of Gorky, got control of this department as of everything else, they instituted a system of repression that made Benckendorff and Nicholas I look like Lorenzo de' Medici. In the meantime, Trotsky, who was Commissar of War but himself a great political writer with an interest in belles-lettres, attempted in 1924, apropos of one of these movements, to clarify the situation. He wrote a brilliant and valuable book called *Literature and Revolution,* in which he explained the aims of the government, analyzed the work of the Russian writers and praised or rebuked the latter as they seemed to him in harmony or in conflict with the former. Trotsky is intelligent, sympathetic; it is evident that he is really fond of literature and that he knows that a work of art does not fulfill its function in terms of the formulas of party propaganda. But Mayakovsky, the Soviet poet, whom Trotsky had praised with reservations, expressed himself in a famous joke when he was asked what he thought about Trotsky's book—a pun which implied that a Commissar turned critic was inevitably a Commissar still; and what a foreigner cannot accept in Trotsky is his assumption that it is the duty of the government to take a hand in the direction of literature.

This point of view, indigenous to Russia, has been imported to other countries through the permeation of Communist influence. The Communist press and its literary followers have reflected the control of the Kremlin in all the phases through which it has passed, down to the wholesale imprisonment of Soviet writers which has been taking place since 1935. But it has never been a part of the American system that our Republican or Democratic administration should lay down a political line for the guidance of the national literature. A recent gesture in this direction on the part of Archibald MacLeish, who seemed a little carried away by his position as Librarian of Congress, was anything but cordially received by serious American writers. So long as the United States remains happily a non-totalitarian country, we can very well do without this aspect of the historical criticism of literature.

Another element of a different order has, however, since Marx's time been added to the historical study of the origins of works of literature. I mean the psychoanalysis of Freud. This appears as an extension of something which had already got well started before, which had figured even in Johnson's *Lives of the Poets,* and of which the great exponent had been Sainte-Beuve: the interpretation of works of literature in the light of the personalities behind them. But the Freudians made this interpretation more exact and more systematic. The great example of the psychoanalysis of an artist is Freud's own essay on Leonardo da Vinci; but this has little critical interest: it is an attempt to construct a case history. One of the best examples I know of the application of Freudian analysis to literature is in Van Wyck Brooks's book, *The Ordeal of Mark Twain,* in which Mr. Brooks uses an incident of Mark Twain's boyhood as a key to his whole career. Mr. Brooks has since repudiated the method he resorted to here on the ground that no one but an analyst can ever know enough about a writer to make a valid psychoanalytic diagnosis. This is true, and it is true of the method that it has led to bad results where the critic has built a Freudian mechanism out of very slender evidence, and then given us merely a romance exploiting the supposed working of this mechanism, in place of an actual study, keeping close to the facts and the documents, of the writer's life and work. But I believe that Van Wyck Brooks really had hold of something important when he fixed upon that childhood incident of which Mark Twain gave so vivid an account to his biographer—that scene at the deathbed of his father when his mother made him promise that he would not break her heart. If it was not one of those crucial happenings that are supposed to determine the complexes of Freudianism, it has certainly a typical significance in relation to Mark Twain's whole psychology. The stories that people tell about their childhood are likely to be profoundly symbolic even when they have been partly or wholly made up in the light of later experience. And the attitudes, the compulsions, the emotional "patterns" that recur in the work of a writer are of great interest to the historical critic.

These attitudes and patterns are embedded in the community and the historical moment, and they may indicate its ideals and its diseases as the cell shows the condition of the tissue. The recent scientific experimentation in the combining of Freudian with Marxist method, and of psychoanalysis with anthropology, has had its parallel development in criticism. And there is thus another element added to our equipment for analyzing literary works, and the problem grows still more complex.

The analyst, however, is of course not concerned with the comparative values of his patients any more than the surgeon is. He cannot tell you why the neurotic Dostoevsky produces work of immense value to his fellows while another man with the same neurotic pattern would become a public menace. Freud himself emphatically states in his study of Leonardo that his method can make no attempt to account for Leonardo's genius. The problems of comparative artistic value still remain after we have given attention to the Freudian psychological factor just as they do after we have given attention to the Marxist economic factor and to the racial and geographical factors. No matter how thoroughly and searchingly we may have scrutinized works of literature from the historical and biographical points of view, we must be ready to attempt to estimate, in some such way as Saintsbury and Eliot do, the relative degrees of success attained by the products of the various periods and the various personalities. We must be able to tell good from bad, the first-rate from the second-rate. We shall not otherwise write literary criticism at all, but merely social or political history as reflected in literary texts, or psychological case histories from past eras, or, to take the historical point of view in its simplest and most academic form, merely chronologies of books that have been published.

And now how, in these matters of literary art, do we tell the good art from the bad? Norman Kemp Smith, the Kantian philosopher, whose courses I was fortunate enough to take at Princeton twenty-five years ago, used to tell us that this recognition was based primarily on an emotional reaction. For purposes of practical criticism this is a safe assumption on which to proceed. It is possible to discriminate in a variety of ways the elements that in any given department go to make a successful work of literature. Different schools have at different times demanded different things of literature: *unity, symmetry, universality, originality, vision, inspiration, strangeness, suggestiveness, improving morality, socialist realism,* etc. But you could have any set of these qualities that any school of writing has demanded and still not have a good play, a good novel, a good poem, a good history. If you identify the essence of good literature with any one of these elements or with any combination of them, you simply shift the emotional reaction to the recognition of the element or elements. Or if you add to your other demands the demand that the writer must have *talent,* you simply shift this recognition to the talent. Once people find some grounds of agreement in the coincidence of their emotional reactions to books, they may be able to discuss these elements profitably; but if they do not have this basic agreement, the discussion will make no sense.

But how, you may ask, can we identify this élite who know what they are talking about? Well, it can only be said of them that they are self-appointed and self-perpetuating, and that they will compel you to accept their authority. Impostors may try to put themselves over, but these quacks will not last. The implied position of the people who know about literature (as is also the case in every other art) is simply that they know what they know, and that they are determined to impose their opinions by main force of eloquence or assertion on the people who do not know. This is not a question, of course, of professional workers in literature—such as editors, professors and critics, who very often have no real understanding of the products with which they deal—but of readers of all kinds in all walks of life. There are moments when a first-rate writer, unrecognized or out of fashion with the official chalkers-up for the market, may find his support in the demand for his work of an appreciative cultivated public.

But what is the cause of this emotional reaction which is the critic's divining rod? This question has long been a subject of study by the branch of philosophy called Aesthetics, and it has recently been made a subject of scientific experimentation. Both these lines of inquiry are likely to be prejudiced in the eyes of the literary critic by the fact that the inquiries are sometimes conducted by persons who are obviously deficient in literary feeling or taste. Yet one should not deny the possibility that something of value might result from the speculations and explorations of men of acute minds who take as their given data the aesthetic emotions of other men.

Almost everybody interested in literature has tried to explain to himself the nature of these emotions that register our approval of artistic works; and I of course have my own explanation.

In my view, all our intellectual activity, in whatever field it takes place, is an attempt to give a meaning to our experience—that is, to make life more practicable; for by understanding things we make it easier to survive and get around among them. The mathematician Euclid, working in a convention of abstractions, shows us relations between the distances of our unwieldy and cluttered-up environment upon which we are able to count. A drama of Sophocles also indicates relations between the various human impulses, which appear so confused and dangerous, and it brings out a certain justice of Fate—that is to say, of the way in which the interaction of these impulses is seen in the long run to work out—upon which we can also depend. The kinship, from this point of view, of the purposes of science and art appears very clearly in the case of the Greeks, because not only do both Euclid and Sophocles satisfy us by making patterns, but they make much the same kind of patterns. Euclid's *Elements* takes simple theorems and by a series of logical operations builds them up to a climax in the square on the hypotenuse. A typical drama of Sophocles develops in a similar way.

Some writers (as well as some scientists) have a different kind of explicit message beyond the kind of reassurance implicit in merely understanding life or in the harmony of artistic form. Not content with such an achievement as that of Sophocles—who has one of his choruses tell us that it is better not to be born, but who, by representing life as noble and based on law, makes its tragedies easier to bear—such writers attempt, like Plato, to think out and recommend a procedure for turning it into something better. But other departments of literature—lyric poetry such as Sappho's, for example—have *less* philosophical content than Sophocles. A lyric gives us nothing but a pattern imposed on the expression of a feeling; but this pattern of metrical quantities and of consonants and vowels that balance has the effect of reducing the feeling, however unruly or painful it may seem when we experience it in the course of our lives, to something orderly, symmetrical and pleasing; and it also relates this feeling to the more impressive scheme, works it into the larger texture, of the body of poetic art. The discord has been resolved, the anomaly subjected to discipline. And this control of his emotion by the poet has the effect at second hand of making it easier for the reader to manage his own emotions. (Why certain sounds and rhythms gratify us more than others, and how they are connected with the themes and ideas that they are chosen as appropriate for conveying, are questions that may be passed on to the scientist.)

And this brings us back again to the historical point of view. The experience of mankind on the earth is always changing as man develops and has to deal with new combinations of elements; and the writer who is to be anything more than an echo of his predecessors must always find expression for something which has never yet been expressed, must master a new set of phenomena which has never yet been mastered. With each such victory of the human intellect, whether in history, in philosophy or in poetry, we experience a deep satisfaction: we have been cured of some ache of disorder, relieved of some oppressive burden of uncomprehended events.

This relief that brings the sense of power, and, with the sense of power, joy, is the positive emotion which tells us that we have encountered a first-rate piece of literature. But stay! you may at this point warn: are not people often solaced and exhilarated by literature of the trashiest kind? They are: crude and limited people do certainly feel some such emotion in connection with work that is limited and crude. The man who is more highly organized and has a wider intellectual range will feel it in connection with work that is finer and more complex. The difference between the emotion of the more highly organized man and the emotion of the less highly organized one is merely a matter of gradation. You sometimes discover books—the novels of John Steinbeck, for example—that seem to mark precisely the borderline between work that is definitely superior and work that is definitely bad. When I was speaking a little while back of the genuine connoisseurs who establish the standards of taste, I meant, of course, the people who can distinguish Grade A and who prefer it to the other grades.

THE AMERICANISM OF VAN WYCK BROOKS (1939, 1946)

F. W. DUPEE

I

NEW ENGLAND has given to the United States its most literate body of native tradition, and educated Americans, regardless of their particular backgrounds, are always tending to become spiritual New Englanders. If the Yankee tradition is no longer very much alive, so much the worse for educated Americans.

Of this type of native mind Van Wyck Brooks is an excellent example. It is true that years ago, as the spokesman of an American city culture which was then just emerging in its strength, Brooks made a great effort to master the spiritual New Englander in himself. He did not quite carry it off; his Yankee alter ego has since taken entire possession of him. It is now clear that he has always owed to the older tradition a great many of his qualities—the restraint and conscience that have marked all his work; the taste for arduous scholarship; the rather elaborate prose which is the conscious register of his highly-organized individuality; but above all the air of unworldliness, of consecration, which comes perhaps from his allegiance to the New England principle of intensive cultivation. "The great thing is to be saturated with something," Henry James, another spiritual New Englander, used to maintain. Brooks has saturated himself with the problems of art and society in the United States. And it was another tendency of the rhapsodic Yankee strain to turn everybody—novelists, philosophers, critics, historians, naturalists—into poets; Brooks, too, admirable though he has been as a scholar and social critic, has always at bottom worked and thought in the manner commonly ascribed to poets. Like them he tends to see all experience in the light of a single overmastering situation. In his case the great situation, the *donnée,* is associated with the vicissitudes of creative inspiration in the United States, with the difficulty of realizing oneself, not only as an artist in America, but as an American artist. The effort to reconcile art and society in terms of our national experience has dominated all his work, both the early and the late, and has given an otherwise episodic career an urgent inner consistency.

II

By working very hard a single important piece of territory a writer may earn, at the very least, the reputation of being a "phenomenon." This has been the case with Brooks, yet it has always been hard to say just what kind of phenomenon he is. During the years when aestheticism was the prevailing literary creed, he used to be called, rather invidiously, a sociologist. But as sociology came to seem to us less alien, less of a mystery, it was decided that Brooks's social insights were the by-products of a temperament primarily ethical. People pointed to his *Freeman* essays, which showed that when hard-pressed by disappointments, as he appears to have been during the post-war years, he was capable of taking up a position of reproachful righteousness barely distinguishable from that of the New Humanists, whom he had always assailed. Let us see to what extent these various distinctions were justified. Morality, it is true, is the socialism of the individualist, who seeks to extend to society at large the codes that have come to govern people in their individual relationships. Brooks has been as consistently an individualist as he has been consistently preoccupied with the larger questions of society. But in deriving his ethical ideas from the new psychology of the Unconscious, he broke in part with the philosophy of traditional moral individualists. Like them he continued to conceive society by analogy with the structure of the human personality, but instead of picturing personality as a complex of higher and lower selves, as a Plato or an Arnold—moralists even in their psychology—normally pictured it, Brooks saw in it the Freudian pattern of repression and sublimation. This pattern, modified as much by vestiges in him of the old ethical severity as by elements of modern materialism, he extended to social experience. Thus, the United States was to him a case of "atrophied personality," a "prodigious welter of unconscious life" which it was the task of the new intelligentsia to bring to consciousness.

In America where the middle class, filling the whole picture, had made life as precarious for specialized types of individuality as it had made it safe for the more standard varieties, it was natural that a critic like Brooks should seize upon the new psychology, apply its insights to American writers of the past, and preach its ethic of self-fulfillment to the writers of the present. His criticism had therefore its intimate connection with his time and place, a connection that we shall presently consider in detail. But let us first look at Brooks's criticism in its more technical aspects. His generation was making a great point of the importance of being "creative," a slogan which Brooks translated into his own medium, developing a criticism that had many of the qualities of imaginative literature. In form it was eloquent, concentrated, boldly thematic; and it carried the biographical method to a higher point of development than it had yet reached in America. In a sense Brooks's approach is merely a variant of methods employed by Sainte-Beuve and Taine, but it has acquired a special character through the intensity both of his individualism and of his preoccupation with psychology. The questions of culture at large he approaches in terms of leading individuals; the work of single writers he considers in the light of their biography. Thus *The Ordeal of Mark Twain, The Pilgrimage of Henry James* and *The Life of Emerson* are all attempts to characterize entire cultural periods through the experience of leading individuals; and even *The Flowering of New England,* as someone has said, is not so much a history as a composite biography. The biographical method is commonly used to cast light on the work of literature. With Brooks, this procedure is usually reversed. When he appeals to the work it is in order to confirm some theory about the man. Literature gets dissolved into biography in such a way that the work itself with its four walls and established furniture as given by its author is often quite lost to view. And this is true concerning his treatment of the intellectual as well as the structural properties of literature. For all his vital interest in the New England tradition, he has never made it very clear just what transcendentalism, considered as a philosophy, really was. And surely it is a paradox of his career that he should have been so warm in his championship of the artist, yet so cold to the work of art, so ready to proclaim America's intellectual poverty, yet in practice so indifferent to ideas.

There have been many instances where Brooks's critical methods involved no particular difficulties. The literary portraits in *Our Poets* were certainly not lacking in a vivid aesthetic concreteness, nor were they demonstrably inconsistent with the actual work of the authors concerned. But other books, notably the *Pilgrimage* and the *Ordeal,* have been deplored because the accomplishment of James and Mark Twain was so largely ignored or distorted. Let us consider these objections, taking up first *The Pilgrimage of Henry James.* This book testifies to Brooks's ability to say things of value and to raise important issues even when in his main argument he appears most mistaken. For the picture of James that emerges from the *Pilgrimage* is a deduction rather from Brooks's general theory of literary nationalism than from the novels themselves, the latter having a complex irony which Brooks fails to take into account and which in the end seriously undermines his thesis. Yet it is curious that in this case Brooks *did* examine the novels, and one concludes, not that his method is necessarily faulty in itself, but that he possesses in any case a strongly metaphysical cast of mind. To the sober scholar in him there is yoked a visionary and the two have some trouble pulling together in harmony. A myth-maker on one side of his nature, he sometimes strikes us as being himself that very poet-prophet, that reincarnated Whitman, which he once had the habit of invoking; but on the other side he is a sceptic, a critic and an historian. Of the effects of this ambivalence there is further evidence in *The Ordeal of Mark Twain.* The general thesis here is much sounder than that of the *Pilgrimage;* and in addition to having been a pioneer in the attempt to fuse the historical and Freudian perspectives, the *Ordeal* was a splendid example of closely-textured argument, analytical wit and the restrained use of local color. It would be hard indeed to forget its picture of Mark Twain, "that shorn Samson, led about by a little child, who in the profound somnolence of her spirit, was simply going through the motions of an inherited domestic piety." Nevertheless the *Ordeal* is full of difficulties. It is one thing to muckrake a period, as Brooks here so effectively muckrakes the genteel era, pointing out its stultifying effects on a writer of genius; but it is another thing again to assume that in happier conditions your writer would have been a Tolstoy. That is more or less what Brooks does assume, with the result that the historical Mark Twain is everywhere dogged by the shadow of an ideal or potential or Unconscious Mark Twain, a kind of spectral elder brother whose brooding presence is an eternal reproof to the mere author of *Huckleberry Finn.* In addition to being highly speculative, Brooks's approach has the disadvantage of diverting him from what Mark Twain really achieved through the cultivation, however fragmentary, of his richly plebeian sensibility. This achievement it was left to Ernest Hemingway and other practicing artists to discover for themselves.

III

Brooks's habit of using the materials of history and biography to construct didactic myths, literary lessons in the shape of parables, was probably the effect of the period in which he came to maturity and of what he was trying to accomplish in that period. Throughout the years of industrial revolution following the Civil War, writers in America had been consigned, some of them to a limbo of servility, others to virtual oblivion, depending on whether they accepted or embraced the prevailing standards of that iron age. But when Brooks's first volume appeared, in 1909, the old exploitative phalanx of American society had been for some years breaking up. There was a great increase of radical consciousness on the part of the working classes, and intellectuals had taken advantage of the general ferment to assert once more the claims of the individual. For the first time since the 1850's, there came into existence a body of professionals sufficiently independent, militant and cohesive to be called an intelligentsia. It had in a sense been the creation of the radical movement; it therefore applied itself to politics, in turn, and evolved a special type in the shape of the muckraker. But this was only the first phase in the career of the new intelligentsia. Later on, in Brooks's generation, a reaction set in against social reformism, which had so plainly missed its mark, and writers turned from politics to literature. The "artist" supplanted the muckraker as the standard intellectual type; consciousness of self was cultivated in place of class consciousness; and writers set out to express and assert and fulfill themselves. Thus the old subjective ethos of romanticism, freshly implemented by modern psychology, was reborn in America some sixty years after the decline of Emersonianism.

Nothing was more remarkable in Brooks than the flair for assimilation and synthesis which permitted him to bring to focus in his criticism all the chief tendencies of those decades. For Brooks, in the long run, art and politics were to seem two separate universes; but his early criticism embodied a notable attempt to bring the two into a better relation and so to combine the ideals of the muckrakers with those of his own primarily aesthetic generation. The actual political content of his criticism was vague and shifting; yet whenever he attempted a definite formulation it became clear that he regarded socialism as a pre-condition of the "creative life" in America. In many respects his early writings provided the United States with its closest parallel to the social-democratic literatures then flourishing in Europe.

Nevertheless Brooks was at heart a psychologist and he was to keep the morality of self-fulfillment squarely in the center of his work. Nor did his socialist convictions in the long run prevent him from conceiving art as a process essentially self-contained, commanding an area of experience to all purposes special and separate. He seems to have taken over from Carlyle and Ruskin the "organic" view of society while rejecting the faith in authoritarian institutions that usually goes with it. The mysticism inherent in this view conflicted all along the line with the scientific perspectives of socialism, forcing upon him a kind of unsystematic dualism. Concerning the relation of politics to literature he tended to conceive the first as a function of a material world, the second as an enterprise connected with a world of the spirit. But Brooks did not exploit the music of antinomies to the extent that it has been exploited by a Thomas Mann, and in practice his dualism merely meant that in his opinion intellectuals ought to keep out of politics. They had, he assured them, a special mission, which was to "articulate the whole life of the people" by supplying the United States with new myths and new values. To this role he advised them to apply themselves with the fervor of a consecrated minority, a priesthood, as he said, or a hierarchy. It was an age that made much of seers and cosmic vocations. Writers were looking for prophets—particularly among themselves. Every nation, every social group, considered itself to have a "special mission." If Brooks was akin to Ruskin and Arnold, he was a Ruskin or an Arnold brought up to date: the *culture* which they had advocated as social medicine, he endeavored to implement in terms of an *organized intelligentsia.* For it was an age, too, of heightened crisis and organized struggle in the field of social relations.

In his preoccupation with the intelligentsia there was a considerable value. More than anyone else, unless it was Randolph Bourne, he grasped the importance to America of the emergence of such a body. He understood what it could mean to the labor movement, and he knew, too, that its absence had for half a century inflicted great hardship on American artists, leaving them solitary and exposed in the arena of a hostile society. It was on the new intelligentsia, then, that Brooks set his hopes for the country's future, to them that he addressed his case histories in literary frustration, his essays in diagnosis and prescription, in short the whole of that prodigious anatomy of the creative life which took shape in his early writings. When, eventually, he ceased to exhort the intellectuals, he lost at the same time a good share of his intellectual vitality.

In view of his socialist professions it is curious that Brooks came to concentrate so exclusively on conditions in a single country. He appears to have felt that in Europe the abuses of capitalism had been somewhat mitigated by the social-democratic movement, a movement whose success he was inclined to attribute to the efforts of literary critics. The United States, on the other hand, was a full-blown capitalist nation which possessed only the weak beginnings of a critical culture. We must develop such a culture if we were ever to experience a genuine social transformation. It was on some such reasoning as this that Brooks tended to justify his exclusive concern with the United States, his tendency to idealize Europe, his habit of ascribing to literary culture the decisive role in reformist politics.

Proceeding always by the rule of opposites, he thought of the United States as the antithesis of Europe in respect to the quality, the unity and the social use-value of its culture. French culture, he pretended, had at the touch of Montaigne fallen together like a single organism. But America had lacked such a master-spirit. Here there had always existed, between literature and experience, theory and practice, a profound cleavage which had affected for the worse both our intellectual and our daily life, condemning the first to impotent idealism and the second to stark materialism. From the beginning the Highbrow and the Lowbrow had divided things between them. An effective middle tradition had failed to appear. In default of the spiritual checks which such a tradition might have exercised, Big Business had got firmly into the saddle and the Acquisitive Life had prevailed over the Creative Life. And with the optimism of a latter-day Whitman—the optimism of a generation pioneering in social aesthetics (they used indeed to declare that social reform constituted the new American "frontier") as their fathers had pioneered in industry—Brooks foresaw a culture which should replace the obsolete hegemony of New England, and represent the country in all its racial, class and sectional complexity.

IV

It is true that on the programmatic side Brooks's early writings were infected with the extravagance that is common to the "organic" conception of society. French critics, we have reason to believe, would be the first to disclaim any super-unity in the culture supposedly begotten by Montaigne. As for America: its intractable minorities and far-flung regions have offered to the literary nationalist a problem so stubborn that it refuses to be solved short of a social reconstruction more profound than any envisaged by Brooks. But on the critical side his work, attracting to it all the severity of a mind divided between poles of scepticism and faith, was of a trenchancy and cleverness rare in American writing. Our culture did actually suffer, as he maintained, from a split personality which expressed itself in various idealistic chivalries on the one hand, and on the other in a plebeian vigor, unlighted by consciousness. Surely, considering the provocation, Brooks was justified in preaching a bold scepticism. "It is of no use," he told the patriots of his day, "to go off in a corner with American literature . . . in a sulky, private sort of way, taking it for granted that if we give up world values we are entitled to our own little domestic rights and wrongs, criticism being out of place by the fireside." Not that Brooks was the only cosmopolitan critic of American letters; but where the New Humanists, for example, took as their standard of comparison the achievements of some remote Periclean or Racinian age, Brooks looked to the European literature of his time. Moreover, in his account of the Genteel Tradition as "the culture of an age of pioneering, the reflex of the spirit of material enterprise," as in a whole range of similar insights, he went far towards situating the country's cultural problems in a concrete atmosphere of social and economic forces. In the long run, however, the value of his early work seems mainly to lie in the skill and courage with which he isolated the data of intellectual maturity in America. In his hands the Highbrow-Lowbrow antithesis served rather as a descriptive than as an analytical tool. And what he really produced was a kind of symptomology sprinkled with clues and half-clues, with partial explanations, with portents adduced as causes and causes in the guise of portents. The materialist in him was always coming into conflict with the "organic" visionary, the social historian with the psychologist. Accustomed to conceiving matter and spirit in the shape of an antithesis, he never attained a stable view of cultural phenomena; and his lack of clarity on this point caused his criticism to veer back and forth between extremes of free will and determinism, so that while it seemed to him at times that the single writer might change the world unaided, at other times it appeared that one was very much at history's mercy. And psychology came to dominate his thought to the extent that he ended by giving the impression that he wanted to fasten upon American writers a cultural inferiority complex.

It was probably this impression rather than simply the severity of his critiques that would help to bring him into partial eclipse in later years. His work would presently appear to belong neither to literary criticism nor to realistic social analysis. When he had finished trying to reconcile politics and literature, mysticism and science, he would be left with an ideology as diffuse as that of an Emerson or a Whitman; and he would seem, like them, to belong to some more primitive stage of American society, the intellectual disorder of whose prophets signified a lack of urgent pressures in the age itself. Even Gide and Mann, accomplished dialecticians and great writers, have not really achieved "universality" in our time: they have merely undergone a series of significant conversions. And Brooks, endeavoring to embrace the Whole, ended by losing touch with its parts; his sensibility acquired a certain abstractness; and in time he was to seem almost the type of that Liberal critic whom Eliot from one angle, and Mencken from another, were to assail with so much effectiveness.

V

The fate of Brooks's ideas was to receive a kind of summing-up, concentrated and dramatic, in the brief career of the *Seven Arts* review. Appearing in the fall of 1916, *The Seven Arts* had Brooks as its chief spokesman; his theme was the necessity of a national literature for an America made acutely conscious of its individuality by the war in Europe. But a year later, America having entered the war, *The Seven Arts* showed a growing distaste for the struggle and was obliged to cease publication. Meanwhile Randolph Bourne had all but replaced Brooks as spokesman, and Bourne's theme was, more and more, the social revolution. What had happened to push *The Seven Arts,* in a single year, from literary nationalism to literary revolutionism? Had we come of age in a world already too far advanced in decay? Had the United States, in attaining to the level of the great powers, likewise fallen heir to a crisis common to the entire capitalist world? This was more or less what had happened, as we can see in retrospect. Nationalism, having simply turned into a sordid imperialism, could no longer inspire a literature. Nor could the idea of the organic society survive the violent manifestations of a period of general revolution. *The Seven Arts,* in its rapid transition, was a fair register of the fact that ideas could appear viable at one moment, only to be swept the next into obsolescence.

The war had witnessed America's maturing as a world power: would we by the same token "catch up" with the elder nations in a cultural sense? To Brooks, at least, it began very shortly to appear that we would not. In America as elsewhere literature's response to war and crisis was both violent and immediate. And the centrifugal tendencies which it developed were the reverse of what Brooks had preached and anticipated. Writers who, like Bourne and Reed, shared his social idealism, were steered by its logic towards socialist theory and politics. There remained the literary majority which, in the main hostile to all politics, was split between two groups. The expatriate generation, addressing themselves to poetry and tradition, pretty much ignored America. The "Titans," who were presently to found the *Mercury,* stayed in this country, as Mencken boldly confessed, solely to make merry at the spectacle of its foolishness. In the United States itself the aftermath of the war witnessed the definitive triumph of Bohemia over the universities and other centers of genteel culture. Instead of merging with the Highbrow to produce a middle tradition, the Low-brow staged a *coup d'état.* Debunking replaced the respectable profession of muckraking. The common man, whom Brooks had respected as an element in his proposed national synthesis, was now to be widely scorned as a simple moron. And if Brooks had taken issue with Dreiser on the grounds that his determinism prevented his fiction from qualifying as healthy social realism, he was now to be faced with a whole generation of Dreisers. In America, in short, there was none of the philosophical scepticism which Brooks had advocated but only the "fashionable pessimism" (as he said) of parvenu plebeians, the coarse laughter of irresponsible satirists. And among the exiles there was an atmosphere of "fashionable pedantry," reactionary metaphysics, symbolist mystification—and Brooks had never cared much for symbolism. The age of prophets and special missions had largely passed. The present age demanded of its artists and critics above all a concrete literary consciousness. Brooks was in no position either to sympathize with its aims or to fulfill its demands. The papers he wrote for the *Freeman* in the early Twenties, and indirectly the biographies of Mark Twain and Henry James, were an index to his opinion of the times. As for the opinion that came generally to be held of him: it was not long before people began to complain that "for all his apparent enthusiasm for the artist, he does not seem vitally interested in art when it appears." He fails to criticize, they said, he merely exhorts. And "the development of young artists is not achieved through exhortation." These strictures were made by Paul Rosenfeld in the mid-Twenties. They reveal the strongly experimental cast of the decade on which Brooks, with his *a priori* temper, had had the misfortune to fall.

VI

In *The Pilgrimage of Henry James* he remarked that to the expatriated author of *The Ambassadors* Europe had remained "a fairy-tale to the end." This was scarcely just to James but it showed the high value which Brooks himself, in 1925, still placed on the critical spirit. The years that followed were to witness his rapid retreat from this position.

In 1920 he had published *The Ordeal of Mark Twain,* which was followed some years later by the *Pilgrimage,* and then after a long interval by *The Life of Emerson.* These books, which, together with the *Freeman* papers, constitute a transition between the earlier and later works, show Brooks in the process of trying to thrash his way out of the isolation in which he has landed. Someone has compared the three biographies to the phases of the Hegelian dialectic, that of Mark Twain being the "thesis," that of Henry James the "antithesis" and that of Emerson the "synthesis." But note that this is a dialectic that opens out towards the past. Brooks is intent not only upon making studies in literary frustration, not only upon furnishing the Twenties with didactic parables (there is reason to think that the *Ordeal,* with its stress upon Mark Twain's immature pessimism, was aimed at the Menckenites, as the *Pilgrimage,* elaborating on the expatriate sensibility, is directed at Eliot's generation), but he is also intent upon discovering the ideal American writer. He finds him at last in the man of old Concord, the "barbaric sage" as W. C. Brownell had called him. And from the rediscovery of Emerson there follows a transfiguration of Emerson's entire society. Brooks has found the key to American literature; he begins to write a cultural history in several volumes, the first of which turns out to be a chronicle, charming as literature, largely fabulous as history, of the creative life in New England. The present has failed us, it is evil; doesn't the past, then, by the law of contraries become good? The modern world has proven to be sadly incoherent; let us seek the organic virtues in the little pre-metropolitan half-agrarian universe of Concord and Boston. It was a Springtime culture and Spring is always virtuous. And if anyone feels disposed to remind us of "world values," let us reply that "we are entitled to our own little domestic rights and wrongs, criticism being out of place by the fireside."

Prefigured in the closing chapters of the *Pilgrimage* (it was Brooks, one feels, much more than it was James who longed to take passage for America), his nostalgia begins to affect his style and the very structure of his work. The pointed, argumentative and analytical manner gives way to a prose of anecdote and local color, a blur of sensuous matter, a dreamlike pastiche of remembered quotations. And one sees that Brooks has affixed to his camera a soft-focus filter.

A comparison of the early and later work reveals, then, an astonishing reversal of opinion in respect to the achievement of New England. "An age of rude, vague, boisterous, dyspeptic causes" was the way he had formerly characterized that time. Its puritanism he had described as "a noble chivalry to which provinciality was almost a condition." Its Ripleys and Danas and Alcotts had seemed "a queer miasmatical group of lunar phenomena." Longfellow had been "an expurgated German student," whom it was foolish to approach critically. And Hawthorne for all his charm had felt life "rather as a phantom than as a man." But already in *The Life of Emerson* Hawthorne has become "a reminder as it were of some vast Cimmerian universe . . . a real Sphinx, with a subterranean self buried fathoms deep in the desert sand." What has happened is that Hawthorne has altered not so much in kind as in scale; he has been blown up to enormous stature in order that he may play the Prince of Darkness to Emerson's Son of Light in a kind of veiled cosmological allegory that runs all through the *Life.* And if Hawthorne, once a little less than a man, is capable of becoming something only short of a god, we can imagine how it will be with Emerson. As New England's chief intelligence Emerson had always figured to Brooks as the personification of a tradition shot through with false sublimities and seriously deficient in experience of life. For Emerson were reserved the most caustic phrases in *America's Coming of Age.* "A strange fine ventriloquism . . . a continual falsetto . . . abstract at the wrong times and concrete at the wrong times . . . he could write page after page about a poet or painter without one intelligibly apt utterance . . . he was not interested in human life; he cared nothing for emotion, possessing so little himself . . . all the qualities of the typical baccalaureate sermon." And so on. But compare this portrait with the estimate of Emerson's virtues implied (for, as in the case of Hawthorne, it is only implied) in the *Life* and *The Flowering of New England.* Here the author of *Representative Men* has become a veritable embodiment of the creative spirit, a Yankee Balder. His prose evokes images of mountain streams, his passage through the New England world is accompanied by the springing up of greenery and flowers.

A few reservations are necessary if we are to see Brooks's two periods in a proper light. Needless to say he was never a debunker, even in his most militant phase, and the severity of his judgments on the New England school was plentifully sweetened with qualification. Indeed he was the writer of his generation who strove hardest to play the mediator between past and present. If he stressed the shortcomings of the Yankee tradition it was because that tradition seemed at best a sectional phenomenon and because it had come to block the growth of a larger intellectual consciousness in America. Nor can we ignore the very considerable merits of Brooks's latest work. The *Life* may seem a rather flimsy performance, but surely the *Flowering* has notable qualities. The opening chapters, dealing with the birth of the artistic spirit in a young nation, and the closing pages, describing Lowell and Holmes as characters of the Yankee twilight, cause the book to be enclosed in a frame of excellent criticism. But in the absence of any such criticism in the case of Emerson, Thoreau, Hawthorne and the rest, the frame only serves to set off a certain sponginess in the picture itself. Here, then, is a New England crowded with creative spirits but virtually bare of masterpieces, for Brooks has given up almost entirely the practice of correlating biography with literature.

Here, above all, is a New England purged of conflict and contradiction, presented as an idyll of single-hearted effort; for Brooks has likewise given up the habit of correlating literary enterprise with social history. His perspective as a man of the twentieth century, his values as a socialist and an historian, have all gone by the board in the interests of an impressionistic *immediacy*. We are invited to survey the New England renaissance as if through the eyes of some actual participant, some breathless Lyceum ticket-holder of the period.

So the *Flowering* represents not so much a frank revision of Brooks's earlier judgments as a shift to a sphere where critical judgment operates only by implication. The Yankee culture has been lifted from the plane of "world values," where it shows a very small and incomplete, into an historical void where it becomes as great as you please. Indeed it is symptomatic of Brooks's present tendency that he nowhere tries to come to terms with his earlier work or to offer a reasonable explanation of the apparent disjunction between his two periods. The most he has done along these lines has been to remark, in the preface to a reissue of three early essays, that the judgments of his first period were the indiscretions of a youth bent on following an iconoclastic fashion. A fashion! So much then for the ardors, the sincerities, the hopes that went into *America's Coming of Age*. In dispensing with a rational view of American history it seem that he has lost the desire to make sense of his own history.

And the once-powerful critic of American life has become the chief curator of its antiquities; the oracle of the intellectuals has turned into the oracle of the book-clubs. He has accomplished his lifelong purpose of reconciling the native artist with the native society—but he has accomplished it in terms of a distant past, an imaginary past. If Europe was a fairy tale to Henry James, what has the United States become to Van Wyck Brooks?

I. A. RICHARDS[1]
(A DENIAL OF THE "PRIME AGENT"; AND THE CONSEQUENCES)
(1937)

D. G. JAMES

> Mr. Bain collects that the mind is a collection. Has he ever thought who collects Mr. Bain?
>
> F. H. BRADLEY—As a footnote to a discussion of Bain's associationism in *Ethical Studies*

. . . . .

III

POETRY . . . is the conveyance, by the imaginative use of language, of imaginative objects, the compulsion upon the reader by the poet of his own imaginative prehension of the world or of some aspect of or object within it. And it is only with poetry in this sense that criticism is concerned. Now the view of poetry as the expression of imaginative prehension is a sufficiently ordinary one, and is certainly not new. But there are grounds for believing that it is not wholly idle to repeat it. For example, a book in which Mr. I. A. Richards undertook to set out the principles of literary criticism seems to be built up out of disregard for this simple and, one would have thought, obvious truth. So completely does Mr. Richards ignore it that his book is for the most part taken up by an attempt to describe the psychological and physiological conditions which he holds are necessary for the writing of great poetry. Now such an inquiry, could it be accomplished with any considerable degree of scientific precision, would have great interest. But such interest as it might have would be irrelevant to what alone is the concern of the critic, namely, poetry. Such knowledge as might be achieved by such an inquiry would have as much relevance to poetry as an attempt to inquire into the psychological and physiological condition of a scientist would have to what we call science. To know the psychology and physiology of a scientist is of no aid to a critic of his work, though it might have interest for him; it certainly would

[1] In Chapter II of *Scepticism and Poetry,* from which the present abridged selection is drawn, James continues his study of the poetic imagination; here he does so by criticizing the aesthetic of I. A. Richards. [*Editor's note.*]

be unimportant for judgment on the adequacy of the work he is criticizing. And it is equally true that in poetry, which is the conveyance of an imagination of the world, either in whole or part, the details of psychological and physiological description are irrelevant. The primary concern of the critic, which is the only strictly literary interest, is with the degree of adequacy with which the poet has conveyed his imaginative object, and with the means he has adopted for such conveyance. There are indeed a hundred and one other matters connected with poetry, historical and perhaps scientific, with which we may busy ourselves. But we should not delude ourselves into thinking that such interests are literary.[2]

This may seem so excessively dogmatic that it may be worth while to consider Mr. Richards' book in more detail, where a quotation from *The Defence of Poetry* sets the theme: "The greatest poets have been men of the most spotless virtue, of the most consummate prudence, and, if we look into the interior of their lives, the most fortunate of men." Mr. Richards is concerned with the "interior of the lives of the poets," that is to say, their mental states, bodies, and nervous systems. And writing of critics, Mr. Richards says: "The qualifications of a good critic are three. He must be an adept at experiencing, without eccentricity, the state of mind relevant to the work of art he is judging. Secondly, he must be able to distinguish experiences from one another as regards their less superficial features. Thirdly, he must be a sound judge of values." [3] (By values here is meant, one supposes, the value or values of the "experiences.") It is to be noted that in this statement of the indispensable qualifications of a good critic (although it is granted, though perhaps incidentally, that the business of a critic is to judge a work of art), it is urged that what the critic has to bear in mind are "experiences"; what he has to judge are "experiences," and their value. And Mr. Richards goes on (p. 226) to eliminate even explicit reference to the work of art by saying, "The critic is throughout judging of experiences, of states of mind," and it is urged that critics are needlessly ignorant of the detailed psychology of such "experiences." It is therefore, if we are to follow Mr. Richards, with states of mind that the critic is concerned—such as are "relevant" to the work of art in question; and it is these states of mind which the critic is to judge.

There can, I think, be no doubt that this is what Mr. Richards intends. And in another chapter he undertakes to define a poem. This definition is of the greatest interest. It is suggested we may define a poem by reference to the poet's "experience," to a qualified reader's "experience," to an "ideal reader's" "experience," or to our own "ex-

[2] To avoid possible misunderstanding, I may add here that it is no part of my purpose to deny (what would obviously be absurd) that emotional endowment and temperament, coupled with the course of the writer's experience, actively determine the nature of his imaginative life. As I have tried to emphasize, the imagination is the organ of the total personality.

[3] *Principles of Literary Criticism,* p. 114.

perience." Mr. Richards, however, refuses to choose any one of them. "We must be more ingenious. We cannot take any single experience as the poem; we must have a class of more or less similar experiences instead. Let us mean by *Westminster Bridge* not the actual experience which led Wordsworth on a certain morning about a century ago to write what he did, but the class composed of all actual experiences, occasioned by the words, which do not differ within certain limits from that experience" (p. 226). This is, incidentally, an astonishing instance of definition-making, for the poet's "experience," by virtue of which it is to be decided whether or not other "experiences" are to be included in the class of "experiences" which is the poem, is unfortunately not known. (Mr. Richards has immediately before refused to define the poem as the poet's experience "since nobody but the artist has that experience.") But our concern is with the definition of a poem as an "experience." And on this definition we are given further enlightenment.

"The process in the course of which a mental event may occur, a process apparently beginning in a stimulus and ending in an act, is what we have called an impulse" (pp. 86-87). An impulse then is the entire process which includes stimulus, mental state and action; it is, that is to say, the causation of a mental event, along with the quality and consequences of that event. (It is particularly to be noted that Mr. Richards likes the "causal" statement of the occurrence of mental experiences.) And "sensation, imagery, feeling, emotion, together with pleasure, unpleasure, and pain are names for the conscious characteristics of impulses." In any given situation, of course, there is no such thing as a single impulse. Moreover, "a stimulus must not be conceived as an alien intruder which thrusts itself upon us, and, after worming a devious way through our organism, as through a piece of cheese, emerges at the other end as an act." The organism is selectively receptive and the resultant action will depend, for its character, upon the organism as well as upon the stimulus, and memory is a constant factor, determining such selection and response. In addition, imagery is constantly substituted for sensation and "incipient activities or tendencies to action" for overt response; the imaginal or incipient action such as occurs in contemplation of works of art is called an "attitude." An attitude is therefore a highly complicated affair, gathering into itself a mass of impulses. Psychology has not as yet achieved any considerable classification of attitudes, on account of their complexity. "Yet it is in terms of attitudes, the resolution, inter-inanimation, and balancing of impulses . . . that all the most valuable effects of poetry must be described" (p. 113). As an illustration of this the effects of tragedy are quoted. Tragedy supplies a poise or balance of two opposed impulses, pity, the emotional accompaniment of an impulse to approach (the word "impulse" is here used apparently of the result of the mental state caused by the stimulus), and terror, the emotional accompaniment of an impulse to retreat. It is in the "attitudes" that value resides; and of attitudes and their value the critic must be an expert judge. Yet since impulses deriving from the stimulus which is the poem are received by the mind, which is an "organized system" of possible impulses, attitudes will vary from reader to reader. It is for this reason that the poem must be defined as a class of "experiences"; and this must mean, in effect, that the poem is not one but many, as many as there are readers.

Valuable attitudes are those in which stability and poise are achieved. Such stability and poise are general characteristics of the most valuable experiences of the arts. But, it must be observed, "we must resist the temptation to analyse its cause into sets of opposed characters in the object. As a rule no such analysis can be made. The balance is not in the structure of the stimulating object, it is in the response" (p. 248). For this reason there is nothing peculiarly "aesthetic" in this poise of impulses; and apparently a large number of stimuli, very different from works of art, can give rise to them. Poems and plays are only among a number of stimuli which can produce such valuable experiences. States of inner harmony or reconciliation of impulses when enjoyed by poets, issue in the writing of poetry; and such states of inner adjustment tend to be accompanied by "transcendental descriptions," of which Wordsworth's *Tintern Abbey* is an example.[4] Such a mental state is apt to cause the poet to look for its origin in a divine source. But such beliefs result from an inner condition, and not vice versa.

IV

This is, I think, the essence of Mr. Richards' aesthetic. And it is summed up by what he has to say of Coleridge's remark that the "sense of musical delight is a gift of the imagination." This, he thinks, is one of Coleridge's "most brilliant feats"; and he goes on to say, "It is in such a resolution of a welter of disconnected impulses into a single ordered response that in all the arts imagination is most shown."[5] The imagination is "most shown in this resolution"; but what the imagination is and how it produces this desirable result we are not told, "for the reason that here its operation is most intricate and most inaccessible to observation"; and the remaining and bigger part of the chapter, which was intended to be a chapter on the imagination, talks of impulses and their resolutions, but not of the imagination. And this is in accordance with Mr. Richards' comparative lack of interest in the act of awareness as contrasted with its volitional and affective accompaniments (the "attitude"); "for a theory of knowledge," he goes on

[4] But to meet all the facts, Mr. Richards should have added that such states may give rise, apparently, to "materialistic descriptions," as in the case of Lucretius.

[5] *Op. cit.*, p. 245. Whether such "resolution" always occurs, and if so, in what sense, is discussed in Ch. IV, Sections 6 and 7.

to say, "is needed only at one point, the point at which we wish to decide whether a poem, for example, is true, or reveals reality, and if so, in what sense; admittedly, a very important question. Whereas a theory of feeling, of emotion, of attitudes and desires, of the affective-volitional aspect of mental activity, is required at all points of our analyses" (p. 91). Mr. Richards' predominant interest in feelings, emotions, attitudes, is at the expense of recognition of the activity of the imagination. He holds the critic to be primarily concerned with the resultant attitudes. "It is the attitudes invoked which are the all-important part of any experiences." What is emphasized is not our awareness of an object or set of objects, but the emotional-volitional results in us of the action of a "stimulus," which acts together with certain subjective conditions. What is important is not what is present to our minds, but what is wrought in our minds in feeling and tendencies to action. The whole regard of this aesthetic is away from the object to its results; his concern is not with the beholdment of an object but with the trains of results set up by the "stimulus." Hence Mr. Richards' love of poetry may be said to be of the cupboard variety; it is a means to an experience which is valuable for life. And his interest in poetry is therefore but an interest in one particular means by which such "experiences" can be produced; for presumably a "balance and reconciliation of impulses," such as great poetry is said to afford, might conceivably be produced by a harmless drug, in which case poetry and drugs are alike stimuli productive of valuable experiences such as it is the business of the critic apparently to judge. Accordingly, what has happened in Mr. Richards' aesthetic is that poetry has simply fallen out of it, and it has become one stimulus among many which can produce desirable results. The qualifications for a poetry-critic and a drug-critic would be, on Mr. Richards' showing, identical; they both would have to be adepts at experiencing states of mind (though for one the states of mind would be "relevant" to a work of art, and for the other those "relevant" to a drug, but such states could conceivably be identical); they would both have to be able to distinguish experiences from one another as regards their less superficial features; and they would both have to be sound judges of value.

Now there is no way in which so impossible a position can be avoided except by giving due recognition to the primacy of the imagination in poetic experience. So long as we fail to do so we necessarily look away from the imaginative object which the poet seeks to make us create, to a number of accompanying effects, emotional and volitional, which, however important, are not the central feature of poetic response. We must, on the contrary, view poetic experience as an awareness of an imaginative object; and the central "experience" is not effects wrought in us, but beholdment by the imagination of an object. It is what is present to our minds which is vital in the experience, and not the emotional-volitional effects. Such effects, of course, there will and must be. But they are attendant upon an act of apprehension which is central. The act of imaginative awareness may indeed be an "incomprehensible ultimate," but it is a unique "incomprehensible ultimate" which cannot be reduced to an effect in the nervous system. "To say," says Mr. Richards, "that the mental (neural) event so caused is aware of the black marks [the poem on paper] is to say that it is caused by them" (p. 90). It is to be noted that "mental" is here, for convenience, equated with "neural"; "for convenience" because Mr. Richards, by his use of the brackets, would have us believe that we can represent mental events as "caused" by physical stimuli in the same way as neural occurrences may be caused by physical stimuli. But in fact this is not possible. The act of awareness has a uniqueness which cannot be summarily dismissed in that fashion. And the whole purpose of Kant's work, which inspired Coleridge, was to insist that this is so, and that the act of awareness is a creative act which may require for its occurrence the presence of certain physical factors, but which cannot be reduced to them. The act of awareness is a unique and creative act, not susceptible of such a convenient reduction to neural events as Mr. Richards would have us believe. Hence the primary situation which we have to bear in mind is not our neural susceptibility to stimuli, but the imaginative synthesis of sensations which are presented to the mind on the occurrence of certain physical and neural processes. Similarly in the arts the vital factor is our imaginative activity in its awareness of an object. In perception and in poetry alike an object is present to the imagination, a presence which, of course, is accompanied by affective-volitional factors, but is nevertheless primary to such factors. In the absence of this recognition Mr. Richards is naturally at a loss to explain Coleridge's statement that a "sense of more than musical delight" is the gift of the imagination. "The sense of more than musical delight" Mr. Richards at once interprets as a poise of impulses; but how is it a "gift of the imagination"? We are not told. Whereas there can be little doubt that Coleridge viewed such affective-volitional effects as incidental ("gifts") to the major fact of the imagination's activity, Mr. Richards' aesthetic concentrates on the gifts. It apparently ignores the giver. No doubt these "gifts" are valuable, and valuable for life; but the critic, if he concentrates on them to the exclusion of the imaginative object, is simply not fulfilling his function. In the "impulse," which is the inclusive name for the entire process from stimulus to attitude, nothing is indicated to show the creative act which is present and fundamental to the rest. We hear a great deal about sensation, tied and free imagery, references, emotions, and attitudes; but nothing of the primary activity without which sensation, imagery, and references are abstractions, and emotions and attitudes impossible. It is all *Hamlet* without the Prince. If we are to remedy this omission, we must cease to speak of the reception of "stimuli" which cause certain results which may be valuable, and speak instead of an "active agency" which creates its object, and in that creation enjoys certain emotional and volitional accompaniments.

V

In a more recently published book, *Coleridge on the Imagination*, Mr. Richards deals at great length with Coleridge's views on the imagination. It is, in the light of what has gone before, of the greatest interest to observe what he has to say, and what validity he is prepared to grant to Coleridge's doctrine. Speaking of Coleridge's desertion of Hartley for Kant, Mr. Richards says that "the two systems (or sets of assumptions), violently opposed though they seemed to him, may each—to a Coleridge—be ways of surveying our mind" (p. 17). Now "materialist associationism" is certainly one way of surveying our mind; it is the way which is dictated by a psychology which sets out to be "scientific." (This we noticed at the end of our first essay, and we shall return to it at the end of this one.) Over against "materialist associationism" Mr. Richards sets "transcendental idealism." But transcendental idealism is not that which is opposed to it. What should be opposed to it, as another "way of surveying the mind," is a psychology which realizes that "materialist-associationism" is not, when clearly understood, anything more than a form of scientific methodology, and which, while admitting that it itself is not "scientific," asserts that the mind is creative in knowledge. This it may clearly do without asserting any epistemological idealism. Now Coleridge once and for all threw over all that Hartley stood for, and ceased to hold an associationism, whether as a "way of surveying the mind" or in any other way; it is true that in so doing he adopted an idealism. But this, for our purpose, can be separated out from his view of the mind as an "active agency." [6] And the choice is not between, as is suggested, the materialist and the idealist. The choice is between a materialistic psychology which does not see its materialism merely as a necessity of scientific inquiry, and a psychology which sees materialism as a necessity to scientific method, and, by rejecting it, is content to be open to the charge of being "unscientific."

Then, at a later stage, after Coleridge's remarks on the primary and secondary imagination have been quoted, come the following astonishing sentences. "Taken as psychology," writes Mr. Richards, "—not as

[6] Although it is true that Coleridge took Kant to be an idealist in the usual sense of the term, it may be emphasized that by "transcendental idealism" Kant intended a doctrine indifferent to both "idealism" and "realism"—a doctrine which regarded idealism and realism as raising (and trying to answer) questions which go "beyond experience" and which therefore should not be discussed. Although Kant certainly gives ground for being regarded as a subjectivist, this was certainly not what he intended. It is probably true to say that there are eminent contemporary writers who, while insisting on "interpretation" and "construction" by the mind in perception, adhere to an uncompromising epistemological realism. But Kant's own view is the most satisfactory.

metaphysics—there is little in such an account of mental *activity* with which a modern psychologist—even though he combines with it a metaphysical materialism, and supposes that the mind is just certain ways of operation in the body—will treat now as other than a commonplace. Data are for him facta; he knows too much about the dependence of every mental event upon former mental events to regard any of their products as simply given to us. For him the activities of the self . . . are results of past activities . . . and this prior experiencing determines how it will experience in the future" (p. 60). What these remarks are apparently intended to convey is that Coleridge, in these sentences, was stating a trivial commonplace and what any associationist could accept. But between all that is implied in Coleridge's view of imagination as the "prime agent of all human perception" and what Mr. Richards reduces Coleridge's remarks to mean, there is, of course, a whole world of difference. This is not the place in which to enter into the detail of the controversy which centres about associationism. But it is plainly absurd to seek to reduce Coleridge's statement, whether taken as psychology or metaphysics, to meaning nothing more than a modern form of associationism could accept. Certainly Coleridge intended something very different from materialistic and associationist psychology. There is reason to believe that Mr. Richards occasionally suspects that this is so; and he then falls back on the suggestion that there is no essential difference between the two views. "We cannot," he says, "reasonably satisfy ourselves, or take either party's word for it, that they are as opposed to each other as they seem to be. We could be satisfied only if we were able to perform a perfect analysis exhibiting them in common terms. We need, in other words, to discover just what each is doing, and a means of comparing these doings—a common framework in which the rival speculative machineries can be examined" (p. 70). Such an analysis and such a technique of comparison are at present beyond our powers. "But we should not," we are told, "hold that there is any irreconcilable clash between their results." This is indeed making the best of two worlds; and doing so on the strength of the lack of an analysis and technique of comparison competent to show how the reconciliation can be made. This kind of argument is, if I may say so, a form of the self-mystification which in his book Mr. Richards attributes to Mr. Herbert Read. It is also a form of "dodging the chief difficulty" which again, in another part of the book, is attributed to others.

There is good reason why Mr. Richards should seek to make the best of the two worlds. For he recognizes, in spite of all his liking for associationism, that Coleridge's view of the mind as active and creative has advantages that "associationism of the Hartley-Condillac type" had not. "As an instrument for exploring the most intricate and unified modes of mental activity—those in poetry—its superiority seems overwhelming." There is indeed little doubt of this; Mr. Richards will hardly allow himself to be drawn into the view of literary creation which Mr. Russell sets out in *An Outline of Philosophy* (p. 200) as resulting from the poets having a store of "unusual associations." Yet, by one of those astonishing reconciliations of opposition which from time to time occur in Mr. Richards' mind, we find him saying on the preceding page that "were Coleridge alive he would, I hope, be applauding and improving doctrines of the type he, as a metaphysician, thought least promising—the very materialistic-mechanistic doctrines that he was attacking." Mr. Richards, therefore, will not have the imagination as Coleridge tried to explicate it; or, rather, he accepts it in the act of saying that it will be shown, by the psychology of years hence, to be at one with "materialist associationism." If he could show how, in but one slightest respect, this is conceivable, we might perhaps take this seriously.

VI

We may now return to the *Principles of Literary Criticism,* in which we are told that the only point at which the theory of knowledge has any relevance for criticism is when we wish to decide whether or not a poem is true or false, or reveals reality. The theory of knowledge has, in Mr. Richards' view, a slighter use in criticism than a theory of feeling, emotion, and attitude, which is required at every point. Now reflection will show that though some theory of apprehension is necessary for criticism, it is not in the least necessary for that purpose which Mr. Richards indicates. In the first place, Mr. Richards apparently believes that *Othello, Tintern Abbey,* or any other poem we wish to mention, is either true or false, does or does not reveal reality. And it is implied that there is at hand a theory of knowledge which can tell us whether or not *Tintern Abbey* does or does not reveal reality. It is a matter of great interest to know that there is such a theory; but if it exists it has not yet come to light. Incidentally, one would have thought that to know whether *Othello* is true or false, or *Tintern Abbey* reveals or fails to reveal reality, a conclusive metaphysic, were such a thing possible, and not only a theory of knowledge, would be necessary. But our present point is that the question of the abstract truth or otherwise of a play or poem simply does not occur in imaginative experience; for poetry is not a number of propositions, but the conveyance of imaginative prehension. The poet sees the world in a certain way; thus has his imagination created it, and thus is it real to him, the world in which he lives and to which in his life he responds. The world as it is represented is the poet's world; and in so far as his poem is successful, he will make it the reader's world by compelling his vision upon him. And this is so whether the poet be a Lucretius or a Wordsworth. In great poetry we at once receive and create an imaginative vision of the world; a new world becomes acutely present to us, or, as Coleridge says, the poet makes us creators, after him, of such a new world. And to ask is *Tintern Abbey* true or false is to put an impossible question from outside the imaginative experience, and, in any case, a question which surely no one can claim to have answered or be able to answer once and for all. Our response to such a world as the poet places compulsion upon us to create may indeed quickly fade after our reading, and that world may soon cease to have a compelling reality for us. But all that is of relevance and importance for criticism is that the poet makes it real for us and compels us to his vision. However Christian a man may be, however much, that is to say, his life may be controlled by the Christian imagination of the world, he may yet enjoy the *De Rerum Natura* as the expression of an amazing vision of the world. It is surely not the business of the critic to make pronouncements upon the "truth" or otherwise of poems and plays; we do not want, say, a Christian critic to point out objections to Lucretius' scheme; we want him to help us enjoy an imaginative synthesis which is not Christian. And if he cannot do that he is no critic; he has to be "chameleon-like," and for the purpose of his work to live in not one world but in a "thousand worlds." [7]

When Mr. Richards undertakes to describe the genesis of the writing of poetry he again shows his interest in "experiences" and "attitudes," not in the object present to imaginative activity. When we read a poem, and enjoy an "experience" of poise of impulses, the stimulus is the poem, though of course the stimulus is complicated in its action by "interior" conditions. What then is the stimulus to the poet which gives him his "experience"? Not, it seems, an imaginative object. Instead, "some system of impulses not ordinarily in adjustment within itself or adjusted to the world finds something which orders it or gives it fit exercise. Then follows the peculiar sense of ease, of free, unimpeded activity and the feeling of acceptance, of something more positive than acquiescence. This feeling is the reason why such states may be called beliefs." [8] Thus we are asked to believe that the labour of imaginative synthesis is a product of a rather mysterious and fortunate adjustment of impulses; and that the literary masterpieces of the world, the *Iliad,* the *Aeneid,* the *Inferno, Paradise Lost, The Tempest,* were stimulated into existence "by something"—possibly a good meal, or a comfortable chair.

We are further told that in order to have "experiences" two conditions are necessary, first mental health, and secondly "frequent occurrence of such experiences in the recent past" (p. 248). These two conditions are interesting. For what, in the first place, is mental

[7] I do not wish to suggest that this is the sole function of the critic; but I do suggest that the critic should avoid the use of the word "truth." Incidentally, in view of Mr. Richards' view of what he calls "revelation theories" of poetry (see later), it is surprising that he should think it worth while to discuss whether or not a poem is "true" or "reveals reality."

[8] *Principles of Literary Criticism,* p. 283.

health? What can it mean for Mr. Richards but the possession of a mental organization which is likely to result in "experiences"? So that, in order to have "experiences" we must have a mind likely to have "experiences." And secondly, in order to have "experiences" in the present and future, we must have had such "experiences" (and frequently) in the past. This is equivalent to saying that in order to have the experience of digesting a meal well we should have a sound constitution, a constitution of the kind likely to digest a meal well; and, secondly, we should have successfully digested meals previously, indeed in the recent past. But all this, to say the least, is not very enlightening.

VII

Mr. Richards, no doubt, is the more willing to take up this attitude because there can be no doubt that a great deal of the world's best poetry is religious—represents, that is to say, a religious imagination of the world. Mr. Richards, however, disapproves of such apprehension of the world. He does so apparently on the basis of his distinction between the scientific and the emotive uses of language, and religious belief is an "emotive" affair. Now as we endeavoured to point out in the previous chapter, this distinction is superficial in comparison with the distinction between language used for mere indication and language used for imaginative conveyance. This failure to see the more significant distinction is again due to a persistent emphasis upon emotional and volitional reactions at the expense of the initial imaginative activity. And when, it is argued, language is used emotively, what is occurring is an effort to bring about "effects in emotion and attitude produced by the reference it occasions." That is to say, a poise or balance of impulses "brought about by something" easily results in a reference being occasioned—in Wordsworth's case, for example, it is God, the immortality of the soul, etc. But these "references" arise out of an emotional-volitional state; they are fictions, and should not therefore be taken seriously—"it is still the attitudes, not the references which are important." "For strong belief-feelings, as is well known, and as is shown by certain doses of alcohol or hashish, and pre-eminently of nitrous oxide, will readily attach themselves to almost any reference, distorting it to suit their purpose."

Now the matter of the explicit expression of belief in poetry is by no means so important as Mr. Richards would have us believe. For the poet's belief can ultimately be interpreted to be only the presence to his imagination of a world which is the world in which he lives, and which, as he responds to it in his life, is his real world.[9] The poet's

[9] A relevant discussion will be found in an essay "The Nature of Believing," by R. B. Braithwaite, in the *Proceedings of the Aristotelian Society* for 1933, where belief is defined as (1) entertainment of a proposition *p*, and (2) a disposition to act as if *p* were true. I suggest that in poetry, whether or not the poet explicitly states propositions which he can be said personally to believe, we have belief-situations.

belief, in other words, is not a matter of mere explicit assertion; it consists in his emotional-volitional response to the world of his imagination, which is shown by that response to be his real world. Whether or not the poet makes formal assertion of belief is not important. Mr. Richards, in accordance with his view of the place of belief in poetry, is strongly opposed to what he calls "revelation" theories—views which hold that poetry can claim to give us truth. For our part, we should agree that the "revelation" theory is a useless and impossible doctrine; but for reasons other than those which Mr. Richards holds. For against the "revelation" theory it is necessary to maintain that, as we do not know "for truth" (as Keats says), the ultimate nature of the universe, we must be content with a situation in which the poet is seen as conveying to us the world as it is for his imagination, which controls his life, and which is thus real to him. Ultimately, whether or not the world is really as it exists for his imagination neither he nor we can in all strictness be said to know.

VIII

But Mr. Richards seeks to elude us by speaking of belief. There are, he says, no "beliefs" in *King Lear*; and music similarly states no "beliefs." In the sense of explicit statements of belief, that is so. Yet to the imagination which is suborned to *King Lear* the world of Lear is a real world; it was for Shakespeare, if only during the time of its composition, the world in which he believed. Similarly, the world of *Tintern Abbey* was for Wordsworth his real world, that to which he responded in behaviour, and it may become so for the reader. The fact that Wordsworth, for obvious reasons, had explicitly to express beliefs to help conveyance of his object, and that Shakespeare, for equally obvious reasons, had not, does not alter the identity of the two situations.[10] Two imaginative apprehensions of the world are being conveyed. That is all that is relevant. Mr. Richards says, and rightly, that in the reading of *King Lear,* no facts verifiable by science, or accepted and believed in, as we accept and believe in ascertained facts, are relevant. But in *Tintern Abbey,* apparently, there are facts verifiable by science

---

King Lear (see later) contains no explicit expression of Shakespeare's belief about human life; but it expresses the kind of world which at the time Shakespeare "entertained" in his imagination and which, as thus entertained, affected his behaviour. If this is true, *King Lear* and, say, *Tintern Abbey* (which contains explicit statements of belief) both alike express belief, and the question of formal expression of belief loses its importance. This is confirmed by the fact that Mr. A. C. Bradley was able to state in propositional form what Shakespeare at the time of writing the tragedies may be said to have believed about human life. No doubt these beliefs were not present in propositional form to Shakespeare's mind; but they are none the less embodied or implicit in the plays.

[10] Of course, if a poet *can* convey his "work" without explicit expression of belief, he should most certainly do so. But clearly there is a large class of poems in which this is impossible. Poetry should *show* and not *say;* expression of belief in poetry is justified only when it is unavoidable.

which are relevant, and which apparently prove that *Tintern Abbey* is a case of distorted reference, of reference to a fiction. If so, we should be glad to know what they are, and to have mention of a single fact "verifiable by science," etc., which is relevant to *Tintern Abbey,* and shows it to have fictitious reference. The fact that in one poem there is, and in the other there is not explicit expression of belief, does not alter the fact that in each case "facts verifiable by science" are irrelevant. In each case language is being used to evoke an imaginative world; and as we have seen, the question of ultimate truth remains unanswered.

There is, however, little doubt as to the source of Mr. Richards' "clear and impartial awareness of the nature of the world." He finds that source in science, a source which apparently, by the information it gives, is able to tell us whether or not an attitude is valuable and "attunes us to existence." In a little book called *Science and Poetry,* Mr. Richards develops this point for us. There he tells us that what he calls the "magical view of nature" (by which is apparently intended the religious view of nature whether primitive or Christian) has been dispelled by the "neutralization of nature," the new "world-picture of science." Science has brought about a "revolution" in these matters, has given us "genuine knowledge," and the former "edifices of supposed knowledge" have simply toppled down. Thus science has apparently told us what sort of a thing "existence" is, and we know now where we stand. Such doctrine, as I have tried to reiterate, is founded on an erroneous view of scientific construction; but in this respect, Mr. Richards not only reveals a failure of comprehension; he adds to such failure self-contradiction of an extreme kind. Having set out such a doctrine as the above, he proceeds to tell us that science "cannot tell us what we are or what this world is; not because these are in any sense insoluble questions, but because they are not questions at all" (p. 53). And this follows the statement on the preceding page to the effect that science has shown us that the "magical" view of nature (which after all is a view of what man and the world are) has been exploded by science. It also immediately follows a statement in which we are told that "science can tell us about man's place in the universe and his chances; that the place is precarious, and the chances problematical." But one would have thought that to tell us this is to tell us a great deal about what we are and what the world is. For what is meant by "chances"? Does Mr. Richards include under "chances" the "chance," for example, of personal immortality or of a supra-temporal existence? One supposes that he must do so, since they are "chances" about which human beings have always been concerned. Does, then, science tell us *nothing* of what man and the world is?

IX

The whole tenor of Mr. Richards' philosophical criticism is due to a very simple failure of discrimination. Building up his views on the misleading distinction between language used for reference and language used emotively, he has failed to realize the imaginative character of scientific construction.[11] And therefore he has failed to see that the "world-picture of science" is an imaginative construction, evolved with a view to the formulation of generalizations of strictest fact. He therefore takes it seriously for an account of the nature of existence. In his psychology, materialistic-associationism accordingly becomes inevitable, the mind becomes for him the nervous system, and it is indifferent to him whether or not we call awareness a mental or a neural event. That being so, Mr. Richards believes that criticism instead of being what it necessarily now is, something vague and uncertain, can be made "scientific" and to consist of precise generalizations and judgments—all that is required is greater knowledge of neurology. When a really adequate knowledge of neurology is obtained, a poem will be susceptible of precise expression; it will be expressible no longer even as an "experience," but as a system of nervous discharges in the mechanical nervous system. No doubt it will be expressible also in mathematical formulae. When poems have thus become reducible to formulae, the critic, who will be an expert neurologist and mathematician, will be able to say, with the utmost precision, which of two poems is the more valuable, which, that is to say, liberates the greatest quantity of nervous energy in the present and for the future. Criticism will thus have become a precise science. It is true that at present neurology is a "jungle." But "it should be borne in mind that the knowledge which the men of A.D. 3000 will possess, if all goes well, may make all our aesthetics, all our psychology, all our modern theory of value, look pitiful." Certainly, this should be "borne in mind." In the meanwhile, it is convenient to regard Coleridge's view of the mind as actively creative as not altogether foolish. But as we saw, in case we should think that Mr. Richards is abandoning his materialistic-associationism, we are assured that an "analysis and technique of comparison" (of which presumably the men of A.D. 3000 will be in possession) will show that there is no irreconcilable clash between James Mill's view of the mind and Coleridge's. It is, no doubt, an advantage to know what knowledge the men of A.D. 3000 will possess; Mr. Richards blandly gives himself the advantage of Coleridge's way of thinking while sublimely assuring us that in a thousand years it will be shown to be a form of materialistic-associationism. I hesitate to describe this kind of argument as unfair. But Mr. Richards

[11] It is only fair to Mr. Richards to point out that in Ch. VII of *Coleridge on Imagination* he shows signs of recognizing this. But as this recognition, if he is to be consistent, involves fundamental changes in his entire aesthetic, I have thought it right to criticize his former view.

would probably have a harder word for anyone who, in discussion, asserted that two utterly different things were really the same, on the grounds that, although he could not for the life of him see how they could be, people of a thousand years hence will be able to.

I have written at such length about Mr. Richards' work in order to bring out the character of the conclusions to which we are brought if we ignore the primacy of the imaginative act in artistic creation and enjoyment. Denying such primacy the virtual result of Mr. Richards' work is to ignore poetry and give us formulae instead. Putting the active agency of the imagination on one side, Mr. Richards introduces us to science and scientific psychology; and we are told a great deal about morals and value. These things are no doubt of great importance, but they are not poetry, and the critic, be he ever so philosophical or scientific, who gives them priority over the activity of the imagination is forgetting the main task of criticism. It is not, of course, the case that matters relating to science, psychology, and problems of morals and value do not arise in the discussion of poetry; and it is of great importance that the inter-relation of these things should be discussed and realized. But it is of still greater importance that we should recognize the arts as the expression of the unique activity of the imagination, instead of setting out to reduce the imagination to something other than it is. And when we say that the imagination is "unique" we do not mean that it is something merely "aesthetic," but that it is an irreducible factor present in all experience whatsoever, yet operative in the arts with a high degree of power and concreteness.

X

It is surprising how, in critics differing radically from Mr. Richards, there is a curious vagueness on the subject of the imagination, and how frequently the use of the word is avoided. For example, we find Mr. Murry writing in *The Problem of Style* (p. 19): "In adopting the notion that style stands in a direct relation to a core or nucleus of emotional and intellectual experience, we have cut away some of the difficulties that seemed to surround one of the most common meanings of the word Style." What is striking in this passage is that Mr. Murry traces back the writing of poetry to "emotional and intellectual" elements. There is no doubt that in the writing of poetry emotional and intellectual elements are present. But surely there is, more important than either, an imaginative element. It may be, of course, that Mr. Murry is using emotion in a very vague way, to include imaginative creation. But if so, this is surely a reprehensible use of a word which carries for everybody, the plain man and the psychologist alike, an indication of forms of feeling which in themselves are not imaginative. And again, in a passage which Mr. Richards quotes from Mr. Lascelles

Abercrombie, we find Mr. Abercrombie speaking of the "quality and force of the *emotion* symbolized by the imagery." But is the main use of imagery to symbolize emotion? One would have thought that its main use was the expression of imaginative idea or object; and Mr. Richards, criticizing Mr. Abercrombie, insists that what is important in imagery is not emotion, but meaning. He falls back from the emotional to the intellectual elements involved.[12] Certainly, again, emotional and intellectual elements are present; but surely they are part of a total experience central to which is imaginative prehension. Such prehension cannot occur in poetry unaccompanied by emotion and thought. But we cannot agree with Mr. Abercrombie to reduce it to emotion or with Mr. Richards to reduce it to meaning. Or again we find it said in a recent work by Mr. John Sparrow [13] that the aim of the poet is to express and create a "state of feeling." It may be that the word "feeling" is being used loosely. But the loose use of a word can be extremely dangerous, and lead to failures to distinguish the important factors in the situation. For "emotion" and "feeling" are in themselves "blind," states of mind which depend for their occurrence upon an activity of mind which is a prehension of an object and carries us outside ourselves. Such activity is creative, in the sense that the object as it is prehended is not given to the mind, but is the outcome of imaginative synthesis. And this activity is necessary in perception, science, and art alike. In the former it is subordinate, functional to certain ends; in the latter it is free and subordinate to neither utility nor abstraction. And the primary fact about poetry is that in and through it an imaginative object is conveyed. This, as it seems to me, is true of all poetry whatsoever, including, as I hope to show, lyrical poetry. And the dangers which accrue to overlooking this seem overwhelming. The weight of emphasis must always be on the vividness with which we grasp an imaginative object or situation, and not on the quality or value of the other aspects of our mental condition associated with that apprehension—"emotion" and "attitudes."

[12] *Coleridge on Imagination,* pp. 35-37.
[13] *Sense and Poetry,* p. 27.

THE NEW CRITICS

(1947)

ROBERT WOOSTER STALLMAN

"Erasmus did not scold his age, he assimilated it."
—ALLEN TATE: review in *New Republic* (June 8, 1927)

I

THERE IS ONE basic theme in modern criticism; it is the dissociation of modern sensibility. The loss of a spiritual order and of integrity in the modern consciousness is T. S. Eliot's major premise. The issue of our glorification of the scientific vision at the expense of the aesthetic vision is the central theme in both the poetry and the criticism of the Southern poet-critics. It is this theme of spiritual disorder which the late Paul Valéry exploited; it shows through the current of the critical writings of I. A. Richards, F. R. Leavis, Yvor Winters, R. P. Blackmur, and the Southern critics. The New Critics, while differing among one another in theory or in practice, are as one through the unifying relation of this obsessive burden.

To what use does the critic put it? My purpose in this essay is to order into a synthesis the critical ideas and methods of the New Critics, and for my starting point I shall trace the ways in which this theme operates at the critical level.

One variation upon the theme is *the loss of tradition.* We lack a religious and a social tradition which would extend moral and intellectual authority to the poet. Dante and the poets of other great ages of poetry had at hand a body of ideas and a faith in them. There is no such agreement today. Never were poets more profoundly divided from the life of society than in our time. The effect upon our Experimental Generation of the loss of an antecedent discipline such as tradition provides forms the subject of Yvor Winters' *Primitivism and Decadence.* The loss has resulted in a poetry of structural confusion. The theme of Eliot's *After Strange Gods* is the limiting or crippling effect upon our literature of our dislocation from a living tradition. The effect is twofold: (1) confusion as to the boundaries of criticism, and (2) extreme individualism in viewpoints—the expression of a personal view of life, the exploitation of personality. Allen Tate, following Eliot, defines tradition as "a quality of judgment and of conduct, rooted in a concrete way of life" that we inherit from our immediate past, or, if we are makers of tradition (and it demands our constant rediscovery), the quality of life that we create and pass on to the next generation. Tradition, no less than religion itself, is formed of a structure of absolutes—points of moral and intellectual reference "implicit and emergent in experience at all times, and under certain conditions, explicit and realized." This conception of tradition is the foundation for the critical outlook of both Eliot and Tate. Eliot's conception of an immutable order is ultimately religious; like Valéry's, Tate's is ultimately aesthetic.

The theme is repeated in other terms—from Hulme to Blackmur—as *the loss of a fixed convention* providing the poet a unifying relation to his society. The modern poet, deprived of some rational structure from which he might derive discipline and authority, is under the constant necessity of either resurrecting a dead convention (Millay) or erecting a new one of his own (Yeats). A tradition or a culture manifests itself in the language, in the medium of the poet's words. It is only in terms of language, which may be defined as the embodiment of our experience in words, that a convention exists or survives. The work of a great poet is the creation of a new convention, a new order of language. A convention is simply the way in which language has been used by the poets of a preceding generation, used so powerfully that we can but carry on its major significance. The operation of this principle in Tate's criticism is best illustrated by his judgment on Millay. By using the language of the preceding generation to convey an emotion peculiar to her own, and by making that language personal, Millay restored life to a dead convention. This is her distinction, but it is also her limitation. She preserved, in the traditional style of the preceding decadent age, the personality of her own age—without altering either. The criticism of Tate, Brooks, and Blackmur is built upon this principle of the language: does the poet make "a genuine attempt to use in his poems the maximum resource of poetic language consonant with his particular talent"?

A third thematic variation is the loss of an objective system of truths imbedded in a homogeneous society—*the loss of belief* in religion and in myth. Eliot claims that what Blake's genius required and lacked "was a framework of accepted and traditional ideas which would have prevented him from indulging in a philosophy of his own, and concentrated his attention on the problems of the poet. . . . The concentration resulting from a framework of mythology and theology and philosophy is one of the reasons why Dante is a classic, and Blake only a poet of genius." Eliot's theme informs Tate's standard for judging such poets as Robinson, MacLeish, and Cummings. Because they had no systematic philosophy or external framework of ideas to sustain them, they substituted their own personality as the core of experience and meaning. MacLeish lacked what Milton had, namely "an objective convention that absorbed every implication of his personal feeling." Lacking an epos or myth, E. A. Robinson had to repeat his ground again and again, writing a poem that would not be written. On Cummings the criticisms of Tate and of John Peale Bishop come to the same point: Cummings' poetry is an image of his unique personality. In ages which suffer the loss of religion there is chaos and violence expressed, and that is what Eliot's *The Waste Land* means. It means "that men who have lost both the higher myth of religion and the lower myth of historical dramatization have lost the forms of human action; it means that they are no longer capable . . . of forming a dramatic conception of human nature . . ." In place of the dramatization of the soul, as we find it in Emily Dickinson's poetry, we get from a contemporary poet like MacLeish the dramatization (in *Conquistador*) of personality against an historical setting.

Another form the theme takes is *the loss of a world order,* a world order which can be assimilated to the poetic vision. Shakespeare had such a world order in his medieval pattern of life, and Emily Dickinson had one in her New England and Puritan Christianity. Without moral and intellectual standards the poet has no means for measuring and testing his personal experience. Our age lacks what Shelley called the "fixed point of reference" for the poet's sensibility. The assumption—a fallacy common to contemporary poets [1]—that order or adequate form can be created simply by the poet's act of self-expression, by his imitation of the world disorder in what Winters has labeled as Expressive or Imitative Form—fails the poet as a solution for the problem of poetic structure. For Winters, Tate, F. R. Leavis, John Crowe Ransom, or R. P. Blackmur—a poem for these critics must have a rational structure, a core of meaning, a scheme of objective reference which orders and gives meaning to the poet's emotions.[2] "Shelley, at his best and worst, offers the emotion in itself, unattached, in the void" (Leavis in *Revaluation*). In MacLeish's *Conquistador* a mechanism of personal sensation is substituted for theme or meaning; the personality attached to Cummings's *Viva* is the only meaning in Cummings's poems; the coherence of *The Bridge* is merely the coherence of the tone or poet's attitude. Tate sets down Crane's career as "a vindication of Eliot's major premise—that the integrity of the individual consciousness has broken down." The failure of *The Bridge,* by virtue of its structural disorder, is symptomatic of the failure of modern poetry generally. Tate's analysis of Crane's poetry extends

[1] Pointed out by Winters in discussing MacLeish's poetry, and by Blackmur on Sandburg's.

[2] For Cleanth Brooks a poem finds its main unity in its tone rather than in its rational structure; "the logical unity does not organize the poem." In *The Well Wrought Urn* he writes: "I question whether the parts of any poem ever attain any tighter connections than the 'psychological' or that the coherence, even of the metaphysical poets, is not ultimately a coherence of attitude." Compare Ransom's views in *The World's Body,* pp. 270-303.

beyond the poems to the outer area of disorder and cross-purposes in the contemporary milieu. Tate relates the world disorder to the poetic one. Likewise, in examining other poets (Eliot, Pound, Dickinson, Bishop), his criticism scrutinizes both the conscious intention of the poet, the intention which is framed within the poem, and the unconscious intention—the cultural mind of the poet's world order as it is expressed in the poetry.

Intellectual chaos has been the background of American poetry and criticism during this period. The problem confronting a poet is to transfer to the poetic process a unified point of view synthesized out of the social and intellectual climate; but in our world today the complexity of these relations is not readily resolvable into a unity. "The modern can never avoid the suspicion," Samuel Hoare observes, "that whatever attitude he takes up is only a partial expression of himself and a partial activity. And he has no scale of values which would justify him in concluding that this part is the most important, that this activity is the fundamental activity. Without this great poetry is impossible." It is a commonplace of criticism, I repeat, that our present-day world is in radical disintegration and that the artist is severed from a living relation to society. Both W. H. Auden and Stephen Spender have explored this theme in their critical writings, Auden pointing out that when there is no organized dogma within society the artist becomes self-consciously didactic. As D. S. Savage says (in *The Personal Principle*), "The modern artist cannot take his values from contemporary society, because that society lacks all coherent standards and values. This it is which explains the artist's isolation from society. In his isolation he is forced to depend upon what values he can find within himself, and this makes a 'classical' art impossible."

The critics tell us that ours is an age of intellectual chaos and spiritual disunity, and yet, despite the prevailing disjuncture between artist and society, it is an age of great poetry. The dilemma of the modern poet, according to Tate, has its counterpart in the disfranchised intellect of the critic. (Blackmur singles out Yvor Winters as a conspicuous example.) It is claimed that the dissociation of sensibility—a theory which has echoed throughout criticism since it first appeared in Eliot's definition of the Metaphysical poets—transposes into the split mind of the critic. And yet it is an age of great criticism. Order, system, and (notwithstanding all the cross-currents of disagreement) unity toolmark the total achievement of the critics of our time.

II

Criticism is the positing and criticizing of dogmas, and its quest is standards of judgment and value. Though Tate disclaims the act of the systematic literary critic, Tate's criticism nevertheless is systematic as an aesthetic theory and as a synthesis of dogmas. The critical ideas do not conflict with each other, as they do in Herbert Read's criticism, but form a coherent system of principles. The system is unified by a single point of view. The point of view, which is that of T. E. Hulme, derives from Bergson. There is a radical division between the realm of faith and the realm of reason; between, on the one hand, the intuitive and qualitative, and, on the other hand, the intellectual and quantitative. It was Hulme's thesis that our spiritual disunity is the result of our failure to recognize the division which exists between the Religious Attitude, which postulates absolute values by which man is judged as limited and imperfect, and the Humanist Attitude, which regards man as fundamentally good and life as the source and measure of all values. Hulme designated the confusion of these two orders as the essence of Romanticism. "The view which regards man as a well, a reservoir, full of possibilities, I call the romantic; the one which regards him as a very finite and fixed creature, I call the classical." Hulme's identification of humanism with romanticism and of the religious attitude with classicism is followed by Eliot, and likewise by Tate.

Classicism means the discrimination between reason and faith; and romanticism, the confusion of reason and faith. This confusion, Eliot complains, has been the background of the modern consciousness since the Renaissance. But as Read remarks, our age "is not clearly either a romantic or a classical age, nor are the categories of a romantic or a classical tradition applicable to it." More significant and fundamental is the dichotomy between art and science. This post-Renaissance dichotomy, which replaces the Renaissance antinomy between faith and reason, represents an opposition between qualitative knowledge (art) and quantitative knowledge (science). The modern problem, as John Middleton Murry sees it, is to reach a synthesis between these two orders of knowledge. He maintains that not until a new synthesis is posed will any work of art of the first magnitude be possible again. In advocating the medieval synthesis as projected into the Thomist system, Murry suggests that "the Classicism of the Middle Ages can serve us only as a symbol, not as a pattern, of a new synthesis" ("Towards a Synthesis," *Criterion:* May, 1927). Tate sums up our modern dilemma through the same perspective and in similar terms. In the decay of Protestantism is to be found the chief clue to our understanding of English literature. Tate's opposition to the modern positivist procedure, the reduction of all knowledge to the quantitative kind, has the same foundation as Murry's opposition to the scientific materialism of our time.

Both Eliot and Tate have thoroughly orientated themselves in Hulme's *Speculations.* As his critics have observed, Hulme's dicta, in the same or in different settings, appear throughout Eliot's writings. They show up also in Tate's. In Hulme is grounded, for instance,

Tate's objection to Emerson's conception of man. (It was Emerson's conception which dissipated all tragic possibilities in that culture for dramatizing the human soul, as Robert Penn Warren points out.) Hulme might have phrased this accounting for the great wastes in Emily Dickinson and Walt Whitman:

> The great bulk of the verse of each appears to have been written on the sustaining pretense that everything was always possible. To see boundless good on the horizon, to see it without the limiting discipline of the conviction of evil, is in poetry as in politics the great stultifier of action. . . . With no criterion of achievement without there could be no criterion of completion within.
>
> (R. P. Blackmur in *The Expense of Greatness*)

Hulme defined the mood and perspective of our age; and this is his importance, almost exclusively. He is important not because he was an original thinker, but because of his influence upon those who have dominated and largely directed the course of contemporary criticism. Tate is a disciple of Hulme in his campaign against scientism, romanticism, and humanism ("the belief that the only values that matter are human values"). Tate accepts as necessary a system of religion because it provides standards by which man can measure his own imperfections. ("The religious unity of intellect and emotion, of reason and instinct, is the sole technique for the realization of values.")

The affinity between the Southern critics and Hulme lies in their common claim that our present disunity has been created by the confusion of two categories: the aesthetic vision, which is concerned with quality, and the scientific vision, which is concerned with quantity. The disunity of the modern mind is the single theme of Tate's *Reason in Madness*. It is the scientism of our age that has forced out the religious attitude and reduced the spiritual realm to irrelevant emotion, under the illusion that all experience can be ordered scientifically. It is the decline of organized religion that has given rise to utilitarian theories of art. Dewey's theory of the integrating power of art attributes to art all the psychological virtues of a religion. Under the formula that all art is action, he identifies art and religion and science as "satisfying the same fundamental needs." Tate, of course, rejects this equation. In *The Aesthetic Emotion as Useful* (in *This Quarter:* Dec., 1932), he exposes the fallacy of the pragmatic aesthetic. Both Tate, in *Reason in Madness,* and Ransom, in *The New Criticism,* attack victoriously the positivists' position and thereby perform for modern criticism, as one of their critics acknowledges, an invaluable service. In line with an aesthetician like Eliseo Vivas, the Southern critics regard the aesthetic and the practical as opposites. Contrary to Dewey's pragmatic aesthetic, art is neither another kind of religion nor another kind of science. Poetry is poetry and not science or religion. The canon of the Southern critics is based upon a division of art and science into two independent, objective and equally valid categories of experience. Science and poetry are the opposite poles of truth; art and religion, though both are the vehicles of qualitative experience, are not identical. It was Arnold's faith that poetry, since religion had yielded to science, could take over the work of religion. (Though the facts of science had undermined religion, they could still support poetry!) Arnold's viewpoint has its contemporary version in I. A. Richards's *Science and Poetry*. Richards here endorsed Arnold's dictum that what is valuable in religion is its aesthetic aspects. Tate's analysis of Arnold shows his position as giving the case for poetry away to the scientist. Arnold's poetics turns poetry into a "descriptive science or experience at that level, touched with emotion." Tate and Ransom attempt to solve anew Arnold's problem. They attempt to place poetry on an equal footing with science. They do so by claiming that poetry is primarily of the intellect and that poetry is "an independent form of knowledge, a kind of cognition equal to the knowledge of the sciences at least, perhaps superior." They claim for art those cognitive ingredients which the early Richards, by his former positivist position, discredited. The knowledge which poetry gives us is a special kind of knowledge and not, as Richards once persuaded us to think, merely an inferior kind of science. Richards misunderstood the aesthetic emotion and equated poetry with life, so Montgomery Belgion declared in his critique, *What Is Criticism?* (*Criterion:* Oct., 1930). The later Richards of *Coleridge on Imagination* (1934), however, has repudiated his former utilitarian theory of art, and with his present definition of poetry—"Poetry is the completest mode of utterance"—Tate acknowledged an essential agreement. (Paul Valéry and T. Sturge Moore have expressed similar insights.) As Tate frames it, "the high forms of literature offer us the only complete, and thus the most responsible, versions of our experience." The arts "give us a sort of cognition at least equally valid with that of the scientific method."

Ransom's theory of poetry as knowledge is fundamentally the same as Tate's. Science and poetry present two different descriptions of the world. Science presents an abstract description, poetry attempts a total description of the object. Poetry's representation of the world is an alternative to that pictured by science. The abstract structures of science sacrifice "the body and substance of the world." Poetry, by virtue of its concrete particulars, restores "The World's Body." (The difference between art and science is marked out in similar terms by Ramon Fernandez: art qualifies, individualizes; whereas science schematizes, collects relations.) "The local, the immediate, and the concrete are the take-off of poetry," Tate remarks (in *Poetry:* May, 1932). The problem of the poet is essentially a problem of aesthetics: what shall the poet "imitate" and to what end? "Art arises in particulars, and it arrives at order at the point of impact between the new particulars and whatever recognized experience the poet has been able to acquire" (*New Republic:* Aug. 2, 1933). Ransom, practising his imitation theory of knowledge upon a poem by Hardy, observes that Hardy's language "is not content with the concepts, but is constantly stopping to insert or to attach the particularity which is involved in images; a procedure which might be called the imaginative realization of the concepts. A genuine poetic energy will work with both these dimensions at once." (*Southern Review:* Summer, 1940). Translated into Tate's terms, the two dimensions embodied in a poem are "extension" and "intension," and the meaning of a poem is its "tension" of these two extremes of language. A good poem achieves a unity or fusion between abstraction and concretion. Idea and image are in tension. On the term *tension* Tate has built his entire aesthetic. (This key word is to Tate's criticism what the term *paradox* is to Brooks's critical theory.)

For Tate, as for Schopenhauer, art aims at nothing outside itself. This formalist creed has brought against the Southern critics the charge of art for art's sake, but their principle of art for art's sake must be interpreted very differently from the aestheticism of the Nineties. Rightly understood, the principle has tremendous implications. Tate's position again squares with John Middleton Murry's: "Art is autonomous, and to be pursued for its own sake, precisely because it comprehends the whole of human life; because it has reference to a more perfect human morality than any other activity of man." Tate's stand puts him at odds with any critical program which inflicts upon art the values of science, or of metaphysics, or of social philosophy. He repudiates, for instance, the program of Edmund Wilson for an art-science. Wilson's view is that art and science, as they come to apply themselves more directly to life, may yet arrive "at a way of thinking, a technique of dealing with our perceptions, which will make art and science one." Wilson's optimism is based on Whitehead's idea that the poetic and the scientific impulses, being radically different, must unite harmoniously in a compromise. This proposal of a compromise is at the heart of Wilson's rejection of the Symbolists (in his *Axel's Castle*). His optimism has kinship with Wordsworth's faith, as Edwin Muir interprets it, that as soon as the world of science becomes somehow as "familiar" as the primitive world of religious myth, our cultural integrity and our literature will be restored. "This belief ignores the hopeless breach between the abstractionism of science and the object itself, for which the abstraction stands and to which it is the business of the poet to return" (Tate in *The Nation:* Nov. 17, 1926).

III

We have discussed the relation of the New Criticism to the spirit of the age, we have traced the central and unifying theme upon which the New Criticism is based, and we have defined the leading dogmas and critical attitudes which have influenced and formed the canons of the New Critics. The most important American critics who have organized our critical attitudes are Eliot, Tate and Ransom, Winters, and Kenneth Burke. Burke is the Aristotle of our criticism, the Aristotle who constructs vast systems. Of all our critics no one has done more towards revolutionizing our reading of a poem than Cleanth Brooks, and no critic has been of greater practical influence. While Brooks and Warren have brought the New Criticism into the universities, it is Tate and Ransom who have furnished it with systematic aesthetic studies. Their critical ideas constitute a single doctrine, their critical positions being basically identical. True, Ransom is the *point de repère* of American letters, as Donald A. Stauffer says; but Tate stakes out the issues more resolutely, and without Ransom's ironic detachment. As the spokesman for the Southern school of poet-critics, he has the greatest eye for the facts of the times and he is downright and persuasive in declaring them. It is this which accounts for my placing of Tate at the center of this present perspective.[3] In these critical cross-currents there are violent disagreements, but, as Ransom remarks, any one of the New Critics shows the influence of the others, and the total effort amounts to a sort of collaboration.

Tate's critical writings constitute a campaign against all schools of critics who judge art for its pragmatic values. Art proves nothing: "it creates the totality of experience in its quality; and it has no useful relation to the ordinary forms of action" (*Reactionary Essays*). According to Tate's theory of art, art springs from the irresistible need of the mind for an absolute experience, one which cannot be adequately satisfied in ordinary experience. The only coherent reality that we can experience is in art, for it is here alone that the disparate elements of our experience attain coherence and form. Art apprehends and concentrates our experience within the limitations of form. The poet as maker strives toward a signification of an experience, emotion or idea, until it becomes, within the dimensions of the poem, "absolute." Poetry is the fusion of "an intensely felt ordinary experience, an intense moral situation, into an intensely realized art." The great poems are absolute: there is nothing beyond the poem. Tate offers the critic no formula for recognizing this quality of absolutism. Ransom follows Tate's doctrine here in his insistence that "Good critical writing is always more or less empirical in method, which means that the critic looks first and last at the poem, while he tries to determine what poetic theory will be the one to accomplish its analysis. Each poem is a new poem, and each analysis is probably the occasion of a new extension of theory in order to cope with it" ("Ubiquitous

[3] This essay attempts to clarify positions rather than to pass judgment upon them. For critiques of the Southern critics, by Roellinger, Trowbridge, and R. S. Crane, see the bibliography (Appendix II).

Moralists," *Kenyon Review:* Winter, 1941). In *Poetry and the Absolute,* which contains the core of Tate's poetics, Tate made the same point, namely that the test of a poem must be applied *a posteriori.*[4]

> One may say that Yeats's poems, *Upon a Dying Lady,* survive the test, in any formulation. . . . He has presented a newly-created *emotion* never before felt by anyone and never to be felt creatively by anyone else; has contributed an absolute signification to an old and relative fact. It is absolute because it is unique and contains no point of relation to any other signification of that fact.

In the perfectly realized poem there is no overflow of unrealized emotion, no emotion or action in excess of the object or situation which should be the objective equivalent for that emotion. Poets must be selected by some absolute, even if it is only a provisional one. If there is any originally ulterior motive, such as Dante's moral contempt for his enemies in Hell, the ulterior motive "is absorbed and becomes implicit in form, rather than explicit and didactic." Paul Valéry has described the perfect poem by way of a simile, comparing it to "a distant sailing-vessel—inanimate but articulate, seemingly with an absolute life of its own."

Eliot's Impersonal Theory of Art, which he announced in *Tradition and the Individual Talent* and elaborated in *The Sacred Wood* (1920), is repeated in scattered instances of Tate's critical dicta. A poem is not the secretion of personal emotions. The emotion or idea embodied in a work of art is impersonal. "The more perfect the artist," Eliot declares, "the more completely separate in him will be the man who suffers and the mind which creates." Contrary to Coleridgean theory, which has led criticism out of the poem and into the mind, Tate's poetics asserts that the specific poetic element is an objective feature of the poem, rather than a subjective effect. We can never determine whether a work is a work of art by establishing its subjective, or purely personal, correlatives. The critic who asserts that he is investigating poetry from the psychological approach is actually leading us away from the fact of the art-work, Tate observes.[5] His stand is poles apart from Herbert Read's "ontogenetic" criticism, as practiced on Shelley in his *In Defense of Shelley,* "which traces the the origins of the work of art in the psychology of the individual and in the economic structure of society." But literary criticism (the definition is Desmond MacCarthy's) is concerned with values, not with the psychological origin of such values. The traditional critic like Tate, as distinguished from the experimental critic like Read, investigates the nature of the poem *as* poem; not the origin of the poem (Read), nor its effect upon the reader (Richards), nor its value for civilization (Dewey).

[4] This important essay is one of Tate's earliest (*Sewanee Review:* Jan., 1926). The core of Ransom's poetics is found in *Criticism as Pure Speculation* (1941).

[5] In his review of Ramon Fernandez' *Messages* (*New Republic:* Aug. 17, 1927), and by way of stating his agreement with Fernandez' critical approach.

For Ransom, likewise, the business of the literary critic is exclusively with an aesthetic criticism. Aesthetic values are anchored within the poem; it is solely the aesthetic structure, the internal organization of the poem, that gives any poem its value. Its value as a poem does not lie in its relation to the mind of the author. In *The Objective Basis of Criticism* (*Western Review:* Summer, 1948), Eliseo Vivas defines an aesthetic structure to be one "which successfully excludes the irrelevant values and controls vigorously the values and meanings it communicates." A work of art, I contend, contains but a single intention, and all the seemingly disparate and conflicting elements which are enclosed within the dimensions of the work accrete around and function towards that one intended end. As for Tate and Eliot, a work of art has a life of its own. True, the ultimate question concerning a work is out of how deep a life does it spring? But the critical question which determines whether it is a work of art is: has it a life of its own? "The life of art is in its form" (Bishop). The difference between art and its germinal event is absolute. The expression of those elements which give art its aesthetic identity and its absolute quality, Roger Fry states in his *Vision and Design,* is never identical with the expression of these elements in actual life. Though Fry limits his discussion to the field of the plastic arts, the concept is open to more general application. Consideration of poetry bears this out. In poetry, life and art can in no way be made equivalent because the emotions or experience which poetry offers are not the actual emotions or experience which everyday life presents, they are specifically aesthetic emotions. (Fry defines the aesthetic experience to be the apprehension of the purely formal relations of a work of art.) This distinction between life and art is also made by Belgion in criticizing Richards' supposition, in *Practical Criticism,* that there is no gap between the two realms. Not only is the aesthetic emotion different from the emotion we should have if we experienced the poem's subject in actual life, but it can be produced without having originated in life at all. And Tate attests to this fact in his Preface to his *Selected Poems:* ". . . that, as a poet, I have never had any [original] experience, and that, as a poet, my concern is the experience that I hope the reader will have in reading the poem." We as readers, T. Sturge Moore comments in his study of Valéry, come to poetry not to know what poets feel; "we read poems because they are wholes, composed of harmonized words and meanings which inter-echo symphonically."

To analyze and elucidate the formed meaning of a poem or novel is the prime job of the critic; but criticism must also make judgments as well as analyses, and therefore criticism cannot stand apart from theory. For technical criticism we look to Brooks, Blackmur, or Empson; for theoretical formulations of the nature of poetry, to Burke, Ransom, Tate, Winters, or Richards. Ransom, like Burke, is a philosophical critic. As critic his prime interest is in the metaphysics of aesthetics; it is only incidentally that he is committed to the technical criticism of poetry. As in *The World's Body,* he begins with aesthetics as the starting point for a philosophical defense of poetry. He gives us a poetics, and the core of it lies in his principle that the differentium of poetry is a metaphysical or ontological one. Poetry is ontology. Poetry, Charles Maurras similarly points out in his Preface to *Musique Intérieure,* is ontology, "for poetry strives . . . towards the roots of the knowledge of Being." Ransom transposes the problem of being, which is for him the basic problem in aesthetics, to the plane of the imaginative content of literature and art. He examines the "ontology" of a work and makes a metaphysical or aesthetic judgment upon it. In the principle that the intellect is the foundation of poetry and that the criterion of judgment is a qualitative one, Ransom and Tate are Aristotelian. To quote Tate, Ransom "has explored possibilities of an Aristotelian criticism of the poetic disorder of our time." He has attempted to establish poetic truth as objective. A poem is a self-enclosed world which "recovers for us the world of solid substance." Its status is "objective," even as the criticism which is a criticism of that poetic structure is objective. Poetry is one way of knowing the world. The knowledge obtainable from poetry is unique. It is radically or ontologically distinct from the prose or scientific formulation. In any scientific formulation objects exist not as solid objects but as points in a structural pattern which controls them. The thought pattern controls and subordinates them to the realization of a thesis. Now in a poem what is analogous to the prose or scientific formulation is its logical structure-meaning. The structure of a poem is its prose argument (the universal); but a poem has not only this determinate meaning, which attaches to the structure, but it has a texture-meaning as well. The texture is the context of indeterminate and heterogeneous details (the concrete). These many-valued texture-meanings are significant since they function in the total meaning of the poem, but they are logically irrelevant to the structure-meaning alone. (This tissue of concrete irrelevance is more valuable for its own sake than for its contribution to the prose argument of the poem.) "A poetic discourse embodies within itself . . . a prose discourse. I think this is a law of poetry. . . . No prose argument, no poem. The prose argument is the poem's 'structure'; and then 'texture' suggests itself for the name of the ubiquitous and unstructural detail" (*The Inorganic Muses*).

The flaw in much of modern poetry, and for Ransom this is the flaw in *The Waste Land,* is that it is all texture and no structure. "Poetic texture without logical structure is not the right strategy." The differentium of poetry is this texture-structure order of objectivity. And the critic's job is to examine and define this texture-structure formulation in individual poems under his scrutiny. To do this, Ransom insists, requires an aesthetician's understanding of what a poem generically "is." "The thing that makes a lyrical poem supreme over other literary forms, and indeed the epitome and standard of literary forms, is its range of content; or, what is the same thing, its density" (*Mr. Empson's Muddles*). It is by the content or subject matter that Ransom differentiates a poetry from a poetry—on the basis of the ontology of the poem, "the reality of its being." In *God Without Thunder,* he poses the view that though poetry and religion are agents of the irrational, they nevertheless yield a greater reality than science does. "Art is radically not science." What distinguishes a poetic discourse from a scientific one is the degree of irrelevant and indeterminate concreteness, the texture.[6]

Permanent poetry, Eliot holds, is a fusion of these two poles of the mind: emotion and thought. For Tate it is a fusion of concretion and abstraction, image and idea, or (to substitute Ransom's dichotomy) texture and structure. Tate reframes Eliot's view: poetry does not give us "an emotional experience," nor "an intellectual experience"; it gives us a poetic experience. In commenting on Wallace Stevens' *Ideas of Order,* Blackmur defines the poetic experience from a parallel viewpoint. Ideas are abstractions, but they are also things seen. "It is the function of poetry . . . to experience ideas of the first kind with the eyes of the second kind, and to make of the experience of both a harmony and an order: a harmonium" (In *The Expense of Greatness*). In all great poetry there is a clash of opposite elements issuing in a tension between abstraction and sensation. In Donne and in Emily Dickinson, "There is no thought as such at all; nor is there feeling; there is that unique focus of experience which is at once neither and both." Dickinson's abstractions are not separately visible from her sensuous illuminations of them; idea and image are in tension. Like Donne, "she *perceives abstraction and thinks sensation*" (Tate in *Reactionary Essays*). The genuine poem embodies both the emotion (or thought) *and* the situation which provokes it. Tate regards Hardy's abstractions as beyond the range of his feelings, since Hardy "rarely shows us the experience that ought to justify them, that would give them substance, visibility, meaning" (*Hardy's Philosophic Metaphors*). He judges Crane and Cummings by the same criterion. (It is the criterion of the Objective Correlative.) Winters' formula that poetry is technique for dealing with irreducible emotion, which Tate attacks in *Confusion and Poetry* (*Sewanee Review:* Apr., 1930), conceals a contemporary version of the romantic dogma that poetry is emotion.[7] Emotion is not the exclusive subject matter

[6] I agree with Stauffer that Ransom's theory goes too far in the separation of texture and structure. "What a poem needs is not the irrelevant word but the relevant word, whether it is expected or unexpected." (*Sewanee Review:* Summer, 1948) The parallel to Ransom's doctrine of Logical Irrelevance is Eliot's doctrine of the Third Dimension, which Eliot made in his critique of Ben Jonson in *The Sacred Wood.*

[7] Compare Burke's theory that a work of art is a psychological machine deliberately designed to arouse emotions.

of poetry. As Auden says, "abstractions are empty and their expression devoid of a poetic value." And the poet's emotions, these too have no value in themselves. In his Preface to Valéry's *le serpent,* Eliot states the point: "Not our feelings, but the pattern which we make of our feelings is the centre of value."

The New Critics have found their standards for great poetry in the seventeenth century Metaphysicals. Using Richards' viewpoint, Brooks defines metaphysical poetry as a poetry of synthesis and claims for it the highest order. It is a poetry which joins widely divergent and conflicting elements in imagery that is functional rather than decorative, and it achieves thus the desired union of emotion and thought. In Donne's poems the comparisons are not illustrations attached to a statement, as they are in Arnold's. In Donne "The comparison *is* the poem in a structural sense." The poetry of synthesis as defined by Richards is synonymous with the poetry of the imagination as defined by Tate (in contradistinction to the poetry of the will—allegory or propaganda art). A poetry of the will, as distinct from a poetry of the imagination, ignores the whole vision of an experience for some special moral, or political, or social interest; the meaning is forced and the total context of the human predicament oversimplified or unexplored. Such didactic poetry is "one-sided"; it is therefore inferior both as a poetic discourse and as a prose or scientific one (*Three Types of Poetry*). "Platonic poetry" is Tate's and Ransom's descriptive term for this didactic poetry which brings poetry into competition with science, falsifying their relationship. Unlike the Metaphysical poet, the Platonic poet discourses in terms of things, "but on the understanding that they are translatable at every point into ideas"; or he elaborates ideas as such, "but in proceeding introduces for ornament some physical properties." Platonic poetry deals with ideas, Physical poetry deals with concrete things. For Ransom, all genuine poetry is a phase of Physical poetry (*A Note on Ontology*).

Brooks's *Modern Poetry and the Tradition* (1939) is a critical synthesis of this modern revolution in our conception of poetry. The revolution, in sum, has consisted chiefly in a return to the Metaphysicals and hence in a repudiation of their heretical deviators: the Augustan Neo-Classicists, who regarded metaphor as a decoration of poetic thought-content; and the nineteenth century Romantics, who discredited irony or wit (the essential ingredient of metaphysical poetry) and regarded poetry as an elevated way of expressing elevated beliefs. Milton and Shelley have been the two main points of attack in this revised perspective of the poetic tradition. We have witnessed the thorough repudiation of Shelley (by Leavis, Tate, and Eliot), and the dislodgment of Milton—for which Eliot was wholly responsible. We have paid homage to Dryden, especially to Dryden the critic, with Eliot and Mark Van Doren as the chief instigators of his ascendant reputation. Pope, placed by Leavis and Brooks in the Metaphysical line (in *Revaluation* and in *The Well Wrought Urn*), has finally come into his own again. But it is Donne who has dominated our poetic and critical climate. While the New Criticism begins with Eliot's *Sacred Wood,* it had its taking-off in Hulme's pronouncement that the Romantic convention had reached a point of exhaustion and that, of immediate necessity, it was now the moment for a new convention or technique to replace the dead one. For the new convention, modern poetry drew upon the school of Donne and, sharing with it, the school of the French Symbolists—both schools representing radical departures from the common poetic tradition. The New Criticism was created out of this new convention—to explain it and to make it accessible.

IV

We have outlined some of the prevailing critical theories on art and the nature of poetry, and we have traced the critical interchanges of principles and methods among the New Critics. What remains to be sketched in are some redefinitions on the nature and function of criticism.

The sole purpose of criticism is to enlighten the reader, to instruct the reader, to create the *proper* reader. The critic prepares the reader to appreciate the ascendant artists of his time by defining for him standards of taste and examples of taste in operation. The chief end of criticism is to elucidate the relation of the poet, or the reader, to the poem. All critical writings can be classified under one or more parts of this three-part poet-to-poem-to-reader relationship. Everything of Richards' criticism, for instance, fits into this framework. This schematic idea is epitomized in his theory of poetry as communication: a poem is an organization of experience, a resolution and "balancing of impulses," and the reader gets the same harmony or "ordering of the mind" as the poet originally experienced. Though neither Brooks nor Tate fully assents to Richards' theory of poetry as communication, Brooks holds similarly that we, as the poet's readers, in a process akin to the poet's exploration of his material, "refabricate from his symbols . . . a total experience somewhat similar, if we possess imagination, to the total experience of the poet himself." Eliot's idea of the Objective Correlative suggests a parallel correlation: the objects or chain of images in a poem, if it is the objective correlative of the poet's original emotion about it, immediately evokes in the spectator the same emotion.

The poet-poem-reader relationship is again illustrated by the Problem of Belief: the question whether it is necessary for the reader to share the poet's beliefs in order to enjoy fully his poetry. The problem of the poem as related to the poet's, or the reader's, beliefs is resolved by Eliot thus: "When the doctrine, theory, belief, or 'view of life' presented in a poem is one which the mind of the reader can accept as coherent, mature, and founded on the facts of experience, it interposes no obstacle to the reader's enjoyment. . . ." With this interpretation, which Eliot makes in *The Use of Poetry* (1933), all later critics concur. The question of the specific merit of a poetic statement as truth or falsehood does not arise when the beliefs of the poet are ordered into an intrinsic whole. It is on this ground that Tate rejects Shelley's poetry, not because Shelley's ideas are immature but because his statements are not an integral part of a genuine poem. As Eliot notes: "Both in creation and enjoyment much always enters which is, from the point of view of 'art,' irrelevant." One irrelevance is the truth or falsity of the belief expressed in the poem *as* poem. It was a mistake of the early Richards to think that what, in the way of acceptance, is demanded of a poem is the poet's own beliefs. All of Spender's best poems convey single emotions, but, as Tate says (in *New Verse:* May, 1933), "these *single emotions* are created, in the sense that a table or chair is created; they are not believed."

Belief, as applied to the arts, is a sociological category. To assign objective status to the content of a poem apart from its form is to reduce the poem's meaning to its original state, and this is to locate it in the historical process. Within terms of this affirmation the critic is testing poetic subject matter by its correlation with the world it represents—the correlations being either historical, psychological, ethical, or economic. This doctrine of relevance is false. The only relevance the New Critics subscribe to is the relevance which subject-ideas have to each other within the formed meaning of the work itself. Poetry, as Blackmur affirms (in *The Double Agent*), "is life at the remove of form and meaning"; criticism has to do with "the terms and modes" by which this remove was made, that is, with the relation between content and form. A work of art is autonomous. It is a construct having a life of its own, and it is limited by its own technique and intention. The New Critics isolate the meaning of a poem only in terms of form.

Their critical practice is consistent with their critical theory. Contrary to Jacques Barzun, Tate does not repudiate the validity of textual exegesis (his own explication of his *Ode to the Confederate Dead* is proof enough). A paraphrase is not the work itself; a paraphrase defines only the poem's structural plan. It is the inferior poem alone that can be replaced by a statement; to paraphrase such a poem is to reduce it to something like its originally unrealized condition. The aesthetic whole, however, resists practical formulation. Tate's whole point is that there is no substitute for the poem itself. The poem "is its own knower, neither poet nor reader knowing anything that the poem says apart from the words of the poem." Brooks and Ransom take of course the same stand.[8]

[8] See Brooks's chapter "The Heresy of the Paraphrase" in *The Well Wrought Urn* (1947). (Yvor Winters' position furnishes "the most respectable example of the paraphrastic heresy.")

In the manner of Empson, Blackmur, or Brooks, who are our most expert technical critics, the critic lets the reader in on the poem's intention. He digs out the facts (and not alone the subsurface ones) and the principle governing the facts; he elucidates the poem's intention (the meaning objectified within the work, which is its form); he analyzes the texture-structure strategy of the poem, and he makes comparative judgments about its technical practice. Such judgments are not abstractions. These critics make analyses and judgments that are informed by a body of principles, but their approach is empirical. The Southern critics and the critics of the *Scrutiny* school are Aristotelian in their method: they analyze the aesthetic object in and for itself. H. A. Mason, in his defense of *F. R. Leavis and 'Scrutiny'* (in *The Critic:* Autumn, 1947), points out that the reader of Leavis' criticism "tends to forget the critic entirely and fails to note that in the process he has appropriated a good number of Mr. Leavis's judgments as his own." The point holds similarly for Empson and for Blackmur. "As there is no Leavisian doctrine or philosophy, there is nothing to seize on in his criticism but the example of first-hand valuation and there is no interference in the triangular interplay between reader, author and critic." The standards of these critics are aesthetic ones, and this sets them apart from other critics whose standards are sociological (Auden), historical (Wilson), psychological (Burke), or ethical (Winters).[9]

The critical writings of Tate and Leavis show a close kinship in their sources, their aims and critical attitudes, and particularly in their conception of the critic's function. Leavis is at one with Tate's rejection of critical relativity, with his dogma of authority in absolute standards which allow the reader no choice in point of view or taste, and with his contention for the values of a tradition as imperative. The critic, directly or by implication, deals with a tradition. He deals with tradition in terms of representative poets (and with individual poets in terms of representative samples of their work). The poet's objective is the same as the critic's. The poet probes the deficiencies of a tradition. As Tate explains, the poet, in the true sense of Arnold's

[9] In experimental critics like Kenneth Burke and Edmund Wilson the aesthetic interests are subordinated to psychological and sociological interests. Their concern is primarily with the nonresident values of a work of art, whereas the Southern and *Scrutiny* critics are concerned almost exclusively with the resident values—the purely formal and aesthetic ones. They attend to the properties of poetry as a fine art. Richards, to the contrary, protests against this isolation of the aesthetic values and argues for the integration of literary and nonliterary disciplines. Auden agrees with this program for the interdependence of ethics, politics, science, and aesthetics. The main difference between them is that Richards finds his standards for judging a work in psychology, Auden finds his in sociology. Auden's claim that aesthetic canons are not absolute is diametrically opposite to Tate's or Ransom's, namely that the "artificial" division between art and life is necessary and worth preserving. Of all critics, Ransom sets the strictest boundaries to criticism. The traditional critic, as distinguished from the experimental critic, aims to clarify the center of criticism rather than to expand its scope and borders. (The distinction between "traditional" and "experimental" critics is made by Eliot in *Experiment in Criticism.*)

dictum that poetry is a "criticism of life," criticizes his tradition "either as such, or indirectly by comparing it with something that is about to replace it . . . he *discerns* its real elements and thus establishes its value, by putting it to the test of experience" (*Reactionary Essays*). Always the business of criticism, Leavis states in his Introduction to *Towards Standards,* is "to define, help form, and organize the contemporary sensibility [the traditional mind which lives in the present or not at all], and to make conscious the 'standards' in it."

Both Tate and Leavis derive their critical position from Eliot. They have crystalized and expanded germinal ideas planted in *The Sacred Wood.* As Leavis makes clear in *Education and the University* (1943), he opposes, however, Eliot's doctrinal approach.[10] Both critics reject Richards' theory of art and, for the past two decades, they have vigorously assaulted his pseudo-scientific, pseudo-psychological, and semasiological approach. It was only in the early Richards that Leavis felt points of agreement, his *Practical Criticism* providing incitement towards Leavis' program for instructing public taste and reforming literary education, for which he pioneered in *Mass Civilization and Minority culture* (1930) and in *How to Teach Reading* (1933). Like Brooks, Leavis insists upon the importance of critical study in the university education of general intelligence, and, like Ransom, he sets strict boundaries to the conception and practice of literary criticism, contending that it "should be controlled by a strict conception of its special nature and methods." Literary criticism "should be the best possible training for intelligence—for free, unspecialized, general intelligence, which there has never at any time been enough of, and which we are peculiarly in need of to-day."

In comparison with Tate, Leavis has more scholarship to buttress his criticism, and, in comparison with Brooks, he has a somewhat wider range. It is Johnson whom Tate and Leavis resemble, for their criticism is a dogmatic and rational criticism. Tate's prose is savage in tone. Where Leavis defends the fort, Tate pursues the enemy. Brooks's debt is chiefly to Empson and Richards, but a striking parallelism is provided by Leavis' work, namely between his *Revaluation* and Brooks's *The Well Wrought Urn,* and again between his *New Bearings in English Poetry* and Brooks's *Modern Poetry and the Tradition.* In the first instance their criticism is technical criticism, in the second instance it is historical rather than critical in approach. The work of Martin Turnell, the leading associate of Leavis' *Scrutiny* school, is likewise both technical and historical criticism. I mention Turnell because I think that he and Leavis represent the two most important critics in England today.

[10] "The debt I recognize is to Eliot's best criticism (*Sacred Wood*),—exemplifying purity of interest ('when you are considering poetry you must consider it as poetry and not as another thing') and the *application,* relevantly, of *intelligence* to poetry. But he left me to work out (a tip or two coming from Middleton Murry) the analytic method" (Leavis in a letter to the author).

Our age is indeed an age of criticism. The structure of critical ideas and the practical criticism that British critics—Leavis, Turnell, Empson, Read—and American critics—Ransom, Tate, Brooks, Warren, Blackmur, Winters—have contrived upon the foundations of Eliot and Richards constitute an achievement in literary criticism which has not been equaled in any previous period of our literary history.

BIOGRAPHICAL NOTES

AND

A SELECTED BIBLIOGRAPHY OF MODERN CRITICISM 1920-1948

BIOGRAPHICAL NOTES

MONROE C. BEARDSLEY, born in Bridgeport, Connecticut, in 1915, is Assistant Professor of Philosophy at Swarthmore College, and author of articles in the *Journal of the History of Ideas, Ethics, Mind, The Journal of Philosophy, Philosophical Review, The Russian Review,* and *The Sewanee Review.*

R. P. BLACKMUR was born in Springfield, Massachusetts, in 1904. One of the editors of *Hound & Horn* (1927-1934), he held a Guggenheim Fellowship in 1937. He has published two influential volumes of criticism—*The Double Agent* (1935) and *The Expense of Greatness* (1940)—and two books of poems—*From Jordan's Delight* (1937) and *The Second World* (1942). His verse and essays have appeared in several books and in many critical journals, first in *The Dial* (1925) and lately in *The Hudson Review* (an essay on Dostoevsky, 1948). Formerly a staff member of the Institute for Advanced Study, he is now a Resident Fellow in Creative Writing at Princeton University.

CLEANTH BROOKS, born in Kentucky in 1906, was educated at Vanderbilt University, Tulane University, and at Exeter College, Oxford University. While teaching at Louisiana State University he edited, with Robert Penn Warren, the famous *Southern Review* (1935-1942) and published, in collaboration with Warren, three analytical anthologies—*Understanding Poetry* (1938), *An Approach to Literature* (1941), and *Understanding Fiction* (1943). These textbooks, together with *Understanding Drama* (1945, 1948), which Brooks co-edited with Robert B. Heilman, are significant contributions in a critical movement in the universities and they have created among younger writers a school of technical critics. His books in criticism are *Modern Poetry and the Tradition* (1939) and *The Well Wrought Urn* (1947). Since 1947 he has held a professorship in English at Yale University. He is also on the staff of the Kenyon School of English.

KENNETH BURKE was born in Pittsburgh, Pennsylvania, May 5, 1897, and was educated at The Ohio State University and at Columbia University. He became music critic for *The Dial* in 1927 and for *The Nation* in 1933. In 1928 he received the Dial Award and in 1935 a Guggenheim Fellowship. He has lectured at the New School for Social Research and at the University of Chicago; he teaches at Bennington College. His major works are *Counter-Statement*

(1931), *Attitudes Toward History* (1937), *The Philosophy of Literary Form* (1941), and, as the first volume in a trilogy, *A Grammar of Motives* (1945). He has translated French and German writings; he has written a book of short stories (*The White Oxen,* 1924), and he has published numerous reviews and articles on music, art, history, fiction, poetry, and criticism. Burke ranks among the most important and most influential critics in America.

F. W. DUPEE, born in Chicago, Illinois, in 1904, was graduated from Yale University. He has taught at Bowdoin and at Bard College, and is now Assistant Professor in English at Columbia University. He was formerly an editor of *Partisan Review* and did reviews in *The Nation* for several years. Editor of *The Question of Henry James* (1945), he is now preparing a life of Henry James for the American Men of Letters Series.

T. S. ELIOT was born in St. Louis, Missouri, September 26, 1888. He was educated at Harvard University (B.A., 1909; M.A., 1910), the Sorbonne, and Merton College, Oxford University. He has worked in London as teacher, bank clerk, as an editor of *The Egoist* (1917-1919), as editor of *The Criterion* which he founded in 1922, and more recently as a member of the editorial board of Faber & Faber, Ltd. He became a British subject in 1927. Holder of the Norton Professorship of Poetry at Harvard, 1932-1933, and other honors, Eliot was awarded the Nobel Prize for Literature in 1948. His most important works in criticism are *The Sacred Wood* (1920), which instigated the modern critical movement as practised by the New Critics; *The Criterion* (1922-1939), which set the standards for other critical journals (such as *Hound & Horn, Scrutiny,* and *The Southern Review*); and *Selected Essays* (1932). He has been the dominant force in modern criticism and poetry. Among poets writing in English, Eliot and Yeats are the two greatest of our time. *The Waste Land* (1922) opened up a new poetic era; *The Four Quartets* (1943) reaffirmed his stature and achievements. Among his other books of poetry are *Prufrock* (1917), *Ash Wednesday* (1930), *Poems, 1909-1935* (1936), *Murder in the Cathedral* (1935), and *Family Reunion* (1939).

WILLIAM EMPSON was born September 27, 1906, at Yorkshire, England. At Cambridge University he took a B.A. degree in mathematics and then studied under Professor I. A. Richards (1925-1929). While at Cambridge he co-edited, with J. Bronowski, *Experiment* (1928-1929). In 1937 he was appointed Lecturer in English literature at the Peking National University, Peiping, and refugeed with the University for two years during the Japanese invasion. After the European War, during which he served in London as Chinese Editor for B.B.C., Empson returned to the Peking National University (1947-1948). In the summer of 1948 he taught at the Kenyon

School of English. He has published two books of poetry—*Poems* (1935) and *The Gathering Storm* (1940)—and two books of criticism—*Seven Types of Ambiguity* (1930), which he wrote while still in his twenties, and *Some Versions of Pastoral* (1935). His forthcoming work, *The Structure of Complex Words,* has to do with a theory about the interaction of literary double meanings.

JOSEPH FRANK was born October 6, 1918, in New York City. He has published critical essays on poetry and fiction in *The Sewanee Review, The Southern Review, The Hudson Review,* and *La Revista Belga.* He is a member of the editorial staff of the Bureau of National Affairs in Washington, D. C. At present he is at work on a study of Flaubert.

HELEN L. GARDNER was born February 13, 1908, in London. She was a lecturer in English literature at the University of Birmingham from 1934 to 1941, and is now Tutor in English literature at St. Hilda's College, Oxford University. She has published articles on fourteenth century English mystics, Elizabethan tragedy, and the poetry of Donne. At present she is preparing a critical edition of the Divine Poems of John Donne.

W. H. GARDNER, born 1902 in London and now living in South Africa, is Senior Lecturer in English at Natal University College. Besides his important critical work, *Gerard Manley Hopkins* (Vol. I, 1944; Vol. II, 1948), he has edited the *Poems of Gerard Manley Hopkins* (1948). Gardner has published *Some Thoughts on 'The Mayor of Casterbridge'* (1930), which is the definitive study of Hardy's novel. He has also published *Salamander in Spring and Other Poems* (1934).

ROBERT B. HEILMAN was born in Philadelphia, Pennsylvania, 1906. He took his B.A. degree at Lafayette College (1927) and his Ph.D. at Harvard University (1935). From 1935 to 1948 he taught English literature at Louisiana State University; he is now Chairman of English at the University of Washington. Author of *America in English Fiction* (1937) and co-editor, with Cleanth Brooks, of *Understanding Drama* (1945, 1948), he has just recently published *This Great Stage,* a book on *King Lear.*

THOMAS ERNEST HULME was born September 16, 1883, in North Staffordshire, England. He attended Cambridge University, traveled through Europe, and finally settled for a while in London, where, as Herbert Read reports, "his forceful personality and witty conversation began to form a group and to influence a generation." He was killed while serving in the artillery during World War I (1917). He did translations of Bergson and Sorel, wrote five imagist poems (first printed in Ezra Pound's *Ripostes,* 1915), and left behind him notebooks and manuscripts, which Read edited in *Speculations: Essays on Humanism and the Philosophy of Art* (1924).

D. G. James was born September, 1905, in Griffithstown, Monmouthshire, Wales. He was educated at the University College of Wales, at University College, London, and at Trinity College, Cambridge University. During the industrial depression he served as warden of a social settlement in South Wales doing educational work for the unemployed. He was Tutor in Adult Education at the University of Birmingham (1934-1937), and next he held a lectureship in English at University College, Cardiff (1937-1941); since 1941 he has been Professor of English at the University of Bristol. He is best known for his distinguished study: *Scepticism and Poetry* (1937). He is also the author of *The Romantic Comedy* (1948), and he has now in the press *The English Augustans: An Introductory Essay*.

G. Wilson Knight was born September 19, 1897, in Sutton, Surrey. He is Reader in English at Leeds University. With the publication of *The Wheel of Fire* (1930), Knight inaugurated a new development in Shakespearean interpretation and criticism. Complementing it, *The Imperial Theme* (1931, 1949) is a further study of the thematic images and contrast patterns which form each Shakespearean play into a poetic whole. *The Shakespearean Tempest* (1932), which draws these two studies together, analyzes the interrelationships which pattern and unify the plays one to another. In *The Burning Oracle* (1939) and *The Starlit Dome* (1941), Knight extends his critical approach into eighteenth and nineteenth century poetry (Milton to Keats).

F. R. Leavis, born in Cambridge, England, in 1895, is a Fellow of Downing College, Cambridge University, and Director of English Studies there. He has been editor of *Scrutiny*—outstanding British critical journal—since he and L. C. Knights founded it in 1932. Author of *Mass Civilization and Minority Culture* (1930), *New Bearings in English Poetry* (1932), *For Continuity* (1933), *Revaluation* (1936), and *Education and the University* (1943), he has edited two anthologies of critical essays—*Towards Standards of Criticism: Selections from The Calendar of Modern Letters, 1925-27* (1933), and *Determinations* (1934)—and has published in *Scrutiny* a great many reviews and essays on poetry and fiction. He has just published a volume called *The Great Tradition. The Importance of Scrutiny,* edited by Eric Bentley (1948), a selection from the *Scrutiny* critics, commemorates the achievement of Leavis and his school.

Elder Olson (born in 1909) took his doctorate at the University of Chicago in 1938, and has since taught at the Illinois Institute of Technology and at Chicago University, where he is now an Associate Professor of English. Along with R. S. Crane and others he has been engaged in inquiries into the philosophic foundations of literary and other forms of criticism. He has published two books of poems—*A Thing of Sorrow* (1934) and *The Cock of Heaven* (1940)—and, in addition to articles and reviews in *Modern Philology* and *Poetry,* has contributed to R. S. Crane's symposium—"Two Essays in Practical Criticism"—which appeared in the *University Review* for Spring, 1942. His "Outline of Poetic Theory" is based on a nearly completed volume to be called *General Criticism and the Shorter Forms of Poetry.*

JOHN CROWE RANSOM was born April 30, 1888, in Pulaski, Tennessee. He was graduated in 1909 from Vanderbilt University and in 1913 took the bachelor's degree at Christ Church, Oxford University. An editor of *American Rhodes Scholars, Oxford* (1913), a founder and editor of *The Fugitive* (1922-1925), and the founder and editor of the *Kenyon Review* (1939—), Ransom taught at Vanderbilt University (1914-1937), and, as Guggenheim Fellow, he was a member of the staff of the University College of the South West, at Exeter, England (1931-1932). He has taught at Bread Loaf Writers' Conferences and he has lectured at the University of New Mexico, the University of Chicago, and recently at Johns Hopkins University (1948). He was Phi Beta Kappa poet at Harvard in 1939. Professor of English at Kenyon College, he is the founder and a Senior Fellow of the Kenyon School of English. A leader of the Southern Agrarian group and of the Southern poet-critics (Bishop, Brooks, Jarrell, Tate, and Warren), he ranks among the important critics and the best poets in America. He is author of two books in criticism—*The World's Body* (1938) and *The New Criticism* (1941)—and of five books of poems—*Poems About God* (1919), *Chills and Fever* (1924), *Grace After Meat* (1924), *Two Gentlemen in Bonds* (1927), and *Selected Poems* (1945).

I. A. RICHARDS, born in Cheshire, England, in 1893, was educated at Magdalene College, Cambridge University, and was a Fellow there in 1926. He taught at Tsing Hua University, Peking (1929-1930), and at Harvard University (1931), where he is again teaching. His four chief works in criticism are the *Principles of Literary Criticism* (1924), *Science and Poetry* (1926), *Practical Criticism* (1929), and *Coleridge on Imagination* (1934).

EDGELL RICKWORD, born in Colchester, England, in 1898, now lives in Deal, Kent. Author of *Rimbaud* (1924), he was editor of *The Calendar of Modern Letters* (1925-1927), and *Scrutinies, First and Second Series* (1928, 1931), and contributed a number of critical articles to *Towards Standards of Criticism: Selections from The Calendar of Modern Letters, 1925-27,* edited by F. R. Leavis (1933). Among these is his essay "The Use of 'Negative' Emotions." He has made translations of Marcel Coulon and of Verlaine, and he has published several books of poetry.

Delmore Schwartz, born in Brooklyn, New York, December 8, 1913, was educated at the University of Wisconsin and at New York University. He did graduate work at Harvard University, where he also taught, and in 1940 received a Guggenheim Fellowship. An editor of *Partisan Review,* he has published critical essays on poets and critics in a number of such journals as *Kenyon Review, Nation, Sewanee Review,* and *Southern Review.* A distinguished poet, his poetic works are *In Dreams Begin Responsibilities* (a story, a verse play, and poems, 1938), *A Season in Hell* (a translation of Rimbaud, 1939), *Shenandoah* (a verse play, 1941), and *Genesis* (a narrative poem, 1946).

Stephen Spender, born in England in 1909, attended University College, Oxford University. While there, with Louis MacNeice he edited the *Oxford Poetry* anthologies of 1929 and 1930. His early poems were published in T. S. Eliot's *Criterion* and in Michael Robert's anthology *New Signatures* (1932). His books of poems include *Poems* (1934), *Vienna* (1934, 1935), *Trial of a Judge* (an allegorical drama, 1938), *The Still Centre* (1939), *Ruin and Visions* (1942), *Poems of Dedication* (1946, 1947). Besides two volumes of critical studies—*The Destructive Element* (1935) and *Life and the Poet* (1942)—he has written two books of short stories: *The Burning Cactus* (1936) and *The Backward Son* (1941). He taught at Sarah Lawrence College, 1947-1948.

Robert Wooster Stallman, born September 27, 1911, in Milwaukee, Wisconsin, was educated at the University of Wisconsin (Ph.D., 1942). He has taught at Wisconsin (1939-1942, 1946), Yale (1943-1944), the University of Kansas since 1946, and at Minnesota, 1947. An associate editor of *Western Review,* he has published essays (on Keats, Hardy, Bishop, Conrad, etc.), poems, and critical checklists (on Bishop, Brooks, Housman, Ransom, Warren, Yeats). He is author of *The Critics' Notebook* (1950) and co-author, with Ray B. West, Jr., of *The Art of Modern Fiction* (1949).

Allen Tate was born in Winchester, Kentucky, November 19, 1899, and was graduated from Vanderbilt University in 1922. A founder and editor of *The Fugitive* (1922-1925), the Southern editor of the *Hound & Horn* (1931-1934), an advisory editor of *The Kenyon Review* (1939-1942), and the editor of *The Sewanee Review* (1944-1946), Tate has done free-lance writing in New York (1924-1928, and 1946—) and, on a Guggenheim Fellowship, lived in France from 1928 to 1930. He has taught at the University of North Carolina and Princeton University and has lectured at the University of Virginia, Southwestern College, Columbia University, and at the University of Kansas. At present he lectures at New York University. He is the author of a dozen books, including two biographies—*Stonewall Jackson* (1928) and *Jefferson Davis* (1929)—and a novel, *The Fathers*

(1938); in criticism—*Reactionary Essays* (1936), *Reason in Madness* (1941), *On the Limits of Poetry* (1948); and *The Hovering Fly* (1948) —and in poetry: *Mr. Pope* (1928), *Poems: 1928-1931* (1932), *The Mediterranean* (1936), *Selected Poems* (1937), and *Poems: 1922-1947* (1948). His wife, who is Caroline Gordon, is the author of *Forest of the South* (short stories, 1945). Tate has edited *The Collected Poems of John Peale Bishop* (1948).

D. A. TRAVERSI was born in 1912 in Montgomery, Wales, and was educated at Merton College, Oxford University. During the war he was Lecturer at the British Institute, Rome (1939-1940); Lecturer at the British Institute, Madrid (1941-1944); Director of the British Institute, Bilbao (1944-1945); Director of the British Institute, Barcelona (1945-1948). At present he is Representative of the British Council in Montevideo. He has published in *Arena, Criterion, Scrutiny,* and *The Dublin Review.* He is author of *An Approach to Shakespeare* (1939).

MARTIN TURNELL was born March 23, 1908, in Birmingham, England. One of the *Scrutiny* critics, he has published critical essays in *Horizon, Modern Language Review,* and in other British journals. Author of *Poetry and Crisis* (1938) and of *The Classical Moment: Studies of Corneille, Molière, Racine* (1947), he has in progress a work on the French novel. The criticism of F. R. Leavis and the writings of Martin Turnell (on the French poets, novelists, and critics) constitute the best criticism that is being done in England today. Regarding his study of Jacques Rivière, he writes: "Along with Eliot and Leavis, I myself have got more out of Rivière than out of any other critic." Turnell at present holds an administrative post with the B. B. C. in London.

ELISEO VIVAS of Venezuela, born in 1901, is a graduate of the University of Wisconsin. He has taught Philosophy at the University of Wisconsin and the University of Chicago. He contributed reviews to *The Nation* for a good many years and served, 1939-1942, as advisory editor to the *Kenyon Review.* His many essays have appeared in books and in critical and learned journals (*Kenyon Review, American Bookman, Western Review, Ethics, The Journal of Philosophy,* etc.). Vivas is Associate Professor of Philosophy at The Ohio State University.

ROBERT PENN WARREN, born in Kentucky in 1905, was educated at Vanderbilt University, the University of California, Yale University, and Oxford University (Rhodes Scholar). He taught at Southwestern College (1930), Vanderbilt University (1931-1934), Louisiana State University (1934-1942), and since 1942, as Professor of English, at the University of Minnesota. In 1945, succeeding Allen Tate, he held the Chair of Poetry in the Library of Congress. A member of the Southern literary group known as the "Fugitive-Agrarians," he was joint editor, with Cleanth Brooks, of *The Southern Review* (1935-1942), and since 1942 an advisory editor of *Kenyon Review*. He has published a biography, *John Brown* (1929); an anthology, *A Southern Harvest* (short stories, 1937), and, in joint authorship with Cleanth Brooks, three textbooks, two of which have won wide recognition: *Understanding Poetry* (1938) and *Understanding Fiction* (1943). Author of three novels and three books of poems, he was awarded the Pulitzer Prize for *All the King's Men* (1945) and the American Academy Prize for his *Selected Poems: 1923-1943* (1944). His previous novels were *Night Rider* (1939) and *At Heaven's Gate* (1943), and his other poetic works: *Thirty-Six Poems* (1935) and *Eleven Poems on the Same Theme* (1942). In 1946 he published a long critical essay on Coleridge's *The Rime of the Ancient Mariner*. While on his second Guggenheim Fellowship, he lived in Italy and there wrote his fourth novel. Warren has taught at Writers' Conferences at the Universities of Montana and Colorado and has lectured at Yale, Indiana, and Kansas.

René Wellek, born in Czechoslovakia in 1903, taught English literature at the University of Prague, Czech at the University of London, and English literature at the University of Iowa (1939-1946). He is Professor of Slavic and Comparative Literature at Yale University. His books are *Kant in England* (1931), *The Rise of English Literary History* (1941), and, in collaboration with Professor Austin Warren, *Theory of Literature* (1949).

Edmund Wilson was born May 8, 1895, in Red Bank, New Jersey. He was editor of the *Nassau Lit* at Princeton, where he was graduated in 1916. Before serving in World War I, he worked as a reporter for the *New York Evening Sun* (1916-1917), was managing editor of *Vanity Fair* (1920-1921), and next an associate editor of the *New Republic* (1926-1931); he is now literary critic of *The New Yorker*. In 1935 and in 1939 he was awarded Guggenheim Fellowships. He has published two books of fiction—*I Thought of Daisy* (1929) and *Memoirs of Hecate County* (1946)—and a book of verse, *Poets, Farewell!* (1929); four works of social reporting—*The American Jitters* (1932), *Travels in Two Democracies* (1936), *To the Finland Station* (1940), *Europe Without Baedeker* (1947); and three books of critical studies: *Axel's Castle* (1931), *The Triple Thinkers* (1938, 1948), and *The Wound and the Bow* (1941, 1947). Wilson has edited *The Collected Essays of John Peale Bishop* (1948).

W. K. Wimsatt, Jr., is Assistant Professor of English at Yale University. He is author of *Prose Style of Samuel Johnson* (1941), and of several articles in scholarly and critical journals. He received a Guggenheim Fellowship in 1947.

YVOR WINTERS, born in Chicago, Illinois, in 1900, was educated at the University of Colorado and at Stanford University, where he now holds an Associate Professorship. His wife is Janet Lewis, a poet and a novelist. His major critical works—*Primitivism and Decadence* (1937), *Maul's Curse* (1938), and *The Anatomy of Nonsense* (1943)—are collected in one volume, *In Defense of Reason* (1947). In 1929-1930 he edited *The Gyroscope,* a mimeographed magazine. He has published eight books of poems, including *The Journey* (1931), *Before Disaster* (1934), *Poems* (1941), and *The Giant Weapon* (1943).

A SELECTED BIBLIOGRAPHY OF MODERN CRITICISM: 1920-1948

This bibliography of modern criticism, selected from a comprehensive compilation of annotated checklists on poets and critics (an unpublished manuscript), brings together significant writings, British and American, appearing since 1920 in the fields of scholarship and the criticism of criticism, poetry, fiction, aesthetics, and art (painting and music), together with certain relevant works on psychology, religion, and history. It includes symposia, critical parodies, anthologies, and bibliographies. It also includes works in translation from such French critics as Remy de Gourmont and Paul Valéry. Authors are listed alphabetically; the author's critical works (books, essays, reviews) are listed chronologically. Critical writings *on* the individual authors are ordered alphabetically. Important writings are cross referenced and occasionally annotated. Many of the poets and critics here included are bibliographed for the first time.

Periodicals are coded thus:

Acc. (*Accent*)
AB (*American Bookman*)
AL (*American Literature*)
Am. Merc. (*American Mercury*)
AR (*American Review*)
AS (*American Scholar*)
Ant. Rev. (*Antioch Review*)
AM (*Atlantic Monthly*)
AP (*American Prefaces*)
B (*Bookman*)
CML (*Calendar of Modern Letters*)
CE (*College English*)
Crit. (*Criterion*)
DR (*Dublin Review*)
EJ (*English Journal*)
ELH (*English Literary History*)
Fur. (*Furioso*)
HM (*Harper's Magazine*)
Hib. Jour. (*Hibbard Journal*)
Hor. (*Horizon*)
H&H (*Hound & Horn*)
HR (*Hudson Review*)
JAAC (*Journal of Aesthetics and Art Criticism*)
JEGP (*Journal of English and Germanic Philology*)
JHI (*Journal of the History of Ideas*)
KR (*Kenyon Review*)
L&L (*Life and Letters*)
Lon. Merc. (*London Mercury*)
MLN (*Modern Language Notes*)
MLR (*Modern Language Review*)
MP (*Modern Philology*)
Mod. Sch. (*Modern Schoolman*)
N (*Nation*)
NEQ (*New England Quarterly*)
NMQR (*New Mexico Quarterly Review*)
NR (*New Republic*)
NS&N (*New Statesman and Nation*)
NV (*New Verse*)
NYTBR (*New York Times Book Review*)
NY (*New Yorker*)
19th Cent. (*Nineteenth Century & After*)
PaR (*Partisan Review*)
PR (*Philological Review*)
PPR (*Philosophy and Phenomenological Research*)
P (*Poetry*)

PULC (*Princeton University Library Chronicle*)
PMLA (*Publications of the Modern Language Association*)
QRL (*Quarterly Review of Literature*)
RES (*Review of English Studies*)
RMR (*Rocky Mountain Review*)
SRL (*Saturday Review of Literature*)
Scr. (*Scrutiny*)
SeR (*Sewanee Review*)
SAQ (*South Atlantic Quarterly*)
SR (*Southern Review*)
Spec. (*Spectator*)
Studies (*Studies: An Irish Quarterly*)
Symp. (*Symposium*)
TLS (*Times Literary Supplement*)
UKCR, UR (*University of Kansas City Review, University Review*)
UTQ (*University of Toronto Quarterly*)
VQR (*Virginia Quarterly Review*)
WR (*Western Review*)
YR (*Yale Review*)

ABERCROMBIE, LASCELLES. *The Idea of Great Poetry.* Secker & Warburg, 1925.
—— "A Plea for the Liberty of Interpreting." *Proc. Brit. Acad.*, 16 (1930).
—— *Poetry: Its Music and Meaning.* Gollancz, 1932.
—— *Principles of Literary Criticism.* Gollancz, 1932, 1935.
On Abercrombie: See T. Armstrong, Jones, Lucas, Monro, Vines, Williams.
Elton, O. *Lascelles Abercrombie: 1881-1938.* Oxford Univ. Press, 1939.
ADAMS, J. DONALD. *The Shape of Books to Come.* Viking Press, 1944.
—— *The Writer's Responsibility.* Secker & Warburg, 1946.
ADLER, MORTIMER. *Art and Prudence.* Longmans, 1937. (Compare Maritain)
—— *How to Read a Book.* Simon & Schuster, 1940.
AIKEN, CONRAD. (See under Bridges, Housman, MacLeish, Winters)
—— *Scepticisms, Notes on Contemporary Poetry.* Knopf; Cape, 1919.
—— "A Plea for Anonymity." NR, 84 (Sept. 18, 1935), 155-7. (Cowley replies, p. 163)
—— "Back to Poetry." AM, 166 (Aug., 1940), 217-23.
—— "Poetry: What Direction?" NR, 104 (May 12, 1941), 670-1.
On Aiken: See Blackmur, Kreymborg, Monroe, M. Moore, Untermeyer, Wilder.
Peterson, Houston. *The Melody of Chaos.* Longmans, 1931. (A critical study)
ALDINGTON, RICHARD. *Literary Studies and Reviews.* Allen & Unwin; Dial Press, 1924.
—— *Life for Life's Sake: A Book of Reminiscences.* Viking Press, 1941. (On Eliot, et al.)
—— (ed.). *The Viking Book of Poetry.* Viking Press, 1941, 1946.
On Aldington: See Daiches, Hughes, Monro, Sparrow, Vines, Winters.
McGreevy, T. *Richard Aldington: An Englishman.* Chatto & Windus, 1931.
ALEXANDER, S. *Beauty and Other Forms of Value.* Macmillan, 1933.
American Caravan. A Year Book of American Literature. Macaulay Co. Edited by Van Wyck Brooks (1927, etc.), A. Kreymborg, Lewis Mumford, Paul Rosenfeld (1929, 1930). See especially No. 1 (1927) for Francis Fergusson's "T. S. Eliot's Impersonal Theory of Art." And No. 3 (1929) for Yvor Winter's important essay: "The Extension and Reintegration of the Human Spirit Through the Poetry Mainly French and American Since Poe and Baudelaire." Pp. 361-404.
"American Poetry: 1930-1940." *Acc.*, 1 (Summer, 1941), 213-28. (Bibliography)
American Writers' Congress. International Publishers, 1935.
AMES, VAN METER. *Aesthetics of the Novel.* Univ. of California Press, 1928.
ARMSTRONG, EDWARD A. *Shakespeare's Imagination.* L. Drummond, 1946.
ARMSTRONG, T. (ed.). *Ten Contemporaries: Notes Towards Their Definitive Bibliographies....* Essays by Abercrombie, H. Palmer, E. Sitwell. E. Benn, 1932.
ARVIN, NEWTON. *Whitman.* Macmillan, 1938.
AUDEN, W. H. "John Skelton." *The Great Tudors,* ed. K. Garvin. Nicholson, 1935.
—— "Psychology and Art To-day." *The Arts To-day,* ed. G. Grigson. Bodley Head, 1935, 1937.
—— "Pope." *From Anne to Victoria,* ed. B. Dobrée. Cassell, 1937. Pp. 89-107.

AUDEN, W. H. Introduction. *Oxford Book of Light Verse,* ed. W. H. Auden. Clarendon Press, 1938.
—— "A Literary Transference (Yeats)." SR, 6 (Summer, 1940), 78-86.
—— "Criticism in a Mass Society." *Intent of the Critic,* ed. D. Stauffer (1941). Pp. 127-47.
—— "The Christian Tragic Hero." NYTBR, Dec. 16, 1945, 1, 21.
—— "The Sea and the Mirror." In *The Collected Poetry of W. H. Auden.* Random, 1945.
—— "The People v. The Late Mr. William Butler Yeats." *Partisan Reader* (1946).
—— "Some Notes on D. H. Lawrence." N, 164 (Apr. 26, 1947), 482-4.
—— "Squares and Oblongs." *Poets at Work.* Harcourt, 1948. Pp. 163-81.
—— "Yeats as an Example." KR, 10 (Spring, 1948), 187-95.

On Auden: See Southworth, Sparrow.
Brooks, Cleanth. *Modern Poetry and the Tradition.* Univ. of North Carolina Press, 1939. Pp. 110-35.
Jarrell, R. "Changes of Attitude and Rhetoric." SR, 7 (Autumn, 1941), 326-49.
Jarrell, R. "Stages of Auden's Ideology." PaR, 12 (Fall, 1945), 437-57.
Mizener, A. "Ideas in Auden." *Accent Anthology.* Harcourt, 1946. Pp. 630-5.
New Verse: Nos. 26-27 (Nov., 1937). "Auden Double Number."
Savage, D. S. In *The Personal Principle.* Routledge, 1944. Pp. 155-82.
Scarfe, Francis. *Auden and After.* Routledge, 1942. Pp. 10-34.
Schwartz, Delmore. "The Two Audens." KR, 1 (Winter, 1939), 34-45.
Stauffer, D. "The Search for Beliefs in Auden's Poetry." VQR, 22 (1946), 570-80.

BABBITT, IRVING. *Rousseau and Romanticism.* Houghton, 1919.
—— "On 'Humanism': An Essay at Definition." *Humanism and America,* ed. N. Foerster. Farrar, 1930.
Rev. by L. Mumford: "The New Tractarians." NR, 62 (Mar. 26, 1930), 162.
—— *On Being Creative and Other Essays.* Houghton, 1932.
Rev. by J. L. Adams in H&H, 6 (Oct., 1932), 173-96.

On Babbitt: See Blackmur, Eastman, Eliot, Elliott, Farrell, Foerster, Grattan, More, Munson, Murry, Ants Oras (under Eliot), Shafer (see More), Spingarn, Tate, Winters.
Cowley, M. "Angry Professors." NR, 62 (Apr. 9, 1930), 207-11.
Fausset, Hugh. *The Proving of Psyche.* Cape, 1929.
See *Crit.,* 9 (Jan., 1930), 349-53.
Manchester, F. & Shepard, O. (eds.). *Irving Babbitt, Man and Teacher.* Putnam's, 1941.
Mercier, L. J. *The Challenge of Humanism.* Oxford Univ. Press, 1933. (On More)
More, P. E. "Irving Babbitt." UTQ, 3 (Jan., 1934), 129-45.
Nickerson, Hoffman. "Irving Babbitt." *Crit.* 13 (Jan., 1934), 179-95. (Biography)
Shafer, R. "The Definition of Humanism." H&H, 3 (July, 1930), 533-57.

BAILEY, RUTH. *A Dialogue on Modern Poetry.* Oxford Univ. Press, 1939.
BAKER, CARLOS. *Shelley's Major Poetry.* Princeton Univ. Press, 1948.
BAKER, DENYS VAL. (ed.). *Little Reviews Anthology.* Allen & Unwin, 1943.
—— (ed.). *Writers of Today.* Sidgwick & Jackson, 1946. (Anthology)
BAKER, HOWARD. "The Contemporary Short Story." SR, 3 (Winter, 1938), 576-96.
—— "An Essay on Fiction with Examples." SR, 7 (Autumn, 1941), 385-406.
BARFIELD, OWEN. *Poetic Diction. A Study in Meaning.* Faber & Gwyer, 1928. (vs. Richards)
Rev. by J. G. Fletcher in *Crit.,* 8 (Sept., 1928), 128-34.

BARNES, A. C. *The Art in Painting.* Barnes Foundation, 1926; Harcourt, 1928.
Rev. by J. Krutch in N, 122 (Mar. 10, 1926), 259.
BARZUN, JACQUES. *Romanticism and the Modern Ego.* Little, Brown, 1943.
BASLER, ROY P. *Sex, Symbolism, and Psychology in Literature.* Rutgers Univ. Press, 1948.
BATES, H. E. *The Modern Short Story: A Survey.* Nelson, 1942.
BATESON, F. W. *English Poetry and the English Language.* Clarendon Press, 1934.
Rev. by F. Leavis in *Scr.*, 4 (June, 1935), 96-100; cf. Bateson: "Criticism and Literary History," *Scr.*, 4 (Sept., 1935), 181-5; Leavis, 185-7; in MP, 33 (Aug., 1935), 87-9.
—— (ed.). *The Cambridge Bibliography of English Literature.* Cambridge Univ. Press; Macmillan, 1940.
BAUDOUIN, CHARLES. *Psychoanalysis and Æsthetics.* Allen & Unwin, 1924.
BEACH, JOSEPH WARREN. *The Outlook for American Prose.* Univ. of Chicago Press, 1926.
—— *The Twentieth Century Novel: Studies in Technique.* Century Co., 1932.
—— *American Fiction: 1920-1940.* Macmillan, 1941.
BELGION, MONTGOMERY. "What Is Criticism?" *Crit.*, 10 (Oct., 1930), 118-37. (On Richards)
—— *The Human Parrot and Other Essays.* Oxford Univ. Press, 1931.
Rev. in *Symp.*, 3 (Jan., 1932), 116-22; by Tate in NR, 70 (Mar. 16, 1932), 133.
—— "The Expression of Emotion." SR, 3 (Spring, 1938), 783-9.
—— "The Poet's Name." SeR, 54 (Autumn, 1946), 635-49.
—— "Heterodoxy on *Moby Dick*?" SeR, 55 (Winter, 1947), 108-25.

On Belgion: Eliot, T. S. "The Modern Mind." *The Use of Poetry*, 1933. Pp. 121 ff.
Richards, I. In *Crit.*, 10 (Apr., 1931), 400-20.

BELL, CLIVE. *Art.* Chatto & Windus, 1914, 1947; Stokes, 1914, 1924.
BELL, ERIC TEMPLE. *The Search for Truth.* Reynal & Hitchcock, 1935.
BELLOC, HILAIRE. *Milton.* Cassell, 1935. (A provocative critical study)
BENÉT, WILLIAM ROSE (ed.). *Fifty Poets. An American Auto-Anthology.* Dodd, Mead, 1932.
——, & PEARSON, NORMAN. *The Oxford Anthology of American Literature.* Oxford Univ. Press, 1938.
BENNETT, JOAN. *Four Metaphysical Poets.* Cambridge Univ. Press, 1934. (On Donne, et al.)
BENNETT, JOSEPH D. *Baudelaire.* Princeton Univ. Press; Oxford Univ. Pr., 1944.
BENTLEY, ERIC. *The Playwright as Thinker.* Reynal & Hitchcock, 1946.
—— *Bernard Shaw.* New Directions, 1947.
—— (ed.). *The Importance of Scrutiny.* George Stewart, 1948. (Essays from *Scrutiny*)
BETHELL, S. *Essays on Literary Criticism.* Dobson, 1948.
BISHOP, JOHN PEALE. "The Discipline of Poetry." VQR, 14 (Summer, 1938), 343-56.
—— "Poetry and Painting." SeR, 53 (Spring, 1945), 247-58.
—— *Collected Essays of John Peale Bishop*, ed. E. Wilson. Scribner's, 1948.

On Bishop: Frank, Joseph. "Force and Form." SeR, 55 (Winter, 1947), 71-107.
Stallman, R. W. "John Peale Bishop: A Checklist." PULC, 7 (Feb., 1946), 62-79.
Stallman, R. W. "The Poetry of John Peale Bishop." WR, 11 (Autumn, 1946), 4-19.
Tate, Allen. In *Reactionary Essays* (1936).
Tate, Allen. "John Peale Bishop, A Personal Memoir." WR, 12 (Winter, 1948), 67-71. Reprinted in *Collected Poems of John Peale Bishop* (1948).

BLACKMUR, R. P. "Conrad Aiken." NR, 61 (Jan. 22, 1930), 255-6.
—— *The Double Agent: Essays in Craft and Elucidation.* Arrow Editions, 1935.

Rev. by M. Roberts in *Crit.*, 15 (July, 1936), 702-5; F. C. Flint: "Contemporary Criticism," SR, 2 (Summer, 1936), 208-24.

BLACKMUR, R. P. "The Instincts of a Bard." (Frost) N, 142 (June 24, 1936), 817-9.

—— *The Expense of Greatness.* Arrow Editions, 1940.

Rev. by Harry Levin in NR, 103 (Dec. 30, 1940), 905-6; H. Muller: "The New Criticism in Poetry," SR, 6 (Spring, 1941), 811-39; Ransom in KR, 3 (1941), 95-100.

—— "Twelve Poets." SR, 7 (Summer, 1941), 187-213.

—— "The Enabling Act of Criticism." *American Issues,* ed. W. Thorp. Lippincott (1941), II. Pp. 876-9.

—— "Between Myth and Philosophy: Fragments of W. B. Yeats." SR, 7 (Winter, 1942), 407-25.

—— "The Economy of the American Writer." SeR, 53 (Spring, 1945), 175-85.

—— "Notes on Four Categories in Criticism." SeR, 54 (Autumn, 1946), 576-89.

—— "In the Birdcage." (Dostoevsky). HR, 1 (Spring, 1948), 7-28.

—— "A Burden for Critics." HR, 1 (Summer, 1948), 170-85.

On Blackmur: Baker, C. "R. P. Blackmur: A Checklist." PULC, 3 (Apr., 1942), 99-106.

Gregory, H. "Two Critics in Search of an Absolute." N, 138 (Feb. 14, 1934), 189-91.

Rice, P. B. "Death on an Island." N, 144 (May 1, 1937), 512-4. (On his poems)

Schwartz, D. "The Critical Method of R. P. Blackmur." P, 53 (Oct., 1938), 28-39.

Tate, A. "R. P. Blackmur." SR, 3 (Summer, 1937), 183-98. (On his poems)

West, Ray. "R. P. Blackmur." RMR, 8 (Summer, 1944), 139-45. (See also Hyman)

BLUNDEN, EDMUND. *Winter Nights: A Reminiscence.* Faber & Gwyer, 1928.

—— *Votive Tablets: Studies.* Cobden-Sanderson, 1931. (Articles from the TLS)

—— *The Mind's Eye: Essays.* Cape, 1934. (Sassoon's poetry, etc.)

—— "Behind the Poem." TLS, 42 (Sept. 25, 1943), 462.

On Blunden: Bridges, R. *The Dialectical Words in Blunden's Poems.* Clarendon Press, 1921.

BOAS, GEORGE. *Philosophy and Poetry.* Wheaton College Press, 1932.

—— *A Primer for Critics.* Johns Hopkins Press, 1937.

Rev. by A. Warren in SeR, 46 (June, 1938), 213-22. (On criticism and meaning)

BODKIN, MAUD. *Archetypal Patterns in Poetry.* Oxford Univ. Press, 1934. (Milton, Eliot, et al.)

BOWMAN, JAMES (ed.). *Contemporary American Criticism.* Holt, 1926. (Anthology)

BOWRA, C. M. *The Heritage of Symbolism.* Macmillan, 1943. (Valéry, Rilke, George, Yeats)

—— *Sophoclean Tragedy.* Oxford Univ. Press, 1944.

—— *From Virgil to Milton.* Macmillan, 1946.

BOYD, ERNEST (ed.). *Criticism in America.* Harcourt, 1924. (Spingarn, Eliot, et al.)

BOYNTON, PERCY. *The Challenge of Modern Criticism.* Rockwell, 1931.

BRADBROOK, M. C. *Themes and Conventions of Elizabethan Tragedy.* Cambridge Univ. Press, 1935.

——, & THOMAS, M. G. L. *Andrew Marvell.* Cambridge Univ. Press, 1940.

—— *Joseph Conrad: Poland's English Genius.* Cambridge Univ. Press, 1942.

—— *Ibsen ... A Revaluation.* Macmillan, 1948.

BRADBY, ANNE (ed.). *Shakespeare Criticism: 1919-1935.* Oxford Univ. Press, 1936.

BRADLEY, ANDREW C. *Oxford Lectures on Poetry.* Macmillan, 1909, 1926.

BRÉMOND, HENRI. *Prayer and Poetry.* Trans. A. Thorold. Oates & Washbourne, 1929.

BRENNER, RICA. *Ten Modern Poets.* Harcourt, 1930.

—— *Poets of Our Time.* Harcourt, 1941.

BREWSTER, DOROTHY, & BURRELL, A. *Dead Reckoning in Fiction.* Longmans, 1924.
BRIDGES, ROBERT. (See under Hopkins)
—— *Milton's Prosody with a Chapter on Accentual Verse.* Oxford Univ. Press, 1921. (Rev. ed.)
—— *Collected Essays, Papers, etc.* Oxford Univ. Press, 1927, 1930. 2 vols.
—— *Correspondence of Robert Bridges and Henry Bradley, 1900-1923.* Clarendon Press, 1940.

On Bridges: See Bush, Carritt, Daiches, Eliot, Evans, Garrod, Gordon, Hamilton. D. G. James, Mégroz, Sélincourt Squire, Stauffer, Williams, Winters, Yeats.
Aiken, Conrad. "Prose and Music." NR, 62 (Mar. 26, 1930), 164-6.
Elton, Oliver. *Robert Bridges and the Testament of Beauty.* Oxford Univ. Press, 1934.
Gordon, G. S. *Robert Bridges.* (The Rede Lecture, 1931) Cambridge Univ. Press, 1946.
Guerard, A. Jr. *Robert Bridges: A Study of Traditionalism.* Harvard Univ. Press, 1942.
McKay, George. *A Bibliography of Robert Bridges.* Columbia Univ. Press, 1933.
Smith, L. P. *Robert Bridges: Recollections.* (S.P.E. tract 35) Clarendon Press, 1931.
Smith, Nowell. *Notes on the Testament of Beauty.* Oxford Univ. Press, 1931, 1940.

BRONOWSKI, JACOB. *The Poet's Defence.* Cambridge Univ. Press; Macmillan, 1939.
—— *A Man Without a Mask.* Transatlantic Arts, 1947. (On William Blake)
BROOKS, CLEANTH. "The Reading of Modern Poetry." AR, 8 (Feb., 1937), 435-49.
——, & WARREN, R. P. *Understanding Poetry.* Holt, 1938.
—— *Modern Poetry and the Tradition.* Univ. of North Carolina Press, 1939.
Rev. by W. Empson in P, 55 (Dec., 1939), 154-6; W. H. Auden: "Against Romanticism," NR, 102 (Feb. 5, 1940), 187; R. Jarrell: "Critical Scholars," NR, 105 (Oct. 6, 1940), 439; H. J. Muller: "The New Criticism in Poetry," SR, 6 (Spring, 1941), 811-39.
—— "The Poem as Organism." *English Inst. Essays, 1940.* Columbia Univ. Press. 1941. Pp. 20-41.
—— "The New Criticism and Scholarship." *Twentieth Cent. Eng.*, ed. W. Knickerbocker. Philosophical Library, 1946. Pp. 371-83.
—— "Criticism and Literary History." SeR, 55 (Spring, 1947), 199-222.
—— *The Well Wrought Urn.* Reynal & Hitchcock, 1947.
Rev. by R. Blackmur in NYTBR, June 8, 1947, pp. 6, 25; Empson in SeR, 55 (Autumn, 1947), 691-7; M. Spears in WR, 12 (Autumn, 1947), 54-8; cf. MLR, 42 (Jan., 1947), 9-24.

On Brooks: Crane, R. "Cleanth Brooks . . . Critical Monism." MP, 45 (May, 1948), 226-45.
Stallman, R. W. "Cleanth Brooks: A Checklist." UKCR, 14 (Summer, 1948), 317-24.

BROOKS, VAN WYCK. *Sketches in Criticism.* Dutton, 1932.
—— *Three Essays on America.* Dutton, 1934.
—— *The Flowering of New England: 1815-1865.* Dutton, 1936.
Rev. by M. Cowley: "The Puritan Legacy," NR, 88 (Aug. 26, 1936), 79-80.
—— *New England Indian Summer: 1865-1915.* Dutton, 1940.
Rev. by D. Schwartz: "Neither Historian Nor Critic," KR, 3 (Winter, 1941), 119-23; Edmund Wilson: "Mr. Brooks's Second Phase," NR, 103 (Sept. 30, 1940), 452-54.
—— "What Is Primary Literature?" YR, 31 (Summer, 1941), 25-37.
—— *The Opinions of Oliver Allston.* Dutton, 1941.
—— *The Times of Melville and Whitman.* Dutton; Dent, 1948.

Rev. by Troy in *New Leader,* 30 (Dec. 13, 1947), 13.

On Brooks: See Blackmur, DeVoto, Rosenfeld, Savage, B. Smith.

"The Brooks-MacLeish Thesis." PaR, 9 (1942), 38-47. (Commentaries)

Dupee, F. W. "The Americanism of Van Wyck Brooks." *Partisan Reader* (1946). Pp. 363-77.

Hyman, Stanley E. In *The Armed Vision.* Knopf, 1948. Pp. 106-26.

BROWNELL, W. C. *The Genius of Style.* Scribner's, 1925.

BUCHANAN, SCOTT. *Poetry and Mathematics.* John Day, 1929.

Rev. by C. Fadiman in N, 130 (May 28, 1930), 629.

BUCK, PHILO, JR. *Literary Criticism: A Study of Values in Literature.* Harper, 1930.

—— *Directions in Contemporary Literature.* Oxford Univ. Press, 1942.

BUCKLEY, J. H. *William Ernest Henley.* Princeton Univ. Press, 1945.

BUERMEYER, LAWRENCE. *The Aesthetic Experience.* Barnes Foundation, 1924.

BULLOUGH, GEOFFREY. *The Trend of Modern Poetry.* Oliver & Boyd, 1934; Rev. ed., 1941.

BURDETT, OSBERT. *Critical Essays.* Holt, 1927. (Shelley, Hawthorne, et al.)

BURGUM, E. B. (ed.). *The New Criticism.* Prentice-Hall, 1930. (Anthology)

—— *The Novel and the World's Dilemma.* Oxford Univ. Press, 1947.

BURKE, KENNETH. *Counter-Statement.* Harcourt, 1931.

Rev. by G. Hicks: "A Defense of Eloquence." NR, 69 (Dec. 2, 1931), 71-6; H. Rosenberg in *Symp.* 3 (Jan. 1932), 116-22.

—— *Permanence and Change.* New Republic Books, 1935.

—— *Attitudes Toward History.* New Republic Books, 1937.

—— *The Philosophy of Literary Form.* Louisiana State Univ. Press, 1941.

Rev. by H. Kuhn in PPR, 2 (Dec., 1941), 223-6.

—— "On Motivation in Yeats." SR, 7 (Winter, 1942), 547-61.

—— "The Tactics of Motivation." *Chimera,* 1 (Spring, 1943), 2 (Summer, 1943), 21-33, 37-53.

—— *A Grammar of Motives.* Prentice-Hall, 1945.

Rev. by J. Ransom: "Mr. Burke's Dialectic," NR, 114 (Feb. 18, 1946), 257-8.

—— "Kinds of Criticism." P, 68 (Aug., 1946), 272-82. (Part of a symposium)

—— "The Imagery of Killing." HR, 1 (Summer, 1948), 151-67.

On Burke: See Hyman, Muller, Munson, Parkes, Ransom, Winters.

Duffey, Bernard. "Reality as Language." WR, 12 (Spring, 1948), 132-45.

Nemerov, Howard. "A Note on the Terms of Kenneth Burke." *Fur.,* 2 (Spring, 1947), 29-42.

BURNSHAW, STANLEY. *André Spire and his Poetry.* Centaur Press, 1933. (2 essays and 40 poems)

BUSH, DOUGLAS. *Mythology and the Romantic Tradition.* Harvard Univ. Press, 1937.

—— "Scholars, Critics, and Readers." VQR, 22 (Spring, 1946), 242-50.

CABELL, JAMES BRANCH. *Some of Us: An Essay in Epitaphs.* McBride, 1931.

CALAS, NICOLAS. *Confound the Wise.* Arrow Editions, 1942. (Artist as rebel and prophet)

CALVERTON, V. F. *The Newer Spirit: A Sociological Criticism of Literature.* Boni, 1925.

—— *The New Grounds of Criticism.* Univ. of Washington Bookstore, 1930.

—— *The Liberation of American Literature.* Scribner's, 1932.

Rev. by G. Hicks: "A Marxian Interpretation." NR, 72 (Sept. 7, 1932), 104-5.

CALVOCORESSI, M. D. *The Principles and Methods of Musical Criticism.* Oxford Univ. Press, 1931.

CAMPBELL, JOSEPH, & ROBINSON, H. M. *A Skeleton Key to Finnegan's Wake.* Harcourt; McLeod, 1944.

CAMPBELL, ROY. *Broken Record.* Boriswood, 1934.

On Campbell: Leavis, F. R. "This Practical Renascence." *Scr.,* (June, 1930), 65-76.

O'Brien, Justin. "Poet on Horseback." KR, 4 (Winter, 1942), 75-86.

Tate, Allen. "Roy Campbell's Poetry." NR, 66 (Mar. 18, 1931), 133.
CANBY, HENRY SEIDEL. *Classic Americans.* Harcourt, 1931. (Irving to Whitman)
CARGILL, OSCAR. *Intellectual America.* Macmillan, 1941. (On Eliot, et al.)
CARNAP, RUDOLF. *Introduction to Semantics.* Harvard Univ. Press, 1942.
CARRITT, E. (ed.). *Philosophies of Beauty from Socrates to Robert Bridges: Being the Sources of Aesthetic Theory.* Foreword by D. Prall. Dutton; Clarendon Press, 1931.
CASSIRER, ERNEST. *An Essay on Man.* Yale Univ. Press, 1944.
CAUDWELL, CHRISTOPHER. *Illusion and Reality.* Macmillan, 1937.
Rev. by H. Gregory: "The Social Sources of Poetry." NR, 98 (Feb. 8, 1939), 25.
CAZAMIAN, LOUIS F. *Criticism in the Making.* Macmillan, 1929.
CENTANO, AUGUSTO (ed.). *The Intent of the Artist,* by Sherwood Anderson, Thornton Wilder, Roger Sessions, W. Lescaze. Princeton Univ. Press, 1941.
CHAMBERS, E. K. *A Sheaf of Studies.* Oxford Univ. Press, 1942.
CHARQUES, R. D. *Contemporary Literature and Social Revolution.* Secker & Warburg, 1933.
CHESTERTON, G. K. *Autobiography.* Hutchison, 1936.
CHILD, RUTH. *The Aesthetics of Walter Pater.* Macmillan, 1940.
CHURCH, RICHARD. *Eight for Immortality.* Dent, 1941.
—— "Art." In *Encyclopedia of the Arts,* ed. D. Runes. Philosophical Library, 1946.
COLLINGWOOD, R. G. *The Principles of Art.* Clarendon Press, 1938.
COLLINS, H. P. *Modern Poetry.* Cape, 1925, 1941; Houghton, 1926.
COLLINS, SEWARD. *"Criticism in America."* B, 71 (June, July, 1930), 241-56; 400-15; 72 (Oct., 1930), 145-64, 209-28. (A survey by a Humanist)
COLUM, MARY M. *From These Roots.* Scribner's, 1938; Columbia Univ. Press, 1945.
CONKLIN, G (ed.). *The New Republic Anthology: 1915-1935.* Dodge Publ. Co., 1936.
CONKLIN, PAUL S. *A History of Hamlet Criticism.* Crown Press, 1947.
CONNOLLY, CYRIL. *Enemies of Promise.* Routledge; Little, Brown, 1939.
—— *The Condemned Playground: Essays, 1927-1944.* Macmillan, 1946.
CONRAD, JOSEPH. *Last Essays.* Dent, 1926.
—— *Conrad's Prefaces to His Works.* Introd. by Edward Garnett. Dent, 1937.

On Conrad: See Bradbrook, Crankshaw, Ford, Guerard Jr., Stallman (under O'Connor), Zabel.
JEAN-AUBRY, G. *Joseph Conrad: Life and Letters.* Doubleday, 1927. 2 vols.

COWLEY, MALCOLM. "Angry Professors." NR, 62 (Apr. 9, 1930), 207-11.
—— "The Poet and the World." (Dos Passos and Cummings) NR, 70 (April 27, 1932), 303-5.
—— *Exile's Return: A Narrative of Ideas.* Norton, 1934.
—— "Literature and Politics." (Strachey and MacLeish) NR, 81 (Jan. 2, 1935), 224.
—— "A Hope for Poetry." (Spender and Lewis) NR, 82 (Feb. 27, 1935), 79.
—— (ed.). *After the Genteel Tradition. American Writers Since 1910.* Norton, 1937.
—— "Sociologists and Symbolists." (Yeats) NR, 96 (Sept. 28, 1938), 218-9.
—— "Poets as Reviewers." (Randall Jarrell) NR, 104 (Feb. 24, 1941), 281-2.
—— Introduction. *The Portable Hemingway.* Viking Press, 1944.
—— "William Faulkner's Legend." SeR, 53 (Summer, 1945), 343-61. In *Southern Vanguard* (1947). Pp. 13-27. In *The Portable Faulkner* (1946).
—— "A Natural History of American Naturalism." KR, 9 (Summer, 1947), 414-35.
—— "Hawthorne in the Looking Glass." SeR, 56 (Autumn, 1948), 545-63.
CRANE, HART. "A Discussion With Hart Crane." P, 29 (Oct., 1926), 34-41.
—— "Modern Poetry." In *The Collected Poems of Hart Crane,* ed. Waldo Frank. Liveright, 1933, 1946. Pp. 175-9.
—— "Two Letters on 'The Bridge.'" H&H, 7 (July, 1934), 677-82.

On Crane: See Blackmur, Cowley, Munson, Riding, Tate, Wilder, Winters.
Fowlie, W. "The Juggler's Dance." *Chimera,* 2 (Autumn, 1943), 3-14.
Horton, Philip. *Hart Crane: The Life of an American Poet.* Norton, 1937.
Savage, D. S. In *The Personal Principle.* Routledge, 1944. Pp. 113-20.
Weber, Brom. *Hart Crane: A Biographical and Critical Study.* Bodley Press, 1948.

CRANE, R. S. "History versus Criticism." EJ, 24 (1935), 645-67.
—— Prefatory Note to "Two Essays in Practical Criticism," by N. F. MacLean and Elder Olson. UR, 8 (Spring, 1942), 199-219.
—— "Cleanth Brooks . . . Critical Monism." MP, 45 (May, 1948), 226-45.

CRANKSHAW, EDWARD. *Joseph Conrad: Some Aspects of the Art of the Novel.* Lane, 1936.

CROCE, B. "The Breviary of Aesthetic." *Rice Institute Pamphlets,* 2 (Dec., 1915), 223-310.
—— *Aesthetics.* Trans. D. Ainslee. Macmillan, 1919, 1922.
—— *The Defense of Beauty.* Trans. E. F. Carritt. Clarendon Press, 1933. (On Shelley)

On Croce: Boas, George: *A Primer for Critics.* Johns Hopkins Press, 1937.
Bosanquet, B. "Croce's Aesthetic." *Proc. Brit. Academy,* 9 (1920).
Elton, Oliver. *The Nature of Literary Criticism.* Manchester Univ. Press, 1935.
Smith, James. "Croce." *Scr.,* 2 (June, 1933), 28-44. (See also Pepper)

CRUM, RALPH. *Scientific Thought in Poetry.* Columbia Univ. Press, 1932. (Relate Crum to Richards)

CUMMINGS, E. E. Introduction, *Collected Poems.* Harcourt, 1938.
Rev. by Paul Rosenfeld in N, 146 (Mar. 26, 1938), 360, 362-3; H. Gregory in NR, 94 (Apr. 27, 1938), 370; M. Zabel in SR, 5 (Winter, 1940), 568 ff.
—— "A Foreword to Krazy." SeR, 54 (Spring, 1946), 216-21.

On Cummings: See Blackmur, Gregory, Riding and Graves, Sparrow, Tate.

CUNLIFFE, J. W. *English Literature in the Twentieth Century.* Macmillan, 1933.

DAICHES, DAVID. *The Place of Meaning in Poetry.* Oliver & Boyd, 1935.
—— *New Literary Values: Studies in Modern Literature.* Oliver & Boyd, 1936.
—— *Literature and Society.* Gollancz, 1938.
—— *The Novel and the Modern World.* Univ. of Chicago Press, 1939.
—— *Poetry and the Modern World.* Univ. of Chicago Press, 1940.
Rev. by A. Tate: "Procrustes and the Poets," NR, 104 (Jan. 6, 1941), 25-6.
—— *Robert Louis Stevenson.* New Directions, 1947.
—— *A Study of Literature.* Cornell Univ. Press, 1948.

DAMON, S. FOSTER. *William Blake: His Philosophy and Symbols.* Houghton, 1924.
—— "The Odyssey in Dublin." (Joyce) H&H, 3 (Oct., 1930), 7-44. (Excellent)
—— *Amy Lowell: A Chronicle.* Houghton, 1935.

DAVIDSON, DONALD. *The Attack on Leviathan.* Univ. of No. Carolina Press, 1938.

DAVIES, W. H. *Later Days.* Cape, 1925.

DAVIS, ROBERT G. "Art and Anxiety." PaR, 12 (Summer, 1945), 310-21.

DAVISON, E. L. *Some Modern Poets and Other Critical Essays.* Harper, 1928.

DAY-LEWIS, C. "Poetry and Revolution." *New Country,* ed. M. Roberts. Hogarth Press, 1933.
—— *A Hope for Poetry.* Blackwell, 1934. "A Hope for Poetry," in *Collected Poems: 1929-1933.* Random, 1935; Oxford Univ. Press, 1936.
Rev. by G. Grigson in *Crit.,* 14 (Jan., 1935), 326-9; Mason in *Scr.,* 3 (1934), 320-2.
—— Introduction. *Selected Poems* by Robert Frost. Cape, 1936. (Essay by Auden also)
—— *The Poetic Image.* (The Clark Lectures, Cambridge Univ., 1946). Cape, 1947.
Rev. in TLS, Apr. 5, 1947, p. 156: "The Image and the Myth."

On Lewis: See Church, Daiches, Flint, Scarfe, Sitwell, Spender, Zabel.
Gregory, H. "The Proletarian Poet." PaR, 3 (May, 1936), 27-8.

DELACROIX, EUGÈNE. *The Journal.* Trans. Walter Pach. Covici Friede, 1937; Crown, 1947.

DE LA MARE, WALTER J. *Behold this Dreamer.* Knopf; Faber & Faber, 1939.

On de la Mare: See Aiken, Brenner, Murry, Palmer, *Scrutinies,* Swinnerton, Williams.

Mégroz, R. *Walter de la Mare: A Biography and Critical Study.* Hodder; Faber, 1924.

Reid, Forrest. *Walter de la Mare: A Critical Study.* Faber & Faber, 1929.

Sherman, S. P. "Walter de la Mare." *The Main Stream,* Scribner's, 1927. Pp. 196-203.

Tribute to Walter de la Mare. Faber & Faber, 1948.

Designed for Reading: The Saturday Review of Literature, 1924-1934. Macmillan, 1934.

DEUTSCH, BABETTE. *"The Future of Poetry."* NR, 60 (Aug. 21, 1929), 12-5.

—— "Poet's Progress." NR, 60 (Oct. 23, 1929), 277-8. (On R. Graves and Ransom)

—— *This Modern Poetry.* Norton, 1935; Faber & Faber, 1936. (On Symbolists, Imagists)

Rev. by R. Cox in *Scr.,* 5 (June, 1936), 98-9. (Severely critical)

DE VOTO, BERNARD. *The Literary Fallacy.* Little, Brown, 1944.

On De Voto: Cowley, M. "In Defense of the 1920's." NR, 110 (1944), 564-5.

Lewis, Sinclair: "Fools, Liars, and Mr. De Voto." SRL, 17 (Apr. 15, 1944), 9, 12.

DEWEY, JOHN. *Art as Experience.* Minton, Balch, 1934.

On Dewey: Goldwater, R. "Professor Dewey on Art." N, 138 (June 20, 1934), 710-11.

Tate, A. "The Aesthetic Emotion as Useful." *This Quarter,* 5 (Dec., 1932), 292-303.

DOBRÉE, BONAMY. *Restoration Comedy.* Oxford Univ. Press, 1924.

—— *Restoration Tragedy.* Oxford Univ. Press, 1929.

—— *The Lamp and the Lute.* Clarendon Press, 1929.

—— "Jules Laforgue." *Symp.,* 1 (Mar., 1930), 458-65.

—— (ed.). *From Anne to Victoria.* Cassell; Scribner's, 1937. (Essays by Auden, Eliot, Spender)

DORNER, ALEXANDER. *The Way Beyond Art.* Wittenborn, 1944.

DRAKE, W. A. (ed.). *American Criticism: 1926.* Harcourt, 1926.

DREW, ELIZABETH. *The Modern Novel: Some Aspects of Contemporary Fiction.* Cape, 1926.

—— *Discovering Poetry.* Norton, 1933.

—— *The Enjoyment of Literature.* Cambridge, 1935.

—— & SWEENEY, J. L. *Directions in Modern Poetry.* Norton, 1940. (Useful)

DRINKWATER, JOHN. *The Muse in Council.* Sidgwick & Jackson; Houghton, 1925.

—— *An Autobiography.* Holt, 1931.

—— *Discovery . . . 1897-1913.* Houghton, 1933.

DUCASSE, JOHN. *The Philosophy of Art.* Dial Press, 1930. (Compare Croce)

—— *Art, The Critics and You.* Askar Priest, 1944.

EASTMAN, MAX. *The Literary Mind: Its Place in an Age of Science.* Scribner's, 1931.

Rev. by F. R. Leavis: "The Literary Mind," *Scr.,* 1 (May, 1932), 20-32; I. A. Richards in *Crit.,* 12 (Oct., 1932), 150-5.

—— *Enjoyment of Poetry.* Scribner's, 1939.

EDGAR, PELHAM. *The Art of the Novel.* Macmillan, 1933.

EDWARDS, W. A. *Plagiarism.* Minority Press, 1933.

ELIOT, T. S. *Ezra Pound: His Metric and Poetry.* Knopf, 1917.

—— *The Sacred Wood: Essays on Poetry and Criticism.* Methuen, 1920, 1928; Knopf, 1921, 1930.

Rev. by J. M. Murry in NR, 26 (1921), 194-5.

Eliot, T. S. "Ulysses, Order, and Myth." (Joyce) *Dial,* 75 (Nov., 1923), 480-3.
—— *Homage to John Dryden.* Hogarth Press, 1924.
Rev. by Edmund Wilson in NR, 41 (1925), 177-8.
—— "A Note on Poetry and Belief." *The Enemy,* 1 (Jan., 1927), 15-7.
—— "Literature, Science, and Dogma." *Dial,* 82 (Mar., 1927), 239-43.
—— "Isolated Superiority." (Ezra Pound) *Dial,* 84 (Jan., 1928), 4-7.
—— "The Poems of Richard Crashaw." *Dial,* 84 (Mar., 1928), 246-50.
—— *For Lancelot Andrewes: Essays on Style and Order.* Faber & Gwyer; Doubleday, 1928.
Rev. by F. Fergusson in H&H, 2 (Apr., 1929), 297-9; C. Aiken in *Dial,* 86 (July, 1929), 628.
—— Introduction. *Selected Poems of Ezra Pound.* Faber & Gwyer, 1928.
—— *Dante.* (Poets on Poets, No. 2) Faber & Faber, 1929.
Rev. by F. Gary in *Symp.,* 1 (Apr., 1930), 268-71; L. Leighton in H&H, 3 (Apr., 1930), 442-4.
—— "Experiment in Criticism." *Tradition and Experiment in Present-Day Literature.* Oxford Univ. Press, 1929. Pp. 198-215. Repr. in *Literary Opinion* (1937). Pp. 11-25. In B, 70 (Nov., 1929), 225-33.
—— Introduction. *London and The Vanity of Human Wishes.* Etchells, 1930.
Repr. in *English Critical Essays, XX Century,* ed. P. M. Jones (World's Classics).
Rev. by A. Tate: "Taste and Dr. Johnson," NR, 68 (Aug. 19, 1931), 23-4.
—— "Poetry and Propaganda." B, 70 (Feb., 1930), 595-602. In *Literary Opinion.* Pp. 25-38.
—— "Donne in Our Time." *A Garland for John Donne: 1631-1931,* ed. T. Spencer. Harvard Univ. Press, 1931. Pp. 1-19.
—— *Selected Essays: 1917-1932.* Faber & Faber; Harcourt, 1932.
Rev. by Waldo Frank: "The Universe of T. S. Eliot," NR, 72 (Oct. 26, 1932), 294-5; R. Blackmur in P, 42 (Apr., 1933), 44-9; H. B. Parkes in H&H, 6 (1933), 350-6.
—— *John Dryden: The Poet, The Dramatist, The Critic.* Holliday, 1932.
—— *The Use of Poetry and The Use of Criticism.* Harvard Univ. Press; Faber & Faber, 1933.
Rev. by D. W. Harding in *Scr.,* 2 (1934), 289-92.
—— *After Strange Gods: A Primer of Modern Heresy.* Faber & Faber; Harcourt, 1934.
Rev. by R. Blackmur in H&H, 7 (July, 1934), 719-26; F. Leavis in *Scr.,* 3 (Sept. 1934), 184; W. Troy in N, 138 (Apr. 25, 1934), 478-9.
—— *Elizabethan Essays.* Faber & Faber, 1934.
Rev. by L. C. Knights in *Scr.,* 3 (Dec., 1934), 306-14.
—— *Essays Ancient and Modern.* Faber & Faber; Harcourt, 1936.
Rev. by F. R. Leavis in *Scr.,* 5 (1936), 84.
—— "Literature and the Modern World." AP, 1 (Nov., 1935), 19-22.
—— Introduction. *Selected Poems* by Marianne Moore. Macmillan; Faber, 1935.
Rev. by P. B. Rice in N, 140 (Apr. 17, 1935), 460.
—— "A Note on the Verse of John Milton." *Essays and Studies,* 21 (1936), 32-40.
—— "Byron." *From Anne to Victoria.* Cassell; Scribner's, 1937. Pp. 601-19.
—— *The Idea of a Christian Society.* Harcourt; Faber & Faber, 1939.
Rev. by R. Blackmur: "It is Later Than He Thinks." *Expense of Greatness* (1940). Pp. 239-44.
—— "The Poetry of W. B. Yeats." SR, 7 (Winter, 1942), 442-54.
—— *Points of View,* ed. John Hayward. Faber & Faber, 1941.
—— Introduction. *A Choice of Kipling's Verse.* Faber & Faber, 1941; Scribner's, 1943.
—— *The Music of Poetry.* Glasgow University. Jackson & Son, 1942. In *Partisan Reader.* Dial Press, 1946. Pp. 494-508.
—— *The Classics and The Man of Letters.* Oxford Univ. Press, 1942.

Eliot, T. S. "Notes Toward a Definition of Culture." PaR, 11 (Spring, 1944), 145-57.

—— "The Social Function of Poetry." *Adelphi,* 21 (July, 1945), 152-61.

—— *What is a classic?* Faber & Faber, 1945.

—— "The Man of Letters and the Future of Europe." SeR, 53 (Summer, 1945), 333-42.

—— "What is Minor Poetry?" SeR, 54 (Jan., 1946), 1-18.

—— "Ezra Pound." P, 68 (Sept., 1946), 326-38.

—— "Milton." SeR, 56 (Spring, 1948), 185-209. Fr. *Proc. Brit. Acad.,* 33. Pamphlet, 1947.

On Eliot: See Aiken, *American Caravan,* 1927 (Fergusson), Bailey, Bateson, Blackmur, Bodkin, Brenner, C. Brooks, V. W. Brooks, Buck, Bullough, Bush, Church, Daiches, Deutsch, DeVoto, Dobrée, Drew, Eastman, Evans, Fergusson, Fernandez, Gregory, Grierson & Smith, Henderson, Hyman, Leavis, Day-Lewis, W. Lewis, Lebowitz, Lucas, MacCarthy, MacNeice, Matthiessen, Monroe, Muir, Nuhn, Parkes, Peacock, Pound, Powell, Ransom, Read, Richards, Riding & Graves, Savage, Sitwell, Slochower, B. Smith, L. P. Smith, Southworth, Sparrow, Spender, Swinnerton, Tate, Tindall, *Towards Standards* (see Leavis), Untermeyer, M. Van Doren, Wheelwright, Wilder, C. Williams, G. Williamson, E. Wilson, Winters, Zabel.

Basler, Roy. "'The Love Song of J. Alfred Prufrock.'" *Twentieth Cent. English* (1946). In *Sex, Symbolism, and Psychology* (1948).

Blisset, W. "The Argument of T. S. Eliot's Four Quartets." UTQ, 15 (1946), 115-26.

Bodkin, Maud. *The Quest for Salvation.* Oxford Univ. Press, 1941. (*Family Reunion*)

Brown, Alec. "The Lyric Impulse." *Scrutinies,* ed. E. Rickword. Wishart, 1931. II.

Campbell, H. "T. S. Eliot." RMR, 8 (1944), 128-37. (Eliot as critic)

Campbell, Roy. "Contemporary Poetry." *Scrutinies,* ed. E. Rickword. Wishart, 1928. I.

Chase, Richard. "The Sense of the Present." KR, 7 (Spring, 1945), 218-31.

Collin, W. E. "T. S. Eliot." SeR, 39 (Jan., 1931), 13-24, 419-24.

T. S. Eliot. Editions Poetry, 1948. (Tributes by Aiken, Empson, MacNeice, Muir, Edith Sitwell, Spender, et al.)

Flint, R. W. "The *Four Quartets* Reconsidered." SeR, 56 (1948), 69-81.

Gallup, D. *Check-List of the Writings of T. S. Eliot.* Yale Univ. Press, 1947.

Grudin, Louis. *Mr. Eliot Among the Nightingales.* Drake, 1932.

Harvard Advocate. 125, No. 3 (Dec., 1938). The T. S. Eliot Number.

Higgins, B. "The Critical Method of T. S. Eliot." *Scrutinies,* ed. E. Rickword. 1931. II.

Hodin, J. "T. S. Eliot on the Condition of Man Today." *Hor.,* 12 (Aug., 1945), 83-9.

Hook, Sidney. "The Dilemma of T. S. Eliot." N, 160 (Jan. 20, 1945), 69-71.

Jack, P. M. "A Review of Reviews." AB, 1 (Winter, 1944), 91-9. (*Four Quartets*)

Kronenberger, L. "T. S. Eliot as Critic." N, 140 (Apr. 17, 1935), 452-3.

Mangan, S. "Apotheosis of Thomas Stearns Eliot." *Pagany,* 1 (1930), 23-36.

Matthiessen, F. O. *The Achievement of T. S. Eliot.* Oxford Univ. Press, 1935, 1947.

McGreevy, Thomas. *Thomas Stearns Eliot.* Chatto & Windus, 1931.

Mesterton, Erick. *The Waste Land: Some Commentaries.* Argus Book Shop, 1943.

Nicholl, A. "Eliot and the Revival of Classicism." EJ, 23 (1934), 269-78.

Nicholson, N. "T. S. Eliot." *Writers of To-day,* ed. D. Baker. Sidgwick & Jackson, 1946.

Oras, Ants. "The Critical Ideas of T. S. Eliot." *Tartu,* B28, No. 3 (1932). (Estonia)
Praz, Mario. "T. S. Eliot and Dante." SR, 2 (Winter, 1937), 525-48.
Preston, R. *'Four Quartets' Rehearsed.* Sheed & Ward, 1946.
Quennell, P. "Mr. T. S. Eliot." L&L, 2 (Mar., 1929), 179-90.
Quiller-Couch, A. "Tradition and Orthodoxy." *The Poet as Citizen.* Macmillan, 1935.
Rajan, B. (ed.). *Focus Three: T. S. Eliot.* Dennis Dobson, 1947. (Critical essays)
Sansom, Clive. *The Poetry of T. S. Eliot.* Oxford Univ. Press, 1947.
Schwartz, D. "T. S. Eliot as the International Hero." PaR, 12 (Summer, 1945), 199-206.
Stephenson, E. M. *T. S. Eliot and the Lay Reader.* Fortune Press, 1944.
Taupin, René. *L'influence du symbolisme français sur la poésie americaine de 1910 à 1920.* Paris: B. Grasset, 1926; Champion, 1929. (See Zukofsky) Rev. by Yvor Winters in H&H, 4 (July, 1931), 607-18.
Taupin, René. "The Classicism of T. S. Eliot." *Symp.,* 2 (Jan., 1932), 64-82.
Unger, L. (ed.). *T. S. Eliot: A Selected Critique.* Rinehart, 1948. (Anthology)
Vivas, Eliseo. "The Objective Correlative." AB, 1 (Winter, 1944), 7-18.
Weiss, Ted. "Eliot and the Courtyard Revolution." SeR, 54 (Spring, 1946), 289-307.
Wheelwright, P. "The Burnt Norton Trilogy." *Chimera,* 1 (1942), 7-18.
Williams, Charles. "A Dialogue on Mr. Eliot's Poem." DR, No. 425 (Apr., 1943), 114-22.
Williamson, H. Ross. *The Poetry of T. S. Eliot.* Hodder, 1932; Putnam, 1933.

ELLIOTT, G. R. *The Cycle of Modern Poetry.* Princeton Univ. Press, 1929.
—— *Humanism and Imagination.* Univ. of North Carolina Press, 1939.
ELLIS, G. W. *Twilight of Parnassus.* Michael Joseph, 1939.
ELTON, OLIVER. *The Nature of Literary Criticism.* Manchester Univ. Press, 1935.
EMPSON, WILLIAM. *Seven Types of Ambiguity.* Chatto & Windus, 1930; New Directions, 1947.
Rev. by James Smith in *Crit.,* 10 (July, 1931), 738-42; H. Rosenberg in *Symp.,* 2 (July, 1931), 412-8; F. Leavis in *Scr.,* 9 (Mar., 1941), 310.
—— *Some Versions of Pastoral.* Chatto & Windus, 1935. Reprinted as *English Pastoral Poetry.* Norton, 1938. See also *Shakespeare Survey,* 1936. (Pamphlet)
Rev. by M. Roberts in *Crit.,* 15 (Apr., 1935), 345-7; K. Burke in P, 49 (Mar., 1937), 347-50; A. Mizener in PaR, 5 (June, 1938), 57-60.
—— "Sense in Measure for Measure." SR, 4 (Autumn, 1938), 340-50.
—— "Basic English and Wordsworth." KR, 2 (Autumn, 1940), 449-57.
—— "The Structure of Complex Words." SeR, 56 (Spring, 1948), 230-50.
On Empson: Bradbrook, M. C. "The Criticism of William Empson," *Scr.,* 2 (Dec., 1933), 252-7.
Brooks, Cleanth. "Empson's Criticism." *Accent Anthology,* 1946. Pp. 496-508.
Ransom, J. C. "Mr. Empson's Muddles." SR, 4 (Autumn, 1938), 322-39.
English Institute Essays. Founded 1939. Columbia Univ. Press. Annual issues.
EVANS, B. IFOR. "The Limits of Literary Criticism." *Essays and Studies,* 18 (1932), 24-52. Clarendon Press, 1933. (On Saintsbury as critic)
—— *Tradition and Romanticism.* Methuen, 1940.
Explicator, The. Vol. I: Oct., 1942—June, 1943. See annual index, 1942-1949.

FALLS, CYRIL. *The Critic's Armoury.* Cobden-Sanderson, 1925.
FARRELL, JAMES T. *A Note on Literary Criticism.* Vanguard Press, 1936.
Rev. by K. Burke in NR, 87 (June 24, 1936), 211; Edmund Wilson: "Novelist Bites Critic," N, 142 (June 24, 1936), 808-10.

FARRELL, JAMES T. *The League of Frightened Philistines.* Vanguard Press, 1945.
—— *The Fate of Writing in America.* New Directions, 1946. (Pamphlet)
—— *Literature and Morality.* Vanguard Press, 1947.
FERGUSSON, FRANCIS. "James's Idea of Dramatic Form." KR, 5 (Autumn, 1943), 495-507.
—— "Action as Passion." KR, 9 (Spring, 1947), 201-21. (On Wagner and Eliot)
—— "D. H. Lawrence's Sensibility." In *Forms of Modern Fiction* (1948).
FERNANDEZ, RAMÓN. *Messages.* Trans. M. Belgion. Cape, 1926; Harcourt, 1927.
Rev. by T. S. Eliot in *Crit.*, 4 (Oct., 1926), 751-7; Edwin Muir in CML, 4 (July, 1927), 161-4; A. Tate in NR, 51 (Aug. 17, 1927), 339-40.
FIRKINS, OSCAR. *Selected Essays.* Univ. of Minnesota Press, 1933.
FITTS, DUDLEY. "Textual Criticism." SR, 7 (Summer, 1941), 217-8. (A parody)
FLACCUS, L. W. *The Spirit and Substance of Art.* Crofts, 1926.
FLETCHER, JOHN GOULD. *Life is my Song.* Farrar & Rinehart, 1937.
FLINT, F. CUDWORTH. "Metaphor in Contemporary Poetry." *Symp.*, 1 (July, 1930), 310-35.
—— "Contemporary Criticism." SR, 2 (Summer, 1936), 208-24.
FLORES, ANGEL. *Literature and Marxism: A Controversy.* Critics Group, 1938.
—— (ed.). *The Kafka Problem.* New Directions, 1946. (Anthology of essays)
FOCILLON, HENRI. *The Life of Forms in Art.* Trans. B. Hogan. Yale Univ. Press, 1942.
FOERSTER, NORMAN. *American Criticism . . . Poe to the Present.* Houghton, 1928.
—— *Towards Standards.* Farrar & Rinehart, 1930. See NR, 65 (Jan. 4, 1931), 249-50.
—— (ed.). *Humanism and America.* Farrar & Rinehart, 1930.
Rev. by H. Hazlitt: "The Pretensions of Humanism." N, 130 (Mar. 5, 1930), 272-3.
—— "The Study of Letters." *Literary Scholarship.* Univ. of No. Carolina Press, 1941. Pp. 3-32.
Rev. by Elder Olson in MP, 40 (May, 1943), 252-4.
FOGLE, RICHARD. "The Imaginal Design of Shelley's 'Ode to the West Wind.'" ELH, 15 (Sept., 1948), 219-26.
FORD, FORD MADOX. Foreword. *Imagist Anthology 1930.* Covici Friede, 1930.
—— "Techniques." SR, 1 (July, 1935), 20-35.
—— *The March of Literature.* Dial Press, 1938.
FORSTER, E. M. *Aspects of the Novel.* Harcourt, 1927, 1947.
—— *Abinger Harvest.* Arnold; Harcourt, 1936.
On Forster: Belgion, M. "The Diabolism of Mr. E. M. Forster." *Crit.*, 14 (Oct., 1934), 54-73.
Brown, E. K. "The Revival of E. M. Forster." YR, 33 (Summer, 1944).
Leavis. F. R. "E. M. Forster." *Scr.*, 7 (Sept., 1938), 185-202.
Traversi, D. A. "The Novels of E. M. Forster." *Arena*, 1 (Apr., 1937).
Trilling, L. "E. M. Forster." KR, 4 (Spring, 1942), 160-73.
Warren, A. "The Novels of E. M. Forster." AR, 9 (Summer, 1937), 226-51.
Woolf, Virginia. In *The Death of the Moth.* Harcourt, 1942.
FOWLIE, WALLACE. *Clowns and Angels.* Sheed & Ward, 1943.
—— *Rimbaud.* Dennis Dobson; New Directions, 1946.
—— *Jacob's Night.* Sheed & Ward, 1947.
FOX, RALPH. *The Novel and the People.* Lawrence & Wishart, 1937.
—— *Ralph Fox: A Writer in Arms.* Ed. John Lehman, 1937. (Fugitive pieces)
FRAENKEL, MICHAEL. *Death is Not Enough: Essays in Active Negation.* Daniel, 1939.
FRANK, J. "Spatial Form in Modern Literature." SeR, 53 (1945), 221-40; 433-56; 643-53.
FRANK, WALDO. *Salvos.* Boni, 1924.
—— *In the American Jungle.* Farrar & Rinehart, 1937.
FRAZER, SIR JAMES. *The Golden Bough: A Study in Magic and Religion.* Macmillan, 1922, 1940.

FREEMAN, JOSEPH. *An American Testament.* Farrar & Rinehart, 1936.
FREUD, SIGMUND. "Dostoevsky and Parricide." PaR, 12 (Fall, 1945), 530-44.
—— *Leonardo Da Vinci: A Study in Psychosexuality.* Trans. A. A. Brill. Random, 1947.
—— *Stavrogin's Confession. By F. M. Doestoevsky. With a Psychoanalytical Study by Sigmund Freud.* Lear Publ., 1947.
Rev. by L. Trilling in *New Leader,* 30 (Dec. 13, 1947), 12.
On Freud: Bartlett, F. H. *Sigmund Freud: A Marxian Essay.* Gollancz, 1938.
Belgion, Montgomery. *Our Present Philosophy of Life.* Faber & Faber, 1929.
Hoffman, F. *Freudianism and the Literary Mind.* Louisiana State Univ. Press, 1945.
"The Legacy of Sigmund Freud." KR, 2 (Spring, 1940), 135-85. (Trilling, Vivas, et al.)
FROST, ROBERT. Introduction. *King Jasper,* by E. A. Robinson. Macmillan, 1935.
—— "Education by Poetry: A Meditative Monologue." AP, 6 (Autumn, 1940), 5-17.
—— "The Figure a Poem Makes." *Collected Poems.* Halcyon House, 1942.
On Frost: See C. Brooks, Church, L. Jones, Monroe, Tate, Warren, Wells, Zabel.
Aiken, Conrad. "Poetry: 1940 Model." NR, 102 (Apr. 22, 1940), 540-1.
Auden, W. H., Lewis, C. Day, Engle, P., Muir, E. Introductory essays to *Selected Poems, by Robert Frost.* Cape, 1936. See *Scr.,* 5 (Mar., 1937), 443-4.
Blackmur, R. P. "Instincts of a Bard." N, 142 (June 24, 1936), 817-8.
Cook, R. L. "Robert Frost: A Time to Listen." CE, 7 (Nov., 1945), 66-71.
Cook, R. L. "Robert Frost as Teacher." CE, 8 (Feb., 1947), 251-5.
Cook, R. L. "Poet in the Mountains." WR, 11 (Spring, 1947), 175-82.
Cook, R. L. "Robert Frost's Asides on his Poetry." AL, 19 (Jan., 1948), 351-9.
Cowley, M. "Frost: A Dissenting Opinion." "The Case Against Mr. Frost: II." NR, 111 (Sept. 11, Sept. 18, 1944), 312-3, 345-7.
Cox, Sidney. *Robert Frost: Original 'Ordinary Man.'* Holt, 1929.
Clymer, W. B. S., & Green, C. R. *Robert Frost: A Bibliography.* Jones Library, 1937.
Hicks, G. "The World of Robert Frost." NR, 65 (Dec. 3, 1930), 77-8.
Jarrell, R. "The Other Robert Frost." N, 165 (Nov. 29, 1947), 588, 590-1.
Mertins, L. & Esther. *The Intervals of Robert Frost.* Univ. of California Press, 1947.
Munson, G. B. *Robert Frost: A Study in Sensibility and Good Sense.* Doubleday, 1939.
Stallman, R. W. "Two Roads Both Taken." NMQR, 17 (Autumn, 1947), 360-1. (Parody)
Thompson, L. *Fire and Ice: The Art and Thought of Robert Frost.* Holt, 1942.
Thornton, Richard (ed.). *Recognition of Robert Frost.* Holt, 1937.
Winters, Yvor. "Robert Frost." SeR, 56 (Autumn, 1948), 564-96.
FRY, ROGER. *Vision and Design.* Chatto & Windus, 1920.
—— *The Artist and Psycho-analysis.* Hogarth Press, 1924. In *Hogarth Essays.* Doubleday, 1928. Pp. 279-303.
—— *Transformations: Critical and Speculative Essays on Art.* Brentano's, 1927.
—— Introduction. *Stéphane Mallarmé: Poems.* Ed. Charles Mauron. Chatto & Windus; Oxford Univ. Press, 1938.
—— *Last Lectures.* Cambridge Univ. Press, 1939.
On Fry: Price-Jones, G. "Roger Fry and Aesthetic Criticism." *Crit.,* 15 (Jan. 1935), 181-92.
Woolf, Virginia. *Roger Fry: A Biography.* Harcourt, 1940.
FRYE. N. *Fearful Symmetry: A Study of Blake.* Princeton Univ. Press, 1947.

GARDNER, HELEN. *Art Through the Ages.* G. Bell; Harcourt, 1926, 1936 (Rev. ed.).
GARROD, H. W. *The Profession of Poetry.* Clarendon Press, 1929.
Rev. by J. Sweeney: "The Click Theory." NR, 62 (Apr. 23, 1930), 279.
—— *Poetry and the Criticism of Life.* Harvard Univ. Press, 1931.
—— *The Study of Poetry.* Clarendon Press, 1936.
—— *Scholarship: Its Meaning and Value.* Cambridge Univ. Press, 1947.
GAUNT, W. *The Aesthetic Adventure.* Harcourt, 1945.
GEISMAR, MAXWELL. *The Last of the Provincials: The American Novel: 1915-1925.* Houghton, 1948.
GIDE, ANDRÉ. *Imaginary Interviews.* Knopf, 1944.
—— *The Journals of André Gide.* Ed. Justin O'Brien. Knopf, Vol. I, 1947. Vol. II, 1948.
On Gide: Ames, Van Meter. *André Gide.* New Directions, 1947.
Lynes, C. "André Gide and the Problem of Form." *Forms of Modern Fiction* (1948).
Mann, Klaus. *André Gide and the Crisis of Modern Thought.* Creative Age Press, 1943.
GILBY, THOMAS. *Poetic Experience: An Introduction to the Thomist Aesthetic.* Sheed & Ward, 1934.
GILKES, M. *A Key to Modern English Poetry.* Blackie, 1937.
GILL, ERIC. *Beauty Looks After Herself.* Sheed & Ward, 1933.
GILMAN, MARGARET. *Baudelaire the Critic.* 1943. Columbia Univ. Press, 1943.
GISSING, GEORGE. *The Immortal Dickens.* Cecil Palmer, 1925.
GLASGOW, ELLEN. *A Certain Measure: An Interpretation of Prose Fiction.* McLeod; Harcourt, 1943.
GOGARTY, OLIVER ST. JOHN. *Phantasy in Fact: As I Was Going Down Sackville Street.* Reynal & Hitchcock; Rich, 1937.
GOLDWATER, ROBERT (co-ed.). *Artists on Art.* Pantheon Books, 1945.
—— "Theme and Form in Modern Painting." *Critique,* 1 (Oct., 1946), 5-12.
GORDON, GEORGE. *Poetry and the Moderns.* Clarendon Press, 1935. (On Eliot)
—— *The Discipline of Letters.* Clarendon Press, 1946. (See Q. D. Leavis)
GORMAN, HERBERT S. *The Procession of Masks.* B. J. Brimmer, 1923. (Hardy, Housman, et al.)
GOTSHALK, DILMAN. *Art and the Social Order.* Univ. of Chicago Press, 1947.
GOULD, GERALD. *The English Novel of Today.* Castle, 1924.
DE GOURMONT, REMY. *Decadence and Other Essays on the Culture of Ideas.* Harcourt, 1921.
—— *Selections from All His Works.* Ed. R. Aldington. Covici Friede, 1928.
On de Gourmont: Taupin, R. "The Example of Remy de Gourmont." *Crit.,* 10 (July, 1931), 614-25.
Turnell, M. "Literary Criticism in France: II." *Scr.,* 8 (Dec., 1939), 231-98.
GRABO, CARL. *The Creative Critic.* Univ. of Chicago Press, 1948.
GRANVILLE-BARKER, H. *Prefaces to Shakespeare.* Princeton Univ. Press, 1947. 2 vols.
GRATTAN, C. H. (ed.). *The Critique of Humanism.* Brewer & Warren, 1930. (Anthology)
GRAVES, ROBERT. *On English Poetry.* Heinemann; Knopf, 1922.
—— *Contemporary Techniques of Poetry: A Political Analogue.* Hogarth Press, 1925.
—— *Another Future of Poetry.* (Hogarth Essays XVIII). L. & V. Woolf; Hogarth Press, 1926.
(A reply to R. Trevelyan's *Thamyris, Or Is There a Future for Poetry?* Kegan Paul, 1925.)
—— *Poetic Unreason and Other Studies.* Cecil Palmer; Harcourt, 1925.
——, & RIDING, LAURA. *A Survey of Modernist Poetry.* Heinemann, 1927; Doubleday, 1928.

GRAVES, ROBERT. "The Future of the Art of Poetry." In *Hogarth Essays.* Garden City, 1928. Pp. 161-93.
—— *Goodbye to All That.* Cape; Seizen Press, 1929. (Autobiography)
—— & HODGE, ALAN. *The Long Week-End.* Faber & Faber, 1941. (Great Britain: 1918-1939)
—— & HODGE, ALAN. *The Reader Over Your Shoulder.* Cape, 1943, 1947; Macmillan, 1943.
GREENE, T. M. *The Arts and the Art of Criticism.* Princeton Univ. Press, 1940.
GREENLAW, EDWIN. *The Province of Literary History.* Johns Hopkins Press, 1931.
GREGORY, HORACE. *The Poems of Catullus.* Trans. fr. the Latin. Covici Friede, 1931.
—— "Wordsworth: An Evaluation." NR, 67 (May 20, 1931), 25-6. (On Frost and H. Read)
—— "Rugged Skeleton." NR, 72 (Nov. 2, 1932), 333-4. (On R. Graves and Skelton)
—— "A Defense of Poetry." NR, 76 (Oct. 11, 1937), 237-8. (On Shelley)
—— *Pilgrim of the Apocalyse.* Viking Pr., 1933. (On D. H. Lawrence)
—— "Two Critics in Search of an Absolute." N, 138 (Feb. 14, 1934), 189-91.
—— "The Man of Feeling." NR, 79 (May 16, 1934), 23-4. (On T. S. Eliot as critic)
—— "Edgar Allan Poe: A Reconsideration." PaR, 10 (May, 1943), 263-74.
—— *The Shield of Achilles: Essays on Belief in Poetry.* Harcourt, 1944.
Rev. by A. Wanning: "Modern Essays," PaR, 11 (Summer, 1944), 350-2.
——, & ZATURENSKA, MARYA. *A History of American Poetry: 1900-1940.* Harcourt, 1946. (1st ed., 1942)
GRIERSON, SIR HERBERT. Introduction. *Metaphysical Lyrics.* Clarendon Press, 1921.
—— *The Background of English Literature.* Chatto & Windus, 1925.
—— (ed.). *The Poems of John Donne.* Oxford Univ. Press, 1929. (1st ed., 1912)
—— *Essays and Addresses.* Chatto & Windus, 1940.
—— "Criticism and Creation: Their Interactions." *Essays and Studies,* 29 (1943), 7-29.
—— & SMITH, J. C. *A Critical History of English Poetry.* Chatto & Windus, 1944, 1947.
On Grierson: See *17th Century Studies: Presented to Sir H. Grierson.* Clarendon Press, 1938.
GRIEVE, C. M. (HUGH MCDIARMID) *Lucky Poet: A Self Study in Literature.* Methuen, 1943.
GRUDIN, LOUIS. *A Primer of Aesthetics.* Covici Friede, 1930.
GUERARD, ALBERT. *Literature and Society.* Lothrop, Lee, & Shepard, 1935.
GUERARD, ALBERT JR. *Robert Bridges: A Study in Traditionalism.* Harvard Univ. Press, 1942.
—— "Criticism and Commodity." NR, 105 (Dec. 8, 1941), 796, 798, 800.
—— *Joseph Conrad.* New Directions, 1947.

HAMILTON, G. *Poetry and Contemplation: A New Preface to Poetics.* Cambridge Univ. Press, 1938
HARDING, D. W. "I. A. Richards." *Scr.,* 1 (Mar., 1933), 327-38. (A summing up)
—— "Aspects of the Poetry of Isaac Rosenberg." *Scr.,* 3 (Mar., 1935), 358-69.
—— "Regulated Hatred: An Aspect of the Work of Jane Austen." *Scr.,* 8 (Mar., 1940), 346-62.
—— "The Psychologist and Criticism." *The Changing World,* No. 4 (May, 1948).
HARDING, ROSAMONDE, M. *An Anatomy of Inspiration.* Cambridge Univ. Press, 1940; W. Heffer, 1948. "Birth of a Poem," by Robert Nichols. Pp. 147-68.
HARDY, JOHN E. "Lycidas." KR, 7 (Winter, 1945), 99-113. Cf. Ransom in *World's Body.* Pp. 1-28.
HARDY, THOMAS. *The Early Life.* By Florence Emily Hardy. Macmillan, 1928.
—— *The Later Years of Thomas Hardy.* By Florence Emily Hardy. Macmillan. 1930

On Hardy: See Blackmur, C. Brooks, Collins, Daiches, Eliot, Evans, Leavis, Murry, Palmer, Richards, Edith Sitwell, L. Strachey, Wells, Williams, Winters.

Abercrombie, L. *Thomas Hardy: A Critical Study.* Secker & Warburg, 1912.

Barton, J. E. "The Poetry of Thomas Hardy." In *The Art of Thomas Hardy,* by Lionel Johnson. John Lane, 1923. (Appendix)

Beach, J. W. *The Technique of Thomas Hardy.* Univ. of Chicago Press, 1922.

Blunden, Edmund. *Thomas Hardy.* Macmillan, 1942.

Bowra, C. M. *The Lyrical Poetry of Thomas Hardy.* Byron Foundation Lecture, 1946.

Chakravarty, A. *The Dynasts and the Post-War Age in Poetry.* Oxford Univ. Press, 1938.

Chapman, Frank. "Hardy the Novelist." *Scr.,* 3 (June, 1934), 22-37.

Gardner, W. H. "Some Thoughts on *The Mayor of Casterbridge." Eng. Ass. Pamphlet,* No. 77. Oxford Univ. Press, 1930.

Lee, Vernon. *The Handling of Words.* John Lane, 1923. Pp. 222-41.

Lawrence, D. H. "Study of Thomas Hardy." *Phoenix.* Viking Press, 1936.

Rutland, W. R. *Thomas Hardy.* Blackwell, 1938.

The Southern Review. 6 (Summer, 1940). *Thomas Hardy Centennial Issue.*

Southworth, James. *The Poetry of Thomas Hardy.* Columbia Univ. Press, 1947.

Stallman, R. W. "Hardy's Hour-Glass Novel." SeR, 55 (Spring, 1947), 283-96.

Trueblood, C. "The Poetry of Thomas Hardy." *Dial,* 82 (June, 1937), 522-5.

Weber, Carl J. *The First Hundred Years of Thomas Hardy.* Colby College, 1940.

HART, J. D. (ed.). *The Oxford Companion to American Literature.* Oxford Univ. Press, 1948. 2nd ed.

HAZLITT, HENRY. *The Anatomy of Criticism.* Simon & Schuster, 1933.

HEILMAN, ROBERT B. "The Unity of King Lear." SeR, 56 (Winter, 1948), 58-68.

—— *This Great Stage.* Louisiana Univ. Press, 1948. (On *King Lear*)

HENDERSON, PHILIP. *Literature and a Changing Civilisation.* John Lane, 1935.

—— *The Novel Today.* Bodley Head, 1936.

—— *The Poet and Society.* Secker & Warburg, 1939.

HEYL, BERNARD. *New Bearings in Esthetics and Criticism.* Yale Univ. Press, 1944.

HICKS, GRANVILLE. *The Great Tradition.* Macmillan, 1933. Rev. ed., 1935.

—— (ed.). *Proletarian Literature in the United States.* International Publ., 1935.

—— *Figures of Transition.* Macmillan, 1939.

—— "The Failure of 'Left' Criticism." NR, 103 (Sept. 9, 1940), 345-7.

HOARE, D. M. *Some Studies of the Modern Novel.* Chatto & Windus, 1939.

HOFFMAN, FREDERICK. *Freudianism and the Literary Mind.* Louisiana State Univ. Press, 1945. (Bibliography)

HOFFMAN, F., ALLEN, C., & ULRICH, C. *The Little Magazine.* Princeton Univ. Press, 1946. New ed., 1947.

See Ezra Pound: "Small Magazines." EJ, 19 (Nov., 1930), 689-704.

See M. Cowley: "Magazine Business: 1910-1946." NR, 115 (Oct. 21, 1946), 521-3.

HOLLINGWORTH, GERTRUDE. *A Primer of Literary Criticism.* Univ. of Toronto Press, 1937.

HONIG, EDWIN. *Garcia Lorca.* New Directions, 1945.

HOPKINS, GERARD MANLEY. *The Letters of Gerard Manley Hopkins to Robert Bridges* and *The Correspondence of Gerard Manley Hopkins and Richard Watson Dixon.* Edited by Claude C. Abbott. Oxford Univ. Press, 1935. 2 vols.

Rev. by Herbert Read in *Crit.,* 14 (Apr., 1935), 478-82; M. Zabel: "Hopkins in His Letters," P, 46 (July, 1935), 210-19; F. Leavis in *Scr.,* 4 (Sept., 1935), 216-31.

—— *The Note-books and Papers of Gerard Manley Hopkins.* Edited by H. House. Oxford Univ. Press, 1937.

—— *Further Letters of Gerard Manley Hopkins.* Oxford Univ. Press, 1938.

On Hopkins: See Deutsch, Empson, Evans, Gordon, Leavis, Day Lewis, MacNeice, Murry, Pepper, Read, Richards, Riding and Graves, Sitwell, Stauffer, Stonier, Austin Warren.

Brockington, A. A. *Mysticism and Poetry.* Chapman & Hall, 1934.

Cohen, S., & Mathison, J. "The Poetic Theory." PQ, 36 (Jan., 1947), 1-20, 21-35.

Collins, J. "Philosophical Themes in G. M. Hopkins." *Thought,* 22 (Mar., 1947), 67-106.

Downey, H. "Gerard Manley Hopkins: A Study of Influences." SR, 1 (Spring, 1936), 837-45.

Gardner, W. H. "The Religious Problem in G. M. Hopkins." *Scr.,* 6 (June, 1937), 32-42.

Gardner, W. H. *Gerard Manley Hopkins (1844-1889).* Secker & Warburg, 1944. Vol. I. Yale Univ. Press, 1948.

Gardner, W. H. *Poems of Gerard Manley Hopkins.* Oxford Univ. Press, 1948. 3rd ed. (With Robert Bridges's Preface and Notes)

Kelly, B. *The Mind and Poetry of Gerard Manley Hopkins.* Humphries, 1935; Pepler & Sewell, 1937.

Kenyon Critics, The. *Gerard Manley Hopkins.* New Directions, 1945.

Lahey, G. F. *Gerard Manley Hopkins.* Oxford Univ. Press, 1930.

New Verse. No. 14 (April, 1935) "Gerard Manley Hopkins Number." Ed. G. Grigson.

Peters, W. A. M. *Gerard Manley Hopkins: A Critical Essay.* Oxford Univ. Press, 1948. (Bibliography)

Phare, E. E. *The Poetry of Gerard Manley Hopkins.* Macmillan, 1933.

Pick, John. *Gerard Manley Hopkins, Priest and Poet.* Oxford Univ. Press, 1942.

Ruggles, Eleanor. *Gerard Manley Hopkins: A Life.* Norton, 1944.

Rev. by W. H. Auden: "A Knight of the Infinite." NR, 111 (Aug. 21, 1944), 223-4.

Trueblood, C. "The Esthetics of Gerard Hopkins." P, 50 (Aug., 1937), 274-80.

Weiss, T. "Gerard Manley Hopkins." *Accent Anthology.* Harcourt, 1946. Pp. 664-77.

Williams, Charles. Introduction. *Poems of Gerard Manley Hopkins.* ed. Robert Bridges. Oxford Univ. Press, 1937. 2nd ed. (1st ed., 1930)

HOSPERS, JOHN. *Meaning and Truth in the Arts.* Univ. of North Carolina Press, 1946.

HOUSMAN, A. E. *The Name and Nature of Poetry.* Cambridge Univ. Press, 1933, 1948.

On Housman: See Blackmur, Bronowski, Connolly, Daiches, Deutsch, Drew, Eliot, *Explicator,* Garrod, Day Lewis, Lucas, MacNeice, Palmer, Pound, I. A. Richards, Rylands, Schneider, Sitwell, M. Van Doren, C. Williams.

Aiken, C. "A. E. Housman." NR, 89 (Nov. 11, 1936), 51-2.

Allison, A. "The Poetry of A. E. Housman." RES, 19 (July, 1943), 276-84.

Bishop, J. "The Poetry of A. E. Housman." P, 56 (June, 1940), 144-53.

Brooks, C. "The Whole of Housman." KR, 3 (Winter, 1941), 105-9.

Dobrée, B. "The Complete Housman." *Spec.,* 164 (Jan. 5, 1940), 23.

Ehrsam, T. *A Bibliography of Alfred Edward Housman.* Faxon, 1941.

Garrod, H. W. "Housman: 1939." *Essays and Studies,* 25 (1939), 7-21.

Gow, A. S. F. *A. E. Housman: A Sketch.* Cambridge Univ. Press, 1936.

Housman, Lawrence. *My Brother, A. E. Housman.* Cape, 1937; Scribner's, 1938.

Jarrell, R. "Texts from Housman." KR, 1 (Summer, 1939), 260-71.

Leighton, L. "One View of Housman." P, 52 (May, 1938), 94-100.

Muir, E. "A. E. Housman." *Lon. Merc.,* 35 (Nov., 1936), 62-3.

Richards, Grant. *Housman, 1897-1936.* Oxford Univ. Press, 1941. (See appendices)

Sparrow, J. "Echoes in the Poetry of A. E. Housman." *19th Cent.,* 115 (Feb., 1934), 243-56.

Spender, S. "The Essential Housman." *Hor.,* 1 (Apr., 1940), 295-301.

Stallman, R. "Annotated Bibliography: A Critical Study." PMLA, 55 (June, 1945), 463-502.

Wilson, Edmund. "A. E. Housman." NR, 92 (Sept. 29, 1937), 206-10.

Withers, Percy. *A Buried Life.* Cape, 1940.

Hughes, Glenn. *Imagism and the Imagists.* Stanford Univ. Press, 1941. (Bibliography)

Hulme, T. E. *Speculations.* Ed. Herbert Read. Kegan Paul; Harcourt, 1924, 1936.

On Hulme: See Eliot, Krutch, Wyndham Lewis, Matthiessen, Riding, Basil Willey.

Coffman, S. *The Making of Imagism: The Contribution of T. E. Hulme and Ezra Pound to English Poetry, 1908-1917.* (Dissertation, Ohio State Univ., 1947).

Roberts, M. *T. E. Hulme.* Faber & Faber, 1938.

Rev. by H. Mason: "The T. E. Hulme Myth," *Scr.,* 7 (Sept., 1938), 215-6.

Tate, A. "Poetry and the Absolute." SeR, 35 (Jan., 1927), 41-52.

Wector, D.: "Hulme and the Tragic View of Life," SR, 5 (Summer, 1939), 141-52.

Humphries, Rolfe. "Poet or Prophet?" (On Jeffers) NR, 61 (Jan. 15, 1930), 228-9.

—— "Miss Millay as Artist." N, 153 (Dec. 20, 1941), 644-5. (On the sonnet as form)

—— "A Disciple of Aristippus." (Housman) N, 154 May 9, 1942), 550-2.

Huxley, Aldous. *Essays Old and New.* Chatto & Windus, 1927; Doran, 1927.

—— *Music at Night and Other Essays.* Fountain Press, 1931.

—— *The Olive Tree.* Chatto & Windus, 1936.

—— *Words and Their Meanings.* Ward Ritchie Press, 1940.

Hyman, Stanley Edgar. *The Armed Vision.* Knopf, 1948. (On Caudwell, Eliot, Empson, V. W. Brooks, Burke, Blackmur, Richards, Wilson, et al.)

Rev. by Irving Howe: "The Critic as Stuffed Head." N, 167 (July 3, 1948), 22-4.

Isherwood, C. *Charles Baudelaire: Intimate Journals.* Blackmore Press; Random, 1930. Introduction by T. S. Eliot.

James, D. G. *Scepticism and Poetry. An Essay on the Poetic Imagination.* Allen & Unwin, 1937.

Rev. by H. Muller in SR, 4 (Summer, 1938), 187-208; in *Hib. Jour.,* 35 (July, 1937), 625-8; Empson in *Crit.,* 16 (July, 1937), 205-7.

—— *The Romantic Comedy.* Oxford Univ. Press, 1948.

James, Henry. *The Letters.* Ed. P. Lubbock. Scribner's, 1920. 2 vols.

—— *Henry James's Criticism.* Ed. M. Roberts. Harvard Univ. Press, 1929.

—— *The Art of the Novel: Critical Prefaces.* Ed. by R. P. Blackmur. Scribner's, 1934.

—— *The Notebooks of Henry James.* Ed. Matthiessen & Murdock. Oxford Univ. Press, 1947.

—— *The Scenic Art: Notes on Acting and the Drama.* Rutgers Univ. Press, 1948.

On James: See Fergusson, Forster, Knights, W. Lewis, Lubbock, Peacock, Pound, H. Read, Spender, Austin Warren, Orlo Williams, Edmund Wilson.

Anderson, Q. "The Two Henry Jameses." *Scr.,* 14 (Sept., 1947), 242-51.

Beach, J. W. *The Method of Henry James.* Yale Univ. Press, 1918.

Beach, J. W. "The Sacred and Solitary Refuge." *Fur.,* 3 (Winter, 1947), 23-37.

Bosanquet, T. "Henry James at Work." *Hogarth Essays.* Doubleday, 1928. Pp. 243-76.

Brooks, V. W. *The Pilgrimage of Henry James.* Dutton, 1925.
Dupee, F. W. (ed.). *The Question of Henry James.* Holt, 1945.
Eliot, T. S. "Henry James." In *Shock of Recognition,* ed. E. Wilson (1943). Pp. 854-65.
Heilman, R. "The Turn of the Screw as Poem." UKCR, 14 (Summer, 1948), 277-89.
Hound and Horn: 7 (April, 1934) Henry James Number. (M. Moore, L. Leighton, et al.)
Kenyon Review: 5 (Autumn, 1943). Henry James Number. (Essays by Barzun, Fergusson, et al.)
Leavis, F. "Henry James and the Function of Criticism." *Scr.,* 15 (Spring, 1948), 98-104.
Matthiessen, F. O. *Henry James: The Major Phase.* Oxford Univ. Press, 1946.
Oliver, C. "Henry James as Social Critic." *Ant. Rev.,* 7 (Summer, 1947), 243-58.
Roberts, M. *Henry James's Criticism.* Harvard Univ. Press, 1929.
Roberts, M. "Henry James and the Art of Foreshortening." RES, 22 (July, 1946), 207-12.
"The Significance of Henry James." TLS, Jan. 6, 1927. (Leading article)
Williams, Orlo. "The Ambassadors." *Crit.,* 8 (Sept., 1928), 47-64. (Excellent)
Zabel, M. "The Poetics of Henry James." P, 45 (Feb., 1935), 270-6.

JARRELL, RANDALL. (Essays under Auden, Frost, Housman, Pound, Yeats)
—— "A Note on Poetry." In *Five Young American Poets.* New Directions, 1940. Pp. 85-90.
—— "The Rhetoricians." NR, 104 (Feb. 17, 1941), 221-2. (On Conrad Aiken)
—— "Contemporary Poetry Criticisms." NR, 105 (July 21, 1941), 88-90.
—— "The End of the Line." N, 154 (Feb. 21, 1942), 222, 224-6, 228.
On Jarrell: Cowley, M. "Poets as Reviewers." NR, 104 (Feb. 4, 1941), 281-2.
Cowley, M. "First Blood." NR, 107 (Nov. 30, 1942), 718-9.

JEFFERS, ROBINSON. (See Cowley, Drew, R. Warren, Wells, Wilder, Winters, Zabel)
On Jeffers: Alberts, S. S. *A Bibliography of the Works.* Random, 1932.
Rev. by M. Zabel: "A Prophet in his Wilderness." NR, 77 (Jan. 3, 1933), 229-30.
Humphries, R. "Poet or Prophet?" NR, 61 (Jan. 15, 1930), 228-9.
Powell, L. C. *Robinson Jeffers: The Man and His Work.* San Paqual Press, 1934.
Rev. by A. Wanning: "Poetry and Belief." KR, 3 (Winter, 1941), 112-5.
Rice, P. B. "Jeffers and the Tragic Sense." N, 141 (Oct. 23, 1935), 480-2.
Schwartz, D. "The Enigma of Robinson Jeffers." P, 55 (Oct., 1939), 30-8; 39-46.
Short, Ray. "The Tower Beyond Tragedy." SR, 7 (Summer, 1941), 132-44.
Sterling, George. *Robinson Jeffers: The Man and the Artist.* Boni, 1926.

Johns Hopkins Symposium on Criticism. Pantheon Books, 1948. (Croce, Read, et al)

JONES, ERNEST. *Essays in Applied Psycho-Analysis.* International Psycho-analytical Press, 1923.
—— *Hamlet: With a Psycho-Analytical Study.* Vision Press, Funk & Wagnalls, 1948.

JONES, HOWARD M. "Literary Scholarship and Contemporary Criticism." EJ, 23 (Nov., 1934), 740-58. Repr. as a pamphlet.
—— "The Limits of Contemporary Criticism." SRL, 24 (Sept. 6, 1941), 3-4, 17. Attacked in Editorial in SR, 7 (Autumn, 1941), iv, vi, viii, x, xii.
—— *The Theory of American Literature.* Cornell Univ. Press, 1948.

JONES, LLEWELLYN. *First Impressions.* Knopf, 1925.
—— *How to Criticize Books.* Norton, 1928. (Book reviews)

JONES, P. (ed.). *English Critical Essays: XXth Century.* Oxford Univ. Press, 1933.

JOSEPHSON, MATTHEW. *Portrait of the Artist as American.* Harcourt, 1930.

JOYCE, JAMES. *Introducing James Joyce: A Selection.* Ed. T. S. Eliot. Faber & Faber, 1942.

On Joyce: See Connolly, Daiches, Damon, Frank, Muir, Read, E. Wilson.

Campbell, J., & Robinson, H. *A Skeleton Key to Finnegan's Wake.* Harcourt; McLeod, 1944.

Eliot, T. S. "Ulysses, Order, and Myth." *Dial,* 75 (Nov., 1933), 480-3.

Gilbert, Stuart. *James Joyce's Ulysses.* Faber & Faber, 1930.

Givens, Seon (ed.). *James Joyce: Two Decades of Criticism.* Vanguard Press, 1948.

Gorman, Herbert. *James Joyce.* Farrar, 1940.

Hendry, Irene. "James Joyce's Epiphanies." SeR, 54 (Summer, 1946), 449-67.

Kain, R. *Fabulous Voyager: James Joyce's Ulysses.* Univ. of Chicago Press, 1947.

Larbaud, Valéry. "The 'Ulysses' of James Joyce." *Crit.,* 1 (Oct., 1922), 94-103.

Levin, Harry. *James Joyce: A Critical Introduction.* New Directions, 1941.

KAZIN, ALFRED. *On Native Grounds.* Reynal & Hitchcock, 1942; Cape, 1944.

KELLETT, ERNEST. *The Whirligig of Taste.* Hogarth Press; Harcourt, 1929.

Rev. by G. Hicks: "De Gustibus." N, 128 (Mar. 27, 1929), 376, 378.

KENMARE, DALLAS. *The Future of Poetry.* Williams & Norgate, 1936.

—— *The Face of Truth.* Shakespeare Head Press, 1939. (On Hopkins, et al.)

KER, W. P. *The Art of Poetry.* Oxford Univ. Press, 1920.

—— *The Collected Essays of W. P. Ker.* Ed. Charles Whibley. Macmillan, 1925. 2 vols.

—— *Form and Style in Poetry. Lectures and Notes.* Ed. E. K. Chambers. Macmillan, 1928.

Rev. by T. Spencer in H&H, 2 (July, 1929), 446-9. See Eliot in *Music of Poetry.*

KIERKEGAARD, SÖREN. *Philosophical Fragments.* Princeton Univ. Press, 1942.

—— *Either/Or.* Vol. I, trans. D. Swenson; II, trans. W. Lowrie. Princeton Univ. Press, 1944.

Rev. by C. Wallis: "The Aesthetic and the Ethical." KR, 6 (Summer, 1944), 454-69.

On Kierkegaard: Channing-Pierce, M. *The Terrible Crystal.* Oxford Univ. Press, 1941.

Lowrie, W. *Kierkegaard.* Oxford Univ. Press, 1938.

KIPLING, RUDYARD. *Something of Myself.* Macmillan, 1937. (Autobiography)

Rev. by Orlo Williams in *Crit.,* 16 (July, 1937), 683-5.

On Kipling: Auden, W. H. "Kipling and Eliot." NR, 110 (Jan. 10, 1944), 55.

Braddy, Nella. *Rudyard Kipling: Son of Empire.* Messner, 1941.

Eliot, T. S. Preface. *A Choice of Kipling's Verse.* Faber & Faber, 1941; Scribner's, 1943. Preface appeared in HM, 1106 (July, 1942), 149-57.

Rev. by Auden: "The Poet of Encirclement," NR, 109 (Oct. 23, 1943), 579-81; Ford Boris: "A Case for Kipling?" *Scr.,* 11 (Summer, 1942), 23-33.

Hopkins, R. T. *Rudyard Kipling: The Story of a Genius.* Palmer, 1930. (Biography)

MacMunn, Sir George. *Rudyard Kipling: Craftsman.* R. Hale, 1937. Rev. ed., 1938.

Scott, Dixon. *Men of Letters.* Hodder, 1917, 1923.

Shanks, Edward. *Rudyard Kipling: A Study in Literature and Political Ideas.* Macmillan, 1940.

Stevenson, L. "The Ideas in Kipling's Poetry." UTQ, 1 (July, 1932), 467-89.

West, Rebecca. "Rudyard Kipling." NS&N, 11 N. S. (Jan. 25, 1936), 112-4.

Williams, Charles. *Poetry at Present.* Clarendon Press, 1930.

Wilson, Edmund. "The Post-War Kipling." NR, 71 (May 25, 1932), 50-1.
Wilson, Edmund. "The Kipling that Nobody Read." *The Wound and The Bow*. Houghton, 1941; Oxford Univ. Press, 1947. Pp. 105-81.

KNICKERBOCKER, W. S. (ed.). *Twentieth Century English*. Philosophical Libr., 1946.

KNIGHT, G. WILSON. *The Wheel of Fire*. Preface by T. S. Eliot. Oxford Univ. Press, 1930; Methuen, 1949.
Rev. by J. Burnham in *Symp.*, 1 (Oct., 1930), 537-41; B. Dobrée in *Crit.*, 10 (Jan., 1931), 342-7. See F. Gary in *Symp.*, 2 (Apr., 1931), 242-52.
—— "The Shakespearean Tempest." *Symp.*, 2 (Oct., 1931), 484-506.
—— *The Imperial Theme*. Oxford Univ. Press, 1931.
Rev. by L. C. Knights in *Crit.*, 11 (Apr., 1932), 540-3.
—— *The Shakespearean Tempest*. Oxford Univ. Press, 1932.
—— *The Christian Renaissance*. Macmillan, 1933. (Contains a note on Eliot)
—— *The Burning Oracle: Studies in the Poetry of Action*. Oxford Univ. Press, 1939.
—— *The Starlit Dome: Studies in the Poetry of Vision*. Oxford Univ. Press, 1941.
—— *Chariot of Wrath*. Faber & Faber, 1942.
—— *The Olive and the Sword*. Oxford Univ. Press, 1944. (Shakespeare studies)

KNIGHT, W. F. JACKSON. *Roman Vergil*. Faber & Faber, 1944.

KNIGHTS, L. C. *How Many Children Had Lady Macbeth?* Minority Press, 1933.
—— *Drama and Society in the Age of Jonson*. Chatto & Windus, 1937.
—— "The Ambiguity of 'Measure for Measure.'" *Scr.*, 10 (Jan., 1942), 222-33.
—— *Explorations: Essays in Criticism*. Chatto & Windus, 1946; George Stewart, 1947.

KORZYBSKI, ALFRED. *Science and Sanity*. Science Press Publ. Co., 1934. 3rd ed., 1948.

KREYMBORG, ALFRED. *Troubadour*. Boni, 1925. (Autobiography)
—— *Our Singing Strength*. Coward-McCann, 1929.

KRIKORIAN, Y. (ed.). *Naturalism and the Human Spirit*. Columbia Univ. Press, 1944.

KRUTCH, JOSEPH WOOD. "A Note on Irony." N, 115 (Nov. 1, 1922), 473-4. (On Huxley)
—— *Comedy and Conscience After the Restoration*. Columbia Univ. Press, 1924, 1948.
—— *Edgar Allan Poe: A Study in Genius*. Knopf, 1926.
—— *The Modern Temper: A Study and a Confession*. Harcourt, 1929.
See K. Burke: "Redefinitions." NR, 68 (Sept. 2, 1931), 74-5.
—— *Experience and Art*. Harrison Smith, 1932.
Rev. by K. Burke: "Belief and Art," N, 135 (Nov. 30, 1932), 536-7; Isador Schneider: "The More Modern Temper," NR, 74 (Mar. 8, 1933), 110.
—— "A Poem is a Poem." N, 137 (Dec. 13, 1933), 679-80. (On T. S. Eliot)
—— "On the Difficulty of Modern Poetry." N, 142 (Mar. 4, 1936), 283-4.
—— "The Half Truth of the Whole Truth." N, 143 (Jan. 2, 1937).
—— "What is a Good Review?" N, 144 (Apr. 17, 1937), 438.
—— "Beauty's Rose." N, 145 (July 31, 1937), 132-3.
—— *Samuel Johnson*. Holt, 1944.
Rev. by Edmund Wilson in NY, 20 (Nov. 18, 1944), 79, 81-2.
See F. Leavis: "Doctor Johnson." KR, 8 (Autumn, 1946), 637-57.

On Krutch: Larrabee, A. "Prufrock and Joseph Wood Krutch." *Acc.*, 3 (Winter, 1943), 115-21.

KUNITZ, STANLEY. *Living Authors*. Wilson, 1931.
—— *Authors Today and Yesterday*. Wilson, 1933.
——, & HAYCRAFT, H. *Twentieth Century Authors: A Bibliographical Dictionary*. Wilson, 1942.

LANGER, SUSANNE. *Philosophy in a New Key*. Oxford Univ. Press; Harvard Univ. Press, 1942.

Rev. by P. B. Rice: "To God via Semantics." N, 155 (Nov. 7, 1942), 486-7.

LANGFELD, H. S. *The Aesthetic Attitude.* Harcourt, 1920. (Defines *empathy*)

LANZ, HENRY. *The Physical Basis of Rime.* Stanford Univ. Press, 1931.

LASKI, HAROLD. *Faith, Reason and Civilization.* Viking Press, 1944.

LAUGHLIN, JAMES (ed.). *New Directions in Prose and Poetry.* New Directions, 1936.

LAWRENCE, D. H. *Studies in Classic American Literature.* Boni, 1923.

Repr. in *The Shock of Recognition,* ed. Edmund Wilson. Doubleday, 1943. Pp. 905-1077.

—— *Fantasia of the Unconscious.* Seltzer, 1922; Secker & Warburg, 1923; Viking Press, 1930.

—— *Assorted Articles.* Secker & Warburg; Knopf, 1930.

—— *The Letters.* Ed. Aldous Huxley. Heinemann; Viking Press, 1932, 1937.

Rev. by F. Leavis in *Scr.,* 1 (Dec., 1932), 273-9; W. Troy in *Symp.,* 4 (Jan., 1933), 85-94.

—— *Phoenix: The Posthumous Papers.* Ed. E. McDonald. Heinemann; Viking Press, 1936.

Rev. by G. Hicks: "D. H. Lawrence as Messiah," NR, 88 (Oct. 28, 1936), 358-9; in TLS, Nov. 21, 1936, 956; K. Quinn in YR, 26 (Jan., 1937), 847-8.

On Lawrence: See Blackmur, Deutsch, Dobrée, Eliot, Fraenkel, Gregory, Hoffman, Hughes, Huxley, Lucas, Muir, Powell, Richards, Savage, Waugh, V. Woolf.

Aldington, Richard. *D. H. Lawrence.* Chatto & Windus, 1930.

Carswell, Catherine. *The Savage Pilgrimage.* Harcourt, 1932.

Ghiselin, B. "D. H. Lawrence's New World." WR, 11 (Spring, 1947), 150-9.

Gregory, H. *Pilgrim of the Apocalypse: A Critical Study.* Viking Press, 1933.

Hoffman, F. "From Surrealism to 'The Apocalypse.'" ELH, 15 (June, 1948), 147-65.

Kingsmill, Hugh. *The Life of D. H. Lawrence.* Dodge Publ. Co., 1938.

Lawrence, Frieda. *Not I, But the Wind.* Rydal Press; Viking Press, 1934.

Leavis, F. R. *D. H. Lawrence.* Minority Press, 1932.

McDonald, D. *A Bibliography of the Writings.* Foreword by D. H. Lawrence. Centaur Book, 1925.

McDonald, D. *A Bibliography of the Writings, 1925-1930.* Centaur Book, 1931.

Merrild, Knud. *A Poet and Two Painters: A Memoir of D. H. Lawrence.* Viking Press, 1939.

Murry, J. M. *The Son of Woman: The Story of D. H. Lawrence.* Cape, 1931. Rev. by T. S. Eliot in *Crit.,* 10 (July, 1931), 768-74.

Murry, J. M. *Reminiscences of D. H. Lawrence.* Cape, 1933.

Murry, J. M. *The Autobiography: Between Two Worlds.* Cape, 1935; Messner, 1936.

Potter, Stephen. *D. H. Lawrence: A First Study.* Cape; Harrison Smith, 1930.

Quennell, P. "The Later Period of D. H. Lawrence." *Scrutinies,* II. Wishart, 1931.

Richards, I. A. "Lawrence as a Poet." NV, No. 1 (Jan., 1933), 15-7.

Rodman, Selden. *Lawrence: The Last Crusade.* Viking Press, 1937.

Rosenfeld, Paul. "D. H. Lawrence." NR, 62 (Mar. 26, 1930), 155-6.

T. E. *D. H. Lawrence: A Personal Record.* Cape, 1935; Knight Publ., 1936.

Tindall, W. *D. H. Lawrence and Susan His Cow.* Columbia Univ. Press, 1939.

Trilling, Diana. (ed.). *The Portable D. H. Lawrence.* Viking, 1947.

Trilling, L. "D. H. Lawrence: A Neglected Aspect." *Symp.,* 1 (July, 1930), 361-70.

Troy, W. "The D. H. Lawrence Myth." *Partisan Reader,* ed. W. Phillips. Dial Press, 1946. Pp. 336-47.

West, Rebecca. *D. H. Lawrence.* Secker & Warburg, 1930.

LAWSON, V. *Dunbar Critically Examined.* Association Publishers, 1941.

LEAVIS, F. R. (See under Bateson, Eastman, Eliot, Hardy, Hopkins, Pound, Yeats)

—— *Mass Civilization and Minority Culture.* Minority Press, 1930. (On Eliot's poetry)

—— "What's Wrong with Criticism?" *Scr.,* 1 (Sept., 1932), 132-46. (On scholar-critics)

—— *New Bearings in English Poetry.* Chatto & Windus, 1932, 1938.

Rev. by Franklin Gary in *Symp.,* 3 (Oct., 1932), 521-34 (Significant).

—— *How to Teach Reading: A Primer for Ezra Pound.* Minority Press, 1933.

Rev. by A. Tate: "How is Writing Taught?" P, 44 (Apr., 1934), 53-5.

—— *For Continuity.* Minority Press, 1933.

—— (ed.). *Towards Standards of Criticism: Selections From the Calendar of Modern Letters 1925-27.* Wishart, 1933. (See for essays by C. H. and Edgell Rickword)

—— (ed.). *Determinations: Critical Essays.* Chatto & Windus, 1934.

——, & THOMPSON, DENYS. *Culture and Environment.* Chatto & Windus, 1933.

—— *Revaluation: Tradition and Development in English Poetry.* Chatto & Windus, 1936; Stewart, 1947.

Rev. by Dobrée in *Spec.,* Oct. 3, 1936, p. 694; Spender in *Crit.,* 16 (Jan., 1937), 350-3.

—— "Arnold as Critic." *Scr.,* 7 (Dec., 1938), 319-32.

—— "Coleridge in Criticism." *Scr.,* 9 (June, 1940), 57-69.

—— "Joseph Conrad." *Scr.,* 10 (June, Oct., 1941), 22-50, 151-81.

—— *Education and the University.* Chatto & Windus, 1943; Stewart, 1948. (On Eliot, Pound, et al.)

—— "Johnson as Critic." *Scr.,* 12 (Summer, 1944), 187-204. See *Scr.,* 11 (1942), 75-8.

—— "'Thought' and Emotional Quality." *Scr.,* 13 (Spring, 1945), 53-71.

—— "Imagery and Movement: Notes in the Analysis of Poetry." *Scr.,* 13 (Sept., 1945), 119-34.

—— "George Eliot." *Scr.,* 13 (Autumn, 1945; Spring, 1946), 172-87; 257-71.

—— "George Eliot." *Scr.,* 14 (Summer, 1946; Dec., 1946), 15-26, 102-31.

—— "Doctor Johnson." KR, 7 (Autumn, 1946), 637-57. (On Krutch's *Johnson*)

—— "The Novel as Dramatic Poem: 'Hard Times.'" *Scr.,* 14 (Spring, 1947), 185-203.

—— *The Great Tradition.* Chatto & Windus, 1948. (Austen, Eliot, James, Conrad)

On Leavis: See Lucas, Edith Sitwell, John Sparrow, Wellek. (See also Bentley)

Mason, H. "F. R. Leavis and Scrutiny." *The Critic,* 1 (Autumn, 1947), 21-34.

Stallman, R. W. "The New Criticism." *A Southern Vanguard,* ed. A. Tate (1947). Pp. 28-51.

LEAVIS, Q. D. *Fiction and the Reading Public.* Chatto & Windus, 1932.

—— "Leslie Stephen: Cambridge Critic." *Scr.,* 7 (Mar., 1939), 404-15.

—— "'The Discipline of Letters': A Sociological Note." *Scr.,* 12 (Winter, 1943), 12-26.

LEBOWITZ, MARTIN. "Thought and Sensibility." KR, 5 (Spring, 1943), 219-26.

LEVIN, HARRY. (ed.). *Selected Works of Ben Jonson.* Random, 1938; Nonesuch Press, 1940.

—— *James Joyce: A Critical Introduction.* New Directions, 1941.

—— "Literature as an Institution." Acc, 6 (Spring, 1946), 159-68. (On Taine)

—— *Toward Stendhal.* New Directions, 1945.

—— *Toward Balzac.* New Directions, 1947.

—— (ed.). *The Portable James Joyce.* Viking Press, 1947. *The Essential Joyce.* Cape, 1948.

LEVIN, HARRY. *The Gates of Horn.* Oxford Univ. Press, 1949. (On Balzac, Stendhal, French novel)

LEWIS, C. S. *The Allegory of Love.* Clarendon Press, 1936.

—— *Rehabilitations.* Oxford Univ. Press, 1939. "Shelley, Dryden, and Mr. Eliot." Pp. 3-34.

—— & TILLYARD, E. *The Personal Heresy.* Oxford Univ. Press, 1939. (See Savage)

—— "Psycho-Analysis and Literary Criticism." *Essays and Studies,* 27 (1941). 1942. Pp. 7-21.

—— *A Preface to Paradise Lost.* Oxford Univ. Press, 1942.

LEWIS, WYNDHAM. *Time and Western Man.* Chatto & Windus, 1927; Harcourt, 1928. (On Eliot, et al.)

Rev. by R. Blackmur: "The Enemy," H&H, 1 (Mar., 1928), 270-3.

See J. Ransom: "Flux and Blur in Contemporary Art." SeR, 37 (July, 1929), 353-66.

—— *Men Without Art.* Cassell; Harcourt, 1934. (On Eliot, Hulme, Romanticism)

—— *Blasting and Bombardiering: Autobiography (1914-1926).* Eyre, 1937.

—— "The Objective of Art in Our Time." In *Wyndham Lewis The Artist.* Laidlaw, 1939.

—— "Picasso." KR, 2 (Spring, 1940), 196-211.

On Lewis: Porteus, H. *Wyndham Lewis: A Discursive Exposition.* Harmsworth, 1932.

Rickword, E. "Wyndham Lewis." *Scrutinies,* II. Wishart, 1931. Pp. 139-61.

Stone, G. "The Ideas of Wyndham Lewis." AR, 1 (Oct., 1933); 2 (Nov., 1933), 578-99; 82-96.

LEWISOHN, LUDWIG. *Expression in America.* Harper, 1932.

Rev. by G. Hicks in NR, 70 (Apr. 13, 1932), 240-1.

——, & GILLIS, ADOLPH. *The Artist and His Message.* Duffield & Green, 1933.

LIDDELL, ROBERT. *A Treatise on the Novel.* Cape, 1947.

LIND, ROBERT. "The Crisis in Literature." SeR, 47 (Jan., Apr., July, Oct., 1939), 35-62, 184-203, 345-64, 524-51; 48 (Jan., Apr., 1940), 66-85, 198-203.

LINDSAY, VACHEL. "What It Means To Be a Poet in America." *Sat. Evening Post,* 199, No. 11 (Nov., 1926), 12-13 ff.

—— "Unpublished Letters of Vachel Lindsay." *Shane Quar.,* 5 (Apr., 1944), 108-17.

On Lindsay: See Gregory, H. Monroe, Lewisohn.

Masters, E. L. *Vachel Lindsay: A Poet in America.* Scribner's, 1935.

Moses, W. "Vachel Lindsay." SR, 1 (Spring, 1936), 828-36.

Wakefield, O. "Vachel Lindsay, Disciple." *Shane Quar.,* 5 (Apr., 1944), 82-107.

Warren, Austin. "The Case of Vachel Lindsay." *Acc.,* 6 (Autumn, 1946), 230-9.

LISTOWELL, W. F. *A Critical History of Modern Aesthetics.* Allen & Unwin, 1933.

Literary Scholarship: Its Aims and Methods. Univ. of North Carolina Pr., 1941.

"Literature and the Professors." KR, 2 (Autumn, 1940), 403-42. (Brooks, Trilling)

"Literature and the Professors." SR, 6 (Autumn, 1940), 225-69. (A Symposium)

Essays by Ransom, Tate, Harry Levin, etc.

See Heilman, R. "Footnotes on Literary History." SR, 6 (1941), 759-70.

See "The Teaching of Literature." SeR, 55 (Autumn, 1947), 569-626. (Symposium)

LOVEJOY, ARTHUR. *The Great Chain of Being.* Harvard Univ. Press, 1936.

—— & BOAS, G. *Documentary History of Primitivism.* Johns Hopkins Press, 1936.

LOWELL, AMY. *John Keats.* Houghton; Cape, 1925. 2 vols.

—— *Poetry and Poets.* Houghton, 1930.

On Lowell: See Aiken, Brenner, Deutsch, Hughes, H. Monroe.

Foster, Damon S. *Amy Lowell: A Chronicle.* Houghton, 1935.

See Fletcher, J. G. "Herald of Imagism." SR, 1 (Spring, 1936), 813-27.

LOWES, JOHN L. *Convention and Revolt in Poetry*. Houghton, 1919, 1922; Constable, 1920.

—— *The Road to Xanadu. A Study in the Ways of the Imagination*. Constable, 1927.

See Warren, R. P. *The Rime of the Ancient Mariner*. Reynal & Hitchcock, 1946.

—— *Essays in Appreciation*. Houghton, 1936.

LUBBOCK, PERCY. *The Craft of Fiction*. Cape; Scribner's, 1921; Peter Smith, 1947.

LUCAS, F. L. *Authors Dead and Living*. Chatto & Windus; Macmillan, 1926.

Rev. by E. Rickword in *Towards Standards,* ed. F. Leavis. Wishart, 1933. Pp. 156-9.

—— "Criticism." L&L, 3 (Nov., 1929), 433-65.

—— "The Criticism of Poetry." *Proc. of Brit. Acad.,* 19 (1933), 167-93.

—— *Ten Victorian Poets*. Macmillan, 1940.

—— *The Decline and Fall of the Romantic Ideal*. Cambridge Univ. Press; Macmillan, 1936.

Rev. by F. Bateson in RES, 14 (Apr., 1938).

LUKACS, GEORGE. "The Intellectual Physiognomy of Literary Characters." *International Literature,* 8 (Aug., 1936), 55-83. (A significant study. Life and art)

MACCARTHY, DESMOND. *Portraits*. Putnam, 1931.

Rev. by Stephen Spender in *Crit.,* 11 (Apr., 1932), 554-7.

—— *Criticism: The Collected Essays of Desmond MacCarthy*. Putnam, 1932. (On Eliot, Yeats)

—— *Leslie Stephen*. Cambridge Univ. Press; Macmillan, 1937.

See Q. D. Leavis: "Leslie Stephen." *Scr.,* 7 (Mar., 1939), 404-15.

On MacCarthy: Little, A. "The Approach to Criticism." *Studies,* 32 (June, 1943), 186-96.

MACKAIL, J. W. *Lectures in Poetry*. Longmans, 1914.

—— "The Study of Poetry." *Rice Institute Pamphlet,* 11 (Sept., 1915), 1-52.

—— *Studies in Humanism*. Longmans, 1938. (On relation of poetry to life)

MACLEISH, ARCHIBALD. "The Social Cant." NR, 73 (Dec. 21, 1932), 156-8.

—— "The Irresponsibles." N, 150 (May 18, 1940), 618-23.

—— *The Irresponsibles*. Duell, Sloan, 1940.

Compare Van Wyck Brooks: "Primary Literature and Coterie Literature" in *The Opinions of Oliver Allston* (1941); and Bernard DeVoto in *The Literary Fallacy* (1944).

—— "Public Speech and Private Speech in Poetry." YR, 27 (Spring, 1938), 536-47.

—— "Poetry and the Public World." AM, 163 (June, 1939), 823-31.

—— *America Was Promises*. Duell, Sloan, 1939.

—— "Post-War Writers and Pre-War Readers." NR, 102 (June 10, 1940), 789-90.

Contrast MacLeish's stand in his review in NR, 76 (Sept. 20, 1933), 159-60.

—— *A Time to Speak: The Selected Prose of Archibald MacLeish*. Duell, Sloan, 1941.

—— *A Time to Act*. Duell, Sloan, 1942.

On MacLeish: See Blackmur, C. Brooks, Deutsch, Gregory, Lind, Stauffer, Strachey, Tate.

Aiken, C. "The Development of a Poet." NR, 77 (Jan. 17, 1934), 287.

Cowley, M. "Poets and Prophets." NR, 104 (May 5, 1941), 639.

Gold, Michael. "Out of the Fascist Unconscious." NR, 75 (July 26, 1933), 295-6. See E. Wilson: "The Literary Class War." NR, 70 (May 4, 11, 1930), 319-23; 347-9.

Mizener, A. "The Poetry of Archibald MacLeish." SeR, 46 (Oct., 1938), 501-19.

Mizener, A. *A Catalogue of the First Editions of Archibald MacLeish*. Yale Univ. Library, 1938.

Rice, P. "Poets and the Wars." N, 140 (Feb. 13, 1935), 189-90, 192.
Wilson, E. "Archibald MacLeish and 'The Word.'" NR, 103 (July 1, 1940).
Zabel, M. "The Poet on Capitol Hill." PaR, 8 (Jan., Mar., 1941), 1, 128.

MacNeice, Louis. "Poetry." *The Arts To-Day,* ed. G. Grigson. Bodley Head, 1935.
—— "Subject in Modern Poetry." *Essays and Studies,* 22 (1936). Clarendon Press, 1937. Pp. 144-58.
—— *Modern Poetry: A Personal Essay.* Oxford Univ. Press, 1938.
Rev. by G. Walton in *Scr.,* 7 (Mar., 1939), 437-40; A. Tate: "Poetry of the Will," NR, 100 (Aug. 16, 1939), 52-3; R. Jarrell in KR, 1 (Autumn, 1939), 468-71.
—— *The Poetry of W. B. Yeats.* Oxford Univ. Press, 1941.
Rev. in *Scr.,* 9 (Mar., 1941), 381-3; by C. Brooks in MLN, 58 (Apr., 1943), 319-20.

On MacNeice: See Aiken, Church, Drew, Scarfe, Southworth, Wilder, Zabel.

Macy, John. *The Critical Game.* Boni, 1922. (On Dante, Hardy, Lawrence, Masefield)

Maier, N. & Reninger, H. *A Psychological Approach to Literary Criticism.* Appleton, 1933.

Malraux, André. *The Psychology of Art.* Chatto & Windus, 1948.

Mann, Thomas. *Essays of Three Decades.* Trans. H. Lowe-Porter. Knopf; Secker & Warburg, 1947.

On Mann: Neider, C. *The Stature of Thomas Mann.* New Directions, 1947.
Blackmur, R. P. "Notes on ... *The Magic Mountain.*" HR, 1 (Autumn, 1948), 318-39.

Mansfield, Katherine. *The Journal.* Ed. J. M. Murry. Knopf, 1927.
—— *Novels and Novelists.* Knopf, 1930.
—— *The Letters.* Ed. J. M. Murry. Constable, 1928; Knopf, 1930.

On Mansfield: See Brewster, Daiches, Drew, Forster, Murry, Richards.
Cox, S. "The Fastidiousness of Katherine Mansfield." SeR, 39 (April, 1931), 158-69.
Explicator, 3 (April, 1945), 49; 5 (Feb., May, 1947), 32, 53. (On *The Fly*)
Friis, Anne. *Katherine Mansfield: Life and Stories.* Copenhagen: Einar Munksgaard, 1946.
Hamill, Elizabeth. "Katherine Mansfield and Virginia Woolf." In *These Modern Writers.* Melbourne: Georgian House, 1946.
Mantz, R. E., & Murry, J. M. *The Life of Katherine Mansfield.* Constable, 1933.

March, H. M. *The Two Worlds of Marcel Proust.* Univ. of Pennsylvania Press, 1948.

Maritain, Jacques. "Poetry and Religion." *Crit.,* 5 (Jan., June, 1927), 7-22, 214-30.
—— *Art and Scholasticism.* Trans. F. S. Flint. Scribner's; Sheed & Ward, 1930. Trans. J. F. Scanlan. Scribner's, 1935, 1942.
Rev. by P. Rice in *Symp.,* 1 (July, 1930), 390-2. (A significant article)
—— "Poetry's Dark Night." KR, 4 (Spring, 1942), 149-59. (Poetry is ontology)
—— *Art and Poetry.* Trans. E. Matthews. Philosophical Library, 1943.

On Maritain: See Eliot, Fernandez, Herbert Read. (Cf. Adler's *Art and Prudence*) Rosenberg, H. "The Profession of Poetry." PaR, 9 (1942).

Marsh, E. M. (ed.). *Georgian Poetry, 1918-1919.* Poetry Bookshop, 1920.

Marx, Karl. (See *American Writers,* Farrell, Edmund Wilson)

On Marxism: Burnham, J. "Marxism and Esthetics." *Symp.,* 4 (Jan., 1933).
Fox, R. "Marxism and Literature." *The Novel and the People.* International Publishers, 1937.
Klingender, F. D. *Marxism and Modern Art.* Lawrence, 1945.
Marshall, M., & McCarthy, M. "Our Critics, Right or Wrong." N, 141 (Oct. 23, to Dec. 18, 1935), 468-72, 542-4, 717-9. Cf. N, 142 (Jan. 1, 1936).
The Meaning of Marx: A Symposium. By Dewey, Hook, Russell, et al., Farrar, 1934.

Parkes, H. P. "The Limitations of Marxism." *The Pragmatic Test.* Colt Press, 1941. Pp. 160-77.
Rowse, A. L. "The Literature of Communism." *Crit.*, 8 (Apr., 1929), 422-36.
Wilson, Edmund. In *The Triple Thinkers.* Harcourt, 1938.
Wilson, Edmund. *To the Finland Station.* Harcourt, 1940.
MASEFIELD, JOHN. *Recent Prose.* Macmillan, 1933.
On Masefield: See Cunliffe, Lucas, Macy, Monro, Murry, Stoll, Charles Williams.
Hamilton, W. H. *John Masefield.* Macmillan; Allen & Unwin, 1922.
Higgins, B. "John Masefield." CML, 1 (May, 1925), 219-25.
Thomas, Gilbert. *John Masefield.* Macmillan, 1933.
MASTERS, EDGAR LEE. "The Genesis of Spoon River." *Am. Merc.*, 28 (Jan., 1933), 38-55.
—— *Vachel Lindsay: A Poet in America.* Scribner's, 1935.
—— *Walt Whitman.* Scribner's, 1937.
On Masters: See Blackmur, Brooks.
Rice, P. B. "Late Flowering." N, 141 (Oct. 16, 1935), 445.
MATTHIESSEN, F. O. *The Achievement of T. S. Eliot.* Oxford Univ. Press, 1935, 1947.
Rev. by R. Blackmur in N, 141 (Oct. 23, 1935), 478-9; G. Grigson in NV, No. 18 (Dec., 1935), 22; F. C. Flint: "Contemporary Criticism," SR, 2 (Summer, 1936), 208-24.
—— *American Renaissance.* Oxford Univ. Press, 1941.
Rev. by B. Smith in VQR, 17 (Autumn, 1941), 625-8; N. Pearson in *Decision,* 2 (Nov., 1941), 107-11; G. Boas in JAAC, No. 4 (Winter, 1942), 88-91.
—— "Eliot's Quartets." KR, 5 (Spring, 1943), 161-78. Cf. *Focus Three,* ed. B. Rajan (1947). "Four Quartets: A Commentary," by Helen Gardner. Pp. 57-78.
—— (ed.). *Selected Poems of Herman Melville.* New Directions, 1944.
—— "Poe." SeR, 54 (Spring, 1946), 175-206.
—— "American Poetry: 1920-40." SeR, 55 (Winter, 1947), 25-55.
MAUGHAM, W. SOMERSET. *The Summing Up.* Literary Guild, 1938.
MAURON, CHARLES. *The Nature of Beauty in Art and Literature.* Hogarth, 1927.
—— *Aesthetics and Psychology.* Trans. by Roger Fry. Hogarth Press, 1935.
MCKEON, RICHARD. "The Philosophic Bases of Art and Criticism." MP, 41 (Nov., 1943; Feb., 1944), 65-87, 129-71.
MCMAHON, PHILIP. *The Meaning of Art.* Norton, 1930. (Introduction to aesthetics)
MÉGROZ, R. L. *Modern English Poetry: 1882-1932.* Nicholson & Watson, 1933.
MENCKEN, H. L. *Prejudices.* 2nd Series, 1920; 3rd Series, Knopf, 1922.
MEYNELL, ALICE. *The Second Person Singular, and Other Essays.* Oxford Univ. Press, 1922.
MILLAY, EDNA ST. VINCENT. *Flowers of Evil. From the French of Charles Baudelaire.* By George Dillon and Edna St. Vincent Millay. Harper, 1936.
On Millay: See Brenner, Cowley, Deutsch, Drew, *Explicator,* Gregory, Ransom, Richards, Tate, Wells, Wilson, Zabel.
Atkins, Elizabeth. *Edna St. Vincent Millay and Her Times.* Univ. of Chicago Press, 1936.
See J. C. Ransom: "The Poet as Woman," *The World's Body,* 1938.
Cowley, M. "Episode in a Poet's Life." NR, 99 (June 7, 1939), 135-6.
Dupee, F. W. In *Symp.,* 2 (July, 1931), 408-11.
Humphries, R. "Miss Millay as Artist." N, 153 (Dec. 20, 1941), 644-5.
Jack, P. M. "An Analysis of the Verse of Edna St. Vincent Millay." NYTBR, Dec. 12, 1943, p. 4.
Rice, P. "Edna Millay's Maturity." N, 139 (Nov. 14, 1934), 568-9.
Schwartz, D. "The Poetry of Millay." N, 157 (Dec. 18, 1943), 735-6.
Walton, Edna. "The Unwise Thrush." N, 132 (Apr. 29, 1931), 480-1.
Yost, Karl. *A Bibliography of Edna St. Vincent Millay.* Harper, 1937.
Zabel, M. "Two Years of Poetry." SR, 5 (Winter, 1940), 568-608.
DE MILLE, GEORGE. *Literary Criticism in America: A Preliminary Survey.* Longmans, 1931.

MILLETT, FRED B. *Contemporary British Literature.* Harcourt, 1939. Rev. ed.
—— *Contemporary American Authors.* Harcourt, 1940. (See introductory essay)
MIZENER, ARTHUR. "The Structure of Figurative Language in Shakespeare's Sonnets." SR, 5 (Spring, 1940), 730-47. See Ransom in *The World's Body* (1938).
—— "The Elizabethan Art of Our Movies." KR, 4 (Spring, 1942), 181-94.
—— "Some Notes on the Nature of English Poetry." SeR, 51 (Winter, 1943), 27-51.
"Modern Poetry." AR, 8 (Feb., 1937), 427-56. (Essays by Tate, Brooks & Warren, M. Van Doren)
MONRO, HAROLD. *Some Contemporary Poets.* Parsons, 1920. (On Pound, Housman, et al.)

On Monro: Eliot, T. S. Introduction. *Collected Poems.* Cobden-Sanderson, 1933.
Pound, Ezra. "Harold Monro." *Crit.,* 11 (July, 1932), 581-92.

MONROE, HARRIET (ed.). *Poetry: A Magazine of Verse.* (See for her reviews)
—— *Poets and Their Art.* Macmillan, 1926, 1932.
—— *A Poet's Life: Seventy Years in a Changing World.* Macmillan, 1938.
MONTAGUE, C. E. *A Writer's Notes on His Trade.* Chatto & Windus, 1930.
MOODY, WILLIAM VAUGHAN. *Letters to Harriet.* Houghton, 1936.

On Moody: Henry, David. *William Vaughn Moody: A Study.* B. Humphries, 1934.
Lovett, R. M. Introduction. *Selected Poems.* Houghton, 1931.
Rev. by R. Blackmur: "Moody in Retrospect." P, 38 (Sept., 1931), 331-7.

MOORE, GEORGE. *Avowals.* Boni, 1919.
—— (ed.). *Pure Poetry: An Anthology.* Nonesuch Press, 1924; Boni, 1925.
—— *Conversations in Ebury Street.* Boni, 1924.

On Moore: Murry, J. *Wrap me up in my Aubusson Carpet.* Greenberg, 1924.

MOORE, MARIANNE (ed.). *The Dial.* (1920-1929) (See Hoffman, *The Little Magazine*)
—— "If a Man Die." H&H, 5 (Jan., 1932), 313-20. (On Conrad Aiken)
—— " 'It is Not Forbidden to Think.' " N, 142 (May 27, 1935), 680-1. (On Eliot)
—— "The Poetry of Wallace Stevens." P, 49 (Feb., 1937), 268-73. See also *Crit.,* 15 (Jan., 1936), 307-9; KR, 5 (Winter, 1943), 144-7. (On Wallace Stevens)
—— "Feeling and Precision." SeR, 52 (Autumn, 1944), 499-507.

On Moore: Blackmur, R. "The Method of Marianne Moore." *Double Agent,* 1935. Pp. 141-71.
Burke, K. "Motives and Motifs." *Accent Anthology,* 1946. Pp. 529-47.
Eliot, T. S. Introduction. *Selected Poems.* Faber & Faber; Macmillan, 1935.
Rev. by P. Rice in N, 140 (Apr. 17, 1935), 458-60; in *Crit.,* 14 (July, 1935), 697-700.
Quarterly Review of Literature: 4, No. 2 (1948). Marianne Moore Issue. (Essays by Fowlie, Ransom, Stevens)
Winters, Y. " 'Holiday and Day of Wrath.' " P, 26 (Apr., 1925), 39-44.
Zabel, M. "A Literalist of the Imagination." NR, 83 (Aug. 7, 1935), 370. See P, 47 (Mar., 1936), 326-36. Repr. in *Literary Opinions,* 1937. Pp. 426-36.

MOORE, MERRILL. (Comp.) *A Miscellany: The Fugitive, Clippings and Comment.* Privately printed, 1939.
MOORE, T. STURGE. *Armour for Aphrodite.* Richards & Toulin, 1929. (On Shelley)

On Moore: See Llewellyn Jones. See Ezra Pound. P, 6 (1915), 139-45.

MORDELL, A. (ed.). *Notorious Literary Attacks.* Boni, 1926.
MORE, PAUL ELMER. *Shelburne Essays.* 1st Series. Putnam, 1904. (11 vols: 1904-1921)
—— *With the Wits.* Houghton, 1920. (Essays on Swift, Pope, et al.)
—— *The Demon of the Absolute.* Princeton Univ. Press, 1928. ("Poe's Literary Method")

MORE, PAUL ELMER. "A Revival of Humanism." B, 71 (Mar., 1930), 1-11.
—— "Irving Babbitt." AR, 3 (Apr., 1934), 22-40. Repr. fr. UTQ, 3 (1934), 129-45.
—— *Selected Shelburne Essays.* Princeton Univ. Press; Oxford Univ. Press, 1936. ("Criticism")
—— *On Being Human.* Princeton Univ. Press, 1936. ("How to Read 'Lycidas'")

On More: See Eliot, Elliott, Matthiessen, Mercier (under Babbitt), Parkes, Sherman.

Bandler, B. "Paul Elmer More." *A Critique of Humanism,* ed. C. Grattan (1930). Pp. 281-97.
Brett, G. S. "Paul Elmer More: A Study." UTQ, 4 (Apr., 1935), 279-95.
Brown, S. G. "Paul Elmer More As Critic." SeR, 47 (Oct., 1939), 476-97.
Gregory, H. "On Paul Elmer More and His Shelburne Essays." *Acc.,* 4 (Spring, 1944), 140-9.
Morrow, Felix. "The Serpent's Enemy." *Symp.,* 1 (Apr., 1930), 168-93.
Parkes, H. B. "Paul Elmer More: Manichean." H&H, 5 (Apr., 1932), 477-83.
Shafer, Robert. *Paul Elmer More and American Criticism.* Yale Univ. Press, 1935.
Wilson, E. "Mr. More and the Mithraic Bull." NR, 91 (May 26, 1937), 64-8.
Young, M. O. *A Bibliography of Paul Elmer More.* Princeton Univ. Press, 1941.
Zabel, M. "An American Critic." P, 50 (Sept., 1937), 330-6. (Excellent)

MORRIS, BERTRAM. *Aesthetic Process.* Northwestern Univ. Press, 1943.
MORRIS, CHARLES. "Foundations of a Theory of Signs." *Encyclopedia of Unified Science.* Univ. of Chicago Press, 1938. I, No. 2.
—— "Aesthetics and the Theory of Signs." *Jour. Un. Science,* 8 (June, 1939), 131-50.
See Allen Tate in *Reason in Madness,* 1941. Pp. 20-61.
MUIR, EDWIN. *We Moderns.* Allen & Unwin, 1918; Free Lance Books, 1921.
—— "T. S. Eliot." N, 121 (Aug. 5, 1925), 162-4. Repr. in *Transition,* 1926.
—— *Transition.* Hogarth Press; Viking Press, 1926. (On Joyce, Lawrence, poetry and fiction)
Rev. by Allen Tate: "Tiresias," N, 123 (Nov. 17, 1926), 509.
—— *The Structure of the Novel.* Hogarth Press, 1928, 1947; Harcourt, 1929.
—— *The Present Age From 1914.* Cresset Press, 1939; McBride, 1940. (Bibliography)
—— *The Story and the Fable.* Harrap, 1940. (Autobiography)
—— *Essays on Literature and Society.* Hogarth Press, 1948.
MULLER, HERBERT J. *Modern Fiction.* Funk & Wagnalls, 1937.
—— "The New Criticism in Poetry." SR, 6 (Spring, 1941), 811-39. (Omnibus Review)
—— *Science and Criticism: The Humanist Tradition.* Yale Univ. Press, 1943.
—— *Thomas Wolfe.* New Directions, 1947.
MUNSON, GORHAM B. *Destinations.* Sears & Co., 1928. (American Literature survey)
—— *Style and Form in American Prose.* Doubleday, 1929.
MURRAY, GILBERT. *The Classical Tradition in Poetry.* Harvard Univ. Press, 1927.
MURRY, JOHN MIDDLETON. *Aspects of Literature.* Collins, 1920; Knopf, 1921; Cape, 1936.
—— *Countries of the Mind.* Collins; Dutton, 1922; Oxford Univ. Press, 1931, 1937.
—— *The Problem of Style.* Oxford Univ. Press, 1922.
—— *Discoveries: Essays in Literary Criticism.* Collins, 1924.
—— *Keats and Shakespeare.* Oxford Univ. Press, 1925.
—— "Towards a Synthesis." *Crit.,* 5 (May, 1927), 297-313.
See Eliot in *Crit.,* 6, 340-7.
—— *Studies in Keats.* Oxford Univ. Press, 1930. 2nd ed., 1939.
—— *D. H. Lawrence, Two Essays.* Minority Press, 1932. (See under Lawrence)
——, & MANTZ, R. *The Life of Katherine Mansfield.* Constable, 1933.

MURRY, JOHN MIDDLETON. *The Autobiography of J. M. Murry: Between Two Worlds.* Cape, 1935; Messner, 1936.
—— *Shakespeare.* Cape; Harcourt, 1936.
——, MACMURRAY, AND OTHERS. *Marxism.* Chapman & Hall, 1936.
On Murry: See Eliot, Fernandez, Rothenstein, Stoll, Swinnerton, Woolf.
Heppenstall, R. *Middleton Murry: A Study in Excellent Normality.* Cape, 1934.

NAHM, MILTON C. *Aesthetic Experience and Its Presuppositions.* Harper, 1946.
NEFF, EMERY. *A Revolution in European Poetry.* Columbia Univ. Press, 1940.
NEIDER, CHARLES (ed.). *The Stature of Thomas Mann.* New Directions, 1947.
—— *The Frozen Sea: A Study.* Oxford Univ. Press, 1948. (On Franz Kafka)
NEWBOLT, SIR H. J. *New Paths on Helicon.* Nelson, 1927.
NICOLL, A. (ed.). *Shakespeare Survey,* I. Cambridge Univ. Press, 1948. Annual.
NOYES, ALFRED. *New Essays and American Impressions.* Holt, 1927.
NUHN, FERNER. *The Wind Blew from the East.* Harper, 1942. (American literature)

O'CONNOR, WILLIAM VAN (ed.). *Forms of Modern Fiction.* Univ. of Minnesota Press, 1948. (Essays by Tate, Beach, R. P. Warren, Troy, et al.)
—— *Sense and Sensibility in Modern Poetry.* Univ. of Chicago Press, 1948.
OGDEN, C. K., & RICHARDS, I. A. *The Meaning of Meaning.* Kegan Paul; Harcourt, 1923.
—— *The Foundation of Aesthetics.* International Publishers, 1925.
OLSON, CHARLES. *Call Me Ishmael.* Oxford Univ. Press, 1947. (On Melville)
ORAGE, A. R. *Readers and Writers.* Knopf, 1922. (On Dowson, Henry James, et al.)
—— *The Art of Reading.* Farrar & Rinehart, 1930. See N, 130 (June 11, 1930), 684-6.
—— *Selected Essays and Critical Writings of A. R. Orage.* Ed. H. Read and Denis Saurat. Stanley Nott, 1935.
Rev. by F. Leavis in *Scr.,* 4 (Dec., 1935), 319.
ORTEGA Y GASSET, JOSÉ. *The Dehumanization of Art* and *Notes on the Novel.* Princeton Univ. Press, 1948.
ORWELL, GEORGE. *Dickens, Dali, and Others.* Reynal & Hitchcock, 1946.
OWEN, WILFRED.
On Owen: See H. P. Collins, Day-Lewis, Murry in *Aspects,* Spender in *Destructive Element.*
Blunden E. Notes to *The Poems of Wilfred Owen.* Viking Press, 1931.
Rev. by Y. Winters in H&H, 5 (July, 1932), 679-81.
Parsons, I. M. "The Poems of Wilfred Owen (1893-1918)." *Crit.,* 10 (July, 1931), 658-69.

PAGET, VIOLET (VERNON LEE). *The Handling of Words.* Lane; Dodd Mead, 1923.
—— *The Poet's Eye.* (Hogarth Essays No. 17) Hogarth Press, 1926.
PALMER, HERBERT. *The Mistletoe Child.* Dent, 1935. (Autobiography)
—— *Post-Victorian Poetry.* Dent, 1938. (See especially for essay on the Georgians)
PANOFSKY, E. "Style and Medium in the Motion Pictures." *Critique,* 1 (1947), 5, 18, 27-8.
PARETO, VILFREDO. *The Mind and Society.* Ed. A. Livingston. Harcourt, 1935. 4 vols.
Rev. by M. Lerner in NR, 83 (June 12, 1935), 135-7; S. Hook in N, 140 (June 26, 1935), 747-8. (Both essays are significant studies)
PARKER, DEWITT. *The Principles of Aesthetics.* Silver, 1920; Crofts, 1946. 2nd ed.
—— *The Analysis of Art.* Yale Univ. Press, 1924; Oxford Univ. Press, 1926.
PARRINGTON, VERNON. *Main Currents in American Thought.* Harcourt, 1927, 1930. 3 vols.

PARSONS, I. M. Introduction. *The Progress of Poetry: An Anthology.* Chatto & Windus, 1936.
PEACOCK, RONALD. *Hölderlin.* Methuen, 1939.
—— *The Poet in the Theatre.* Harcourt, 1946. (Essays on Eliot, Yeats, et al.)
PEPPER, S. C. *Aesthetic Quality: A Contextualist Theory.* Scribner's, 1938.
Rev. by Eliseo Vivas: "Beauty as Quality," N, 146 (Apr. 23, 1938), 480-1.
—— *The Basis of Criticism in the Arts.* Harvard Univ. Press, 1946.
PEQUY, CHARLES. *Men and Saints.* Pantheon, 1944. (Essay by Julian Green)
PEYRE, HENRI. *Writers and Their Critics.* Cornell Univ. Press, 1944.
PHILLIPS, WILLIAM, & RAHV, PHILIP (eds.). *The Partisan Reader.* Dial Press, 1946.
On Partisan Review: See M. Cowley: "Partisan Review," NR, 96 (Oct. 19, 1938), 311-2.
PLEKHANOV, GEORGE. *Art and Society.* Trans. by P. Leitner. Critics Group, 1936.
Poets At Work: Essays by W. H. Auden, Karl Shapiro, Rudolf Arnheim, Donald A. Stauffer. Introd. Charles D. Abbott. Harcourt, 1948. (On the creative process)
POLLOCK, THOMAS. *The Nature of Literature.* Princeton Univ. Press, 1942.
POTTER, STEPHEN. *The Muse in Chains.* Cape, 1937. (Compare Leavis's *Education*)
POTTLE, FREDERICK. *The Idiom of Poetry.* Cornell Univ. Press, 1942. Rev. ed., 1946.
See R. P. Warren: "Pure and Impure Poetry." KR, 5 (Spring, 1943), 228-54.
POUND, EZRA. *The Spirit of Romance.* Dutton, 1910; Dent, 1911. (See Praz)
—— "A Few Don'ts By an Imagiste." P, 1 (Mar., 1913), 200-6. (In *Make It New.*)
—— *Pavannes and Divisions.* Knopf, 1918. (See "A Retrospect")
—— *Instigations.* Boni, 1920. (Analyses of Eliot and Henry James)
Rev. by Mark Van Doren: "England's Critical Compass." N, 112 (May 4, 1921), 669-70.
—— "On Criticism in General." *Crit.*, 1 (Jan., 1923), 143-56.
—— "Small Magazines." EJ, 19 (Nov., 1930), 689-704. (Best essay on the subject)
—— *How to Read.* Harmsworth, 1931. With *The Spirit of Romance, Part I,* 1932.
See Leavis, F. *How to Teach Reading: A Primer for Ezra Pound.* Minority Press, 1933.
—— *The A. B. C. of Reading.* Routledge; Yale Univ. Press, 1934.
Rev. by K. Burke: "Gastronomy of Letters," N, 139 (Oct. 17, 1934), 458-9; H. Gregory: "The A. B. C. of Ezra Pound," P, 46 (Aug., 1935), 279-85.
—— *Make It New: Essays.* Faber & Faber, 1934; Yale Univ. Press, 1935.
Rev. by B. Dobrée in *Crit.*, 16 (Apr., 1935), 523-6; in NR, 85 (Nov. 27, 1935), 80-1.
—— *Polite Essays.* Faber; New Directions, 1937. (On Eliot, Housman, W. C. Williams)
—— *Culture.* New Directions, 1938.
Rev. by J. V. Healy: "The Pound Problem," P, 57 (Dec., 1940), 200-14.
On Pound: See Aiken, Blackmur, Bullough, Bush, Drew, Deutsch, Eliot, Hughes. Leavis, W. Lewis, Matthiessen, Monro, Monroe, Riding and Graves, Sitwell, Sparrow, Stoll, Tate, Taupin, Tillyard, Wells, Winters, Zabel.
Amdur, A. S. *The Poetry of Ezra Pound.* Oxford Univ. Press, 1936. (Pamphlet)
Bishop, J. P. "The Talk of Ezra Pound." N, 151 (Dec. 21, 1940), 637-9.
Blackmur, R. "The Masks of Ezra Pound." H&H, 7 (Jan., 1934), 177-212.
Blackmur, R. "An Adjunct to the Muses' Diadem." P, 68 (Sept., 1946), 338-47.
Bottrall, Ronald. "XXX Cantos of Ezra Pound." In *Determinations,* ed. F. R. Leavis (1933). Pp. 179-98.
Eliot, T. S. *Ezra Pound: His Metric and His Poetry.* Knopf, 1917 (Publ. anon.)
Eliot, T. S. "Isolated Superiority." *Dial,* 84 (Jan., 1928), 4-7.
Eliot, T. S. Introduction. *Ezra Pound: Selected Poems.* Faber & Gwyer, 1928.

Rev. by J. G. Fletcher in *Crit.,* 8 (Apr., 1929), 513-24.
Eliot, T. S. "Ezra Pound." P, 68 (Sept., 1946), 326-38. (A tribute)
Gregory, H. "The Search for a Frontier." NR, 75 (July 26, 1933), 292-4.
Highet, Gilbert. "Homage to Ezra Pound." N, 154 (Feb. 21, 1942), 228, 230. (Parody)
Praz, Mario. "T. S. Eliot and Dante." SR, 2 (Winter, 1937), 525-48. (Important)
Tate, Allen. "Ezra Pound's Golden Ass." N, 132 (June 10, 1931), 632-4.
Williams, W. C. "The XXX Cantos of Ezra Pound." *Symp.,* 2 (Apr., 1931), 257-63.
Yale Poetry Review: No. 6 (1947). Ezra Pound Issue. (Essay by H. H. Watts)
Yeats, W. B. *A Packet for Ezra Pound.* Dublin: Cuala Press, 1929.
Zabel, M. "Varieties of Poetic Experience." SR, 3 (Spring, 1938), 799-819.
Zukofsky, L. "The Cantos of Ezra Pound." *Crit.,* 10 (Apr., 1931), 424-40.

POWELL, DYLIS. *Descent from Parnassus.* Crescent Press, 1934. (On Eliot, Lawrence, et al.)

PRALL, D. W. *Aesthetic Judgment.* Crowell, 1929.
—— *Aesthetic Analysis.* Crowell, 1936.

PRAZ, MARIO. *The Romantic Agony.* Trans. by A. Davidson. Oxford Univ. Press, 1933.
Rev. by W. Troy: "The Romantic Agony," N, 137 (Oct. 11, 1933), 417-8.

PRESCOTT, F. C. *The Poetic Mind.* Macmillan, 1922.
—— *Poetry and Myth.* Macmillan, 1927.

PRIESTLEY, JOHN. *Figures in Modern Literature.* Lane, 1924.

PRIOR, MOODY E. *The Language of Tragedy.* Columbia Univ. Press, 1947.

PRITCHETT, V. S. *The Living Novel.* Reynal & Hitchcock, 1947.

Proletarian Literature in the United States: An Anthology. Ed. Granville Hicks and others. Introd. Jos. Freeman. International Publishers, 1935. (On M. Gold, M. Cowley, et al.)

QUENNELL, PETER. *Baudelaire and the Symbolists.* Chatto & Windus, 1929.

QUILLER-COUCH, SIR ARTHUR. *Studies in Literature.* Cambridge Univ. Press, 1933. 3rd Ser.
—— *The Poet as Citizen and Other Papers.* Cambridge Univ. Press; Macmillan, 1935.

QUINN, K., & SHATTUCK, C. (eds.). *Accent Anthology: 1940-1945.* Harcourt, 1946.

QUINTANA, RICARDO. Introduction. *Two Hundred Poems.* Longmans, 1947.

RADER, M. (ed.). *A Modern Book of Esthetics.* Holt, 1935. (Bibliography)

RAJAN, B. (ed.). *Focus Three: T. S. Eliot.* Contains C. Brooks on *The Waste Land,* E. Jones on *Ash Wednesday,* Helen Gardner on *Four Quartets,* Philip Wheelwright on Eliot's Philosophical Themes, etc., and a Checklist. *Focus Four: The Novelist as Thinker.* Dennis Dobson, 1947, 1948.

RALEIGH, WALTER. *Some Authors: Literary Essays.* Oxford Univ. Press, 1923.
—— *On Writing and Writers.* Ed. George Gordon. Arnold, 1926.

RANDALL, JOHN. *The Making of the Modern Mind.* Houghton, 1941. (Rev. ed.)

RANK, OTTO. *Art and Artist.* Trans. C. Atkinson. Knopf, 1932.
Rev. by J. Krutch: "What Is Art?" N, 135 (Dec. 7, 1932), 569-70.

RANSOM, JOHN CROWE. *God Without Thunder.* Harcourt, 1930.
—— "The Aesthetic of Regionalism." AR, 2 (Jan., 1934), 290-310.
—— "Characters and Character." AR, 6 (Jan., 1936), 271-88. (On the novel)
—— "Mr. Empson's Muddles." SR, 4 (Autumn, 1938), 322-39.
—— *The World's Body.* Scribner's, 1938. (On Milton, Millay, Richards, et al.)
—— "Yeats and His Symbols." KR, 1 (Summer, 1939), 309-22.
—— "Honey and Gall." SR, 6 (Summer, 1940), 2-19. (On Hardy and Housman)
—— "The Pragmatics of Art." KR, 2 (Winter, 1940), 76-87. (Significant item)

RANSOM, JOHN CROWE. "The Irish, the Gaelic, the Byzantine." SR, 7 (Winter, 1942), 517-46. (Yeats)
—— "Criticism as Pure Speculation." *Intent of Critic,* ed. D. Stauffer (1941).
—— *The New Criticism.* New Directions, 1941. (On Richards, Eliot, Winters)
—— "Poetry: The Formal Analysis." KR, 9 (Summer, 1947), 436-56. (On Brooks' *Urn*)
—— "Poetry: The Final Cause." KR, 9 (Autumn, 1947), 640-58.
—— "The Literary Criticism of Aristotle." KR, 10 (Summer, 1948), 382-402.

On Ransom: See C. Brooks, V. W. Brooks, Deutsch, Drew, Gregory, Heyl, Hoffman, Kazin, Kreymborg, Monroe, Muller, Riding, Stauffer, Tate, Untermeyer, Wells, Wilder, Williamson, Winters, C. & M. Van Doren.

Burgum, E. B. "John Crowe Ransom." RMR, 8 (Spring, 1944), 87-93.
Roellinger, F. "Two Theories of Poetry as Knowledge." SR, 7 (Spring, 1942), 690-705.
Schwartz, D. "Instructed of Much Mortality." SeR, 54 (Summer, 1946), 438-48.
Sewanee Review: 56 (Summer, 1948). Dedicated to Ransom. Essays by Brooks, Jarrell, Stauffer, Van O'Connor, Eliseo Vivas, et al.
Stallman, R. W. "The New Criticism." *A Southern Vanguard,* ed. A. Tate. Prentice-Hall, 1947. Pp. 28-51.
Stallman, R. W. "John Crowe Ransom: A Checklist." SeR, 56 (Summer, 1948).
Stauffer, D. "Critical Principles and a Sonnet." AS, 12 (Winter, 1942), 52-62.
Trowbridge, H. "Aristotle and the 'New Criticism.'" SeR, 52 (Autumn, 1944), 537-55.
See Ransom's rejoinder: "The Bases of Criticism." SeR, 52 (Autumn, 1944), 556-71.
Warren, R. P. "A Note on Three Southern Poets." P, 40 (May, 1932), 103-13.
Warren, R. P. "John Crowe Ransom." VQR, 11 (Jan., 1935), 93-112.
Winters, Yvor. "John Crowe Ransom." *The Anatomy of Nonsense,* 1943. Pp. 168-228.

READ, HERBERT (ed). *Speculations, by T. E. Hulme.* Kegan Paul; Harcourt, 1924; 1936.
—— "Psycho-Analysis and the Critic." *Crit.,* 3 (Jan., 1925), 214-30.
—— *Reason and Romanticism: Essays in Literary Criticism.* Faber & Gwyer, 1926.
Rev. by T. S. Eliot in *Crit.,* 4 (Oct., 1926), 750-7.
—— *In Retreat.* Hogarth Press, 1925. (Autobiography)
—— *Phases of English Poetry.* Hogarth Press, 1928; Harcourt, 1929.
Rev. by T. Spencer in H&H, 2 (July, 1929), 447-9. (Also on W. P. Ker)
—— *English Prose Style.* Bell, 1928. (On metaphor, imagery, tradition)
—— *The Sense of Glory.* Cambridge Univ. Press; Harcourt, 1929. (On Henry James, et al.)
Rev. by F. C. Flint in *Symp.,* 1 (Apr., 1930), 276-9.
—— "Tolstoy's Theory of Art." *The Listener,* Apr. 2, 1930, 592.
—— "The Form of Modern Poetry." *Symp.,* 1 (July, 1930), 293-309.
—— *Wordsworth.* Cape, 1930; Harrison Smith, 1931.
Rev. by H. Gregory: "Wordsworth: An Evaluation," NR, 67 (May 20, 1931), 25-6.
—— *The Meaning of Art.* Faber & Faber, 1931.
—— *The Anatomy of Art.* Dodd Mead, 1932.
—— *Form in Modern Poetry.* Sheed & Ward, 1932.
Rev. by James Smith in *Scr.,* 1 (Mar., 1932), 393-6.
—— "Poetry and Belief in Gerard Manley Hopkins." NV, No. 1 (Jan., 1933). 11-5.
—— "Surrealism and the Romantic Principle." In *Surrealism.* Faber & Faber, 1936.
—— (comp.) *Essays and Studies,* 21 (1935). Clarendon Press, English Association essays: Eliot on Milton, W. H. Gardner on Hopkins, C. S. Lewis, and Tillyard.

READ, HERBERT. *In Defense of Shelley and Other Essays.* Heinemann, 1936.
Rev. by M. Roberts in *Spec.*, 156 (Feb. 28, 1936), 358; W. H. Auden in NV, No. 20 (Apr., 1936), 22-4; Hugh Porteus in *Crit.*, 15 (July, 1936), 724-30.
—— *Five on Revolutionary Art.* Wishart, 1936. (Towards Marxist art criticism)
—— *Art and Society.* Heinemann; Macmillan, 1937.
—— *Collected Essays in Literary Criticism.* Faber & Faber, 1938.
—— *Poetry and Anarchism.* Faber & Faber, 1938.
Rev. by A. Tate: "The Poetry of the Will," NR, 100 (Aug. 6, 1939), 52-3; A. Mizener in SR, 5 (Autumn, 1939), 376-400; cf. Burke in KR, 1 (Summer, 1939), 272-82.
—— "The Present State of Poetry." KR, 1 (Autumn, 1939), 359-69.
—— *Annals of Innocence and Experience.* Faber & Faber, 1940, 1947. (Autobiography)
—— "Coleridge as Critic." SeR, 56 (Autumn, 1948), 597-624.

On Read: See Eliot, Muir, Muller, Murry, Savage, L. P. Smith, Sparrow, Vines.
Blackmur, R. "The Criticism of Herbert Read." *Larus,* 1 (Apr., 1928), 45-58.
Greene, Graham. "Herbert Read." *Hor.*, 3 (Mar., 1941), 213-8.
Häusermann, H. "The Development of Herbert Read." *Herbert Read,* ed. H. Treece (1944).
Ramsay, A. "Psychology and Literary Criticism." *Crit.*, 15 (July, 1936), 627-43.
Treece, Henry. *Herbert Read: An Introduction to His Work by Various Hands.* Faber & Faber, 1944. (Select Bibliography, pp. 116-20)

REID, LOUIS. *A Study in Aesthetics.* Macmillan, 1931.
REINHARDT, K. "Basic Principles in Literary History." JEGP, 30 (July, 1931), 385-91.
RICE, P. B. "Paul Valéry." *Symp.*, 1 (Apr., 1930), 206-20. In *Literary Opinion,* ed. M. D. Zabel. Harper, 1937. Pp. 455-66.
—— "A Modern Poet's Technique: Guillaume Apollinaire." *Symp.*, 2 (Oct., 1931), 468-83.
—— "Subtle Artificer." (Robert Fitzgerald) N, 142 (Feb. 9, 1936), 222-8.
See J. Krutch: "On the Difficulty of Modern Poetry." N, 142 (Mar. 4, 1936), 283-4.
—— "George Santayana: The Philosopher as Poet." KR, 5 (Autumn, 1940), 460-75.
—— "Thomas Mann and the Religious Revival." KR, 7 (Summer, 1945), 361-77.
RICHARDS, I. A. *Principles of Literary Criticism.* Kegan Paul, 1924; Harcourt, 1925, 1929. 5th ed., 1934. Re-issued 1938, 1948.
Rev. by E. Rickword in CML, 1 (Apr., 1925), 164-6; H. Read in *Crit.*, 3 (Apr., 1925), 444-9; Edwin Muir in SRL, 1 (June 6, 1925), 807. See K. Burke in *Permanence and Change,* 1935. P. 320 ff.
—— OGDEN, C. K., & WOOD, JAMES. *The Foundations of Aesthetics.* Allen & Unwin, 1922; International Publishers, 1925; Lear, 1948. (2nd ed., rev.)
Rev. by V. Calverton: "Aesthetics," SRL, 2 (Jan. 2, 1926), 464.
——, & OGDEN, C. K. *The Meaning of Meaning.* Harcourt, 1923, 1925, 1936.
—— "Gerard Hopkins." *Dial,* 81 (Sept., 1926), 195-203.
—— *Science and Poetry.* Kegan Paul; Norton, 1926.
See A. Tate: "Revolt Against Literature," NR, 44 (Feb. 9, 1927), 329-30; Eliot: "Literature, Science, and Dogma," *Dial,* 82 (Mar., 1927), 239-43.
—— *Practical Criticism: A Study of Literary Judgment.* Kegan Paul; Harcourt, 1929. 2nd ed., 1930.
Rev. by J. G. Fletcher in *Crit.*, 9 (Oct., 1929), 162-4; A. Tate: "Poetry in the Laboratory," NR, 61 (Dec. 18, 1929), 111-3; J. Burnham in *Symp.*, 1 (Jan., 1930), 115-24; R. Blackmur in H&H, 3 (Apr., 1930), 451-3.
—— *Mencius on the Mind.* Kegan Paul, 1932.
Rev. by K. Burke: "The Technique of Listening," N, 136 (Apr. 12, 1933), 416.
—— "Lawrence as a Poet." NV, No. 1 (Jan., 1933), 15-7.

RICHARDS, I. A. *Coleridge on Imagination.* Kegan Paul, 1934; Harcourt, 1935.
Rev. by F. Leavis: "Dr. Richards, Bentham and Coleridge," *Scr.,* 3 (Mar., 1935), 382-402; cf. Empson in *Scr.,* 4 (June, 1935), 65-7; W. Empson in *Crit.,* 14 (Apr., 1935), 482-85; R. Blackmur: "The Imagination Crowned," N, 140 (Apr. 10, 1935), 423-4; C. Brooks: "The Poet's Fancy," NR, 85 (Nov. 13, 1935), 26-7.
—— *The Philosophy of Rhetoric.* Oxford Univ. Press, 1936.
Rev. by F. Leavis in *Scr.,* 6 (Sept., 1937), 211-7; W. Empson in *Crit.,* 17 (Oct., 1937), 127-9; A. Warren in SeR, 46 (Apr., 1938), 213-22.
—— *Interpretation in Teaching.* Harcourt, 1938; Kegan Paul, 1939.
—— *How to Read a Page.* Norton, 1942.
Rev. by E. Olson in MP, 40 (Feb., 1943), 275-83. (Reviews also *Language of Poetry*)
—— "The Interaction of Words." *The Language of Poetry,* ed. A. Tate. Princeton Univ. Press, 1942.
—— "*Troilus and Cressida* and Plato." HR, 1 (Autumn, 1948), 362-76.
On Richards: See Barfield, Belgion, Blackmur, Bodkin, Bronowski, C. Brooks, Burke, Eastman, Eliot, Empson, Fausset, D. G. James, F. R. Leavis, C. S. Lewis, Day Lewis, Muir, Murry, Pollock, Ransom, Read, Riding & Graves, M. Roberts, Scott-James, Spender, Stoll, Tate, Urban, Vines, Wheelwright.
Belgion, M. "What Is Criticism?" *Crit.,* 10 (Oct., 1930), 118-39; reply by Richards: "The Practice of Interpretation," *Crit.,* 10 (Apr., 1931), 410-20; cf. Bronowski in *Crit.,* 11 (Jan., 1932), 322-4; cf. Tate in NR, 70 (Mar. 16, 1932), 133.
Bentley, Eric. "The Early I. A. Richards." RMR, 8 (Winter, 1944), 29-36.
Bethell, S. "Suggestions Towards a Theory of Value." *Crit.,* 15 (Jan., 1935), 239-50.
Eliot, T. S. "The Modern Mind." *The Use of Poetry,* 1933. Pp. 124-37.
Hamilton, G. R. *Poetry and Contemplation.* Cambridge Univ. Press, 1938.
Harding, D. W. "I. A. Richards." *Scr.,* 1 (Mar., 1933), 327-38. (Excellent)
James, D. G. *Scepticism and Poetry.* Allen & Unwin, 1937. (Important)
Ong, W. "The Meaning of the New Criticism." *Mod. Sch.,* 20 (May, 1943), 192-209.
Phillips, W. "Categories for Criticism." *Symp.,* 4 (Jan., 1933), 31-47.
Pollock, T. C. "A Critique of I. A. Richards' Theory of Language and Literature." In *A Theory of Meaning Analyzed.* Institute of General Semantics. Chicago, 1942. Pp. 1-25.
Spaulding, J. G. "Richards' Theory of Poetic Value." In *A Theory of Meaning Analyzed.* Institute of General Semantics, 1942. Pp. 26-35.
Urban, W. T. *Language and Reality.* Macmillan, 1941. (Cf. C. Brooks in *Urn*)
RICKWORD, C. H. "A Note on Fiction." *Towards Standards,* ed. F. R. Leavis (1933). Repr. in *Forms of Modern Fiction,* ed. W. Van O'Connor. Univ. of Minn. Press, 1948. Pp. 294-305. In CML, 2 (July, 1926).
RICKWORD, EDGELL. *Rimbaud: the Boy and the Poet.* Heinemann; Knopf, 1924.
—— (ed.). *Scrutinies,* by Various Hands. Wishart, 1928, 1931. 2 Series. II: Essays on the Poetry of Eliot, by Alec Brown; on Eliot's critical method, by B. Higgins; "Wyndham Lewis," by E. Rickword; "Virginia Woolf," by W. Empson.
—— "The Use of 'Negative' Emotions." *Towards Standards,* ed. F. Leavis (1933). Pp. 71-8. In CML, 1 (May, 1925), 236-41.
RIDING, L., & GRAVES, R. *A Survey of Modernist Poetry.* Heinemann, 1927; Doran, 1928.
RIDING, LAURA. *Contemporaries and Snobs.* Doubleday, 1928. (On Hulme, Stein)
—— "Poems and Poets." *Epilogue,* ed. Laura Riding. 1 (Autumn, 1935).
—— Foreword. *The Collected Poems of Laura Riding.* Random, 1939.
Rev. by M. Zabel in SR, 5 (Winter, 1940), 568-608. See Blackmur in *Expense.*
RIDLEY, M. R. *Poetry and the Ordinary Reader.* Dutton, 1939.

RILKE, RAINER MARIA. *Notebooks of Malte Laurids Brigge.* Hogarth Press, 1930.
—— *The Journal of My Other Self.* Trans. J. Linton. Norton, 1930. (Autobiography)
—— *Letters to a Young Poet.* Trans. M. D. Norton. Norton, 1934.
—— *Wartime Letters: 1914-1921.* Trans. M. D. Norton. Norton, 1940.
Rev. by W. H. Auden: "Poet in Wartime." NR, 103 (July 8, 1940), 59-60.
On Rilke: Bowra, C. M. *The Heritage of Symbolism.* Macmillan, 1943. Pp. 56-97.
Butler, E. M. *Rainer Maria Rilke.* Cambridge Univ. Press; Macmillan, 1941.
Rev. by P. Horton in KR, 3 (Summer, 1941), 516-9; in *Scr.*, 10 (Jan., 1942), 298-304.
Mason, Eudo C. *Rilke's Apotheosis.* Basil Blackwell, 1938.
Pickman, H. "Rainer Maria Rilke." H&H, 4 (Spring & Summer, 1931), 325-65; 512-55.
Rose, W., & Houston, G. (eds.). *Rainer Maria Rilke: Aspects of His Mind and Poetry.* Introd. by Stefan Zweig. Sidgwick & Jackson, 1938.
ROBERTS, MICHAEL. "Notes on English Poets," P, 39 (Feb., 1932), 271-9. (On belief)
—— "The Categories of T. E. Hulme." *Crit.*, 11 (Apr., 1932), 375-85.
—— Preface. *New Signatures.* Hogarth Press, 1932. (Anthology: Auden, Day Lewis, Spender)
—— (ed.). *New Country: Prose and Poetry by Various Authors.* Hogarth Press, 1933.
—— *Critique of Poetry.* Cape, 1934. (On critic's function, symbolism, pure poetry, etc.)
—— (ed.). *The Faber Book of Modern Verse.* Faber & Faber, 1936.
—— *The Modern Mind.* Faber & Faber, 1937.
—— *T. E. Hulme.* Faber & Faber, 1938.
—— "The Critic and the Public." SR, 4 (Autumn, 1938), 368-81.
ROBERTSON, RT. HON. J. M. "On Criticism." *Crit.*, 4 (Apr., 1926), 244-61.
ROBINSON, EDWIN ARLINGTON. *Selected Letters.* Comp. R. Torrence. Macmillan, 1940.
On Robinson: See Blackmur, Brenner, V. W. Brooks, Drinkwater, *Explicator*, Gregory, Hicks, L. James, Kreymborg, Lewisohn, Lowell, Monroe, Munson, Squire, Tate, Ward, Wells, Whipple, Winters, C. Wood, C. & M. Van Doren, Untermeyer.
Bates, W. *Edwin Arlington Robinson and His Manuscripts.* Colby College Libr., 1944.
Brown, R. Walter. *Next Door to a Poet.* Appleton-Century, 1937.
Cestre, C. *An Introduction to Edwin Arlington Robinson.* Macmillan, 1930.
Hagedorn, H. *Edwin Arlington Robinson.* Macmillan, 1938.
Hogan, C. B. *A Bibliography of Edwin Arlington Robinson.* Yale Univ. Press, 1936.
Hudson, Hoyt. "Robinson and Praed," P, 41 (Feb., 1943), 612-20.
Kaplan, Estelle. *Philosophy in the Poetry of E. A. Robinson.* Columbia Univ. Press, 1940.
Richards, L. E. *Edwin Arlington Robinson.* Harvard Univ. Press, 1931.
Van Doren, Mark. *Edwin Arlington Robinson.* Literary Guild, 1927.
Waggoner, H. H. "E. A. Robinson and the Cosmic Chill." NEQ, 13 (Mar., 1940), 65-84.
Winters, Yvor. *Edwin Arlington Robinson.* New Directions, 1946. (Important)
Zabel, M. D. "Robinson." In *Literary Opinion* (1937). Pp. 397-406.
ROSENBERG, HAROLD. "Myth and Poem." *Symp.*, 2 (Apr., 1931), 179-91. (Freud and myth)

ROSENFELD, PAUL. *Port of New York. Essays on 14 American Moderns.* Harcourt, 1924.
—— *Men Seen.* Dial Press, 1925. (Critical Essays on Stevens, Lawrence, et al.)
On Rosenfeld: Mellquist, J., & Wiese, L. (eds.). *Paul Rosenfeld.* Creative Age Press, 1948.
ROTHENSTEIN, WILLIAM. *Men and Memories, 1910-1922.* McCann, 1932.
—— *Since Fifty: Men and Memories, 1922-1938.* Macmillan, 1940.
ROURKE, CONSTANCE. *American Humor: A Study of the National Character.* Harcourt, 1931.
ROUTH, H. V. *Towards the Twentieth Century.* Macmillan; Cambridge Univ. Press, 1937.
RUNES, D., & SHRICK, E. (eds.). *Encyclopedia of the Arts.* Philosophical Library, 1946.
RUSSELL, B. *An Inquiry into Meaning and Truth.* Norton, 1940.
RUSSELL, GEORGE W. ("A. E.") *Song and Its Fountains* by A. E. Macmillan, 1932.
—— *The Living Torch.* Macmillan, 1937. (Selections from his criticism)
On Russell: Eglinton, J. *A Memoir of A. E.* Macmillan, 1938.
Rev. by P. Colum in NR, 94 (Mar. 30, 1938), 228-9.
Figgis, D. *A. E.: a Study of a Man and a Nation.* Maunsel, 1916.
RYLANDS, GEORGE. *Words and Poetry.* Introduction by L. Strachey. Hogarth Press, 1928. (Useful)

SAINTSBURY, GEORGE. *The Collected Essays: 1875-1920.* Dent; Dutton, 1923-24. 4 vols.
—— *Prefaces and Essays.* Macmillan, 1933.
—— *A Saintsbury Miscellany.* Oxford Univ. Press, 1947. (With portraits by Grierson, et al.)
SAMPSON, GEORGE. *The Concise Cambridge History of English Literature.* Macmillan, 1941.
SANDBURG, CARL. See Aiken, Blackmur, Brenner, Cowley, Deutsch, *Explicator,* Kreymborg, Lowell, MacLeish, Monroe, Rosenfeld, Untermeyer, Van Doren, Whipple, Zabel.
SANTAYANA, GEORGE. *Little Essays.* Ed. L. P. Smith. Scribner's, 1920, 1934.
—— *Winds of Doctrine: Studies in Contemporary Opinion.* Dent, 1913; Scribner's, 1926.
—— *Three Philosophical Poets.* Harvard Univ. Press, 1927.
—— *The Genteel Tradition at Bay.* Scribner's, 1931.
—— *Obiter Dicta.* Ed. J. Buchler and B. Schwartz. Scribner's, 1935. ("What is Aesthetics")
—— *Persons and Places: The Background of my Life.* Scribner's, 1944.
On Santayana: See Backmur, MacCarthy, Oras (on Eliot), Ransom, P. B. Rice.
Howgate, G. W. *George Santayana.* Univ. of Penn. Press, 1939.
Leavis, Q. D. "The Critical Writings of George Santayana." *Scr.,* 4 (Dec., 1935), 278-95.
SASSOON, SIGFRIED. Introduction. *Poems,* by Wilfred Owen. Huebsch, 1921.
—— *The Old Century and Seven More Years.* Faber & Faber, 1938. (Autobiography)
—— *On Poetry.* Arrowsmith, 1939.
—— *The Weald of Youth.* Viking Press, 1942. (Biography of his youth)
On Sassoon: Blunden, E. *The Mind's Eye: Essays.* Cape, 1934.
SAURAT, DENIS. *Milton, Man and Thinker.* Cape, 1925.
—— *Blake and Modern Thought.* Constable, 1929.
SAVAGE, D. S. *The Personal Principle: Studies in Modern Poetry.* Routledge, 1944.
—— "E. M. Forster." WR, 10 (Summer, 1946), 190-204.
—— "Ernest Hemingway." HR, 1 (Autumn, 1948), 380-401.

SCARFE, FRANCIS. *Auden and After: The Liberation of Poetry: 1930-1941.* Routledge, 1942.

SCHACK, W. "A Critique of Art Criticism." VQR, 18 (Winter, 1942), 93-109.

SCHELLING, FELIX. *Appraisements and Asperities.* Lippincott, 1922. (Masefield, et al.)

SCHNEIDER, ELIZABETH. *Aesthetic Motive.* Macmillan, 1939.

SCHOEN, MAX (ed.). *The Enjoyment of the Arts.* Philosophical Library, 1944. (Daiches, et al.)

SCHORER, MARK. *William Blake: The Politics of Vision.* Holt, 1946.

—— (co-ed.). *Criticism: The Foundations of Modern Literary Judgment.* Harcourt, 1948. (Anthology: "Aristotle to Wimsatt")

SCHUCKING, LEVIN L. *The Sociology of Literary Taste.* Oxford Univ. Press, 1944.

SCHWARTZ, DELMORE. See under Auden, Blackmur, Eliot, Jeffers, Millay, Ransom, Tate, Edmund Wilson, Winters, Yeats.

—— "John Dos Passos . . ." SR, 4 (Autumn, 1938), 351-67.

—— Introduction. . *A Season in Hell* by Arthur Rimbaud. New Directions, 1939.

—— "Poetry and Belief in Thomas Hardy." SR, 6 (Summer, 1940), 64-77.

—— "The Isolation of Modern Poetry." KR, 3 (Spring, 1941), 209-20.

—— "Anywhere Out of the World." N, 157 (July 24, 1943), 102-3. (Eliot's *Four Quartets*)

On Schwartz: O'Donnell, G. "Delmore Schwartz's Achievement." P, 54 (May, 1939), 105-8.

SCOTT-JAMES, R. *The Making of Literature: Some Principles of Criticism.* Secker & Warburg, 1938.

SEDGWICK, W. E. *Herman Melville: The Tragedy of Mind.* Harvard Univ. Press, 1945.

DE SÉLINCOURT, E. *Oxford Lectures on Poetry.* Clarendon Press, 1934.

SHANKAR, SHAWANI. *Modern English Poetry.* Student's Friends, 1937.

SHANKS, EDWARD. *Baudelaire: Flesh and Spirit.* Little, Brown, 1930.

SHAPIRO, KARL. *Essay on Rime.* Reynal & Hitchcock, 1945.

—— "English Prosody and Modern Poetry." ELH, 14 (June, 1947), 77-92.

—— "A Farewell to Criticism." P, 71 (Jan., 1948), 196-217. See P, 71 (Feb., 1948), 257-9.

—— "The Meaning of the Discarded Poem." *Poets at Work.* Harcourt, 1948. Pp. 83-121.

SHAW, BERNARD. *Portraits and Reviews.* Constable, 1931.

SHERMAN, STUART P. *Americans.* Scribner's, 1922.

—— *The Main Stream.* Scribner's, 1927. (Sandburg, P. E. More, et al.)

On Sherman: *The Life and Letters.* By J. Zeitlin & H. Woodbridge. Farrar, 1929.

Rev. by F. Matthiessen: "Sherman and Huneker," NR, 61 (Dec. 18, 1929), 113-4, 115.

SHIPLEY, JOSEPH T. *The Quest for Literature: A Survey of Literary Criticism.* Smith, 1931.

—— (ed.). *Dictionary of World Literature.* Philosophical Library, 1943.

—— (ed.). *Encyclopedia of Literature.* Philosophical Library, 1946.

SITWELL, EDITH. (See under Armstrong)

—— "Experiment in Poetry." *Tradition and Experiment.* Oxford Univ. Press, 1929. Pp. 74-97.

—— *Alexander Pope.* Faber & Faber; Cosmopolitan Book Corporation, 1930.

Rev. by C. Aiken: "Edith Sitwell's Pope," NR, 62 (May 14, 1930), 358-9.

—— (ed.). *The Pleasures of Poetry.* Norton, 1934. 3 vols. (Anthology)

—— *Aspects of Poetry.* Duckworth, 1934. (On Eliot, Hopkins, Leavis, Pound, Sparrow, Yeats)

—— *Selected Poems: With an Essay on Her Own Poetry.* Duckworth, 1936; Houghton, 1937.

Rev. by P. Horton in NR, 91 (Aug. 4, 1937), 369-70; in P, 50 (June, 1937), 161-4.
SITWELL, EDITH. "Three Eras of Modern Poetry." In *Trio,* by Edith, Osbert, & Sacheverell Sitwell. Macmillan, 1938. Pp. 97-139, 143-187. (On Whitman, Housman, the Georgians, et al.)
—— "Lecture on Poetry Since 1920." L&L, 39 (Nov., 1943), 70-97.
—— *A Poet's Notebook.* Macmillan, 1943. (On Chaucer, Shakespeare, Wordsworth, Hopkins, et al.)

On Sitwell: See Bullough, Monro, Muir, Powell, Riding & Graves, Sparrow, Gertrude Stein, Wells, Williams.

A Celebration for Edith Sitwell. Ed. José Garcia Villa. New Directions, 1948. (Essays by Spender, Bowra, Gregory, et al.)
Lewis, Wyndham. *The Apes of God.* 1930. McBride, 1931.
Little, A. "The Approach to Criticism." *Studies,* 32 (June, 1943), 186-96.
Mégroz, R. *The Three Sitwells: A Biographical and Critical Study.* Richards Press, 1927.
Muir, Edwin. "Edith Sitwell." N, 120 (Apr. 15, 1925), 426-7.
Vines, S. "The Three Sitwells." *Scrutinies,* ed. E. Rickword. Wishart, 1931. II. Pp. 164-82.

SLOCHOWER, H. *No Voice Is Wholly Lost.* Creative Age Press, 1945.
SMITH, BERNARD. *Forces in American Criticism.* Harcourt, 1939. (Marxist criticism)
Rev. by M. Cohen in JHI, 1 (Apr., 1940), 240-51; Zabel in N, 149 (Oct. 7, 1939), 381-2.
SMITH, CHARD POWERS *Pattern and Variation in Poetry.* Scribner's, 1932. (On aesthetics)
—— *Annals of the Poets.* Scribner's, 1935. (Biographical data)
SMITH, D. N. *Some Observations on Eighteenth Century Poetry.* Oxford Univ. Press, 1937.
See *Essays on the 18th Century Presented to David Nichol Smith.* Clarendon Press, 1945.
SMITH, GREGORY. *Ben Jonson.* Macmillan, 1920.
SMITH, JAMES. "On Metaphysical Poetry." *Scr.,* 2 (Dec., 1933), 222-39.
—— "Burns." *Scr.,* 2 (Mar., 1934), 334-47.
—— "Wordsworth: A Preliminary Survey." *Scr.,* 7 (June, 1938), 33-35.
—— "Baudelaire." *Scr.,* 7 (Sept., 1938), 145-66. (Compare Turnell's essay)
—— "Marlowe's 'Dr. Faustus.'" *Scr.,* 8 (June, 1939), 36-55.
—— "The Tragedy of Blood." (Webster) *Scr.,* 8 (Dec., 1939), 265-80.
—— "'As You Like It.'" *Scr.,* 9 (June, 1940), 9-32. (Technical criticism)
—— "'Much Ado About Nothing.'" *Scr.,* 13 (Spring, 1946), 242-57.
SMITH, LOGAN PEARSALL. *Words and Idioms.* Constable, 1925. (Repr. *Four Words,* 1924)
—— *On Reading Shakespeare.* Harcourt; Constable, 1933. (Interpretations)
—— *All Trivia: Trivia, More Trivia, etc.* Harcourt, 1934. (*Trivia,* 1st ed., 1917)
—— *Reperusals and Re-Collections.* Constable, 1936. (Vs. Read and J. M. Murry)
—— *Unforgotten Years.* Constable, 1938; Little, Brown, 1939.
—— *Milton and His Modern Critics.* Oxford Univ. Press, 1940; Little, Brown, 1941. (Eliot)
SMITH, S. STEPHENSON. *The Craft of the Critic.* Crowell, 1931.
SNELL, GEORGE. *The Shapers of American Fiction.* Dutton, 1947.
SONNENSCHEIN, E. A. *What Is Rhythm?* Oxford Univ. Press, 1925.
SOUTHWORTH, J. G. *Sowing the Spring: Studies in British Poets.* Blackwell, 1940.
SPARROW, JOHN. *Sense and Poetry.* Constable; Yale Univ. Press, 1934.
Rev. in *Scr.,* 2 (Mar., 1934), 141-9; in SR, 6 (Spring, 1941), 811-39.
SPEARS, M. K. "The Meaning of Matthew Prior's *Alma.*" ELH, 13 (Dec., 1946), 266-90.
SPEIRS, JOHN. *The Scots Literary Tradition.* Chatto & Windus, 1940.

SPIERS, JON. "Chaucer." *Scr.,* 11 (Dec., 1942; Spring, 1943), 84-108; 189-211; 12 (Winter, 1943), 35-57.
SPENCER, T. (ed.). *A Garland for John Donne.* Harvard Univ. Press, 1931.
—— "The Critic's Function." SeR, 47 (Oct., 1939), 552-8.
—— "The Central Problem in Literary Criticism." CE, 4 (1942), 159-63.
—— "How to Criticize a Poem." NR, 109 (Dec. 6, 1943), 816-8. (Parody)
—— *Shakespeare and the Nature of Man.* Macmillan, 1942.
SPENDER, STEPHEN. "The Artistic Future of Poetry." NR, 88 (Apr. 18, 1934), 268-70.
—— *The Destructive Element.* Cape, 1935; Houghton, 1936. (On Eliot, James, Yeats, et al.)
Rev. by G. Stone in AR, 6 (Feb., 1936), 506-12; Krutch in N, 142 (Mar. 18, 1936), 352-3.
—— "Keats and Shelley." *From Anne to Victoria,* ed. B. Dobrée. Cassell, 1937. Pp. 574-87.
—— "The Creative Imagination in the World To-day." *Folios of New Writing: 1940.* Hogarth Press, 1940. (Compare Pound on the poet's function in *How to Read*)
——, & GILI, J. L. (Trans.) *Poems, by F. Garcia Lorca.* Oxford Univ. Press, 1940.
—— "The Year's Poetry: 1940." "Poetry in 1941." *Hor.,* 3 (1941), 138-49; 5 (1942), 96-111.
—— *Life and the Poet.* Secker & Warburg, 1942. (The poet in modern society)
—— "Modern Writers in the World of Necessity." PaR, 12 (Summer, 1945), 352-60.
—— "The Making of a Poem." PaR, 13 (Summer, 1946), 294-308. (Significant)
On Spender: See Bullough, Daiches, Lind, Scarfe, Southworth.
Flint, F. C. "New Leaders in English Poetry." VQR, 14 (Summer, 1938), 502-18.
Lehman, J. "Revolutionary Trends in English Poetry." *Internat'l. Lit.,* 4 (1936), 60-83.
Mayberry, George. "Objects of Contemplation." NR, 116 (Mar. 3, 1947), 33-4.
Tate, Allen. "A New Artist." NV, 3 (May, 1933), 21-3. (On belief)
Zabel, M. "The Purpose of Stephen Spender." P, 45 (Jan., 1935), 208-13.
SPENGLER, OSWALD. *The Decline of the West.* Knopf, 1926; Allen & Unwin, 1930. 2 vols.
Rev. by Tate in N, 122 (May 12, 1926), 532-4; Burke in *Dial,* 81 (Sept., 1926), 242-8.
On Spengler: Pringle-Pattison, A. "The Philosophy of History." *Proc. Brit. Academy,* 8 (1933). Oxford Univ. Press, 1933. (A refutation)
SPINGARN, J. E. (ed.) *Criticism in America.* Harcourt, 1924. (Anthology)
—— "The New Criticism." In *The New Criticism,* ed. E. Burgum. Prentice-Hall, 1930. Pp. 3-25.
—— *Creative Criticism.* Harcourt, 1931. Rev. ed.; 1st ed., 1917.
SPITZER, LEO. *Linguistics and Literary History.* Princeton Univ. Press, 1948.
SPURGEON, CAROLINE. *Leading Motives in the Imagery of Shakespeare's Tragedies.* Oxford Univ. Press, 1930.
See *Symp.,* 2 (Apr., 1931), 242-52.
—— *Shakespeare's Imagery and What It Tells Us.* Cambridge Univ. Press; Macmillan, 1935.
Rev. by M. Zabel in MP, 34 (Aug., 1936), 78-83. See Hyman's *The Armed Vision* (1948).
SQUIRE, SIR JOHN C. *Books Reviewed.* Doran, 1922. (De la Mare, Gosse's criticism)
—— *Essays on Poetry.* Doran; Hodder & Stoughton, 1923. (On Bridges, Yeats, et al.)
—— *Contemporary American Authors.* Holt, 1928.
—— *The Honeysuckle and the Bee.* Heinemann, 1937. (Autobiography)
STALLMAN, R. W. *"Bibliography of A. E. Housman."* PMLA, 55 (June, 1945), 463-502.

STALLMAN, R. W. "Keats the Apollinian." UTQ, 16 (Jan., 1947), 143-56.
—— "The New Criticism and the Southern Critics." *A Southern Vanguard,* ed. A. Tate. Prentice-Hall, 1947. Pp. 28-51.
—— "Life, Art, and 'The Secret Sharer.'" *Forms of Modern Fiction,* ed. W. Van O'Connor. Univ. of Minn. Press, 1948. Pp. 229-42.
—— "A Note on Intentions." CE, 10 (Oct., 1948), 40-1.
—— *The Critics' Notebook.* Foreword by R. P. Warren. Univ. of Minn. Press; Oxford Univ. Press, 1949.
——, & WEST, RAY B., JR. *The Art of Modern Fiction.* Rinehart, 1949.
STARKIE, ENID. *Baudelaire.* Putnam, 1933.
—— *Rimbaud in Abyssinia.* Oxford Univ. Press, 1937.
—— *Arthur Rimbaud.* Faber & Faber, 1938. Rev. ed., 1947.
Rev. by Turnell in *Scr.,* 7 (Sept., 1938), 220-3; Zabel in PaR, 7 (July, 1940), 268-82.
"The State of American Writing: A Symposium." PaR, 15 (Aug., 1948). (By Blackmur, Fiedler, Stevens, L. Trilling, et al.)
STAUFFER, DONALD A. (ed.). *The Intent of the Critic.* By E. Wilson, Foerster, Ransom, Auden. Princeton Univ. Press, 1941.
Rev. in N, 153 (Oct. 18, 1941), 376-8; in MP, 40 (Feb., 1943), 275-80.
—— "Critical Principles and a Sonnet." AS, 12 (Winter, 1942), 52-62.
—— *The Nature of Poetry.* Norton, 1946. (Useful as introduction to poetry)
—— "The Modern Myth . . ." *English Inst. Essays,* 1947. Columbia Univ. Press, 1948. Pp. 23-49.
—— "Genesis, Or the Poet as Maker." *Poets at Work.* Harcourt, 1948. Pp. 37-82.
STEIN, GERTRUDE. *Portraits and Prayers.* Random, 1934. (On Eliot, Sitwell, et al.)
STEIN, LEO. *The A. B. C. of Aesthetics.* Horace Liveright, 1927.
STEVENS, WALLACE. See Benét & Pearson's *Oxford Anthology* (Comment by Stevens).
—— Preface. *Collected Poems, by W. C. Williams.* Objectivist Press, 1934.
—— "The Noble Rider and the Sound of Words." *The Language of Poetry,* ed. A. Tate (1942).
—— "The Figure of the Youth as Virile Poet." SeR, 52 (Oct., 1944), 508-29.
On Stevens: See Blackmur, Gregory, M. Moore, Riding & Graves, Wells, Winters.
Harvard Advocate: 127 (Dec., 1940). Wallace Stevens Number. "Statements."
O'Connor, W. Van. "Wallace Stevens and Imagined Reality." WR, 12 (Spring, 1948), 156-63.
Simons, Hi. "'The Comedian as the Letter C.'" SR, 5 (Winter, 1940), 453-68.
Simons, Hi. "The Genre of Wallace Stevens." SeR, 53 (Oct., 1945), 566-79.
Simons, Hi. "Wallace Stevens and Mallarmé." MP, 43 (May, 1946), 235-59.
Sypher, W. "Connoisseur in Chaos." PaR, 13 (Winter, 1946), 83-95.
Voices: 121 (Spr., 1945). Wallace Stevens Number. Essays by Various Hands.
Zabel, M. "The Harmonium of Wallace Stevens." P, 39 (Dec., 1931), 148-54.
STEWART, JEAN. *Poetry in France and England.* Hogarth Press; Harcourt, 1931.
STOLL, E. E. *Art and Artifice in Shakespeare.* Macmillan; Cambridge Univ. Press, 1933.
—— *From Shakespeare to Joyce.* Doubleday, 1944.
STONIER, G. W. *Gog Magog: and Other Critical Essays.* Dent, 1933. (On Hopkins, et al.)
STRACHEY, JOHN. *Literature and Dialectical Materialism.* Covici Friede, 1934.
Rev. by M. Cowley: "Literature and Politics." NR, 81 (Jan. 2, 1935), 224.
STRACHEY, LYTTON. *Characters and Commentaries.* Harcourt, 1933; Chatto & Windus 1936. (On Pope, et al.)
STRONG, LEONARD A. G. *Common Sense About Poetry.* Gollancz, 1931.
SUTHERLAND, JAMES. *The Medium of Poetry.* Hogarth Press, 1934. (Wordsworth, Keats, et al.)
SWINNERTON, FRANK. *The Georgian Scene: A Literary Panorama.* Farrar & Rinehart, 1934.

SYMONS, ARTHUR. *The Symbolist Movement in Modern Literature.* Dutton, 1919; 1st ed., 1899.
—— *Dramatis Personae.* Bobbs-Merrill, 1923; Faber & Gwyer, 1926. ("On Criticism")
—— *The Collected Works of Arthur Symons.* Secker & Warburg, 1924. 16 vols.
—— "Edgar Allan Poe." *Life and Letters,* 2 (Mar., 1929), 163-78. (On his influence)
—— *A Study of Walter Pater.* Sawyer, 1932.

On Symons: See T. S. Eliot in *Selected Essays.*

Waugh, Arthur: "Symon's Criticism." *Tradition and Change.* Chapman & Hall, 1919.

Welby, T. E. *Arthur Symons: A Critical Study.* Philpot, 1925; Adelphi Press, 1926.

SYMONS, JULIAN. "Restoration Comedy." KR, 7 (Spring, 1945), 185-97. (Cf. Knights)

TAGGARD, GENEVIEVE (ed.). *Circumference: Metaphysical Verse, 1456-1928.* Covici Friede, 1929.
—— *The Life and Mind of Emily Dickinson.* Knopf, 1930.

TATE, ALLEN. "Poetry and the Absolute." SeR, 35 (Jan., 1927), 41-52.
—— *Reactionary Essays on Poetry and Ideas.* Scribner's, 1936.
Rev. by G. Stone in AR, 7 (Summer, 1936), 341-52; Flint in SR, 2 (Summer, 1936), 208-24.
—— "Modern Poets and Convention." AR, 8 (Feb., 1937), 427-35. (Part I, symposium)
—— *Reason in Madness: Critical Essays.* Putnam, 1941.
Rev. J. Barzun in SRL, 24 (May 31, 1941), 7; Burke in KR, 1 (Winter, 1942), 126-32.
—— (ed.). *The Language of Poetry.* Princeton Univ. Press; Oxford Univ. Press, 1942. (Essays by Cleanth Brooks, I. A. Richards, Wallace Stevens, Philip Wheelright)
—— "The Fugitive 1922-1925: A Personal Recollection." PULC, 3 (Apr., 1942), 75-84.
—— "Dostoevsky's Hovering Fly." SeR, 51 (Summer, 1943), 353-69.
—— *Sixty American Poets: 1896-1944.* Library of Congress, 1945. (Notes and Bibliography)
—— "A Reading of Keats." AS, 15 (Winter, 1945), 55-63; 15 (Summer, 1946).
—— (ed.). *A Southern Vanguard.* (The Bishop Memorial Volume). Prentice-Hall, 1947.
—— "Techniques of Fiction." *Forms of Modern Fiction,* ed. W. Van O'Connor. Univ. of Minn. Press, 1948.
—— *On the Limits of Poetry: Selected Essays.* Swallow Press-Morrow Co., 1948.
—— *The Hovering Fly.* Cummington Press, 1948. (Critical essays, reprints)
—— "Longinus." HR, 1 (Autumn, 1948), 344-61.

On Tate: See Cleanth Brooks, Riding & Graves, Ransom, Winters.

Abrams, E. "The Reading of Poetry." ELH, 9 (Sept., 1942), 235-44. (An attack)

Dupee, F. W. "Frost and Tate."' N, 160 (Apr. 21, 1945), 464, 466.

Flint, F. C. "Five Poets." SR, 1 (Winter, 1936), 650-74. (Excellent essay)

Horrell, Joe. "Notes on Conversion in Poetry." SR, 7 (Summer, 1941), 119 ff.

Mizener, A. "'The Fathers' and Realistic Fiction." *Acc.,* 7 (Winter, 1947), 101-9.

Roellinger, F. "Two Theories of Poetry as Knowledge." SR, 7 (Spring, 1942), 690-705.

Stallman, R. W. "The Southern Critics." *A Southern Vanguard.* Prentice-Hall, 1947. Pp. 28-51.

Schwartz, D. "The Poetry of Allen Tate." SR, 5 (Winter, 1940), 419-38.

Thorp, Willard. "Allen Tate: A Checklist." PULC, 3 (Apr., 1942), 85-98.
Trowbridge, H. "Aristotle and the 'New Criticism.'" SeR, 52 (Autumn, 1944), 537-55.

TAUBER, HERBERT. *Franz Kafka: An Interpretation of His Works.* Secker & Warburg; Yale Univ. Press, 1948.

TAUPIN, RENÉ. *L'influence du symbolisme français sur la poésie américaine de 1910 à 1920.* Paris: B. Grasset, 1926; Champion, 1929.

TEETER, LOUIS. "Scholarship and the Art of Criticism." ELH, 5 (Sept., 1938), 173-94.

THOMAS, DYLAN. *Selected Writings.* Introd. J. Sweeney. New Directions, 1946.
On Thomas: Fiedler, L. "The Latest Dylan Thomas." WR, 11 (Winter, 1947), 103-6.
Horan, R. "In Defense of Dylan Thomas." KR, 7 (Spring, 1945), 304-10.
Savage, D. S. "The Poetry of Dylan Thomas." NR, 114 (Apr. 29, 1946), 619-22.
Scarfe, Francis. *Auden and After.* Routledge, 1942. Pp. 101-17.
Symons, Julian. "Obscurity and Dylan Thomas." KR, 2 (Winter, 1940), 61-70.

THOMAS, EDWARD. *The Childhood of Edward Thomas.* Faber & Faber, 1938.
On Thomas: See Bullough, Davies, Monro, Murry.
De La Mare. Foreword. *Collected Poems of Edward Thomas.* Selwyn, 1920; Seltzer, 1921.
Eckert, R. P. *Edward Thomas: A Biography and a Bibliography.* Dent, 1937.

THOMAS, WRIGHT, & BROWN, S. G. *Reading Poems.* Oxford Univ. Press, 1941 (Explications)

THOMPSON, DENYS. *Reading and Discrimination.* Chatto & Windus, 1936.

THORPE, C. D. "Coleridge as Aesthetician and Critic." JHI, 5 (Oct., 1944), 387-414

TILLOTSON, GEOFFREY. *On the Poetry of Pope.* Clarendon Press, 1938.
—— *Essays in Criticism and Research.* Cambridge Univ. Press; Macmillan, 1942.

TILLYARD, E. M. W. *Poetry Direct and Oblique.* Chatto & Windus, 1934, 1945.
—— *The Miltonic Setting Past and Present.* Cambridge Univ. Press; Macmillan, 1938.
Rev. by F. Leavis: "In Defence of Milton," *Scr.*, 7 (June, 1938), 104-14.
——, & LEWIS, C. S. *The Personal Heresy. A Controversy.* Oxford Univ. Press, 1939.
See D. S. Savage in *The Personal Principle.* Routledge, 1944.

TINDALL, WILLIAM. *Forces in Modern British Literature: 1885-1946.* Knopf, 1947.
—— "Scholarship and Contemporary Literature." *English Inst. Annual,* 1940. Pp. 42-60.

TOBIN, J. E. *Alexander Pope: A List of Critical Studies . . . 1895 to 1944.* Cosmopolitan Service Co., 1945.

TOVEY, DONALD F. *Essays in Musical Analysis.* Oxford Univ. Press, 1941.

Tradition and Experiment in Present Day Literature. Oxford Univ. Press, 1929.

TRAVERSI, D. A. "The Vision of Piers Plowman." *Scr.*, 5 (Dec., 1936), 276-91.
—— "Coriolanus." *Scr.*, 6 (June, 1937), 43-58.
—— *Approach to Shakespeare.* Sands: Paladin Press, 1939.
—— "Henry the Fifth." *Scr.*, 9 (Mar., 1941), 352-74.
—— "The Development of Modern Italian Poetry." *Scr.*, 10 (Oct., 1941), 143-56.
—— "Measure for Measure." *Scr.*, 11 (Summer, 1942), 40-58. See *Scr.*, 10 (Jan., 1942), 234-47.
—— "Henry IV—Part II." *Scr.*, 15 (Spring, 1948), 117-22.

TRILLING, LIONEL. *Matthew Arnold.* Allen & Unwin; Norton, 1939.
Rev. by R. P. Warren in KR, 1 (Spring, 1939), 217-21; H. Muller: "Matthew Arnold: A Parable for Partisans." SR, 5 (Winter, 1940), 551-67.
—— "Literary and Aesthetic." KR, 2 (Spring, 1940), 152-73. (Freud and literature)
—— "The Sense of the Past." PaR, 9 (May, 1942), 229-41.
—— *E. M. Forster.* New Directions, 1943.
—— "Sermon on a Text from Whitman." N, 160 (Feb. 24, 1945), 215-6, 218, 220.

TRILLING, LIONEL. "A Note on Art and Neurosis." PaR, 12 (Winter, 1914), 41-8.
See Robert Gorham Davis: "Art and Anxiety." PaR, 12 (Summer, 1945), 310-21.
—— "The World of Sherwood Anderson." NYTBR, Nov. 9, 1947, 1, 68f.
—— "The Princess Casamassima." *Hor.*, 17 (Apr., 1948), 267-95.
—— "Manners, Morals, and the Novel." *Forms of Modern Fiction*, ed. O'Connor (1948). Pp. 144-60.
TROTSKY, LEON. *Literature and Revolution*. International Publishers, 1925.
—— "Art and Politics." PaR, 5 (Aug., 1938), 3-10.
TROY, WILLIAM. "Paul Valéry and the Poetic Universe." QRL, 3, No. 3 (1946), 232-9.
—— "The D. H. Lawrence Myth." *Partisan Reader* (1946). Pp. 336-47.
TUCKER, T. F. *Judgment and Appreciation of Literature*. Melbourne Univ. Press, 1926.
TURNELL, MARTIN. "Tristan Corbière." *Crit.*, 15 (Apr., 1936), 393-417.
—— "The Poetry of Jules Laforgue." *Scr.*, 5 (June, 1936), 128-49. (Excellent survey)
—— "Mallarmé." *Scr.*, 5 (Mar., 1937), 425-38. (On R. Fry's trans. *Poems of Mallarmé*)
—— "The Poet of Revolution." *Scr.*, 7 (Sept., 1938), 223-34. (Starkie's *Rimbaud*)
—— *The Poetry of Crisis*. Sands: Paladin Press, 1938. (Beliefs in modern poetry)
—— "Literary Criticism in France." *Scr.*, 8 (Sept., Dec., 1939), 167-83; 281-98.
—— "The Criticism of Jacques Rivière." MLR, 35 (Oct., 1940), 470-82.
—— "Postscript on Verlaine." *Scr.*, 9 (Dec., 1940), 249-58.
—— "Flaubert." *Scr.*, 13 (Autumn, 1945; Spring, 1946), 200-18; 272-91. (Excellent)
—— "Stendhal." *Hor.*, 16 (July, August, 1947), 50-75, 121-39.
—— *The Classical Moment. Studies of Corneille, Molière, Racine*. Hamilton, 1947; New Directions, 1948.
TUVE, ROSEMOND. *Elizabethan and Metaphysical Imagery*. Univ. of Chicago Press, 1947.
TYLER, PARKER. *Magic and Myth of the Movies*. Harcourt, 1947. (Cf. Panofsky)

UNTERMEYER, LOUIS. *American Poetry Since 1900*. Holt, 1923. (A treatise and anthology)
—— *Modern American and British Poetry*. Harcourt, 1936. (Biography and critical introductions)
—— *From Another World*. Harcourt, 1939. (Autobiography)
URBAN, W. M. *Language and Reality: The Philosophy of Language*. Macmillan, 1939. (Symbolism)

VALÉRY, PAUL. *Variety*. Trans. M. Cowley. Harcourt, 1927. *Variety: 2nd Series*, 1938.
Rev. J. Krutch: "Paul Valéry and Intellectualist Critics." N, 125 (Oct. 12, 1927), 377-8.
—— *Introduction to the Method of Leonardo da Vinci*. John Rodker, 1929.
—— "Art and Progress." YR, 19 (June, 1930), 749-53.
—— *Eupalinos, Or the Architect*. Trans. W. McStewart. Oxford Univ. Press, 1932.
—— "Concerning the 'Cimetière Marin.'" SR, 4 (Summer, 1938), 156-65. (Significant)
—— "A Course in Poetics: First Lesson." SR, 5 (Winter, 1940), 401-18.
—— "Things Left Unsaid." KR, 10 (Spring, 1948), 228-39. (Trans. W. Geoffrey)
On Valéry: See Bishop, Bowra, Monro, Monroe, Shipley, Symons, Tate, E. Wilson.
Fay, Bernard. *Since Victor Hugo*. Trans. Paul Doolin. Little, Brown, 1927.
Fowlie, Wallace. "Homage to Valéry." SeR, 54 (Spring, 1946), 250-7.
Gide, André. "Paul Valéry." KR, 8 (Spring, 1946), 277-90.
Hoare, Samuel. "Paul Valéry." *Towards Standards*, ed. F. Leavis (1933). Pp. 127-38.

Lalou, René. "The Importance of Paul Valéry." N, 123 (Dec. 1, 1926), 597-8.
Moore, T. Sturge. "A Poet and his Technique." *Crit.*, 4 (Oct., 1926), 680-93.
More, P. E. "The Modernism of French Poetry." AR, 5 (Summer, 1935), 329-48.
Quarterly Review of Literature: 3, No. 3 (Autumn-Winter, 1946). Paul Valéry Number.
Rice, P. B. "Paul Valéry." *Symp.*, 1 (Apr., 1930), 206-20. In *Literary Opinion* (1937)
Roditi, E. "Paul Valéry: Poetics as an Exact Science." KR, 6 (Summer, 1944), 398-408.
Zabel, M. D. "Paul Valéry." P, 45 (Nov., 1934), 90-99.

VAN DOREN, CARL. *The Roving Critic.* Knopf, 1923. (Articles and reviews)
—— *Many Minds.* Knopf, 1924. (On Lindsay, Millay, et al. Holds that life and art are one)
—— *Three Worlds.* Harper, 1936. (Autobiography)
——, & MARK VAN DOREN. *American and British Literature Since 1890.* Appleton, 1939. (Rev. ed.)

VAN DOREN, MARK. *The Poetry of John Dryden.* Harcourt, 1920; Minority Press, 1931; Holt, 1946.
Rev. by Sharard Vines: "Dryden Redivivus." *Scr.*, 1 (Dec., 1932), 283-5.
See Samuel Monk: "Dryden Studies: A Survey." ELH, 14 (Mar., 1947), 46-63.
—— *Shakespeare.* Holt, 1939; Allen & Unwin, 1940. Foreword by Hugh Walpole.
—— "Good Critics Rare and Common." N, 154 (Jan. 24, 1942), 94-5. Repr. in *Reader.*
—— *The Private Reader.* Holt, 1942. ("What Is a Poet?" On Whitman, Frost, et al.)
—— *The Noble Voice.* Harcourt, 1946. (A study of ten literary works)
On Van Doren: Bishop, H. "The Poetry of Mark Van Doren." N, 149 (Dec. 23, 1939), 714-6.
Matthiessen, F. "A Good Workman." KR, 1 (Autumn, 1939), 453-7. (Cf. M. Zabel)

VEBLEN, THORSTEIN. *The Theory of the Leisure Class.* Vanguard Press, 1926.
Rev. by Lewis Mumford in NR, 67 (Aug. 5, 1931), 314-6.

VENTURI, LIONELLO. *Art Criticism Now.* John Hopkins Press, 1941.
—— *Painting and Painters.* Scribner's, 1945.

VINES, SHERARD. *Movements in Modern English Poetry and Prose.* Oxford Univ. Press, 1927.

VIVAS, ELISEO. "The Objective Correlative of T. S. Eliot." AB 1 (Winter, 1944), 7-18.
—— "Kafka's Distorted Mask." KR, 10 (Winter, 1948), 51-69.
—— "The Objective Basis of Criticism." WR, 12 (Summer, 1948), 197-210. (Significant)

WALDOCK, A. J. *'Paradise Lost' and Its Critics.* Cambridge Univ. Press; Macmillan. 1947.

WARD, A. C. *Twentieth Century Literature.* Methuen, 1929; Longmans, 1940.
—— *The Nineteen-Twenties: Literature and Ideas...* Methuen, 1930.

WARNER, REX. *The Cult of Power.* Lippincott, 1947. ("The Allegorical Method")

WARREN, AUSTIN. "The Criticism of Meaning." SeR, 46 (June, 1938), 213-22.
—— *Richard Crashaw: A Study in Baroque Sensibility.* La. Univ. Press, 1939.
—— "Literary Criticism." *Literary Scholarship.* Univ. of N. C. Press, 1941. Pp. 133-74.
—— *Rage for Order: Essays in Criticism.* Univ. of Chicago Press, 1948.
Rev. by A. Stein in SeR, 56 (Autumn, 1948), 697-703.
——, & WELLEK, RENÉ. *The Theory of Literature.* Harcourt, 1949.

WARREN, R. P. "The Hamlet of Thomas Wolfe." *Literary Opinion*, ed. M. Zabel (1937). Pp. 359-72.
——, & BROOKS, CLEANTH. "The Reading of Modern Poetry." AR, 8 (Feb., 1937), 435-49.
—— "Katherine Anne Porter." KR, 4 (Winter, 1942), 29-42.
—— "Pure and Impure Poetry." KR, 5 (Spring, 1943), 228-54.
—— *The Rime of the Ancient Mariner: An Essay.* Reynal & Hitchcock, 1946.
—— "Hemingway." KR, 9 (Winter, 1947), 1-28. In *Hor.*, 15 (Apr., 1947), 156-79.
On Warren: O'Connor, W. "'Provincial Poet.'" *A Southern Vanguard*, ed. A. Tate (1947). Pp. 92-9.
Stallman, R. W. "Robert Penn Warren: A Checklist." UKCR, 14 (Autumn, 1947), 78-83.
WATKINS, W. B. "Shakespeare's Banquet of Sense." SR, 7 (Spring, 1942), 706-34.
WAUGH, ARTHUR. *Tradition and Change: Studies in Contemporary Literature.* Chapman, 1919.
WELLEK, RENÉ. "Literary Criticism and Philosophy." *Scr.*, 5 (Mar., 1937), 375-83.
—— "Periods and Movements in Literary History." *English Inst. Annual, 1940.* Columbia Univ. Press, 1941. Pp. 73-93.
—— "The Parallelism Between Literature and the Arts." *English Inst. Annual, 1941.* Columbia Univ. Press, 1942. Pp. 29-63.
—— "Literary History." *Literary Scholarship.* Univ. of No. Carolina Press, 1941. Pp. 89-130.
—— "The Mode of Existence of a Literary Work of Art." SR, 7 (Spring, 1942), 735-54.
—— "Six Types of Literary History." *English Inst. Essays, 1946.* Columbia Univ. Press, 1947. Pp. 107 ff.
——, & WARREN, AUSTIN. *The Theory of Literature.* Harcourt, 1949.
WELLS, HENRY W. *Poetic Imagery.* Columbia Univ. Press, 1924.
—— *The Judgment of Literature: An Outline of Aesthetics.* Norton, 1928.
—— *New Poets From Old: A Study in Literary Genetics.* Columbia Univ. Press, 1940.
—— *The American Way of Poetry.* Columbia Univ. Press, 1943.
We Moderns. Gotham Book Mart: 1920-1940. No. 42. (Checklists and critical notes)
WEST, ALICK. *Crisis and Criticism.* Lawrence & Wishart, 1937. (A Marxist critic)
WEST, RAY B., JR. "Truth, Beauty, and American Criticism." UKCR, 14 (Winter, 1947), 137-48.
—— *Writing in the Rocky Mountains.* Univ. of Nebraska Press, 1947. (Checklist and essays)
——, & STALLMAN, R. W. *The Art of Modern Fiction.* Rinehart, 1949.
WEST, REBECCA. *The Strange Necessity.* Garden City: Doubleday, 1928.
WESTON, JESSIE L. *From Ritual to Romance.* Cambridge Univ. Press, 1920.
WEYGANDT, C. *The Time of Yeats. English Poetry of To-Day.* Appleton-Century, 1937.
WHEELWRIGHT, PHILIP. "Poetry and Logic." *Symp.*, 1 (Oct., 1930), 440-57. (On belief)
—— "On the Semantics of Poetry." KR, 2 (Summer, 1940), 247-51. (On Richards)
—— "Poetry, Myth and Reality." *The Language of Poetry*, ed. A. Tate (1942).
—— "Eliot's Philosophical Themes." *Focus Three: T. S. Eliot*, ed. B. Rajan (1947).
WHIPPLE, T. K. *Spokesmen: Modern Writers and American Life.* Appleton, 1928.
—— *Study Out the Land.* Univ. of California Press, 1943. (American literature 1920-40)
WHITEHEAD, ALFRED N. *Science and the Modern World.* Macmillan, 1925; Cambridge, 1926.
—— *Symbolism: Its Meaning and Effect.* Macmillan, 1927, 1937.
—— *The Function of Reason.* Princeton Univ. Press, 1929.

On Whitehead: Smith, James. "Alfred North Whitehead." *Scr.*, 3 (June, 1934), 2-21.
Wilson, Edmund. In *Axel's Castle.* Scribner's, 1931. (See index)
WILDE, OSCAR. *Intentions.* McIlvaine & Co., 1891; Brentano's, 1907.
—— *A Critic in Pall Mall.* Sel. by E. V. Lucas. Methuen, 1922. (Reviews, etc.)
On Wilde: Roditi, Edouard. *Oscar Wilde.* New Directions, 1947.
Symons, Arthur. *A Study of Oscar Wilde.* Sawyer, 1930.
WILDER, AMOS. *The Spiritual Aspects of the New Poetry.* Harper, 1940.
WILKINSON, L. P. *Horace and His Lyric Poetry.* Cambridge Univ. Press, 1945.
WILLEY, BASIL. *The Seventeenth Century Background.* Chatto & Windus, 1934.
WILLIAMS, CHARLES. *Poetry at Present.* Clarendon Press, 1930. (An introduction)
—— *The English Poetic Mind.* Clarendon Press, 1932.
—— *Reason and Beauty in the Poetic Mind.* Clarendon Press, 1933.
Rev. by James S. Wilson: "Faculty of Poets," VQR, 10 (July, 1934), 475-80.
—— "A Dialogue on Mr. Eliot's Poem." DR, 425 (Apr., 1943), 114-32. (*Four Quartets*)
WILLIAMS, ORLO. *Contemporary Criticism of Literature.* Parsons, 1925.
WILLIAMS, OSCAR (ed.). *New Poems: 1940.* Yardstick Press, 1941.
—— (ed.). *New Poems: 1942.* Peter Pauper Press, 1942.
—— (ed.). *New Poems: 1943.* Howell, 1943.
—— (ed.). *New Poems: 1944.* Howell, 1944.
—— (ed.). *A Little Treasury of Modern Poetry.* Scribner's, 1946.
WILLIAMS, W. CARLOS. *Kora in Hell: Improvisations.* Four Seas, 1920.
—— "A Note on Poetry." In *Oxford Anthology,* eds. Benét & Pearson (1938). Pp. 1313-4.
—— "Frederico Garcia Lorca." KR, 1 (Spring, 1939), 148-58.
—— "An Approach to the Poem." *English Inst. Essays, 1947.* Columbia Univ. Press, 1948. Pp. 50-75.
On Williams: See Blackmur, Pound, Rosenfeld, Winters, Zabel.
Morgan, F. "William Carlos Williams." SeR, 55 (Oct., 1947), 675-90.
Stevens, Wallace. Preface. *Collected Poems (1921-1931).* Objectivist Press, 1934.
Rev. P. Rice in N, 138 (Mar. 28, 1934), 365-6; Aiken in NR, 78 (Apr. 18, 1934), 289-90.
Winters, Yvor: "Poetry of Feeling." KR, 1 (Winter, 1939), 104-7.
WILLIAMSON, GEORGE. *The Donne Tradition.* Harvard Univ. Press, 1930.
WILSON, EDMUND. See on V. W. Brooks, Farrell, Housman, *Literary Opinion* (1937), MacLeish, P. E. More, *Tradition and Experiment* (1929).
—— "Notes on Babbitt and More." *Critique of Humanism.* Ed. C. Grattan (1930). Pp. 39-60.
—— *Axel's Castle: A Study in the Imaginative Literature of 1870-1930.* Scribner's, 1931; 1947.
Rev. H. Hazlitt in N, 132 (Mar. 4, 1931), 245-6; F. Dupee in *Symp.*, 2 (Apr., 1931), 264-7; cf. E. K. Brown: "The Method of Edmund Wilson," UTQ, 11 (1941), 105-11; Tate in H&H, 4 (July, 1931), 619-24.
—— "The Literary Class War." NR, 70 (May 4, May 11, 1932), 319-23, 347-9. (On M. Gold)
—— "Art, the Proletariat and Marx." NR, 76 (Aug. 23, 1933), 41-5. (On Hicks, et al.)
—— "The Ambiguity of Henry James." H&H, 7 (Apr., 1934), 385-406.
—— "The Canons of Poetry." AM, 153 (Apr., 1934), 455-62. In *Triple Thinkers* (1938).
See J. Bishop: "The Discipline of Poetry." VQR, 14 (Summer, 1938), 343-56; and Paul Rosenfeld: "What Happened to the Prose Poem?" SRL, 26 (July 24, 1943), 9-11.
—— "The Literary Left." NR, 89 (Jan. 20, 1937), 345-8; cf. Cowley in NR, 89, 348-50.

WILSON, EDMUND. "The Oxford Boys Becalmed." (Auden & Isherwood) NR, 90 (Feb. 24, 1937), 77-8.
—— "Flaubert's Politics." PaR, 4 (Dec., 1937), 13-24. (See M. Turnell on Flaubert)
—— *The Triple Thinkers.* Oxford Univ. Press, 1938, 1948. (On Samuel Butler, John Chapman, et al.)
Rev. by F. Matthiessen: "In the Tradition of Emerson." NR, 94 (Apr. 6, 1938), 279-80; Zabel: "What Is the Artist?" N, 146 (May 21, 1938), 590-2; Blackmur in VQR, 14 (Summer, 1938), 445-50; F. Dupee in PaR, 4 (May, 1938), 48-51. (Excellent)
—— "The Myth of the Marxist Dialectic." PaR, 6 (Fall, 1938), 66-81. Cf. 82-90.
—— *To the Finland Station.* Harcourt, 1940. (On Anatole France, Taine, et al.)
—— *The Boys in the Back Room. Notes on California Novelists.* Colt, 1941.
—— *The Wound and the Bow: Seven Studies.* Houghton, 1941; Secker & Warburg, 1942; Oxford Univ. Press, 1947. Title Essay in NR, 104 (Apr. 21, 1941), 548-55.
Rev. by Zabel in N, 153 (Oct. 11, 1941), 348-50; Leavis in *Scr.*, 11 (Summer, 1942), 72-3; Fiedler in *New Leader,* 30 (Dec. 13, 1947), 15.
See H. M. Jones: "The Limits of Literary Criticism." SRL, 24 (1941), 3, 4, 17;
See L. Trilling: "Art and Neurosis." PaR, 12 (Winter, 1945), 41-8.
—— "The Historical Interpretation of Literature." *Intent of Critic* (1941). Pp. 39-62. Reprinted in *Triple Thinkers* (1948).
—— "Poe as a Literary Critic." N, 155 (Oct. 31, 1942), 452-3.
—— (ed.). *The Shock of Recognition.* Doubleday, 1943. (Anthology, criticism)

On Wilson: See Cowley, Guerard, Hyman, P. E. More, Savage, Shafer, Stauffer.
Adams, R. "Masks and Delays: Edmund Wilson as Critic." SeR, 56 (Spring, 1948), 272-86.
Fiess, Edward. "Edmund Wilson: Art and Ideas." *Ant. Rev.,* 1 (Fall, 1941), 356-67.
Howe, I. "Edmund Wilson." N, 167 (Oct. 16, 1948), 430-1.
Mizener, A. "Edmund Wilson: A Checklist." PULC, 5 (Feb., 1944), 62-78.
Schwartz, D. "The Writing of Edmund Wilson." *Acc.,* 3 (Summer, 1943), 177-86.
Snell, George. "Edmund Wilson: The Historical Critic." RMR, 8 (Winter, 1944), 36-44.

WILSON, J. DOVER. *What Happens in 'Hamlet.'* Cambridge Univ. Press, 1935.
See Brooke, Tucker: *Essays on Shakespeare.* Yale Univ. Press, 1948.
—— *The Fortunes of Falstaff.* Macmillan, 1944. (Explicates *Henry IV,* etc.)
WILSON, KATHERINE. *Sound and Meaning in Poetry.* Cape, 1931.
WIMSATT, W., & BEARDSLEY, M. "The Intentional Fallacy." SeR, 54 (Summer, 1946), 468-88.
—— "The Affective Fallacy." SeR, 56 (Winter, 1949).
WIMSATT, W. "The Structure of the 'Concrete Universal.'" PMLA, 62 (Mar., 1947), 262-80.
—— "Poetry and Morals." *Thought,* 23 (June, 1948), 281-99.
WINTERS, YVOR. (See under *American Caravan,* 1929; W. C. Williams)
—— "'Holiday and Day of Wrath.'" (Marianne Moore) P, 26 (Apr., 1925), 39-44.
—— "The Poetry of Louise Bogan." NR, 60 (Oct. 16, 1929), 247-8.
—— "Notes on Contemporary Criticism." In *The Gyroscope.* Nov. 1929. Ed. Y. Winters.
—— "Poetry, Morality and Criticism." *Critique of Humanism,* ed. C. Grattan (1930).
—— "Robinson Jeffers." P, 36 (Feb., 1930), 153-65. In *Literary Opinion* (1937).
—— "The Progress of Hart Crane." P, 36 (June, 1930), 152-65. In *Primitivism* (1937).
—— "The Lyrics of Robert Bridges." H&H, 5 (Jan., 1932), 321-8. In *Primitivism.*
—— "Poets and Others." (Allen Tate's *Poems*) H&H, 5 (July, 1932), 675-9.
—— "T. Sturge Moore." H&H, 7 (Apr., 1933), 534-45.
—— (ed.). *Twelve Poets of the Pacific.* New Directions, 1937.

WINTERS, YVOR. *Primitivism and Decadence.* Arrow Editions, 1937.
Rev. by G. Stone: "Poetry and Morals." AR, 9 (Apr., 1937), 58-79; F. C. Flint in VQR, 13 (Summer, 1937), 453-7; D. Schwartz in SR, 3 (Winter, 1938), 597-614.
—— *Maul's Curse: Seven Studies.* New Directions, 1938. (On Hawthorne, H. James)
Rev. R. Jarrell: "The Morality of Mr. Winters." KR, 1 (Spring, 1939), 211-5.
—— "The 16th Century Lyric in England." P, 53 (Feb., 1939), 258-72.
—— *The Anatomy of Nonsense.* New Directions, 1943. (On Stevens, Eliot, Ransom)
Rev. by A. Mizener in *Acc.*, 4 (Spring, 1944), 185-7; T. Weiss in QRL, 1 (1944), 212-34.
—— *Edwin Arlington Robinson.* New Directions, 1947.
—— *In Defense of Reason.* Swallow-Morrow, 1947. Repr. *Primitivism, Maul's Curse,* and *The Anatomy.* New essay is "The Significance of *The Bridge* by Hart Crane."

On Winters: See Blackmur, C. Brooks, Flint, Hyman, Ransom, Tate, Ray West.
Aiken, Conrad: "The Careful Rapture." NR, 104 (Apr. 21, 1941), 539-40. (His *Poems*)
Barrett, William. "Temptations of St. Yvor." KR, 9 (Autumn, 1947), 532-51.
Swallow, Alan. "Yvor Winters." RMR, 9 (Fall, 1944), 31-7.

WOLFE, HUMBERT. *Notes on English Verse Satire.* Hogarth Press; Harcourt, 1929.
—— *Romantic and Unromantic Poetry.* Univ. of Bristol Press; Arrowsmith, 1933. (Vs. Eliot, et al.)
—— *Now a Stranger.* Cassell, 1933. (Autobiography)
—— *Portraits by Inference.* Methuen, 1935.

WÖLFFLIN, HEINRICH. *Principles of Art History.* Trans. M. D. Hottinger. Holt, 1932.

WOOD, CLEMENT. *Poets of America.* Dutton, 1925.
—— *The Craft of Poetry.* Dutton, 1929.

WOODBERRY, G. E. *Literary Memoirs, Studies, Heart of Man and Other Papers.* Harcourt, 1922.
Rev. by M. Van Doren in N, 114 (Mar. 1, 1922), 261-2.

The Yale Review Anthology. Edited by Wilbur Cross & Helen MacAfee. Yale Univ. Press, 1942.

WOOLF, VIRGINIA. *The Common Reader.* Hogarth Press, 1925, 1929. ("Modern Fiction," etc.)
—— *A Room of One's Own.* Harcourt, 1929.
—— *The Second Common Reader.* Harcourt; Hogarth Press, 1932. Combined with *The Common Reader.* One vol. Harcourt, 1947.
—— *Reviewing.* Hogarth Press, 1939.
—— *The Death of the Moth.* Harcourt, 1942. (Includes "Letter to a Young Poet," 1932)
Rev. by L. Kronenberger: "Virginia Woolf as Critic,'" N, 155 (Oct. 17, 1942), 382-5.
—— *The Moment and Other Essays.* Harcourt, 1948.

On Woolf: See Burgum, Daiches, Forster.
Bennett, Joan. *Virginia Woolf: Her Art as a Novelist.* Harcourt, 1945.
Blackstone, Bernard. *Virginia Woolf.* Hogarth Press, 1948.
Brace, M. "Worshipping Solid Objects." *Accent Anthology,* eds. K. Quinn & C. Shattuck. Harcourt, 1946.
Chambers, R. L. *The Novels of Virginia Woolf: A Critical Study.* Oliver & Boyd, 1947.
Daiches, David. *Virginia Woolf.* New Directions, 1942.
Empson, W. "Virginia Woolf." *Scrutinies,* ed. E. Rickword. II, 1931.
Forster, E. M. "The Novels of Virginia Woolf." *Crit.*, 4, (Apr., 1926), 277-86
Forster, E. M. "The Art of Virginia Woolf." AM, 170 (Sept., 1942), 82-90

Horizon: 3 (May, 1941), 313-27. Tributes by four authors (Eliot, V. S. West, et al.)

Quennell, Peter. *Letter to Mrs. Virginia Woolf.* Hogarth Press, 1932.

Roberts, John H. "'Vision and Design' in Virginia Woolf." PMLA, 61 (1946), 835-47.

Savage, D. S. "The Mind of Virginia Woolf." SAQ, 46 (Oct., 1947), 556-73.

Toynbee, Philip. "Virginia Woolf: A Study." *Hor.*, 14 (Nov., 1946), 290-304.

Troy, William. "Virginia Woolf." *Symp.*, 3 (Jan., Apr., 1932), 53-63, 153-66.

Wilson, James S. "Time and Virginia Woolf." VQR, 18 (Spring, 1942), 267-76.

YEATS, WILLIAM BUTLER. *Essays.* Macmillan, 1924.

—— *A Vision.* T. Werner Laurie, 1925; Macmillan, 1938.

—— *Autobiographies.* Macmillan, 1926.

—— *Dramatis Personae: 1896-1902.* Macmillan, 1936.

—— Introduction. *The Oxford Book of Modern Verse.* Oxford Univ. Press, 1936.

—— *Letters on Poetry from W. B. Yeats to Dorothy Wellesley.* Oxford Univ. Press, 1940.

Rev. by M. Zabel: "The Last of Yeats." N, 151 (Oct. 12, 1940), 333-5.

—— *Florence Farr, Bernard Shaw, W. B. Yeats: Letters.* Dodd Mead, 1942.

On Yeats: See Bentley, Blackmur, Bowra, Brenner, Brownowski, Bullough, Bush, Church, Collins, Cunliffe, Daiches, Deutsch, Drew & Sweeney, Eliot, Empson, Evans, Gogarty, Gregory, Grierson, L. Jones, F. R. Leavis, Day Lewis, MacCarthy, More, Murry, Orwell, Palmer, Peacock, Ransom, Richards, Savage, Sitwell, Southworth, Sparrow, Spender, Squire, Stauffer, Swinnerton, Tindall, Tuve, C. & M. Van Doren, A. Warren, Wells, Weygandt, Wilder, C. Williams, E. Wilson, Winters, Zabel.

Auden, W. H., & Schwartz, D. "Two Essays." PaR, 6 (Spring, 1939), 46-59.

Auden, W. H. "Yeats as an Example." KR, 10 (Spring, 1948), 187-95.

Blackmur, R. "Between Myth and Philosophy." SR, 7 (Winter, 1942), 407-25.

Brooks, Cleanth. "The Vision of William Butler Yeats." SR, 4 (Summer, 1938), 116-42.

Eglinton, John (*pseud.*) *Irish Literary Portraits.* Macmillan, 1935.

Ellmann, R. "W. B. Yeats: Magician." WR, 12 (Summer, 1948), 232-40.

Green, H. M. *The Poetry of W. B. Yeats.* Australian English Assn., 1931.

Gwynn, Stephen (ed.). *Scattering Branches.* Macmillan, 1940. (Tributes)

Haydn, Hiram. "The Last of the Romantics." SeR, 55 (Spring, 1947), 297-323.

Hone, Joseph. *W. B. Yeats: 1865-1939.* Macmillan, 1942. (Biography)

Houghton, W. "Yeats and Crazy Jane." MP, 40 (May, 1943), 316-29.

Jeffares, A. "The Byzantine Poems of W. B. Yeats." RES, 22 (Jan., 1946), 44-52.

Knights, L. C. "Poetry and Criticsm." *Explorations.* Chatto & Windus, 1946. Pp. 170-85.

Leavis, F. "The Great Yeats, and the Latest." *Scr.*, 8 (Mar., 1940), 437-40.

Macdonagh, T. *Literature in Ireland: Studies.* Talbot Press, 1939.

MacNeice, Louis. *The Poetry of W. B. Yeats.* Oxford Univ. Press, 1938.

Masefield, John. *Some Memories of W. B. Yeats.* Macmillan, 1940; Cuala Press, 1941.

Menon, V. K. N. *The Development of William Butler Yeats.* Oliver & Boyd, 1942.

O'Donnel, J. P. *Sailing to Byzantium.* Harvard Univ. Press, 1939.

Olson, Elder. "Sailing to Byzantium." UR, 8 (Spring, 1942), 209-19.

Pollock, J. H. *William Butler Yeats.* Duckworth, 1935 (Biographical and critical)

Ransom, J. C. "Yeats and His Symbols." KR, 1 (Summer, 1939), 309-22.

Southern Review: The William Butler Yeats Memorial Issue: 7 (Winter, 1942). (Dated also Winter, 1941) Essays by Blackmur, Burke, Eliot, Gregory, Jarrell, Matthiessen, Mizener, Ransom, Schwartz, Tate, Austin Warren, M. D. Zabel, et al.

Spencer, T. "The Later Poetry of W. B. Yeats." H&H, 7 (Oct., 1933), 164-75.

Strong, Leonard A. G. *A Letter to W. B. Yeats.* Hogarth Press, 1932.

ZABEL, MORTON DAUWEN. See under Hopkins, James, Jeffers, MacLeish, More, Valéry. Yeats.

—— "The Lyrics of James Joyce." P, 36 (July, 1930), 206-13.

—— "Baudelaire." P, 43 (Oct., 1933), 38-46.

—— "Towards Standards of Criticism." P, 45 (Oct., 1934), 40-6. (Jonson as critic)

—— "Poets of Five Decades." SR, 2 (Summer, 1936), 160-86. (Omnibus review)

—— (ed.). *Literary Opinion in America.* Harper, 1937. (See Zabel's Introduction) Rev. by James Burnham in PaR, 5 (June, 1938), 49-53.

—— "Four Poets in America." *Literary Opinion,* ed. M. D. Zabel. Harper, 1937. Pp. 397-436. (On Robinson, Sandburg, MacLeish, M. Moore)

—— "The Century of Leopardi." P, 50 (Aug., 1937), 270-3.

—— "Varieties of Poetic Experience." SR, 3 (Spring, 1938), 799-819. (On Pound, et al.)

—— "The Condition of American Criticism." EJ (June, 1939), 417-28.

—— "The Whole of Housman." N, 150 (June 1, 1940), 684-6. (A good essay)

—— "Hardy in Defense of His Art." SR, 6 (Summer, 1940), 125-49. (Excellent)

—— "Two Years of Poetry: 1937-1939." SR, 5 (Winter, 1940), 568-608.

—— "The Secret Sharer." NR, 104 (Apr., 21, 1941), 567-74. (On Conrad)

—— "The Thinking Body: Yeats in the Autobiographies." SR, 7 (Winter, 1942), 562-90.

—— "The Contemporary Period." *A Book of English Literature.* Macmillan, 1943.

—— "Joseph Conrad: Chance and Recognition." SeR, 53 (Winter, 1945), 1-22. (Excellent)

—— "Rimbaud: Life and Legend." *Partisan Reader,* ed. W. Phillips. Dial Press, 1946.

—— (ed.). *The Portable Conrad.* Viking Press, 1947. See Introduction.

—— "Graham Greene." In *Forms of Modern Fiction* (1948). Pp. 287-93.

ZUKOFSKY, LOUIS. "American Poetry: 1920-1930." *Symp.,* 2 (Jan., 1931), 60-84.

—— (ed.). *An 'Objectivists' Anthology.* Humphries, 1932.